Social and Political Implications of Data Mining:
Knowledge Management in E–Government

Hakikur Rahman
SDNF, Bangladesh

INFORMATION SCIENCE REFERENCE

Hershey • New York

Director of Editorial Content: Kristin Klinger
Director of Production: Jennifer Neidig
Managing Editor: Jamie Snavely
Assistant Managing Editor: Carole Coulson
Development Editor: Julia Mosemann
Typesetter: Jeff Ash
Cover Design: Lisa Tosheff
Printed at: Yurchak Printing Inc.

Published in the United States of America by
        Information Science Reference (an imprint of IGI Global)
        701 E. Chocolate Avenue, Suite 200
        Hershey PA 17033
        Tel: 717-533-8845
        Fax: 717-533-8661
        E-mail: cust@igi-global.com
        Web site: http://www.igi-global.com

and in the United Kingdom by
        Information Science Reference (an imprint of IGI Global)
        3 Henrietta Street
        Covent Garden
        London WC2E 8LU
        Tel: 44 20 7240 0856
        Fax: 44 20 7379 0609
        Web site: http://www.eurospanbookstore.com

Library of Congress Cataloging-in-Publication Data

Social and political implications of data mining : knowledge management in E-government / Hakikur Rahman, editor.
      p. cm.
Includes bibliographical references and index.

Summary: "This book focuses on the data mining and knowledge management implications that lie within online government"--Provided by
publisher.

ISBN 978-1-60566-230-5 (hardcover) -- ISBN 978-1-60566-231-2 (ebook)
1. Electronic government information. 2. Data mining. 3. Knowledge management. I. Rahman, Hakikur, 1957- II. Title.

JF1525.A8S63 2009
352.3'802854678--dc22

                              2008041370

British Cataloguing in Publication Data
A Cataloguing in Publication record for this book is available from the British Library.

All work contributed to this book set is original material. The views expressed in this book are those of the authors, but not necessarily of the
publisher.

Nasser Ayoub, *Institute of Technology, Japan*

Yuji Naka, *Institute of Technology, Japan*

Rodrigo Sandoval-Almazán, *Autonomous University of the State of Mexico, Mexico*

Mario A. Gutiérrez A., *Digital Animation Research Center, Mexico*

Abdul Raufu Ambali, *University Technology MARA (UiTM), Malaysia*

Angela. M. Chailla, *Sokoine University of Agriculture, Tanzania*

Andrew W. Malekani, *Sokoine University of Agriculture, Tanzania*

Frank W. Dulle, *Sokoine University of Agriculture, Tanzania*

Table of Contents

Section I
Content Management and Knowledge Management

Section II
Universal Access to Social Services

Section III
Security, Safety, and Trust

Section IV
E-Governance and Artificial Intelligence

Section V
Virtual Communities and Cases

Detailed Table of Contents

Section I
Content Management and Knowledge Management

Chapter I

Shamsul I. Chowdhury, Roosevelt University, USA

Chapter I of this book presents various data warehousing methodologies along with the main components of data mining tools and technologies, and discusses how they all could be integrated together for knowledge management in a broader sense. The chapter also focuses on how data mining tools and technologies could be used in extracting knowledge from large databases or data warehouses. The chapter further focuses on the reusability issues of knowledge management and presents an integrated framework for knowledge management by combining data mining (DM) tools and technologies with case-based reasoning (CBR) methodologies.

Chapter II

Kostas Metaxiotis, National Technical University of Athens, Greece

Arguing that most of the prior research studies have investigated the possible application of knowledge management in the public sector, Chapter II focuses on the application of knowledge management in e-government. Recognizing the importance of e-government and knowledge management (KM) to delegate into the public administration sector, the chapter is a continuation of a previous research related to the application of knowledge management in e-government. This chapter discusses various important issues of KM in e-government and presented a framework for application of KM in e-government, including hints for carrying out future research. Moreover, the chapter, by positioning the proposed framework of KM in e-government, discusses about its application in a Greek municipality.

Chapter III

LuAnn Bean, Florida Institute of Technology, USA
Deborah S. Carstens, Florida Institute of Technology, USA
Judith Barlow, Florida Institute of Technology, USA

Chapter III examines e-government challenges regarding the linkages between data mining and knowledge management (KM) over time, discusses the organizational development of e-government applications, and details out both general and specific issues, as such social, ethical, legislative, and legal issues that impact effective implementations of e-government. A final focus of the chapter is the potential strategic benefits of a risk-based approach that can be used to enhance the core synergy of KM and data mining applications in e-government operations.

Chapter IV

Hakikur Rahman, SDNF, Bangladesh

Chapter IV is focusing on knowledge management issues for developing knowledge management portals to empower citizens and societies. In this context, the chapter introduced a few critical aspects of knowledge management perceptions, justified establishment of knowledge management portals acting as a tool of empowerment, provided insight on data mining as a technology of implementation, suggested a solution by introducing Semantic Web Technologies as an essential technology for establishing knowledge management portals, puts forward contemporary challenges during the establishment of knowledge management portal, illustrated a few cases that are acting as knowledge management portals, and concluded before giving a few hints on future research issues for empowering common element of the society.

Section II
Universal Access to Social Services

Chapter V

Stefano De Luca, Evodevo s.r.l., Italy
Enrico Memo, Ca' Foscari University, Italy

Chapter V of the book is dealing with a methodology, Health Discoverer, and consequential software, aiming at disease management and measurement of appropriateness of healthcares. This chapter particularly focuses on data mining techniques that can be used to verify Clinical Practice Guidelines (CPGs) compliance and the discovery of new, better guidelines. The research work is based on Quality Records, episode parsing using Ontologies and Hidden Markov Models.

Chapter VI of this book introduces hospital governance as a policy domain in which data mining methods have a potential to provide insight and practical knowledge. The chapter starts by exploring the essentials of the concept, by analyzing the root notion of governance and comparing it with applications in other sectors of social services. The chapter also outlined the recent developments and examples in this sector from the UK, France and The Netherlands. Furthermore, a research agenda has been developed based on an evaluation of the current state of affairs. The chapter concludes with an introduction to the European Hospital Governance Project, which follows the outlines of the described research agenda.

Chapter VII focuses on data mining techniques that are being used to extract large quantity of livelihood data to extract useful information. In this chapter the data mining approach is proposed for the characterization of family consumptions in Italy. For this purpose, a series of statistical techniques are being used in sequence and different potentialities of selected methods for addressing these kinds of issues are highlighted. This study may be considered an example of operational and concrete approach of managing of large data-sets in the social-economical science, from the definition of goals to the evaluation of results.

Chapter VIII provides a general overview on contemporary electronic payment systems, focusing developing countries and tried to relate electronic payment systems as an enabler of financial empowerment. This chapter reiterated that by raising economic activities via electronic means, as a component of electronic commerce, could augment the electronic governance system of a country. It has also put forward various issues, challenges, methods and tools needed to implement electronic payment systems, especially focusing developing countries.

Section III
Security, Safety, and Trust

Chapter IX
Arla Juntunen, University of Helsinki, Finland

Chapter IX discusses how a public sector organization made an effort to enhance their collaborative processes and organizational knowledge base in a specific functional area and how they implemented KM-tools to improve knowledge and information sharing and transferal both within the organization and among partners. This chapter aims to promote knowledge management and KM-tools usage in government and to identify the challenges and benefits gained by an implementation of analytical solutions. It also describes the managerial and organizational implications on the usage of analytical solutions and the effects on political decision-making and government programs.

Chapter X
Shuting Xu, Virginia State University, USA
Xin Luo, Virginia State University, USA

Chapter X addresses a variety of technological applications of text mining on security issues. In this chapter, it is argued that the text mining technology has become vital in the arena of information systems security (ISS), especially after the 9/11 tragedy. This chapter tends to shed light on the correlation between text mining and ISS, and thereby addresses various text mining applications in ISS. It has tried to put forward various text mining applications, including social network analysis, abnormal detection, topic discovery and identity detection, and also discusses on social perspective of text mining. The chapter has also presented a section on future analysis of text mining for ISS research.

Chapter XI
Reima Suomi, Turku School of Economics, Finland
Olli Sjöblom, Turku School of Economics, Finland

Chapter XI introduces aviation safety data analysis as an important application area for data mining. The chapter begins with the introduction of the basic concepts of data mining, and afterwards, the field of aviation safety management is discussed. In that connection, data mining is identified as a key technology to study through flight incidents reports. Later on, the test runs for four data mining products, for possible use in the Finnish civil aviation authority, are described in detail. The chapter ends with conclusions, which convey that even sophisticated data mining tools are just tools: they do not provide any automatic gears, but skilled users can use them for searching potential clues in the data.

Section IV
E-Governance and Artificial Intelligence

Chapter XII

Chapter XII uses Dynamics Causal Mining as the technique for modeling and analyze E-government, where Dynamics Causal Mining is a combination of System Dynamics and Data Mining. This chapter suggests an integration of System Dynamics and Association Mining for identifying causality and expanding the application area of both techniques. This gives an improved description of the target system represented by a database; it can also improve strategy selection and other forms of decision making.

Chapter XIII

Touching upon all knowledge management processes from knowledge capture, knowledge sharing, to knowledge creation, Chapter XIII goes beyond the methodology and tools used for developing such a system for the Greek Government, to the integration and the diffusion of e-Government knowledge with the help of formal ontology definitions - capturing the core elements of the domain together with their main relationships.

Chapter XIV

Chapter XIV presents data mining, as a planning and decision support tool for biomass resources management to produce bio-energy. Furthermore, the chapter has tried to define the decision making problem for bio-energy production. The Decision Support System, that utilizes a data mining technique, e.g. clustering, integrated with other group of techniques and tools, such as Genetic Algorithms, Life Cycle Assessment, Geographical Information System, etc, is presented. Finally, a case study has been included that shows how to tackle the decision making problem.

Section V
Virtual Communities and Cases

Chapter XV

Rodrigo Sandoval-Almazán, Autonomous University of the State of Mexico, Mexico
Mario Arturo Gutiérrez Alonso, Tecnológico de Monterrey Campus Morelia, Mexico

Chapter XV provided an example of a user-friendly interface for knowledge management and information retrieval, through the use of virtual assistants in E-government applications. The chapter has also presented a short state of the art on-line virtual assistants technology, highlighting the knowledge management aspects. Along this perspective, two case studies from the Mexican state of Guanajuato, and the Federal Government Citizen's Web Page are being presented and discussed. These case studies provided new insights into access methods, interfaces and ways to query and present information in e-government applications.

Chapter XVI

Abdul Raufu Ambali,University Technology MARA (UiTM), Malaysia

Chapter XVI seeks to address the digital divide associated with e-government, which can serve as impediment for application of information and communication technology (ICT). As a case study, the chapter explores the various initiatives that have been undertaken by the Malaysian government to bridge the newly evolved digital gap.

Chapter XVII

A. M. Chailla, Sokoine University of Agriculture, Tanzania
F. W. Dulle, Sokoine University of Agriculture, Tanzania
A. W. Malekani, Sokoine University of Agriculture, Tanzania

Chapter XVII discusses the problems of digitization, challenges and future opportunities for East African university libraries with focus on collaborative efforts and strategies backed up with policies for investments in ICTs training and integration of ICTs into the core university activities for effective knowledge management (KM) and information dissemination. It is argued in the chapter that digitization of library information will add value to more effective university KM, faster information access and better use in multidisciplinary fields including local content.

Businesses are now facing globalized competition and are being forced to deal with an enormous amount of data. The vast amounts of data and the increasing technological ability to store them also facilitated data mining. In order to gain a certain level of competitive advantage, businesses now commonly adopt a data analytical technology called data mining. Nowadays, data mining is more widely used than ever before, not only by businesses who seek profits, but also by nonprofit organizations, government agencies, private groups, and other institutions in the public sector. Organizations use data mining as a tool to forecast customer behavior, reduce fraud and waste, and assist in medical research.

Foreword

Knowledge management has become an essential element of this contemporary world that is driven by information and knowledge. Knowledge management is needed to facilitate information exchange, content management, service delivery and transaction processes with the citizens, as well as inter-governmental activities, inter alia. Furthermore, adopting innovative information and communication technology (ICT) methods diversified applications are being carried across the globe to upgrade capacity, learning skill and knowledge acquisition by the common people of the society. In this way, many countries have reached to an elevated platform of knowledge dynamics.

Knowledge acquisition processes require manipulation and handling of huge amount of information and data for appropriate management and thereby, assist the end-user to take knowledgeable decisions. Intelligent decision-making techniques, in effect, directly and indirectly assist the stakeholders to upgrade their governance system, be it a government, a business or a society.

Nowadays, governance system in a large extent depends on the information delivery performance, thereby, influence strengthening of electronic governance in the society. Thus, knowledge management in electronic government (e-government) deserves appropriate manipulation of information, data and content utilizing pertinent technologies. In this aspect, data mining is an emerging technology, which is being used by concurrent researchers for developing necessary tools and techniques in the intelligent decision making processes.

A book focusing knowledge management in e-government through application of data mining techniques inflicting social, economical, technological and political implications for overall society development is a very crucial and timely achieved output. Such a book will generate tremendous impetus, not only for general research, but also will create enormous research initiations, and at the same time will act as a potential guideline for the development practitioners. This book will find its usefulness to academia, development agencies, government and non-government organizations and policy initiators.

Prof. Dr. A.M.M. Safiullah
Vice Chancellor
Bangladesh University of Engineering and Technology (BUET)
Dhaka, Bangladesh

Preface

Data mining can be termed, as the *extraction process of hidden predictive information from huge databases. In a sense, data mining* is a powerful emerging technology with enormous potential to assist communities focus on the most important information in their livelihoods. Utilizing data mining tools trends, patterns and behaviors of data can be monitored, and at the same time assist to predict future trends and behaviors of data. This allows societies/ entrepreneurs/ agencies to make proactive, intelligent, and knowledge-driven decisions. Furthermore, the automated and prospective analyses offered by data mining budge beyond the analyses of past events provided by demonstrative tools typical of decision support systems. Foremost, data mining tools can respond to diversified questions that traditionally were too time consuming to resolve. They scour databases for hidden patterns, finding predictive information that experts may miss because they lies outside their normal expectations (DIG White Paper, 1995).

Nowadays, data mining can also be termed as knowledge discovery processes, and increasingly becoming one of the most acknowledged topics in information technology. Much of it deals with the process of automatically retrieving essential information and discovering hidden relationships that is crucial in making knowledgeable decisions (Chen & Liu, 2005). During the last decade, data mining has been used in diversified application domains and has proven the ability to support various types of critical applications under knowledge discovery.

As an emerging field, data mining attracted potential researchers in this community, and at the same time, many have endorsed its diversified utilizations. Among several trends of its utilizations, archival of high-dimensional data; incorporation of semantic search; rapid data-driven analysis; knowledge-driven end products are phenomenal. In these contexts, social and political implications of data mining are important, especially in the realm of knowledge management in e-government. Ranging from providing value added social services, knowledge acquisition processes to electronic government initiatives, and content management systems implication of data mining converges. However, by far political implications of data mining in the knowledge management processes remain confined in the central bodies and corporate agencies. For proper knowledge development at the grass roots and for homogeneous distribution of knowledge acquisition system, bi-directional thoroughfare is desired in terms of policy initiations.

As Chaterjee (2005) outlines, data mining techniques are the outcome of an extensive process of study, research and product development. In essence, this evolution began when entrepreneurs started archiving business data in computers, efforts continued with improvements in easier data access, and more recently, researches generated technologies that allow users to navigate through their data in real time. Over the time, data mining takes this evolutionary development beyond retrospective data access, thus routing the expansion towards proactive information delivery for the management of human livelihood through improved intelligentsia.

Eventually, data mining is becoming a significant tool in science, engineering, industrial processes, healthcare, medicine, and other social services for making intelligent decision. However, the datasets in these fields are predominantly large, complex, and often noisy. Therefore, extracting knowledge from data requires the use of sophisticated, high-performance and principled analysis techniques and algorithms, based on sound statistical foundations. These techniques in turn necessitate powerful visualization technologies; implementations that must be carefully tuned for performance; software systems that are usable by scientists, engineers, and physicians as well as researchers; and infrastructures that support them (Mueller, 2004; SIAM, 2006).

Well developed information and communication network infrastructure and knowledge building applications, adapted to regional, national and local conditions, easily accessible and affordable, and making greater use of locally available technologies and other innovative methods where possible, can accelerate the social and economic progress of countries, and the well being of all individuals and communities. However, knowledge acquisition from crude data mostly depends on social, cultural, economical and political aspects of a country, rather than pure technology. It requires incorporation of intricately built knowledge management tools and techniques, archival of discrete data or information to feed the knowledge acquisition system and management of very superficial and complicated data or information within the system.

The issues and aspects of archiving scientific data include the discipline specific needs and practices of scientific communities as well as interdisciplinary values and methods. However, when this archival process is targeted to improve the livelihood of common people of the community, increase their knowledge level and eventually enhance the governance system, the tasks of data archiving ranges from accumulating, digitizing, preserving, providing security to providing easy accessibility. Thus, data archiving amalgamates with social diversifications, economic variations, cultural conjunctures, political peripheries and foremost, deals with human psychology. Data archiving becomes part and parcel of day-to-day activities of human life and management of these data reflects variation of human endeavors.

The leveraging of data mining tools to facilitate knowledge management and e-governance incorporates contexts of health care, literacy, governance issues, civic responsiveness, environment issues, climate changes and most importantly, equitable access for economic opportunities by creating social capital that are essential for the holistic deployment of economic development activities of a society. These issues are intricately intermingled with social and political environment of a nation. This book has tried to include issues, aspects, features, experiments, projects and cases related to socio-political enhancements among connected communities utilizing data mining techniques in the context of knowledge discovery and knowledge enhancement processes.

WHERE THIS BOOK STANDS

In this interconnected world, where information is an essential element of community empowerment, capacity development and socio-economic development, data mining is widening emerging and relatively a new area of research and development, which can provide important outcomes to the common citizens. It can yield substantial knowledge from even raw data that are primarily gathered for wider range of applications. In this context, various institutions have already started to derive considerable benefits from its diversified applications and at the same time, many other industries and disciplines are applying the technique in increasing effect for their own development.

However, the challenge of equitable distribution of resources for homogenous development taking into account the social, cultural, political and economic background protecting everyone's interest confronts policy initiators, academics and researchers, including government and non-government agencies, and development partners for taking attempt to create a development dynamics. Data mining would assist this evolutionary process beyond retrospective data access and routing to potential and proactive information delivery. This book includes various aspects of existing data mining and decision support techniques and their requirements to improvise the development of such information system at each tier of the governance structure. It also incorporated global initiatives and highlight their capabilities depicting real life cases to act as role models. The cases are on improvement of governance system, enhancement of peace building effort, electoral up-gradation, improvement of learning mechanism, scientific perfection, interactive imagery, or simple content repository for knowledge building.

Primary objective of this publication is to promote knowledge management in e-government, identify knowledge management technologies, and highlight the challenges in the implementation of e-government systems and especially knowledge management solutions at the grass roots. Moreover, as the contemporary world has began to realize that the political and economic significance of the more than half of the world's population are living in largely untapped rural setting, realization of pragmatic knowledge acquisition processes to improve e-governance has become prime importance for every nation. For this reason, Governments and nongovernmental organizations, including development agencies are increasingly concerned with addressing economic development goals and stability, stubborn deficit in rural health and learning, urban migration, environmental degradation, and other related trends. In these circumstances, a publication on knowledge management processes focusing e-governance featuring emerging technology like data mining deserves primary importance among the academia, researchers, development practitioners, policy initiators and individuals.

Today many research communities, including informatics, systematics, academics, phylogenetics, ontologists, physicians, scientists and ecologists, are on the verge of transformation as a consequence of network capability that enable a new class of research dimension based on instant interaction with networked information servers and computational services, in a newly evolved paradigm known as 'grid computing.' High-throughput information backbones linking data enabled desktops of scientists around the globe assist to launch a new class of research collaboration with 'wired together' in a virtual and global environment. These processes are generating remarkable amount of data/content to be capitulated for effective deployment of knowledge acquisition system, and, therefore demand competent data/info mining techniques at the both end of usage (generator and end user). The book included conceptual framework, various analysis and synthesizes a variety of data mining techniques for improvement of social and political systems, varying from healthcare services, bio-energy database, crime analysis, and aviation safety to learning, portal management system, e-government modeling, and ontology.

The major asset of this book is the accumulation of several theoretical researches, case analysis, and a few practical implementation processes accompanying profound discussions and techniques for accomplishing tasks that one could easily adopt even in a non-technical environment. In fact, this book will act, not only as a research guide but also as an implementation guide in the longer run.

ORGANIZATION OF THE BOOK

The book is organized into five sections with seventeen chapters. A brief description of each of the chapters follows:

In recent years data warehousing and data mining are being used as unique tools in decision support, business intelligence and other kind of social and economic applications. **Chapter I** of this book presents various data warehousing methodologies along with the main components of data mining tools and technologies, and discusses how they all could be integrated together for knowledge management in a broader sense. The chapter also focuses on how data mining tools and technologies could be used in extracting knowledge from large databases or data warehouses. The chapter further focuses on the reusability issues of knowledge management and presents an integrated framework for knowledge management by combining data mining (DM) tools and technologies with case-based reasoning (CBR) methodologies.

While current literature on knowledge management has been addressing issues, challenges and opportunities for the private sector initiatives, little has been discussed for the public sector, and even less in the aspect of e-government. Acknowledging the fact that the implementation of a framework for the application of knowledge management in e-government is a challenging task that requires coordination and contribution from many agencies, departments and policy makers, **Chapter II** tried to put forward a framework for knowledge management in e-government for better e-government management. Furthermore, recognizing the importance of e-government and knowledge management (KM) to devolve into the public administration sector, the chapter put forward the continuation of a previous research related to the application of knowledge management in e-government. This chapter discusses important issues of KM in e-government and presented the framework for application of KM in e-government as a basis for future research. Finally, by positioning the proposed framework of KM in e-government, the chapter discusses about its application in a Greek municipality.

It is evident that appropriate data mining models and applications in e-government settings have the potential to bring major benefits to wider range of stakeholders. Furthermore, as these models evolve, structural transitions occur within e-government that includes an evolution of managerial practices through knowledge management (KM). **Chapter III** examines e-government challenges regarding the linkages between data mining and KM over time, discusses the organizational development of e-government applications, and details out both general and specific issues, as such social, ethical, legislative, and legal issues that impact effective implementations of e-government. A final focus of the chapter is the potential strategic benefits of a risk-based approach that can be used to enhance the core synergy of KM and data mining applications in e-government operations.

Knowledge management is not just a simple technology driven process, rather it is policy driven issue that is intermingled with technology, decision, management and intellectuality. Along this way, empowering common citizens utilizing knowledge development utilities is a challenge to the researchers and development practitioners. Furthermore, dissemination of intellectual content for public view, their understanding, capacity development, and specifically for being utilized as a tool to increase their social, educational, political and economic ability is by far the most difficult part of the system. **Chapter IV** of the book is focusing on knowledge management issues for developing knowledge management portals to empower citizens and societies. In this context, the chapter introduced a few critical aspects of knowledge management perceptions, justified establishment of knowledge management portals acting as a tool of empowerment, provided insight on data mining as a technology of implementation, suggested a solution by introducing Semantic Web Technologies as an essential technology for establishing knowledge management portals, puts forward contemporary challenges during the establishment of knowledge management portal, illustrated a few cases that are acting as knowledge management portals, and concluded before giving a few hints on future research issues for empowering common element of the society.

Utilizing data mining techniques, knowledge management in e-government is enhanced that evidently augments provision of improved social services by the government and other actors in the society. Along this perspective, the importance of various social services including education and health is constantly increasing. Simultaneously, as the societies are growing older, the awareness of a proper social care is spreading among citizens. However, the central issue, here is the increasing cost of maintaining such social care systems, especially the expenses in healthcare are an important portion of the overall expenses of a country. Therefore, it is very important to determine if the given cares are the appropriate ones. **Chapter V** of the book is dealing with a methodology, *Health Discoverer*, and consequential software, aiming at disease management and measurement of appropriateness of cares. This chapter particularly focuses on data mining techniques that can be used to verify Clinical Practice Guidelines (CPGs) compliance and the discovery of new, better guidelines. The work is based on Quality Records, episode parsing using Ontologies and Hidden Markov Models.

As discussed in Chapter five, governance in healthcare refers to the complexity of checks and balances that determine how decisions are made within the top structures of hospitals. In this aspect, **Chapter VI** of this book introduces hospital governance as a policy domain in which data mining methods have a potential to provide insight and practical knowledge. The chapter starts by exploring the essentials of the concept, by analyzing the root notion of governance and comparing it with applications in other sectors of social services. The chapter also outlined the recent developments and examples in this sector from the UK, France and The Netherlands. Furthermore, a research agenda has been developed based on an evaluation of the current state of affairs. The chapter concludes with an introduction to the European Hospital Governance Project, which follows the outlines of the described research agenda.

Along the context of universal access to social services, apart from education and healthcare improved livelihood is important for better governance. **Chapter VII** focuses on data mining techniques that are being used to extract large quantity of data to get useful information. In this chapter the data mining approach is proposed for the characterization of family consumptions in Italy. The research has found that Italian expenditures form a complex system, and to mitigate this, the Italian National Bureau of Statistics (ISTAT) carries out a survey each year on the expenditure behaviour of Italian families. The survey enumerates household expenditures on durable and daily goods and on various services. For this purpose, a series of statistical techniques are used in sequence and different potentialities of selected methods for addressing these kinds of issues are pinpointed. This study recommends that, further investigation is needed to properly focalize on service usage for the characterization, for example, of the nature of investigated services (private or public) and, most of all, about their supply and effectiveness across the national territory. Still this study may be considered an example of operational and concrete approach of managing of large data-sets in the social-economical science, from the definition of goals to the evaluation of results.

Apart from education, healthcare, and livelihood services stable economic transactions is an important component of the governance system of a country. In this aspect, payment processes are the core of the economic transactions, whether the transaction is national or global. Payment system is an age-old system of transfer of properties. It has taken diverse forms depending on demand, usage, acceptability, tradition, culture, methods, technology and availability. Recently evolved payment systems varied from commodity transfers, physical financial transactions (traditional payment systems) to virtual payment transactions (electronic payment systems). Utilizing modern day technologies, electronic payment systems have also taken various forms in varying environments and societies. **Chapter VIII** provides a general overview on electronic payment systems, focusing developing countries and tried to related electronic payment systems as an enabler of financial empowerment. In this context, this chapter reiterated that by raising economic activities via electronic means, as a component of e-commerce, could augment the electronic governance system of a country. It has also put forward available issues, challenges, methods and tools needed to implement electronic payment systems, especially focusing developing countries.

Chapter IX discusses how a public sector organization made an effort to enhance their collaborative processes and organizational knowledge base in a specific functional area and how they implemented

KM-tools to improve knowledge and information sharing and transferal both within the organization and among partners. The implementation of KM-tools in the crime analysis function as part of intelligence-led policing assisted in preventing more crimes and creating safer communities. The use and recognition of the benefits of KM-tools also facilitated the development of continuing learning and education in all the levels and in all the fields and locations of the organization. This chapter aims to promote knowledge management and KM-tools usage in government and to identify the challenges and benefits gained by an implementation of analytical solutions. It also describes the managerial and organizational implications of the usage of analytical solutions and the effects on political decision-making and government programs.

In the arena of information security and knowledge management, text mining has becoming instrumental in extracting pertinent information to create valuable knowledge for more effective knowledge management. **Chapter X** addresses various technological applications of text mining in information systems security (ISS) issues. The techniques are being categorized according to the types of knowledge to be discovered and the text formats to be analyzed. The chapter also focuses on privacy issues of text mining, which are social aspects of text mining, and also discusses on future trends of text mining research.

Security, safety and trust are important components of a governance system, and as long as they are being managed by electronic means, they form quite a potential platform of electronic governance system. Along these issues, **Chapter XI** establishes aviation safety as a social service, forming part of e-governance and introduces a data analysis as an important application area for data mining. In this chapter, the reader is introduced to the basic concepts of data mining. After that, the field of aviation safety management is discussed, and in that connection, data mining is identified as a key technology to study through flight incidents reports. Afterwards the test runs for four data mining products, for probable use in the Finnish civil aviation authority, are described in detail. The chapter ends with conclusions that tell that even sophisticated data mining tools are just tools: they do not provide any automatic tools, but skilled users can use them for searching clues in the data.

It is apparent that, electronic government or digital government is not a simple or well-defined theoretical concept; rather it is a complex phenomenon, which involves technical, organizational, institutional and environmental aspects. Researchers from different disciplines are trying to model the E- government using combinations of various methods from different areas, which can help to deal with complexity and obtain explanations that are more comprehensive. **Chapter XII** uses Dynamics Causal Mining as the technique for modeling and analyze E-government, where Dynamics Causal Mining is a combination of System Dynamics and Data Mining. This chapter suggests an integration of System Dynamics and Association Mining for identifying causality and expanding the application area of both techniques. This gives an improved description of the target system represented by a database; it can also improve strategy selection and other forms of decision making. The aim is to identify causal factors hidden in the data and discover the underlying causality between the observed data.

In an effort to follow the new public administration roadmap and invest in the sharing of knowledge, most of the governmental organizations appear in a crossroad. A lot of knowledge has been created, organized and even digitized but still it cannot be considered available anywhere, anytime, for any citizen, business or other organization. Making governmental knowledge available to its beneficiaries requires the design, development and deployment of a Knowledge Registry, as the platform to cater for the formal description, composition and publishing of the governmental services canvas. Touching upon all knowledge management processes from knowledge capture, knowledge sharing, to knowledge creation, **Chapter XIII** goes beyond the methodology and tools used for developing such a system for the Greek Government, to the integration and the diffusion of e-Government knowledge with the help of formal ontology definitions - capturing the core elements of the domain together with their main relationships.

Chapter XIV presents data mining, as a planning and decision support tool for biomass resources management to produce bio-energy. Furthermore, the chapter has tried to define the decision making problem for bio-energy production. The Decision Support System, that utilizes a data mining technique, e.g. clustering, integrated with other group of techniques and tools, such as Genetic Algorithms, Life Cycle Assessment, Geographical Information System, etc, is presented. Finally, a case study has been included that shows how to tackle the decision making problem using this technique.

The objective of **Chapter XV** is to provide an example of a user-friendly interface for knowledge management and information retrieval, through the use of virtual assistants in E-government applications. The chapter has also provided a short state of the art on-line virtual assistants technology, highlighting the knowledge management aspects. Two case studies from the Mexican state of Guanajuato, and the Federal Government Citizen's Web Page are being presented and discussed. These case studies provide new insights into access methods, interfaces and ways to query and present information in e-government applications.

There is no doubt that e-government application in public administration and its productive use of ICTs would improve the interface between respective governments and their citizens in both service deliveries and provisions of basic needs. However, it is recognized that while there are many benefits that have been obtained by implementing e-government, there are many sectors of society that are not part of this growing electronic culture. Perhaps, economics, lack of access to the Internet and other technologies, low literacy levels and often lack of interest or willingness to use the new technologies, contributes to a country's disparities in e-government practices. This way a gap is being created among the digitally reached and un-reached communities. **Chapter XVI** seeks to address the digital divide associated with e-government, which can serve as impediment for application of ICT. As a case study, the chapter explores the various initiatives that have been undertaken by the Malaysian government to bridge the digital gap.

Digitization initiatives and knowledge management have become an integral part in the changing global information society, where knowledge management comprises a range of practices used by organizations to identify, create, represent, and distribute knowledge. However, digitization initiatives refer to either jointly or collaborative efforts to translate existing library holdings whether in print, graphical, audio or combination of all, into digital format commonly known as electronic resources. As a case study, **Chapter XVII** discusses the problems of digitization, challenges and future opportunities for East African university libraries with focus on collaborative efforts and strategies backed up with policies for investments in ICTs training and integration of ICTs into the core university activities for effective knowledge management (KM) and information dissemination. It is argued in the chapter that digitization of library information will add value to more effective university KM, information access and use in multidisciplinary fields including local content.

Finally, as a case of social and political implications of data mining, Chapter XVIII put forwards application of data mining techniques in public sector administration. In the public sector, data mining was used as a means to detect fraud and waste, but in time it emerges as a measuring tool and means for improving program performance. This chapter discusses on issues like, improving services or performance, helping customer relations management, managing human resources, and detecting fraud, waste and abuse in the public sector administration. It also discusses on analysis of scientific and research information, detection of criminal activities, and detection of terrorist activities in public administration before providing future research directions on predictive analysis and diversity of data mining application domains.

CONCLUSION

The growing interest of contemporary researchers in data mining is motivated by a common problem across multifaceted disciplines, as how does one store, access, model, and ultimately illustrate and understand very large data sets? Historically, different aspects of data mining have been addressed by diverse disciplines. But, as a truly interdisciplinary text on data mining with social and political implications focusing knowledge management in e-government, blending the contributions of information science, computer science, social science, knowledge management, ontology, and algorithms deserves further studies and researches (Hand, Mannila & Smyth, 2001; Han & Kamber, 2005).

As unique its name carries, the book incorporates methodical and pragmatic research outcomes in the aspect of data mining accommodating socio-political interests. Implementation of knowledge based e-government plan to reach common citizens through ICT mediated techniques, especially utilizing data mining modus operandi may be directed toward the key target audiences, as such the community people. But, they would include decision-makers and policy initiators; the general public; industry and service communities; scientific and technical communities; academics; government and non-governmental organizations; public interest advocacy groups; civil society advocacy groups, donor agencies and development partners and international financial institutions.

In addition to these, as researches revealed data mining is the process of automatic discovery of patterns, transformations, associations and anomalies in massive databases, and is a highly interdisciplinary field representing the confluence of multiple disciplines, such as database systems, data warehousing, machine learning, statistics, algorithms, data visualization, and high-performance computing (COMP 290, 2003). Utilizing data mining techniques with social and political implications to improve e-governance require methodical knowledge management. Furthermore, knowledge management is desirable to facilitate information exchange and transaction processing with citizens, as well as to enable inter-government knowledge sharing and integration.

However, the core content generators (data generators) are the appropriate knowledge systems that connect people to reach other despite barriers of time, geography, culture, literacy, and even ownership of a telephone or computer or Internet. Therefore, broader audiences of this book will widely vary from individuals, researchers, scientists, academics, politicians, students, librarians, journalists and development practitioners. Finally, this book will generate tremendous impetus in terms of knowledge-based research initiations, thus will have highly acceptable scholarly value and at the same time potentially contribute to this very specific sector of research.

REFERENCES

Chen, S.Y. & Liu, X. (2005). Data mining from 1994 to 2004: an application-orientated review, International Journal of Business Intelligence and Data Mining, Vol.1: 4-21(18).

COMP 290 (2003). Research Seminar theme of Data Mining: Concepts, Algorithms, and Applications. Department of Computer Science, The University of North Carolina at Chapel Hill, NC.

DIG White Paper (1995). An Overview of Data Mining at Dun and Bradstreet, Data Intelligence Group, Dun & Bradstreet, Inc., USA.

Hand, D.J., Mannila, H. & Smyth, P. (2001). Principles of Data Mining (Adaptive Computation and Machine Learning). The MIT Press (August 1, 2001)

Chaterjee, J. (2005). Using Data Mining for Business Intelligence, Retrieved June 15, 2008 from http://www.aspfree.com/c/a/MS-SQL-Server/Using-Data-Mining-for-Business-Intelligence/

Han, J. & Kamber, M. (2005). Data Mining : Concepts and Techniques, Second Edition, The Morgan Kaufmann Series in Data Management Systems, Morgan Kaufmann; November 3, 2005

Mueller, J.P (2004). Mining Amazon Web Services: Building Applications with the Amazon, Sybex, January 23, 2004

SIAM (2006). Excerpts from the 2006 SIAM Conference on Data Mining, Society for Industrial and Applied Mathematics (SIAM), April 20, 2006 – April 22, 2006, Bethesda, MD, USA.

Acknowledgment

I am pleased to acknowledge the support from all involved in the entire accretion of manuscripts, review process, revision and finalization of the book, without which the project could not have been satisfactorily completed. I am highly grateful to all the authors who provided their relentless and generous assistance, but reviewers who were most helpful and provided inclusive, thorough and creative comments are, Arla Juntunen, Shamsul Chowdhury and Paola Annoni. Thanks go to my close friends and colleagues at SDNF and ICMS for their wholehearted encouragements during the entire process.

Special thanks also go to the dedicated publishing team at Idea Group, Inc. Particularly to Jessica Thompson, Julia Mosemann, Heather Probst and Joel Gamon for their continuous suggestions, relentless supports and timely feedbacks via e-mail for keeping the project on schedule, and to Mehdi Khosrow-Pour and Jan Travers for their enduring professional guides. Finally, I would like to thank my family members for their love and support throughout this period.

Hakikur Rahman, *PhD*
ICMS, Bangladesh
August 2008

Section I
Content Management and Knowledge Management

Chapter I
A Conceptual Framework for Data Mining and Knowledge Management

Shamsul I. Chowdhury
Roosevelt University, USA

ABSTRACT

Over the last decade data warehousing and data mining tools have evolved from research into a unique and popular applications, ranging from data warehousing and data mining for decision support to business intelligence and other kind of applications. The chapter presents and discusses data warehousing methodologies along with the main components of data mining tools and technologies and how they all could be integrated together for knowledge management in a broader sense. Knowledge management refers to the set of processes developed in an organization to create, extract, transfer, store and apply knowledge. The chapter also focuses on how data mining tools and technologies could be used in extracting knowledge from large databases or data warehouses. Knowledge management increases the ability of an organization to learn from its environment and to incorporate knowledge into the business processes by adapting to new tools and technologies. Knowledge management is also about the reusability of the knowledge that is being extracted and stored in the knowledge base. One way to improve the reusability is to use this knowledge base as front-ends to case-based reasoning (CBR) applications. The chapter further focuses on the reusability issues of knowledge management and presents an integrated framework for knowledge management by combining data mining (DM) tools and technologies with CBR methodologies. The purpose of the integrated framework is to discover, validate, retain, reuse and share knowledge in an organization with its internal users as well as its external users. The framework is independent of application domain and would be suitable for uses in areas, such as data mining and knowledge management in e-government.

INTRODUCTION

People have been collecting and organizing data from stone ages. In the earlier days data were collected and recorded in one way or the other mainly for record keeping purposes. With the advancement in computational technology in general and storage technology in particular data collection and their storage in large data warehouses have become an integral part of the data processing and decision-making environment of today's organizations. Over time people have learned to value data as an important asset.

Reliable data in a database or a data warehouse could be used for decision-making purposes by appropriately analyzing the data and making them more meaningful and useful. In other words data could be analyzed to find hidden patterns and foresee trends. The process is broadly being called data mining.

Data mining usually starts with a hypothesis or an assumption and ultimately creates new information or knowledge. In order to survive and succeed in the tough business world of today it is also very important to store and manage the evolving knowledge within an organization. Knowledge management is the overall activities of creating, storing, re-using and sharing the new knowledge. Knowledge management increases the ability of an organization to learn from its environment and to incorporate knowledge into the business processes by adapting to new tools and technologies, for example; data warehousing, data mining and case-based reasoning.

The chapter presents the necessary fundamentals of data warehousing (DW), data mining (DM) (methodology, tools, techniques, systems and terminology) and related technologies. One of the purposes of the chapter is to develop and gain an understanding of the principles, concepts, functions and uses of data warehousing and data mining for knowledge management in a broader sense. Data modeling in data warehousing plays a vital role in successful utilization of the data

resources as an organizational asset. The data quality is also an important aspect in the process. The following topics have been addressed:

- DW methodology
- DW data modeling
- DW data quality issues
- DM – techniques and uses
- DM and Business intelligence – From findings to application
- DM and CBR (Case-based Reasoning) for knowledge retention and reuse.

The work falls into the category of content management of data from database/data warehouse using data mining and other intelligent techniques like expert system, CBR, etc. The purpose is to make the extracted knowledge available to the users (both internal and external) in organizations of different structure and forms, including e-government. In e-government one of the most important benefits would be citizen empowerment through access to information/knowledge (The World Bank Group 2008).

In the work the term *business* and *customer* has been used in a broader sense. By *business* and *customer* is meant the core activities that take place and the consumer of information respectively in an organization.

BACKGROUND

Over the years data warehousing and data mining tools have evolved into a unique and popular business solutions to attain business understanding and decision-making. Decision makers already consider these systems to be the corner stone in their IT system portfolio. Data and the knowledge derived from the data and sharing them within an enterprise and its business partners and collaborators is a key success factor in today's complex business world, and hence flexible tools are needed to deal with the evolving complexities.

Different business solutions need to be derived to cope with the ever-changing business need. Furthermore, Business problems and solutions not only affect people within an organization, but also other people outside the organization, like customers and suppliers (Chan, Witte and Chowdhury, 2004). Data and related technology for data access, analysis and delivery are the driving factors in data warehousing. It is implemented to attain competitive advantage and is a valuable core competency (Atre, 2003a; Montalbano and Chowdhury, 2006). Data warehousing is not a destination – it is a journey and projects as such should be treated as continuous projects where newer and newer functionalities are being added incrementally (Lawyer and Chowdhury, 2005).

A well designed data warehouse with all needed data is helpful in answering relevant questions, for example; for better customer relationship management (CRM). The importance of relationship marketing and the use of CRM systems as a valuable tool for retaining customers have been well recognized by decision makers (Chan, Witte and Chowdhury, 2004). In e-government the purpose of data warehousing would be to centralize all relevant data and make them accessible to the population in a timely and convenient manner. In fact, organizations have been building data warehouses centralizing organizational data since the early 1990's and still there is a lack of common agreement regarding the appropriate design and architecture for a data warehouse (Chowdhury, 2005; Inmon, 2002; 2004). Idea behind a data warehouse is to centralize company wide information to create and deliver the necessary analytical environment (for data mining or knowledge discovery) to meet the changing needs of business. A data warehouse environment could be implemented using any of the four main existing approaches, namely (Agosta, 2005; Breslin, 2004; Fang and Tuladhar, 2006): i. the top-down, ii. the bottom-up, iii. the hybrid and iv. the federated approach.

The top-down also known as Inmon's approach focuses on the data warehouse as the nerve center of the entire analytic environment. This is a multi-tier environment consisting of dependent data marts (smaller subject-specific warehouses) that use a dimensional model. This approach may or may not use an initial staging area depending on the amount of data involved.

The bottom-up also known as Kimball's approach focuses on delivering business value by deploying dimensional data marts as quickly as possible. In the hybrid approach both the top-down and bottom-up theories are combined. In this design, the enterprise and data mart models are developed simultaneously.

Finally, in the federated approach guidelines, procedures, and best practices of building a data warehouse are identified and outlined, and the focus is on doing whatever is necessary to deliver an analytical environment (for data mining) to meet the changing needs of the business, for example; improved customer service.

There are considerable philosophical debates, obstacles, and pros and cons as to the selection of a data warehousing methodology (Lawyer and Chowdhury, 2005). However, the method chosen must meet business requirements, and be flexible and scalable. In other words the methodology must minimize the gaps between the business processes and the technology that are being used to run the business in the organization. In the next section, discussions will be limited to the bottom-up (Ralph Kimball's) approach commonly know as dimensional data modeling for creating a data warehouse (Kimball and Ross, 2002) with some explanatory examples.

DATA WAREHOUSE DATA MODELING

An Entity Relationship (ER) diagram is the backbone for implementing a transaction-oriented relational database application to run the day-today operation of the business usually known as on-line transaction processing (OLTP) system. These types of system rely on a relational database that must efficiently update highly normalized, referentially integrated tables based on an ER model. As an example of an ER model let us take the case of the hypothetical NorthWind Traders Database implemented in MS ACCESS2003 relational DBMS (Alley et. al, 2006). NorthWind Trading Company is a business-to-business (B2B) enterprise and stocks 77 products from 29 suppliers in 8 categories of food-related products. In 8 quarters, the company has received 830 orders from 91 customers around the world through 9 employees during the last two years. The firm shipped these orders by using 3 shipping companies. The company's OLTP system employs an entity relationship (ER) model to process transactional data. Uses of this model help eliminate redundancies and contribute to data integrity, completeness, and consistency in the OLTP system (Kroenke,

2002; Gillenson, 2005). Figure 1 presents an ER model of NorthWind Traders OLTP system. The ER model contains eight entities (tables) that are related with one another and the model also shows the type of relationship in between the entities. For example, the type of relationship in between suppliers and products is of type 1: N (many) and so on (Alley et. al, 2006; Chowdhury, 2005; 2006).

Star or dimensional modeling is used for implementing data warehouses. In a Star model a central fact table is surrounded by a set of dimension tables (Figure 2). There are two main arguments in favor of Star models: i. they are easy for business people to understand and use, and ii. retrieval performance is usually effective (Todman, 2001). Moreover, Star Model has replaced ER diagramming as the most effective choice for data warehouse design (Jukic, 2006; Kimball and Ross, 2002; Sen and Sinha, 2005).

Three approaches are generally in use for star modeling (Chenoweth et al, 2003; Chowdhury,

Figure 1. An example of an ER model

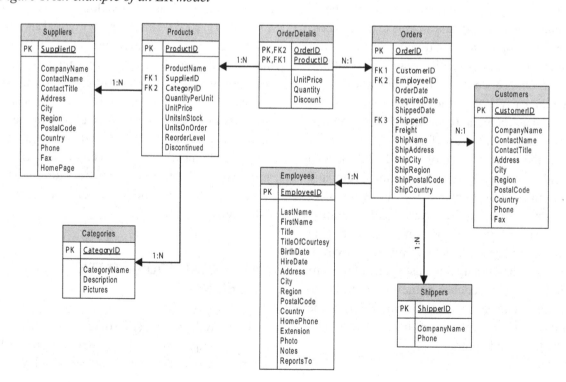

2007a; 2007c; Sperley, 1999): i. development by modification, for example; buy a home that is constructed and knock some walls to add new walls, etc. ii. development from template, for example; buy some existing home plans and has a house built to the plans or a modified version of the plans and iii. full custom development, for example; contact an architect and start from scratch.

In development by modification the existing ER model is modified and reorganized in the form of a Star model by deleting the operational information and adding more of decision making information to accommodate the decision making needs of the business.

Modification or conversion of the ER diagram to a star schema is a step-by-step process and usually begins with a conversation between end users and IT professionals to discover a list of *burning or critical business questions.* This list consists of a set of analytical problems that decision makers feel are important success factors to the future direction of the business.

Data modeling is as much art as science; many possibilities may exist for a successful conversion to Star models. To understand and explain the processes, this research has formed a JAD (Joint Application Development) team to study the ER model of the NorthWind Traders database and formulate a set of critical questions, which are important for the success and survival of the hypothetical NorthWind enterprise. The JAD team comprised business expertise, IT expertise and also members who were familiar with DBMS ACCESS and NorthWind Trading database. The list of critical questions as perceived by the JAD team is summarized in Table 1.

The conversion process can take a good amount of discussion in the form of JAD sessions for a correct determination of the information the system should provide. Planning is the key to successful design and could likely involve a few iterations before the converted model could be accepted. The model that emerges from this conversion forms the Star model showing relationship between entities.

The resulting Star model proposed and implemented by the team member in the project to find answers to their burning questions are presented below in Figure 2.

During the conversion the JAD team also followed useful guidelines based on the Ten Commandments of Dimensional Data Modeling. The ten commandments summarizes as to what needs to be done for a successful and useful conversion (Chowdhury, 2006). The team followed them

Table 1. Critical business questions

Critical business questions	Why they are important?
1. How can the company analyze sales by quantity based on region and time?	This question is a very important one to ask because it will enable one to understand the overall performance of the company.
2. What are the top and bottom 5% of products sold over time and region?	This may be one of the most important questions that any business should ask. A company should keep record of the fluctuation of sales per product category per year to understand the trends of when these items are purchased and where they are purchased.
3. Who are the top 10% of the customer base over time and category?	A business should know its top customer and try to retain them by establishing good relationship with them.
4. Which employees are most productive related to sales, time, product, and region?	Here the question is to understand employee performance, which is valuable to compare the sales per employee for product, region and time. For example, a company sometimes may want to provide incentives to the top employee, which encourages the sales force to increase their performance.
5. What suppliers deliver the best-selling products?	The business also should know their top selling products and their suppliers.

into practical realization in the form of teamwork and has been described elsewhere (Chowdhury, 2005; 2007a).

The approach taken in the JAD team was based on lessons learned in research and teaching practices in the field for many years. Development by modification was found to be useful and is becoming a common acceptable (best) practice for star modeling. Success with this approach depends on factors, such as: the ER models are relatively new, well designed and normalized; the IT staff (for the new DW project) is very familiar with the source system OLTP models; the IT staff also understands the data that is already in the database; and many data warehouse reference and fact tables are already in the OLTP model in a different form.

The resulting Star model (Figure 2) reduces the number of tables from eight (in the ER diagram – Figure 1) to seven by removing the Categories, Order Details, and Orders tables and replaces them to form a Sales Fact table, and Time dimension table, which simplified the model. A great benefit of this star diagram is that the diagram includes a new table called Time (dimension) and this table includes facts such as the day, month, year, quarter, and time, which can be very helpful when using as a reference to a sale.

The next step in the process is to populate the star model with data (from source system/s) and test it by making sql queries/data mining to validate that the model satisfy the information requirement of the enterprise by providing answers to the critical business questions. The usefulness and effectiveness of the star model

Figure 2. A Star model

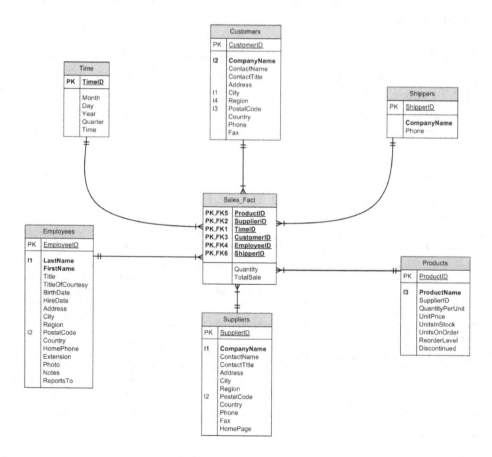

depends on how accurately it has addressed the Ten Commandments of Star Modeling (Alley et. al, 2006; Chowdhury, 2005; Garcia, Janjua, and Galvan, 2006;. Rieger, 2006).

DW DATA QUALITY ISSUES

Data quality is a key issue when an organization implements an enterprise wide data warehouse, for example for customer relationship management (CRM) or other purposes. Utilizing CRM requires that customer information be of high quality, in order to identify, validate and consolidate customers within an organization. Quality of the data will determine the quality of the data warehouse as well as the quality of the decision-making. In other words data quality is an investment in future. Data warehouses allow firms to learn more about their customers so that they can develop strategies to maximize services, profits and minimize cost. Some of the characteristics of data warehouse data are that (Chowdhury, 2005; Laudon and Laudon, 2004):

- The data is subject oriented, meaning it comes from different sources including external sources,
- The data is integrated,
- The data is non-volatile, meaning it is not changed,
- The data is time variant, meaning it is time stamped,
- The data must be of high quality, meaning the data is error-free,
- The data is aggregated or summarized,
- The data is often de-normalized to make queries run quicker, and
- The data is not necessarily absolutely current, meaning it does not have the most current piece of information. To get the most current piece of information, the data has to be refreshed more often.

This research has addressed and examined the aspects of ensuring data quality in a data warehouse by utilizing mainly a revised process flow model (Chowdhury, 2005; 2007b; Sperley, 1999). The purpose was to recommend the suitability and usability of the process flow model for ensuring quality data in data warehouses. The ultimate goal was to recommend a methodology for the highest possible data quality in a data warehouse. The research came to the following findings:

- The first step in the data quality improvement program needs to discover where data quality problems exist in the source systems. When sources for problems are identified, methods must be developed to improve data quality.
- Data quality improvement should be a continuous process. The sooner the process starts the better are the chances to have quality data. Data quality improvement program may be started prior to building a data warehouse.
- It has also been observed that people, collecting and recording data must be trained and well motivated to do a good job. Business and other data should be carefully gathered and recorded as it is being done in the field of medicine.

DATA MINING VS. KNOWLEDGE DISCOVERY IN DATABASES (KDD)

Data mining is a process that uses statistical, mathematical, artificial intelligence and machine-learning techniques to extract and identify useful information and subsequent knowledge from large databases (Berry and Linoff, 2004). The main steps in the process are shown in Table 2.

Knowledge discovery in databases (KDD) is a comprehensive process of using data mining methods to find useful information and patterns in

Table 2. Data mining vs. knowledge discovery

Main Data Mining Steps	Steps in Knowledge Discovery in Data bases (KDD)
Data preparation Defining a study Reading the data and building a model Understanding your model Prediction	Selection (of data) Preprocessing or cleansing Transformation or conversion Data mining (selecting data mining methods and performing the mining) Interpretation/evaluation

data. KDD is a multi-disciplinary field of research, which includes machine learning, statistics, database technology, expert systems (ES) and data visualization. KDD steps are shown in Table-2.

If the definitions and the different steps are compared in DM and KDD, some commonalities can be seen, as well as certain differences. In KDD, data mining is being considered as one step in the processes. In other words Knowledge discovery is the whole process and in it Data Mining is the discovery stage. The KDD process involves evaluation, and possibly interpretation of patterns extracted by data mining to decide which subsets of patterns constitute knowledge. Data mining also requires significant data "preprocessing", choice of algorithms, and assumes information "post-processing". Even though there are differences between DM and KDD, often DM is used as a synonym for KDD in the literatures. In this work, that convention was followed. Over the years the differences between them are getting blurred (smaller and smaller). Alternative names used in the past are data archaeology, data dredging (badly done), functional dependency analysis and data harvesting (Desai and Chowdhury, 2003; Chowdhury, 2005).

In these contexts, data mining could broadly be classified into two broad categories (Turban, Aronson and Liang, 2005):

- **Hypothesis-driven data mining:** Begins with a proposition by the user, who then seeks to validate the truthfulness of the proposition. This category of data mining may use a model-driven approach.

- **Discovery-driven data mining:** Finds patterns, associations, and relationships among the data in order to uncover facts that were previously unknown or not even contemplated by an organization. This category uses a data driven approach.

Moreover, data mining is useful for:

- **Classification:** Supervised induction used to analyze the historical data stored in a database and to automatically generate a model that can predict future behavior
- **Clustering:** Partitioning a database into segments in which the members of a segment share similar qualities
- **Association:** A category of data mining algorithm that establishes relationships about items that occur together in a given record
- **Sequence discovery:** The identification of associations over time
- **Visualization:** used in conjunction with data mining to gain a clearer understanding of many underlying relationships.

However, a good tool may accommodate both these approaches. With increased sophistication in data collection and storage facilities, data driven form of data mining is becoming more common. Available data mining tools offer a wide variety of algorithms. The most common are decision trees, artificial neural networks, regression analysis, genetic algorithm, Bayesian belief networks.

DM tools and technologies have evolved during the last decade and now are extensively been used by different organizations. The strength of today's DM tools and technologies is due to – increasing computing power, improved data collection, statistical and learning algorithm and also advances in user's interface design. A general methodology for data mining is given in Figure-3. This research has implemented a system based on the above framework and it was proven successful in mining data from a large database described elsewhere (Chowdhury, 1990; 2005). Most data mining tools of today use a similar framework.

With the help of the system as depicted in Figure-3 a user with his/her domain specific knowledge would be able to create an analytical model from the existing data repository. Once the user accepts the analytical model the system can help with the statistical analysis/data mining. Statistical expertise is incorporated in SES (Statistical Expert System) to provide necessary

help to the users in the process of analytical design and choose an appropriate statistical technique/algorithm relevant to the data and provide help in conducting the analysis/data mining. The user may be an expert in his or her domain (for example business, medicine, economics, politics, e-governance, etc.) but may not be familiar with statistical know how to design and conduct an analysis. The system would also support the user to conduct data driven data mining, where analytical model building is not necessary.

The outcome of the statistical analysis needs to be validated before it could be incorporated into the knowledge base. For a successful validation of a data material, one need knowledge in three different contexts, namely: data context, statistical/methodological context, domain context. The data context utilizes some general knowledge of the data and application domain to transform or structure the data into a model, which could be

Figure 3. A Data mining framework: supporting both model and data driven approaches

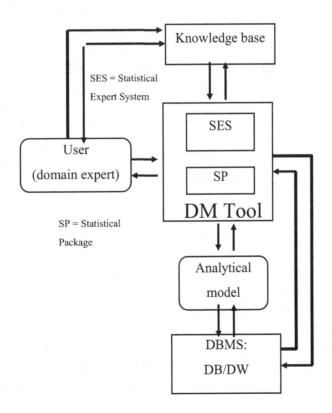

statistical or analytical and conduct the analysis. The domain context, in addition to the above, should have more deep and specific knowledge of the application domain to be able to interpret the results appropriately and draw conclusions from the statistical analysis.

DM AND BUSINESS INTELLIGENCE

Current trends in today's complex business environment include collecting and analyzing information regarding customers, products, and processes in order to increase profit and reduce expenses. Businesses are gathering and analyzing these data by implementing various systems to make up a suite of Business Intelligence System. Business intelligence (BI) is a conceptual framework for decision support. A BI architecture would include databases (or data warehouses), analytical tools, applications and methodologies. The purpose is to enhance data into information and then into knowledge to be able to address business issues and concern successfully. The steps can be summarized in the following scheme:

Data --> Information -- > Understanding --> Knowledge --> Business (Process) Intelligence

From the steps above, it is seen that the data needs to be analyzed, validated and interpreted to gain an understanding and increase our knowledge, which could be utilized to address relevant business situation.

BI is carried out to gain sustainable competitive advantage and is a valuable core competence in today's complex world. BI needs access to combined and centralized business data/information. Data warehousing is being used by many organizations as a way to pull all related data together in order to successfully answer relevant business questions. Idea behind a data warehouse is to centralize company wide information to create and deliver the necessary analytical environ-

ment (for data mining or knowledge discovery) to meet the changing needs of business (Atre, 2003b; Montalbano and Chowdhury, 2006) . Data warehouse data can be compared with the metaphor of the crystal river with its pure life-giving water, which always reflects the stone over which it flows. Similarly data warehouse data would reflect the organizational activities (Desai and Chowdhury, 2003). Business must treat user data with the same care that physicians apply to patient information (Chowdhury, 2006).

Business intelligence system can best be defined as a broad category of applications and technologies for gathering, storing, analyzing, and providing access to data to help enterprise users make better business decisions. BI applications include the activities of decision support systems, query and reporting, online analytical processing (OLAP), statistical analysis, forecasting and data mining (Berry and Linoff, 2004; Turban, Aronson and Liang, 2005).

DATA MINING AND CBR

CBR (Case-based Reasoning) has been defined as an artificial intelligence technique for learning and reasoning from experiences. It is a technology for solving new problems by adapting the known solutions of previous similar problems. In CBR the knowledge gained over time is related to specific cases to form a case-base. Cases are situation-specific knowledge, stored in a structured base (case database or case-base) together with the necessary general knowledge (Chan and Chowdhury, 2005; Chowdhury, 2005; Laudon and Laudon, 2004; Sankar, Pal, and Shiu 2004).

A new problem is solved by trying to describe what the problem is. This description is then used to retrieve old cases from the case database. The retrieved case is compared with the new case to reuse the previously gained knowledge. This process creates a suggested solution to the problem, which is compared with the real world example and tested. During this revision, useful experience from the test is added and forms a new tested solution. This tested solution gives a confirmed solution, which is then retained in the case database as a new case (Laudon and Laudon 2006) . The problem solving steps have been schematically represented in Figure-4.

Case-Bases

Usually a database contains one type of information, i.e., the facts or problem descriptions. In a case-base each case contains at least two types of information: i. facts, describing a problem situation and also ii. a solution, or a methodology to derive a solution. In other words the problem description together with the solution makes a case – a complete story (Chowdhury, 2001; 2005; 2007d; Sankar, Pal, and Shiu 2004). Case-bases can be developed, maintained and updated in four steps.

i.   Building a well-organized database of cases (usually called a case-base), which contains description of earlier cases (problem descrip-

tions and possible solutions or a methodology to derive a solution). Searching after cases from the case-base that are similar to a present case. An index mechanism supports efficient retrieval.

ii.   Adjusting the earlier solution to the present situation;

iii. Validating the adjusted solution; and

iv.   Updating the case base. If the solution is valid it is saved in the case base for future use.

DM and CBR technologies can be combined together into an integrated knowledge management framework for attaining BI by performing data mining and retaining the BI by using CRR technology (Chowdhury, 2005a). A framework for integration is presented in Figure-5. System implemented based on the framework would help to acquire new knowledge through iterations of analysis and operations (data mining). Further the knowledge that is being discovered/captured by performing extensive analysis would be represented, retained and reused by employing CBR technology to solve future problems. In other

Figure 4. Steps in a CBR system development cycle

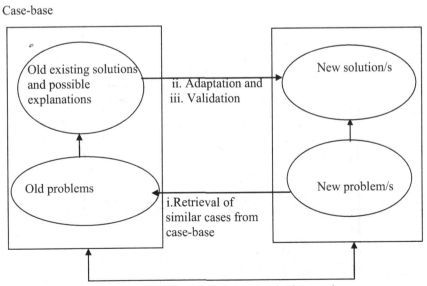

words the knowledge (discovered and stored by the DM part – Figure-5) in *knowledge base* would be used as a front-end by the CBR technology component (Figure-5) to create reusable CBR applications.

Data mining is used to support the acquisition of knowledge from databases. DM integrated with CBR (Figure 5) can be viewed as a general knowledge management and also a problem-solving tool. Knowledge Management is also the practice of treating knowledge as a corporate asset. Knowledge assets are equally important for competitive advantage and survival as physical and financial assets (Desai and Chowdhury, 2003). Data mining and CBR can be seen as complimentary methodologies and integration of the two would help to implement powerful and reusable systems for better knowledge management as well as to address future problems (Chowdhury and Chan, 2007). One of the key benefits of combining DM with CBR would be to enhance organization's knowledge base

by generating solutions to specific problems that are too massive and complex to be analyzed by human beings in a short period of time.

FUTURE RESEARCH DIRECTIONS

Over the years, data warehousing grew from a simple reporting database to an analytic application that provide static information to help users track trends, including profitability analysis, sales forecasting, customer segmentation, financial and other form of analyses. However, this static information does not provide end-users with the most recent information in order to perform business analyses on real-time or near real-time data. This lack of information is because of the batch mode process (extract, transform and load) that provides a snapshot of information reflecting the data at the time the last file was loaded. As a result of this time delay in information, the available data is not sufficient to respond to current business situations (Galvan, 2006).

Figure 5. An integrated framework for knowledge management

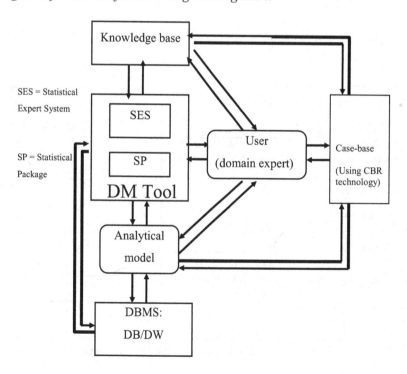

To take DW, DM and KM to the next level, it will be necessary for a business to alter their strategy to include at least near real-time (NRT) update of the data in a data warehouse. Access to more current information from the source system would empower end-users. It would allow them to increase the speed and accuracy of analytic and strategic business decisions based on information across departments, enterprises and external systems. As a result, users would be able to generate timely and relevant reports across all data facets of an organization (Agosta, 2005; Galvan, 2006). Future directions of research would be to study how best the real-time or the near-real time update could be accommodated in the proposed framework.

DISCUSSION

One of the main focuses of the chapter has been the presentation of an integrated framework for data mining with other related technologies. In the framework DM has been seen as a link between DW and CBR. Further DM is not an end in itself. The knowledge gained and business intelligence attained by using DW and DM could be retained and reused by using CBR technology. It is the technology based on AI for solving new problems by adapting the known solutions of previous similar problems.

Data mining and CBR can be seen as complimentary methodologies for knowledge management in a broader sense. DM tools can help us extensively to learn and gain knowledge from the data sets. Still the reusability of the knowledge that is being extracted/gained is not very common. One way to improve the reusability is to use this knowledge base as front-ends to CBR applications.

In other words DM tools and technologies need to be integrated with CBR tools and technologies to reuse the knowledge in addressing identical

future problems. CBR is an artificial intelligence technology that uses previous knowledge from solved problems in order to give suggestions to the solution of new problems. In CBR, descriptions of previous expert experiences are represented as cases in a knowledge base, new problems are solved by adapting to solutions of similar cases in the past (Chowdhury, 2005).

Therefore, data mining is considered to be one of the ten most important technologies, in terms of the potential impact on wide-range of scientific, economic, socio-political and diverse other applications. Data mining focuses on the process of discovering knowledge while CBR focuses on the management and application of knowledge through representation, retrieval, re-use, revision and retention of case knowledge. However, knowledge management has not been central to data mining research so far. Data mining combined with CBR could be viewed as a general knowledge management and problem-solving tool. The resulting benefits could be better management of resources, greater efficiency and growth (Chan and Chowdhury, 2005).

REFERENCES

Agosta, Lou. (2005). Data Warehousing Lessons Learned: Hub-and-Spoke Architecture Favored. *DM Review*, March 2005.

Alley, M., Alonso, PJ., Womack, C & Yao, Y. (2006). Star or Dimensional Modeling. Assignment in Data Warehousing and Data Mining, *Term Paper*, WEHCBA, Roosevelt University, Summer 2006.

Atre, S. (2003a). The Top 10 Critical Challenges for Business Intelligence Success; *Computerworld;* June 30, 2003.

Atre, S. (2003b). Business Intelligence Success is Never an Accident; *Computerworld*; September 15, 2003.

Berry, M.J.A. & Linoff G.S. (2004). *Data Mining Techniques: For Marketing, Sales, and Customer Relationship Management* (paperback), 2nd Edition. ISBN: 0-471-47064-3, Wiley.

Breslin, M. (2004). Data Warehousing: Battle of the Giants; *Business Intelligence Journal*, pp 6-20; Winter 2004.

Chan, J., Witte, C. & Chowdhury, S. (2004). *Information Architecture for Electronic Customer Relationship Management*. Paper presented at the American Society of Business and Behavioral Sciences (ASBBS) conference, 2004.

Chan, J and Chowdhury, S. (2005). Enhancing Customer Services using Case-based Reasoning. Published in the communications of the ICISA – *the official journal of the International Chinese Information Systems Association*, Vol VII. Number 1, pp 53-61.

Chenoweth, T., David, S & Robert SL. (2003). A Method for Developing Dimensional Data Marts. *Communications of the ACM*, Vol. 45, No. 12, pp.93-98.

Chowdhury, S.I. (1990). Computer-Based Support for Knowledge Extraction from Clinical Databases, *Linköpings Studies in Science & Technology*. Dissertations No. 240, Linköping University.

Chowdhury, S. (2001). From Databases to Casebases: What, Why and How?" presented at the MBAA (Midwest Business Administration Association) –*SAIS (Society for the Advancement of Information System)* Conference, 2001.

Chowdhury, S. (2005). Lecture Notes on *A course on Data Warehousing and Data Mining*, WE-HCBA, Roosevelt University, 2005.

Chowdhury, S. (2005a). Tools and Techniques for Exploring Business Problems and Solutions and Attaining as well as Retaining Business Intelligence. presented at the MBAA (Midwest Business Administration Association) –*SAIS (Society for the Advancement of Information System)* Conference, 2005.

Chowdhury, S. (2006). *Project description in Data Warehousing and Data Mining Course*, WE-HCBA, Roosevelt University, Summer 2006.

Chowdhury S. (2007a). A Research Proposal on Model Conversion: E-R to Star Model. Roosevelt University, Spring 2007.

Chowdhury, S. (2007b). Methodology for Ensuring Data Quality in Data Warehouses, *Paper published in the Proceedings of the MBAA-SAIS (Midwest Business Administration Association - Society for the Advancement of Information System)*, March 28-30, 2007.

Chowdhury, S. (2007c). From ER to Star Data Modeling - A Methodology, Paper accepted for publication in the *Journal of American Society of Business and Behavioral Sciences* (ASBBS). Fall 2007.

Chowdhury, S. (2007d). Trends in Database Tools and Technologies, paper accepted for publication in the *Journal of The Business Review*, Cambridge, Vol. 7, No. 1, Summer 2007.

Chowdhury, S and Chan, J. (2007). *Data Warehousing And Data Mining: A Course In MBA And MSIS Program From Uses Perspective*. Paper presented at the 18th Annual Conference of IIMA (International Information Management Association), Beijing, China, October, 2007.

Desai, N. and Chowdhury, S. (2003). Data Mining for Competitive Business Advantages: Present and Future Implications. Published in the *Journal of American Society of Business and Behavioral Sciences* (ASBBS). Vol. 10, N0. 1, pp62-71, Spring 2003.

Fang, R., & Tuladhar, S. (2006). Teaching Data Warehousing and Data Mining in a Graduate Program of Information Technology. In *The*

Consortium for Computing Sciences in Colleges, pp. 137-144.

Galvan M. (2006). *Active Data Warehousing*. Term-paper in INFS413-X5: Data Warehousing and Data Mining, Roosevelt University, summer 2006.

Garcia, C., Janjua, T. & Galvan, M. (2006). *Northwind Traders Star Schema Model. Assignment in Data Warehousing and Data Mining*, Term Paper, WEHCBA, Roosevelt University.

Gillenson, M. (2005). *Database Processing: Fundamentals of Database Management Systems*, ISBN – 0-471-26297-8, Wiley, 2005.

Inmon, W. (2002*). Building the Data Warehouse*. 3rd ed. John Wiley and Sons.

Inmon, Bill. (2004). Information Management: Charting the Course: The Virtual Data Warehouse – Transparent and Superficial. *DM Review* March 2004.

Jukic, N. (2006). Modeling Strategies and Alternatives for Data Warehousing Projects. *Communications of the ACM*, Vol. 49, No. 4, pp. 83-88.

Kimball, R and Ross, M. (2002). *The Data Warehouse Toolkit*. 2nd ed. John Wiley & Sons.

Kroenke, D. (2002). Database Processing – *Fundamentals, Design and Implementation* (8th ed.). Pearson Education, Inc.

Laudon, K.C and Laudon, J.P. (2004). *Managing the Digital Firm*, Eigth Edition, Prentice Hall, Upper Saddle River, New Jersey.

Laudon, K.C and Laudon, J.P. (2006). *Managing the Digital Firm*, Tenth Edition, Prentice Hall, Upper Saddle River, New Jersey.

Lawyer, J and Chowdhury, S. (2005). Data Warehousing Practices – A success Story. *Published in GESTS (Global Engineering, Science and Technology Society) International Transactions on Computer Science and Engineering*, Paper field: Computer and its Application. Vol. 21 and No. 1. Nov. 2005.

Montalbano, J.P & Chowdhury, S.I. (2006). Business Intelligence Systems: Critical Considerations. Paper published in the *Proceedings of the MBAA-SAIS (Midwest Business Administration Association - Society for the Advancement of Information System)*, 2006.

Rieger, M. L. (2006). *Star Database Model: A comparison of 3 Alternatives with a Recommended Solution*. Assignment in Data Warehousing and Data Mining, Term Paper WEHCBA, Roosevelt University.

Sankar K. Pal, S. & Shiu C. K. (2004). *Foundations of Soft Case-Based Reasoning*. Wiley-IEEE, ISBN 0471086355.

Sen, A. & Sinha, AP. (2005). A Comparison of Data Warehousing Methodologies. *Communications of the ACM*, Vol. 48, No. 3, pp. 79-84.

Sperley, E. (1999). *The Enterprise Data Warehouse: The Planning, Building & Implementation*. Volume I: 1st edition, ISBN 0139058451, Prentice Hall.

The World Bank Group (2008). E-Government Definitions. Retrieved May 10, 2008, from http://go.worldbank.org/M1JHE0Z280.

Todman, C. (2001). *Designing a Data Warehouse: Supporting Customer Relationship Management (Paperback)*. ISBN: 0-13-089712-4. Prentice Hall.

Turban, E., Aronson, J.E., & Liang T.P. (2005). *Decision Support Systems and Intelligent Systems*, 7th Edition. Upper Saddle River, NJ: Prentice Hall.

Chapter II
A Framework for Knowledge Management in E-Government

Kostas Metaxiotis
National Technical University of Athens, Greece

INTRODUCTION

E-government, driven by an ever-increasing and pervasive use of information and communication technologies, is affecting the public sector more and more (Bannister, 2005; Eyob, 2004; Metaxiotis & Psarras, 2004). Many governments across the globe have resorted to instituting e-government initiatives as a way of better positioning themselves in the Information Age (Information for Development Programme [InfoDev], 2004), or seem at least to be showing commitments in redressing the imbalances resulting from the low utilization of knowledge resources and ICT in the economy and governance (Joi, 2004). E-government is enabling government organizations to provide better services to their constituents. The ability to improve citizens' access to services has made e-government an attractive investment for government organizations, fueling worldwide implementation of such applications (Amaravadi, 2005; Scherlis & Eisenberg, 2003). As an emerging practice, e-government seeks to realize processes and structures for harnessing the potentialities of information and communication technologies at various levels of government and the public sector for the purpose of enhancing good governance. The key issues in transformation are the adoption and uptake of interoperable standards, the development of appropriate business models, the legal and policy frameworks that will facilitate integration, and governance arrangements that support both enterprise responsibilities and cross-agency approaches and responsibilities.

On the other hand, in order to gain competitive advantage for their survival, most of the large companies in the private sector have been actively taking initiatives to adopt new management tools, techniques, and philosophies. Governments always follow suit. History shows that most of the management philosophies were first practiced in large companies; once they gained foot in the field, they became adopted in other sectors. Enterprise resource planning (ERP), business process reengineering (BPR), and total quality management (TQM) are indicative examples. Now comes the turn of knowledge management (KM). Governments are now realizing the importance of KM to their policy making and service delivery to the public, and some of the government departments are beginning to put KM high on their agenda.

Public administrations are knowledge-intensive organizations. They host a particularly high percentage of professionals and specialized staff who command important domains of knowledge. This is particularly the case in ministerial departments and in the judiciary and regulatory agencies. Many public organizations are chiefly "intelligence organizations" where human actors cooperate in order to store and process information and to produce information output for further use. If we ask the question, "How does the public administration know what it knows?" it becomes immediately evident that even though there is indeed a lot of knowledge in the organizations, it is not necessarily available anywhere, anytime for anybody. Not all parts of a public organization or even citizens can necessarily benefit from that knowledge. This means that a lot of "wheel reinventing" is going on in public administration.

Not only does the trend toward the knowledge society call for KM solutions (Davenport & Prusak, 1998; Metaxiotis, Ergazakis, & Psarras, 2005; Wiig, 1993) but also current e-government developments significantly influence the public sector. E-government implies fundamental knowledge redistribution and requires a careful rethinking of the management of information resources and knowledge bases.

Implementing a framework for the application of KM in e-government is a very challenging task as it requires many agencies, departments, and policy makers to coordinate their efforts in addition to preparing the technology and supporting the infrastructure—the soft infrastructure, meaning the laws, rules, and regulations that must be changed—in order to facilitate the development of both the new infrastructure and information and knowledge services. While most of the prior research studies have investigated the possible application of KM in the public sector, none have focused on the application of KM in e-government; this is done in this chapter. In this chapter, the author, recognizing the importance of e-government and KM to devolve into the public administration sector, continues his previous research related to the application of KM in e-government (Metaxiotis & Psarras, 2005), discusses key issues, and presents a framework for the application of KM in e-government as a basis for future research.

KNOWLEDGE MANAGEMENT IN E-GOVERNMENT: BACKGROUND

While literature on KM has been addressing issues, challenges, and opportunities for the private sector, little has been discussed for the public sector, and even less in e-government. Frank (2002) reported that several e-government initiatives in USA are using knowledge management principles as the way to knock down the stovepipes that keep government from operating as efficiently as it could....The idea of "collect once, use many" is a common theme in several of the 24 e-government initiatives led by the Office of Management and Budget...

Lenk (2003) presented typical situations in order to stress the specific significance of KM for the public sector.

- Clerical and professional work concerning individual cases to be decided upon
- Individual services to citizens
- Pursuit, by citizens or enterprises, of business or personal affairs involving public bodies
- Management of administrative work and organizations
- Policy formulation by ministerial departments and other public bodies
- Parliamentary work

Other researchers (Stracke, 2002; Bresciani, Donzelli, & Forte, 2003; Palkovits, Woitsch, & Karagiannis, 2003) recognized that in order to efficiently manage e-government evolution, it is fundamental to transform the public administration into a learning organization, characterized by a high level of sharing, reuse, and strategic application of the acquired knowledge and lessons learned. A learning organization is an organization that facilitates the learning of all its members and continuously transforms itself. The basic idea behind it is to create a knowledge chain (collection, production, customization, and delivery) suitable to support and improve the whole organization functioning.

Bruecher (2003) presented the development of a requirement analysis for a KM system in the field of e-government; the objective of the analysis was to figure out the various requirements of the heterogeneous user group and to provide the basis for a more detailed blueprint of the system. Key issues, challenges, and opportunities of KM in the public sector were addressed by Cong and Pandya (2003).

According to Liebowitz (2004), KM in an e-government environment can be a powerful tool for reformers, inside and outside government. Recently, Metaxiotis and Psarras (2005) discussed the application of knowledge management in e-government initiatives and described a knowledge model as a basis for future research in the field.

THE PROPOSED FRAMEWORK FOR KNOWLEDGE MANAGEMENT IN E-GOVERNMENT

The Positioning of Knowledge Management in E-Government

Nowadays, it is quite clear that the traditional bureaucratic model of government is no longer functional. E-government can contribute to better functioning of democracy by online provision of reports and other government information (open government) that would otherwise be difficult to obtain or be unavailable, and through online debates and plebiscites. It can bring efficiency through providing citizens with relatively inexpensive, real-time access to consistent, up-to-date information and transaction facilities, and in parallel can enable governments to disseminate information at lower costs than ever before. Simultaneously, modernization and reorganization of governmental work and responsibilities imply significant changes to knowledge resources. KM concepts and tools can really provide great support to exploit the huge knowledge and information resources, and assist e-government introduction to a modern public administration in an effective way. The positioning of a KM system in an e-government environment is presented in Figure 1, adopted by Manuel (2005).

A good e-government model provides a platform where various communities and special-interest groups represent themselves; it builds an environment with specialized expertise that can help answer questions and guide people to find solutions. This is called the community management system of e-government. E-government is a transition process from a conventional to a people-oriented proactive electronic system. To accept this transition process, the communities need to be trained and educated, and in addition the model should be accessible by different communities including the disabled and the underprivileged. This is called the transition management system of e-government. A knowledge management system provides an environment where knowledge flows from a source with knowledge to a destination that needs knowledge and/or captures knowledge and creates new knowledge. Finally, a good e-government environment needs to maintain a powerful integrated hardware and software network so that several billions of information and knowledge pieces can be found in this system by users. This is called the infrastructure management system of e-government.

Figure 1. The positioning of knowledge management in e-government

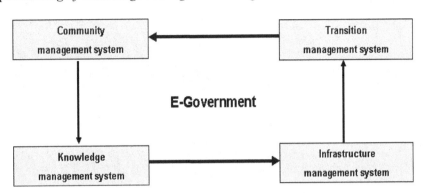

The Proposed Framework

As e-government implementations progress, the focus shifts from simply providing access to services in electronic form to actively engaging citizens or empowering various stakeholders to create an electronic, knowledge-based democracy. Increasingly knowledgeable citizens require governments to be on top of newly created knowledge as it is increasingly rapidly produced by more differentiated actors. Malhotra (2000) has stressed that a new perspective of KM is to be effectively deployed in the world of e-business.

Due to the fact that public administrations and their organizational environments are characterized by the presence of very diverse kinds of actors (e.g., citizens, employees, businesses, politicians, and decision makers), the critical point for applying a KM concept to e-government is principally to build a suitable knowledge model (Metaxiotis & Psarras, 2005) and then to create an appropriate framework for the application of KM in e-government environments, having in mind the positioning of KM in e-government (Figure 2).

We used the following main principles for deriving our framework.

Universal access. Every citizen has the right to access basic and relevant knowledge of all aspects of society; therefore, the framework should offer knowledge-sharing services that can be accessed through multichannels and multidevices.

Public education and training. Every citizen should be equipped with skills to be independently involved in the knowledge-based society.

Infrastructure development. An affordable, secure, and reliable information, knowledge, and communication infrastructure should be developed on a local, regional, and national level with an efficient connectivity to global networks. The hard infrastructure will create a broadband system linking every home, school, and public institution within the community.

Unified KM portal. Portal technologies should integrate content, applications, and processes together. Hence, the portal can deliver better communications and collaboration between citizens, businesses, suppliers, public institutions, and so forth, providing real-time access to knowledge stored in various systems and knowledge bases to push citizens to store, apply, or create new knowledge.

Customer-centric communication and knowledge sharing. Is knowledge provided based on customer-perceived preferences, needs, and desires? Does the definition mention customer focus or customer preferences? Is there an avenue for customers to address their preferences, needs, and desires?

Based on the above-mentioned principles, we have conceptualized our framework for the application of KM in e-government, which is presented in Figure 2.

Figure 2. The proposed framework

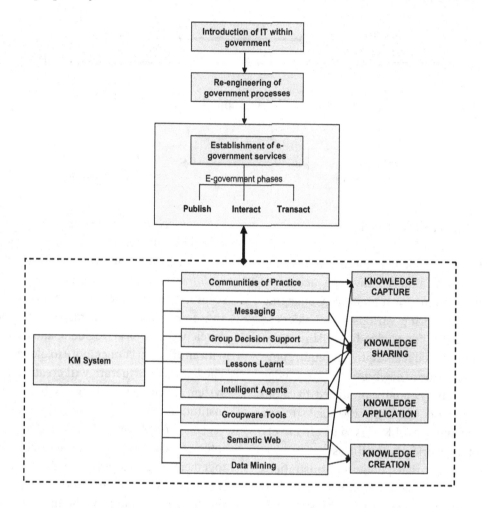

The proposed framework points that the gradual development of e-government environments in public-sector organizations is similar to the one in private-sector organizations. "If you automate inefficient processes, they will become more inefficient" is a well-known adage in the IT community. Reengineering is in many instances necessary to align an agency's internal processes with those of other agencies or governments and thus facilitate cooperation. Without this, e-government will remain only partial and therefore is likely to be an unsuccessful exercise.

In the phase of the establishment of e-government services, we follow the World Bank's (Center for Democracy and Technology [CDT], 2002) model, which defines three stages.

- **Publish:** Broadening access to government information
- **Interact:** Increasing public participation in government decision making
- **Transact:** Making government services more readily available to the public

Due to the high complexity in e-government applications and sometimes the "fuzziness" in public administration procedures, the application of KM principles is a difficult task that should be combined with traditional business process management actions. The development of a KM system in an e-government environment can touch each of the above-mentioned stages and can be related to any of the KM processes: knowledge capture, knowledge sharing, knowledge application, and knowledge creation. Knowledge identification and capture refer to identifying the critical competencies, types of knowledge, and the right individuals (civil servants) who have the necessary expertise that should be captured. Then, this captured knowledge is shared between individuals, departments, and the like. The knowledge application involves applying, which includes retrieving and using, knowledge in support of decisions, actions, and problem solving, and which ultimately can create new knowledge. As new knowledge is created, it needs to be captured, shared, and applied, and the cycle continues.

Depending on which KM process or function we want to apply to an e-government phase, we can use the appropriate technology, as shown in Figure 2. It is obvious that the application of KM in e-government, based on the proposed framework, should be necessarily characterized by the "divide and conquer" rule; due to the high risk involved, the government organizations need to modularize the KM initiative efforts and implement them one piece at a time.

It is important to be stressed that the supply side of such a framework requires a range of legislative changes, which is a key issue. Legislative changes could include the recognition of electronic documents in courts of law, electronic signatures, data matching, knowledge protection, the certification of knowledge, and intellectual property rights legislation. Regulatory changes are also required for a host of activities from knowledge capture to knowledge creation and knowledge-based service delivery. On the other hand, the demand side of the framework gives customers access to online knowledge-based services through multiple channels and systems. This framework includes developing a critical mass of manpower and knowledge sufficient to support an e-governance strategy. Unless citizens are trained and have requisite skills to participate in e-governance, citizens' participation and engagement would be a difficult task for evolving electronic, knowledge-based democracy.

Applying the Proposed Framework in a Greek Municipality

The application of the proposed framework to the Greek municipality is, according to our best knowledge, the first attempt to bring KM into e-government in real practice.

The municipality of Maroussi is located in the north suburbs of Athens, about 11 km from Athens' center, at the foot of Penteli Mountain. About 70,000 inhabitants live in the municipality and its area is 16.2 m². In economical terms, it is one of the most important municipalities in Greece. It is the center of financial and cultural development. The city's infrastructure is well developed and a series of quality services are offered to the citizens. Some of the city's most important assets are the following.

- In its premises lies the main complex in which the majority of the Olympic Games 2004 activities have taken place, such as the opening and closing ceremony and a series of important field sports. This was a major event for the local region, as well as the whole country. Due to the Olympic Games, many of the city's infrastructures (e.g., road axes, public transportation, and sports installations) have been significantly improved. Many other positive interventions have also taken place.

- Due to the Olympic Games, the whole region gained publicity and reputation outside the country, something that created new ways of cooperation with other cities.

- Maroussi is the heart of the modern economic life in Athens since it hosts the offices of many innovative and hi-tech enterprises. There are more than 1,800 medium and large companies that are based in the city representing the following sectors: telecommunications, IT, financial services, insurance, construction, and so forth. More than 33,000 people are working in these companies.

- It is one of the largest commercial centers in Greece, with many stores and shopping malls.

- The municipality offers to all of its citizens, through a series of innovative (compared to other municipalities in Greece) lifelong learning initiatives, the possibility to acquire a high level of skills and knowledge so as to remain competitive in the contemporary, competitive environment.

- The local government is very active in various sectors. It tries to implement new and modern methods of organization and to improve the municipality's infrastructure so as to attract businesses and offer a high quality of life.

It is true that not every city in the world can pursue strategies and undertake initiatives so as to be transformed successfully into a KM-based e-governed city. In other words, these strategies will not eventuate into the desired results for every city, at least to the extent in which they would permit one to characterize their use as a successful case. A city should have the necessary level of development, on the basis of which the proposed framework will be applied, so the whole effort will bring successful results. Although all urban regions contain knowledge activities, not all cities can be knowledge centers.

The application of the proposed framework to Maroussi started in early 2006 and is still ongoing. The results until now show that the proposed framework is being successfully applied and put into practice in spite of the given constraints (e.g., limited funding, political will, public bureaucracy, and so forth). The pilot project began with a period of familiarization of the municipality's local government with the concepts of KM and knowledge-based development (KBD), and continued with the diagnosis of its current status as an e-governed city. This diagnosis constituted the main input for the next stage: the definition of the implementation strategy. An analytical action plan was prepared, incorporating a detailed description of needed actions or projects (for each year). The results, outcomes, and lessons learned at the end of this pilot project will be used in order to assess the applicability of the framework and fine-tune the implementation methodology.

MEASURING KNOWLEDGE MANAGEMENT IN E-GOVERNMENT

Measuring KM is a difficult task. During the E-Gov Institute Knowledge Management 2004 Conference, the American Productivity & Quality Center (APQC) focused on how some government organizations implement KM initiatives, mobilize resources, and measure and evolve their KM programs (APQC, 2004) by stressing that "[j]ust because knowledge is intangible does not mean that its impact is."

Some of the very important measurement points from the APQC study include the following.

- Cost reduction
- Quality improvement
- Increase in services provided
- Citizen satisfaction
- Time saved
- Quick problem resolution

Detailed discussion on the above measurement points and proposed models for the measurement of knowledge are not in the scope of this chapter.

FUTURE TRENDS

The above described framework is quite comprehensive and is helpful in identifying measures to assess knowledge-based e-government implementation for e-participation and e-democracy. Future research should focus on examining the effectiveness of the proposed framework. Detailed questionnaires and other survey instruments could be developed from this framework to assess citizens' participation and engagement.

Finally, a major future challenge is the application of the framework to a big city, which will incorporate structures missing from our case (e.g., hospitals, universities) and at the same time, it will be able to make available larger amounts of funds from the beginning of the initiative. Concluding, we can say that the application of knowledge management in e-government is clearly an area that needs to be more fully addressed.

CONCLUSION

E-government is the latest buzzword for governments trying to involve people in administration, address transparency in their bureaucracies, and make themselves more responsive to their citizens. It has become an everyday reality, but still needs to be shaped with vision and long-term planning. E-government success requires changing how government works, how it deals with information and knowledge, and how officials view their jobs and interact with the public.

Knowledge management is the mental, behavioral, and cultural shift from the old adage "Knowledge is power" to the new mindset "Sharing knowledge is power." It is important to note that acting and decision making in the public sector is not a prerogative of management. Complex decisions are made at the operational level, and it is precisely here that most knowledge demands originate. In general, knowledge management is not only required to know which rules and regulations to apply, but also to be able to reconstruct afterward whether the right procedures were followed.

This chapter has attempted to integrate the two fields of KM and e-government into one singular focus to foster new strategic thinking in KM-based e-government. A framework for the application of

KM in e-government was presented and discussed. Since most products of public administration and governance work are delivered in the shape of information and knowledge themselves, KM concepts and tools can really provide great support to the introduction of e-government into a modern public administration. In addition, the retirement of civil servants and frequent transfer of civil servants across government departments also create new challenges for the application of KM in the public sector. Knowledge management is a promising way to enlarge the scope of e-government and improve the modernization and reorganization of governmental work.

FUTURE RESEARCH DIRECTIONS

Visions of knowledge-based e-government or a global-knowledge government are being discussed in the scientific community. There is a common agreement that KM can offer many advantages in e-government. However, as it also happened in the early stages of the evolution of KM, there is neither a coherent framework nor a unified methodology for the design and implementation of successful KM applications in e-government. Consequently, a major stream of future research is to propose coherent frameworks and methodologies for the design, development, and operation of successful KM applications in e-government.

Undoubtedly, there is need for concerted efforts toward the direction of formulating a generally accepted, comprehensive framework for KM in e-government. However, the role of technology in this effort should not be underestimated. This is reflected by the fact that according to recent studies, the technologies used to support KM initiatives are evolving rapidly. Consequently, another stream of future research is to use advanced KM technologies and tools for the proper development of successful KM applications in e-government. In what follows, there is a classification of KM tools that is available in the market and could be used.

- Knowledge Mapping
- Data Mining
- Information Retrieval
- Knowledge Discovery
- Document Management
- Organizational Memory

On the other hand, any KM initiative that is driven purely by technology, without a corresponding change in the culture of the organization, is certain to eventually fail. Too often, organizations implement state-of-the-art technology and then discover that culture and behavior are slow to change. The success of KM initiatives in many fields (including e-government) depends equally to the active involvement of everyone throughout the organization as well as to their consistency with the organization's broader business strategy and culture. Technologies and social systems are equally important in KM. Organizations that follow the KM program with clear objectives and approaches and that manage to coordinate their social relations and technologies tend to be more successful, whereas some other organizations that implement a KM initiative with focus on IT in order to reap some quick benefits without having focus on the human side and a long-term strategy fail. This is the case for KM initiatives in e-government, and consequently more research should be directed in this specific subfield.

REFERENCES

Amaravadi, C. (2005). Digital repositories for e-government. *Electronic Government: An International Journal, 2*(2), 205-218.

American Productivity & Quality Center (APQC). (2004, April). *Measuring the impact of knowledge management*. Proceedings of the E-Gov Institute Knowledge Management 2004 Conference.

Bannister, F. (2005). E-government and administrative power: The one-stop-shop meets the turf war. *Electronic Government: An International Journal, 2*(2), 160-176.

Bresciani, P., Donzelli, P., & Forte, A. (2003). *Requirements engineering for knowledge management in egovernment*. Proceedings of the Fourth Working Conference on Knowledge Management in Electronic Government, Rhodes Island, Greece.

Bruecher, H. (2003). *Requirement analysis for a knowledge management system in egovernment*. Proceedings of the Fourth Working Conference on Knowledge Management in Electronic Government, Rhodes Island, Greece.

Center for Democracy and Technology. (2002). *2002 digital state survey*. Retrieved from http://centerdigitalgov.com

Cong, X., & Pandya, K. (2003). Issues of knowledge management in the public sector. *Electronic Journal of Knowledge Management, 1*(2), 25-33.

Davenport, T., & Prusak, L. (1998). *Working knowledge: Managing what your organisation knows*. Boston: Harvard Business School Press.

Eyob, E. (2004). E-government: Breaking the frontiers of inefficiencies in the public sector. *Electronic Government: An International Journal, 1*(1), 107-114.

Frank, D. (2002). *E-gov theme: "Collect once, use many."* Retrieved from http://www.fcw.com/fcw/articles

Information for Development Programme (InfoDev). (2004). *E-government handbook for developing countries*. Retrieved from http://www.infodev.org

Joi, L. (2004). Bridging the digital divide: Some initiatives in Brazil. *Electronic Government: An International Journal, 1*(3), 300-315.

Lenk, K. (2003). *Relating knowledge management in the public sector to decision-making and administrative action.* Proceedings of the Fourth Working Conference on Knowledge Management in Electronic Government, Rhodes Island, Greece.

Liebowitz, J. (2004). Will knowledge management work in the government? *Electronic Government: An International Journal, 1*(1), 1-7.

Malhotra, Y. (2000). Knowledge management for e-business performance. *Information Strategy: The Executives Journal, 16*(4), 5-16.

Manuel, P. (2005). A model of e-governance based on knowledge management. *Journal of Knowledge Management Practice*, pp. 1-10.

Metaxiotis, K., Ergazakis, K., & Psarras, J. (2005). Exploring the world of knowledge management: Agreements & disagreements in the research community. *Journal of Knowledge Management, 9*(2), 6-18.

Metaxiotis, K., & Psarras, J. (2004). E-government: New concept, big challenge, success stories. *Electronic Government: An International Journal, 1*(2), 141-151.

Metaxiotis, K., & Psarras, J. (2005). A conceptual analysis of knowledge management in e-government. *Electronic Government: An International Journal, 2*(1), 77-86.

Palkovits, S., Woitsch, R., & Karagiannis, D. (2003). *Process-based knowledge management and modelling in e-government: An inevitable combination.* Proceedings of the Fourth Working Conference on Knowledge Management in Electronic Government, Rhodes Island, Greece.

Scherlis, W., & Eisenberg, J. (2003). IT research, innovation and e-government. *Communications of the ACM, 46*(1), 67-68.

Stracke, J. (2002). *E-government: Supporting knowledge and information flows with supply chain management.* Proceedings of the Third Working Conference on Knowledge Manage-

ment in Electronic Government, Copenhagen, Denmark.

Wiig, K. (1993). *Knowledge management foundations: Thinking about thinking. How people and organizations create, represent and use knowledge.* Arlington, TX: Schema Press.

FURTHER READING

Amidon, D. M. (2004). *In the knowledge-zone: Architecting a blueprint for the World Trade of Ideas.* Retrieved from http://www.inthekzone.com

Amin, A., & Thrift, N. (1995). The globalisation of the economy: An erosion of regional networks? In G. Grabher (Ed.), *The embedded firm.* London: Routledge.

Arboníes, A. L., & Moso, M. (2002). Basque Country: The knowledge cluster. *Journal of Knowledge Management, 6*(4), 347-355.

Asheim, B. T. (1996). Industrial districts as learning regions: A condition for prosperity. *European Planning Studies, 4*, 379-400.

Bailey, C., & Clarke, M. (2000). How do managers use knowledge about knowledge management? *Journal of Knowledge Management, 4*(3), 235-243.

Baqir, M. N., & Kathawala, Y. (2004). "Ba for knowledge cities: A futuristic technology model. *Journal of Knowledge Management, 8*(5), 83-95.

Carrillo, F. (1999). *The knowledge management movement: Current drives and future scenarios.* Paper presented at the Third International Conference on Technology, Policy and Innovation: Global Knowledge Partnerships. Creating Value for the 21st Century, Austin, TX. Retrieved from http://www.knowledgesystems.org

Carrillo, F. J. (2002). Capital systems: Implications for a global knowledge agenda. *Journal of Knowledge Management, 6*(4), 379-399.

Carrillo, F. J. (2004). Capital cities: A taxonomy of capital accounts for knowledge cities. *Journal of Knowledge Management, 8*(5), 28-46.

Chatzkel, J. (2004). Greater Phoenix as a knowledge capital. *Journal of Knowledge Management, 8*(5), 61-72.

Davenport, T., & Prusak, L. (1998). *Working knowledge: Managing what your organisation knows.* Boston: Harvard Business School Press.

DeLong. (1996). *Endogenous growth: Economic theory and faster growth.* Retrieved from http://econ161.berkeley.edu/OpEd/endo

Drucker, P. (1998). From capitalism to knowledge society. In D. Neef (Ed.), *The knowledge economy* (p. 15). Woburn, MA: Butterworth.

Ergazakis, K., Karnezis, K., Metaxiotis, K., & Psarras, J. (2005). Knowledge management in enterprises: A research agenda. *Intelligent Systems in Accounting, Finance and Management, 13*, 17-26.

Ergazakis, K., Metaxiotis, K., & Psarras, J. (2004). Towards knowledge cities: Conceptual analysis and success stories. *Journal of Knowledge Management, 8*(5), 5-15.

Ergazakis, K., Metaxiotis, K., & Psarras, J. (2005). An emerging pattern of successful knowledge cities' main features. In J. Carrillo (Ed.), *Knowledge cities: Approaches, experiences and perspectives.* Academic Press, Butterworth-Heinemann/Elsevier.

European Commission. (2000). *Innovation policy in a knowledge-based economy.* Brussels, Belgium: Office for Official Publications of the European Communities.

Gibbons, J. H., & Malone, T. F. (2001). Intergenerational ethics. *New Ethical Challenges in Science and Technology: Proceedings of a Sigma Xi Forum in Albuquerque NM, 9-10 November 2000* (pp. 149-161, 180).

Komninos, N. (2002). *Intelligent cities: Innovation, knowledge systems and digital spaces.* Routledge.

Laszlo, K. C., & Laszlo, A. (2002). Evolving knowledge for development: The role of knowledge management in a changing world. *Journal of Knowledge Management, 6*(4), 400-412.

Laszlo, K. C., Laszlo, A., Campos, M., & Romero, C. (2002). Evolutionary development: An evolutionary perspective on development for an interconnected world. *World Futures.*

Maier, R., & Remus, U. (2003). Implementing process-oriented knowledge management strategies. *Journal of Knowledge Management, 7*(4), 62-74.

Malone, T. F. (1995). Reflections on the human prospect. In R. H. Socolow (Ed.), *Annual review of energy and the environment* (pp.1-19). Palo Alto, CA: Annual Reviews.

Malone, T. F. (1998). A new agenda for science and technology for the twenty-first century. *Proceedings of the KOSEF's 20th Anniversary Symposium on Issues of Science and Technology in the 21st Century* (pp. 67-90).

Malone, T. F., & Yohe, G. W. (2002). Knowledge partnerships for a sustainable, equitable and stable society *Journal of Knowledge Management, 6*(4), 368-378.

Mansell, R. (2002a). Constructing the knowledge base for knowledge-driven development. *Journal of Knowledge Management, 6*(4), 317-329.

Mansell, R. (Ed.). (2002b). *Inside the communication revolution: Evolving patterns of social and technical interaction.* Oxford: Oxford University Press.

Mansell, R., & Steinmueller, W. E. (2002). *Mobilising the information society: Strategies for growth and opportunity.* Oxford: Oxford University Press.

Metaxiotis, K., Ergazakis, K., & Psarras, J. (2005). Exploring the world of knowledge management: Agreements and disagreements in the academic/practitioner community. *Journal of Knowledge Management, 9*(2), 6-18.

Milton, N., Shadbolt, N., Cottman, H., & Hammersley, M. (1999). Towards a knowledge technology for knowledge management. *International Journal of Human-Computer Studies, 51*, 615-641.

Rubenstein-Montano, B., Liebowitz, J., Buchwalter, J., McGaw, D., Newman, B., & Rebeck, K. (2001). SMARTVision: A knowledge-management methodology. *Journal of Knowledge Management, 5*(4), 300-310.

TERMS AND DEFINITIONS

Collaborative Tools: Collaborative tools are electronic tools that support communication and collaboration: people working together; essentially they take the form of networked computer software.

Community Management System: This is a platform where various communities and special-interest groups with specialized expertise represent themselves and try to find solutions to specific problems.

Data Mining: Data mining is a process of automatically searching large volumes of data for patterns such as association rules. It is also called knowledge discovery in databases (KDD).

Distributed Knowledge Management Model: This is the model that combines the interdependence of one partial product state model to others with the idea of knowledge acquisition rather than just an operational exchange relationship.

Groupware Tools: These are specific software tools that allow groups of people to share information and to coordinate their activities over a computer network.

Intelligent Agents: This is a software agent that exhibits some form of artificial intelligence that assists the user and will act on his or her behalf in performing repetitive computer-related tasks.

Semantic Web: The Semantic Web is a new technology that intends to create a universal medium for information and knowledge exchange by putting documents with computer-processable meaning (semantics) on the World Wide Web.

Chapter III
E–Government Knowledge Management (KM) and Data Mining Challenges:
Past, Present, and Future

LuAnn Bean
Florida Institute of Technology, USA

Deborah S. Carstens
Florida Institute of Technology, USA

Judith Barlow
Florida Institute of Technology, USA

ABSTRACT

Powerful data mining models and applications in e-government settings have the potential to bring major benefits to a wide range of stakeholders. As these models evolve, structural transitions occur within e-government to which include an evolution of managerial practices through knowledge management (KM). Unfortunately these efforts are vulnerable to a number of critical human interaction and behavioral components. This chapter examines e-government challenges regarding the linkages between data mining and KM over time, discusses the organizational development of e-government applications, and details both general and specific social, ethical, legislative, and legal issues that impact effective implementations. A final focus of the chapter is the potential strategic benefits of a risk-based approach that can be used to improve the core synergy of KM and data mining operations in e-government operations.

INTRODUCTION

Data mining in both the private and public sectors has focused on its ability to reveal patterns, relationships, and connections between behaviors or variables. From an e-government standpoint, data mining has the potential to bring major cost and convenience benefits to all stakeholders, including citizens and businesses. While the proliferation of data mining applications can provide very powerful data management tools, organizations employing these initiatives have been vulnerable to misunderstanding implementation limitations and oversight issues. When examined more closely, the majority of these limitations are closely linked to miscalculations about the human components that interface with these systems rather than the technology capabilities of a computer network. These human interaction and behavioral issues include such vulnerabilities as: (1) a dependence on data pattern and relationship determinations by analysts, (2) varying competencies and deficient analytic skills of specialists interpreting the data for knowledge management (KM) purposes, (3) falsely identifying relationships between variables that do not necessarily equate with causation, (4) misunderstanding information awareness issues of data quality and integrity, (5) mission creep (or the use of data for purposes beyond its primary collection), (6) privacy of data, (7) inadequate security of data (based on the interoperability needs of several organizations and user groups and the complexity of the distribution), (8) ethical breaches of users and suppliers of information, and (9) inadequate attention to laws and insufficient policies (Seifert, 2004).

In order to examine e-government's challenges regarding the linkages between data mining and KM over time, this chapter focuses on the organizational development of e-government applications that have evolved and currently interface with both general and specific social, ethical, legislative, and legal issues. The chapter also concludes with a future perspective regarding a risk-based approach for e-governments – one that improves the core synergy of KM and data mining operations.

BACKGROUND AND EVOLUTION OF E-GOVERNMENT AND DATA MINING

The history of e-government computing architectures and applications has seen similar developments to those evolving in the corporate world. While large, expensive mainframe computers of the 1960s and 70s were programmed to process inventory control and materials management data, the majority of costs were simply focused on capturing data in a machine-readable format and getting it into the system, accounting for over 80% of software project costs in the period from the 1960s through the early 1990s (Hazzan, Impagliazzo, Lister & Schocken, 2005).

Emphasis on data integrity concerns about the proper handling of data containing dates reached a climax in the late 1990s, causing many organizations to invest in high-performance database systems to avoid potential catastrophic errors when the year 2000 rolled around. A side effect of the rush to avoid Y2K problems, whether real or imagined, caused firms to implement large, expensive database management systems that led to better data capture, data storage, data processing and data sharing capabilities (Robertson & Powell, 1999).

With this new found wealth of cheap, accurate, timely, accessible and processable data from post-2000 information systems, the costs of deploying data mining applications was reduced, leading to new methods of explicitly capturing "knowledge" or "intelligence" from the large (and growing) data stores (Schwaig, Kane & Storey, 2005). The result is that data mining methods can be applied not only to an organization's own data stores but also to data copied, purchased or stolen from external sources or other government agencies.

TRANSFORMING DATA MINING EFFORTS THROUGH KNOWLEDGE MANAGEMENT

As Wagner, Cheung, Lee, and Ip (2003) note, e-governments most likely concentrate their data mining efforts as part of an evolutionary model, which moves their managerial practices toward knowledge management (KM) through four distinct structural transformations. In the first mode (known as broadcasting), governments initially present a web presence, which is limited to static web pages and one-way communication. From there, e-governments transition to the second mode, known as interaction, whereby websites exchange information or services with citizens, which allows them to inquire and obtain limited database resources from websites located behind a portal. The third stage, or transaction structure, allows users to execute financial matters with the governments and, therefore, requires more advanced processing capabilities and security measures. Finally, at the integration stage, the e-government environment evolves to a single contact point for all involved departments, so that no duplication of efforts exists.

Within these e-government stages, knowledge management becomes the most critical focus of data mining when it surpasses the broadcasting level, where citizens can inquire, officials respond to public needs, and there is interoperability between government offices or departments. Wagner et. al (2003) explain that e-governments must focus on different goals for KM needs that bridge relationships with the public, as well as those interactions within and between governmental departments. Essentially, transactions with the public, whether they are about a payment or a question about a regulation, must be focused on addressing an inquiry with a knowledgeable response that reflects the integrity of the system. In a slightly different vein, the relationship within a governmental department must focus on the improvement of the efficiency in providing knowledge, such that speed and accuracy are improved. Finally, the sharing effect of knowledge between departments has even a different goal, which is the objective of improving the reusability of knowledge without unnecessary duplication. Given these varied models and objectives, the mining of data combined from unrelated sources becomes a particularly critical e-government challenge which may potentially lead to legal disputes, persistent inaccuracies, violations of privacy, and other ethical concerns (Pollach, 2007; Taipale, 2003).

MAXIMIZING KM PRACTICES: ORGANIZATIONAL FACTORS

In order to achieve maximization of these goals and avoid the pitfalls mentioned, e-government must leverage knowledge assets through: (1) organizational adaptation and development of a knowledge culture, (2) continual reexamination of how the data and information technologies are used, (3) close attention to external risks (both general and specific) that reflect social, political and legal challenges, and (4) forward-looking planning for dealing with risks that will impact future practices.

As a critical foundation for achieving maximum knowledge performance and effectiveness supported by data mining applications, several researchers (Oliver & Kandadi, 2006; Batra, 2006) point to organizational culture and strategic flexibility. According to Batra (2006), innovative design of KM systems in these types of environments are more closely aligned with business strategies and ensure that IT is used for acquiring, consolidating, transferring and utilizing organizational knowledge in a strategic manner.

Oliver & Kandadi (2006) present ten factors that mold and develop this innovative knowledge culture. They include leadership, organizational structure, evangelization, communities of practice, reward systems, time allocation, business processes, recruitment, infrastructure and physical attributes. In many respects, the first factor for e-government initiatives, which is leadership, must reflect the "tone at the top" or a supportive environment that emphasizes senior management goals. The key to this factor is empowerment of primarily middle and front-end managers that can help make necessary changes that drive the improvement and success of KM implementations.

The second factor that is important to a forward-thinking KM environment in e-government is the development of an organizational structure that effectively embeds KM roles into core functional areas, such as service delivery, citizen empowerment, or exposure and outreach. Using a blended approach of embedding KM functions within positions throughout the organization allows for an integration of KM programs that makes knowledge management a part of everyone's position and department. Thus, it allows for an overall enhanced knowledge culture.

Evangelization, a third factor, requires the spreading of information about how KM is transforming the e-government process. As such, this factor requires various communication channels to convey the significance of processes and achievement outcomes resulting from KM and touts its mutual benefits to all users. Within an organization, this factor is advanced by such measures as regular identification and rewards for employees who make a difference in knowledge sharing and improvement.

A fourth factor, originally coined by Lave and Wenger (1991), suggests that communities of practice (or CoPs) strengthen knowledge cultures. These CoPs are commonly defined as overlapping functional departments within government organizations that work to solve collective problems with knowledge.

Reward systems (mentioned in connection with evangelization) comprise a fifth factor, which must be fine-tuned to foster a knowledge culture. As noted in a number of KM studies,

the review of human resource management practices that appraise knowledge contributions and directly or indirectly reward employees for these efforts should be maximized—even to the point of weighting overall performance appraisals up to 20 percent for these knowledge initiatives (Ardichvilli, Page, & Wentling, 2003; Malhotra and Galletta, 2003; McLure and Faraj, 2000).

A predominant sixth factor is the allocation of time necessary for developing a knowledge culture. While senior management may give lip service to knowledge creation strategies, without time devoted to employee learning and collaborative activities, KM targets cannot be achieved. Within an e-government environment, this may be more effectively achieved through a pilot project approach, as is promoted by researchers Paul (2003) and Reinhardt (2005).

The seventh factor for development of data mining within a sustainable e-government KM culture is the key focus on business processes. As experts note, an analysis of the core processes along the value chain indicating how data flow is provided to users should focus on the standardization in capturing and reusing functional knowledge (Nissen and Levitt, 2004; Wenger, 2004).

Recruitment is the eighth factor affecting KM and a culture that propagates it. E-governments should strive to find potential employees that have aptitudes and positive attitudes toward improving knowledge sharing as part of a team.

Without infrastructure (the ninth factor), which includes adequate data mining technologies and intranets and extranets that allow for efficient and effective collaboration, power grabs of hoarding information or inaccessible pockets of information will inhibit KM culture.

Finally, the physical attributes of a workspace can be very important in promoting knowledge sharing. Structural environments housed within physical locations that have common or shared meeting rooms and open spaces encourage social networking and can heighten the advancement of KM practices among employees.

MAXIMIZING KM PRACTICES: INFORMATION TECHNOLOGIES

Organizations must continually reexamine how their data and information technologies are used from the aspect of internal operations within the government as well as external interactions with citizens, businesses and other governments (Ray & Mukherjee, 2007). This enables e-government initiatives to avoid failures resulting from a techno-centric focus rather than a governance-centric or stakeholder focus (Saxena, 2005). In other words, failed e-government systems typically concentrate on the quantity of technological capabilities rather than the quality of service outcomes and goal effectiveness. A number of KM studies note that most knowledge initiative failures are due to an under-emphasis on the human interaction, quality planning, and behavioral vulnerabilities in knowledge sharing (previously discussed) and a disproportional over-emphasis on the information technology (Moffett, McAdam & Parkinson, 2003; Mohamed, Stankosky, & Murray, 2006; Smith, McKeen & Singh, 2006).

This is not to say that the information technology is not important. As a supportive function, it can enhance knowledge creation, storage/retrieval, transfer, and application. Automating internal operations can improve operating costs, response times, resource utilization and overall efficiency and effectiveness in delivery of public services, transparency and accountability in government processes, and increased information flow (both internally and externally). External operations can be maximized through development of accurate and quality system information, multiple different access or touch points for users (mobile devices, public kiosks, Internet, etc.), user-friendly user interfaces, access to training programs, and support to assist users. With regard to enhancing human interaction, systems should be built to ensure that interfaces have the ability to work with the user in presenting and getting information at a level that matches their competency (Vouros,

2003). Furthermore, maximizing KM practices through information technologies also require that these systems be flexible in design and able to support interoperability, scalability, and high performance (Ray & Mukherjee, 2007).

The key point is that technology is only one part of the equation and must ultimately be viewed as a way to effectively deliver knowledge to be used in an active manner. As Smith et. al (2006) notes, when users experience problems with this delivery system, they lose faith in the integrity of the e-government implementation and, in many cases, avoid any future ordeals by opting out of the process. In this all too often failed IT scenario, the results are that active knowledge sharing breaks down and cannot be leveraged for maximum e-government advantage.

GENERAL RISKS AND CHALLENGES: SOCIAL, ETHICAL, LEGISLATIVE AND LEGAL

Numerous social, ethical, political, and legal risks and challenges in connection with information transformations are causing all organizations, including e-governments, to examine privacy, piracy, safety, data security, data integrity, competence, honestly, loyalty, and fairness (Himma, 2007; Chow, 2001). Furthermore, government is under continuous scrutiny to increase its effectiveness or accountability, while reducing or eliminating decision-making risks associated with transactions. Within the e-government realm, development of socially responsible policies is required to ensure effective knowledge management in public services (Riege & Lindsay, 2006). These social responsibilities must include building trust and confidence from citizens that use e-government services and transactions (Ebrahim & Irani, 2005).

In the last few years, many government departments and agencies have created innovative and complex systems connecting people to information by focusing on knowledge management practices. The result is that e-government has emerged as a defining force by replacing traditional means of accessing public services. For example, Ray and Mukherjee (2007) report that national e-government health initiatives in India must address such social challenges as how to provide access to individuals below the poverty line and in rural communities, as well as maintain sustainability of this private-public partnership. This common problem, not limited to any one country, faces primary or underlying social concerns, including what levels of education, training and support are needed for current and potential users of e-government systems. Researchers note key social paradoxes in creating these systems and point to implementation failures that: (1) cater to a population of literate individuals only, (2) do not consider other communication issues (such as language barriers or provide English-only systems), or (3) do not consider integration of conventional norms of the populations, such as an assimilation of ancient practices with traditional medicine (Ray & Mukherjee, 2007; Gasson & Shelfer, 2007).

Beyond these social challenges are the potential for ethical breaches. These remain fundamental problems for e-government implementations due to the vast amount of information maintained, the size and complexity of governmental structures, and a lack of standards (Koh, Ryan & Prybutok, 2005). Since every level of government uses, collects, processes and disseminates sensitive information containing personal, financial and medical data, this has enabled organizations to too easily reprocess the information and disseminate it (Hewett & Whitaker, 2002). Unfortunately, as Ebrahim & Irani (2005) state, the benefits gained by data mining and knowledge management practices in e-government can all be erased when organizations do not view the information as confidential but instead as a commodity to be bought and sold. Therefore, a higher standard of ethics in e-government knowledge management practices must be supported by the continued development of codes of conduct and governance policies on data banks (Verschoor, 2000).

To fill the social and ethical voids of organizations with limited or deficient knowledge policy development, legislators and the legal profession have stepped in to help control the dissemination of information by addressing: (1) what data can be collected, (2) who should be notified of collected data, (3) under what conditions can collected data be stored, (4) the right of individuals to access and call for corrections to the stored data, and (5) the limits to use and disclosure of the stored data (Hewett & Whitaker, 2002). This is by no means limited to e-government practices but encompasses the corporate world as well. One example is the United State's Health Insurance Portability and Accountability Act (HIPPA) of 1996. This legislation spans both business and government protection of individuals' data privacy. Included in the Act are directives regarding which patient data can be used or disclosed, the identification of individuals or organizations that will authorize patient information, requirements about patient authorization signatures, and information about the initial and expiration dates of patient agreements (Rafalski & Mullner, 2003).

Finally, it is interesting to see how the legal profession is currently struggling with the proliferation and accumulation of electronic data within all corporate and government organizations—tremendous data stores amassed for various purposes, including data mining. While many government agencies are immune to lawsuits, recent rulings in the U.S. court system may have a "seachange" effect on the interface of data mining/KM projects for certain e-government entities, as well as the data privacy and enforcement policies. The balance of this chapter examines specific new quagmires for increased e-government data mining/KM policies and presents a risk-based approach to deal with them.

SPECIFIC RISKS:
E-DISCOVERY RISKS
SPILLOVER TO E-GOVERNMENT

One of the most recent changes for some e-governments is analogous to having government organizations create a treasure map detailing where all the electronic records are buried. This was the result of the Civil Rules Advisory Committee of the U.S. Judicial Conference, who crafted a proposed amendment to address the fact that traditional paper rules were too outdated to apply to unprecedented electronic data problems facing our legal system. In particular, their proposal addressed the legal treatment of automatically created metadata, the retrieval of "deleted" data, and, most urgently, the sheer volume of electronic information collected, which may or may not be used for data mining purposes (U.S. Judicial Conference, 2005). This proposal resulted in the newly revised Federal Rules of Civil Procedures (FRCP), which went into effect on December 1, 2006. Under these procedures, both private and public organizations must be able to provide electronically stored data in e-discovery lawsuits or face the prospect of penalties and courtroom losses. In addition, these rules go on to clarify that document metadata is also part of e-discovery and must be considered in every case. Basically, the courts are saying that if data are digital and deemed relevant, they are discoverable. Thus, as discoverable, all the data must be found, preserved, and examined.

Two key court cases provide relevant background leading to these new rules. Experts consider the most influential case on e-discovery rules to be Zubulake vs. UBS Warburg, 217 F.R.D. 309 (S.D.N.Y. 2004). The central focus of this case was: How do you determine what electronic evidence is accessible? In a series of rulings, this discrimination case addressed the questions of what electronic evidence was discoverable, how the cost of discovering electronic records should be shared among parties, and whether sanctions

should be imposed on the defendants for failing to produce evidence. Before this opinion, most companies or government organizations did not have document retention programs. Laura Zubulake, a former UBS employee, was awarded $29 million in 2005 in her sexual discrimination lawsuit. (Krause, 2007; Rodier, 2007).

The second case was that between Morgan Stanley vs. Ronald Perelman, where Perelman charged the company with deceiving him about Sunbeam's financial success in order to gain his acceptance of the stock for a buyout offer of his company, Coleman. In this case, Morgan Stanley essentially claimed that they were unaware of the situation and the $1.57 billion jury ruling against them hinged almost completely on their lax e-discovery procedures (Rodier, 2007).

According to Gibson (2006), the risk for organizations, including governments, is that the proliferation of data mining and computer storage vehicles, as well as unyielding growth of electronically stored information (ESI) and system architectures, may now result in just as critical an issue for enterprise content management (ECM) as previous legislation enacted under the Sarbanes-Oxley (SOX) Act. As data repository capacities continue to swell through additional devices, like a wide range of handheld PDAs to thumb drives to cell phones, many organizations may not even be aware of their risk exposure. (Although a bit dated, one can get an idea of the magnitude of this data explosion by looking at the report from the School of Information Management and Sciences (SIMS) at the University of California at Berkeley (Lyman & Varian, 2003). This SIMS study found that about five exabytes of new data were created worldwide in 2002 alone, which is equivalent to half a million new libraries the size of the Library of Congress print collection. Of this new information, ninety-two percent was electronic and stored primarily on hard disks.)

Interestingly, changes in these federal rules that govern civil litigation have prompted state and local governments to take a closer look at their electronic data stores. In the event that they become litigants in federal courts, the rules will apply to e-government entities, particularly those for cities and school districts.

As consolidation of knowledge assets/data mining initiatives have been implemented to help government agencies examine programs and improve services, the risk exposure associated with e-government and these data warehouses has increased. Britt (2007) notes that the city of Minneapolis ramped up its knowledge management efforts in February 2007 with a new ECM system, when its e-government development manager calculated that research for a single litigated investigation under the new FRCPs would cost the city as much as $100,000.

In the face of these new court challenges, several critical issues were faced by organizations employing significant data stores. These include the following:

1. Organizations must consider proactive measures with a long-term, integrated approach to e-records management policies. According to Cummings (2007), many organizations must recognize the fine line of data with no relevant business use and those processes that identify preferred supplier/client relationships and pilot-tested workflows. This requires a records-retention policy focused on information you cannot justify keeping or potentially mining. A well-planned policy will eliminate unexpected "dormant liabilities" in the form of unnecessary data and create a standardized way to preserve relevant information, through audit trails that prevent spoliation (or the alteration of ESI or its metadata). Thus, a risk-based approach is recommended, which assesses all data exchange relationships.

2. Many vendors see the FRCPs as the next big "gold rush." As Eden (2007) points out, firms purporting to have a quick fix for getting informational data houses in order

actually released more than 4,000 press releases after the Morgan Stanley case (noted earlier). In these instances, organizations must do their homework about a vendor's search capabilities, financial health, security measures that preserve privacy, insurance coverage maintained, and potential legal conflicts. While some vendors offer tools that institute litigation holds (which may include audit trails that support policies for the collection and preservation of relevant ESI), many do not offer strong search or culling tools that are context sensitive and customizable for an organization. The greater capabilities that these solutions can supply, as far as indexing, clustering, search and retrieval, and context support, the more benefit they are to the organization.

A RISK-BASED APPROACH FOR E-GOVERNMENTS: FUTURE PLANNING FOR IMPROVED SYNERGY OF KM AND DATA MINING OPERATIONS

As with any endeavor, clear articulation of goals, plans and strategies are necessary for success. The following discussion presents a basic risk-based planning approach for achieving dynamic knowledge transfers through KM and data mining operations in e-government.

First, planning for KM and data mining operations should clearly identify the essential goals to be achieved in the e-government setting. This means that planning must consist of establishing commitment and governance procedures, identifying stakeholders, defining the mission and value, identifying governance issues such as with efficiency or effectiveness, and determining the scope of the e-government system(s) (Saxena, 2005). As with any project plan, other basic components of these efforts consist of cost, quality, and time (or what Nemanti and Barko (2003) refer to as the Iron Triangle). Each of these three factors can be further broken down. In evaluation of cost, technology should be looked at from the standpoint of the costs affiliated with maintaining a system. There should also be a link between costs and the benefits associated with improved efficiency as well as satisfied users. The second factor, quality, should be examined to ensure that a system is reliable. Furthermore, the technologies must be effective and have a social, ethical, and environmental impact. The third factor, time, should analyze the validity of a system to produce information of appropriate quality while recognizing how the information itself will be used. This factor positively impacts organizational learning, strategic goals, and recognizes questions of privacy and security.

Second, the common technological issues in KM and data mining operations should be examined as part of risk-based planning. By understanding these issues in advance, unexpected risks can be prevented or avoided all together. Initially, the KM system being developed needs to be designed to adequately address user requirements. This necessitates understanding the diverse use of each knowledge asset and, in simple terms, means that the user community must first be defined. Within most e-government applications, the user community is generally comprised of citizens, government employees, other governments, and businesses. Once this is done, Bose (2002) suggests this understanding should be broadened to include a perspective of how, when and where the system will be interacting with users, as well as identifying the type of decision support processes involved. Other researchers further recommend that the development and maintenance of information repositories and collaborative applications should selectively target the types of information that are easily available, find knowledge within organizations that can be developed and maintained in a cost-effective manner, foster an environment that supports user feedback, and be

engineered to automatically acquire new knowledge sources and check for consistency of this information (Abecker, Bernardi, Hinkelmann, Kuhn & Sinteck, 1998; Vouros 2003). Addressing the technological risk of not only finding the knowledge but also delivering the knowledge for individual consumption is also imperative. Therefore, the interfaces for these technologies must be developed as user-friendly functions, if e-government systems are to be adopted, accepted and ultimately used (Ray & Mukherjee, 2007). Finally, proposals to secure funding for the technological requirements of KM and data mining operations should recognize the critical establishment of system maintenance and upgrades, as well as proper infrastructure, physical housing, and internal training (Gao, Li & Nakamori, 2002; Gasson & Shelfer, 2007).

Third, a study of the social aspects of KM and data mining efforts should be undertaken to ensure success of e-government systems. A wide range of social issues associated with users of e-government systems can include language barriers, literacy levels, and technical skills (Ray & Mukherjee, 2007). Researchers note that access points (such as the web, public kiosks, information centers and mobile devices) as well as the makeup of citizen communities can significantly impact successful implementations (Nemati & Barko, 2003; Ray & Mukherjee, 2007). Whenever possible, it is advisable to establish partnerships to enhance community support and ensure success of these e-government efforts. Additional training initiatives to help bridge the gap of the digital divide, such as basic e-literacy or Internet training, can enhance adoptions and the number of participants reached through these systems. As outlined above, these three basic considerations for risk-based planning are critical for managing e-government KM challenges and should be part of the continual improvement and monitoring phases for systems, even after implementation.

CONCLUSION

Over the last decade, the list of government departments and agencies with innovative and complex systems to connect people to information through KM practices continues to grow (Ebrahim & Irani, 2005). Leveraging knowledge assets within government requires examination of internal organizational and technology factors, as well as external risks associated with social, ethical, political and legal challenges. As the popularity of e-government information systems and data mining efforts increases, storage of greater amounts of potentially sensitive data face the same issues as purveyors of sensitive data in the public section—primarily those related to data accuracy and data accessibility (Himma, 2007).

KM and data mining go beyond concerns of data accuracy and data access in search of intelligence or meaning gleaned from its data stores. KM and data mining applications need to address privacy and security issues and move beyond technical systems toward social systems that ensure the human, social and organizational aspects (Rogerson, Weckert & Simpson, 2000). In e-government, social responsibilities are targeted toward the development of policies that ensure effective knowledge management in public services (Riege & Lindsay, 2006). To fill the social and ethical voids of organizations with limited or deficient knowledge policy development, legislators and the legal profession have stepped in to help control the dissemination of information by addressing: (1) what data can be collected, (2) who should be notified of collected data, (3) under what conditions can collected data be stored, (4) the right of individuals to access and call for corrections to the stored data, and (5) the limits to use and disclosure of the stored data (Hewett & Whitaker, 2002). As noted in this chapter, the benefits of data mining and knowledge management may all be lost when organizations view the minable data as a commodity to be bought and sold (Ebrahim & Irani, 2005). Instances of mining data from unrelated sources may lead to legal disputes, persistent inaccuracies, violations of privacy, and other ethical concerns (Pollach, 2007; Taipale, 2003). With the rise of e-commerce, e-government and the affordable, yet sophisticated features of data mining software, personal information have become an easy target of sharing or cross-referencing across networks (Forcht & Thomas, 1994). It has been noted how legislation and the legal profession have taken the role of "putting out brushfires" created by a lack of data governance policies. In particular, this research detailed the legal profession's most recent introduction of new e-discovery rules that will impact enterprise content management for e-government applications.

This research has also addressed strategic issues to ensure successful leveraging of knowledge assets which were through: (1) organizational adaptation and development of a knowledge culture, (2) continual reexamination of how the data and information technologies are used, (3) close attention to external risks (both general and specific) that reflect social, political and legal challenges, and (4) forward-looking planning for dealing with risks that will impact future practices. Authors promote a proactive risk-based planning approach for the integration and continuous improvement of KM and data mining operations in e-government – one that addresses current and future challenges. From a strategic standpoint, incorporating the risk-based planning into a continual feedback loop for improvement is the best way to address the fundamental challenges of e-government KM and data mining efforts. Despite the fact that it can be a relatively lengthy process, it stimulates new concepts, as well as accelerates their definition and development. E-government stakeholders who participate in this feedback gain insights into the technology, but more importantly provide new ideas that can accelerate and influence their future transactions. Drawing from a white paper by the Computer Science and Telecommunications Board (2002), authors believe the following three-pronged strategy in coordination with the risk-based planning approach that were presented should be considered. This strategy by e-government entities would include: (1) a longitudinal analysis of past programs, including both positive and negative experiences of stakeholders, as well as expectation fulfillments of users, (2) identification of other program management models that provide a good comparative approach for alternative directions, and (3) identification of proven program strategies that are in sync with management's evaluation of acceptable risks and time horizons.

A wealth of opportunities exists for research related to applications of KM in e-government. General research in KM and data mining applies to the public sector in much the same way as it does in the public sector, including more efficient algorithms for data matching across independent data stores. Future research should evaluate the efficacy and accuracy or KM applications in e-government and examine their impacts on citizen privacy. Survey research examining strategic implementations of KM in various government settings and their implications for citizens and their governments would be a good starting point for further study. Further research could target and identify e-governance initiatives that have been undertaken to best meet citizens' needs. Finally, network analysis research methods could provide an interesting measurement approach for future studies, thereby helping to understand and enhance the variety, strength, content, and structure of adopters or users of e-government applications. By coupling best practices research with a better understanding of stakeholder linkages (through link tracing studies or snowball sampling techniques), data mining and KM processes could be further explored for purposes of fine-tuning operational efficiency, effectiveness, and excellence in e-government.

REFERENCES

Abecker, A., Bernardi, A., Hinkelmann, K., Kuhn, O., & Sintek. M. (1998). *Techniques for Organizational Memory Information Systems.* DFKI GmbH: DFKI Document D-98-02.

Ardichvilli, A., Page, V. & Wentling, T. (2003). Motivation and barriers to participation in virtual knowledge-sharing communities of practice. *Journal of Knowledge Management, 7*(1), 64-77.

Batra, S. (2006). Impact of information technology on organizational effectiveness: a conceptual framework incorporating organizational flexibility. *Global Journal of Flexible Systems Management 7*(1/2), 15-25.

Bose, R. (2002). Customer relationship management: key components for IT success. *Industrial Management & Data Systems, 102*(2), 89-97.

Britt, P. (2007). Government gets a grip on knowledge sharing. *KMWorld*, April 1. Retrieved September 3, 2007, from http://www.kmworld.com/Articles/ReadArticle.aspx?ArticleID=35777&PageNum=1

Chow, W. S. (2001). Ethical belief and behavior of managers using information technology for decision making in Hong Kong. *Journal of Managerial Psychology, 16*(4), 258-267.

Cummings, Joanne. (2007). How e-discovery can save you big bucks. *Network World*, May 22. Retrieved September 6, 2007, from http://www.itworldcanada.com/Pages/Docbase/ViewArticle.aspx?id=idgml-5ae90c98-4918-4e2d-b8aa-9be-1611fe6f2

Computer Science and Telecommunications Board. (2002). *Information technology research, innovation, and e-government.* Retrieved May 14, 2008, from http://books.nap.edu/openbook.php?record_id=10355&page=R1

Ebrahim, Z. & Irani, Z. (2005). E-government adoption: architecture and barriers. *Business Process Management Journal, 11*(5), 58-611.

Eden, S. (2007). Vendors jump on e-discovery bandwagon. *Intelligent Enterprise, 10*(1), 9.

Forcht, Karen A., & Thomas, Daphyne S. (1994). Information compilation and disbursement: moral, legal and ethical considerations. *Information Management and Computer Security, 2*(2), 23-28.

Gao, F., Li, M. & Nakamori, Y. (2002). Systems thinking on knowledge and its management: systems methodology for knowledge management. *Journal of Knowledge Management, 6*(1), 7-17.

Gasson, S. & Shelfer, K.M. (2007). IT-based knowledge management to support organizational learning Visa application screening at the INS. *Information Technology & People*, *20*(4), 376-399.

Gibson, S. (2006). The urgent need for e-data management at the enterprise level: the impending implosion of electronic stored information. *Computer and Internet Lawyer, 23*(8), 5-8.

Hazzan, O., Impagliazzo, J., Lister, R. & Schocken, S. (2005). Using history of computing to address problems and opportunities. In J. Dougherty (Ed.), *Proceedings of the 36th SIGCSE technical symposium on computer science education* (pp.126-127). New York, NY: Association for Computing Machinery, Inc.

Hewett, W. G. & Whitaker, J. (2002). Data protection and privacy: the Australian legislation and its implications for IT professionals. *Logistics Information Management, 15* (5/6), 369-76.

Himma, K. E. (2007). Foundational issues in information ethics. *Library Hi Tech, 25*(1), 79-94.

Koh, C. E., Ryan, S. & Prybutok, V. R. (2005). Creating value through managing knowledge in an e-government to constituency environment. *The Journal of Computer Information Systems, 45*(4), 32-42.

Krause, J. (2007). E-discovery gets real. *ABA Journal, 93*, 44-51.

Lave, J. & Wenger, E. (1991). *Situated Learning: Legitimate Peripheral Participation.* New York, NY: Cambridge University Press.

Lyman, P. & Varian, H.R. (2003). *How much information?* Retrieved September 6, 2007, from http://www2.sims.berkeley.edu/research/projects/

Malhotra, Y. & Galletta, F.D. (2003). Role of commitment and motivation in knowledge management systems implementation: theory, conceptualization, and measurement of antecedents of success. In R.H. Sprague (Ed.), *IEEE Computer Society Proceedings of the 36th Annual Hawaii International Conference on System Sciences (HICSS'03)* (Track 4, Volume 4, page 115.1) Washington, D.C.: IEEE Computer Society.

McLure, W. & Faraj, S. (2000). It is what one does: why people participate and help others in electronic communities of practice. *The Journal of Strategic Information Systems, 9*(2/3), 155-73.

Moffett, S., McAdam, R. & Parkinson, S. (2003). An empirical analysis of knowledge management applications. *Journal of Knowledge Management, 7*(3), 6-26.

Mohamed, M., Stankosky, M. & Murray, A. (2006). Knowledge management and information technology: can they work in perfect harmony? *Journal of Knowledge Management, 10*(3), 103 – 116.

Nemati, H.R. & Barko, C.D. (2003). Key factors for achieving organizational data-mining success. *Industrial Management & Data Systems, 103*(4), 282-292.

Nissen, M.E., & Levitt, R.E. (2004). Agent-based modeling of knowledge dynamics. *Knowledge Management Research & Practice, 2*(3), 169-183.

Oliver, S. & Kandadi, K.R. (2006). How to develop knowledge cultures in organizations? A multiple case of large distributed organizations. *Journal of Knowledge Management, 10*(4), p. 6-24.

Paul, L.G. (2003). Why three heads are better than one: how to create a know-it-all company. *CIO Magazine, 17*(5), 94-106.

Pollach, I. (2007). What's wrong with online privacy policies? *Communications of the ACM 50*(9), 103-108.

Rafalski, E. & Mullner, R. (2003). Ensuring HIPAA compliance using data warehouses for healthcare marketing. *Journal of Consumer Marketing, 20*(7), 29-633.

Ray, S. & Mukherjee, A. (2007). Development of a framework towards successful implementation of e-governance initiatives in health sector in India. *International Journal of Health Care Quality Assurance, 20*(6), 464-483.

Reinhardt, R. (2005). Implementation of an intellectual capital management system: advantages of a "bottom-up" approach. *Journal of Universal Knowledge Management, 0*(1), 67-73.

Riege, A. & Lindsay, N. (2006). Knowledge management in the public sector: stakeholder partnerships in the public policy development. *Journal of Knowledge Management, 10*(3), 24-39.

Robertson, S. & Powell, P. (1999). Exploiting the benefits of Y2K preparation. *Communications of the ACM, 42*(9), 42-48.

Rodier, M. (2007). E-Discovery: a daunting task -- as electronic data proliferates, complying with e-discovery rules becomes more difficult - and more costly. *Wall Street & Technology, 25*(9), 23.

Rogerson, S., Weckert, J. & Simpson, C. (2000). An ethical review of information systems development – the Australian computer society's code of ethics and SSADM. *Information Technology & People, 13*(2), 121-136.

Saxena, K.B.C. (2005). Towards excellence in e-governance. *International Journal of Public Sector Management 18*(6), 498-513.

Schwaig, K. S., Kane, G. C., & Storey, V. C. (2005). Privacy, fair information practices and the fortune 500: the virtual reality of compliance. *SIGMIS Database 36*(1), 49-63.

Seifert, J.W. (2004). Data mining: an overview. *CRS Report for Congress, December 16.* Retrieved December 1, 2007, from http://www.fas.org/irp/crs/RL31798.pdf

Smith, H., McKeen, J., & Singh, S. (2006). Making knowledge work: five principles for action-oriented knowledge management. *Knowledge Management Research and Practice, 4(*2), 116 – 124.

Taipale, K. (2003). Data mining and domestic security: connecting the dots to make sense of data. *Columbia Science & Technology Law Review, 5(2).* Retrieved September 11, 2007, from http://www.stlr.org/html/volume5/taipaleintro.php

U.S. Judicial Conference. (2005). *Report of the Civil Rules Advisory Committee 40 (amended July 25, 2005).* Washington, D.C.: Reprinted in Communications on the Rules of Practice and Procedure of the Judicial Conference of the U.S., Summary of Committee on Rules of Practice and Procedure: Agenda E-i8 app. C.

Verschoor, C. (2000). Can an ethics code change behavior? *Strategic Finance, 82*(1), 26-28.

Vouros, G.A. (2003). Technological issues towards knowledge-powered organizations. *Journal of Knowledge Management, 7*(2), 114-127.

Wagner, C., Cheung, K., Lee, F., & Ip, R. (2003). Enhancing e-government in developing countries: managing knowledge through virtual communities. *The Electronic Journal on Information Systems in Developing Countries 14*(4), 1-20.

Wenger, E. (2004). Knowledge management as a doughnut: shaping your knowledge strategy through communities of practice. *Ivey Business Journal, 68*, 1-7.

Chapter IV
Knowledge Management Portals for Empowering Citizens and Societies

Hakikur Rahman
SDNF, Bangladesh

ABSTRACT

Knowledge management is not a simple technology driven modus operandi, rather it is policy driven issue that is intermingled with technology, decision, management and intellectuality. Along this route, empowering common citizens utilizing knowledge development utilities is a challenge to the researchers and development practitioners. Furthermore, dissemination of intellectual content on the Web for public view, their understanding, capacity development, and specifically for being utilized as a tool to increase their social, educational, political and economic ability is by far the most difficult part of the system. The process complicates further, when emerging technologies are being adopted to provide the solution, especially for the common people of the community with their social and political implications. However, in recent years, knowledge management has become a new branch of system management for achieving breakthrough in entrepreneurship, social and governance performance synergizing people, process, technology and policy. At the same time, emerging technologies like, data mining are being utilized for carrying out intelligent decision among dispersed source of huge data. Semantic Web Technologies are also being incorporated in the decision making processes. This chapter is focusing on knowledge management issues for developing knowledge management portals to empower citizens and societies. In this context, the chapter introduced critical aspects of knowledge management perspectives, justified establishment of knowledge management portals acting as a tool of empowerment, provided insight on data mining as a technology of implementation, throws a solution by introducing Semantic Web Technologies as an essential technology for establishing knowledge management portals, puts forward contemporary challenges during the establishment of knowledge management portal, illustrated a few cases that are acting as knowledge management portals, and concluded before giving a few hints on future research issues for empowering common element of the society.

INTRODUCTION

Knowledge Management (KM) is not merely a technology-driven process rather a policy imperative, facilitated by technology for better management and a system with increased utilization of the system's intellectual and business assets. Usually, KM decisions are based on who (people), what (knowledge) and why (objectives); leaving the how (technology) to be derived from the first three parameters. In this perspective, the basic aim is to leverage wealth of information that are currently available within a system to maximize impact and results. Moreover, critical sets of data, information and knowledge assets should be identified, captured and effectively disseminated within and outside the system (UN, 2005).

Knowledge, information and data are considered to be a system's principal assets and a main source of its comparative advantage (UN, 2005). Management of knowledge is, therefore, becomes essential to make the system more valuable to the stakeholders. Management of knowledge or knowledge management is primarily evolves within the society by the cumulative desire of the common citizens. These are indigenous knowledge. As time proceeds, technology advances, complexity of storage of huge data or information becomes simpler, dissemination process become more efficient, KM systems turned towards promoting their economic value. Gradually, KM systems could able to grasp attention of business communities.

The role of relevant information, knowledge and communication in development is at the core of attention. With regard to access to information, it appreciates the importance of access to the global information pool, but attaches equal importance to feeding local content into the system, based on the right of social and cultural appearance, diversity and communication (Fust, 2003).

In recent years, Knowledge Management has become a new branch of business management for achieving breakthrough in business performance

through the synergy of people, processes and technology. It evolved from the need for advancing beyond the failing paradigm of information and communications technology (ICT) management that accounts for over 70%-80% system failures. As 'ICT' becomes more of a commodity and endowed with more complex 'potential' capabilities, the need for re-focusing on its strategic execution emerges. Furthermore, during this transition process from an era of information scarcity to information overload, there is a need to re-focus on human sense-making processes underlying decisions, choices, and performance. In this new paradigm of increasingly uncertain and complex business environments, dynamically evolving performance outcomes are the key drivers of how 'smart minds' use 'smart technologies' to leverage strategic opportunities and challenges (Brint dot com, 2007; Berry & Linoff, 2004).

Along these contexts, not only development of KM systems is important, but also dissemination of knowledge through pertinent KM systems is essential. Despite the newly evolved technologies, not many methodologies or algorithms are available in the contemporary field for providing solutions to manage huge sets of content. Furthermore, algorithms complicate further with scarcity of known methodologies, when the contents are being utilized to produce knowledge, especially for the common masses. Therefore, knowledge management to empower the common citizens remains an intricate issue to all involved in this field.

The complicacy deepens further while researchers incorporate methodologies, as such data mining to extricate accurate information from a set of huge data. There are Bayesian, apriori, decision-tree, clustering, prediction, neighbor and similar algorithms are available to provide solutions for generating knowledge from data synthesizing their inherent content. Data mining products are taking the knowledge management field by strong thrust. Major research houses and entrepreneurs in this arena are incorporating data mining techniques in their knowledge acquisition processes (Jin & Agrawal, 2003).

However, accumulation and dissemination of knowledge through appropriate knowledge management system remains a challenge to the agents who are actively involved in establishing knowledge banks. The knowledge bank usually takes the form of traditional print, data driven content or web based portal. Given the diverse nature and hugeness of data and information, a web-based portal is the best solution to reach the increasing on-line communities across the world. A portal that is easily accessible to the end user, understood by most of them, creates positive attitude towards livelihood and foremost, adds value to their life acting as a knowledge enhancement gadget is a knowledge management portal.

Knowledge management portals are a common form of knowledge management system and act as simplified and standardized platform of common interface to all. In Figure-1, portal interface to a knowledge management system has been illustrated, where data is the core element of the management system, though knowledge management system has been shown as four separate entities, but they should be interpreted as a conglomerated entity, as a whole. Similarly, Table-1 illustrated different possible component of a knowledge management portal.

As evident from Table 1, a KM portal enclave could almost all the possible component of soceity activities. Through appropriate tools and techniques, these faculties of knowledge paradigm belonging to communities can add, knowledge gain to the common elements of the society. These tools could be data mining, techniques could be Semantic Web Technologies and solution could be holistic KM portal.

A typical knowledge management system largely depends on data acquisition techniques and data mining is one of the important components to tackle. However, due to the nature and scopes of this chapter, detail on data mining techniques will not be covered, rather a few definition points will be touched in the background section while justifying the relationship of data mining as an

Figue 1. Interface between a portal and the knowledge management system (Source: author)

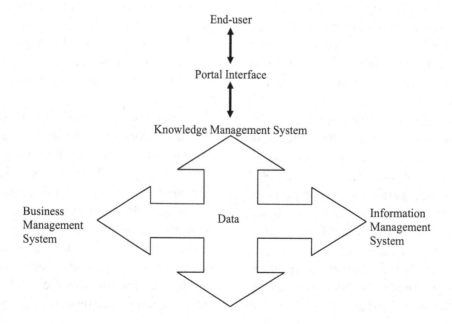

Table 1. Different probable components of a knowledge management portal (Source: author)

Knowledge Management		
Financial Services	Social Services	**Government Sector Services**
Accounting	Healthcare	Government
Banking	Hospitality	Public sector
Customers	Medicine	Human resources
Consulting	Agriculture	Logistics
Manufacturing	Education	Military
Marketing	Entertainment	Engineering
Supply chain	Environment	Legal issues
Small business		Technology

important technique in the knowledge management system. For sake of generalized concept, the relationship between data mining and KM portal will be figured out, data mining techniques and their potentialities will be discussed and adoption of KM portal in the empowerment process of common citizens and societies will be outlined.

This chapter emphasizes on issues related to the management of KM portals that are used to create and generate knowledge among citizens and societies. By societies, it is meant that a group of people with common interest and gathered in terms of similar social, cultural, political and economic ranking. This chapter will outline implication of data mining and incorporation of appropriate tools in the development of knowledge management portals, justification and challenges in developing knowledge management portals, illustrate a few cases and finally put forward some recommends in the form of hints for future researches.

BACKGROUND

Information is a basic need of life. With growing interdependence of information in human life, access to information becomes crucial for people who have to adapt their livelihood strategies in dynamic information-based environments. Ac-

cess to information is a prerequisite for survival in the modern world that is characterized by global economic and political dynamics relevant for each and every component of the society. Access alone is, however, not sufficient. Adequately utilizing information, transforming it and creating knowledge out of it requires scopes, competencies and opportunities. Being empowered incorporates being capacitated for making meaningful use of information in view of improving and sustaining ones livelihoods. Empowerment, therefore, is a second prerequisite for survival and for socio-economic development as the fundamental paradigm for a surviving global society (Fust, 2003).

Knowledge refers to the totality of attained information and skills that an individual utilizes in solving various problems. This encompasses theoretical insights, as well as practical day-to-day rules and behavior. Knowledge is information perceived and utilized by individuals in guiding their proceedings. Information can be used by an individual only in the form of knowledge in contrast to information, whereas knowledge is bound to the person and always structured by the individual so as to perceive his or her expectations in terms of causes, effects, and connections. Pieces of information can be processed automatically, and may, establish an enhancement of value and/or a contribution to the task of converting it to knowledge. Perhaps, knowledge can either consciously be formulated or able to be formulated in language/expressible form (explicit knowledge) or not (implicit knowledge)[1].

Information and knowledge are crucial assets of the global information-based society. Nowadays, knowledge is increasingly produced within the private sectors. With the emergent tendency of privatized media, knowledge and information are being transformed into a private good for exclusive use (Fust, 2003). However, knowledge and its management have become more relevant in their business usage in terms of economic values.

Knowledge Management (KM) thinking within development partners has come a long way since the concept first crossed over from the private sector in the late 1990s. The World Bank was the first to embark on an ambitious KM programme. Since then most other development agencies have taken crucial steps, though with have varied approaches in terms of the terminology and the levels of investment (Barnard, 2003).

The need for better knowledge sharing within and among development agencies is an essential element of project management. There are familiar problems that most agencies are only too aware of. Project documents getting lost, data are not updated, evaluation lessons being ignored, consultant reports getting buried, research being bypassed, lessons learned are ignored, field experiences being wasted when staff move on, organizational learning being blocked by hierarchies or internal structures, agencies not knowing what each other are doing, partnership or sharing of information among similar agencies being ignored, and foremost, local stakeholders being left out of the loop. In addressing these challenges, the starting point for most agencies has been to begin management at the organization level by getting their own house in proper order. This should be the default approach within the corporate sector. Many corporate houses are adopting KM within their agencies first and reaping its benefits. But,

still the question remains as, is it necessarily the best way of encouraging knowledge sharing in a development context? And, even if the answer is yes, what could be the other alternatives (Barnard, 2003)? Should an organization depend on a single channel of information for its development? Perhaps, these issues will be taken care of in the future research section.

KM, a recent megatrend in business administration, emphasizes the asset-character of knowledge and, thus, of the new perception of human elements as being knowledgeable. This insight coincides with a second megatrend, originating in the development world; the acknowledgement of the crucial role of knowledge and expertise, especially in local knowledge, for securing sustainable livelihoods (Fust, 2003).

In its first generation KM concentrated on the organizations and analysis of data and information, on archiving documents and making them available through search and retrieval, whereas in second generation KM focuses on people. Skills of using information purposefully, storing information as knowledge in human brains and making knowledge available in human interactions are largely becoming key aspects of the present-day view of KM. (Sharp, 2003)

Knowledge management is a responsive strategy aimed at obtaining the right knowledge to the right people at the right time, and assisting people share and put information into action in ways that strive to improve organizational performance. At the same time, KM needs to focus on creating a culture of knowledge sharing and learning. Eventually, KM is a permanent contend for learning, in adapting new conditions and challenges, and accordingly changing practices (including programmes, procedures, organizational structures) with a view to improve these practices, doing job better, and increasing efficiency[2].

KM PORTAL AND THEIR SOCIAL IMPLICATIONS

This section comprises the main thrust of this chapter. In this section, application of data mining techniques in society development processes will be introduced; the relationship of data mining and KM portals will be justified; utilization of KM portal in the empowerment process of societies and citizens will be illustrated and finally, how Semantic Web technologies are being utilized in establishing KM portals will be put forward.

KM Portals and their Social Responsibilities

A Web site or service that offers a broad array of resources and services like e-mail, forums, search engines, and on-line shopping malls. The first Web portal, America Online (AOL) offered online services, and also provided access to the Web. But by now most of the traditional search engines have transformed themselves into Web portals to attract and keep a larger audience[3]. Among recent portals, Goggle, Yahoo, Voila, Lycos, MSN, Go and My Netscape are popular. A portal is a Web site that provides a uniform interface with the ability to use a secure username/ password to access customized content based on specific end-user interests and demands. Integrating information (data, content) with proper coordination, processing and expertise a knowledge management portal may improve accountability; able to analyze a program's effectiveness; promote standardized data-collection methodology; facilitate timely feedback; generate useable reports; combine multiple forms into a single on-line channel; identify training needs.

Web portals provide a single point of access to a variety of content and core services, and ideally offer a single verifiable entry point. Portals offer a managed online experience, and can be particularly helpful as a start and return point for people who are new to the web. Portal content can be dynamically managed through databases, application windows, and sometimes cookies. Portals often include calendars and to-do lists, discussion groups, chats, messaging, announcements and reports, searches, email and address books, and access to news, weather, maps, and shopping, as well as bookmarks. There are other types of Web portals that can organize information into specific channels, customizable page containers where particular information or an application appears. Channels make it easy to locate information of interest by categorizing appropriate content. Moreover, Web portals offer advantages over home pages because they can offer user-specific and customized views. For example, a university's web portal could offer customized, specific content based on end users' roles (e.g., faculty, student, staff, administrator, admission seekers). Roles help the portal determine their privileges for reading, searching, updating, adding channels, and personalizing content. The portal, then uses the information stored in the roles to offer the appropriate content and service choices. The user can then create more specific content organization by selecting from the personalized material and services by making the portal work in their own way[4].

Again, in a very common sense, a Web portal is a site that functions as a single point of access to information on the World Wide Web. Portals present information from diverse sources in a unified way. Furthermore, in addition to the search engine facility, web portals offer other services such as e-mail, news, stock prices, infotainment and other features. As a whole, portals provide a way for enterprises to provide a consistent look and feel with access control and procedures for multiple applications, which otherwise would have been different entities altogether[5]. Therefore, a portal is a web site that provides uniform interface to all with the ability to access customized content based on specific end-user interests and demands. Sometimes, it may offer secured entry by using username and password. Typically a "portal site" has a catalog of web sites (site map), a search engine, or both[6].

A portal can be static (htmls and non-interactive) or dynamic (eXtensible Markup Languages and interactive). By integrating information (data, content), a knowledge management portal evolves. A knowledge management portal supposed to:

- Provide useful information in a simplified format through a single channel;
- Combine multiple forms of output into a single on-line channel;
- Identify end-user demands (knowledge needs);
- Promote standardized data collection methodology;
- Facilitate timely feedback and coordination;
- Assist to analyze a program's effectiveness;
- Generate useable reports through aggregate data;
- Streamline and tracks reporting approval process; and
- Improve accountability of the system.

By maintaining a composite Web site comprised of knowledge content, a KM portal can support:

- Single or multiple archived mailing lists (e-groups, blogs),
- Web based collaborative tools for promoting partnership among its stakeholders (forms, guest books),
- Conduct on-going debate and dialogue for promoting better governance (blogs, e-polls),
- Create employment opportunities by bridging between job seekers and job providers (jobsite),
- Increase investment opportunities by providing information related to financial matters (tenders, bids, procurements),

- Develop mechanism by establishing common platform of dialogue for improved government policies and services (e-polls, on-line/off-line surveys),
- Focus on legal and regulatory aspects by raising voices of common citizens (blogs, e-polls),
- Accommodate knowledge acquisition and learning system for knowledge gain of citizens (content, data bank, document bank, news, articles, products, best practices, KM related content, e-learning), and
- Establish a common platform for capacity development of citizens (human resource development) (Pastor, 2002; ECA, 1999).

Figure 2 illustrates a KM portal architecture and its interfaces with the end user for knowledge development or empowerment.

In this perspective, KM portals establish a form of knowledge management system and act as a common platform of interface that is visible to all. KM portal provides the ability to expose the capability of a system by forming a centralized location and adopting ubiquitous technologies, as such a simple Web browser, each and every member of the community can access it. Be it a society member or a government employee or a business entrepreneur, all may have the same accessibility to a well defined KM portal.

Furthermore, KM portal promotes knowledge sharing and better content dissemination in database driven environment, where data mining techniques can be applied (faster search, intelligent search, adoptive algorithm, improved decision making, etc.). At the same time, use of Web technique, like Semantic Web technologies can assist KM portal developers in designing their portals in more intelligent way (Web-based collaborative tools, user-friendly plug-ins, faster front-end-back-end interaction, increased personalization, etc.). As Louisiana (2002) stated, KM portal allows for content aggregation, taxonomy generation, data capture, filtering and data mining.

Figure 2. Basic KM Portal Architecture (Source: Adopted from Cantu, et. al., 2005)

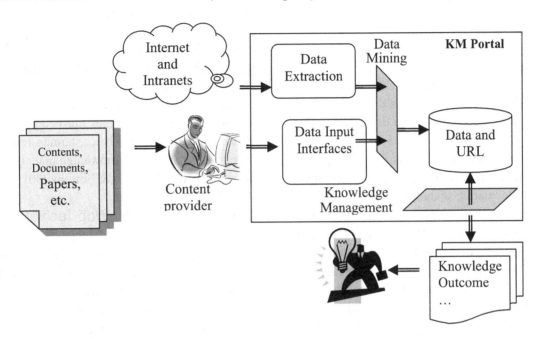

Adoption of data mining in knowledge discovery system and thereby in the KM system provides practical and multidisciplinary approach in solving activities related to knowledge development (Bozdogan, 2003). However, sometimes the use of data mining techniques becomes difficult due to the lack of a knowledge discovery in the database system (Viglioni, 2007). This demands further research and study in the aspect of incorporating appropriate data mining tools in the knowledge acquisition system.

Data Mining in Social Advancement System

Society development activities are dynamic processes that are intended to raise the livelihood of society and thereby empower each and every members of the society. Raising of their livelihood, mainly related to upgrade their economic capacity and empowering is related to increase their knowledge capacity. In these days of modernization and inclination of society members towards the use of technology adopted innovations for their social

activities, collective action of societies are more or less turning to be technology driven.

Activities ranging from broader access of information related to education, health, environment, public content, public services, decision support system, general commodity, small and medium sized entrepreneurship, e-commerce, tourism, ecosystem management, natural resources management to biodiversity, earth science and scientific research (Rahman, 2008a) are nowadays incorporate utilization of information and communication technology driven methods. In this context, utilization of data mining tools and techniques for preservation of data, utilization of acquired data in making knowledgeable decision, increasing the return of investment (ROI), establishment of web intelligence and acquisition of learning system are extremely essential.

According to Rahman (2008b), data mining is all about acquisition, assessment and analysis of data in assisting the social elements to take knowledgeable decision. Thus, the data be so small or huge; automated or semi-automated can help to uncover meaningful patterns and sequences in establishing decision support systems, such as the KM portals.

KM Portals and Data Mining

In this Internet driven data abundance world, knowledge management tools demands proper data handling mechanism, so that simple algorithms can be applied to gather data and information to be regarded as useful components in the knowledge acquisition process. Looking at the complex nature of data acquisition and huge amount of data, data mining is one of the best solutions to approach. Data mining (or data acquisition) is the process of autonomously retrieving useful information or knowledge ("actionable assets") from large data stores or sets. Data mining can be performed on a variety of data stores, including the World Wide Web, relational databases, transactional databases, internal legacy systems, pdf documents, and data warehouses. Nowadays, many agencies use automated data mining or information retrieval techniques[7].

Furthermore, data mining may be considered as the artificial intelligent portion of knowledge accumulation, as it deals with learning, classification and analysis that are parameters of artificial intelligence. It does not lead to just a mere thinking machine, but also explore solutions through numerous techniques. Thus, data mining has become an enormous industry, even in the context of socio-political and legal issues, where governments are utilizing archived data for evaluating the behaviors of their citizens (Kimball & Merz, 2000; Mueller, 2004; Tan, Steinbach & Kumar, 2005; Feldman & Sanger, 2006).

Speaking in a loose sense, the goal of data mining is to find intelligent patterns among massive amount of data. This entails on how intelligent a data is in terms of its usefulness and value addition. Moreover, when one is dealing with huge amount of data, incorporation of statistical and preprocessing techniques would strengthen the sampling, and thereby the characteristics of the data (Mueller, 2004).

However, the growing interest in data mining is motivated by a common problem across various disciplines, as how to store, retrieve, synthesize, utilize and disseminate with a huge pattern of data sets? Traditionally, different aspects of data mining can be addressed independently by different disciplines. But, to provide value added services for society development, they must contribute to information science, statistics, human resource development and other knowledge management faculties (Hand, Mannila & Smyth, 2001).

A Solution: Semantic Web Technologies

There is no burgeoning technology when data mining techniques are being used to raise the knowledge capacity of a social element. By setting up simple algorithms, of even minor complicacy, hidden patterns from huge amount of data can be revealed and useful information can be extracted from raw data (Witten & Frank, 2005). However, development of knowledge dynamics from intelligent information and dissemination of knowledge through appropriate methodologies remain challenged. The situation aggravates further, when the question arises, as how to develop the capacity of common citizen with proper knowledge content.

In this aspect, the Semantic Web provides an appropriate platform not only for knowledge exchange, but also knowledge management. The benefits of implementing Semantic Web technologies can be easily translated into various knowledge management processes. Furthermore, Semantic Web technologies have the potential to increase the information consistency and the information processing quality of Web portals (Argüello, El-Hasia & Lees, 2006). The semantic web is an elongation of the existing web that appends a layer of information semantically unfolding the data on the web (Crean, 2003). Technologies currently involved in the development of the Semantic Web are predominantly aimed at providing easy and effective access, search and selection of quality content driven by the desire of the user. They are related to developing methods, tools and systems to give services for accessing, filtering and retrieving intelligent content from the World Wide Web or from the major corporate repositories. The main technologies incorporated are those of knowledge representation, ontologies and intelligent agents (Pastor, 2002).

There are many ways by which information may reach to the common people, but their appropriateness and knowledge level remained questioned. Contents perish as days pass by, or become outdated without regular updates. Given the best solution at hand, designing, mapping, accessing and archiving are quite difficult to carry on for knowledge content. A KM portal can act as the stand-alone milestone in this aspect. As introduced earlier, a KM portal can provide a common interface among designer, developer, researcher and user, and at the same time can enrich knowledge content for all, including the portal itself.

Clearly, management of KM portal is critical, especially when data and contents are interrelated to empower knowledge of human. Similarly, a computer can search for desired document using a search engine, but it cannot read or interpret for extrapolating it to be usable. In this aspect, Semantic Web technologies can provide solutions (Fensel, Wahlster, Lieberman & Hendler, 2002; Cardoso & Sheith, 2006; Cardoso, 2007). KM portal designers can adopt these technologies for better knowledge diffusion. Semantic Web technologies applications ranges from knowledge exchange (Semantic exchange), knowledge acquisition (ontology), knowledge enhancement (learning) to knowledge dynamics (KM portal) (Pan & Thomas, 2007; Crean, 2003; Jovanović, et. al., 2007). Figure 3 illustrates the application of Semantic Web for knowledge management processes.

Despite the importance of Semantic Web technologies, in establishing KM portals, this chapter will not conduct extensive research on

Figure 3. Application of SWTs for KM processes (Source: Adopted from Pastor, 2002)

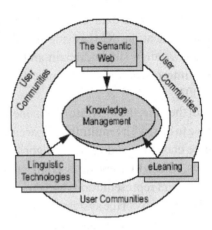

this issue due to its technical nature and theme of this chapter. Only the applicability factors of Semantic Web technologies will be discussed. Later in the chapter, a few cases of KM portals will be illustrated. However, it is mentioned that these KM portals are not necessarily being made up by using Semantic Web technologies.

As mentioned by Tim Berners-Lee, the inventor of the World Wide Web that Semantic Web is the next step in web evolution. Eventually the web based data can be processed directly and indirectly by machines. In the Semantic Web data itself becomes part of the web and can be processed independently of application, platform, or domain. With the data on the web, machines can process, transform, assemble, and even act according to the instruction given by the data to make intelligent decision.

However, implementing the Semantic Web requires adding semantic metadata, or data that describes data, to information resources. This allows machines to effectively process the data based on the semantic information that describes it. After obtaining huge semantic information associated with the data, computers can make inferences about the data. It understands what the data source is and how to relate them to other data. In this regard, eXtensible Markup Language

(XML) can offer some metadata in the form of human-readable tags that describes data. Before XML, data was stored in flat file and database formats, where most data was customized to particular application. XML made the data interoperable within a single domain and provide syntactic interoperability (Daconta, Obrst & Smith, 2003).

Most of the time, the software maintainers routinely have to deal with a multitude of parameters, like source code or pseudo code or algorithms or documents, which often end up disconnected, due to their different representations and the size and inherited complexity of the system. Therefore, one of the main challenges in software maintenance is to create and maintain the semantic connections among all the different components. In this aspect, Semantic Web technologies can deliver a unified representation to explore, query and argue about a multitude of software parameters (Witte, Zhang & Rilling, 2007).

Technically speaking, the first step required for a machine to understand data is to get the data into a uniform format. For example, a field labeled "weather_forecast" always should have the same format and contain the same type of information. This type of functionality is easily available on web sites that use forms which allow users to enter information and run a query. Many applications are nowadays running live on different servers interconnected around the globe, providing support to airlines industry, online banking, weather monitoring, geographical information system (GIS), satellite system, remote sensing, tele-health, semantic data grid and others. Even, search engines like Google or Yahoo uses thousands of interconnected servers running under a common platform of firmware providing service to numerous clients at the same time. They could be considered as important primary tools for opening knowledge dimension of their users. The next step towards Semantic Web demands that data from multiple domains is classified based on its properties and its relationship with other

data. This is an elongated dimension of Semantic Web technologies, where technologies as such resource description framework (RDF)[8], RDF Schema (RDFS)[9] and web ontology language (OWL)[10] evolved.

In order to learn more about how to interrelate social service systems development with the power of information and knowledge management related to different social service, including e-government service provision of ontology-driven application based on Semantic Web technologies came into focus. In this context, Semantic Web turned to be a document-oriented approach, where Web pages are treated as informational resources rather than simple data outlets. However, designing and using information resources is not only a technical and organizational challenge, but also it must take into account the socio-cultural-political-economic aspects of information. In fact the concept of a unit of information is vital, not only in the technical architecture, but also in society's concepts of information. A document may be treated as a unit of information and is not only the unit for reference, retrieval and presentation, but also the unit of ownership, license to use, scalability of payment, level of confidentiality, and degree of endorsement (Carter & Belanger, 2004; Sharma, 2004; Jovanovic, et. al., 2007; Lacy, 2005).

Along this concept, Ontologies are regarded as a key in solving interoperability problems. The standardization of ontologies used within an accessible network provides a common platform for cross-organizational applications. Even if such an agreement is not possible, then there are scopes to bridge semantic gaps through mapping and reconciliation of ontologies. Nowadays, most Web-based applications desire that the information architecture should be implemented along with the architecture of software components. Applying Semantic Web technologies opens the gateway to enrich the information architecture through the use of ontology or other semantic concepts as indicated above. Here, the ontology serves as the core semantic expression to support the retrieval/production/re-production and display of contexualized information. However, the choice of technology and architecture will largely be influenced by the requirements for incorporating and processing semantic expressions. Increased sophistication of the technical implementation may amplify the quality of service application, but at the same time it deserves augmented effort for mastering the technology (in terms of required knowledge, components to be integrated, refinement of software process, complicated algorithms, etc.) (Klischewski & Jeenicke, 2004; Staab & Studer, 2004; Sharma, 2004; Davies, Studer & Warren, 2006). Finally, adoption of appropriate technology, especially for the improved knowledge enactment of common citizens of a community would strive to prosper prominently around this newly emerged research dimension.

KNOWLEDGE MANAGEMENT PORTALS: A FEW CASES

This section briefly describes a few portals on knowledge management, comprising of learning, entrepreneurship, research and knowledge development.

Suzlon Energy, a global manufacturer of wind turbine with operation in over 11 countries and 236 locations, has introduced knowledge management portal in March 2007 and registered a 108% increase in sales in the last financial year. They mainly focus on sharing information and making connections among the employees that gave rise to the need of managing data and at the same time increased the knowledge generation (Suzlon Energy, 2008).

ViciDoc's enterprise document management and workflow automation system is providing knowledge management portal services to various government agencies, including Singapore (SPRING, Singapore) and India (Government of Kerala and State Bank of India, India), where web interfaces have been created to submit document, search through content, collaborate for updating the knowledge base of corporate users. In this way users can use single document for multipurpose applications and without any third party intervention. Service cost has been drastically reduced. Moreover, decision making has also been faster in many cases (ViciDocs, 2008).

Responding to the needs of knowledge based organizations and cope up with the emerging Caribbean information society, the Economic Commission for Latin America and the Caribbean has recently reorganized its Caribbean documentation center into the Caribbean Knowledge Management Center. Eventually, this has lead to establish them the Caribbean Centre of Excellence for E-Governance Developing an activity-based knowledge management system for contractors to increase knowledge and build capacity in the Caribbean by using ICT in government and governance (Caribbean KD Center, 2008a;b;c).

Construction Activity-Based Knowledge Management (ConABKM) is a concept of knowledge management to construction projects during the construction phase and this system may be usable for general contractors. Integrating IDEF (Integrated DEFinition function modeling) modeling methods the system develops a prototype for designing construction knowledge management systems. Applying the ConABKM system in highway construction projects demonstrates the effectiveness of sharing knowledge in the construction phase. Furthermore, the combined result of the prototype and the ConABKM reveal that by utilizing the latest web technology, knowledge exchange and storage concepts and modes of implementation, a ConABKM system can be an effective tool for all experts and engineers participating in the construction phase of a project (Tserng, & Lin, 2004).

In terms of e-Governance, KISSAN of Kerala, India has set a unique platform of knowledge portal. Karshaka Information Systems Services and

Networking (KISSAN) is providing integrated services through its agri-information portal to the Kerala government, including added services like toll-free call centre and awareness raising TV programs. Furthermore, this services are not only restricted to Kerala, but also being disseminated to other Indian states. It is a partnership programme of the Kerala Agricultural University and the Farm Information Bureau (Kissan, 2008).

At the University of Queensland, USA, the Distributed Systems Technology Centre and the Centre for Microscopy and Microanalysis are working in partnership on a project that is applying Semantic Web technologies to optimize fuel cell design. The project, namely the FUSION (Fuel Cell Understanding through Semantic Inferencing, Ontologies and Nanotechnology) project applies, amplifies, and merges Semantic Web technologies and image analysis techniques to develop a knowledge management system for optimizing the design of fuel cells. As fuel cell efficiency depends on the fuel cell layers' internal structure and the interfaces between them, an analysis of electron-microscopy images of cross-sectional samples through fuel cells can reveal precious information. In this context, simple macro-level information such as the thickness, surface area, roughness, and densities of the cell layers can help to determine gas permeation of the electrode materials (Hunter, Drennan & Little, 2004).

VISION is a European Union funded knowledge management roadmap project that initially describes state-of-the-art of knowledge technologies and then develops a roadmap for future research and development in this field. The state-of-the-art report with pertinent projects, organizations and software has been also represented in the form of ontology and associated cases and a semantics-driven access to this data has been made available via a Web portal (Maedche & Staab, 2003).

Knowledge management is a critical part of any corporate body or an institution. Tata Management Training Centre's (TMTC) experts

have recognized this fact and as a follow up, the organization aspires to become a repository and disseminator of best practices and values in the Tata Group. It has developed a knowledge management portal that initially contained company-specific information and practices. After collecting numerous relevant information from a number of global databases on teaching, problem-solving and even leisure reading, the portal became a platform to share best practices and even case studies (Ramswamy, 2004).

Megacycle.net is a knowledge portal and intended for use by Primary Health Care Practitioners of Bristol and South Gloucestershire, UK., acting as the stand-by knowledge facilitator. Someone working in Primary Health Care in that geographical area, can avail the service from this portal through simple registration[11]. This knowledge facilitation portal is part of the Knowledge Resource and Information Service (KRIS) that provides other services like, books and journals available on all aspects of healthcare, leaflets and posters on healthcare topics, videos, teaching packs, displays and models available to be borrowed, Internet access and inter library loan service.

In the form of for-profit entity, Hyperwave, a leading provider of collaborative knowledge management and e-learning solutions has the advanced base platform IS/6 R2. This platform enhances the ability to rapidly develop flexible collaborative knowledge management, portal and e-learning solutions. Furthermore, Hyperwave offers information management and software solutions to empower information distribution, team collaboration and continuous learning across the extended enterprise. Dedicated to unleashing the potential of organizational learning, Hyperwave delivers the means to use corporate information most effectively through its four key offerings: Smart Information Distribution, Smart Collaborative Workspace, Smart Collaborative Learning and Interactive Knowledge Center[12].

As an example in the defense sector, Defense Threat Reduction Agency (DTRA) may be cited here. They have developed the DTRA Acquisition Web ToolBook, a KM portal that represents accumulation of knowledge management, process management, and operational simplicity which are basic ingredients of a successful end-user information system. It is not a huge system, but acts as comprehensive repositories of acquisition information and collaboration for access, simple techniques and finite searches. Moreover, incorporating graphic interfaces, it provides user-friendly look at the desktop. DTRA AWT also adopted the key principles of a successful knowledge management system, as such minimizing clicks; maximizing access; simplifying operation; reducing search tiers; increasing graphical interfaces; simplifying designs; providing better accuracy in contents; extenuating better accuracy in contents; and justifying the demand of the end-users (Avery, 2008).

In the field of healthcare, NHS24, as a KM portal delivers healthcare information through partnership among public sector healthcare providers. NHS24 provides national healthcare information, clinical assessment, advice and referral service for Scotland. This service is available to the entire population of the country 24hours a day, especially when General Practitioners' (GPs) surgeries are closed. This portal aims to provide access to local healthcare services and health related information, thus allowing patients and their families to access necessary health advice during patient's journey to a nearby healthcare outlet. Among other features, NHS24 offers platform independent, easily accessible, locally relevant heterogeneous information in a managed way, targeted to the local people, as an Online e-Health Information Service. Over 1000 staffs are working under this system providing healthcare services to the entire population of Scotland (BEA, 2006).

More citations and information from similar successful cases could elongate this chapter.

However, a future research could closely monitor one or two cases, collect their performance data, analyze their effectiveness, and finally could assess their impact in the empowerment process of the society. It has been observed that a wholesome KM portal to strengthen the intellectual capacity of individual element of a society is still missing at large. There is a potential vacuum in the aspect of accumulating appropriate content, process them to fit into the knowledge portal, present them in simpler format, and update the entire system according to the desire and demand of the end-user. Furthermore, despite huge success in establishing knowledge management portals utilizing newly evolved tools and techniques, design, development and operation of knowledge management portals remain a challenge to the developers and researchers, especially when they are used to deal with contents related to knowledge development processes for general community people.

CHALLENGES OF KM PORTALS

During the operation and maintenance of knowledge management systems, major data on socio-economic development processes remain scattered and nobody archive those important primary data or their sources. Most of the time, after a few months or at the year end, they are being deleted from the source computer or their documentations get lost. Furthermore, though primary data are being accumulated during establishment and operation of many innovative projects around the world, but, due to lack of incentives, or management, most of the time those data or records are not being archived or preserved. At the end of the project period, everything gets lost. Researchers in the field when look for any potential data in that particular expertise, they do not find any alternative than to re-generate the raw data. By that time many scenario changes, including the socio-economic, political, and population sets.

Analysis of primary data, most of the time reflects the impact of development projects at that region, if they would be collected and processed through experimentally verified methods and techniques. Policy makers, researchers, academics and development actors can take benefit out of the research outcome comprising analytical benchmarking and periodical data accumulation through proper data acquisition processes. Often these results can pin point the stakeholders at the national level to take decisions or steps, at short-medium-longer term perspective. A community with an intrinsic nature or behavior may be reflected through a thorough data acquisition survey, which may or may not be reflected in a traditional census.

Main deficiencies of a knowledge management system are well known. Management of information and documents gets more importance than the way how people interact, pool their knowledge and learn mutually from one another. Experts leaving means knowledge leaving and critical knowledge are not available when decisions are being taken. KM portals may facilitate the communication among the collaborators, in particular when they work at distant places. Exchanging and sharing of information are also important, but they pose a question of mutual trust and confidence, which is essentially a critical issue.

As said earlier, KM on global level is closely linked to empowering the poor. Aiming at valorizing their competencies and allowing them to build on a knowledge base to overcome poverty and social injustice is another challenge for a KM portal. Here, civil society organizations can take a central role. They could act as the interface of the global world on one side, characterized by global access through the Internet and similar technologies, but, on the other side of the digital divide, the local world rarely connected and habitually ignored. For that matter, everybody is to develop its particular competencies, to link up with their partners, to network with each other in order to create alliances and communities, to participate in different platforms and to promote multi-stakeholder initiatives. Problems the global society faces require working in dynamic clusters, varied geographies, and constricted access. Added to these, further, is the strive for a culture of non-sharing, even in a world that is built on open competition. A KM portal can work here as a common platform, can provide information to the accessed communities through even constricted bandwidth and if designed properly through appropriate tools, may even stand as a substantive replacement of paper-based documents that are not easily available to those remote communities.

In this context, connectivity alone will not be sufficient. It will demand integrated approach accompanied by capacity building and institutional strengthening. At the same time, it is also crucial to address the soft factors pertaining to information, communication and knowledge. They would include the quality and relevance of information, the recognition and protection of indigenous knowledge, the establishment of communication rules and rights, the protection of cultural diversity, the ability to use ICT or the ability to make use of the information provided, and many more. Otherwise, only technical access will translate into acquired imbalances, as the South simply becomes a consumer of information produced and owned by the North. To overcome all these, it is vital to promote the creation and exchange of local content, based on local cultures and languages, and a properly designed KM portal acting as a common platform.

The Semantic Web initiative of the World-Wide Web Consortium (W3C) has been active for the last few years. It has attracted interest and skepticism in equal measure. The initiative was inspired by the overwhelming vision of its founder, Tim Berners-Lee, of a more flexible, integrated, automatic, and self-adapting Web, providing a richer and more interactive experience for its users. They were real challenges for the researchers and users in this field. However, till date, the W3C has developed a set of standards and tools to support his vision. Through several years of extensive research and development, these are now in usable form and could make a real impact. Using Semantic Web technologies, KM portals can easily be developed, and disseminated to their target users. However, people are still inquiring how they can be used in real life cases to solve real life problems.

Despite their immense potential, Semantic Web technologies are still largely ignored in the business enterprises. Very often their potentials are overlooked, or mistaken for text-analysis techniques by the misconception of the term "semantic". Moreover, not being popularized through advertisement by their solution providers, they are at best being considered as "a promising technology", but not ready to be used right now. In addition to these, they may even suffer from a negative prejudice, being perceived as yet another technological hype, whose promises, such as the easy exchange of information, have already been heard many times before. Also, current focus is about Web portal services, and people do not quite understand what Semantic Web technologies add to the ground. In this context, people awareness of the potential of Semantic Web technologies faces a difficult challenge (Servant, 2007).

Apart from those mentioned above, the challenges will remain, especially related to knowledge management portals and among many a few are infrastructure barrier, content barrier, operational barrier, managerial barrier, social barrier, economic barrier, cultural barrier, and political barrier. Table 3 has tried to put forward a few challenges at the left and their corresponding output, if the challenges can be overcome.

FUTURE DIRECTIONS

In a representative enterprise, around 75% of internal knowledge is circled within the organization's email and desktop PCs. It seems good information is everywhere, but if someone looks for a reliable information, it is hard to find. Furthermore, it is harder to find a portal who could enlighten its users through knowledge content. A knowledge management portal should be able to address need-based, role-based, and workflow-based content with flexible indexing and searching, and capable of easy document conversion providing turn-key customized solution. Future knowledge portal should not only serve the enterprises and corporate houses, but also academics, entrepreneurs, researchers, development actors, industrial users, knowledge seekers, and policy makers.

Creating knowledge management portals using the Semantic Web technologies could be treated as the next generation web with the vision of having background knowledge about the meaning of web sources stored in a machine-processable and -interpretable way, and at the same time can act

Table 3. Common barriers/challenges of knowledge portals and their corresponding outcomes (Source: Author)

Challenge Component	Output/Outcome
Psychological	Strengthened Foundation
Social	Empowerment
Cultural	Ethical
Political	Enactment
Technological	Virtual Networking
Service	Economic benefit

as the high graded interface for empowering the human knowledge skills. Semantic Web technologies could be used for next-generation knowledge and information system, including tourism, life science project, health endeavors, edutainment, learning and research.

The area of modern day tourism is highly dynamic area that already extensively uses the available Internet technologies. However, the shortcomings of the existing technology are that information finding and extraction as well as the interpretation of the information contained in the web sources is mostly left to the interpretation of the human user. In the Semantic Web based portals, background knowledge about the meaning of web resources can be stored as machine-processable meta-data. Thereby, services for finding, integrating, or connecting information may be based on these semantic descriptions.

As an example, the semantic description of Ryokans as a Japanese style of lodging returns their existence and the corresponding tourism offers even to the novice Japan visitor who is looking for accommodations and who did not know about their existence before. Analogously, the search for *classical music festivals* with corresponding travel arrangements and checking of availabilities could be integrated by semantic means such that the *opera event* in Usedom, a German island in the Baltic Sea will return with corresponding travel and lodging arrangements though it has not been explicitly enquired (Mädche &. Staab, 2002).

Though knowledge portals utilizing different tools, including the Semantic Web is turning towards a global database with their evolutionary features and distributed nature, but issues of accessibility, trust and credibility remain their. Not all the data sources have universal access, especially primary data sources. Even if they would be given restricted access, the issue of security will come next. At the same time, sources of database and data itself may be questionable in terms of reliability. Furthermore, utilizing Semantic search,

abundance of relevant information deserves very methodical filtration and intelligent representation that emerges as new challenges to the researchers. At the very remote corners where majority of the population resides, reaching out there with these innovative knowledge tools will remain very interesting future research areas for quite a few years to come.

There are areas of future research in establishing huge datasets using eXtended Markup Language (XML), eXtensible Hypertext Markup Language (XHTML), Extensible Stylesheet Language Transformations (XSLT), Resource Description Framework (RDF), HyperRDF, RDF Schema (RDFS), Web Ontology Language (OWL), OWL Lite, OWL Description Logistics, and OWL full documents for providing tools to create and edit RDF instance documents or RDFS vocabularies or OWL ontologies graphically with context sensitive entry and full syntax checking. Merging those features to a knowledge management portal would be the next generation web service empowering the citizen of the future world.

CONCLUSION

In today's all-inclusive, hyper-competitive marketplace, generation and dissipation of knowledge can no longer be understood from within the boundaries of formal organizational mechanisms (Awazu, 2004). Development of knowledge is not a superfluous concept, but an omni-potent subject in the arena of learning processes. However, tools related to the development of knowledge, especially for common citizen is hardly present in contemporary researches, and even concurrent research agencies or academics are lacking in concepts on how to yield better output from knowledge dissemination systems, or how to realize the output at the grassroots, or how to reach the masses. At the outset, any measuring tools are also missing in global market through which knowledge management systems could be measured.

Moreover, the concept of knowledge management is not novel in information systems practice and research. But, radical changes in the business environment have suggested boundaries of the traditional information-processing view of knowledge management. New business environments are characterized not only by rapid pace of change, but also discontinuous character of dynamic changes, and require a re-conceptualization of knowledge management as it has been understood in information systems practice and research (Malhotra, 2000).

Content management tools need to incorporate synchronized multimedia, including information management, digital libraries, community bulletin board, and last but not the least, a Semantic grid. Knowledge management is increasingly becoming an important strategic instrument for sustaining the competitive advantage of societies. Community based entrepreneurs are undertaking knowledge management initiatives and making significant investments. However, there is relatively little empirical support for the impact of knowledge management on the performance of those agencies (Choi & Jong, 2005).

Time has come to think globally and act locally. The same applies to knowledge management portals too. By setting boundaries of KM systems at the organizational level have obvious pragmatic advantages. The audience is well defined, contents are manageable and most personnel can be reached these days using common ICT systems, wherever they are in the world. Furthermore, personnel usually go through periodic training, appraisal and career development scheme, and if the KM portal could be tied into these by providing some kinds of incentives to them, monitoring their performances and encouraging good knowledge sharing practices, the system would acquire huge knowledge content in a short period. Keeping boundaries close also allows KM systems to be closely matched to institutional set goals and agendas, either at the institute or department level.

However, there is no need to filter material from stakeholders outside the organization, negotiate priorities, or enter into complicated cost sharing arrangements. But, at the same time, it is necessary to share sensitive material, which may be particularly important when one is trying to encourage learning from failures, not just successes, and where confidentiality is essential in building trust. These provide good reasons for keeping KM within the family to a considerable extent, and this is the route that most development agencies have gone now. So, there are also drawbacks in this approach that need to be considered, notably the problem of duplication of efforts, and the knowledge fortification tendency (Barnard, 2003). Therefore, a KM portal needs to adopt a compromised balance of internal and external content depending on local need, knowledge acquisition capacity of local community, and adaptability of the society.

REFERENCES

Argüello, M., El-Hasia, A. & Lees, M. (2006). A Semantic Web Portal to construction knowledge exchange, In Zanasi, A., Brebria, C.A. & Ebecken, N.F.F. (Eds.). *Data Mining VII: Data, Text and Web Mining and their Business Applications* 417-427, WIT Transactions on Information and Communication Technologies, Vol 37, WIT Press.

Avery, J.P. (2008). A different kind of Web-based knowledge management: "Little A" Principles Apply to "Big A" Portals, Defense AT&L, May-June 2008: 30-33.

Awazu, Y. (2004). Knowledge Management in Distributed Environments: Roles of Informal Network Players, A Proceedings of the 37th Hawaii International Conference on System Sciences, Hawaii.

Barnard, G. (2003). Knowledge Sharing in Development Agencies: Knowledge Fortress or Knowledge Pool?, a paper presented at the EADI/MWG Conference, Dublin.

BEA (2006). NHS24: Knowledge Management Portal Delivers High Quality Healthcare Information, BEA Systems, Inc., CA, USA.

Berry, M.J.A. & Linoff, G.S. (2004). Data Mining Techniques: For Marketing, Sales, and Customer Relationship Management, Wiley Computer Publishing, 2004.

Bozdogan, H. (2003). (Ed.). Statistical Data Mining and Knowledge Discovery, Chapman & Hall/CRC.

Brint dot com (2007). Retrieved December 28, 2007 from http://www.brint.com/km/

Cantu, et. al. (2005). A Knowledge-based entrepreneurial approach for business intelligence in strategic technologies: Bio-MEMS, *Proceedings of the Eleventh Americas Conference on Information Systems,* Omaha, NE, USA August 11th-14th 2005: pp: 1327-1340.

Choi, B. & Jong, A.M., (2005). An Examination of KM Strategies and the Market Value of the Firm: Based on the Event Study Methodology, A proceedings of Knowledge Management in Asia-Pacific 2005, Building a Knowledge Society: Linking Government, Business, Academia and the Community, Victoria University of Wellington, New Zealand.

Cardoso, J. & Sheth, A. (2006). Semantic Web Services, Processes and Applications, Springer, 2006.

Cardoso, J. (2007). Semantic Web Services: Theory, Tools and Applications, Idea Group.

Carter, L. & Belanger, F. (2004). Citizen Adoption of Electronic Government Initiatives, A Proceedings of the 37th Hawaii International Conference on System Sciences, Hawaii.

Caribbean KD Center (2008a). Accessed February 02, 2008 from http://ckmportal.eclacpos.org/;

Caribbean KD Center (2008b). Accessed February 02, 2008 from http://eceeg.dec.uwi.edu/drupal/

Caribbean KD Center (2008c). Accessed February 02, 2008 from http://ckmportal.eclacpos.org/dev/suriname

Crean, M. (2003). *A Weblog Recommender using Machine Learning and Semantic Web Technologies*, White paper, University of Bristol, UK.

Daconta, M.C., Obrst, L.J., & Smith, K.T. (2003). The Semantic Web: A Guide to the Future of XML, John Wiley & Sons.

Davies, J., Studer, R. & Warren, P. (2006). Semantic Web Technologies: Trends and Research in Ontology-based Systems, Wiley.

ECA (1999). Economic Commission for Africa (ECA), 1999 available at http://www.uneca.org/adf99/thewayforward.htm

Feldman, R., & Sanger, J. (2006). The Text Mining Handbook: Advanced Approaches in Analyzing Unstructured Data, Cambridge University Press.

Fensel, D., Wahlster, W., Lieberman, H. & Handler, J. (2002). Spinning the Semantic Web: Bringing the World Wide Web to Its Full Potential, MIT Press.

Fust, W. (2003). Knowledge Society, Knowledge Management and ICT, an Editorial contribution to a publication edited by the Community Development Library, Dhaka, Bangladesh.

Hand, D.J., Mannila, H. & Smyth, P. (2001). Principles of Data Mining (Adaptive Computation and Machine Learning), The MIT Press.

Hunter, J., Drennan, J. & Little, S. (2004). Realizing the Hydrogen Economy through Semantic Web Technologies, E-Science, IEEE Intelligent System, January-February 2004, pp. 1-9.

Jin, R. & Agrawal, G. (2003). Efficient Decision Tree Construction on Streaming Data, in the Proceedings of 9th International Conference on

Knowledge Discovery and Data Mining (SIG-KDD), August.

Jovanović, et. al. (2007). Using Semantic Web Technologies to Analyze Learning Content, In *Internet Computing*, September/October 2007 (Vol. 11, No. 5): 45-53.

Klischewski, R. & Jeenicke, M. (2004). Semantic Web Technologies for Information Management within e-Government Services, In *Proceedings of the 37th Annual Hawaii International Conference on System Sciences (HICSS'04) - Track 5 p. 50119b*, Hawaii.

Kimball, R. & Merz, R. (2000). The Data Webhouse Toolkit: Building the Web-Enabled Data Warehouse. Wiley.

Kissan (2008). Accessed February 02, 2008 from http://www.igovernment.in/site/KISSAN-to-offer-agri-portal-platform-to-other-indian-states/).

Lacy, L.W. (2005). OWI: Representing Information Using the Web Ontology Language, Tratfford Press, 2005.

Lousiana (2002). *The State IT Master Plan*, Office of Information technology, State of Lousiana, Baton Rouge, Lousiana.

Mädche, A., & Staab, S. (2002). Applying Semantic Web Technologies for Tourism Information Systems,. In: K.Wöber, A. Frew, M. Hitz (eds*.), Proceedings of the 9thInternational Conference for Information and Communication Technologies in Tourism, ENTER 2002*. Springer Verlag, Innsbruck, Austria, 23 - 25th January 2002, pp. 311-319

Mädche, A. & Staab, S. (2003).The Karlsruhe Ontology and Semantic Web Meta Project, KAON: The Karlsruhe Ontology and Semantic Web Meta Project, Special issue on Semantic Web, *Künstliche Intelligenz* (3): 27-30.

Malhotra, Y. (2000). Knowledge Management and New Organization Forms: A Framework for Business Model Innovation, *Information Resources Management Journal*, 13(1), January-March, 2000, pp. 5-14.

Mueller, J.P. (2004). Mining Amazon Web Services: Building Application with the Amazon API, Sybex.

Pan, J.Z. & Thomas, E. (2007). Approximating OWL-DL Ontologies. *Proceedings of the Twenty-Second AAAI Conference on Artificial Intelligence*, July 22-26, 2007, Vancouver, British Columbia, Canada. AAAI Press 2007: 1434-1439.

Pastor, F.G. (2002). *Knowledge Management: A Trip Round Europe, Knowledge Management and Information Technology*, UPGRADE Vol. III, No. 1, February 2002, pp. 66-71.

Rahman, H. (2008a). Prospects and Scopes of Data Mining Applications in Society Development Activities, In: Rahman, H. (Ed.). *Data Mining Applications for Empowering Knowledge Societies*, IGI References, Hurshey, PA, USA: 159-185.

Rahman, H. (2008b). Application of Data Mining Algorithms for Measuring Performance Impact of Social Development Activities, In: Rahman, H. (Ed.). *Data Mining Applications for Empowering Knowledge Societies*, IGI References, Hurshey, PA, USA: 135-158.

Ramswamy, S. (2004). Changing the learning curve, accessed from http://www.tata.com/0_our_commitment/employee_relations/articles/20040629_tmtc.htm on March 04, 2008.

Servant, François-Paul (2007). Semantic Web Technologies in Technical Automotive Documentation, Proceedings of the OWLED 2007 Workshop on OWL: Experiences and Directions, Vol. 258, Innsbruck, Austria, June 6-7, 2007. Edited by Christine Golbreich,

Aditya Kalyanpur, & Bijan Parsia, Technical University of Aachen, Germany.

Sharma, S. (2004). E-Governance: An Approach to Manage Bureaucratic Impediments, in the *Proceedings of the E-Governance: challenges and opportunities for democracy, administration and law*, Seoul, S. Korea, p. 11.

Sharp, D. (2003). Knowledge Management Today: Challenges and Opportunities, Information Systems Management, Vol. 20, Issue 2, pp. 32-37.

Staab, S., & Studer, R. (2004). Handbook on Ontologies, Heidelberg: Springer Verlag.

Suzlon Energy (2008). Accessed on February 02, 2008 from http://www.tech2.com/biz/india/casestudies/computing/suzlon-energy-knowledge-management-portal-energises-employees/1522/0

Tan, Pang-Ning, Steinbach, M., Kumar, V. (2005). Introduction to Data Mining, Addison Wesley.

Tserng, H.P. & Lin, Yu-Cheng (2004). *Developing an activity-based knowledge management system for contractors*, Automation in Construction Volume 13, Issue 6, November 2004, Pages 781-802, Elsevier B.V.

UN (2005). Information and Communication technologies for development: Progress in the implementation of General Assembly resolution 57/295, report of the Secretary-General, General Assembly, A/60/323, United Nations.

ViciDocs (2008). Accessed on February 02, 2008 from http://www.vicidocs.com/govtpub.asp

Viglioni, G.M.C. (2007). *Methodology for Railway Demand Forecasting using Data Mining*, SAS paper 161-2007, SAS Institute Inc., USA.

Witte, R., Zhang, Y. & Rilling, J., (2007). Empowering Software Maintainers with Semantic Web Technologies, In Franconi, E., Kifer, M. & May, W. (Eds.), *The Semantic Web: Research and Applications*, 4th European Semantic Web Conference, ESWC 2007, Innsbruck, Austria, June 3-7, 2007, Proceedings of , Springer, pp. 37-52.

Witten, I.H. & Frank, E. (2005). Data Mining: Practical Machine Learning Tools and Techniques, Morgan Kaufmann.

ADDITIONAL READINGS

Brian Matthews (2005), Semantic Web Technologies, JISC Technology and Standards Watch , TSW0502, Ireland, available at http://www.jisc.ac.uk/uploaded_documents/jisctsw_05_02pdf.pdf

Brooks, C., Kettel, L. & Hansen, C. (2005). "Building a Learning Object Content Management System," *Proc. 10th World ELearn Conference,* Assoc. for the Advancement of Computing in Education, 2005, pp. 2836–2843.

Caragea, D., Silvescu, A., and Honavar, V. (2004). A Framework for Learning from Distributed Data Using Sufficient Statistics and its Application to Learning Decision Trees. In: *International Journal of Hybrid Intelligent Systems.* Vol. 1. No. 2. pp. 80-89.

Jovanović, J. et al. (2006). "Learning Object Context on the Semantic Web," *Proceedings of the 6th IEEE International Conference on Advanced Learning Technologies,* IEEE Press, 2006 pp. 669–673.

Kernaghan, K. (2004). Moving Toward the Virtual State: Integrating services and Service Channels for Citizen-Centred Service Delivery, a paper from 20th International Congress of Administrative Sciences, Seoul, July 2004.

Knight, C., Gašević, D. & Richards, G. (2006). "An Ontology-Based Framework for Bridging Learning Design and Learning Content," *Educational Technology & Society,* vol. 9, no. 1, 2006, pp. 23–37.

Linoff, G.S. & Berry, M.J.A. (2002). Mining the Web: Transforming Customer Data into Customer Value, Wiley, 2002.

Malhotra, Y. (2000a). From Information Management to Knowledge Management: Beyond the 'Hi-Tech Hidebound Systems', In K. Srikantaiah & M.E.D. Koenig (Eds.), *Knowledge Management for the Information Professional.* Medford, N.J.: Information Today Inc. (American Society for Information Science and Technology Monograph Series), 2000, pp. 37-61.

Malhotra, Y. (2000b). Knowledge Assets in the Global Economy: Assessment of National Intellectual Capital, *Journal of Global Information Management*, 8(3), July-Sep, 2000, pp. 5-15.

Malhotra, Y. (2001a). How to Enable Next Generation e-Business Architectures for Business Transformation, Expert Paper, Intel Corporation, June 2001.

Malhotra, Y. (2001b) Organizational Controls as Enablers and Constraints in Successful Knowledge Management Systems Implementation, In Y. Malhotra (Ed.), *Knowledge Management and Business Model Innovation.* Hershey, PA: Idea Group Publishing, 2001, p. 326-336.

Malhotra, Y. (2002). Is Knowledge Management Really an Oxymoron? Unraveling the Role of Organizational Controls in Knowledge Management, In D. White (Ed.), *Knowledge Mapping and Management*, Hershey, PA: Idea Group Publishing, 2002, pp. 1-13.

Rud, O.P. (2000). Data Mining Cookbook: Modeling Data for Marketing, Risk and Customer Relationship Management, Miley, 2000.

Winter, M. et al. (2004). "Using Semantic Web Methods for Distributed Learner Modelling," *Proc. 2nd Int'l Workshop Applications of Semantic Web Technologies for E-Learning,* 2004; available at www.win.tue.nl/SW-EL/2004/ISWC-SWEL-Camera-ready %236-Winter-CR.pdf

ENDNOTES

1 Glossary Knowledge Management and Capacity Development, available from Swiss Agency for Development and Cooperation (SDC)'s web site http://www.sdc.admin.ch/

2 Glossary Knowledge Management and Capacity Development, available from Swiss Agency for Development and Cooperation (SDC)'s web site http://www.sdc.admin.ch/

3 http://webopedia.internet.com/TERM/W/Web_portal.html

4 http://kb.iu.edu/data/ajbd.html

5 http://en.wikipedia.org/wiki/Web_portal

6 http://www.matisse.net/files/glossary.html#P

7 http://www.xsb.com/glossary.aspx

8 RDF is an XML-based standard for describing resources that exist on the web, intranets and extranets.

9 RDFS is used to create vocabularies that describes groups of related RDF resources and the relationships between those resources.

10 OWL is a third W3C specification for creating Semantic Web applications.

11 http://www.megacycle.net/; http://www.avon.nhs.uk/kris/default.htm

12 http://findarticles.com/p/articles/mi_m0EIN/is_2002_Oct_28/ai_93425618

Section II
Universal Access to Social Services

Chapter V
Better Knowledge for Better Health Services:
Discovering Guideline Compliance

Stefano De Luca
Evodevo s.r.l., Italy

Enrico Memo
Ca' Foscari University, Italy

ABSTRACT

The expenses in Health Care are an important portion of the overall expenses of every country, so it is very important to determine if the given cares are the right ones. This work is about a methodology, Health Discoverer, and a consequent software, aimed to disease management and to the measure of appropriateness of cares, and in particular is about the data mining techniques used to verify Clinical Practice Guidelines (CPGs) compliance and the discovery of new, better guidelines. The work is based on Quality Records, episode parsing using Ontologies and Hidden Markov Models.

INTRODUCTION

The importance of health and social services is constantly increasing as global societies grow older and the awareness of a proper care is spreading between citizens. Central point of this issue is the increasing cost of maintaining such health and social care systems. As reported by OECD (OECD Health Data 2007), the GDP (Gross Domestic Product) used in the health care varies from 5.5% (Korea) up to 15.5% (USA), in Italy we score a 8.7%. This research used the last complete data, on year 2004. In 2005, 2006 and 2007 this research assisted to a substantial growth, in Italy it expect a raise from 8.7% up to 9%.

The research's purpose was to reach the definition of a valid and applicable method for inappropriateness reduction in medical praxis.

Table 1. Health expenditure %GDP

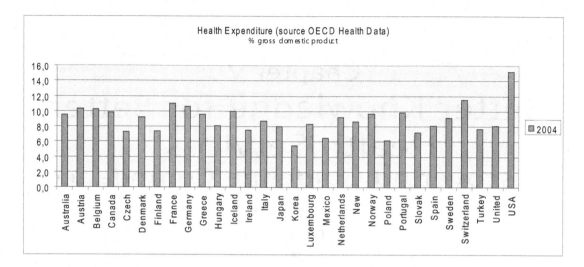

Being sanitary economy a relatively young science, authors were sure that the quest wouldn't be easy and, being the *inappropriateness* recognized as one of the main resource waste causes within health care services, they were also sure that their search wouldn't be a trivial one.

The measure of appropriateness is strongly related to the use of Health Information Technology (HIT); use of HIT is seen as a way to increase the general quality of medical care and a way to reduce its cost (Welch et al. 2007); the clinical decision support systems increase guideline adherence in the clinical practice, thus improving health status and improving the financial elements on the long term.

The EPR (Electronic Patient Records, or Electronic Health Records) are the most discussed form of HIT. USA's Institute of Medicine (www.iom.edu) states eight core functionalities describing EPR:

- Health information and data storage,
- Management of results from laboratory and imagingtests,
- Electronic ordering (e.g., prescription drugs and referrals),
- Clinical decision support (e.g., guideline reminders),

- Interoperability, and
- Administrative processes such as billing.

The research intend to start from existing EPR software systems by improving their ability to manage guidelines and to discover important health properties, hidden in the health data.

This chapter describes the process and technologies authors used to approach the inappropriateness, choosing within different instruments the more suitable one, and presents the model developed starting from their consideration.

Because it is very hard to define when a care is appropriate, guidelines usage has been seleceda a metric to measure the appropriateness. The way a care is given mainly depends on the processes defined by medical institution as the correct one, and formalized as medical guidelines. So it is very important to know if the medics are following one of the possible guideline, because if it is so there are strong chances that the given care are appropriate, with greater results for the patient and lower expense for the medical institution (and typically for the government).

In section 2 it'll be discussed the process followed to establish an acceptable (by medics, institutions, government) way to measure care rightness and other, yet established metrics; this section is very important because there is a strong resistance bye medics and medical institution to measure the quality of given cares. Hence in section 3 it'll be proposed a generalized software architecture able to cope with the problems shown in section 2. Section 4 is focused on the clinical guidelines, entering in the core of this paper, i.e., how to determine if the medics are following them. Section 5 introduces data mining techniques and process (CRISP-DM) when is applied to medical data. Section 6, Guidelines adherence discovery using Markov Chains, describes in detail the new algorithms and tools realized to effectively answer the goal: discovering guideline compliance. Last section 7 draws some conclusion.

THE PROCESS

The study started on 2004 with a project named *Health Mining* (Bei, A., De Luca, S., Ruscitti, G. and Salamon, D., 2005, De Luca S., Memo, E. et al. 2005). The goal of this study was to define a disease management methodology acceptable and approvable by the government levels and by doctors and their structures. Being disease management, and inappropriateness computation in particular, an important element in economic rate of hospitals' work, it was essential to count on a large base to support the methodology, otherwise it'd be easy to experience a reject of the entire process.

National and international instruments recognition represented the first step of followed process. The survey emphasized the following instruments:

- **PRUO:** Protocol for Hospital's Usage Revision and his American version AEP (Appropriateness Evaluation Protocol) are two measure/classification instruments aimed to split the days spent in the hospital in "appropriate" and "inappropriate";

- **Disease Staging:** a classification system for in-patients developed in the USA by prof. Gonnella, from Thomas Jefferson's University of Philadelphia. The classification algorithm evaluates patient's pathological condition and its gravity homogeneously and strictness;

- **AP Pro:** evaluates acute patient's admissions on the basis of discharge forms, it discovers low-complex assistance admissions and minimal severity admissions that, for their characteristics, are suitable for a Day Hospital treatment;

- **LEA:** Essential Assistance Levels are Italian limits established by National Sanitary Service (SSN), defining uniformity for granted cares, based on the constitutional principle that enacts health right for all citizens.

All these instruments, variously used on the Italian territory, missed one of the main characteristics we were searching for: the usefulness of the method for many different user levels.

That's why it has been chosen to proceed with an international comparison, arranging three different expert commissions coming from Sweden, United Kingdom and Germany and asking them which kind of instruments the three different nations were using to cope with inappropriateness at a national and local level. Thanks to this comparison an extremely interesting instrument used by Sweden Health Ministry at a national level since the 80's was discovered: the national quality registers.

National Quality Registers: The Swedish Model

Sweden started more than 15 years ago a specific process trying to answer the following questions: how to enhance quality? How to reduce medical practice variability? How to reduce costs?

The answer has been mainly found in the institution of pathology-specific digital registers.

These registers collect data on patients, treatments and subsequent results and outcome. At the present days Sweden can count on over 40 registers and call them "Quality Registers", emphasizing the scope they are built for.

National Quality Registers are basically databases collecting:

- Patient personal data
- Diagnosis
- Treatments
- Results

These kinds of data, variously aggregated and statistically analyzed, represent a precious instrument to promote and to monitor the quality enhancing in national health systems.

Different registers can all provide the following data:

- Register starting date
- Approximate volume of interventions
- Register's Patient Coverage on Total Patient for a given pathology
- Register's patient inclusion criteria
- Brief list of register's variables
- Feedbacks: data reports and statistical analysis of data
- Results: conclusions emerging from reports and statistics
- Publications
- Contact information for data insertion referent and data transfer criteria

The greatest register value comes from the large amount of homogenous data collected yearly on all the national territory on different pathologies. These data analysis permits the easy, immediate and economic dissemination of new best practices. Registers can also provide a sort of alarm system for defects causing problems to patients, representing a learning and medical decision support system.

Registers are useful if, and only if, each single health unit can monitor provided services' quality in time, comparing reached level with other structures and national average. Many Swedish registers still show great variability moving from region to region: however these kind of instruments can emphasize and disseminate the best performing regional model.

In Sweden Quality Registers are not obligatory, Swedish strategy is to maintain the register participation free and voluntary-based, while maintaining anonymous the data input and publication. In these way non-excellent health units are not discriminated, but fostered in register participation (free and useful for guideline design and best practices individuation).

Registers were born at a local level, but nowadays have been adopted at a national and centralized level. Few, but essential are the register creation and maintenance rules, they must:

- Contain individual data on diagnosis, medical intervention and relative results;
- Preview doctor participation;
- Preview meetings and feedback procedures;
- Facilitate collaboration between health structures;
- Face nationally relevant themes;
- Try to involve private structures;
- Be able to generate relevant and credited information.

In Sweden registers are public and can count on a common system and software, all the data must be inputted immediately and only the complications are lately inserted. Periodically, all data are transmitted from the local database to the national one and yearly each single health unit receives his own report. General data are published yearly and used in national and international meetings.

These were the reason to focus on this instrument, but enriching it at a new level. This process ended his first run with a web based, emphasized version of a quality register based on pacemaker and AICD (Automatic Implantable Cardioverter Defibrillators) implants.

Main features of the system were:

- **Web based interface:** no need for installing software on different PC and possibility of older hardware systems utilization;
- **Different user level access:** we previewed Regional, Hospital and single Doctor access to data, each level was characterized by different statistical tools;
- **Architecture flexibility:** for an easy application to any disease.

Health Mining project evolved then in a new project, **Health Discoverer**, that enhanced Health Mining with a Service Oriented Architecture, a stronger data mining level and ontology support.

Expected Outcome

The quality register model, based on international standards, lets surgeons to input detailed data regarding patients, symptoms, implants, administered drugs and follow-up. In the original Health Mining, we used CARDS data standard for cardiology audit.

The system offers a large range of statistical analysis on recorded data and previews different user levels: region, hospital and single doctor. The register has been thought to assure regional statistics on the observed medical care and to foster a sharper phenomenon perception; at the hospital level, statistics may be used to compare values with regional averages and to support budget making. Last but not least, the systematic data recording and the statistics availability may be able to cope with medical praxis variability, reducing it.

Process Components

The main process components are the followings:

- **Disease selection:** while Disease Management can be applied to all kind of diseases, the assuption is that it's better to mainly cope with the most interesting illness, in term of social relevance and cost reduction, notwithstanding more managed diseases mean more reuse of medical data and better context for data mining extractions.
- **Guidelines selection:** after a specific disease selection, this step involves the selection of (a set of) field-relevant international guidelines.
- **Quality records selection and adaptation:** given the guidelines, variables referred by inappropriateness studies have been chosen, in order to compose a quality record; the system can use existing international quality records, but they must be localized and adapted to Disease Management purposes.
- **Business intelligence, Data Mining and rule extraction, new guidelines discovery:**

Figure 1. Disease management process

after the process phase, the technical ones. Here data are collected and used to calculate statistical groups and process/results variance, to extract rules about the care process and new approach to guidelines or part of them.

Given the task complexity, different tools were used: statistical analysis of deviance is useful to turn off the noise, while Knowledge Discovery in Database (KDD) is critical to extract valuable insights about the best practice or problems in the managed context; so typical business intelligence, statistical tools, specific data mining and rule inference tools were used. **Health Discoverer** adds to this layer an ontological discoverer that enable the model to use logical inference reasoners.

- **Results evaluation:** the last step consists in Evidence Based Medicine usage, exploiting the results to re-plan actions, changing (if necessary) the used guidelines and improving the general process. At this stage the system is ready to re-start the process, with better confidence and control over the way health care can be managed.

All the above phases involve a validation by the scientific committee in order to avoid naïve choices or to avoid confusion between localized improvements and general ones. In this way the system is able to produce a higher quality process, to minimize the possible physicians resistance to the control tool, to design the DM tool in a doctors' positively perceived way.

SOFTWARE ARCHITECTURE

Main goal of Health Discoverer is the collection of all the relevant medical data and their analysis by data mining tools and techniques to discover Clinical Practice Guidelines (CPG) adherence

and the reasons resulting in good or bad disease management. In doing so, the interest focuses in sharing knowledge on existing or discovered Guidelines and in the other kinds of knowledge, in particular derived rules, clusters and simpler statistics – including Key Performance Indicators (KPI) as usual in Business Intelligence.

Health Discoverer has three main components: the Input Front-End sub-system, that collects all the information and give users the possibility to input data and view discovered results, the Storage sub-systems, where a Medical Data Warehouse is built, the Engine sub-system, where multiple data mining algorithms and the Guidelines discovery are applied. Health Discoverer is based on a Service Oriented Architecture (SOA), where all components are joined by an Enterprise Service Bus (ESB); the communications are carried out by standard web services and specific medical protocols, as DICOM or HL7 (e.g., for Electronic Patient Record data gathering). The flow of information and services is managed by a standard BPEL engine and a rule engine, both driving the ESB communications.

The architecture is based on these macro components:

- **Front end:** is a web based front-end for input patient data and dissemination of the results. It receives data from:
  - **Forms,** generated by a generalized Form Management System which allows to rapidly create a web based way to obtain quality record data;
  - **EPR data stored in HIS system,** usingweb service and HL7/DICOM protocols to pass on EPR, this way supporting the interoperability with other products;
  - **Tree Input Management,** to manage the disease's process tree created by the guidelines, graphically represented in the front-end; the user can select the

Figure 2. Health discoverer architecture

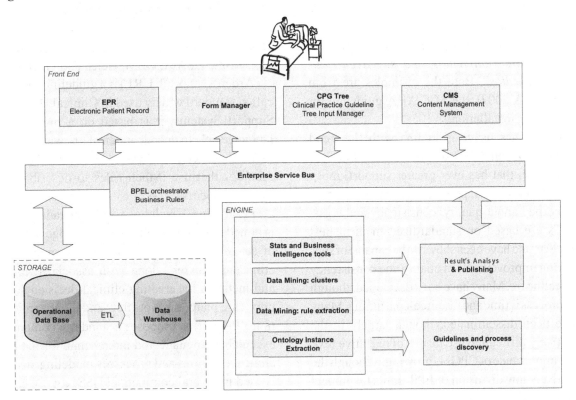

branch related to the real process of the illness cure and indicate the possible divergence. In this way alternate guidelines can be discovered or, if the guideline does not exists for the chosen illness, it can be anew created.

A **CMS** is used to disseminate results.

- **Storage:** receive the information from the Front End and collected them through an ETL (Extract, Transform and Load); once in the sub-system, the data will be used to populate a data warehouse, optimized for statistical and data mining purposes.
- **Engine:** core of Health Discoverer, includes the statistical components, the data mining tools, the ontology instance extraction and guideline and process discovery.

CLINICAL PRACTICE GUIDELINES (CPGS)

Clinical Practice Guidelines (CPGs) are a method for standardization and uniform improvement of the quality of medical care. CPGs describe plans and processes aimed to cure a specific illness.

As stated by the International Organization OpenClinical (URL: www.openclinical.org), "Guidelines are designed to support the decision-making processes in patient care. The content of a guideline is based on a systematic review of clinical evidence - the main source for evidence-based care."

According the Institute of Medicine definition, clinical guidelines are "systematically developed statements to assist practitioner and patient decisions about appropriate health care for specific clinical circumstances".

The guidelines are composed by decision trees, as in *Figure 3*, and descriptive text as "*Under certain circumstances, an implanted pacemaker may be useful for treating patients with recurrent symptomatic ventricular and supraventricularlartachycardias*". Both the examples are from (ACC/AHA 2002), the ACC/AHA guideline for pacemaker installation.

Guidelines usage is in line with the trend towards evidence-based medicine (EBM) and healthcare, that has ever-greater support, motivated by clinicians, politicians and management concerned about quality, consistency and costs. CPGs are based on standardized medical best practice, and have been shown to be capable of supporting improvements in quality and consistency in healthcare. Many have been developed, though the process is time and resource-consuming. Many have been disseminated, though largely in the relatively difficult to use format of narrative text. The importance of CPGs is growing, although the relatively low diffusion of EPR limits the impact on the medical practice.

Indeed, CPGs are mostly in textual form, that is impracticable by the EPR and by automatic system able to verify guideline' application. There are several systems aimed to formalize CPGs: Arden, PROforma, USAM, GEM, Helen and GLIF.

Arden Syntax (cf. URL) is a guideline specification standard widely used in Clinical Decision Support Systems; it is based on a procedural language able to encode medical knowledge and logic. Knowledge is defined in *Medical Logic Modules* that use if-then rules to describe the medical process.

PROForma (Fox, Johns & Rahmanzadeh 1998) is aimed to represent clinical knowledge in form of set of tasks; it is a language for modelling clinical processes, along with associated tools and methods for creating clinical decision support, care planning, workflow and other applications. PROforma proposes a standard, computer executable language and interchange format for clinical decisions and processes modeling, and it is used in several commercial DSS, e.g., Arezzo or Cocoon.

Figure 3. Selection of pacemaker systems for patients with atrioventricular (AV) block (excerpt ACC/AHA Pacemaker Installation Guideline)

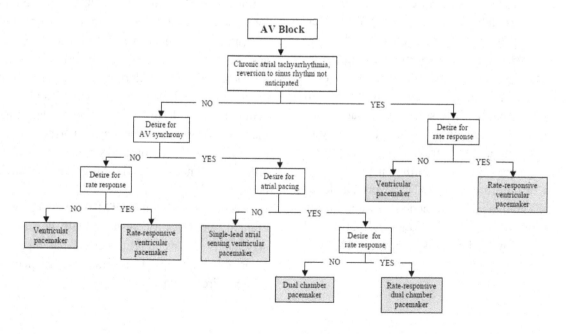

The Guideline Elements Model (GEM) is an XML-based guideline document model designed to organize all the life-cycle of guidelines. It is intended to facilitate translation of natural language guideline documents (i.e., the "natural" form of CPGs) into a format that can be automatically processed by machines. GEM is intended to be used throughout the entire guideline lifecycle to model information pertaining to guideline development, dissemination, implementation, and maintenance. GEM is document-centric and want to use the guideline document as a knowledge source to promotes authentic translation of domain knowledge.

GLIF is being described just below, 'cause it has been choosedas a standard for this work.

All these standards, and hence the guidelines "formally" described using them, start from the idea that there are persons designing them, and so are unable to encode the knowledge extracted from data mining algorithms (as acknowledged too by Kazemzadeh et al. 2006).

GLIF

The Guideline Interchange Format (GLIF) is a language for structured representation of guidelines, developed to facilitate sharing clinical guidelines.

The GLIF model (Peleg et al., 2000) allows the specification ofa guideline as a flowchart of temporally ordered steps, representing *clinical decision* and *action steps*. Concurrency was modeled using branch and synchronization steps. GLIF's guideline class also can manage authoring information, as the author, the status, the modification date and version, the scope of the guideline, eligibility criteria, and so on.

While developing a guideline, it is important to model not only the knowledge and the task involved in the care giving, but also to manage the guideline maintenance and the instantiation of a CPG in a real clinical environment, e.g., how to get patient data from EPR or to alert medics

in case of problems, and, last but not the least, the retrospective assessment of the quality of the application of the guidelines.

The modeling language of GLIF, in particular GLIF3 – its current version, permits to model the actions needed to describe a clinical guideline, using as a low level language a form of XML and an UML-like object oriented structure that permits to have different levels of description, using *classes*. In particular, GLIF3 offers:

- **Action steps:** recommendations for clinical actions to be performed (e.g., prescribe a medicine, order a test, start a treatment).
- **Decision steps:** decision criteria for conditional flowchart traversal (e.g., if-then decisions, as *if patient has high fever then do this*).
- **Branch and synchronization steps:** allow concurrency starting two or more concurrent decision flows, e.g., prescribing a medicine and a laboratory test at the same time. Synchronization reunify different branches in one single flow, e.g., receiving different tests in order to chose the next step.
- **Patient-state step:** characterizes patient's clinical state, the clinical history and diagnoses etc.

Indeed, to extract knowledge from the clinical database and then verify the adherence to the CPGs, GLIF3 has been used to model a flowchart diagram or, better, a finite state automaton with these basic modeling constructs, derived by the GLIF3 steps. This approach is similar to that of Kazemzadeh and Sartipi (2006), although the built automaton is needed to compare with discovered one and not (or at least *not only*), as in cited paper, to incorporate data mining task in a formal guideline.

Using these constructs, a CPG can be represented as a flowchart representation of a temporal sequence of clinical steps. In the following, these steps will be related to *events* to be discovered by the data mining process.

GLIF has three Representation levels: the *Author/viewer*, meant to describe the medical guideline for human understanding; the *Abstract machine*, that can be executed by an interpreter and used to analyze the correctness of guideline application; the *Integration into application environments*, to adapt to specific environments and contexts.

In this work, only the Abstract machine is mainly used, it is defined by logical expressions and actions that refer to defined concepts (medical ontology). The ontology can be formally defined by using the semantic web standards, as RDF and, more interesting, OWL (Web Ontology Language) that supersedes RDF including Description Language constructs and then allowing logical reasoning.

The GLIF standard has been chosen 'cause it is based on ontology, has a clear semantic and it can be based on OWL, that permits to extend the initial knowledge with new rules, although limited by the expressivity of Description Logic (a subset of First Order Logic).

DATA MINING IN CLINICAL CONTEXT

There is not a shared view of the adequacy of therapy, nor there is sufficient evidence of the right way to manage health care. Hence there is a strong need in having predictive modeling on Disease Management and data mining from the collected clinical work is proposed to start the process. On the other hand, this process needs to be an iterative, human-controlled one to permit the physician the evaluation of automatically generated results (clusters, trends, rules).

To remark the importance of knowledge discovery and modeling, the important Disease Management Association of America (DMAA) has a specific committee named "predictive modeling": "The mission [...] is to educate the health care community about analytic tools available for increasing the efficiency and effectiveness of disease management programs." (May, J. (2006), pg. 374).

Data mining is mainly used in the process of guidelines evaluation and new best practice process discovery, although, once the needed data warehouse is complete, it is possible to work on other goals too.

An interesting improvement area is the use of temporal data mining for extraction of long processes and geographical data mining for insights from the hospitals and patients geographical positioning. This is a new frontier of data mining, and there are virtually no works on the health area (except for Rohan. B et al. (2001)).

At last, the goal is to unify the results of the data mining rule extraction with an ontology description of the guidelines; these are formalized by GLIF (GuideLine Interchange Format, for a description see (Kazemzadeh and Sartipi 2006)). The outcome consists in enriching the ontology with logic rules descriptions derived by data mining, so that inference engines, i.e., reasoners, can use them to extend the knowledge discovered by the data mining process.

Definitions

Hand, Mannila& Smyth, in their *Principles of Data Mining*, define Data Mining (DM) as *"the analysis of (often large) observational data sets to find unsuspected relationships and to summarize the data in novel ways that are both understandable and useful to the data owner."*

In this case, clinical data are used to verify the appropriateness of the given cares, and in particular if these cares are following standard guidelines or, in case the cares are particularly successful, to extract a better guidelines. So, the goal is the building of a Clinical Decision Support System that, by interpreting the patient data using the mined knowledge within the context of the clinical guidelines, will be able to assist the decision makers and the medics to evaluate the

Figure 4. CRISP-DM life cycle

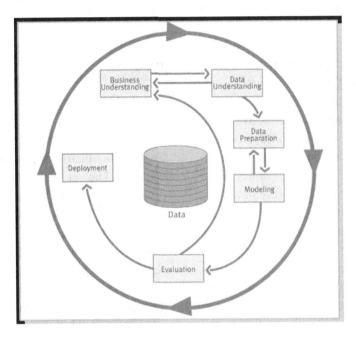

current way of giving care and then make better decision about the process and the enforcement of the following standard CPGs.

Applying data mining in health care is not a novelty. However, there are some issues that make DM in this scientific field particular. Medical data sets are typically too large or too sparse. When data from medical machines (e.g., an ECG or a PET) or from an epidemiological study on a country are collected, millions of records, typically low-detailed, may result; for instance, in Italy all the implantations of pacemakers and AICD are registered in a large National records, but the information are limited to the initial diagnosis, personal data and the model of pacemaker installed – really too few information to state care appropriateness. On the other side, if we collect detailed data within a single Hospital, we will have lots of columns, but a small patient populations – in this study more than 300 columns (fields) are filled, but only about a hundred of patients recorded.

Both cases require pushing data mining algorithms and processes to their limits (Roddick 2003).

All the most typical data mining techniques were applied to clinical data, in particular the macro areas of classification, clustery analysis and rule discovery. CRISP-DM process manages the application of these algorithms.

KDD Process: CRISP-DM

The KDD process is formalized in an industrial standard, CRISP-DM, that models the life cycle of a data mining project.

The steps of CRISP's life cycle, are:

- *Business Understanding:* Understanding the project objectives and requirements from a business perspective, then converting this knowledge into a data mining problem definition and a preliminary plan. The steps in this phase are: Determine the Business Objectives, Determine Data requirements for Business Objectives, Translate Business questions into Data Mining Objective.
- *Data Understanding:* characterize data available for modelling. Provide assessment and verification for data.

- ***Data Preparation:*** In this phase a set of examples is generated (choose sampling method, consider sample complexity, deal with volume bias issues), the attribute dimensionality is reduced (remove redundant and/or correlating attributes, combine attributes eg. sum, multiply, difference etc.) attribute value ranges are reduced (group symbolic discrete values, quantify continuous numeric values), data are transformed (de-correlate and normalize values, map time-series data to static representation).

- ***Modelling:*** In this phase, various modelling techniques are selected and applied and their parameters are calibrated to optimal values. Typically, there are several techniques for the same data mining problem type. Some techniques have specific requirements on the form of data. Therefore, stepping back to the data preparation phase is often necessary.

- ***Evaluation:*** At this stage in the project a model (or models) appearing to have high quality from a data analysis perspective is built. The model must be evaluated and reviewed to be certain it properly achieves the business objectives. A key objective is to determine if there is some important business issue that has not been sufficiently considered.

- ***Deployment:*** The knowledge gained will need to be organized and presented in a way that the customer can use it. It often involves applying "live" models within an organization's decision making processes, for example in real-time personalization of Web pages or repeated scoring of marketing databases. It can be as simple as generating a report or as complex as implementing a repeatable data mining process across the enterprise. In many cases it is the customer, not the data analyst, who carries out the deployment steps.

In the following subsection, the main DM techniques in health care are reviewed. An interesting more lengthy source is the paper "Selected techniques for data mining in medicine"(Lavra, 1999).

Classification

In classification the interest is focused in modelling the boundaries between classes (Hand et al. 2001). The act of classification is the training of a function to classify data item into, usually pre-defined, classes. Most popular algorithms in this class are: probabilistic learners as the Naïve Bayesian classifiers, decision tree learner as C4.5, Artificial Neural Networks.

In medicine, an evident use of classification is the partition of the all-patient group in affected and not affected by a disease. This group of algorithms are widely used in medicine, for instance in (Huang et al. 2007) to classify diabetic patients, or (Delen et al. 2005) in predicting breast cancer survivability.

Cluster Analysis

The idea in cluster analysis is to partition data (related to patients, to diseases etc.) to identify groups with a mapping function from a training sample to one of the identified groups. The algorithms in this group usually minimize a distance measure between a new item to be clusterized and the item in the yet classified cluster (e.g., using centroids). Although the goal is the same of classification, usually classification is supervised (i.e., the classification for the training samples is known) while clustering is unsupervised (the algorithms discover *per sé* the groups).

Popular algorithms for clustering are KNN – K-nearest neighbour algorithm, Kohonen maps – or SOM – Self Organizing Maps.

As stated by (Kazemzadeh. and Sartipi 2006), an application of clustering in the clinical care domain might be to perform risk analysis and assess patients' risk factors. (Churilov et al. 2004) have carried out a similar study to assign patients to three disjoint clusters of high, intermediate, and low risk patients.

Association Rules

The goal of association rule mining is the extraction of *if... then...* rules from the data, where *if A then B* will means that items of group A implies items of group B with a certain percentage *confidence*.

Association rules are very general, and can be employed in healthcare for identify patterns in data set; you can say that association rules *explain* the reasons of data, e.g., identify that a disease arises from two composed symptoms. association rules are employed for detecting when medics used a particular type of pacemaker, and then the soundness of the choice can be evaluated.

Each rule of the form $A \rightarrow B$ is characterized by the rule support, i.e., the total number of occurrence of the rule, and the confidence, i.e., the ratio of occurrence where A and B applies to the number of occurrence where only A applies. High confidence will mean that the causal relation between A and B is strong; high support will mean that the given rule that there are many sample of them can be trusted.

Rules are a form of knowledge stating the hidden relations, and so they are very important in clinical data mining. Figure 5 shows some rules extracted with C4.5 algorithm to identify the type of pacemaker medics will use and why.

There are lots of works on this subject; a new interesting one is by (Feng et al., 2006), on rule extraction in traditional Chinese medicine.

Temporal and spatial data mining

Another important point is the need in analysing data within a spatial and temporal framework. This is very important in case of epidemiological studies or syndromic surveillance (cf. URL: www.syndromic.org). This type of surveillance involves collecting and analyzing statistical data on health trends – such as symptoms reported by people seeking care in emergency rooms or other health care settings – or even sales of medicines to early detection of bio terrorism attacks or diffusion of epidemics. Within the context of appropriateness, it is very interesting to discover if there are local differences in managing a specific clinical illness.

Temporal analysis is even more important, given that is important to study the order in which cares are provided. E.g., an important case of inappropriateness arises from two sequential hospital admissions related to the same illness: if the patient was correctly healed in the first admission, there were no raison to admit him again, so it is evident the care from the first admission were faulty.

Usually, in data mining temporal data are flattened in a single row that presents all the data together. This is a oversimplification that can hinder the discover of temporal relationships between cares, and it is inherently hard given the

Figure 5. Example of extracted rule

```
    R1: IF CONFSYS=VDD and ISCHEMIA=no THEN
Pacemaker= KVDD701
    R2: IF CONFSYS=VDD and
    ISCHEMIA=IMA_Q THEN
Pacemaker= KVDD901
    R3: IF CONFSYS=CSVD THEN
        Pacemaker=EntityDC
```

wide degree of freedom in giving care also for the same clinical condition. On the other hands, *real* temporal and spatial mining involves algorithms and processes that are heavy in computation time and not yet so reliable.

An intermediate way to approach temporal data is the segmentation in discrete *episode events*.

Of course, to discover guidelines application, temporal analysis is *needed*, so the choice fallen on episode estimation that permits us to really discover CPGs uses.

Episodes

Episodes are well known in healthcare, and are the base of popular instruments as Diagnosis-Related Group (DRG) or Episode Treatment Groups (ETGs).

Diagnosis-related groups (DRGs) are a classification of hospital case types into groups expected to have similar hospital resource use. Medicare uses this classification to pay for inpatient hospital care. The groupings are based on diagnoses, procedures, age, sex, and the presence of complications or comorbidities. The DRGs may be assigned using different grouper, besides comparisons among different DRG versions should be done with caution since criteria are revised periodically.

Following Williams and Solon (Williams et al., 2002 - Solon et. al., 1967) episodes of care can be defined as "*A block of one or more medical services, received by an individual during a period of relatively continuous contact with one or more providers of service, in relation to a particular medical problem or situation*".

Although the definition is very general, it is still useful for defining how to partition the semi-continuous data found in the database. To define a block of cares as a single episode it is necessary to know the specific cares applied to the monitored disease: different diseases can have different way to compute blocks and episodes.

A transformation phase computing episodes from the database is applied. To define an episode

a *key element* that identify a clinician (medic, nursery) giving an evaluation or a treatment to a patient is needed; to this key element we can link other elements (as drug prescriptions, tests and so on). In this way a fixed frame window is not used, but the construction of the episode on the relevance of care. This work is based on inpatient cares, so the construction starts from the admission to the hospital and ends with the discharge from the hospital and the subsequent patient recalls – the idea is that the sequence is relative to a complete disease management.

This is coherent with the quality records too, so we have a long sequence of more simpler episodes, each one can be atomic or a simple composition of atomic acts. The episodes are chosen to match the steps in the guidelines.

To have a sound appropriateness instrument, relevant aspects must be included in the episodes, as complications, comorbidities, important treatment as surgery.

Clinical complications: are complications arising during disease treatment that can change significantly the cares; complications can be related to the main disease, and described by the CPG. For instance, after a pacemaker installation can arose a haematoma; complication of a bronchitis can result in a pneumonia.

Comorbidities: it describes the effect of all other diseases or previous medical history (treatment, drugs etc.) an individual patient might have other than the primary disease of interest. For instance, a patient that needs a pacemaker implants *and* have HIV, requires different treatment from a patient without HIV. Comorbidities can impact heavily on the care plans, and it is important to record all the elements that can permit to differentiate patients with or without comorbidities, otherwise data mining will produce incorrect results.

Surgery and other important treatments: in this case, surgery can be considered as a single step in the main guideline, while a specific protocol or guideline are applied to the surgery

Figure 6. Action records of patient cares

Time	Episode	Episode event #	Patient	Context	Action	Parameters-1	Parameters-2	Parameters-3
0	1	1	id-p$_{300}$	inpatient	admission	initial patient's clinical state and history		
1	1	2	id-p$_{300}$	inpatient	prescription	medicine$_1$		
1	1	2	id-p$_{300}$	inpatient	prescription	medicine$_2$		
1	1	2	id-p$_{300}$	inpatient	prescription	test$_1$		
2	1	3	id-p$_{300}$	inpatient	action	test$_1$		
3	1	4	id-p$_{300}$	inpatient	patient-step	patient's clinical state resulting from test1		
2	1	5	id-p$_{300}$	inpatient	action	assumption	medicine$_1$	quantity
3	1	5	id-p$_{300}$	inpatient	action	assumption	medicine$_2$	quantity
4	1	6	id-p$_{300}$	inpatient	prescription	test$_2$		
5	1	7	id-p$_{300}$	inpatient	action	test$_1$		
5	1	8	id-p$_{300}$	inpatient	action	assumption	medicine$_1$	quantity
5	1	8	id-p$_{300}$	inpatient	action	assumption	medicine$_2$	quantity
5	1	8	id-p$_{300}$	inpatient	action	assumption	medicine$_3$	quantity
6	1	9	id-p$_{300}$	inpatient	action	treatment$_2$		
6	1	10	id-p$_{300}$	inpatient	patient-step	patient's clinical state resulting from test$_2$		
7	1	10	id-p$_{300}$	inpatient	patient-step	clinical state		
7	1	11	id-p$_{300}$	inpatient	dismission	from admission		
8	1	12	id-p$_{300}$	recall	admission	to recall		
9	1	13	id-p$_{300}$	recall	action	test$_3$		
9	1	13	id-p$_{300}$	recall	patient-step	patient's clinical state resulting from test$_3$		
10	1	14	id-p$_{300}$	inpatient	dismission	from recall		
11	1	15	id-p$_{300}$	recall	admission	to recall		
12	1	16	id-p$_{300}$	recall	action	test$_3$		
12	1	16	id-p$_{300}$	recall	patient-step	patient's clinical state resulting from test$_3$		
13	1	17	id-p$_{300}$	recall	action	treatment$_3$		
14	1	18	id-p$_{300}$	recall	patient-step	clinical state		
15	1	19	id-p$_{300}$	inpatient	dismission	from recall		

itself. So the analysis is simplified by managing this sequence of care not a single, complex, one but as the sum of two simpler sequences.

Figure 6 shows a simplified view of the data at the beginning of episode event counting process: each row contains the time when information are recorded, patient id (for privacy reason, his/her name is not used but an id only), the action type, the action parameters.

The data table contains information about a patient (id-p$_{300}$) admitted to the hospital, the relative given cares and two sequences of recall, the first with only a test and the second with a treatment too.

A tool is applied to this initial table to determine the episodes, *E²T* or *Episode Extraction Tool*. E²T uses episode discrimination criteria borrowed by the CPGs and by the medical ontology used as reference. It is useful to note that the column "action" is not present in the initial data, but was derived from the ontology too. This ontology permits to derive that to take a drug or make a

test are all "action", while the test results or a screening are "patient-step"; as you can see, the concept "action", "patient-step" and so on come from GLIF3 ontology, extended to suite the needs. In the database, we don't find the "branch step" and the "synchronization steps", because there are no explicit data to identify the start of parallel actions (*branch*) and the subsequent unification (*synchronization*); how explained below, this void has impact in the next step.

Once E²T computed the episodes and its events in the clinical lifetime of a patient, the adherence to the applied therapy to official guidelines can be extracted.

GUIDELINES ADHERENCE DISCOVERY USING MARKOV CHAINS

All the elements needed to compute the guideline adherence by medics are now defined. Indeed we have:

- **Databases** with all recorded cares for each patients; these databases are derived by EPR, quality records, doctors' annotations and so on;
- **A data warehouse** that unify all the collected data in homogeneous views (data marts) and permits to analyze data efficiently and with focus the subsequent data mining operations; ETL tools are used to create the data warehouse and in the process inconsistencies are cleaned and reduced and errors in the data cleared;
- **Rules and clustering** computed by "traditional" data mining; these results can be used *per se* or as annotation of the discovered CPGs;
- **Episodes**, extracted by a parser in accord to events and episode definition; these sequences are specific to each patient cares (in this case, the inpatient cares plus the hospital recalls);
- **Formalized clinical practice guidelines**, in GLIF3 format; we can have more than one CPG for each disease, for instance we can have an European, Italian, USA, specific medical association guidelines: these guidelines are all correct, and a medic can chose one of them or no one, preferring to decide itself.

From these key elements, a way to compute the adherence to each possible guideline and, in case is needed, the *real* guideline that the hospital (or the medic) is *really* using.

Hidden Markov Models

As noticed in last paragraph, database shows only the episode events (and hence the episodes), but has no information on the process flow. The moments when clinical personal (medics, nurses and so on) operates a choice is *hidden*: we can watch the observable output of a black box, but we have no (direct) knowledge of how the box

Figure 7. A Markov chain

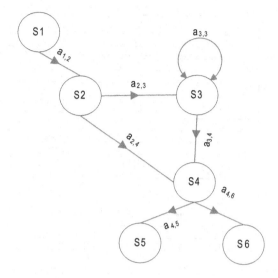

operates, i.e. we don't know the *model* of the black box. This is common situation, and there is a strong formalism used to model it: Markov Hidden Models (HMM).

HMM are related to Markov chains. The idea is to have a system that can be modelled any time as being in one of n distinct states s_1, s_2, ..., s_n, as illustrated by Figure 7. The system changes from a state to another according to a set of probabilities associated with each state. The time associated with state changes is denoted as $t = 1, 2, ..., m$ and the actual state at time t is denoted as q_t. To have a sound probabilistic description of this system the current state at time t and all the predecessor states are needed; for Markov chains, this probabilistic description is reduced to the current and the predecessor state only (Rabiner 1988, a very good introduction to Markov chains and Hidden Markov Models).

$$P[q_t = S_j \mid q_{t-1} = S_j, q_{t-2} = S_k, ...]$$
$$= P[q_t = S_j \mid q_{t-1} = S_i] \tag{1}$$

Only the process in which the right hand side of previous equation is independent of time is considered, and so the probability of the transition a_{ij}, i.e., moving from state s_i to state s_j is:

$$a_{ij} = P[q_t = S_j \mid q_{t-1} = S_i] \qquad (2)$$

where

$$a_{ij} \geq 0 \qquad (3)$$

and

$$\sum_{j=1}^{N} a_{ij} = 1 \qquad (4)$$

Formally, a Markov chain is a triple $\langle E, \{p(p_1 = s)\}, A \rangle$ where:

- $E = \{1,2,...,k\}$ is finite set of states (or events); each state is a symbol generated by the alphabet S
- p is the set of the initial probabilities;
- A is the set of transition probability a_{st} for each s, t in E; as it said, the transition probability a_{st} is $a_{st} = P(p_i = t \mid p_{i-1} = s)$

More informally, a (first order) Markov chain is a probabilistic automaton where the probability of state change is related only to the previous state. A Markov chain is also an *observable* Markov model, because each state is related to an observable world event (an event of the world being modelled).

Hidden Markov Models deal with the modeling of situation where the world events cannot be observed; this is our case, because the transition is known, i.e., the effects of the state changing, but not the states themselves.

A HMM is a stochastic process determined by the two interdependent mechanisms, an underlying Markov chain having a finite number of states and a set of random functions (the black box). At each time step, the process modelled by the HMM is in a specific state and an observation is given by the random functions related to the current state. The Markov chain that is hidden to the observer changes state in accord to the transition probability from the current state to the next (using the probability matrix that describe each transition from i to j). The observer sees only the output of the random functions associated with each state and so cannot observer the Markov chain and does not observe its states – indeed, the chain is *hidden* to the observer, while the outputs are known.

A formal definition of a HMM, using Rabiner notations is:

1. N is the number of states in the model; although the states are hidden, a certain correspondence between these states and world events can be assumed, in this case states of a CPG;
2. M is the number of distinct observation symbols per state, i.e., the discrete alphabet size; in this case, the types of given cares, the types of tests and so on;
3. A the transition probability matrix $A = \{a_{ij}\}$, where a_{ij} is the transition probability of the underlying Markov chain to move to state j from the (current) state i, as in eq. 2.
4. B the observation symbol probability distribution matrix $B = \{b_j(k)\}$ where $b_j(k)$ is the random function associated with state j and where
   $b_j(k) = P[v_k \text{ at } t \mid q_t = S_j]$ $1 \leq j \leq N \text{ and } 1 \leq k \leq M$ (5)
5. Initial distribution $\pi = \{\pi_i\}$ where
   $\pi_i = P[q_1 S_j]$ $1 \leq j \leq N$ (6)

Hence the elements of an HMM are the model parameters of N, M, A, B, and π. N and M, that are implicit in the dimensions of the matrices A and B, can be removed simplifying the formula. So , a HMM is defined by the notation $\lambda = (A, B, \pi)$.

In conclusion, HMM is used to model the data collected about the CPGs use and discover real practice adherence, using the principles of Evidence Based Medicine: data evidence is exploited to extract knowledge about the appropriateness of (hospital) practice cares and their compliance with one of the CPGs designed by healthcare associations.

Last step to reach the goal is the computation of CPG adherence, as described in the next subsection

Chain Discoverer Tool (CDT)

In the last step in compliance discovering, there are two distinct problems: the first is computing how specific CPG are compliant with the training set, i.e., the collected data marked with episodes and episode events; the second is the discover of the best, possibly new, CPG as determined by the clinical follows up.

There is an important difference in the formalism used in the two problems: the first is a known Markov model, and so known is the underlying Markov chain, i.e., the probabilistic automaton derived by the CPG. Looking at the segment of a hearth CPG in *Figure 3*, it emerges an evidence of a tree that is the base of such automaton: remember, the only observable elements in database are the grey boxes while the branches (e.g., "Deside for rate response") are used by medics but otherwise hidden.

However, if only the compliance must be checked, known sources (from the patient-state step nodes) can be used to verify if the medic followed this particular guideline; e.g., the "chronic a trial tachyarrhythmia" can be verified by the state of the patient, and so the hidden elements

are known, and a "simple" Markov chain can be used instead of an HMM.

In the second case, the free search for a good CPG, there is no prepared CPG, and so a full HMM must be used (no CPG, hence no evident Markov chain).

The *Chain Discoverer Tool* (CDT) is used to accomplish both these operations. From the E^2T the care data labelled with episodes are discovered, and CDT emits the percentage of compliance with a set of CPGs, and, if requested, the real automaton that describes (probabilistically) the cares given in accord to the database.

Compliance of a Specific CPG

Verification of the degree of compliance with some CPG is a useful tool to verify if a medic and his team are following one of the official guideline; it is important to remember that each disease can have more that a CPG, produced by European medic associations, or American ones or a National associations; hence, while the protocols are mandatory, the guidelines are discretionary. However, for a Clinical Decisional Support System, it is important to know if a medic are using one of the official guidelines or a new (possibly better) guideline.

To compute the distance between a specific care and one of the possible CPGs Laxman's work (Laxman et al. 2005) can be useful, talking about the discover of frequent episodes and learning hidden Markov models. An episode sequence is an ordered tuple of event types, with a time label, for instance:

Figure 8. CPG compliance discovery

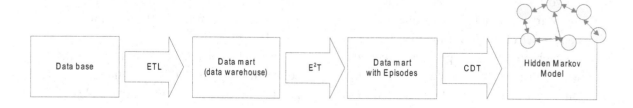

$$\langle (E_1, t_1), (E_2, t_2), \ldots, (E_n, t_n) \rangle$$

Removing the time label, an episode can b defined as a sequence of events

$$E_1 \rightarrow E_2 \rightarrow \ldots \rightarrow E_n$$

First step is the counting of non-overlapping episode frequency. Two occurrences of an episode are said to be non-overlapping if no event associated with one appears in between the events associated with the other. The *frequency* of an episode is defined as the maximum number of non-overlapping occurrences of the episode in the event sequence.

The overlapping can happen in clinical data if a patient receive care for two distinct diseases: the two event sequences are overlapping but they belongs to distinct process and CPGs; this differentiation is carried out by the E_2T tool.

To determine the adherence to a CPG, the counting of episodes compatible with each CPG must be measured, that is given by algorithm 1:

This algorithm is a much simplified version of that in (Laxman et al. 2005), because we split the episode counting in the two tools, one step in E^2T and one in CDT.

Discovery of a New CPG

The discovery of a new CPG is equivalent to the discovery of the parameters of a HMM. The parameters that we are looking for are the number N of states, the transition probabilities matrix A – for each a_{ij} and hence the topology of the Markov chain, i.e., starting to a full connected graph, we want to remove the connections a_{ij} where the probability of the transition a_{ij} is 0. The topology of the HMM is defined by the type and the size of the HMM (Kwong et al. 2001). The type of HMM describes the connections between the states in the HMM and the size of HMM is the number of states used in the HMM.

There are several algorithm to compute and optimize the model parameters (the a_{ij}), in particular the Baum-Welch algorithm (Baum 2003), a specialized version of hill climbing. "Optimize" means to discover the most fit parameters compliant with the training set, i.e., the observed data.

This task is a simplified version of the general one. We can estimate the number N of states deriving it from the existing guidelines, and then start from a random probabilities matrix. We used a standard Baum-Welch algorithm although it suffer by sub-optimal optimization (given his hill-climbing derivation). A better, although more complex, solution is to use genetic algorithm that are able to optimize the model parameter *and* the topology at same time; details of such methods are described in (Kwong et al. 2001). We have planned the switch to genetic algorithms in the next version of CDT.

We can derive different HMM from the initial data. We are interested in these cases:

Algorithm 1. CPGs episode occurrence counting

```
INPUT: C is the set of candidate episodes, i.e., the training data for a single episode
       for all episodes e[i] in C
           for all event A[j] in e[i] do
               for all possible automaton α_x
                   if A[j] is acceptable by the automaton α_x at step j then increment freq_αk
OUTPUT: frequencies freq_αk for all automata a_x (i.e., all the computed CPGs)
```

- **The totality of the training sample,** i.e., collected data: this experiment gives us an idea of the real process flow medics are using.
- **Only the training sample with a positive outcomes,** i.e., resulting in a successful disease management and less expensive cares; this is a very important process description, because it can be better than the "official" CPGs.
- **Only the training sample with a negative outcomes,** the inverse of the last case, i.e., resulting in unsuccessful disease management and/or expensive cares; this model is important too, because it gives us hint of how improve the cares.

The data set can be computed using filters as:

- Specific hospital;
- Specific department;
- Specific region etc.

For privacy and legal reason, it is impossible to apply the algorithm to one specific medic/team, although the instrument can be used as an improvement tool by the interested medic (and only from him/her).

CONCLUSION AND FUTURE RESEARCH

This research has moved from a Health-Mining project that gave interesting results, especially thanks to wide consensus gained among physicians. The objective was to put the basis for a generic disease management support system, establishing the workflow process and the needed software tools, directly reusable when moving to other diseases. In this sense, Health-Mining was a generalized framework involving not only software elements but also actors (physicians, managers, etc.).

Assuming the process has been correctly developed, actively involving relevant actors, we set-up appropriate instruments to harvest data, copying with frequent and well-known issues related to medical data collection.

Authors were sure that classical statistical analysis of patient records (as in Swedish National Quality Register) would provided us with a large amount of useful information, but they knew that this kind of process is human driven and, being a simple mechanism, would have not been able to discover unknown, probably useful, Guidelines. In fact, thanks to Gödel proof (K. Gödel, 1931), authors know that in a logic-formal system not all the true sentences can be deducted using the given rules. So, they used appropriate languages and algorithms to implement a system free to search for different kind of associations in a given database. Thanks to appropriate interpreters and Clinical Practice Guidelines discoverers they build a system able to focus data mining discovery into understandable and applicable Guidelines, going far beyond the simple statistical analysis of data and avoiding both incompleteness problems and user driven limitations. Concluding, Health Discoverer adds to Health-Mining project new temporal data mining algorithms, ontology extraction capabilities, and a better integration with standard data format for Guidelines.

As future works, authors expect to incorporate this system in the management process of large hospitals. The application to a larger set of illnesses has a direct managerial implication, because the system can act a meter and recommender on a larger audience, and can strengthen the algorithm too, because it will be challenged by more data, and they know how noise, missing data etc. can impact on an algorithm performance.

For the management side, this research has experimented the system (a simpler version) on a real project (pacemaker installation, as reported above), and it got some important results – especially for the extraction rule. Now the researchers want to measure how the system really impacts on the care and cost improvement, and if it is possible to extract better guidelines from the concrete hospital life: it has been theoretically supposed, but a concrete proof will represent a success for the entire theory.

REFERENCES

ACC & AHA, "ACC/AHA/NASPE 2002 Guideline Update for Implantation of Cardiac Pacemakers and Antiarrhythmia Devices", (2002) American College of Cardiology Foundation and the American Heart Association, ; 106:2145-2161, URL: http://www.americanheart.org/downloadable/heart/1032981283481CleanPacemakerFinalFT.pdf

Arden Syntax for Medical Logic Systems, web site: http://cslxinfmtcs.csmc.edu/hl7/arden

Baum, L.E. (2003) "Hidden Markov Models and the Baum-Welch Algorithm", IEEE Information Theory Society Newsletter, Vol. 53, No.4, December 2003, pp. 1-1

Bei, A., De Luca, S., Ruscitti, G. and Salamon, D. (2005) Health-Mining: a Disease Management Support Service based on Data Mining and Rule Extraction. In *Proceedings of the 2005 IEEE Engineering in Medicine and Biology 27th Annual Conference Shanghai, China*, IEEE.

Churilov, L., Bagirov, A. M. , Schwartz, D. , Smith, K. A. & Dally. M. (2004) "Improving risk grouping rules for prostate cancer patients with optimization". In *HICSS*, 2004.

Data Mining Group, PMML, web site: http://www.dmg.org/v3-1/GeneralStructure.html

De Luca, S., Memo, E., Santesso. E. et al.(2005) *L'appropriatezza dei ricoveri ospedalieri: analisi e proposte*, (in Italian: *Appropriateness of hospital admissions: analysis and proposals*), 2005 Libreria Editrice Cafoscarina (Venice).

Delen, D., Walker, G. & Kadam, A. (2005) "Predicting breast cancer survivability: a comparison of three data mining methods", in *Artificial Intelligence in Medicine* (2005) 34, pp. 113—127

EMCC (European Monitoring Centre on Change) (2003), *The future of health and social services in Europe*, European Foundation for the Improvement of Living and Working Conditions. URL: http://www.eurofound.europa.eu/emcc/publications/2003/sf_hss_1.pdf

Feng, Y., Wu, Z., Zhou, X., Zhou, Z., Fan, W. (2006) "Knowledge discovery in traditional Chinese medicine: State of the art and perspectives", in *Artificial Intelligence in Medicine* (2006) 38, pp. 219—236

Field M., Lohr K. (1992) Clinical Practice Guidelines: Directions for a New Program, I.o.M., editor. Committee to Advise the Public Health Service on Clinical Practice Guidelines; 1992.

Fox J., Johns N., Rahmanzadeh A. (1998) Disseminating medical knowledge: the PROforma approach. Artificial Intelligence in Medicine 1998;14:157–81.

Forthman, M.T., Dove, H.G., Wooster, L.D. "Episode Treatment Groups (ETGs): A Patient Classification System for Measuring Outcomes Performance by Episode of Illness", *Top Health Inform Manage*, 2000, 21(2), 51–61

Gödel K., *Über formal unentscheidbare Sätze der Principia Mathematica und verwandter Systeme*, Monatshefte für Mathematik und Physik, vol. 38 (1931).

Hand, D. Mannila H. & Smyth, P. (2001), *Principles of Data Mining*, MIT Press, Cambridge, MA, 2001.

Huang, Y., McCullagh, P., Black, N & Harper, R. (2007) "Feature selection and classification model construction on type 2 diabetic patients' data", in *Artificial Intelligence in Medicine*, Volume 41, Issue 3, November 2007, Pages 251-262

Kazemzadeh, R.S. and Sartipi, K. (2006), Incoporating Data Mining Applications into Clinical Guildelines. In *Proceedings of the 19th IEEE Symposium on Computer-Based Medical Systems (CBMS'06)*, IEEE.

Kwong, S., Chau, C.W., Man, K.F., Tang, K.S, (2001) "Optimisation of HMM topology and its model parameters by genetic algorithms", Elsevier, *Pattern Recognition* 34 (2001), pp. 509 – 522

Lavrač, N. (1999) "Selected techniques for data mining in medicine", in *Artificial Intelligence in Medicine* Vol. 16 (1999) pp. 3–23

Laxman, S. Sastry, P.S., Unnikrishnan, K.P. (2005) "Discovering Frequent Episodes and Learning Hidden Markov Models: A Formal Connection", in *IEEE Transactions On Knowledge And Data Engineering*, vol. 17, no. 11, November 2005, pp. 1505 – 1517

Mattke, S., Seid, M. & Ma, S. (2007) "Evidence for the Effect of Disease Management: Is $1 Billion a Year a Good Investment?" in *The American Journal Of Managed Care*, Vol. 13, No. 12, pp. 670–6

May, J. (2006) DMAA: Defining Quality in Health Care Coordination. In Disease Management, vol. 9, n. 6., pp 371-375.

Mörchen, F. (2006) "Algorithms for time series knowledge mining". In Eliassi-Rad, T., Ungar, L. H. , Craven, M., Gunopulos, D. editors, *Proceedings The Twelveth ACM SIGKDD International Conference on Knowledge Discovery and Data Mining*, pages 668–673, 2006.

Mörchen, F. (2007), "Unsupervised pattern mining from symbolic temporal data", in *SIGKDD Explorations* Volume 9, Issue 1, pp. 41 – 55

OECD - Organization for Economic Co-operation and development (2007), *OECD Health Data 2007 - Frequently Requested Data*, URL: http://www. oecd.org/document/16/0,2340,en_2649_34631_ 2085200_1_1_1_1,00.html

Openclinical, clinical Practice Guidelines, web site: http://openclinical.org/guidelines.html

Peleg M, Boxwala A. A., Omolola O., Zeng Q., Tu, S.W, Lacson R., Bernstam, E., Ash, N., Mork, P., Ohno-Machado, L., Shortliffe, E.H., and Greenes, R.A. (2000). "GLIF3: The Evolution of a Guideline Representation Format" In Overhage M.J.,, Ed., *Proceedings of the 2000 AMIA Annual Symposium (Los Angeles, CA, 2000)*, Hanley & Belfus, Philadelphia.

Proforma, web site: http://www.acl.icnet.uk/lab/ proforma.html

Rabiner, L. R. (1989) "A tutorial on hidden Markov models and selected applications in speech recognition," *Proc. IEEE*, vol. 77, no. 2, pp. 257–286, Feb. 1989.

Roddick, J.F., Fule, P., Graco, W.J., (2003) "Exploratory Medical Knowledge Discovery Experiences and Issues", in *ACM SIGKDD Explorations Newsletter*, Volume 5 , Issue 1 (July 2003), pp. 94 – 99

Rohan. B., Graham. W., and Hongxing, H. (2001) Feature Selection for Temporal Health Records. In Cheung, D., Williams, G.J. and Li, Q. (Eds.): *PAKDD 2001, LNAI 2035*, pp. 198-209.

Shahar, Y., Young. O, Shalom, E., Galperin, M., Mayaffit, A., Moskovitch, R., Hessing, A., (2004) "A framework for a distributed, hybrid, multiple-ontology clinical-guideline library, and automated guideline-support tools", Elsevier, Journal of Biomedical Informatics 37 (2004) 325–344

Shahar, Y., Miksch, S., Johnson, P., (2006) "A task-specific ontology for the application and critiquing of time-oriented clinical guidelines", in *Artificial Intelligence in Medicine*, Springer, Lecture Notes in Computer Science, Volume 1211/1997

Shiffman, R.N, Michel, G., Essaihi, A., Thornquist, E, (2004), "Bridging the Guideline Implementation Gap: A Systematic, Document-Centered Approach to Guideline Implementation", in *Journal of the American Medical Informatics Association* Volume 11 Number 5 Sep / Oct 2004

Solon,J.A., Feeney,S.H., Jones,S.H., Rigg,R.D., Sheps,C.G. (1967) "Delineating episodes of medical care". *American Journal of Public Health*, 57 (1967) 401–408

Solon,J.A.,Feeney, S.H., Jones, S.H., Rigg,R.D., Sheps,C.G. "Delineating episodes of medical care" in *American Journal of Public Health*, 57 (1967) pp. 401–408

Tu, S. W., Kahn, M. G., Musen, M. A., Ferguson, J. C., Shortliffe, E. H., and Fagan, L. M. (1989). "Episodic Skeletal-Plan Refinement on Temporal Data". *Communications of ACM*, 32:1439-1455.

Welch, W.P., Bazarko, D., Ritten, K., Burgess, Y., Harmon, R., Sandy, L.G., (2007) "Electronic Health Records in Four Community Physician Practices: Impact on Quality and Cost of Care", *Journal of the American Medical Informatics Association*, Volume 14, Issue 3, May-June 2007, Pages 320-328

Williams, G., Baxter. R., Kelman, C., Rainsford, C., He, H., Gu, L., Vickers, D., Hawkins, S., (2002), "Estimating Episodes of Care Using Linked Medical Claims Data", in R.I. McKay and J. Slaney (Eds.): *AI 2002*, LNAI 2557, Springer, pp. 660–671, 2002.

Won, K-J., Prügel-Bennett, A., Krogh, A., (2006) "Evolving the Structure of Hidden Markov Models", *IEEE Transactions on Evolutionary Computation*, vol. 10, no. 1, February 2006, pp. 39–49.

Chapter VI
Governance in European Hospitals:
Analysing Governance Practices Using Data Mining and Information Visualisation

Kristof Eeckloo
Centre for Health Services and Nursing Research, Belgium

Luc Delesie
Centre for Health Services and Nursing Research, Belgium

Arthur Vleugels
Centre for Health Services and Nursing Research, Belgium

ABSTRACT

Hospital governance refers to the complex of checks and balances that determine how decisions are made within the top structures of hospitals. In this chapter, authors introduce hospital governance as a policy domain in which data mining methods have a large potential to provide insight and practical knowledge. The chapter starts by exploring the essentials of the concept, by analysing the root notion of governance and comparing it with applications in other sectors. Recent developments and examples from the UK, France and The Netherlands are outlined. Based on an evaluation of the current state of affairs, a research agenda is developed. The chapter concludes with an introduction to the European Hospital Governance Project, which follows the outlines of the described research agenda. Methods of data mining and information visualisation that are used in this project are explained by means of a real data example.

INTRODUCTION:
A STRAIGHTFORWARD
THEORY OF GOVERNANCE

The term governance has a strong intuitive appeal: it is easily associated with attributes such as accountability, transparency and participation. Yet, when it comes to a definition, governance seems to turn into a rather complex and versatile notion (European Commission, 2001). Illustrative for its versatility are the many concepts and neologisms in which the term is used. *Corporate governance* is probably the best known. It stands for the system by which a private corporation is directed and controlled by its share- and stakeholders (Cadbury, 1992). Other examples are *clinical governance, cultural governance, social governance, E-governance, global governance, government governance*, etc. At the Birbeck University of London there is even a research centre on 'football governance'. All of these concepts put forward their own definitions, all shaping – and blurring – for their part, the root notion of governance.

However, despite this breadth and ambiguity of definitions and wide scope of applications, governance essentially refers to the means for achieving direction, control and coordination of wholly or partially autonomous individuals or organizational units, on behalf of interests to which they jointly contribute (Lynn et al., 2001). It takes shape in the complex of rules, values, procedures and structures, usually referred to as *"checks and balances"*, that determine how decisions are taken by these individuals or units (Rozman, 2000).

As such, it has a social, a political and an economic dimension. And it can be encountered at all levels of human activity: for example, at state level, at the level of the local community or at the level of a corporation.

Already within the world of health, Preker and Harding (2003) identify four levels of governance. First, there is the global or cross-national level.

An example of a specific topic at this level are the procedures to address international pandemics. Second, there is multi-sectoral (or 'macro') governance. This level addresses policy sets that control the behaviour and use of resources in the broader economy of a nation. Third, there is sectoral (or 'meso') governance, where the ministry of health seeks to promulgate policies and allocate resources among providers, payers, and technology-pharma producers to not just restore health, but to protect and promote health. And finally, there is institutional (or 'micro') governance, which deals with the control of a specific organization's (for example a hospital, pharmaceutical company or health insurance plan) resources for mission accomplishment.

This chapter will focus on the application of the governance-concept within the organisational context of a hospital: commonly referred to as "hospital governance".

In many European countries, the governing bodies of hospitals are increasingly recognised as key actors in the health care systems. As decentralised health care agents, they are thought to embody both entrepreneurial dynamism and societal legitimacy. The challenge many health care systems currently face is to achieve a "fit" between the changing context of health care and the key configurations of these governing bodies of hospitals: structure and composition (who), role (what) and functioning (how).

Meeting this challenge is no easy task and depends on three intertwined prerequisites. The first is a solid and valid conceptual model for the delineation and testing of the many diverse characteristics and variables at play. The second is close observation in a wide range of hospitals in different socio-cultural and economic-political settings which will result in reliable experimental data. The third is a method of analysis and synthesis for the myriad of relationships that are undoubtedly at the basis of the actual situation. Data mining and information visualisation can support this challenge, as these can help targeting governance configurations to the characteristics of the health care systems and care settings in which they are embedded.

The chapter provides a real data example of such use of data mining and information visualisation, based on the data of a recent research project on hospital governance. Preceding this example, an overview is given of the changing characteristics of hospital governance in Europe, followed by a proposed research agenda.

BACKGROUND: GOVERNANCE IN HOSPITALS, A COMPLEX REALITY

Hospital governance shares with corporate governance the institutional approach. However, it also has some important distinguishing characteristics (Miller, 2002; Brickley & Van Horn, 2002; Beekun et al., 1998).

First, there is the fact that the overall majority of hospitals (certainly in Europe) are public or non-profit private institutions (Yuen, 2005). As a consequence they have no *shareholders*. The emphasis has therefore shifted to the large diversity of *stakeholders* (tax payers, patients, G.P.'s, government authorities, health insurers, etc.). They are *de facto* the owners of the hospital (Carver, 2006). This makes the task of the hospital board and other governing bodies within the hospital more complex, as they lack the profit-maximisation principle as a clear-cut touchstone for evaluating decisions.

Hospitals are also more complex than most other organisations. As a consequence, the outcomes of their transactions are less transparent and more difficult to assess (Djellal & Gallouj, 2005).

But probably the most distinguishing characteristic lies in the fact that the locus of the decision-making process itself - the place and the context in which decisions take shape - is much more diffuse than in most other organisations. To the extent even, that Glouberman and Mintzberg,

in their well-known article "Managing the Care of Health and the Cure of Disease", use the metaphor of the "four worlds" of the hospital (Glouberman & Mintzberg, 2001).

First, there is the world of cure. It consists of the medical community, with its different "professional chimneys", representing the different specialities and corresponding hierarchical lines. Supporting this world is the world of care, in which nurses play a central role. Characteristic for this world are the many workflows around the patient. Its organising principle is based on the coordination of these workflows. Then there is the world of the administrative hierarchy, the management of the hospital. Its function is to control and rationalise. Paradoxically, they are responsible for the entire institution, but also removed from direct involvement in the operations in the world of cure and care.

Finally, there is the world of the trustees, usually represented in a formal board. Their task is overseeing the management and the hospital activities. Through their functioning and composition they should embody the legitimacy of the hospital. Therefore they often have a strong link with the local community.

As Glouberman and Mintzberg describe with great sense for figurative language, these four worlds correspond to four sets of activities, four ways of organising, four unreconciled mindsets. As a result, the hospital ends up being not one organisation but four.

It is clear that this situation enhances considerably the odds and possible impact of the agency problem. As a result of the "walls" between the different worlds, the *checks and balances* are very fractional. The oversight function of a traditional hospital board, for instance, is mainly on financial parameters. It hardly interferes with the world of cure and care.

It has also been argued that this state of affairs makes the hospital sector a difficult setting to implement E-Government initiatives (Tuohy, 2003). As result of the fragmentation, multiple information gaps exist between the different actors in the sector. Changes in the technology of information handling and transfer have to a certain extent been successful in reducing these gaps. However, these information systems are costly to implement and are often confronted with risk-adjustment and related problems (Arrow, 2003).

The model described by Glouberman and Mintzberg has grown organically in the second half of the past century. Despite the obvious problems resulting from it, one could even argue that for many decades, it has proved to bring security and stability.

However, in recent years this traditional model has been put more and more under pressure. The latter is the subject of the next paragraph.

A GROWING NEW PARADIGM

Many factors are driving the hospital systems, and the decision-making processes within it, to change (McKee et al., 2002): financial pressures, changing clinical knowledge, changes in demography and - the related - shifting patterns of disease, changing expectations from the public, changes in the workforce (e.g. EU working time directive), internationalisation of health systems, etc.

All these changes in the external and internal environment are putting pressure on the traditional decision-making system within hospitals. From an organisational point of view, the system will therefore have to react, if it wants to keep or re-establish its equilibrium. In physiology this process is called "homeostasis": this is the property of an open system (especially living organisms) to regulate its internal environment to maintain a stable, constant condition, by means of multiple dynamic equilibrium adjustments, controlled by interrelated regulation mechanisms (Langley, 1973).

Translated in governance terms: a shift is needed in the *checks and balances* that determine how the decision-making processes in the hospital are directed, coordinated and evaluated.

This "organisational homeostasis" is an ongoing process. To illustrate this, some examples have been summarized. And the best way to look at them is from the perspective of the traditional model, since the examples have one important characteristic in common: they seem to break down the walls between the different worlds.

A first example is the development and implementation of *clinical pathways*. Clinical pathways can be described as multidisciplinary plans that map the care process for a defined patient population (De Bleser et al., 2006). They are increasingly used in European hospitals, primarily to improve the efficiency of hospital care while maintaining or improving quality of care (Hindle & Yazbeck, 2005; Vanhaecht et al., 2006). They support the operational decision-making process within hospitals. As multidisciplinary plans they interconnect the different professional chimneys within the world of cure. At the same time, they also take over the main organising principle of the world of care: coordination of workflows. Clinical pathways are therefore a good example of the gradual break down of the walls between the cure and care worlds of the hospital.

Two other examples are *evidence based-medicine (EBM)* (Scalise, 2004) and *clinical performance indicators* (Mainz, 2003). Two different concepts, but in a sense, they both cause the same shift in the traditional decision-making model: a shift from the world of management to the worlds of cure and care. This does not mean that managers will now take the decisions within these two worlds. It refers to the fact that one important "function" of the world of management becomes more and more present within the cure and care world, namely, the principle of rationalisation. EBM is essentially about rationalising clinical practice. Clinical performance measurement is about making clinical practice visible and, thus, subject to improvement.

Shifts are also occurring between the world of trustees and the world of management. They go in both directions. First, there is the tendency in many countries that the traditional organisers of hospital care, such as congregations and local communities, are willing to take a step back from direct participation in running the hospital (White, 2000). The growing complexity of hospital care has caused that these parties, which are usually represented in the hospital board, are no longer able to fulfil their function of overseeing hospital performance. They tend to leave this task, at least in part, to the management. To achieve this task, the latter uses management tools such as the Balanced Scorecard (Chow et al., 1998; Oliveira, 2001), or the EFQM-model (Nabitz et al., 2000; Moeller, 2001). By doing so, managers become able to "share" part of the oversight function with the trustees.

Next example is the integration of healthcare professionals in the worlds of trustees and management. In recent years, many hospitals in Europe have redesigned their organisational structure around patient groups: clusters, divisions or care centres (Lega & DePietro, 2005). Within these more or less autonomously working entities, it is seen that quite often physicians and nursing leaders taking up the management positions. And increasingly, healthcare professionals are also called upon to bring their knowledge and experience to the hospital board. Due to developments like DRG-financing, clinical expertise has proved to be indispensable at board level as well (Mark et al., 1998; Silverman & Skinner, 2004; Cardinaels et al., 2004).

The last example is of a somewhat different nature: *patient empowerment* and the concept of the "open" hospital (Powers & Bendall, 2003; Holt et al., 2000; Quetzal Tritter & McCallum, 2006; Tomes, 2006). It is at the same time the least visible and the most powerful change factor. Traditionally, hospitals were merely accountable to the government and to the trustees. Today, hospitals and the people working in it, are ex-

pected to give directly account to the patients, to the local community and to society at large. The patient is no longer considered as a passive "user" of hospital care, but as a real actor within the health care market and the decision making structures of the hospitals. This is the most powerful change factor because it has an impact on the hospital as a system. It interferes simultaneously within all the "worlds" of the hospital: in the form of increased competition, shared clinical decision making, public rating systems, health services integration, case management, patient representation and patient rights.

All of the described developments are significantly changing the decision-making configurations within hospitals. If one would depict all developments within the framework of the traditional model, the result would be a crisscross of transfers, connections and decision-making "hubs". In times where allusions to the airline industry are the order of the day in the hospital sector (Bion & Heffner, 2004; Trask, 2002; Pape, 2003; Singh et al., 2003) one critical question would then soon come up: *Where is the pilot?*

It used to be easy: the four worlds had their own logic, their own steering mechanisms, their own pilots. To a certain extent, this brought security and stability, as it maintained the "span of control" at manageable dimensions.

As a result of the ongoing developments the decision-making processes within the hospital are increasingly interconnected. As much as this is a positive step on the way to integration, it also raises new challenges. If we want to prevent our hospitals from becoming self-steering monoliths, the adequate tools to steer, coordinate and evaluate the different interconnected decision-making processes within the hospital, need to be installed. This will be one of the major challenges for the hospital of the future: it is about governance of the hospital as an integrated and accountable actor in the health care system. The questions that remain are *who, what* and *how?*

The *who*-question relates to the actors within the new governance configurations, the structure and the composition of the governing bodies and the competencies required.

The *what*-question is about the roles and the tasks of the different actors and their mutual adjustment.

The *how*-question deals with the techniques that should be used and the non-structural checks and balances that should be in place: internal control procedures, reporting systems, risk management, etc.

Some aspects of these questions can be dealt with at the micro level of individual hospitals. Homeostasis will further do its work. Others will need an intervention at macro (government) or meso level (professional organisations, local health networks, etc.), aiming at steering, stimulating, supporting and/or harmonising the adaptation processes within hospitals. The three questions are currently on the agenda in many European healthcare systems, in varying ways, with varying priorities, at varying levels (micro, meso and/or macro), and leading to varying – sometimes even opposing – solutions. By way of illustration, the next paragraph gives three examples from three different health care systems.

RECENT DEVELOPMENTS IN THREE EUROPEAN COUNTRIES

NHS Foundation Trusts

Foundation trusts are the most recent type of National Health Services (NHS) trusts in England (Busse et al., 2005; Dixon, 2002). They are set up under the Health and Social Care (Community Health and Standards) Act of 2003 as legally independent organisations, called "Public Benefit Corporations". Becoming a foundation trust provides trusts with some additional freedoms including less control by central government and greater access to borrowing for capital investment (DoH, 2005).

Foundation trusts attract most attention because of their particular governance arrangements (Klein, 2004). First, every foundation trust must identify a "community of members", made up of individuals who live in the area, patients and staff. Members can expect to receive regular information about their trust and be consulted on plans for future development.

However, the main prerogative of the members is that they are able to vote – and stand for election themselves – for the board of governors, which is the second governance level. The main role of the board of governors is in the strategic planning of the organisation. The board of governors also appoint the chair and non-executive directors of the board of directors, which is the third governance level. Public members are eligible to be appointed as non-executive director (which means that they can be represented at all three governance levels). The executive directors are appointed through open competition.

The first independent reviews, carried out by the Healthcare Commission have shown that foundation trusts are making progress in developing new services and improving accountability to their local populations. However, no significant differences were found on readily available indicators of quality of, and access to, care between NHS foundation trusts as a whole group, and other acute NHS trusts (Healthcare Commission, 2005; Lewis, 2005).

Critical analyses have mainly focused on the governance arrangements of the foundation trusts (Rowe & Bond, 2003; Klein, 2003). These arrangements would confuse principal-agent configurations, as they create a set of relationships which are incoherent and mutually conflicting (Wilmoth, 2004). More specifically, they are deemed to be compromised by: the ability of staff to become members of trusts; boards bearing risks of decisions outside their control while simultaneously being insulated from the consequences of their decisions by budget constraints; and conflicts of interest as boards simultaneously act as agents of both central regulators and local beneficiaries (Howell, 2004).

French Hospital 2007 Plan

At the end of 2002 the reform plan "Hospital 2007" was launched by the then French Minister of Health, Jean-François Mattei. One of the immediate causes was the release of the "Piquemal-report" (on the reduction of working time), earlier that year (Piquemal, 2002). This report described the state of the internal functioning of the French public hospitals as extremely worrying, as it lacks flexibility and constitutes a great source of frustration for the professionals that work in it. New working time regulations were expected to even worsen this state of affairs. Subsequent reports emphasised serious capacity problems and financial inefficiencies within the French health care system (Bosh, 2004).

The Hospital 2007 Plan constituted a far-reaching restructuring plan, including important capital investment measures, new financing techniques, a more transparent planning policy and incentives for better cooperation between private and public institutions.

The plan also included an important section on hospital governance, which aimed to reform the internal organisation of public hospitals (DHOS, 2004). Before the reform, their governance structure consisted of a hospital board (*conseil d'administration*), which had important, but restrictively enumerated decision-making prerogatives, and a director, whose competence was general. They were assisted by two advisory bodies: the hospital medical committee (*CME*), ensuring the representation of physicians, and the hospital technical committee (*CTE*), assembling the representatives of trade union organisations.

The Ordinance of May 2th, 2005, one of the legislative texts implementing the Hospital 2007 Plan, has significantly modified this structure. A new body, the executive committee, now has to be installed, assembling an equal number of admin-

istrative and medical representatives (including the president of the hospital medical committee). The Ordinance also imposes a modification of the composition and competences of the hospital board and a reorganisation of the CME and the CTE (which can now hold joint meetings).

Furthermore, the organisational structure of the hospital has been completely redesigned with the rearrangement of clinical departments in "activity centres" (*pôles d'activité*) (Moliniè, 2005). These activity centres are headed by physicians. The latter are *ex officio* member of the CME and must embody at least half of the physician-section within the executive committee. All physician heads are assembled in a strategic committee, covering all activity centres. Within their activity centres, they are assisted by an administrative and a paramedical manager. The principal innovation in comparison to the traditional departmental structure is that the centres dispose of management autonomy which is based on an internal contract. Most hospitals retain the subsidiarity principle: what falls within the management of "proximity" is delegated to the centres: staff, small equipment, medico-pharmaceuticals. Henceforth the department heads are no longer responsible for the management of resources, but must refocus on their specialties: continuity of care, evaluation of quality, development of protocols.

The plan is considered a real revolution and difficult to implement (Debrosse, 2006; Clement, 2004). Therefore, it is accompanied by extensive communication and training plans. Critics focus on the rigidity of the plan: the measures (e.g. restructuring in activity centres) are applicable to all public hospitals, irrespective of their size and context. The reform has been launched, there is no plan B.

Dutch Integration Act and Governance Codes

In February 2000, the Dutch Integration Act was brought into force which formalised by law the financial and organisational integration of specialists into the hospital organisation.

The following, rather enigmatic, phrase in article 3 of the act explains the principle (Kruijthof, 2005): "Notwithstanding the responsibility of the board of directors of a hospital, the responsibility for the medical treatment and care of a patient in a hospital rests with the specialist. The specialist will obey the organisational and financial framework set by the board. The board will obey the framework of specialist care, set by the specialists. The board will consult the specialists before negotiating with insurers."

To understand the importance of the above stipulations of the Integration Act, in particular the last sentence, one has to take in mind the characteristics of the Dutch health care system, which is to a large extent market-driven. Within legal limits (maximum prices), private insurers and sickness funds negotiate with health care providers about prices and fees (Wasem et al., 2004).

After the Integration Act, far-reaching reforms of the financing system were carried through which tend to further enhance the market forces between patients, care providers and insurers: e.g. output pricing based on Diagnosis and Treatment Combinations (DTCs), abolishment of the distinction between private insurers and sickness funds, etc (Hendrikse et al., 2004).

All these developments have emphasised the need for a strong governance framework within hospitals. Dutch hospitals (of which the overall majority are non-profit private institutions) are typical examples of the "two-tier"-board model: they have a board of directors, which is responsible for the day to day running of the hospital and an independent board of supervisors. Although medical specialists often take positions in the lower management echelons of hospitals, they usually have no formal role within this governance structure (Scholten & van der Grinten, 2005).

The applicable legislation leaves a lot of freedom as to the composition, role and functioning of both boards. However, also typical for the

Netherlands is the role played by the sector itself and in particular the professional organisations, in supporting and assessing governance practices in hospitals. As a method of self-regulation several governance codes have been published in recent years, by various organisations "from the field".

The first Code on Health Care Governance was published by the Meurs Commission in 1999 (Hoek, 1999). It was to a large extent inspired by the code on corporate governance which was published in 1997 by the Peters Commission. The focus of the code was on the roles of the board of supervisors, remuneration of board members and transparency of public reporting. The recommendations of the Meurs code were further specified by the code of the Dutch Association of Supervisors of Care Institutions in 2000 and by the code of the Dutch Hospital Association in 2004 (Besouw & Noordman, 2005). In 2005, a Uniform Care Governance code was published, applicable to all six care sectors and established on explicit demand of the Minister of Health and Welfare (BoZ, 2005).

The example of the Netherlands is particularly interesting because it illustrates perfectly how governance reforms can take shape simultaneously at the micro, meso and macro level. It also shows how the changes in the internal and external environment of hospitals have a direct impact on its governing configurations.

DEVELOPING A RESEARCH AGENDA

Learning from Diversity

The described developments in England, France and the Netherlands illustrate that governance is at the core of attention within the European hospital sector. Yet, they merely serve as examples. Also in other European countries, governments, researchers and hospital leaders are attempting to find the right "fit" between the changing context of health care and the key configurations of the governing structures and processes within hospitals (Eeckloo et al., 2004; Ditzel et al., 2006; OPSS, 2006). Many of them are looking at examples from abroad to learn from the innovative solutions, the achievements and the mistakes of their European colleagues.

However, the variety of approaches as already illustrated in the three examples reveals that no uniform scenario, or route map for governance reforms, applicable to all hospitals in all European health care systems, is available (nor would be useful). This is due to the very nature of hospitals itself. On the one hand, hospitals constitute more or less autonomous business entities and therefore require a well-adjusted internal administrative framework. But at the same time, they are deeply embedded in, and influenced by, the health care system of which they form part.

The resulting duality of 'object of entrepreneurial autonomy' and 'instrument of public health policy' is characteristic for hospital governance and its applicable legislation. In other (for profit) sectors the legal framework of governance aims mainly at protecting the rights of the shareholders and some central stakeholders. In the health care sector, and especially in hospitals, this legal framework is usually much more substantial and intrinsically linked to the tasks, the financing and the functioning of the institutions. It is also to a large extent determined by the social security system and the national or regional social policy.

This state of affairs creates two fallacies: 1) reference data for structural governance problems are usually the same within one single health care system, and thus of little practical use; and 2) innovative solutions from abroad are not helpful either, unless they are cautiously examined against the background of the wider governance configuration in which they are embedded.

Both fallacies provide arguments why comparative research is needed to develop a European research framework on hospital governance.

The European Hospital Governance Project

In line with the proposed research agenda, a pioneering project on hospital governance has recently been launched as a joint initiative of the European Hospital and Healthcare Federation (HOPE), the European Association of Hospital Managers (EAHM) and the Centre for Health Services and Nursing Research of the K.U.Leuven (www.hospitalgovernance.org).

The principal aim of the project is to compare governance practices across Europe. The study uses the data of a comprehensive survey of individual CEOs, which was organised by HOPE and EAHM in the spring of 2005. The focus of the survey was on Western Europe. By the intermediary of the national partner organisations of HOPE and EAHM, a representative sample was achieved, which counts in total 519 hospitals. Preliminary results confirmed that the governance practices within hospitals, based on generic descriptions of structures, processes and relationships, were highly correlated with the wider characteristics of the healthcare system in which they are embedded. For an overview of these results, based on descriptive statistics: see Eeckloo et al. 2007a & Eeckloo et al., 2007b.

A DATA MINING APPROACH

Data Analysis

Subsequent to a general descriptive analysis of the data, in depth analyses have been performed in order to obtain more refined knowledge on hospital governance practices in Europe. Rather than making general observations and identifying general trends, these analyses aimed to reveal and explain specific patterns of hospital governance. To make this possible, methods of data mining and knowledge discovery (Hand et al., 2001; Jain et al., 2000) were used. The methods are all based on computer algorithms calculating iteratively the "best" 3D information visualisation for the selected variables.

In the next paragraphs, an example of such analysis is presented. The example uses the survey data relating to the function of the hospital board. The main purpose is to introduce the reader to the syntax and the semantics of the information visualisation and to explain how it is used in processing the survey data. It is not within the scope of this contribution to discuss in detail the content of the survey results.

The Function of the Hospital Board: Total Activities Analysis

The function of the hospital board is not easily translated into research variables. Most existing studies focus on specific aspects: e.g. strategic decision-making (Judge & Zeithaml, 1992; Alexander & Weiner, 1998; Alexander et al. 2006) CEO-evaluation (Young, 1996; Young et al., 2000) and monitoring clinical performance (Prybil, 2006; Joshi & Hines, 2006; Vaughn et al., 2006); or use rather abstract notions of the board's function: e.g. analytical, political, contextual (McDonagh, 2006). In the present study, the aim was to gain insight into the function of the hospital board, without limiting the latter to one ore more specific aspects.

To fulfil this aim, the so called "Total Activities Analysis"-approach (TAA) was used (Harris, 1993). Characteristic of TAA is that it identifies the tasks of the board in the context of the "total spectrum" of possible tasks. To that purpose, each respondent was asked to list the governing bodies of his or her hospital. In a subsequent question the respondent was asked to mark the tasks of each of the listed bodies within a closed list of 25 tasks, ranging from adopting and/or amending the bylaws of the hospital to operational decision-making. For each body identified as a hospital board[2] this results in a task profile composed of 25 dichotomous (yes/no) answers.

Information Visualisation: Syntax and Semantics

Our goal is to gain insight into the range of tasks among the hospital boards in Europe by visual means: what range of tasks typifies what type of board? Figure 1 displays the information visualisation that was constructed on the basis of the task profiles for all hospital boards in the data set (292 in total). The specific method that was applied here is *multidimensional scaling* (MDS) (Cox & Cox, 2001)[3]. Other methods applied in the project are non-linear optimally transformed vector, centroid and monotone regression models, and combinations thereof.

In the following paragraphs, the syntax and the semantics of the visualisation will be explained stepwise.

First, the degree of similarity between any two boards with respect to their profile of tasks (25 yes/no answers) was defined and measured. To that purpose, a Kullback-Leibler type measure (Kullback, 1959) of similarity between every possible pair of boards was standardised: this measure considers the absence of any task as informational as its presence. A degree of 0 implies that the two boards have the exact same tasks, a degree of 1 implies that the two boards differ completely: one board has exactly those tasks that the other board does not have and conversely. The calculations are rather voluminous, since the 292 governing bodies result in 292 x 291/2 or 42,486 possible pairs of boards.

Subsequently, the calculated similarity indexes were used to calculate the position of each board in the visualisation. This is an iterative process: a computer algorithm calculates step by step the position of each board so that the resulting visualisation represents best the relations (as expressed in the similarity indexes) between the different boards. Best is a rather tricky concept: Kruskal's stress-1 measures 0.195 but is not an adequate indicator as it does not take into account the "quality" of the monotone transformation of

Figure 1. Hospital board function

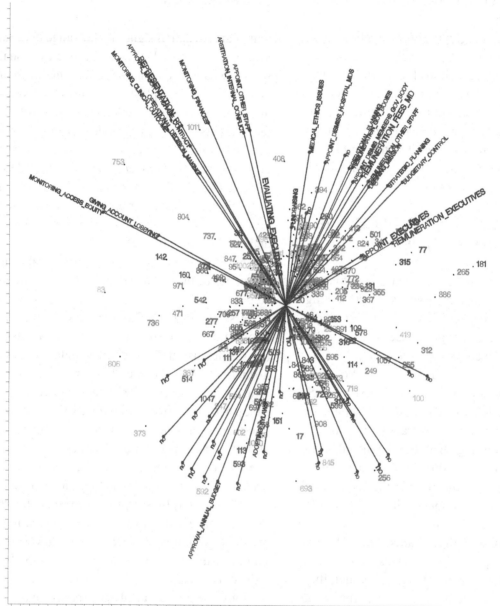

the similarity indexes on which the visualisation is based. A better indicator of best is the plain Kendall rank order correlation coefficient (Tau-b) between all similarity index values and their corresponding distances in the visualisation. It's value in Figure 1 is +0.710.

Three boards could not be significantly represented in the visualisation. In a nutshell, the visualisation positions boards sharing exactly the same task profile at the same spot, while boards with strongly diverging tasks profiles are positioned "far" from each other. In reality, the tool uses 3D representations, whereas this book format only allows 2D projections. The numbers in the visualisation identify the hospitals, the colours correspond to the countries in which the hospitals are located: France = ink blue, Belgium = red, UK = pink, Germany = dark brown, The Netherlands = beige, Switzerland = moss-green, Portugal = bright blue, Spain = purple, Ireland = dark green, Greece = orange, Austria = bright green.

As distance does not depend on rotation, the axes play a subordinate and purely technical role. More important are the lines with the blue labels. They represent the 25 tasks. Each was constructed using non-linear statistical regression analysis based on smoothing (Breiman & Friedman, 1985) between the 3D coordinates of the boards in the visualisation and their dichotomous (yes/no) value with respect to each task. They allow tracing back the task profile of each board, within the synthesis of 292 boards.

To that end, the boards must be projected perpendicularly on the line corresponding to all tasks at study. Boards that score a particular task "yes" will be positioned on the side of the corresponding line with the MAX-label; boards that score the task "no", will be positioned on the side with the not-label. Their exact position in relation to each task line is a best position in relation to all other tasks and in relation to all other 292 boards and their 25 task profiles. Thus, this means that the position of the lines is based on the task profile of all boards included in the sample. Important

for the comprehension of the visualisation is the fact that the lines are positioned independently of the process of positioning the boards. The latter are positioned first. The lines are then "entered" within the existing visualisation of boards, in a way that they best represent the task profiles of the boards.

The consequence of this approach is that also the relative position of the lines is meaningful. The angles between the lines visualise the degree of association between the respective tasks. Two lines that run parallel or close to each other indicate that the corresponding tasks are highly correlated among all boards: this means that if a random participant allocates one of these tasks to the board, the odds are high that he will also allocate the other task to the board (only if the MAX-label of the two lines are at the same side, if not, the opposite is true: the odds will be high that they do not allocate the other task to the board!). Perpendicular lines indicate that the corresponding tasks are not correlated.

Applications for Governance Research

The visualisation allows gaining insight within the wide-ranging task profiles of hospital boards.

Table 1. Taxonomy function hospital board

Fragmented, non-strategic tasks	Strategic tasks
Giving account to and lobbying with government authorities	Adopting and/or amending the bylaws of the hospital
Representation and maintaining public relations	Defining the hospital mission
Monitoring accessibility, equity and legitimacy of services	Strategic planning
Monitoring financial performance	Evaluating performance of executive management
Monitoring clinical outcome	Intervention in medical ethics issues
Fundraising	Approval of the annual budget
Appointment and dismissal of employees	Budgetary control
Arbitration of internal conflicts	Appointment and dismissal of hospital physicians
Approval of purchase, service and/or credit contracts	Appointment and dismissal governing bodies
Operational planning	Appointment and dismissal of executive management
Operational decision-making	Setting remuneration and/or fees of hospital physicians
	Setting remuneration of members of governing bodies
	Setting remuneration of executive management
	Setting remuneration of employees

Particularly interesting is that the visualisation reveals clear patterns corresponding to the countries in which the hospitals are located. A contrast can for instance be distinguished between the position of French boards (mainly at the left side) and Belgian boards (mainly at the upper right side) [Fisher exact $p \leq 0.0001$][4]. These different positions indicate that boards of Belgian hospitals have a clearly different task profile then those of French hospitals: as most of the MAX-labels of the lines are at the upper side of the visualisation, the task profile of the former is more comprehensive. Also the boards of Portuguese hospitals (mainly at the top in the middle) appear to have a comprehensive task profile. The board of supervisors of Dutch hospitals are clustered at the right side at the bottom. This means that they have a limited task profile in comparison with the complete data set. This is in accordance with the logic of described "two-tier"-board model.

A second application of the visualisation is that it allows synthesizing the function of the board taxonomically. This implies a reduction or *classification* of the 25 task variables into a limited set of variables. The latter is necessary to integrate the function of the hospital board into further empirical analyses. "Taxonomically" means that the classification is derived from the empirical data (*inductive*). In a second phase, the derived classification is conceptually interpreted. This approach differs from a "typological" classification, which is first delineated conceptually (*deductive*) and in a second phase tested empirically.

As the lines are based on the empirical task profile of the hospital boards, they offer the tools for this taxonomic classification. Particularly the angles between the lines are an important indication: where these angles are small, the corresponding tasks are related. On analysis of the visualisation a dichotomy can be distinguished between a bundle of closely joined lines at the right side, and a group of more dispersed lines at the left side.

After having identified this dichotomy inductively, a conceptual difference between the corresponding tasks can be identified. Analysis of the lines at the right learns that all corresponding tasks relate to overall strategic policy. The lines at the left are more specific and have a less strategic focus. Herein a distinction can be recognized which is well-known within the governance-literature, namely the distinction between "general governance technology" and "specific governance technology" (Williamson, 1999; Van Hulle et al., 2002). In this literature, the board is acknowledged as an instrument of general governance technology. It is considered not cost-efficient to involve the board in more fragmented tasks where more "specific" governance technology is appropriate (e.g. contracts, delegation to management or special purpose vehicles).

The visualisation enables to make a taxonomical distinction between the tasks that are related to both governance-technologies (see Table 1). Linking this distinction with the position of the boards in the visualisation reveals for instance that most UK hospital boards (pink) have a large share of fragmented tasks, combined with a moderate or limited strategic focus: i.e. at the left side of the visualisation. The few boards of governors of hospitals that already had a Foundation status at the time of the survey are located more to the right in the visualisation.

In the project, two aggregate variables were constructed based on the distinction between both types of tasks, and integrated in further empirical analyses.

FUTURE RESEARCH DIRECTIONS

In the preceding paragraphs, an example was given of the innovative use of data mining and information visualisation in a pilot study on the comparison of hospital governance practices.

The same methods should now be applied in practice-oriented empirical studies on hospital governance. The added value of these studies will only increase, as in the near future, there will be an urgent demand for empirical studies testing how the gradual changes in the configurations of hospital governance affect performance, both in terms of efficiency of the governing bodies and of overall hospital outcomes. Without seriously taking into account the specificities of the context by using the adequate methods, the relevance of these empirical studies will not exceed the setting of – the fictitious – "average" or "typical" hospital.

E-Government initiatives by definition deal with data handling and transfer by electronic means. The diffusion of the basic technology, procedures and skills to safeguard integrity, accessibility, security, privacy, etc of such huge volume as is required in the health care sector is slow and disappointing. A minority of health care workers are yet convinced of the return on investment of moving from the old paper, pencil and telephone approach to the modern electronic means. The creation and demonstration of added-value is crucial: in the front office: safety and quality of care and level of satisfaction, as well as in the back office: improved care delivery systems, including the governance of each hospital.

CONCLUSION

Since new patient demands, budgetary constraints and increased competition set the tone at the European hospital scene, hospital governance is subject to increasing public interest. In many European countries the governing bodies of hospitals have been recognised as key actors in the health care system. As decentralised health care agents they are thought to embody both entrepreneurial dynamism and societal legitimacy. The challenge is now to match the configurations of these governing bodies with the changing context of health care and health care organisation. To succeed in this challenge, practice-oriented research is needed

to support and counsel the ongoing process of transition.

Governance is inherently complex and multi-dimensional. The suggested research should take this into account. Data mining methods provide the appropriate tools, as they allow revealing and explaining complex and multi-dimensional patterns in research data. In the present chapter, a real data example was introduced to explain the syntax and semantics of such data mining approach to governance.

ACKNOWLEDGMENT

The authors wish to thank the organisations HOPE and EAHM, and their respective national partner organisations, for their important role in the coordination and dissemination of the European Hospital Governance Project. They specially would like to thank the Scientific Committee of EAHM for its valuable input in validating the survey used in the project and helping to form the ideas presented in this chapter.

REFERENCES

Alexander, J.A., Weiner, B.J. (1998), The Adoption of the Corporate Governance Model by Nonprofit Organizations. *Nonprofit Management & Leadership*, 8(3), 223-242.

Alexander, J.A, Ye, Y., Lee, S.D., Weiner, B.J. (2006), The Effects of Governing Board Configuration on Profound Organizational Change in Hospitals. *Journal of Health and Social Behavior*, 47(3), 291-308.

Arrow, K. (2003), Reflections on the Reflections. In: Hammer, P.J., Haas-Wilson, D., Peterson, M.A., Sage, W.M., editors. *Kenneth Arrow and the changing economics of health care*. Durham: Duke University Press.

Beekun, R.I., Stedham, Y., Young, G.J. (1998). Board Characteristics, Managerial Controls and Corporate Strategy: A Study of U.S. Hospitals. *Journal of Management*, 24(1), 3-19.

Besouw, S.M., Noordman, T.B.J. (2005). *Non-Profit Governance. Zicht op de stand van zaken.* Delft: Eburon.

Bion, J.F., Heffner, J.E. (2004). Challenges in the care of the acutely ill. *Lancet*, 363, 970-7.

Bosh, X. (2004), French health system on verge of collapse, says report. *Lancet*, 363, 376.

Brancheorganisaties Zorg. (2005). *Zorgbrede Governancecode.* Utrecht: BoZ.

Breiman, L., Friedman, J. (1985). Estimating Optimal transformations for Multiple Regression and Correlation, *Journal of the American Statistical Association*, 80(394), 580-598.

Brickley, J.A., Van Horn, L. (2002). Managerial incentives in nonprofit organizations: evidence from hospitals. *J Law Econ*, 45, 227-249.

Busse, R., Schlette, S., Weinbrenner, S., editors. (2005). *Health Policy Developments. Issue 4. Focus on Acces, Primary Care, Health Care Organization.* Gütersloh: Verlag Bertelmann Stiftung.

Cadbury, A. (1992). *Report of the Committee on the Financial Aspects of Corporate Governance.* London: Gee.

Cardinaels, E., Roodhooft, F., Van Herck, G. (2004). Drivers of cost system development in hospitals: results of a survey. *Health Policy*, 69(2), 239-52.

Carver, J. (2006). *Boards That Make a Difference. 3th edition.* San Francisco: Jossey-Bass.

Chow, C.W., Ganulin, D., Teknika, O., Haddad, K., Williamson, J. (1998). The balanced scorecard: a potent tool for energizing and focusing healthcare organization management. *Journal of Healhtcare Management*, 43, 263-80.

Clement, J.M. (2004). *Hôpital 2007: Les répercussions dans le champ du droit hospitalier.* Bordeaux: Les études hospitalières.

Cox, T.F., Cox, M. (2001), *Multidimensional Scaling.* London: Chapman and Hall.

De Bleser, L., Depreitere, R., De Waele, K., Vanhaecht, K., Vlayen, J., Sermeus, W. (2006). Defining pathways. *Journal of Nursing Management*, 14(7), 553-63.

Debrosse, D. (2006). New Governance. Creation of an executive committee and regrouping by centres. *Hospital*, 8(2), 45-6.

Department of Health. (2005). *A Short Guide to NHS Foundation Trusts.* London: Department of Health.

Direction de l'hospitalisation et de l'organisation des soins. (2004). *Circulaire DHOS/E1 n°61 du 13 février 2004 relative à la mise en place par anticipation de la nouvelle gouvernance hospitalière.*

Ditzel, E., Štrach, P., Pirozek, P. (2006). An inquiry into good hospital governance: A New Zealand-Czech comparison. *Health Research Policy and Systems*, 4, 2.

Dixon, J. (2002) Foundation hospitals. *Lancet*, 360, 1900-1.

Djellal, F., Gallouj, F. (2005). Mapping innovation dynamics in hospitals. *Res Pol*, 34, 817-35.

Eeckloo, K., Delesie, L., Vleugels, A. (2007a). Hospital Governance: Exploring the European Scene – Part I, *Hospital*, 9(2), 14-16.

Eeckloo, K., Delesie, L., Vleugels, A. (2007b). Hospital Governance: Exploring the European Scene – Part II, *Hospital*, 9(3), 30-32.

Eeckloo, K., Van Herck, G., Van Hulle, C., Vleugels, A. (2004). From Corporate Governance To Hospital Governance. Authority, transparency and accountability of Belgian non-profit hospitals' board and management. *Health Policy*, 68, 1-15.

European Commission (2001). *White paper on European governance*. Brussels: European Commission of the European Union.

Glouberman, S., Mintzberg, H. (2001). Managing the Care of Health and the Cure of Disease. Part I: Differentiation & Part II: Integration. *Health Care Management Review*, 26(1), 56-84.

Hand, D., Mannila, H., Smyth, P. (2001). *Principles of Data Mining (Adaptive Computation and Machine Learning)*. Massachusetts: MIT Press.

Harris, M. (1993). Exploring the Role of Boards Using Total Activities Analysis. *Nonprofit Management & Leadership*, 3(3), 269-281.

Healthcare Commission. (2005). *The Healthcare Commission's review of NHS foundation trusts*. London: Commission for Healthcare Audit and Inspection.

Hendrikse, G.W.J., Schut, F.T. (2004). Naar nieuwe beheersstructuren in de Nederlandse gezondheidszorg? *Acta Hospitalia*, 44(1), 5-20.

Hindle, D., Yazbeck, A.M. (2005). Clinical pathways in 17 European Union countries: a purposive survey. *Aust Health Rev*, 29, 94-104.

Hoek, H. (1999). The art of governance of Dutch hospitals. *World Hosp Health Serv*, 35(3), 5-7.

Holt, N., Johnson, A., de Belder, M. (2000). Patient empowerment in secondary prevention of coronary heart disease. *Lancet*, 356, 314.

Howell, B. (2004). Lessons from New Zealand for England's NHS Foundation Trusts. *J Health Serv Res Policy*, 9(2), 104-9.

Jain, A., Duin, R., Mao, J. (2000). Statistical Pattern Recognition: A Review, *IEEE Transactions on Pattern Analysis And Machine Intelligence*, 22, 4-37.

Joshi, M.S., Hines, S.C. (2006). Getting the board on board : Engaging hospital boards in quality and patient safety, *Jt Comm J Qual Improv*, 32(4), 179-187.

Judge W.Q., Zeithaml C.P. (1992). An Empirical Comparison between the Board's Strategic Role in Nonprofit Hospitals and in For-Profit Industrial Firms. *Health Services Research*, 27(1), 47-64.

Klein R. (2004). The first wave of NHS foundation trusts. *BMJ*, 328, 1332.

Klein, R. (2003). Governance for NHS foundation trusts. *BMJ*, 326, 174-5.

Kullback, S. (1959) *Information Theory and Statistics*, New York: Wiley.

Kruijthof, K. (2005). *Doctors' Orders. Specialists' Day to Day Work and their jurisdictional Claims in Dutch Hospitals*. Rotterdam: Erasmus Universiteit Rotterdam.

Langley, L.L., editor. (1973). *Homeostasis: origins of the concept*. Stroudsburg: Dowden, Hutchinson and Ross.

Lega, F., DePietro, C. (2005). Converging patterns in hospital organization: beyond the professional bureaucracy. *Health Policy*, 74(3), 261-81

Lewis, R. (2005) NHS foundation trusts. The Healthcare Commission's review offers something for both proponents and detractors. *BMJ*, 331, 59-60.

Lynn, L.E., Heinrich, C.J., Hill, C.J. (2001). *Improving Governance: A New Logic for Empirical Research*. Washington DC: Georgetown University Press.

Mainz, J. (2003). Developing evidence-based clinical indicators: a state of the art methods primer. *Int J Qual Health Care*, 15(Suppl 1), i5-i11.

Mark, T.L., Evans, W.N., Schur, C.L., Guterman, S.M.A. (1998). Hospital-Physician Arrangements and Hospital Financial Performance. *Med Care*, 36(1), 67-78.

McDonagh, K.J. (2006). Hospital governing boards: a study of their effectiveness in relation to organizational performance. *Journal of Healthcare Management*, 51, 377-391.

McKee, M., Healy, J., Edwards, N., Harrison, A. (2002). Pressures for change. In: McKee, M., Healy J., editors. *Hospitals in a changing Europe*. Buckingham: Open University Press.

Miller, J.L. (2002). The Board as a Monitor of Organizational Activity. The Applicability of Agency Theory to Nonprofit Boards. *Nonprofit Management & Leadership*, 12, 429-450

Moeller J. (2001). The EFQM Excellence Model. German experiences with the EFQM approach in health care. *Int J Qual Health Care*, 13(1), 45-9.

Molinié, E. (2005). *L'Hôpital public en France: Bilan et perspectives*. Paris: Conseil Economique et Social.

Nabitz, U., Klazinga, N., Walburg, J. (2000). The EFQM excellence model: European and Dutch experiences with the EFQM approach in health care. *Int J Qual Health Care*, 12(3), 191-201.

Observatório Português dos Sistemas de Saúdo. (2006). *Um Ano de Governação em Saúdo*. Coimbra: CEIS-UC.

Oliveira, J. (2001). The balanced scorecard: an integrative approach to performance evaluation. *Healthc Financ Manage*, 55(5), 42-6.

Pape, T.M. (2003). Applying airline safety practices to medication administration. *Medurg Nurs*, 12(2), 77-93.

Piquemal, M. (2002). *Rapport de mission*. Paris: Mission Nationale d'Evaluation de la mise en place de la R.T.T. dans les établissements de santé.

Powers, T.L., Bendall, D. (2003). Improving health outcomes through patient empowerment. *J Hosp Mark Public Rel*, 15(1), 45-59.

Preker, A.S., Harding, A. (2003). *Innovations in Health Service Delivery: The Corporatization of Public Hospitals*. Washington DC: The World Bank.

Prybil, L.D. (2006). Size, composition, and culture of high-performing hospital boards. *American Journal of Medical Quality*, 21, 224-229.

Quetzal Tritter, J., McCallum, A. (2006). The snakes and ladders of user involvement: Moving beyond Arnstein. *Health Policy*, 76(2), 156-68.

Rowe, R., Bond, M. (2003). Foundation trusts. Hitting the big time. *Health Serv J*, 113, 30-1.

Rozman, R. (2000). The organizational function of governance: development, problems, and possible changes. *Management*, 5(2), 94-110.

Scalise, D. (2004). Evidence-based medicine. *Hosp Health Netw*, 78(12), 32-7, 2.

Scholten, G.R.M., van der Grinten, T.E.D. (2005). The integration of medical specialists in hospitals. Dutch hospitals and medical specialists on the road to joint regulation. *Health Policy*, 72, 165-73.

Silverman, E., Skinner, J. (2004). Medicare upcoding and hospital ownership. *J Health Econ*, 23(2), 369-89.

Singh, R., Saleemi, A., Walsh, K., Popert, R., O'Brien, T. (2003). Near misses in bladder cancer – an airline safety approach to urology. *Ann R Coll Surg Engl*, 85, 378-81.

Tomes, N. (2006). The patient as a policy factor: a historical case study of the consumer/survivor movement in mental health. *Health Aff*, 25(3), 720-9.

Trask, C. (2002). The lot of airline pilots and consultants is not so different. *BMJ*, 13, 105.

Tuohy, C.H. (2003). Agency, Contract, and Governance: Shifting Shapes of Accountability in the Health Care Arena. *Journal of Health Politics, Policy and Law*, 28(2-3), 195-215.

Vanhaecht, K., Bollmann, M., Bower, K., Gallagher, C., Gardini, A., Guezo, J. et al. (2006). Prevalence and use of clinical pathways in 23 countries - an international survey by the European Pathway Association (www.E-P-A.org). *J Integ Care Pathways*, 10, 28-34.

Van Hulle, C., Eeckloo, K., Van Herck, G., Vleugels, A. (2002). Governance bij Belgische ziekenhuizen: analyse en optimalisering. In: Peeters, L., Matthyssens, P., Vereeck, L., editors. *Stakeholder Synergie*. Leuven: Garant.

Vaughn, T., Koepke, M., Kroch, E., Lehrman, W., Sinha, S., Levey, S. (2006), Engagement of leadership in quality improvement initiatives: executive quality improvement survey results. Journal of patient safety, 2, 2-9.

Wasem, J., Greβ, S., Okma, K.G.H. (2004). The role of private health insurance in social health insurance countries. In: Saltman, R.B., Busse, R., Figueras, J., editors. *Social health insurance systems in western Europe*. Berkshire: Open University Press.

Wearing, R. (2005). *Cases in corporate governance*. London: SAGE Publication.

White, K.R. (2000). Hospitals sponsored by the Roman Catholic Church: separate, equal, and distinct? Milbank Q, 78(2), 213-39.

Williamson, O.E. (1999). *The Mechanisms of Governance*. New York: Oxford University Press.

Wilmoth, S. (2004). Foundation trusts and the problem of legitimacy. *Health Care Anal*, 12(2), 157-69.

Young, G.J. (1996), Insider Representation on the governing boards of nonprofit hospitals: trends and implications for charitable care. *Inquiry*, 33(4), 352-362.

Young, G.J., Stedham, Y., Beekun, R.I. (2000), Boards of Directors and the Adoption of a CEO Performance Evaluation Process. *Journal of Management Studies*, 37(2), 277-296.

Yuen, P. (2005). *Compendium of health statistics. 17ᵗʰ edition*. London: Office of Health Economics.

ADDITIONAL READING

Lynn, L.E, Heinrich, C.J, Hill, C.J. (2001). *Improving Governance: A New Logic for Empirical Research*. Washington DC: Georgetown University Press.

Rozman, R. (2000). The organizational function of governance: development, problems, and possible changes. *Management*;5(2), 94-110

ENDNOTES

[1] The content of this chapter has partly been published in Eeckloo, K., Delesie, L. & Vleugels, A. (2007). Where is the pilot? The changing shapes of governance in the European hospital sector. *Journal of The Royal Society for the Promotion of Health*, 127(2), 78-86. Permission for incorporation in this chapter was obtained by the Royal Society for the Promotion of Health.

[2] For this identification, the following criteria were used: name, composition, meeting frequency and characteristics of other listed bodies.

[3] In this particular dichotomous case, a multiple correspondence analysis would have been as helpful to generate a meaningful information visualisation. We preferred our two-step method as the similarity index step allowed us to order the 25 tasks with respect to their information for the taxonomy of hospital boards.

[4] Statistical significance of a hypothesis concerning the position of specified subjects (i.e. hospital boards) in specific areas of the visualisation is tested in relation to the null hypothesis of a maximally proportional distribution of all subjects in the same areas of the visualisation.

Chapter VII
A Data Mining Approach to Advance Knowledge in Public Government:
Profiling Households

Paola Annoni
University of Milan, Italy

Pieralda Ferrari
University of Milan, Italy

Silvia Salini
University of Milan, Italy

ABSTRACT

Data mining is the process of 'mining' into large quantity of data to get useful information. It comprises a broad set of techniques originated within different applicative fields to solve various types of issues. In this chapter the data mining approach is proposed for the characterization of family consumptions in Italy. Italian expenditures are a complex system. Every year the Italian National Bureau of Statistics (ISTAT) carries out a survey on the expenditure behaviour of Italian families. The survey regards household expenditures on durable and daily goods and on various services. Here the goal is twofold: firstly it describes the most important characteristics of family behaviour with respect to expenditures on goods and usage of different services; secondly possible relationships among these behaviours are highlighted and explained by social-demographical features of families. To this purpose, a series of statistical techniques are used in sequence and different potentialities of selected methods for addressing these kinds of issues are pinpointed. This study recommends that, further investigation is needed to properly focalize on service usage for the characterization, for example, of the nature of investigated services (private or public) and, most of all, about their supply and effectiveness across the national territory. Still this study may be considered an example of operational and concrete approach of managing of large data-sets in the social-economical science, from the definition of goals to the evaluation of results.

INTRODUCTION

Over the last years, due to the development and the diffusion of the Information and Communication Technology, Public Administrations are getting in short time large quantitative of data about the services (i.e. education, health, public utilities, etc.), that are provided by themselves as well as about characteristics of citizens: who they are, what they get, do, need, think about and so on. These data can be fruitfully used by government to analyze, asses and improve inventions and services. One can think, for example, to the more and more increasing interest on the evaluation and comparison of public service utilities, also because of privatization processes which were carried out or are still in progress in many countries. In this case, strategy choices about how, when and at which cost to provide a public service, customer expectations towards service availability and price, workers expectation towards occupational level and payments are all crucial elements which have to be taken into account in decision making policy.

This shows how the process of decision making in the public management is undoubtedly complex and needs to be properly founded on scientific bases requiring a good knowledge of statistical and computational methods. Therefore, data mining techniques seem especially suitable for this kind of analysis, provided that data mining is intended as a process that, mining into a large quantities of data, allows to discover new information translatable in decisions.

Born in the private sector as a tool to improve the business process, data mining has soon become a competitive weapon which can ensure the profitability of a company. To that purpose, the Nobel Prize winner Dr. Penzias comments in 1999 (see for example Groth, 2000): "Data mining will become much more important, and companies will throw away nothing about their customers because it will be so valuable. If you're not doing this, you're out of business".

Most significant applications of data mining are customer relationships, quality control and forecasting in financial marketing, but the fields where data mining techniques are nowadays used with full success are numerous.

In spite of, or perhaps because of, its origin in private sector, in more recent years the need to extend this approach to the public sector is felt. Nevertheless there are some differences between private and public setting. The most important differentiation is that public management has to take into account specific variables in the process evaluation. In fact, variables connected with social utility, risk and benefit for the collectivity are of primary importance and should be included in the analysis. That makes the analysis more complex, for example, with regards to public services aforementioned. These services are often intangible, the customer satisfaction is not so easy to quantify, the definition of specific targets may be difficult, the comparison between different public services might not be a simple task, due also to different geographic locations or heterogeneity of populations, the public nature of services and so on. For this reason, the problems of public management are "intrinsically" multi-way and standard techniques could not take advantage of this "richness" of data, while 'ad-hoc' techniques and simultaneous models might be more suitable.

Furthermore, communication problems are also substantial in government management. In fact, it is important to dedicate particular attention in conciliating the need of complex and sophisticated statistical methods with an easy communication and understanding of the results, because they must be shared by service providers, decision makers, operators, users and citizens.

Despite the relevance of decision support in the public sector, the measuring process is still not completely explored. This chapter is a proposal in this direction. It is devoted to demonstrating how tools of data mining can be used to obtain useful information for government in order to make duly decision according to some aims of economical or social policy. The focus is on the analysis of Italian families expenditures through a CRISP-DM, i.e. a CRoss Industry Standard Process model for data mining (Perner, 2002). As well known, the microeconomic theory of consumption tries to explain how a consumer spends his own income on goods and services and how his behaviour is oriented to maximise his total utility (for a review see for example Blundell 1988). Here the approach is completely different since it is purely data driven and not based on specific econometric models. In this respect, authors are applying statistical models to make 'data speak' with the final aim of exploring data from different points of view and for summarizing them into useful information.

In Section 2 the definition of the problem is canvassed; Section 3 is devoted to data understanding and preparation: Association Rules, factor analysis and k-means cluster are implemented in order to reduce the high dimensionality of data and to go further into data comprehension. Peculiar models, Decision Trees and Canonical Correspondence Analysis, are detailed in Section 4, while in Section 5 the evaluation of selected models are described and results are shown and discussed. In the end, Section 6 highlights some conclusions and future perspectives.

THE CASE STUDY

Analyses are based on data from the 'Household Expenditure Survey 2003' by the Italian National Bureau of Statistics (*ISTAT*), which is a yearly survey for the analysis of expenditures of Italian families. The survey covers about 28000 Italian families. The aim is to collect the amount of household expenditure on durable and daily goods and on various other services. Particular focus is on social and economical aspects of the household way of life. The survey is repeated each year, thus allowing for comparative analyses and data update.

As a first step, the analysis here presented aims to describe the most important characteristics of family behaviour with respect to expenditures on goods and usage of services. As a second step, every relationship among these behaviours have to be highlighted and eventually explained by social-demographical characteristic of families.

Furthermore, regarding to public services it is relevant to identify prospective lacks or deficiencies in order to properly plan public interventions. The final goal is to detect the presence of critical situations and/or social risk factors.

PRELIMINARY PROCESSES OF DATA-HANDLING

As mentioned above, the data-set is very large: about 28000 records with 400 fields. Each record represents a statistical unit (a family) while each field represents a variable collected for the family. Variables have different measurement scales, as such; categorical, ordinal, numerical and dichotomous. Variables comprised of social-demographical characteristics of the family (number of components, age, education, etc.); household preferences on durable goods (property of a car, house, computer, etc.); household preferences on services (transport, health, insurances, school, entertainment, culture, etc.); household expenditures on daily goods (foods, drinks, cigarettes, newspapers, etc.). Data are provided in standard ASCII format and data manipulation is needed in order to obtain a *customer table* structure.

Due to the nature of collected variables, the data-set is characterized by prevalence of zeros and of spurious information. As it is always the case in data-mining analyses, data cleaning and filling methods are applied.

However, peculiar aspects of the problem suggest the researchers to divide variables into three groups, as sketched in Figure-1: (a) expenditures on daily goods (continuous scale of measurement); (b) preferences on services (dichotomous); and (c) social-demographical characteristics of the family (categorical, ordinal, and numeric variables).

This classification is due to various reasons. First of all variables play different roles. Expenditures are response variables which are driven by social-demographical features and, furthermore, they reflect personal choices of the family components. On the contrary, social-demographical variables are explanatory variables and play the role of risk factors. Preferences on services are placed at an intermediate level with respect to the previous variable typologies, because the preference is related on one hand to the effective need of that service (school, mobility, health-care, etc.), which depends on customers, and on the other hand to the service availability, which depends on practical politics.

In addition, statistical issues contribute in discriminating among these different sets of variables. In particular scales of measurement and different variable roles should lead to the proper choice of methods and techniques. Because of both problem complexity and variable typologies, different models have to be alternatively or jointly used. With this regard, data-mining appears particularly suitable.

Once variables have been divided into the sets, as explained above, within each set explorative analyses are applied in order to keep non-redundant data and discard sources of misleading noises. In particular, Association Rules (Agrawal et al., 1995) are employed to define different combination of services usage by households (here called 'service profile'), while factor and cluster analysis are used in sequence to identify different combinations of expenditures which characterize families (here called 'expenditure profile'). Service and expenditure profiles actually represent new variables which will be used with social-demographical variables to the final purpose. Methods for setting-up service and expenditure profiles are described in the following sub-sections.

Association Rules for the Setting-Up of Family Service Profiles

Authors concentrate on the family usage of various types of private or public services. In particular, the focus is on *means of transport, instruction & culture, household & babysitting*. Data are of binary type (family uses or not). The goal is to find relevant relationships among preferences on different services.

In the sample, for each of the different type of service, many variables are available for each

Figure 1. Data structure of the case study: three sets of variables are defined

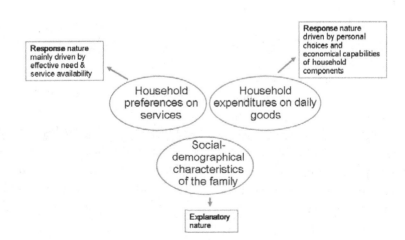

family. For example for the service *means of transport* the following variables are collected: property of a car, a motorcycle, a scooter, a camper or a bicycle, subscription/tickets for buses, trains, airplanes or ferries. In order to identify significant links into multi-ways cross tables, classical approaches involve log-linear models. In this case dimensionality is too high and a classical approach is evidently wasteful, both from the computationally and from the interpretative point of view, hence alternative explorative techniques are needed. The choice is Association Rules since it is based on the same starting point as log-linear models, i.e. the odds ratio.

Association Rules, usually employed to obtain Market Basket Analyses (Perner, 2002), is applied here by taking families as customers and different household preferences on services as products. The algorithm of Association Rules automatically finds associations which can be manually detected using visualization techniques, such as the Web node. An *A-Priori* algorithm is used to extract a set of rules from the data, pulling out those rules with the highest information content. As known, Association Rules are based on statements of the form:

"if antecedent then consequent"

say $A \Rightarrow B$ where A is the *antecedent* and B the *consequent*. To create an *A-Priori* rules set, one or more Input fields and one or more Output fields are to be defined. Categorical variables can be Input (antecedent), Output (consequent) or Both. *A-Priori* algorithm is particularly suitable in this case because it is fast and it considers various antecedents at a time. The steps here undertaken are as follows: (a) selection of all the variables which indicate household preferences on services, among those indicated above; (b) detection of the most important linkages between antecedents and consequents by symmetric approach, so as not imposing any constraints on the

choice of both antecedents and consequents; (c) particular regard to specific groups of preferences by asymmetric approach in order to discard non informative variables.

However, the main problem in association rule modelling is to find, from the available database, subsets of association rules that are interesting. Interestingness can be measured according to various criteria, the measures commonly used to assess the strength of an association rule are the indexes of support, confidence, and the lift.

Statistical interestingness is related to the observed frequency of the rules. For a given rule, say $A \Rightarrow B$, indicate with $N_{A \to B}$ its absolute frequency (count), that is, the number of times in which this rule is observed, at least once. In other words, $N_{A \to B}$ measures the number of transactions in which the rule is satisfied. The 'support' for a rule $A \Rightarrow B$ is obtained dividing the number of transactions which satisfy the rule by the total number of transactions, N.

$$support\left\{A \to B\right\} = \frac{N_{A \to B}}{N} \qquad (1)$$

From the previous expression, the support of a rule is a relative frequency that indicates the proportion of transactions in which the rule is observed. When a large sample is considered, the support approximates the probability of occurrence of the rule:

$$support\left\{A \to B\right\} = Prob\left\{A \to B\right\} = Prob\left\{A \text{ and } B \text{ occur}\right\} \qquad (2)$$

The support is a quite useful measure of interestingness of a rule: it is typically employed to filter out the rules which are less frequent.

The 'confidence' of the rule $A \to B$ is instead obtained by dividing the number of transactions which satisfy the rule by the number of transactions which contain the body of the rule, A:

$$confidence\{A \rightarrow B\} = \frac{N_{A \rightarrow B}}{N_A} = \frac{\frac{N_{A \rightarrow B}}{N}}{\frac{N_A}{N}} =$$

$$\frac{support\{A \rightarrow B\}}{support\{A\}} \tag{3}$$

From the previous expression, the confidence expresses a relative frequency (a probability in the limit) that indicates the proportion of times that, if a rule contains the body A, it will also contain the head B. In other words, it is the frequency (or probability) of occurrence of B, conditionally on A being true. Association rules are required to satisfy both a minimum support and a minimum confidence constraint at the same time. At medium to low support values, often a great number of frequent item-sets are found in a database. A popular measure for this purpose is 'lift' (Brin et al., 1997). The lift of a rule is defined as:

$$lift\{A \rightarrow B\} = \frac{confidence\{A \rightarrow B\}}{support\{B\}} =$$

$$\frac{support\{A \rightarrow B\}}{support\{A\}support\{B\}} \tag{4}$$

and can be interpreted as the deviation of the support of the whole rule from the support expected under independence given the supports of A and B. Greater lift values indicate stronger associations: a value greater than one expresses the fact that there is a positive association, while a value less than one a negative one.

In addition to these classical measures, further measures of interestingness could be considered, such as Chi-Square statistic, Gini Index, Odds Ratio, Linkage Disequilibrium, etc.

Antecedents/Consequent associations are computed imposing an antecedent support higher than 2% and 10% of minimum rule confidence. A maximum number of five antecedents is imposed. Rules are selected looking at the lift value (lift > 1).

Analysis results suggest to recode different types of preferences into two categorical macro-variables *transport* and *instruction&house*. Variable *transport* is defined to have four categories: public, private, both, none, which indicate the preference of the family towards private or public means of transport. Variable *instruction&house* is defined to have the following categories: school, house, both, none, in order to describe the household behaviour with respect to expenditures related to instruction, school fees, school-buses, private lessons, etc. and house-care, which include both domestic care and baby-sitting. Unlikely data do not allow for discriminating between public or private school preference.

Family preferences behaviour is described by every possible combination of categories of the two new macro-variables. Hence, sixteen family profiles are defined as all possible combinations of the macro-variables: PUblic-School (PU-S), PUblic-House (PU-H), Private-School (P-S), Both-None (B-N), etc.

Factor and Cluster Analysis for the Setting-Up of Expenditure Profiles of Families

As just mentioned variables which describe family expenses refer to the whole household and not to every single component. In order to identify expenditure profiles, expenses have to be reduced to per-capita amounts.

If a per-capita amount of a household is computed by simply dividing the total by the number of components, the implicit assumption is that economies of scale do not exist. That is, each component has equal weight in the computation. However, larger households generally have an actual advantage over smaller households as they can benefit from sharing commodities (such as housing, stoves, furniture, etc.) or from purchasing products in bulk, which is usually cheaper. Hence economies of scale have to enter the analysis. There is no single agreed-upon method to estimate economies of scale in consumption. Equivalence scales are used to enable welfare comparisons across heterogeneous households. Since the study is analyzing the Italian scenario the following equivalence scale has been applied:

$$X_e = X/(nc)^{0.65} \qquad (5)$$

where X is the total expenses of the household and nc is the number of components who belong to the household. The equivalence coefficient 0.65 was specifically estimated for Italian families on the basis of Engel's method (Carbonaro, 1985). In the following, all expenditures on daily goods are transformed into 'equivalent expenditures' X_e, according to eq.(5) and direct comparisons are feasible.

Factor analysis was applied to 'equivalent expenditures' in order to detect specific combinations of daily consumptions. On the basis of the scree-plot, eight factors are selected. These factors are characterized as follows: 1. primary goods (sugar, bread, oil, milk, etc.); 2. cultural goods (newspapers, books, theatre, etc.); 3. domestic goods (soaps, washing powder, toilet paper, etc.); 4. fast food goods (cheese, cold cut, deep-frozen, etc.); 5. vegetables; 6. fresh fruit; 7. luxury goods (champagne, shellfish, caviar, etc.); 8. idle-hours goods (cigarettes, lottery, pubs, etc.). Each family is now described by a particular expenditure profile which is defined by a string of the above factors.

Successively, cluster k-means algorithm is applied to define groups of families homogeneous with respect to expenditure profiles. It emerges that families can be divided into six groups as shown in Table 1. Each group is characterized by a typical expenditure behaviour as evident from Figure 2.

Furthermore, it is easily observable that, all groups, but the third one, show a particular expenditure behaviour since one factor is clearly predominant. Specifically the first group represents families whose preference is towards fast food; the second group towards primary goods; the forth towards goods typically consumed during idle-hours. In the fifth group the predominant factor is the fresh fruit factor, while the sixth group is characterized by high values of the cultural factor. The only exception is the third group which is composed by families with low values for every factor.

Taking into account the distribution of factors within clusters (Figure 2) we named the six groups as follows: 'Sophisticated', 'Classical', 'Poor', 'Vicious', 'Naturist', 'Intellectual'.

MODELING

Since data mining is generally employed to handle large or even massive data-sets, the preparatory step of data understanding and data preparation is a key-point for good and efficacious results.

Table 1. Frequency distribution of clusters

Cluster	Frequency	Percentage
Sophisticated	4688	16.8
Classical	2442	8.7
Poor	13742	49.1
Vicious	2857	10.2
Naturist	2993	10.7
Intellectual	1259	4.5

It has been seen that for the case study under investigation this preparatory step is carried out as a first phase with the main target of resuming information and simplifying data. Specifically this first phase consists on data handling within each of the three sets of variables: service usage, daily expenditures and social-demographical characteristics. In this phase new aggregated variables are built, service and expenditure profiles (see Sect.3), and replace original variables in subsequent analyses.

The second step in most data mining approaches is the modelling step, where the analyst tries to get a deeper insight into the data and their mutual relationships.

In this case the attention is paid at the joint analysis of the three variable sets taken pair wise: service profiles vs social-demographical characteristic and expenditure profiles vs social-demographical characteristics. In fact, given that social-demographical characteristics of a family have an explanatory meaning, it is interesting to pinpoint every possible association between services usage or expenditures and family charac-teristics. As will be shortly shown, to this purpose authors use two different approaches for services usage and for expenditures according to variable roles and scale of measurements. Furthermore, given the particular nature of the case under investigation, a third phase is provided where an overall analysis is carried out. Specifically the three sets of variables have been considered together as a triple to find out possible thrusting characteristics which induces a certain type of family to choose a certain type of service. Such an overall analysis can be performed following a twofold approach: indirect or direct. Indirect approaches are those which enables only indirect interpretation of family types and family service choices, by eventually superimposing the value of selected explanatory variables one at a time. Direct approaches are those which embed explanatory variables into the analysis of associations between family typology and service usage. As will be shortly discussed (Sect. 4.3) a direct approach is by far recommended since it allows for detecting patterns of variation that may be 'best' explained by selected predictors.

Figure 2. Means of first eight factors within clusters

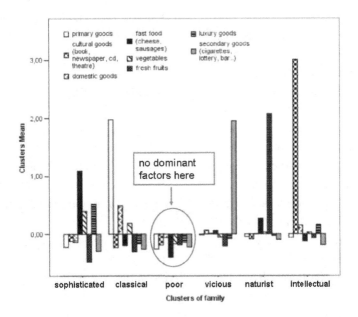

For the purposes of analysis as outlined above three different statistical methods are being adopted:

1. Correspondence Analysis for discovering patterns of service profiles;
2. Decision Tree for classifying expenditure profiles; and
3. Canonical Correspondence Analysis for jointly investigating the three sets of variables.

Since the modelling part is the core of the study, it is worthwhile to provide a brief description of selected statistical methods, which is separately provided in next subsections. Specific applications of these methods under this case study are shown and discussed in the next Section.

Correspondence Analysis

Correspondence Analysis (CA) is an ordination technique which may be applied in general to contingency tables (Clausen, 1998; Greenacre, 1984). The goal of CA is to reduce dimensionality providing a map, usually in two dimensions, of row and column points where Euclidean distances are proportional to c^2 distances between rows or columns.

Methods for ordinations, such as PCA and CA, can be simply considered techniques for matrix approximation, as data are usually organized in two-way matrices, but also, more ambitiously, as techniques for discovering underlying structures (Prentice, 1977). In the latter case, it is supposed that the particular configuration of observed data is caused by underlying unobserved variables and that the ordination technique provides an insight into relations with latent variables from the observed data only. From this point of view both PCA and CA can be considered as ordination techniques able to detect different types of underlying structure of data. On the one hand, PCA relates to a linear response model whereas on the

other hand CA is related to a unimodal response model, since it assumes bell-shaped relationships between variables. This kind of model has been considered ideal to describe biological species behaviour along an environmental gradient (Austin, 1976; Gauch, 1982) and is here adapted to shape family behaviour (Sect. 5.1).

For a very brief technical description of CA, let Y_{mxn} be the data-matrix, with $M_{mxm} = \mathrm{diag}\,(y_{k+})$ and $N_{nxn} = \mathrm{diag}\,(y_{+i})$. Various approaches can be applied to reach CA ordination axes. One of them is called optimal scaling which computes standardized typology scores $\mathbf{x}_{nx1}$ that maximize the dispersion d of service profile scores $\mathbf{u}_{mx1}$. In matrix notation:

$$\delta = (\mathbf{u}^T \mathbf{M} \mathbf{u}) / (\mathbf{x}^T \mathbf{N} \mathbf{x}) \qquad (6)$$

where T stands for transpose and $\mathbf{u} = \mathbf{M}^{-1}\mathbf{Y}\mathbf{x}$. Denominator of the right hand side of eq.6 takes into account the standardization of $\mathbf{x}$, provided $\mathbf{x}$ is centered. Dispersion d represents the inertia of row scores. The problem of maximizing d with respect to $\mathbf{x}$ has as a solution the second root l_2 of the following equation:

$$\mathbf{Y}^T \mathbf{M}^{-1} \mathbf{Y} \mathbf{x} = l\,\mathbf{N}\mathbf{x} \qquad (7)$$

Hence $\delta = \lambda_2$. The first eigenvector of CA is thus the solution related to the second root of eq.(7), i.e. its first non-trivial solution (Greenacre, 1984).

Decision Tree

Decision trees belong to the wide group of methods for addressing classification-type issues, which are generally those where predictions of a categorical dependent variable Y are based on various continuous and or categorical factors X_1, $X_2,\ldots, X_n$.

There are various methods for analyzing classification-type problems, either from simple continuous predictors, such as binomial or multinomial logit regression, from categorical predictors, as for instance Log-Linear analysis of multi-way frequency tables, or both such as designs based on analysis of covariance, ANCOVA (Agresti, '90; Takeuchi et al., '82).

Regression approaches, such as logistic regression, or classification approaches, such as linear discriminant analysis (Mardia et al., '79), play an important role in many data analyzes, providing prediction and classification rules for understanding the importance of different predictors. Although attractively simple, the traditional parametric linear model may fail in various situations: in real life in general and in social science in particular, effects are often non linear (Hastie et al., 2001). Non parametric learning methods, for instance neural networks and support vector machine (Vapnik, 1995; Smola, 1999), are flexible and provide powerful approximation for any type of relationships among any type of variables. The drawback of this approach is the difficult interpretability of the mapping function that is often a sort of black-box.

The choice is here towards tree-based methods which are flexible and easy-to-interpret tools for looking at data (Breiman et al., 1984; Hastie et al., 2001). Tree classification techniques have two major advantages over many alternative techniques: firstly they produce simple and efficacious outputs, secondly they do not underlie on any implicit assumptions on data structure (e.g. linearity or monotonicity of the relationship between the dependent variable and factors). This makes tree-based techniques particularly useful when real life data are to be analyzed and interpreted.

The most popular method for tree-based is the Classification and Regression Tree, C&RT[1] (Hastie et al., 2001). The CART procedure is a stepwise top-down method which performs binary splits of the starting population P into smaller and smaller sub-sets. The fundamental idea is to select each split of a subset so that the data in each descendent subset have less 'impurity', or in other words are purer, than the data in the parent subset. At each step one factor at a time is analyzed and the best one is selected. The optimal criteria is in terms of factors which mostly decrease the impurity level of the parent subset.

When a certain stopping rule is achieved, terminal subsets form a partition of P and are called terminal nodes or also *leaves*. The starting node, which comprises the whole sample, is called *root* and at each step only binary uni-variate splits of nodes are performed. At a certain node m, the impurity level is measured in terms of heterogeneity of categories of the response variable Y. Different measures of node impurity can be used. The Gini index is here adopted:

$$G = \sum_{k=1}^{K} \hat{p}_{mk}(1 - \hat{p}_{mk}) \qquad (8)$$

where K is the number of different categories of response variable Y and $\hat{p}_{mk}$ is the proportion of cases in class k for node m. Apart from the fact that Gini index is easy to compute, it is more sensitive to changes in node probabilities and has a twofold meaning: misclassification rate and node variance. The G index can assume only non negative values, with minimum value 0 representing homogeneity, that is only one category represented. In a tree setting-up the top down direction, from root to leaves, is towards decreasing values of G index, that in the seeking of homogeneity or, in other words, of 'purity'.

A key advantage of recursive binary splits is that it avoids data fragmentation. Multiway splits, such as the splitting of each node in more than two groups, fragment data very quickly, thus leaving not enough data for the next split. Since the C&RT algorithm allows for recursive splits, that is each factor can re-enter the splitting process at various different splits, multi-way splits can be achieved by a series of binary splits, and this is generally preferred (Hastie et al., 2001).

One of the attractive features of C&RT is the *pruning* procedure which provides an objective and efficacious stopping rule for the tree growing. To say it simply, a large tree T_0 is firstly built, then it is pruned using cost-complexity pruning, which is a way to cope with trade-off between tree size (number of leaves) and its goodness of fit to the data. A common practice is to choose as a stopping rule the 'one SE rule' whose description is beyond the target of the paper (a full description of the stopping rule can be found for example in Breiman et al., 1984).

After the optimal tree is set-up, each leaf is assigned a class of the response category according to the so called *plurality rule*: each node is classified in class k ($k=1, ... K$) if k the most frequent class of that node.

The goodness of fit of the tree can be measured by the misclassification rate R, that can be estimated in various ways. The most common used indicator is the re-substitution estimate of R, that is defined as the proportion of cases misclassified (Breiman et al., 1984). The problem with re-substitution estimate of R is that it is computed using the same data used to construct the tree, instead of an independent sample. Still it is broadly used and, specially when small samples are available, it is the only feasible estimate for tree accuracy. If large data-sets are available, a validation process can be undertaken with either split-sample or cross-validation misclassification rates. In the split-sample case, the tree is generated using a training sample and the misclassification rate is computed on the remaining sample. For cross-validation, the sample is divided into a number of sub-samples and in turn, the tree is generated excluding the data from each sub-sample.

Furthermore, due to the iterative procedure and its stopping rules the tree-based algorithm automatically selects only discriminant factors. Discriminant variables are ranked during selection, and hence as a rank of factor relevance is also obtained.

Canonical Correspondence Analysis

Canonical type analysis was originally developed for biological community data (Makarenkov & Legendre, 2002) as a tool; to relate species abundance data as response variables, and to a set of environmental variables as predictors. The main goal of canonical analysis is to obtain an ordination of the response variables whose axes are maximally and linearly related to predictors.

Two main forms of this type of canonical analysis are Redundancy Analysis (RDA) and Canonical Correspondence Analysis (CCA). RDA, invented by Rao (1964), can be considered a constrained extension of Principal Component Analysis (PCA) and uses a linear model both to relate response variables within themselves and to relate response variable with predictors. In this sense RDA can be considered doubly linear. On the other hand CCA, introduced by ter Braak (1986), is the constrained version on Correspondence Analysis (CA). It models unimodal responses to latent gradients, as the parent analysis CA, while assuming linearity of the relationships between response variables and predictors. As shown in next section, the unimodal approach is chosen to describe families. Hence CCA, rather than RDA is adopted for this research.

A crucial feature of canonical ordination analysis deserves a better explanation at this point. The fact that CCA and RDA are able to detect patterns best explained by external covariates (predictors) refers to direct gradient ordination techniques. As aforementioned at the beginning of this section, this approach is called a direct gradient approach in contrast to the indirect gradient approach which is a two-step analysis of different sets of variables.

Direct gradient methods directly include covariates into the algorithm that computes variables ordination. That allows for detecting patterns of variation in the response variables which are best related to covariates, solving the problem of covariates which explain residual variation. To put it simple, this research considers the case where selected covariates cannot explain the main variation but they still explain some remaining variation, which can nevertheless be substantial, especially in data mining analysis where large data sets are analyzed. For instance covariates might be strongly related to the fourth ordination axis and this is not highlighted because usually two or at the most three ordination axes are extracted. This constraint is generally overcome by canonical ordination techniques which, in this sense, stand between regression and ordination (Jongman et al., 1995).

CCA is a restricted version of CA. In fact it maximizes eq.(6), provided $\mathbf{x}$ is centered, subject to the constraint $\mathbf{x} = \mathbf{Z}^T \mathbf{c}$, where $\mathbf{Z}_{2xn}$ is the matrix of standardized values of the two covariates and $\mathbf{c}$ is the vector of unknown weights. By inserting $\mathbf{x} = \mathbf{Z}^T \mathbf{c}$ in eq.(6) and maximizing δ with respect to $\mathbf{x}$, it is possible to find the solution of CCA. More precisely, the roots of the following equation:

$$\mathbf{Z}\mathbf{Y}^T\mathbf{M}^{-1}\mathbf{Y}\mathbf{Z}^T\mathbf{c} = I\ \mathbf{Z}\mathbf{N}\mathbf{Z}^T\mathbf{c} \qquad (9)$$

provide the maximization of δ with respect of $\mathbf{x}$, where the maximum δ equals the maximum λ. For each ordination axis corresponds an eigenvalue that represents the amount of inertia explained by the axis. The total inertia being the sum of eigenvalues calculated by the unrestricted procedure, that it those provided by CA.

EVALUATION AND RESULTS INTERPRETATION

Within each phase of this study, authors need to choose among different models. The choice is based on various criteria. First of all proper statistics criteria (lift, percentage of explained variance, misclassification rate, etc.) are to be taken into account. At the same time, informative criteria (nice interpretability of results) and models compatibility (models can be used in sequence and/or in a jointly way) are adopted. Last but not least, model results should allow for direct and effective communication and these choices take into account also this non trivial aspect. In fact, for most people, graphical display are more ef-

fective than mathematical formula (Kennet and Thyregod, 2006).

In the previous Section authors separately describe adopted methods from a general perspective with the aim of explaining their general features. In the following subsections the specific application of them for the case under study is provided.

Relating Service Usage and Family Characteristics by CA

Patterns and possible relationships between family typologies and their preferred services usage are highlighted by CA. In this specific case the method is employed to get an ordination of service profile and family type points. Focusing on service profiles, in the unimodal CA model they occur in limited range of values for each latent variable (or, re-write, please). The assumptions underlying this type of model are that there exists a set of unobserved variables which characterize each family typology and are strictly related to the family service profile. The method is then here adopted to model the behaviour of families with respect to service usage, assumed to have an unimodal shape.

To this aim a contingency table of service profiles by family typologies is set up. Service profiles are built in earlier Section, while family typologies are taken from *ISTAT* survey. Then the starting data-matrix Y_{mxn} is being treated as the service profiles-by-family typologies matrix. Following these, the classification of family typologies is shown in Table 2.

Results of Correspondence Analysis are shown in Fig.3, which shows the two-dimensional map of service profile and family typology scores.

In CA computations an asymmetric approach is chosen in order to assign more importance to spatial distribution of service profiles (differences and similarities between family typologies are trivial). Following the 'centroid rule' (Greenacre, '84; ter Braak & Verdonschot, '95), family

Table 2. Classification of family typologies

Family type	Code
couple with one child	couple_1
couple with two children	couple_2
couple with three or more children	couple_3
only one parent	1_parent
couple without children with reference component of age under 35	two_35
couple without children with reference component of age between 36 and 64	two35_64
couple without children with reference component of age over 64	two_65
single of age under 35	one_35
single of age between 36 and 64	one35_64
single of age over 64	one_65
other typology	Other

typologies are seen to be scattered around points of service profile that are mainly chosen by those families.

The cumulative percentage of total inertia explained by the first two CA axes is 96.8% thus indicating a satisfactory representative power of the reduced space.

As evident from the map in Figure 3, two groups of profiles are prominant: the one on the right side of diagram, which represents households with low mobility needs and without school expenditures (family who prefer public means of transport, spend money for domestic cares but not for schools); on the other hand, the group on the left side is composed by families who have high mobility and school needs. Accordingly, the mutual position of service profile and family typology points shows that the group on the right is composed by older families or families without children, while the group on the left is evidently mostly composed by families with children.

Relating Expenditures and Family Characteristics by Decision Tree

One of the study goals is to establish whether it is possible to classify Italian households by means of social-demographical variables, having profiled them into different expenditure groups. Given the nature of expenditure profiles and social-demographical variables, respectively response and explanatory variables, the best approach is to choose among classification-type analyzes, with family expenditure profile as nominal response and various social-demographical characteristics of households as predictors. The CART approach is then adopted. In particular, since the frequency distribution of expenditure profiles is highly concentrated on the 'poor' category (Table 1), that is indeed the most interesting category form this research's point of view, the response variable was recoded into a binary response 'poor'/'not poor'. Selected predictors, both of quantitative and qualitative type, include family type (Table 2), geographical area of residence of the family and the following variables related to the reference person in the family: professional condition, professional position, age, sex, status, level of education were considered.

The summary of options and final characteristics of the tree are comprised of:

- Minimum number of cases in parent node: 1000
- Minimum number of cases in child node: 500

Figure 3. CA results: biplot of service profiles and family typologies

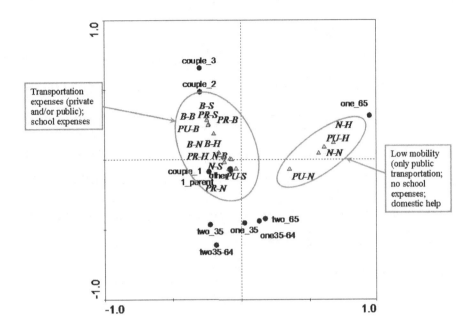

- Included variables (% normalized impor-tance): Family type (100%), Geographical Area (36%), Age number (26.1%), Education (17.3%), Professional Position (8.7%), Pro-fessional Condition (7.2%), Sex (0.2%)
- Number of nodes: 29
- Number of terminal node : 15
- Depth of Tree: 5.

In Figure 4 the tree map is represented. The focus is on the final node number nineteen, which is associated to the maximum conditional frequency of 'poor', as can be seen in Table 3 that shows final nodes ordered by Response (conditional frequency of poor) and Index (ratio between Response value in the node and Response in the root node).

The tree expenditures vs social-demographi-cal characteristics provides a cross-validation classification error of 0.41, with twenty splits (see Section on Decision Tree). Since the intent of this research is purely explorative, the tree can be considered as having a good classification performance. This means that the expenditure choices of the families mainly depend on their

characteristics.. As shown in Table 1 and in Figure 5 (see Root Node) the total percentage of 'poor' is 49.1%. The CART algorithm identifies a leaf where the percentage of 'poor' is about 70.8%. The leaf represents almost 4.5% of overall population and 6.5% within cluster 'poor' (see Table 3). A capture of the rule that describes this segment is shown in Figure 5. It emerges that expenditure profiles are mostly driven by family type, geographical area of residence and professional position. In particular the tree detects a critical segment of population which includes families with more than one child, living in the Southern part of Italy and where the reference person in the family is a worker[2] or does not have a stable job.

Three-Way Analysis by CCA

In order to get a better understanding of patterns of service profiles versus family typologies, some explanatory variables could be integrated into the ordination technique described in sub-section on Correspondence Analysis and sub-section on Relating Service usage and Family characteristics

Figure 4. Tree map

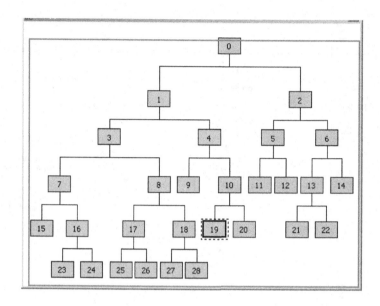

Table 3. Terminal node ordered by Response and Index

Terminal node	Overall Population		Cluster Poor		Response	Index
	N	%	N	%		
19	1260	4,5%	892	6,5%	70,8%	144,1%
23	982	3,5%	658	4,8%	67,0%	136,4%
20	1631	5,8%	1032	7,5%	63,3%	128,8%
9	4586	16,4%	2671	19,4%	58,2%	118,6%
24	585	2,1%	334	2,4%	57,1%	116,3%
28	2668	9,5%	1390	10,1%	52,1%	106,1%
15	2223	7,9%	1142	8,3%	51,4%	104,6%
26	2601	9,3%	1304	9,5%	50,1%	102,1%
27	914	3,3%	417	3,0%	45,6%	92,9%
12	795	2,8%	340	2,5%	42,8%	87,1%
25	5632	20,1%	2297	16,7%	40,8%	83,0%
14	859	3,1%	308	2,2%	35,9%	73,0%
11	1245	4,4%	417	3,0%	33,5%	68,2%
21	553	2,0%	180	1,3%	32,5%	66,3%
22	1447	5,2%	360	2,6%	24,9%	50,7%

Figure 5. Capture of leaf for Node 19. In the top left there is the Root (Node 0). In the bottom left there is Node 1 that represent the first split (see Tree Map, Fig. 4), the excluded family types are singles and young couples without children. The right part is the final part of the leaf with the most interesting Node.

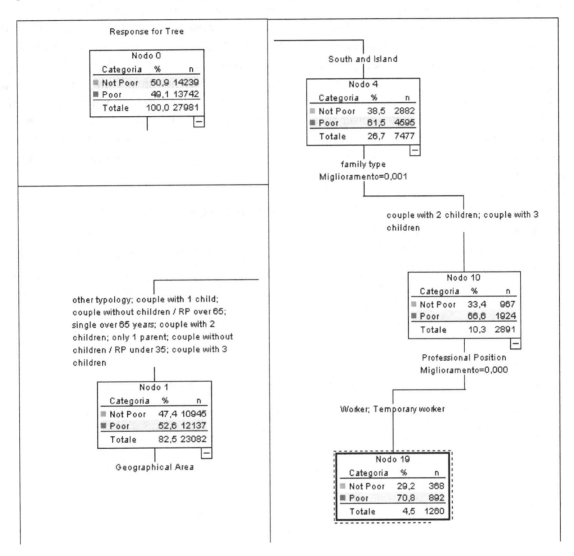

by CA. The goal is to detect patterns of variation in service profiles that are best explained by 'external' variables (covariates). Since this step of the analysis involves three groups of variables, it is called a 'three way' analysis. To this purpose CCA approach is preferred to the RDA one (subsection on Canonical Correspondence Analysis) having assumed an unimodal shape for family behaviour.

Two variables are considered as covariates for family service preferences: the average age of the reference person in the family, as an indicator of 'generation' and the average equivalent expenditure X_e (eq. 5), as a rough indicator of richness. CCA embeds the two covariates into the bi-dimensional map of service profiles vs family typologies. As discussed shortly above, the method was originally developed to detect relationships between biological species composition and environmental gradients. In this case service profiles play the role of biological species and environmental gradients are defined as 'generation' and richness' indicators.

Results of CCA are illustrated in Fig.6. As for CA, the type of scaling is asymmetric, hence service profile points are located at the centroid of family typology points. The cumulative percentage of total inertia explained by the two-dimensional space is now 70.3%, i.e. it is lower than the percentage inertia explained by the two axes of CA (see Sect.5.1). This is concordant with the constrained nature of CCA with respect to CA. Since CCA axes are obtained by a constrained maximization problem, eigenvalues of CCA are generally lower than those of CA, thus leading to a lower percentage of explained variability.

Two major groups are still well recognizable. Now households with low mobility needs and no school expenses are on the left side and the complementary one is on the right side (signs of scores

are not uniquely identified in CA and CCA). It is interesting to note that the two groups are mainly explained by the age of the reference component of the family, thus suggesting that the usage of services is mainly driven by the actual household needs of that service and not by economical capabilities. The richness indicator, taken as the average equivalent expenditure, does not seem to influence service profiles pattern. Yet, family typologies could be ordered along the richness axis making evident that young singles have more money to burn than older or numerous families.

CONCLUSION

This research shows how to use various data-mining techniques for providing solutions and generating knowledge from huge data-sets at an operative level, by synthesizing their relevant content. Despite the constant transition from

Figure 6. CCA results: triplot of service profiles and family typologies with two covariates

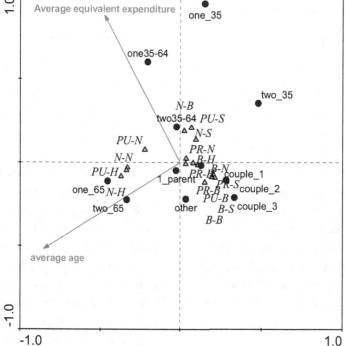

information deficiency to information overload, which every field of research is experimenting, many issues are still open from methodological and practical points of view. The steps from data to information to knowledge represent a challenge for both the researcher and the manager.

Within this perspective the present study aims at providing an empirical example of data-mining from an official data-set regarding Italian household expenditures. The goal of the research is to profile families from the point of view of their consumptions and service usage. Authors identified relevant expenditure patterns and their links to family characteristics. They adopt a data-driven process based on multivariate analysis. It has been observed that, mono-variate and marginal views miss important relations. On the contrary multivariate approach aims at discovering and highlighting relationships and 'hidden evidences'. The analysis highlights two major aspects: on one hand three-way analysis points out that service usage is mainly driven by the effective household needs and not by its economical capabilities, on the other hand critical situations can be detected within the population which include families with more than one child, living in the Southern part of the country and with a precarious job or a low level of professional position.

Results may be particularly useful to public administrators and managers for planning actions and investments, as they provide an insight into family expenditure behaviour and the most influencing factors. In addition this research investigated household actual preference for services, which is relevant for avoiding situations of social deficiencies and/or economical hotspots. If intervention policy and/or prioritization are to be planned, such aspects should be taken into account and further investigations, if necessary, could be properly focused.

FUTURE RESEARCH DIRECTIVES

Possible future developments and improvements of the presented research may be twofold: one related to the data used and the other to the methods. In fact, from one hand it is of primary interest to integrate results with other sources of data. In particular it emerges the need of collecting more information about the nature of services (private or public), their supply and effectiveness. From the other hand, variants of adopted methods could be useful to get a more precise insight into data. For example continuous rules based on intervals and not on dichotomous variables could catch more information and allow for a more proper decision process.

Last but not least, the analysis may be enriched by means of a predictive part, which is indeed the ultimate task of data mining. Data mining tasks comprise gaining insights into data, extract relevant information and knowledge, finding-out patterns and relationships between variables and, eventually, making predictions. This research accomplishes some of these tasks, letting prediction as a possible future step. As an instance, having highlighted specific critical situations, future analyses may be devoted to the prediction of different impacts of possible intervention policies.

REFERENCES

Agrawal, R., Mannila, H., Srikant, R., Toivonen, H., & Verkamo, A. I. (1995). *Fast discovery of association rules. Advances in Knowledge Discovery and Data Mining.* Cambridge, MA: AAAI/MIT Press.

Agresti, A. (1990). *Categorical Data Analysis.* New York: John Wiley & Sons.

Austin, M.P. (1976). On nonlinear species response models in ordination. *Vegetatio, 33,* 33-41.

Berry, M.J.A., & Linoff, G. (1996). *Data Mining Techniques: for marketing, sales, and customer support.* New York: John Wiley and Sons.

Blundell, R.W. (1988). Consumer Behaviour: Theory and Empirical Evidence – A Survey. *The Economic Journal, 98*,16-65.

Breiman, L., Friedman, J. H., Olshen, R., & Stone, C. J. (1984). *Classification and Regression Trees.* Pacific Grove, CA: Wadsworth & Brooks.

Brin S., Motwani R., Ullman J.D., Tsur S.(1997, May) *Dynamic itemset counting and implication rules for market basket data.* Paper presented at the ACM SIGMOD International Conference on Management of Data, Tucson, Arizona.

Carbonaro, G. (1985). *La Povertà in Italia – Studi di Base: Nota Sulle Scale di Equivalenza.* Roma, IT: Istituto Poligrafico dello Stato.

Clarke, K.R., & Warwick, R.M. (1994). *Change in Marine Communities: an Approach to Statistical Analysis and Interpretation.* Plymouth, UK: Plymouth Marine Laboratory, Natural Environment Research Council.

Clausen, S.E. (1998). *Applied Correspondence Analysis. An Introduction.* Thousand Oaks, CA: SAGE Publications, Inc.

Gauch, H.G.Jr (1982). Noise reduction by eigenvector ordinations. *Ecology, 63*(6), 1643-1649.

Greenacre, M. J.(1984). *Theory and Applications of Correspondence Analysis.* London: Academic Press.

Groth, R. (2000). *Data Mining: Building Competitive Advantage.* New Jersey : Prentice Hall PTR.

Hastie, T., Tibshirani, R., & Friedman, J. (2001). *The Elements of Statistical Learning: data mining, inference and prediction.* New York: Springer-Verlag.

Jongman, R.H.G., Ter Braak, C.J.F., & Van Tongeren, O.F.R. (1995). *Data Analysis in Community and Landscape Ecology*, Cambridge, UK: Cambridge University Press.

Kenett, R., & Thyregod, P. (2006) Aspects of statistical consulting not taught by academia. *Statistica Neerlandica 60*(3), 396-411.

Makarenkov, V., & Legendre, P. (2002). Nonlinear redundancy analysis and canonical correspondence analysis based on polynomial regression. *Ecology, 83*(4), 1146-1161.

Mardia, K.V., Kent, J.T., & Bibby, J.M. (1979). *Multivariate Analysis.* San Diego, U.S.:Academic Press, INC.

Perner, P.(2002). *Advances in Data Mining.* Berlin-Heidelberg : Springer Verlag.

Prentice, I.C. (1977). Non-metric ordination methods in ecology. *The Journal of Ecology, 65*(1), 85-94.

Rao, C.R. (1964). The use and interpretation of principal component analysis in applied research. *Sankhyaá, A 26*, 329-358.

Takeuchi, K., Yanai, H., & Mukherjee, B. N. (1982). *The Foundations of Multivariate Analysis.* New Delhi: Wiley Eastern Limited.

ter Braak, C.J.F. (1986). Canonical correspondence analysis: a new eigenvector technique for multivariate direct gradient analysis. *Ecology 67*, 1176-1179.

ter Braak, C.J.F., & Verdonschot, P.F.M. (1995) Canonical Correspondence Analysis and related multivariate methods in aquatic ecology. *Aquatic Sciences, 3*, 255–289.

ENDNOTES

[1] 'Classification' tree for categorical response variable and 'Regression' tree for continuous response variable.

2   Please note that 'worker' is here intended as a low level kind of occupation which differentiates from higher levels of professional positions such as 'employee', 'manager', etc.

Chapter VIII
Electronic Payment Systems in Developing Countries for Improved Governance System

Hakikur Rahman
SDNF, Bangladesh

ABSTRACT

Payment system is an age-old system of transfer of properties. It has taken different forms of transactions depending on demand, usage, acceptability, tradition, methods, technology and availability. Payment systems varied from commodity transfers, physical financial transactions (traditional payment systems) to virtual payment transactions (electronic payment systems). Electronic payment systems have also taken various forms in varying environments and societies. This chapter provides a general overview on various electronic payment systems, focusing developing countries and tried to relate electronic payment systems as an enabler of financial empowerment. In this context, this chapter reiterated that by raising economic activities via electronic means, as a component of e-commerce, could enhance the electronic governance system of a country. It has also put forward available issues, challenges, methods and tools needed to implement electronic payment systems, especially focusing to developing countries.

INTRODUCTION

Electronic commerce and its related services over the Internet could be the engines that improve economic well-being of a nation through liberalization of local services, rapid integration into globalization, and leap-frogging through evolved technology. As electronic commerce, from its very inception, integrates the domestic and global markets by negotiating on trade issues in more elaborated ways, it demand re-investigation of key domestic policies, specifically in telecommunications, financial systems, and distribution and delivery mechanisms of a nation. These sectors are considered as intrinsic factors to the development of a modern economy. Liberalization of policies will rebound to greater economic welfare than restriction in more narrowly focused sectors. Thus, the e-commerce wave can act as a powerful force to erode domestic barriers that have slowed the liberalization of this sector in many countries (Mann, 2000)

Among various aspects of electronic commerce, its operational complexity and inherited characteristics of network externalities are the two prime features that are hindering its implementation. More specifically, the complexities of negotiations require cooperative efforts among operators inside and outside their countries through national and regional platforms. These processes demand policy upgradation at the local level, including the regional contexts, such as following WTO charters. Secondly, by nature, electronic commerce is characterized by network externalities and developing countries rather by not taking advantage of the technical leadership coming out of the private sector are mostly lagging behind. In this respect, Mann (2000) indicated that network externalities and interoperable standards are key in maximizing the benefits of e-commerce. Moreover, developing countries should not try to develop domestic standards. Adopting the old technique of import substitution to develop a domestic industry is even more economically wasteful in the context of the Internet and electronic commerce. They would be benefited more, if they could localize the globally available successful policies, rules and techniques fitting into their national contexts.

However, development of e-commerce in developing countries is not only restricted by local policy and financial laws, but also compounded by many visible and invisible impediments; such as infrastructure, consumers' habit, local culture, trust, awareness, security, and many other issues. The situation aggravates further, when specific issues on electronic payment systems come into focus for enhancing economic activities of developing nations to foster their economic growth.

The electronic payments networks that are available in many countries, are created mainly by the initiatives of private entrepreneurs, such as the issuing and acquiring agencies of corporate debit/credit card systems. In fact, these are ever innovative systems, which connect buyers, sellers, the banking system and other specialized operators like, card issuers and processors. However, the evolution of such networks demands better technologies to offer growing efficiency and security, convenience and value creation, consumer empowerment and greater transparency in the fees, including standardization and regulation (Hnatyuk, Marur & Patrzalek, 2001; Mazzi, 2006).

In recent years, the widespread adoption of digital payment systems is rapidly expanding the sales volume of goods and services, and reducing the barriers of immediate credit and liquidity and the geographic boundaries to trade and exchange. Therefore, huge amount of data traffic is flowing across localities, nations and regions, demanding incorporation of efficient data handling mechanisms. The statistics data confirms that the volumes of the transactions carried out through credit and debit cards are at a very high rhythm, and the cards are more frequently used as efficient payment tool incorporating data mining techniques for the cross-border transactions. Adopting EMV[1] standards, the payment cards are becoming more secure and 'intelligent' and are going to exploit the microchip technology. The microchip card, created mainly in order to reduce the frauds, also allows the development of new multiple functions that are going to transform the card concept and are heavily changing the daily consumers' usage of these payment tools. Furthermore, globalization of the banking and financial institution through enhanced market competitiveness with more evolutionary services have generated both the birth of new actors and the improved specialization of the old operators (Mazzi, 2006). As long as growths of e-commerce continue, electronic payment systems will prosper, as an inherent part of the system. Eventually, national economic growth will find impetus in various sectors, thus improving socio-economic status of their societies. By virtue of strong economic growth, rapid financial transit and confident socio-economic system, the overall governance system of a country is going to be improved.

This chapter will focus on electronic payment systems (EPSs) as a part of electronic commerce, provide general overview of EPS, discuss issues and challenges related to implementation of affordable EPS, utilization of data mining techniques in establishing EPS, implication of EPS in the e-governance, and future issues related to assist good financial governance through efficient electronic payment systems.

BACKGROUND

Electronic Commerce can be referred to general exchange of goods and services via the Internet[2]. It is a generic term denoting business done over the web and/or processed electronically[3]. This includes any on-line transaction of buying and selling where business is done via Electronic Data Interchange (EDI)[4], i.e., e-commerce is the process of buying or selling goods or services via the Internet[5]. In holistic sense, e-commerce is a general concept covering any business transaction executed electronically between parties such as companies (business-to-business- B2B), companies and consumers (business-to-consumer – B2C), consumers and consumers (C2C), business and the public sector (B2G), and consumers and the public sector (C2G). The digital or electronic payments can be defined as all the payment transactions that can be processed through the exchange of digital information and data among terminals and information systems capable to perform authorization and authentication procedures that enable money transfer. (Hnatyuk, Marur & Patrzalek, 2001; Federal Reserve Bank of Boston, 2002; Reserve Bank of Australia, 2006)

A few examples of e-commerce transactions could be:

- An individual purchases a book on the Internet.
- A person reserves a hotel room over the Internet.
- A buyer calls a toll free number and orders a computer using the seller's interactive telephone system.
- A businessman buys office supplies on-line or through an electronic auction.
- A retailer orders merchandise using an EDI network or a supplier's extranet.
- A manufacturer orders electronic components from another plant within the company using the company's intranet, or outside the company using the Internet.
- An individual withdraws funds from an automatic teller machine (ATM)[6], etc.

Nowadays usage of plastic money (credit and debit cards) and electronic banking systems is progressively becoming popular among people to conduct their financial transactions. Going by this trend usage of Internet based payment system to send and receive money online would be the next logical step in monetary transactions. The Electronic Payment Systems (EPS) come in two categories namely, cash-like or debit payment systems and check-like or credit payment systems. Major players in this field are bankers, the third parties and mobile communication network operators, including ISP providers. More specifically, the digitalization of the retail payment systems, or the payments of good and services enabled by the usage of credit, debit, prepaid, and commercial (both branded and private label cards), is becoming one of the driving forces of the entire financial and economic market. (Hnatyuk, Marur & Patrzalek, 2001; Federal Reserve Bank of Boston, 2002; Reserve Bank of Australia, 2006)

Using the Internet, user in the Customer-to-Customer payment systems can transfer money to each other from their checking, credit cards or other accounts. The first C2C payment system was developed in 1999 in USA. Currently, the largest and the most popular e-payment system is Pay Pal. In autumn 2000 Pay Pal broadened its scope of business activity to some European countries. At present, it offers worldwide service.

Over the past decades and years, the payment systems have been evolving in order to cope with the growing international and national demands of the economic actors, such as companies providing goods and services, travelers and consumers, banking and financial institutions. Consumers, entrepreneurs and governments have continued to increase their use of electronic payments. At the same time, advances in computer processing, telecommunications, and data storage have contributed to a wider range of payments system innovations. Although only a limited number of these innovations have seen commercial accomplishment, there has been advances toward expanding the range of options and techniques for making electronic payments globally to increase the overall efficiency of payment systems (Ferguson, Jr. & Minehan, 2002; May, 2000; Sato & Humphrey, 1995; Humphrey, 1995; Abrazhevich, 2004). Nowadays, all over the world, the digital payment systems are rapidly increasing.

During the past years, the credit card industry moved fast to facilitate on-line payments in retail electronic commerce, and credit cards continue to be the dominant payment instrument. Major debit cards that clear through the credit card networks are also being used for on-line transactions, thereby providing cardholders with an additional means of making payments than using traditional deposit-account balances at banks. Several innovators have attempted to create completely new payment instruments for use in electronic commerce, although most typically offer a new interface for end users to the payments system while relying on existing electronic systems, such as the automated clearinghouse (ACH), for clearing and settlement (Federal Re-

serve Bank of Boston, 2002). These operations demand secured and bug-free firmware, high-speed data network and capability in handling huge amount of transactional data. In terms of physical or logical acquisition, these involve sophisticated technologies, skilled work force and efficient control systems. Most of the developing countries are in a state of establishing laws and regulations related to overall ICT development issues, whereby specific development leading to electronic payment systems, by far will take longer period of implementation. The developed world is already at their matured state of operation and therefore, this gap will grow exponentially unless the developing countries would carry out effective instrumentation in this aspect (Brenner & Brenner, 2006; Johnson, 1998).

Along these contexts, Figure 1 would like to justify how electronic payment systems could assist in improving governance in developing countries. Similarly, in Table 1, factors related to payment system, finance, EPS, e-commerce and e-governance have been put forward with possible relationship among them. Figure 2 illustrates how the impacts of communication system for social services promote e-services, and in turn geared towards an improved e-governance system. The next section would like to discuss issues, developments, controversies and challenges in this aspect, and provide recommendations and solutions.

* Payment system is a component of Finance[φ, ρ]

\# Electronic payment system is a component of E-commerce[φ, ρ]

Φ E-commerce is a component of E-governance[φ, ρ]

α E-governance is an emerging issue in Developing countries fostering economic growth and sustained development[φ, ρ]

β Improved electronic payment system can provide impact in the improved e-governance in developing countries[φ, ρ]

Figure 1. Relationship among factors between payment system and e-governance (Source: Author)

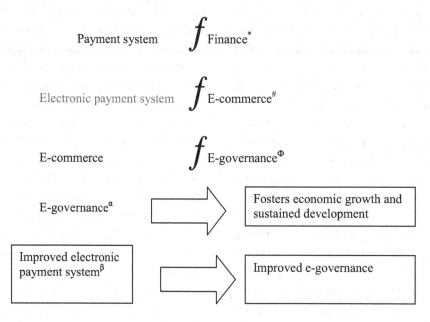

φ: *factors concerning these terms-* technology, the Internet, economics, marketing, information science/information technology, accounting, privacy, intellectual property, equity, governance; technology change, business development, and social controversies; Internet Protocol, computer law, commercial law, banking, tax and insurance law; Electronic Communications Act, Financial Services and Markets Act, National-regional-international Directives and Legislations; E-governance, data warehousing, E-readiness, data mining, VSATs[7], data mart, OLAP, application software, Local Area Network; Social, cultural, organizational, and cognitive impacts of e-commerce technologies and advances on organizations and societies around the world.

ρ: (Humphrey, 1995; Rubin & Cooter, 1994; Traylor, et.al., 1998; Groppelli & Nikbakht, 2006; Downes & Goodman, 2006; Tyson, 2006; Smith, 2001; Laudon & Traver, 2001; Constance H. McLaren & McLaren, 2000; York, Tunkel, Chia & Edge, 2000; Prabhu, 2006; Bhatnagar, 2004; Khosrowpour, 2005a;b; Prins & Prins, 2001; Al-Hakim, 2006).

- **Electronic money** (also known as **e-money**, **electronic cash**, **electronic currency**, **digital money**, **digital cash** or **digital currency**) refers to money or scrip which is exchanged only electronically.
- **Scrip** is any substitute for currency which is not legal tender and is often a form of credit.

MAIN THRUST

In recent years, market, technologies, and legal developments have contributed to a surge of novelty and change in payment systems, including the development of new means of making payments and the alteration of existing means. Traditional payments service providers such as banks and bank associations have been involved in a large number of challenging initiatives. A significant

Table 1. Relationships among finance, EPS and e-governance (Source: Google and Wiki definitions, and author)

Terms	Factors effecting their development
Payment System	Transfer of ownership and settlement of obligations arising from the exchange of goods and services
	Processing payment instruments and settling consequential debts among parties to the system
	Mechanisms, rules, institutions, people, markets, and agreements concerned with the exchange of possible payment
	Transfer of money by providing settlement services between credit card issuer and acquirer
	Transfer funds between financial institutions
	Procedures and associated computer networks used to settle financial transactions in bond markets, currency markets, and futures, derivatives and options markets
Financial System	Collecting, processing, maintaining, transmitting, and reporting data about financial events
	Supporting financial planning or budgeting activities
	Accumulating and reporting cost information
	Supporting the preparation of financial statements
	Purchasing, Accounts Payable, Accounts Receivable/Cash Receipts, General Ledger, Pooled Investments, Budget Management, Fixed Assets, Inventory and Facilities Management
	Organize the settlement of payments, raise and allocate, and manage the risks associated with financing and exchange
Electronic Payment System	A payment system operating with electronic money
	Payment of money or scrip which is exchanged only electronically
E-commerce	On-line transaction of buying and selling where business is done via Electronic Data Interchange
	Business done over the web and/or processed electronically
	Exchange of goods, information products, or services via an electronic medium such as the Internet
	Shop and exchange funds electronically online via the Internet or a network; buy and sell on the Internet.
	Buying and selling of goods by way of electronic media, such as telephones, fax machines, computers, and video-teleconferencing equipment
E-government	Use of the Internet technology as a platform for exchanging information, providing services and transacting with citizens, businesses, and other arms of the government.
	Applied by the legislature, judiciary, or administration, in order to improve internal efficiency, the delivery of public services, or processes of democratic governance.
	Primary delivery models are Government-to-Citizen or Government-to-Customer (G2C), Government-to-Business (G2B) and Government-to-Government (G2G) & Government-to-Employees (G2E).
E-governance System	Network of organizations to include government, nonprofit, and private-sector entities
	One-stop portal, where citizens have access to a variety of information and services.

Figure 2. Social and Financial service promotion can assist in improving e-governance (Source: Adopted from ePSO, 2001)

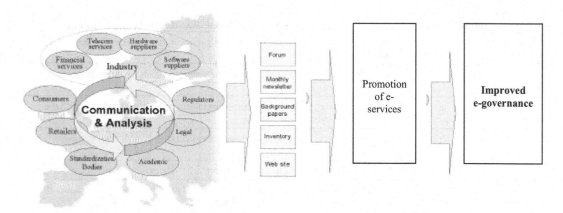

amount of creativity has also emerged from new entrants into various parts of the traditional payments system, including data processing and transaction-processing firms, technology firms, and retailers. The number of similar initiatives was particularly high during the technology boom of the 1990s. A few of these have become relatively successful, but others have failed. However, the use of electronic instruments for making retail payments has become much more common in many developed countries in the past ten years. On-line commerce and banking continue to grow. Over the longer term, however, the sustained development of safe and efficient electronic commerce and finance demanded continuous development of safe and efficient retail electronic payments systems (Federal Reserve Bank of Boston, 2002; Loshin & Vecca, 2003).

On the contrary, on-line commerce and banking has not been flourished in developing countries, and they are falling behind in this competition. In terms of infrastructure (technical infrastructure to create an Internet marketplace), innovation (process, product, market), process automation (hardware, software, human skill), legislation (protocols, laws, regulations), globalization (adoption of international standards), and localization (awareness among common citizens) most of the developing countries are yet

to take off (Mann, 2000; Mann, Eckert & Knight, 2000). While flourishing of common e-commerce activities in many developing nations is at the preliminary stage, specific focus on electronic payment system deserves more sophisticated investigation and literature review. Scope of this chapter would restrict a very in-depth search on this issue, however, as a research publication and be valuable to its readers, generic discussion will be made emphasizing issues on EPS in developing countries.

Among world population of 6,070,581 in 2000, there were 360,985,492 Internet users on December 31, 2000. The figure rises to 1,458,632,361 as on June 30, 2008 (estimated world population in 2008 is 6,676,120,288),with an Internet penetration rate of 21.8% and a usage growth rate of 304.1% between 2000 and 2008. However, the Internet penetration rate in Africa is the lowest (5.3%) despite the growth rate of 1,031.2 % and Asia (15.2%) with growth rate of 401.8%[8]. Among other issues, Internet penetration is an important component in advancing electronic payment systems. Most of the developed world has taken this opportunity to flourish their electronic means of financial transaction and enhance their economic empowerment. According to a forecast by Forrester Research, Inc. made in 2005 that only in the United States the on-line retail sales (B2C sales of goods including auctions and travel) will grow from $172 billion in 2005 to $329 billion in 2010 with a 14% compound annual growth rate (CAGR) (Johnson & Tesch, 2005). Adopting this emerging technology, On-line debit system has been developed in many countries, including Austria, Canada, the Czech Republic, Denmark, Finland, Germany, India, Japan, Korea, Malaysia, the Netherlands, Singapore, Sweden and the United States (Lowe, 2006).

On the other hand, in Asia, China, India, Hong Kong, Japan, and Singapore are major players in e-commerce and thus plays important role in promoting electronic payment systems. Japan alone represents over 60% of all of Asia's economy, but most of the remaining countries in South Asia, except India are far behind in the scenario. According to Far Eastern Economic Review[9], within Asia the borderless world of the Internet could not translate well into reality, where physical products still had to be shipped. With complex and rapidly fluctuating currency conversions, exorbitant shipping costs, and excessive delays in delivery, the added costs of shopping online at international business sites tended to be prohibitive. As a result, the majority of Internet businesses in Asia trafficked only within their own countries. Simultaneously, e-commerce proponents claim that trade and economic growth could flourish only if African governments gave up protectionist measures and point to successes like the tourism industry, where the opening of e-markets has produced positive results[10].

In terms of building technical infrastructure, performing economic reconstruction, articulating social changes, introducing new laws and legislations (Intellectual Property Laws, Copyright Laws, Electronic Signature Law, Trademark Law, Patent Law, Regulation for the Protection of Computer Software and Copyrights, etc.), promoting e-commerce and EPSs, introducing electronic services delivery systems, promoting public key infrastructures, deploying electronic transaction bills, providing adequate funding,

and mostly building trust and confidence among common citizens on the benefits of e-commerce and electronic payment systems, majority of the developing countries are lagging behind the developed ones.

Furthermore, different characteristics of the local environment, both infrastructural and socioeconomic, including diversified cultural differences have created a significant level of variation in the acceptance and growth of ecommerce in different regions of the world, especially in developing countries. As revealed by Wiki[11], many developing countries are still cash-based economies. Cash is the favored mode of payment not only because of security but also because of anonymity, which is useful for tax evasion purposes or keeping secret what one's money is being spent on. Therefore, establishment of e-commerce or introduction of electronic payment systems in developing countries needs to be devised through judgment, analysis and methods among technological, social, cultural, psychological, and political dimensions.

As a developing nation or a transitional economy, one has to look into more in-depth issues to implement electronic payment systems; for example:

- Existing monetary rules on financial transactions,
- Laws pertaining to electronic payment systems (for example, digital signature provisions or dual-currency cross-border electronic financial transactions),
- Available information infrastructure to carry out flawless transactions,
- Habit and culture of local community to use this alternate form of payment system;
- Trust and security surrounding each and every transactions (for attracting returning clients on the system),
- Any sort of incentives (to attract new clients),

- Transactional costs (should be minimized to reduce burden on existing clients or encourage new clients),
- Simplified operational procedures (less complicated procedures during each transaction),
- Inter-operability (all ATMs should allow all cardholders to transact barrier free),
- Transparent accounting (no hidden cost or non-transparent cut at the operator's end), etc.

However, to be optimistic, if one would really like to establish workable EPS in developing countries, utilizing available information infrastructure and data grid, it is expected that major elements of e-commerce applications can easily be developed. All these require secured, electronic data interchange (EDI), more flexibility (operational and procedural), and negotiated interchange. By encouraging entrepreneurial activity, e-marketplace can be a beginning of an enormous repository of data and information. Use of WWW metadata technologies, as RDF (Resource Description Framework) and XML (eXtensible Markup Language) in technical, scientific and engineering applications could become paramount and they could be used in e-commerce applications (Rahman, 2008). Recent researches integrated within the scientific process associated with metadata encourage researchers assisting in the development of wealth creation processes, including technology transfer, and effectively transmutes across directly into e-Commerce. Furthermore, beyond metadata-based cataloguing of knowledge assets, incorporating recent data mining techniques, it is possible to do text- or multimedia- data mining to extract further refined knowledge on transactions / communications across the entire system (Jeferry, 2000).

Next, a few issues on establishment of EPS, challenges they face, methods that may be adopted and tools or instruments that may be incorporated in electronic payments systems are being discussed. They have been highlighted in the perspective of a generic environment. However, as this research has been emphasizing situations in developing countries, discussion on advanced technologies, cases or contexts have been minimized.

Issues

Timing of Settlement

Timing of settlement is an important parameter in EPS. As the time between the clearing and settlement of a payment lengthens, the risk to the payments participants also increases. Though real-time or near-real-time clearing and settlement is always preferable, but to complete the entire process the system should be faster and the deal should be final. Furthermore, faster clearing and settlement should be not only for payment instructions but also for return instructions. Returns are an important part of the payments process, and there is room for improvement in return times, essentially for ACH debit transactions. Improvements in returns could reduce risk and help participants more effectively manage it. Originators of ACH debit transfer instructions could manage their risks more effectively if they did not have to wait three or four days to receive notification that such an instruction will have to be returned.

A Common Standard

The development and adoption of standards are key in achieving widespread use of electronic payments as well as other goals such as payments system safety and accessibility. A common standard can enable the straight-through processing of electronic payments files from the originator of the transfer to the receiver. Open standards, such as eXtensible Markup Language, or XML, can further promote interoperability by enabling systems based on different standards to communicate more readily. Moreover, the lack of a common standard for a payments system and its participants at various levels can increase the cost of participating in the system and introduce inefficiencies such as format translation and manual processing. The lack of standards, primarily in payment-message formats, contributes significantly to the cost and complicacy of cross-border electronic payments. There is a need to harmonize the message formats for file and wire transfers across countries or regions. Greater standardization of formats has the potential to reduce costs for correspondent banks, increase straight-through processing, and improve service for their customers across the regions (Fry, et. al., 1999).

Improved Processing

On the assumption that checks will continue to play a significant role in the financial payments system in the developing countries for some time, banks, third-party processors, payments associations, and retailers may deploy new electronic tools for the collection of check payments. These organizations are motivated by a desire to reduce the cost of check collection, but they also see the deployment of these new electronic tools as a transition step until there is greater acceptance of payments that are initiated electronically. In this respect, *improved processing efficiencies* will reduce the handling of paper, enable faster clearing and return of checks (Federal Reserve Bank of Boston, 2002).

Secured and Trustworthy Web Site

Users of electronic payment system prefers a secured web site with product information on its pages, different ordering methods offered by the site, different payment methods, a shipping cart with tax calculation, some form of money back guarantee, clear privacy policy, and a minimum security measure. As a matter of fact, a web site

running electronic payment should be trustworthy (transactions should not be fraudulent with minimum financial risk) and secured (personal information should not be given to any third party with no identity risk).

From the technical viewpoint, implementing sophisticated authentication and security mechanisms can solve both of the above-mentioned problems. However, they do not automatically make the web site trustworthy. The implemented security techniques should be transparent and clearly explained to the user. In addition, there are other factors that influence trust in a payment system, as such, privacy, information credibility and ease-of-use. People are a bit sensitive about privacy of their personal information. Therefore, the company should only ask for minimum and necessary information, explain, why the requested data is needed and assure properly about security of personal information given by the user. Company (address, contacts, history, products) information and information about the offered services should be clear, ease to find and up-to-date. Good presentation, navigation and professional design make the web site ease-to-use and appealing. (Hnatyuk, Marur & Patrzalek, 2001; Bauknecht, Madria & Pernul, 2000; Umar, 2003).

Laws, Regulations, and Private-Sector Rules

As it is viewed that payment-related laws and regulations are complex, confusing, and causing uncertainty, the developing countries should pursue regulatory changes for improving the legal and regulatory environment to foster greater innovation. As Geva (2001) stated laws pertaining to the disposition of funds by checks and credit transfers, covering both paper-based and electronic payments addressing common law, civilian, and `mixed' jurisdictions need to be incorporated in the electronic payment systems.

Periodic Assessments

Periodic assessment of laws and regulations is required in light of transforming market developments to allow for innovation and improvements in the payments system to encourage open dialog and to adjust the regulatory structure to accommodate reasonable change.

Trust Definition

For e-commerce trust means a person's motivation to invest time, money and personal data in a e-commerce site in return for goods and services that meet certain expectations. However, the more a person trusts a web site, the larger the risk he or she is willing to take when dealing with the web site. In this context, the users of e-payment systems are mostly afraid of two types of risks: financial risks (whether the transaction can be fraudulent) and identity risks (the possibility of error or fraudulent use of personal information).

Challenges

Among many challenges of the electronic payment systems and their implementation processes, a few are being discussed here.

Innovation

Although the use of electronic payments systems has grown considerably, the basic design of clearing and settlement systems for electronic retail payments has not changed that much. In this respect, innovation may strengthen the safety and efficiency of electronic payments systems. However, innovators are likely face numerous business challenges, including slowly changing payments practices by users of payments systems. Hindering innovations puts significant barriers for improvement or lack of flexibility in markets. From the standpoint of public policy, it is vital to identify barriers to innovation and, where

appropriate, to search for ways to address them (Federal Reserve Bank of Boston, 2002).

Technology Challenge

In spite of the benefits of the Internet to the banking industry, sometimes it may prove a double-edged sword. For instance, banks may gain revenue advantages on the retail side by charging for services such as electronic bill presentment and payment (EBPP) and may improve cross selling of products. On the other hand, the effect of the Internet on the commercial side of the bank may be negative as well. Cash managers are worried about potential revenue decreases as the processing of paper bills declines and third parties attract customers with more competitive services.

Furthermore, the Internet poses a range of risks and threats, including:

- security risks (may arise due to hacking or unauthorized access to a bank's key information like the accounting system, risk management system and portfolio management system);
- internal breach or fraud (employees may acquire the authentication data in order to access customer accounts, causing losses to the bank);
- operational risks (may arise due to inaccurate processing of transactions, non-enforceability of contracts, compromises in data integrity, data privacy and confidentiality, unauthorized access/intrusion to bank's systems and transactions, etc.);
- risk of the wrong choice of technology (improper system design, outdated technology and inadequate control processes);
- legal risks (arises when violation of laws, rules and regulations or prescribed practices takes place, or when the legal rights and obligations of parties to a transaction are not well established);

- cross-border risks (the geographic reach of banks and customers beyond national borders may lead to cross border risks, and this risk involves legal and regulatory risks, as there may be uncertainty about legal requirements in some countries and jurisdiction ambiguities with respect to the responsibilities of different national authorities);
- reputation risks (getting significant negative public opinion, and main reasons for this risk may be the system or product not working to the expectations of the customers, system deficiencies, security breaches, inadequate information to customers about product use and problem resolution procedures, problems with communication networks that impair customers' access to their funds or account information);
- money laundering risks (as transactions are conducted remotely, banks may find it difficult to apply traditional method for detecting and preventing undesirable criminal activities, which may lead to money laundering risk)[12].

Systems Constraints

System constraints and the lack of system integration affect both corporations' and banks' ability to use on-line payments information services. Corporations' accounts payable, accounts receivable, payments, and reconcilement systems continue to be less integrated than necessary for seamless handling of invoice and electronic payments information. In addition to these, the legacy systems are generally not structured to handle electronic payments. This situation is not likely to be overcome in a short time and system and organizational changes may be necessary before significant progress is made (Federal Reserve Bank of Boston, 2002).

Regulatory Challenges

A sensible balancing among satisfactory functioning of an electronic payment, operational elements of the transaction, security of the payment transactions, privacy protection of the processed and exchanged data, regulatory issues related to the transaction, coping up with the technological changes and overall satisfaction of all stakeholders within the system (government, financial agencies, banks, users) will always remain as challenges. Among these parameters, regulatory issues are the most critical one to hinder the development of electronic payments system in the developing countries. Many of them are new in this field, regulatory bodies of them are weak or not so well established, and many lack a longer-term vision (Hnatyuk, Marur & Patrzalek, 2001).

Cross-Border Payments

Cross-border payments are quite costly and cumbersome. Cross-border payments include business and personal payments, such as money transfers by overseas residents to family members in resident countries. These payments, mainly personal payments, typically involve an explicit fee in addition to implicit or explicit charges for foreign exchange conversions. The principal amount of the payment may also be subject to deductions by parties to the transaction. Additionally, interchange fees for cross-border credit card payments are also perceived to be costly. For these reasons, some retailers and financial services providers prefers alternatives to credit card payments for international on-line commerce, particularly when it involves countries in which the use of credit cards is not widespread (Federal Reserve Bank of Boston, 2002).

Moreover, the speed, cost, and reliability of payments that must cross national borders are a critical concern for consumers and businesses that have international relationships. There is a need for further enhancements in the payments system to improve the variety of *cross-border payments* services offered to end users. In this respect, private-sector organizations can play a key role in promoting faster, safer and cheaper cost cross-border payments.

Security, Fraud, and Privacy Risks

Security, fraud, and privacy risks are the three important challenges that an EPS is facing. To minimize these risks, the system should be easily deployable, able to provide cost-effective methods for authenticating and authorizing retail payments transactions in real time to manage security and at the same time confine on line fraud risks. A session would comprise all activities, from entering into the system to making a payment transaction, from the moment the user's identity is verified in the browser until the communication is broken. Some major card associations are using techniques that authenticate only the individual payment transaction and not the entire session (for example, Verified-by-Visa and Secure Payment Application by MasterCard). Other techniques for authorization and authentication are less technology intensive. For example, some end users and processors search commercial databases to authenticate users or provide for authorization of ACH payments. These searches are expensive, and not foolproof. For the future, some infrastructure providers proposed preserving the underlying ACH infrastructure but adding on a system for authentication or authorization, or both. One approach is to use real-time PIN-based debit card authorization, in conjunction with an ACH transfer. Application of data mining techniques has real significance in

this respect (Atkins, 1995; Cirasino, 2007; Federal Reserve Bank of Boston, 2002).

Fees and Incidental Costs

The costs of Internet use are a major barrier to the rapid growth of e-commerce in many developing countries, and at the same time, people are reluctant to transmit credit card information across the net. These are mainly related to the cost element, rather than the habit. If costs could be minimized, habits would be improved radically. Moreover, the interchange fee is another prime factor for credit card schemes. It is an issue for all in a four-party system (payer, payee, issuer, and acquirer) (see Figure 3). Most of the time, high interchange fees are discouraging end-users to enter frequently into the system. Moreover, the issue arises because in a four-party system two players, the issuer and the acquirer jointly produce a service for the payer and the payee (ePSO, 2001:56).

Methods

The electronic payment system uses various methods for effective payments, such as:

- Loading the terminal accepting payment instruction details,
- Ensuring authentication of the terminal user,
- Securing personalized secure use of the payment system,
- Encrypting the payment instructions,
- Exchanging payment instruction messages through the telecommunications network,

Figure 3. Payment flow in a Four-Party System (Source: ePSO, 2001)

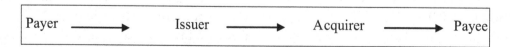

- Exchanging messages with the telecommunications network,
- Decrypting the payment instruction messages,
- Creating records of payment system users in the payment system server,
- Processing payment instructions,
- Exchanging payment instructions with payment clearance systems,
- Registering transactions in subscribers' respective accounts,
- Composing respective acknowledgement and information messages to payers and payees,
- Sending out transaction and statement reports for subscribers,
- Billing subscribers,
- Handling subscribers' claim,
- Payment server data mining, and
- Third-party use of subscriber transactions' data for promotion[13].

A few of these methods are being discussed below:

Real-Time Transaction Processing, Clearing, and Settlement

Normally, in electronic payment systems clearing and settlement should always occur immediately to reduce risk. However, when cost considerations are weighed against real-time functionality in instances where alternative, less-costly solutions could achieve similar results. Lack of adequate and advanced information infrastructures are restricting developing countries to come forward in real-time transaction system (Federal Reserve Bank of Boston, 2002).

A Universal Payment System

The future EPS envisage an advanced system that will give end users options in such areas as timing, completeness, information capability, and fees. Such systems might incorporate tools for managing the risk of originating and receiving payments, including tools for authenticating and authorizing end users in real time. In this aspect, a *universal payment system* with interoperability among existing payments systems will increase the processing flexibility and efficiency. The system should also accommodate more-efficient, more-reliable means for transferring and integrating payments and payment-related information. Currently, incomplete integration of technology (mainly due to lack of appropriate technology and skills) widely affects the ability of banks, corporations, and consumers to develop and use new payments and information services. This sort of incompatibility has always hindered development of electronic payment system in the past and is likely to do so in the future.

Demand Deposit

There are a number of options available for making payments using the demand deposit accounts, which represent the predominant medium of exchange. However, the demand may be insufficient for alternative on-line payment instruments, and security issues may have held back the development. Moreover, the existing clearing and settlement infrastructure may need to be conducive to *true on-line environment*. Secure on-line payment instruments that use demand deposit accounts is potentially important for fostering electronic commerce in the long term, and it will continue to safeguard the progress of initiatives in this area.

Universal Format

The system requires a universal payment-message format, i.e., a common format for several types of electronic payments but with separate clearing channels or business rules for each type. Existing multiple payment-message formats, such as the formats for ACH, wire transfers, and other electronic payments, increases the cost and complexity of payments processing. In contrast, a universal payment-message format could improve efficiency and reduce cost. Using XML a universal format can be defined, and the use of a common set of XML message tags would allow inconsistent message formats to be understood and processed. However, further research is needed to allow XML-based payments standards that could yield more benefits (Federal Reserve Bank of Boston, 2002).

Virtual Account

Many users of EPS system prefer a virtual account, where they can store some money for Internet transactions. This service makes them feel more confident than using the credit card or the personal bank accounts for each transaction. The main advantage of the virtual account is, in the users' opinion, lower financial risk as if they can loose only the money, which they have stored on the account. Therefore, there should have a possibility to use the Internet based payment system without necessity of using credit cards, and the system should work all over the world (Hnatyuk, Marur & Patrzalek, 2001).

Online Bank Transfer

This system uses the Internet to transfer funds among the participants of the system, which is termed as Internet banking.

Prepaid Card System (Scratch Cards)

This is a very flexible method of financial transaction among specific clienteles of the system. Using some form of distinct numbers verified by secured servers, companies (especially mobile operators) and agencies are providing this easily available payment service to their customers. Recently several systems for low-value payments on the Internet/WiMax based on 'scratch cards' have been very popular in many countries. Scratch cards, used for pre-paid mobile phones are easy to use, can be bought by anyone, and are gaining popularity among their clients.

Third Party Billing Systems

Telephone companies (TELCOs)[14] in many countries are acting as intermediaries for providing payment of utility services, and this would save time and money in paying utility bills. However, this sort of payment systems needs security, trust and confidence among the participants.

Mobile Payment

Payment methods by mobile phone have gone a step further in the development of electronic payment systems. Nowadays, banks, TELCO operators and ICT-services companies are striving to develop all kinds of mobile phone payment solutions. As mobile telephones are becoming easily available and accessible to the majority of the population in the developing countries, more structured ways of mobile payment solutions can form a larger share of the electronic payment systems. In many countries, they are being used to pay the utility bills.

On-line Payments from Deposit Accounts

Development of low-cost payment instruments that would permit consumers and businesses to make real-time inter-bank fund transfers for conducting electronic commerce. The most widely available option is the signature-based debit card (for example, the Visa Check Card or Debit MasterCard Card), which allows a cardholder to draw on a deposit account to pay a merchant that accepts cards issued by the sponsoring card association (Federal Reserve Bank of Boston, 2002).

Electronic Bill Presentment and Payment (EBPP)

Electronic bill payment system is becoming popular in many countries. These have been developed more rapidly than B2B payments products, as fewer parameters are necessary to reconcile payments against accounts receivable data. The most recent accomplishment in C2C payments is the Electronic Bill Presentation and Payment (EBPP) systems that allow customers to view and pay their bills over the Internet. According to Terplan (2003) electronic bill presentment and payment (EBPP) is revolutionizing the electronic billing process by offering online and real time presentment of bill content and payment choices. EBPP is the easy way of viewing billing status, remittance items, and presenting balances using a universal browser from any location. Furthermore, these systems consists of value added capabilities like personalization, up-selling, online dispute management, and better control of the accounts payable and receivable process can significantly improve customer care and customer relationship management on behalf of service providers.

In Australia, the market for bill payment services provides consumers with a number of choices through the services of BPay, Australia Post and BillExpress. Both BPay and Australia Post extended their electronic bill payment in 2004, by offering to a full EBPP service. Japan, Taiwan and Malaysia have the most advanced chip migration programs in the Asia Pacific. In those countries, migration for credit cards has been complete and other point-of-sale systems are emerging. A number of other countries, like Hong Kong, India, Indonesia, Pakistan, the Philippines, Singapore and Thailand are supposed to have migrated their credit card systems by 2007. China, South Korea and New Zealand are not expected to migrate until 2000. In North America, the Canadian EFTPOS/ATM system, Interac has planned to be able to process chip transactions from 2007. Examples of other available chip-based prepaid

systems include Proton in Belgium, the K-Card in Korea and Chipknip in the Netherlands. In Finland, for consumer payments to Internet merchants, online bank transfer is the most frequently used methods after the credit card payment. In the United States, MasterCard has incorporated the PayPass chip into mobile phones (Hnatyuk, Marur & Patrzalek, 2001; Federal Reserve Bank of Boston, 2002; ePSO, 2001; Böhle, 2002; Böhle, Rader & Riehm, 1999).

Tools/Instruments

Available popular tools/instruments used in the electronic payment systems are given below:

Online Credit Card System (Credit and Debit Cards)

National and international debit and credit cards are becoming increasingly popular among city dwellers for making payment of regular expenditures or acquiring funds as desired at their flexibility.

Smart Cards

Smart cards are being used not only to ensure fair commercial access to all kinds of merchants throughout the world, but also for non-financial applications.

E-Purses and Chip Cards

A more advanced technology in the electronic payment systems arena, and going to be dominant in near future replacing currently available debit/credit cards.

ACH Checks[15]or E-Checks

Electronic checks offer businesses and consumers a convenient and flexible ACH payment processing. The correct positioning of electronic check processing reduces operating expenses, improves cash flow, lowers administrative costs, streamlines business operations and enables multiple channel order processing and payment. Similarly, ACH e-Check is a solution/service that allows accepting e-checks with specific processing gateway server. However, this service is more or less geographically confined.

Electronic Payment Systems and Data Mining

Traditional direct marketing strengths, emerging electronic payments systems and newly evolved data mining experiences provide a solid base for moving the electronic payment products more into the consumer-direct distribution channel. Use of data mining techniques can identify segments within the potential customer base that are best qualified for a targeted, specific product offer. Furthermore, corporate houses and financial agencies can also mine the database of non-respondents to market new products after completion of an initial product offering. Various data mining strategy allows to reduce acquisition costs and maximize enrollment responses per marketing campaign[16]. Data mining techniques can assist to improve fraud detection, improve EPS practices, analyze massive amounts of data for taking intelligent decision, reduce transaction time of data, enhance security of the system and increase credibility of electronic payments system.

By improving information quality for complex and distributed event based systems, and applying data mining methodology to electronic payments systems, exploratory data analysis can be conducted to identify key features of the data; develop analytical models that detect statistically significant changes from baselines for data fields and attributes derived from data fields; monitors baselines and sending alerts when operational data or data derived from operational data deviates from baselines; conduct root cause analysis to determine why a statistically significant change

has occurred and measure its impact; and develop formal business and technical reference models so that information quality problems are less likely to occur in the future (Bugajski, Grossman, Sumner & Zhang, 2005).

Electronic Payment Systems and e-Governance

In a knowledge-based society, e-governance and e-commerce should run as a day-to-day practice with emerging and existing cutting-edge technologies to achieve competitiveness, economic stability and sustainable development. As a component of e-commerce, electronic payments system, and their auxiliaries, such as the electronic utility bill payment system or on-line payments from deposit accounts may lead to financial empowerment for the common element of a society, which in turn will lead to the overall development of the e-Governance in a country. Government services can be put into web based servers from where common citizens can gain access to those services as a part of e-governance, including payment of funds for various purposes through electronic means. This will eventually raise the economic stability of a country, reduce the transactional delay in the financial management, increase the transparency of the governance system and enhance the credibility of the governance system.

However, for the promotion of e-commerce and e-governance, Information and Communications Technology Act of a country should accommodate the following major provisions:

- Legal validity of electronic contracts
- Legal recognition of digital signatures
- Accepted security procedure for electronic records and digital signatures
- Appointment of authenticating authorities, including recognition of foreign endorsing authorities
- Types of computer crimes being defined and stringent penalties need to be incorporated under the Act

- Establishment of Cyber Appellate Tribunal under the Act
- Act to be able apply for offences or contraventions committed inside the countries and outside their own national territories
- Constitution of Cyber Regulations Advisory Committee to advise the Government and Agencies for promotion of electronic based financial transactions
- Provisions of digital copyright
- Appropriate consumer protection
- Sale or the transfer of immovable property through electronic means (Sengupta, Mazumdar & Barik, 2005; Thorpe & Horman, 2000).

FUTURE RESEARCH

Worldwide payment systems are so diversified that they vary greatly from country to country and region to region, a book chapter on electronic payment system focusing developing country contexts is not so simple. This need a continuous research on this specific subject and updated information from those countries. The subject area should cover issues related to standard development and deployment, legislation and implementation, methods and technologies, means and instruments, process and validation and various other issues. A few of future research issues are being discussed below:

- **SET- Secure Electronic Transaction:** A standard for public key encryption intended to enable secure electronic commerce transactions lead developed by MasterCard and Visa;
- **SSL - Secure Socket Layer:** A protocol that provides a secured communication on the Internet by encrypting the information;
- **CEPS - Common Electronic Purse Specifications:** Established in June 1998 to define

requirements for electronic purse schemes, it is expected that CEPS will lead to cross border interoperability;
- **EMV - Europay International, MasterCard and Visa:** The Europay-MasterCard-Visa specifications for chip-based payment cards. EMV is a standard for interoperation of IC cards ("Chip cards") and IC capable POS terminals and ATM's, for authenticating credit and debit card;
- **FINREAD - Financial transactional IC card reader:** An European solution to meet the need for advanced security for smart card transactions via public networks;
- **HBCI - Home Banking Computer Interface:** A bank-independent protocol for online banking, developed for and used by German banks; and
- **OFX - Open Financial Exchange:** A specification for the electronic exchange of financial data between financial institutions[17] (Hnatyuk, Marur & Patrzalek, 2001; Federal Reserve Bank of Boston, 2002).

These solutions designed by combining applications, databases, networks, computing platforms, and middleware services into a working system that would deliver economic value to the customers, such as:

a. Component-based architectures,
b. XML Web Services, Sun's J2EE, and Microsoft's .NET in building component-based architectures for enterprise applications,
c. Enterprise data architectures in Web-XML environments,
d. Architecture implementation concepts using XML Web Services, Sun's J2EE, Microsoft's .NET, and other platforms, and
e. State of the practice (case studies), market (commercial products), and art (research and development trends) of component-based architectures (Umar, 2003).

Moreover, a future electronic payments system should be able to answer the following questions:

- How the information technology is transforming the financial services to improve the payments systems?
- How to revolutionize and advance the ways by which the financial services make and receive payments?
- What are the barriers to these innovations that have been encountered?
- What are the issues that should be brought to the attention of the appropriate organizations? (Federal Reserve Bank of Boston, 2002)

The Internet based payment system may drive through a paradigm shift from a decentralized to a central server approach. All account-based payment instruments could be channeled through a payment host providing necessary instructions for all transactions between customers and merchants on the one hand and the banking networks on the other hand. Future research should take initiatives to foster innovation, and works leading to reduce potential barriers to innovation and at the same time provide support in formulating legislation to address any perceived barrier in greater use of electronic check presentment.

To cope with the services by introducing digital certificates, future developments need to be fully anticipated. There are several private-sector service providers, including Identrus and Verisign, currently providing a range of services related to digital certificates. However, the national or international electronic payment systems may act as a general root authority for digital certificates issued by the financial industry. By serving as the root authority for issuing digital certificates the system can authenticate their own customers' access to this web-based services; and at the same time by serving as the root authority for such certificates security issues are improved.

Furthermore, issues like cross country disparity of payment culture (e-purses, credit card use), impact of cross-border trade on e-commerce and e-payment methods, regulation, innovation, and legislation (new directives, rules, laws); e-money and near-money (bonus points, loyalty schemes); competition between banks, near-banks and non-banks; approaches to micro-payments, etc. could be taken into consideration (Anik & Pathan, 2004).

CONCLUSION

E-commerce can have positive effects on all economies contributing to the mutually supportive goals of sustainable economic growth by enhancing the public welfare, and fostering social harmony. It also can be instrumental in assisting developing economies participate in the multilateral trading system. Benefits ensuing from the rapid growth of e-commerce will help them meet more effectively their vital development goals, such as poverty reduction, health and education (METI, 2004).

Primarily, three factors influence the electronic payments system. The terminals (hardware, software), added economic value to businesses (reduced fraudulent transactions), and reduced transaction time (instant authentication). Conversely, payment instruments or services that require significant changes to internal business processes or computer systems, and modest improvement in payments practices, may be too costly or complex to succeed. Simultaneously, instruments or services requiring modifications to several systems overseen by several departments in a single organization can fall victim to conflicting priorities and incentives within that organization. Furthermore, a requirement for significant or costly actions by large numbers of consumers, such as upgrading personal computers or downloading software, can be costly and inconvenient and imply very low rates of adoption. (Federal Reserve Bank of Boston, 2002)

Advances of ICTs have created new forces in managing organizations. These forces are leading modern organizations or corporate houses to reassess their current structures to become more effective in the growing global economy (Khosrowpour, 1995). Similarly, designing a well-functioning intergovernmental fiscal system is a prerequisite for achieving other reform objectives, such as macroeconomic stability, private sector development, and a social safety net for those affected by the transition. At the same time, a broader analytical framework that is conventionally involved in the process of intergovernmental finance is needed for analyzing fiscal issues in those economies (Sato & Humphrey, 1995). Electronic payment systems in developing countries has to go a long way in achieving sustained economic empowerment and thus steer the governance system for improved e-governance.

REFERENCES

Abrazhevich, D. (2004). Electronic Payment Systems: a User-Centered Perspective and Interaction Design, Dennis Abrazhevich publication.

Al-Hakim, L. (2006). Global E-government: Theory, Applications and Benchmarking, Idea Group Publication.

Anik, A.A. & Pathan, Al-Mukaddim K. (2004). A Framework for Managing Cost Effective and Easy Electronic Payment System in the Developing Countries, In Proceedings of International Conference on Intelligent Agents, Web Technology and Internet Commerce (IAWTIC'04), Gold Coast-Australia, 12-14 July, 2004. pp. 112-119.

Atkins, R.D. (1995) (Ed.), The Alleged Transnational Criminal: The Second Biennial, Martinus Nijhoff Publishers.

Bauknecht, K., Madria, S.K. & Pernul, G. (2000). (Eds.) Electronic Commerce and Web Technolo-

gies: First International Conference on Electronic Commerce and Web Technologies, EC-Web 2000, Springer.

Bhatnagar, S.C. (2004). E-government: From Vision to Implementation : a Practical Guide with Cases, Sage Publications.

Böhle, K. (2002). Integration of Electronic Payment Systems into B2C Internet Commerce: Problems and Perspectives, Background Paper #8, European Communities.

Böhle, K., Rader, M. & Riehm, U. (1999). (Eds.) Electronic Payment Systems in European Countries: Country Synthesis Report, European Commission, ECSC-EEC-EAEC, Brussels, Luxembourg.

Brenner, P. DeCoster & Brenner, P. (2006). Central America: Structural Foundations for Regional Financial Integration, International Monetary Fund, World Bank. International Monetary Fund.

Bugajski, J., Grossman, R., Sumner, E. & Zhang, T. (2005). A Methodology for Establishing Information Quality Baselines for Complex, Distributed Systems, 10th International Conference on Information Quality (ICIQ), November 4th - 6th 2005, MIT, Cambridge, MA.

Cirasino, M. (2007). Reforming Payments and Securities Settlement Systems in Latin America and the Caribbean, World Bank Publications.

Downes, J. & Goodman, J.E. (2006). Dictionary of Finance and Investment Terms, Barron's Educational Series, Incorporated.

ePSO (2001). Electronic Payments Systems Observatory, ePSO Newsletter Issues no. 1-8, July 2000-September 2001, Institute for Prospective Technological Studies, European Commission, pp.3.

Federal Reserve Bank of Boston (2002). The Future of Retail Electronic Payments Systems: Industry Interviews and Analysis, Staff Study #175,

Federal Reserve Staff for the Payments System Development Committee, Board of Governors of the Federal Reserve System, Federal Reserve Bank of Boston, USA.

Ferguson, R.W. Jr. & Minehan, C.E. (2002). In Foreword: The Future of Retail Electronic Payments Systems: Industry Interviews and Analysis, Staff Study #175, Federal Reserve Staff for the Payments System Development Committee, Board of Governors of the Federal Reserve System, Federal Reserve Bank of Boston, USA.

Fry, M.J. et. al. (1999). Payment Systems in Global Perspective, Routledge.

Geva, B. (2001). Bank Collections and Payment Transactions: Comparative Study of Legal Aspects, Oxford University Press.

Groppelli, A.A. & Nikbakht, E. (2006). Finance, Published 2006, Barron's Educational Series, Inc.

Hnatyuk, Y., Marur, M. & Patrzalek, E. (2001). Money Mover, Electronic Payment System, available from http://www.telono.com/research/MOMO.pdf

Humphrey, D.B. (1995). Payment Systems: Principles, Practice, and Improvements, World Bank Technical Paper #260, World Bank, World Bank Publications.

Jeffery, K.G. (2000). The Grid for e-Science: e-Commerce Benefits, Information technology Department, CLRC, ITD.

Johnson, C. & Tesch, B. (2005). Forrester Research, (2005). US eCommerce: 2005 To 2010, A Five-Year Forecast And Analysis Of US Online Retail Sales, Retrieved June 16, 2008 from http://www.forrester.com/Research/Document/Excerpt/0,7211,37626,00.html

Johnson, Omotunde E. G. (1998). Payment Systems, Monetary Policy, and the Role of the Central Bank, International Monetary Fund.

Khosrowpour, M. (1995). Managing Information and Communications in a Changing Global Environment, International Conference of Management Association, Information Resources Management Association, Idea Group Inc (IGI).

Khosrowpour, M. (2005a). Practicing e-government: A Global Perspective, Organisation for Economic Co-operation and Development, 2005, Idea Group Publication.

Khosrowpour, M. (2005b). Advanced Topics in Electronic Commerce: V. 1., 2005, Idea Group Publication.

Laudon, K.C. & Traver, C.G. (2001). E-commerce: Business, Technology, Society, 2001, Addison Wesley.

Loshin, P. & Vacca, J.R. (2003). Electronic Commerce, Charles River Media.

Lowe, P. (2006), 'Payment Systems Developments and Architecture: Some Background', speech to the Australian Bankers' Association and APCA Forum on 'Payment Systems Evolution: Where to From Here?', 27 September.

Mann, C.L. (2000). Electronic Commerce in Developing Countries: Issues for Domestic Policy and WTO Negotiations, Peterson Institute Working Paper Series #WP00-3, Peterson Institute for International Economics, Washington, DC.

Mann, C.L., Eckert, S.E. & Knight, S.C. (2000). Global Electronic Commerce: A Policy Primer, Institute for International Economics, Washington, DC.

May, P. (2000). The business of ecommerce: from corporate strategy to technology, Cambridge University Press.

Mazzi, G.B. (2006). The European Vision for digital payment systems. In: Pacifici, G., Pozzi, P. (Eds.), Money-On-Line.eu: The European Scenario of Digital Payment Systems and Smart Cards, FrancoAgneli, Milan, Italy.

McLaren, C.H. & McLaren, B.J. (2000). E-commerce: Business on the Internet, 2000, South-Western, Educational Publishing.

METI (2004). Towards eQuality: Global E-Commerce Presents Digital Opportunity to Close the Divide Between Developed and Developing Countries, METI's Proposal for WTO E-Commerce Initiative, Ministry of Economy, Trade and Industry, Japan.

Prabhu, C.S.R. (2006). E-governance: Concepts and Case Studies, 2006, Prentice Hall of India.

Prins, J.E.J. & Prins, C. (2001). Designing E-government: On the Crossroads of Technological Innovation and Institutional Change, Published 2001, Kluwer Law International.

Rahman, H. (2008). Prospects and Scopes of Data Mining Applications in Society Development Activities, In Rahman, H. (Ed.) Data Mining Applications for Empowering Knowledge Societies, IGI Global, Information Science Reference, Hershey: pp. 159-185.

Reserve Bank of Australia (2006). Payment Systems Developments and Architecture: Some Background, Payments Policy Department, Reserve Bank of Australia.

Rubin, E.L. & Cooter, R. (1994). The Payment System: Cases, Materials, and Issues, 1994, West Publishing Company.

Sato, S. & Humphrey, D.B. (1995). Transforming Payment Systems: Meeting the Needs of Emerging Market Economies, World Bank Publications.

Sengupta, A., Mazumdar, C. & Barik, M.S. (2005). e-Commerce security – A life cycle approach, *Sadhana* Vol. 30, Parts 2 & 3, April/June 2005, pp. 119–140, India.

Smith, B.W. (2001). *E-Commerce: Financial Products and Services*, 2001, Law Journal Press.

Terplan, K. (2003). Electronic Bill Presentment and Payment, CRC Press.

Thorpe, R. & Horman, G. (2000). Strategic Reward Systems, Financial Times.

Traylor, N.T. et.al. (1998) Payments, Clearance, & Settlement: A Guide to the Systems, Published 1998, DIANE Publishing.

Tyson, E. (2006). Personal Finance for Dummies, Published 2006, John Wiley & Sons.

Umar, A. (2003). E-Business and Distributed Systems Handbook: Architecture, NGE Solutions, Inc., USA.

USCH (1995). The Future of Money: Hearing Before the Subcommittee on Domestic and International Monetary Policy, Trade, and Technology, Committee on Banking and Financial Services, Subcommittee on Domestic and International Monetary Policy, United States Congressional House, Congressional Sales Office, United States.

York, S., Tunkel, D., Chia, K. & Edge, H.S. (2000). E-commerce: A Guide to the Law of Electronic Business, Butterworths.

ADDITIONAL READINGS

Chowdary T. H. (2002). E-governance in India experienced in AdnhraPradesh. Global e-Policy e-Gov Forum proceeding, Seoul, R.O.K: Global e-Policy and e-Government Institute: 262-278.

Grabner-Kraeuter, S. (2002). The role of consumers' trust in online shopping. Journal of Business Ethics 39: 43-50.

Hennock, M., (2002). China's Baby Steps in E-Commerce, BBC Online News September 24,2002, Retrieved 2nd November 2002 from the World Wide Web http://news.bbc.co.uk/1/hi/business/2276360.stm

Juliussen, E., (2002). Internet Users by Country Retrieved 13th December 2002 from the World Wide Web http://www.etforecasts.com

Kraemer, K.L. & Dedrick, J., Melville, N.P. & Zhu, K. (2006). (Eds) Global e-commerce: Impacts of National Environment and Policy, Cambridge University Press; 1st edition.

Lee, M. and E. Turban, (2001). "A trust model for consumers Internet shopping." International Journal of Electronic Commerce 6: 75-91.

McKnight, D. and N. Chervany. (2001). "What trust means in e-commerce customer relationships: An interdisciplinary conceptual typology." International Journal of Electronic Commerce 6: 35-59.

McKnight, D., L. Cummings, and N. Chervany. (1998). "Initial trust formation in new organizational relationships." Academy of Management Review 23: 473-490.

Rose, B., Rosin, L., (2002). "Internet 9: The Media and Entertainment World of Online Consumers" Arbitron/Edison Media Research.

Travica, B., (2002). "Diffusion of electronic commerce in developing countries: The case of Costa Rica." Journal of Global Information Technology Management, 5(1), 4-24.

Urban, G., F. Sultan, and W. Qualls. (2000). "Placing trust at the center of your Internet strategy." Sloan Management Review 42: 1-13.

Wolcott, P., Press, L., McHenry, W., Goodman, S. E., Foster, W., (2001). "A framework for assessing the global diffusion of the Internet." Journal of the Association for Information Systems, 2(6).

Zwass, V., (1996). "Electronic commerce: Structure and issues." International Journal of Electronic Commerce, 1(1), 3-23.

ENDNOTES

[1] **EMV** is a standard for interoperation of IC cards ("Chip cards") and IC capable *POS terminals* and ATM's, for authenticating credit and debit card payments. The name EMV comes from the initial letters of Europay, MasterCard and VISA, the three companies which originally cooperated to develop the standard.

[2] www.hostingconsumerreports.org/glossary.php

[3] www.paytran.com/glossary.html

[4] www.wnd.com/mediakit/glossary.asp

[5] www.merchant-accounts.com/merchant-account-glossary.htm

[6] http://www.census.gov/epcd/www/ebusines.htm

[7] Very Small Aperture Terminal

[8] Source: www.internetworldstats.com

[9] http://ecommerce.hostip.info/pages/486/Global-E-Commerce-Asia-E-COMMERCE-HURDLES-IN-ASIA.html

[10] http://ecommerce.hostip.info/pages/483/Global-E-Commerce-Africa-ONGOING-DEBATE.html

[11] http://en.wikibooks.org/wiki/E-Commerce_and_E-Business/E-Commerce_Applications:_Issues_and_Prospects

[12] http://www.webdomaindesignhosting.com/key-issues-e-banking.html

[13] http://gauss.ffii.org/PatentView/EP1334475

[14] A **telephone company** (or **telco**) provides telecommunications services such as telephony and data communications

[15] The Automated Clearing House (ACH) is a network of regional associations, inter–bank associations, and private–sector processors. ACH payments are processed and settled electronically, thereby increasing reliability, efficiency and cost effectiveness. ACH payments are generally settled in one day or more.

[16] http://ipoportal.edgar-online.com/ipo/textSection.asp?cikid=73633&fnid=2256&IPO=1&sec=bd&coname=PAYMAP+INC

17   http://www.freshpatents.com/On-line-cred-
      it-information-system-dt2.html; On-line
      Credit Information System; http://www.
      freepatentsonline.com/20060064306.html

Section III
Security, Safety, and Trust

Chapter IX
Data Mining as Part of Intelligence–Led Policing in the Finnish Police

Arla Juntunen
University of Helsinki, Finland

ABSTRACT

The field of knowledge management has emerged in response to organizational needs to capture and manage what they know. This chapter discusses how a public sector organization made an effort to enhance their collaborative processes and organizational knowledge base in a specific functional area and how they implemented KM-tools to improve knowledge and information sharing and transferal both within the organization and between partners. The main expectations for the information management included the specific knowledge of its own area as well as core competencies created and systematically developed around its own areas of expertise. The implementation of KM-tools in the crime analysis function as part of intelligence-led policing assisted in preventing more crimes and creating safer communities. Decision-making in the police changed gradually from just analyzing and following past events to predicting and preventing crimes. The use and recognition of the benefits of KM-tools also facilitated the development of continuing learning and education in all the levels and in all the fields and locations of the organization. This chapter aims to promote knowledge management and KM-tools usage in government and to identify the challenges and benefits gained by an implementation of analytical solutions. It describes the managerial and organizational implications of the usage of analytical solutions and the effects on political decision-making and government programs.

INTRODUCTION

This chapter introduces data mining in a criminal investigation context as part of intelligence-led policing strategies and discusses its political, managerial and societal implications. This chapter depicts the issues and challenges of the adoption, implementation, social and political outcomes of various data mining analysis techniques, and how these techniques are used in analyzing the different operations of the daily police work, and discusses the increased efficiency and productivity in the Finnish police organization. In general, data mining can provide value to different governmental and police operations by extracting useful information out of vast amounts of collected data. In addition, data mining can be predictive and uncover hidden patterns that the police can strategically use to reduce costs, detect fraud and reveal different criminal activities. Data mining tools predict future trends and behaviors, allowing different organizational units to make proactive, knowledge-driven decisions. Data mining analysis moves beyond the analyses of past events provided by retrospective tools typical of decision support systems. The expression "Data Mining" can refer to the whole process of knowledge discovery and sometimes to the methods that used in the knowledge discovery phase. In this chapter, d*ata mining can be defined as "the application of database technology and techniques — such as statistical analysis and modeling — to uncover hidden patterns and subtle relationships in data and to infer rules that allow for the prediction of future results."* as defined by U.S. General Accounting Office (GAO; 2004). The concept of intelligence-led policing in this chapter refers to *"the application of criminal intelligence analysis as an objective decision-making tool in order to facilitate crime reduction and prevention through effective policing strategies and external partnership projects drawn from an evidential base."* (Ratcliffe, 2003).

Moreover, the recent increasing interest in crime analysis and studies of crimes' societal implications as part of internal security started in 2003 in Finland. Finland's Prime Minister Matti Vanhanen's Government decided in its 2003 Government Program to start preparations for a program concerning internal security. It was deemed necessary to start a multi-organizational development plan that would extend over a period of several years in order to ensure long-term decision-making and development in this area. When adopting the Government Program on the 24th June 2003, the Government's idea was to increase public safety and security by reducing drug-related, violent and financial crimes and to improve the citizen's safety in everyday life situations. Crime prevention and investigation were seen as important in enhancing internal security. Fear of crime or perceptions of insecurity are not a simple phenomenon (Bilsky & Wetzels, 1997) but a multi-element issue that has been divided into fear, anxiety, vulnerability, risk assessment, concerns and perceptions of safety and insecurity (Ferraro & LaGrange, 1987; Hollway & Jefferson, 2000; Mawby et al., 2000). Therefore, this goal of increasing public safety and security required new decision support tools, knowledge management practices within governmental agencies and inter- and intra-organizational knowledge transfer and collaborative networks with the police, customs and boarder control.

Furthermore, it is claimed that Finland is one of the safest countries in Europe. The most significant exception is the amount of violent crime. In fact, the number of violent offences, for example homicide, is the largest in Western Europe in relation to the population. Another important exception is the number of home and leisure accidents, which is considerably higher than in the other Nordic countries. To improve internal security it is necessary to reduce the number of homicides, the amount of violent crime in general, as well as the number of accidents, particularly home and leisure accidents. It is also vital to prepare for future trends by combating threats and challenges that may affect internal security. (Ministry of the Interior, 2004, pp.5-6). Thus, crime analysis and data mining were needed for crime prevention as well as the enhancement of internal security.

This study will next discuss previous research in this area. Secondly, it will describe the analysis and the methodology of the study, and finally, it will discuss the implications of this study and the use of data mining in criminal investigation as part of internal security.

BACKGROUND OF THE STUDY

Similar to the private sector, today's police organizations face a rapidly changing operating environment and a great deal of challenges. They must deal with the changes while answering to demands for increased service, reduced costs, use of fewer resources and, at the same, time increased efficiency and accountability. The police organization as part of national security, must deal with the changing expectations of multiple contact groups, emerging regulation, growing international threats, changes in politics and political leaders, decentralization of organization and centralization of certain functions providing similar services, as well as increasing demand for better accountability. Collaboration between different organizations, citizens and networks demands a collaborative culture (Blomqvist et al., 2007). It also requires trust, supporting both individual achievement and intrapreneurship but also community, with collectively shared values and norms to cope with complex interdependency and high uncertainty at the operating environment. (Adler & Heckscher, 2006; Blomqvist et al., 2007). The experts in the police identified several areas in which more support of collaborative tools and knowledge sharing were required.

The public administration literature has a plethora of scholars who claim that the public

sector should adopt business-like techniques in order to increase efficiency (Khademian, 1995). This is also true of the data warehouse and mining technologies. Some of the key challenges that the police face in their effective and professional information gathering include: the consolidation of dispersed information, development and maintenance of smooth processes among various communities and law enforcement personnel, and effective communication with targeted groups that are important to the commonly agreed strategies and goals. The increase of data allows more opportunities to identify different trends and changes in crimes within the operating environment. This study attempts to show that the role of knowledge and knowledge support tools such as data mining can be triggers for organizational change and resource reallocation.

The knowledge based view of the organization depicts organizations as repositories of knowledge and competencies (Kogut & Zander, 1992), and also highlights the increase of knowledge workers in organizations that are heavily reliant on knowledge and information (see e.g. Stewart, 2001; Blomqvist & Levy, 2006). From this viewpoint, organizational 'advantage' arises from an organization's superior capability in creating, sharing and transferring knowledge to use the knowledge in different situations.

Furthermore, the volume and value of information is growing exponentially, and, therefore, one of the main challenges facing organizations today is how to uncover the hidden value in its collective databases, to separate critical information from inconsequential information, and uncover the tacit knowledge veiled in the minds of their employees – the intellectual capital of the organization. Because knowledge can take on both tacit and explicit manifestations, organizational knowledge can be created through both experimental learning, and information acquisition and processing. New problems and situations trigger search heuristics, during which novel explanations are located and innovative solutions developed. These solutions are stored in the organization's 'solution set' and their repeated use results in their becoming part of organizational practices and processes (Cyert & March 1963; Walsh, 1995).

In addition, innovations are becoming a critical part of the government manager's role (Altschuler & Zegans, 1997). Citizens are rapidly losing patience with governmental agencies, such as police departments, that do not recognize the growing and shifting needs of their communities and private citizens, and that continue to retain outmoded or ineffective routines (Osborne & Gaebler, 1992). Moreover, entrepreneurial spirit and organizational renewal are also required in the public sector. Therefore, citizens require new ideas of action in the public administration (Altschuler & Zegans, 1997).

The concept of intelligence-led policing (Peterson, 2005) is a collaborative effort based on improved intelligence operations, community-oriented policing and problem solving. The term "intelligence-led policing" originated in Great Britain (The Kent Policing Model). The Kent Constabulary developed the concept in response to rapid increases in property-related offenses (e.g., burglary and automobile theft) at a time when resources were scarce. This model resulted in more police time being available to create intelligence units to focus, initially, on property-related offenses , resulting a 24-percent drop in crime over 3 years (Anderson, 1997).

According to Peterson (2005), historically, the following have been the most common forms of data collection used in police organizations: Physical surveillance (either in person or by videotape),electronic surveillance (trap and trace or wiretap), informants, undercover operators, newspaper reports (now also Internet sources), and public records (e.g., deeds and property tax records). Today, a broad range of analytic techniques and methods are available to support intelligence efforts (Peterson, 2005): (1) **Crime analysis:** Crime pattern analysis, geographic analysis, time-series analysis, frequency-distribu-

tion analysis, behavioral analysis, and statistical analysis; (2) **Investigative (evidential) analysis:** Network analysis, telephone record analysis, event, commodity, and activity-flow analysis; timeline analysis, visual investigative analysis, bank record analysis, net worth analysis, business record analysis, content analysis, post seizure analysis, case and conversation analysis; and (3) **Strategic analysis:** Threat assessments, vulnerability assessments, risk assessments, estimates, general assessments, warnings, problem profiles, target profiles, and strategic targeting.

This qualitative study of the Finnish Police and the development and implementation of the KM-tools as part of intelligence-led policing strategies in an internal security context is an instrumental case study. It is important, therefore, to remember the instrumental character of a case study in generating theory. The study was stimulated by the need to understand the logic of a public organization's attempt to adopt new tools and methods and to enhance knowledge management both within the organization and between its partners. The study period was from 1997 to 2007, during which time both the data warehouse and traditional decision support system were developed, as well as new crime analysis methodology based on KM-tools such as data mining.

Empirically this study is limited to the Finnish Police and its crime analysis function. The findings and implications of this study may not be universally applicable; the organizational and cultural contexts are issues, which can have a notable impact on the results generated. The study presents only a limited part of the report material. The researcher's interpretation concentrated on findings from a mass of information at a more specific level. The researcher's role was as a participant-researcher. This particular research approach was chosen as it provided optimal access and the incorporation of multiple resources and views. Naturally, the objectivity of the study may be questioned as the researcher has a position-related bias, being involved in the study organization. To decrease the degree of subjectivity, the topic of the study has been chosen in a manner to create neutrality and to hold an ethically acceptable status; it does not enhance the position of the researcher nor does it harm the position of the organizational functions involved.

The internal validity of the study is enhanced through careful data handling with consistent analysis and organization of the research. Validity is improved by including participants' comments and corrections. The research audit system also improved the quality of the study. The material and data would generate similar results if re-studied, although the researcher's pre-knowledge and area specific experience remarkably assisted in the planning, analysis and reporting of this study.

Several scholars see advantages in the use of a longitudinal process in this research in that it provides a more in-depth dimension by inserting the research into a rich temporal setting (Elo, 2005; Perry, 1998; Vincze, 2004;). Process-based analysis is a method that allows a continuous research process in real time and monitors the overall evolution of the issues under study. However, Tsoukas (1989, p.551) argues that even idiographic studies can generate explanations that are externally valid. He also states that idiographic research conceptualizes the causal structures, while clarifying the contingent manner through which a set of postulated causal powers interact and gives rise to the flux of the phenomena studied. Eisenhardt (1989, p.532) considered, for example, convincing evidence as a key criteria when evaluating inductive theory. This study did not aim to develop new theories or models but, rather, derived from the empirical material, new findings to synthesize at the end of the research process with the existing theories of knowledge management and strategic management.

DEVELOPMENT AND IMPLEMENTATION PROCESS OF THE CRIME ANALYSIS BASED ON KM-TOOLS

The Finnish Police have highly efficient methods for processing large volumes of data that can be useful even at the level of a local police station. These include data warehousing, reporting and analyzing tools that also include possibilities for data mining with Map Info -tool and various analysis techniques, such as the, decision tree. However, the value of such analysis systems lies in the fact that they can provide records which can be easily searched for target items. Furthermore, they offer a method of data security that can be demonstrated to the users, whilst assuring the user that he still has the opportunity to make his or her own conclusions of the data before any operation.

There are also systems being developed and evaluated for coordination and effective communication among local actors, such as law enforcement, fire departments and local health facilities and national agents, like the National Bureau of Investigation and National Traffic Police. However, the issue of protection of confidentiality and data security, while providing important information to those who need it most, is an issue that is defined either in law or with user and data access restrictions.

The process of collecting data for analyzing and predicting trends and changes in the operational environment was not easy. There were several old legacy systems and local databases within the organization. The process of creating a data warehouse took a couple of years. However, updating and adding new data to the warehouse was a continuous process that had lasted since 1997. The organization had collected data from different areas to monitor, report and guide the organization towards its agreed goals.

Figure 1. The Reporting Database stores data from different operational databases and external data sources. The information is used to monitor and analyze the data for the daily police operations. The management can use the data stored to steer the organization towards its goals and react timely to the changes in the operating environment. It is used also on a daily basis to assess the situation in field operations and have a live video from the scheme.

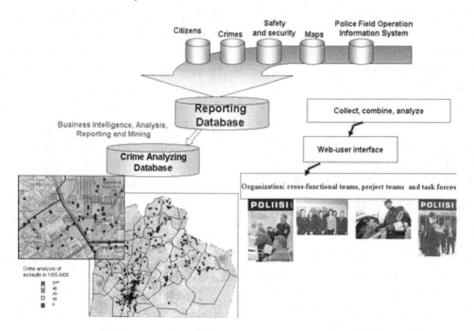

Methodologies for combining information from the legacy systems and supporting existing organizational and business processes were essential. It required identification of key processes and essential information to support existing strategies within the organization. It also required estimating the cost of developing, deploying and maintaining knowledge intensive collaborative applications and empirically validating their usability, including the capability of analyst-workgroups to use the systems with minimum involvement from their IT support team.

Moreover, it was noted that the traditional reporting tools were not sufficient in estimating and predicting future trends and that they did not assist in picking up weak signals and slow changes in operational environment in different parts of the country. The use of data mining tools also showed the way to use other knowledge management tools, such as document management and expertise knowledge bases within the organization. Moreover, the automated analyses offered by data mining tools moved beyond the analysis of past events typical for traditional reporting and decision support tools. Data mining in crime analysis showed new connections in crimes and potential suspects that the conventional tools were not able to show or proved too time consuming. For example, there were similar crimes committed within a city area. However, there were no suspects or eyewitnesses. There were rumors of a potential suspect, and data mapping showed that the crimes were done within a certain area. Data mining tools were able to connect the tenant information within the certain area of the city with the crime locations. The police was able to find the named person in one of the buildings within the search area.

Data mining can improve intelligence efforts in analyzing and solving different criminal activities and help allocate scarce police resources to where they are most needed. The concerns of data mining in respect of secure access and privacy issues were also dealt with by specific data mining technologies including rule-based processing, selective revelation, and secure creditentialing and constant auditing to ensure privacy and information protection in the data warehouse. In general, common uses of data mining in the police force include knowledge discovery, improving service or performance in processes and tasks, detecting fraud, analyzing and managing human resources, detecting criminal activities or patterns and analyzing intelligence and detecting terrorist activities. The application of data mining in the context of counterterrorism and criminal activities is intended to automate certain processes and tasks and to facilitate the identification and cataloguing of definite threads and pieces of information that otherwise would have remained unnoticed using manual or other traditional means of investigation.

RESULTS AND BENEFITS

The data mining tool accelerated the creation and acquisition of new knowledge. It allowed the development of knowledge communities within the organization. These communities were capable of analyzing crimes based on the data of legacy systems, weak signals and other external data sources. The implementation of crime analysis assisted in preventing more crimes, creating safer communities and tracking crime trends and changes in the operational environment. Decision making in the police changed gradually from just analyzing and following past events to predict and prevent crimes. The use and recognition of the benefits of using KM tools also facilitated the development of continuing learning and education in all levels and in all the fields and locations of the organization.

The accelerating knowledge distribution and diffusion developed the information structure (so called *info structure*) and connectivity possibilities on the broadest possible geographical scale. The accelerated knowledge consumption in crime analysis was through the creation of a culture of innovation and through experimentation and the reward of success in the work place.

The ICT (information, communication and technology)-solutions encouraged collaboration, the sharing of information and knowledge and accelerated the process of the distribution of new knowledge and information within the organization. Crime analysis based on data mining and new decision support tools created the procedures, methods and rules to store and archive information and knowledge, and to continue the process of refining knowledge and information from existing legacy systems by incorporating experiences from field operations to the development of the analysis and the decision support tools. In this aspect, the data quality of the current legacy systems is important.

Moreover, the result of reviewing the processes and practices within the whole organization required a common framework and methods. The Finnish Police used the Common Assessment Framework (CAF) in its self-assessment process. This CAF method is widely used in the public sector in Europe. The CAF-model is a total quality management tool inspired by the Excellence Model of the European Foundation for Quality Management (EFQM) and the model of the German University of Administrative Sciences in Speyer. Its basic argument is that excellent results in organizational performance, citizens and society can be achieved through leadership driving strategy and planning, partnerships, organizational resources and processes. It has a holistic approach to the public sector organization and its performance analysis. The CAF-model is applicable to public organizations at the national, federal, regional and local level. (Ministry of Finance, 2008)

Furthermore, e-police as part of e-government was also an additional goal considered when developing crime analysis. It also included specifically designed, customized services to assist citizens in certain areas of police work by phone and by internet.

In addition, extranet and intranet tools were created to assist collaboration across the organizational boundaries of different governmental agencies as part of the community partnership strategies. Collaboration, and information and intelligence sharing are the keys to reduce and prevent crimes. This supports the studies of Ericsson and Haggerty (1997). Readiness for collaboration with external and internal partners was essential in knowledge transfer and sharing, and creating crime analysis based on KM-tools. Readiness for collaboration included the activity of seeking collaboration, policies and practices to support collaboration and resources for collaboration, such as technology, money and people. In addition, project management across organizational boundaries required collaboration capabilities to create the data warehouse and crime analysis and a decision support portal to support different organizational needs and requirements to be used by internal customers as well as the external partners, including customs and border control. In networking, strong collaborative relationships enhanced the utilization of area specific and experiential knowledge, experience and learning (Elo, 2005; Juntunen, 2005). The more transactional relationships remain influential only at the operational level and were easily terminated or changed (Elo, 2005).

Police command also wanted a management reporting and decision support portal that would enhance their access to different information on events within the country and between international partners. The organizational implications were to create a knowledge team to analyze and provide weekly and monthly reports for the police command. The teams were divided into specific knowledge working groups according to their specific area of expertise. Their tasks were to provide real-time knowledge and information support for the police command based on the data mining and other KM-tools. Assumptions were also made based on weak signals and global trends' surveillance. They were also responsible for the collaboration within external and internal partners. They also suggested developmental objectives to the management according to their own expertise area.

The beneficiaries of the system are mostly management and analysts, who can acquire more real-time data for operational and strategic planning. It also assisted the whole organization in their information needs by collecting and combining the data from several sources into one data warehouse.

One result was that the Finnish police viewed the intelligence-led policing as knowledge-led policing and started to train analysts throughout the nation in a similar way. It also started a new working group to create the "Analysts' Handbook" in which the analysts gathered commonly agreed terms and concepts, processes and best practices in order to help new-comers to the analyst field to have easier access to information and to know the best way to do analysts' work. The handbook is located online. It is accessible by any analysts within the organization.

The managerial implications of the implementation and development of the new kind of decision support system based on KM tools were that the managers focused more on receiving and reviewing intelligence reports about the status of their own organization and of the external environment than before when they were acting based on past events. It was also seen as important to deliver the intelligence reports to the ones who need it most, usually located outside the intelligence or analyst unit. It was also of great value to discuss and get feedback of intelligence reports delivered in order to refine the process and to make it more effective and more accurate concerning the needs of the users of the intelligence report. The benefits of the new decision making process, based on data mining, improved managerial knowledge of the operational environment. It assisted in developing and implementing new information transfer processes, methods and tools to manage and expand the available knowledge in such a way as to make it available and easy to distribute to all the managers. As a summary, achieving an integrated, knowledge-based culture was an additional goal. It assisted in increasing both predictability of services, activities and reinforced the stability and status of police and its administration in a changing social and operational environment.

CONCLUSION

The development and implication of KM-tools as part of intelligence-led policing strategies enhanced the KM initiatives within the organization: for example, the KM was taken into the agenda of the analysts meetings and their development program. It was also seen that knowledge-based organizational management and direction is necessary. The political implications of more accurate information and knowledge of security issues led to the continuance of the Internal Security program from 2007 until 2011 as it was seen necessary to gather more information on the situation of security issues. Furthermore, to enhance and maintain the safety level gained during the previous years, it was suggested that the security issues involve and address every citizen, business and government itself. In addition to these, in Finland, as in many other countries, a system of governance seems to consist of multiple overlapping negotiation system networks between the various actors.

The expectations on the knowledge management of the government agency included the specific knowledge of its own area, core competencies created and systematically developed around its own expertise areas. They included strategic capabilities for management of the organization

and interconnectedness with both internal and external partners and innovativeness in processes, methods, tools practices and services to meet the fast pace changes of operational environment.

The environmental dynamics thrive from the market, political and social structures, technical development and values and actions of citizens. In this context, technological change plays an important role in altering organizational practices, processes and changing tasks (Porter, 1985: 175).

The self renewal of the organization through innovations and intrapreneurship and the co-evolution of knowledge and competence management are essential in a rapidly changing competitive environment (Tuomi, 1999; Hong & Ståhle, 2005; Weiss, 1998) of rationalized and embedded knowledge (see Figure 2). The very survival of organizations facing rapid changes depends upon their ability to renew what they offer the world and the ways in which they operate and deliver their services (Francis & Bessant, 2005). Moreover, strategy and policy aimed at sustainable development particularly strengthens the innovativeness and change management capabilities of the organization. Renewable capabilities are used for activities that require sustaining from today to the future so that the present organization will not deplete the chances of success for the future organization. The most significant challenges that the police will face include changes that might come because of global economic, political, climate and socio-demographic changes. Climate changes will affect resources, such as cars, tyres, bikes, clothing, as well as what crimes become more popular during certain seasons. It can also influence certain seasonal crimes, including "summer festival –related crimes" or "summer cottage" crimes if summer cottages are only used for a few summer months. Nowadays, these cottages are empty during the colder months of the year and form an easy target for burglars. The global economic and political situation can effect immigration and organized crime movements.

Figure 2. The knowledge management of a public organization: from organizational competence to organizational renewal

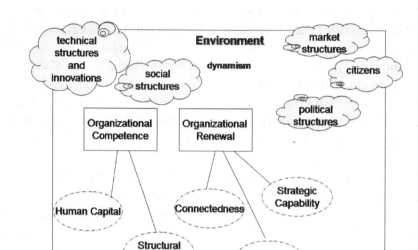

These are all environmental and external changes that can affect the organization and its workload. However, there may also be internal changes that can reduce resources, the amount and location of police stations and the organizational structure of the police.

According to Tuomi (1999) the learning process within an organization and the need for new information and knowledge can be triggered by three different sources: the environment, the society, or the learning unit itself. Information technology. and the KM-tools especially, can assist in transferring, storing and sharing the information and encoded knowledge between different parts of organization.

Organizations face rapid technology and other operational environmental changes with limited ability to react due to the fast pace of technological development, financial commitments or managerial decision processes. In these situations, organizations should have the ability to innovate and to be flexible in their managerial processes and structures. By focusing on knowledge management, an organization can uncover innovations in processes and practices that can assist in the changing environment. Simply having KM-processes to produce knowledge and information of a certain area or service could assist enough to sustain an existing status. Yet, collecting knowledge and experiences of others, their problems and problem solving methods could assist in creating similar best practices processes within the organization as well as facilitate knowledge transfer and sharing between communities of practice (Wenger et al., 2002).

Moreover, success, performance and efficiency are still the key topics when discussing public sector agencies. Therefore, by crime analysis, the case organization managed to create a knowledge base and new capabilities related to crime analysis and KM-tools within one function of an agency, and thus, increase the knowledge of changes in the operational environment and assist in the prevention of crimes. According to Mintzberg, Ahlstrand and Lampel (1998, pp. 175-231) in organizations that operate in highly complex environments, such as the police, collective learning and knowledge management are essential as the knowledge required to create strategy is widely dispersed. Furthermore, organizations facing new situations usually have to engage in a process of learning to understand emerging change as exemplified by the introduction of technological breakthroughs such as the Internet and mobile-technologies.

It is also argued that knowledge sharing in organizations and communities of practice is facing major challenges due to a misalignment between the incentives within the system and the objective of creating value through knowledge sharing (Kondratova & Goldfarb, 2003). Therefore, improvements are suggested for virtual collaborative spaces on the Internet that are intended to serve as knowledge creation and sharing spaces, not only for employees of the individual organization but also by diverse participants of communities of practice.

Furthermore, interaction in ICT-developmental projects between different government agencies is undertaken with the intention of achieving a strategic objective to enhance knowledge transfer and sharing between the different parties involved. As a summary, globalization and increasing networking within the organizations (cf. Tuomi, 2002) and between the public and private sector requires more analytical and political tools to better conceptualize the government-citizen-business relationships and networking among the different actors. Due to this networked environment, we also need tools to evaluate the processes and working methods across different governmental agencies and organizational boundaries.

FUTURE RESEARCH DIRECTIONS

Concerns about the effectiveness of providing e-services in government agencies have mushroomed in the last decade. In part, this was due to the fast pace of technology development, globalization and increasing networking between the private and public sector. In Finland, the government aims to ensure good quality services are available for citizens. This is quite a challenge because of the demographic differences in various parts of the country. Therefore, the government encourages the development of more collaboration between different municipalities and also between private and public sector, and the creation of efficient and easy-to-use e-government services so that citizens will have basic services regardless of where they live. The police has organized the crime analyzing function across the country so that each area of the country has its own analysis team and so that the network of analyzers keep frequent contact with each other and with international colleagues to update their knowledge of types of crimes both locally and internationally. Collaboration between the police and social workers, border control and customs is also frequent and organized,: for example, the police-border-customs cooperation (so called PBC cooperation) in which they have co-training, disaster practice situations and other cooperative meetings.

ICT (information-communication-technology) is said to be a major catalyst for socioeconomic development, therefore, the experiences and information on the usage of ICT are of key importance. ICT can be used in service of broader strategic objectives in a number of development sectors to codify knowledge, for example: in education, e-commerce, and e-government. The collaborative networking that is increasingly emerging in our society requires efficient knowledge sharing and transferring which can be achieved using KM-tools like for example, data mining.

In addition, we also need to acquire better ways to develop such competencies in employees and organizations that will facilitate the creation and use of new information and knowledge. As with any competence learned, it can erode and the information can become outdated. For example, in crime analysis one needs to update knowledge on crimes and the operational environment as well as key actors in the field so that one know what to do and what to look for.

Furthermore, more knowledge on the grass root solutions made for e-government to increase the efficiency and learning in teams and networks of different actors is still needed. Moreover, an essential part of decision making is a collective decision making process and idea sharing in which the decisions and ideas are transmitted from one individual to another in a manner reminiscent of disease. In the context of innovations and competing and supplemental technologies (see e.g. Tushman & Anderson, 2004) individuals and also organizations pay frequent attention to the actions and decisions of other actors (see Watts, 2003).

The findings of this study show the value and benefits of data mining as part of intelligence-led policing in the criminal investigation and internal security context. The study proposes further research on knowledge management and e-government issues due to the interdisciplinary requirements of networking society, and the new analytical techniques with greater computing power that allows an unprecedented volume of data to be analyzed. It also suggests that new studies are required for network-related research, like the cooperation of different governmental actors. not only in crime analysis but also in sharing information on other related topic areas. It is seen that a long-term effect in reducing and preventing crime depends on the efficient collaboration and cooperation of different public sector and local actors. It also requires intelligence and information sharing between and within the network of law enforcement and other local actors.

REFERENCES

Adler, P.S. & Heckscher, C. (2006). Towards Collaborative Community, In The Firm as a Collaborative Community. In Charles Heckscher and Paul S. Adler (Eds.) *Reconstructing Trust in the Knowledge Economy*, 11-101.

Altschuler, A. & Zegans, M. (1997).Innovation and Public Management: Notes from the State House to City Hall. in A. Altschuler and R. Behn (Eds.), *Innovation in American Government*, Washington D.C.: Brookings Institution.

Anderson, Richard (1997). Intelligence-Led Policing: A British Perspective. In *Intelligence Led Policing: International Perspectives on Policing in the 21st Century*. Lawrenceville, NJ: International Association of Law Enforcement Intelligence Analysts.

Blomqvist K., & Levy, J. (2006). Collaboration Capability – A Focal Concept in Collaborative Knowledge Creation And Innovation in Networks. *International Journal of Management Concepts and Philosophy* 2: 1, 31-48.

Blomqvist, K., Miles, G., Miles, R.E. & Snow, C.C. (2007). *Critical Factors and Organizational Processes in Continuous Collaborative Innovation*. Paper submitted to the Copenhagen Conference on Partnerships: Achieving Collaborative Advantage, 30th - 31st of August 2007, Copenhagen Business School, Denmark.

Cyert, R. & March, J. (1963). *A Behavioral Theory of the Firm*. Englewod Cliffs: Prentice Hall.

Elo, M. (2005). *SME Internationalization from Network Perspective – Empirical Study on a Finnish-Greek Business Network*. A doctoral dissertation, Publications of Åbo Akademi University, Finland.

Ferraro, K. F. & LaGrange, R. (1987). The measurement of fear of crime. *Sociological Inquiry* 57, 70–101.

Francis, D. & Bessant, J. (2005). Targeting innovation and implications for capability development. *Technovation*, 25, 171–183.

Hollway, W. and Jefferson, T. (2000). The role of anxiety in fear of crime. In T. Hope and R. Sparks (Eds.) *Crime, risk and insecurity*. London: Routledge.

Hong, J. & Ståhle, P. (2005). The Coevolution of Knowledge and Competence Management,

Int. J. *Management Concepts and Philosophy*, Vol. 1, No. 2.

Juntunen, A. (2005). *The emergence of a new business through collaborative networks: a longitudinal study in the ICT sector.* Acta Universitatis Oeconomicae Helsingiensis. Printed in HSEPrint. A-series, no 256, ISSN 1237-556X. ISBN: 951-791-957-3/1.

Kogut, B. & Zander, U. (1992). Knowledge of the Firm, combinative capabilities and the replication of technology. *Organization Science* 3(3): 383-397.

Kondratova, I. & Goldfarb, I. (2003). Design concepts for Virtual Research and Collaborative Environments, in J. Cha, R. Jardim-Gonçalves, & A. Steiger-Garção (Eds.) *Knowledge Management in Architectural, Engineering and Construction, 10th ISPE International Conference on Concurrent Engineering: The Vision for Future Generation in Research and Applications.* Madeira Island, 26-30 July 2003. Portugal, A.A. Balkema Publishers, 797-803.

Mawby, R. I., Brunt, P. & Hambly, Z. (2000). Fear of crime among British holidaymakers. *British Journal of Criminology* 40, 468–79.

Ministry of the Interior (2004). *A Safer Community. Internal Security Programme Summary.* Ministry of the Interior publications 2004. Retrieved August 13, 2007, from www.intermin.fi

Mintzberg, H., Ahlstrand, B. & Lampe, J. (1998). *Strategy Safari. The complete guide through the wilds of strategic management.* Prentice Hall Financial Times. London.

Osborne, D. & Gaebler. T. (1992). Reinventing Government: How the entrepreneurial spirit is transforming the public sector. *Plume*, 1992. p. 87.

Perry, Chad (1998). Processes of a case study methodology for postgraduate research in marketing, *European Journal of Marketing.* Vol. 32: 9/10.

Peterson, Marilyn (2005) Intelligence-Led Policing: The New Intelligence Architecture. NCJ 210681. September 2005.

Porter, M. (1985). *Competitive Advantage. Creating and Sustaining Superior Performance.* The Free Press. NY.

Ratcliffe, Jerry (2003). Intelligence-led policing. *Australian Institute of Criminology – trends and issues in crime and criminal justice*, no 248.

Stewart, T.A. (2001. *The Wealth of Knowledge: Intellectual Capital and the Twenty First Century Organization.* First edition. New York, NY: A Currency Book: Doubleday; A division of Random House, Inc.

Tuomi, I. (1999). *Corporate Knowledge: Theory and Practice of Intelligent Organizations.* Helsinki: Metaxis.

Tuomi, I. (2002). *Networks of Innovation: Change and Meaning in the Age of the Internet.* Oxford: Oxford University Press.

Tushman, Michael L., & Anderson, Philip (2004). (Eds.) *Managing Strategic Innovation and Change: A Collection of Readings.* 2nd ed. N.Y.: Oxford University Press.

U.S. General Accounting Office (GAO) (2004), "*Data Mining: Federal Efforts Cover a Wide Range of Uses,*" GAO-04-548, May 2004.

Vincze, Z. (2004). *A Grounded Theory Approach to Foreign market expansion in newly emerging market. Two Finnish Companies in the Visegrád countries.* Series A-4:2004. Doctoral dissertation. Publications of the Turku School of Economics and Business Administration, Turku, Finland.

Walsh, J.P. (1995). Managerial and organizational cognition: Notes from a trip down memory lane. *Organization Science*, 6: 280-321.

Watts D. J. (2003). *Six Degrees: The Science of a Connected Age.* New York: Norton.

Weiss, L. M. (1998). *Collection and Connection: Rationalized and Embedded Knowledge in Knowledge-Intensive Organizations (Rationalized Knowledge).* Ph.D dissertation, Harvard University.

Wenger, E., McDermott, R. & Snyder, W.M. (2002). *Cultivating Communities of Practice.* Boston, MA: Harvard Business School Press.

Chapter X
Current Issues and Future Analysis in Text Mining for Information Security Applications

Shuting Xu
Virginia State University, USA

Xin Luo
Virginia State University, USA

ABSTRACT

Text mining is an instrumental technology that today's organizations can employ to extract information and further evolve and create valuable knowledge for more effective knowledge management. It is also an important tool in the arena of information systems security (ISS). While a plethora of text mining research has been conducted in search of revamped technological developments, relatively limited attention has been paid to the applicable insights of text mining in ISS. In this chapter, we address a variety of technological applications of text mining in security issues. The techniques are categorized according to the types of knowledge to be discovered and the text formats to be analyzed. Privacy issues of text mining as well as future trends are also discussed.

INTRODUCTION

Text mining is an instrumental technology that today's organizations can employ to extract information and further evolve and create valuable knowledge for more effective knowledge management. The deployment of text mining technology is also of vital importance in the arena of information systems security (ISS), especially after the 9/11 tragedy which galvanized the government to increasingly spend resources pursuing hardened homeland security. Furthermore, providing security to computer information systems and communications infrastructures is now one of the national priorities. While a plethora of text mining or data mining research has been conducted in search of revamped technological development, relatively limited attention has been paid to the applicable insights of text mining in ISS.

In an effort to fill the void, this article tends to shed light on the correlations between text mining and ISS and to address a variety of technological applications of text mining in ISS privacy issues as well as future trends related to security. As such, this article is organized as follows: after an introduction section, the second section presents the background of text mining and its application in security; the third section addresses different categories of techniques used for text mining in ISS, including social network analysis, abnormal detection, topic discovery, and identity detection; section four discusses social perspectives of text mining versus privacy violation and section five presents future analysis of text mining for ISS research.

BACKGROUND

Defined as "*the discovery by computer of new, previously unknown, information by automatically extracting information from different written resources*"(Fan et al. 2006), text mining is an emerging technology characterized by a set of technological tools which allow for the extraction of unstructured information from text. With the exponential growth of the internet, it is literally cumbersome for individuals as well as companies to process all the overwhelmed information. Not like some data mining techniques discovering knowledge from only the structured data, such as numeric data, text mining is related to finding knowledge from the unstructured textual data including e-mails, Web pages, business reports, and articles, etc. Leaping from old-fashioned information retrieval to information and knowledge discovery, text mining applies the same analytical functions of data mining to the domain of textual information and replies on sophisticated text analysis techniques that distill information from free-text documents (Dörre et al. 1999).

As voluminous corporate information must be merged and managed and the dynamic business environment pushes decision makers to promptly and effectively locate, read, and analyze relevant documents to produce the most informative decisions, discovering hidden patterns from the structured data plays an important role in business where patterns are paramount for strategic decision making. Text mining pursues knowledge discovery from textual databases by isolating key bits of information from large amounts of text, by identifying relationships among documents, and by inferring new knowledge from them (Durfee 2006). Furthermore, (Fan et al. 2006) indicated that the key to text mining is creating technology that combines a human's linguistic capabilities with the speed and accuracy of a computer. Gluing the generic process model for text-mining application proposed by (Fan et al. 2006) and general text mining framework suggested by (Durfee 2006), we think that the following model can capture the processes involved in text mining from text collection and distillation to knowledge representation (see Figure 1).

Figure 1. Processes involved in text mining(Adapted from (Durfee 2006; Fan et al. 2006)

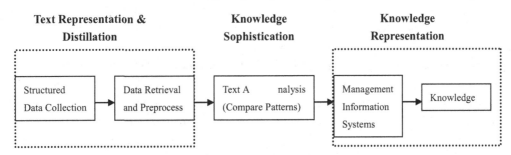

TEXT MINING IN SECURITY APPLICATIONS

There is an increasing demand to apply text mining in information system security issues, for example, corporations wish to survey large collection of e-mails to identify illicit activities; counterterrorism analysts want to review large amounts of news articles to identify information relevant to potential threats, etc. One of such application is ECHELON (European 2001), which is a world-wide signal intelligence and analysis network run by the UKUSA Community. It can capture radio and satellite communications, telephone calls, faxes, e-mails and other data streams nearly anywhere in the world. Text mining is used by ECHELON to search for hints of terrorist plots, drug-dealers' plans, and political and diplomatic intelligence.

Various text mining techniques have been proposed in literature for different security applications. The text formats to be mined may include:

- E-mail
- Web page
- News article
- Web Forum Message / Instant Message

The types of knowledge to be discovered in security applications may include:

- Connections among people, groups, and objects
- Abnormal behavior/interest of people under surveillance
- Topic/theme of text
- Author of text

The knowledge to be discovered above like topic/theme of text is also one of the main goals for main stream text mining research. However, compared with other general text mining application goals like clustering or classifying related texts, or finding the matching texts for the given key words or key sentences, the security applications focus more on discovering the hidden relationships of objects mentioned in the texts.

Text corpus, in any format, can be used to discover any of the aforementioned types of knowledge. However, different kind of format may facilitate the discovery of different type of knowledge. For example, the sender and receiver of an e-mail may reveal the relationship among people. By inspecting the Web page browsing history, we may find out a person's change of interests. Many techniques have been proposed to discover different types of knowledge, which we introduce in details in the following four categories. Techniques used in one category can be used in another, and the functions in each category may overlap.

Social Network Analysis

Social Network Analysis (SNA) is the study of mathematical models for interactions among people, groups, and objects (McCallum, 2005). It has recently been recognized as a promising technology for studying criminal and terrorist networks to enhance public safety and national security. It can be applied to the investigation of organized crimes by integrating information from multiple crime incidents or multiple sources and discovering regular patterns about the structure, organization, operation, and information flow in criminal networks (Xu et al. 2005). It can also be used to study the change and evolvement of the organizational structure in a corporation. It is currently one of the most important techniques applied in text mining for security applications.

Social Network Characteristics

In Social Network Analysis, some sophisticated structural analysis tools are needed to discover useful knowledge about the structure and organization the networks. The following social network characteristics are usually calculated and analyzed: the overall structure of the network, the subgroups and their interactions, and the roles of network members (nodes).

Overall Structure

Generally the following graph metrics are considered to compare the characteristics of social networks (Chapanond et al., 2005):

- *Degree distribution* is the histogram of the degree of vertices in the graph.
- *Diameter* is the longest of the shortest paths between any pair of vertices in a connected graph. It reflects how far apart two vertices are (from each other) in the graph.
- *Average Distance* is the average length of shortest path between each vertex in the graph.

- *Average Distance Ratio* is defined as (total number of vertices in a graph – Average Distance) / total number of vertices in a graph.
- *Compactness* is the ratio between the number of existing edges and the number of all possible edges.
- *Clustering Coefficient* of a vertex is defined as the percentage of the connections between the neighbors of a vertex. Clustering Coefficient of a graph is the average value of Clustering Coefficient for all vertexes.
- *Betweenness* of an edge is defined as the number of shortest paths that traverse it.
- *Relative Interconnectivity* between two clusters is defined as the normalized absolute interconnectivity between the two clusters.
- *Relative Closeness* between two clusters is the normalized absolute closeness between the two clusters.

Relative interconnectitity and relative closeness are metrics used to determine the similarity in graph structure between two clusters.

The overall structure of one social network can be compared with another to show the similarities and differences between them. For example, Chapanond et al. compared the graph properties of Enron e-mail graph with the RPI e-mail graph and found that degree distributions in both graphs obeyed the power law but the density of connectivity among communities of practice were different (Chapanond et al., 2005).

The overall structure of social network usually changes over time. Snapshot of network at different times may be compared to find the changes or trends in the structure of an organization. Diesner et al. compared a network from a month during the Enron crisis with a network from a month in which no major negative happenings were reported and where the organization seemed to be on a successful path (Diesner et al. 2005). The results indicated that the during the Enron crisis the network had been denser, more centralized and more connected than during normal times. Such kind of knowledge is of potential benefit for modeling the development of crisis scenarios in organizations and the investigation of indicators of failure.

Subgroups

A social network usually consists of subgroups of individuals who closely interact with each other, such as cliques whose members are fully or almost fully connected. Some data mining techniques like clustering can be used to find out such subgroups (Han et al. 2006).

Pattern of Interaction

Blockmodeling (Wasserman et al. 1994) can be used to discover patterns of interaction between subgroups in SNA. It can reveal patterns of be-tween-group interactions and associations and can help reveal the overall structure of the social network under investigation. Given a partitioned network, blockmodel analysis determines the presence or absence of an association between a pair of subgroups based on a link density mea-sure. If the density of the links between the row subgroups is greater than a threshold value, which means the two subgroups interact with each other constantly, then the two subgroups have a strong association.

Role of Node

Several graph metrics such as degree, between-ness, and closeness can denote the importance of a node in a social network. A node with high degree may imply the individual's leadership, whereas a node with high betweenness may be gatekeeper in the network (Xu et al. 2005). We can find those particular nodes with inordinately high degree, or with connections to a particularly well-connected subset of the network (McCallum, 2005). As an

example, Krebs employed these metrics to find the central individuals in the electrical network consisting of the 19 hijackers in the 9/11 attacks (Krebs 2002).

Application Examples

Based on different text formats, the methods ad-opted to construct social networks and conduct analysis may be quite different. Next we will use some examples to explain how Social Network Analysis is applied to various text formats.

E-Mail

An e-mail usually contains the following parts: Sender, Recipient, Date and Time, Subject and Content. A directed simple graph can be con-structed in which vertices represent individuals and directed edges are added between individuals who correspond through e-mail. An undirected graph can also be constructed as described in (Chapanond et al., 2005): If the individuals must have exchanged at least *threshold1* e-mails with each other and each member of the pair has sent at least *threshold2* e-mails to the other, then the two individuals will be connected by an edge in the graph. Here *threshold1* and *threshold2* are predefined threshold values. Changing the value used for each threshold will change the structure of the graph. Sometimes nodes and edges can have multiple attributes such as the position and loca-tion of an employee or the types of relationships between two communication partners.

An Author_Recipient_Topic (ART) model was proposed in (McCallum, 2005) for social network analysis. The ART model captures topics and the directed social network of senders and receivers by conditioning the multinomial distribution over topics distinctly on both the author and one recipi-ent of a message. It takes into consideration both author and recipients distinctly, and models the e-mail content as a mixture of topics. The ART model is a Bayesian network that simultaneously models message content, as well as the directed social network in which the messages are sent. In its generative process for each message, an author, a_d, and a set of recipients, r_d, are observed. To generate each word, a recipient, x, is chosen at uniform from r_d, and then a topic z is chosen from a multinomial topic distribution $\varphi_{ad,x}$, where the distribution is specific to the author-recipient pair (a_d, x). Finally, the word w is generated by sampling from a topic-specific multinomial distribution θ_z. The result is that the discovery of topics is guided by the social network in which the collection of message text was generated.

Web Page

To apply social network analysis to Web site data like Web pages, the first step is to harvest related Web sites (Zhou et al. 2005, Reid et al. 2005). A focused Web crawler can be employed to automatically discover and download relevant Web sites by following the HTML links from a starting set of pages (Albertsen 2003). Metadata then can be extracted and used to rank the Web sites in terms of relevance. Once the Web sites are harvested, Web link and content analysis are used to study how a group is using the Web.

Web link analysis is based on hyperlink structure and is used to discover hidden relationships among communities (Givson et al. 1998). There are two classes of Web link analysis studies: relational and evaluative (Borgman et al. 2002). Relational analysis gives insight into the strength of relations between Web entities in particular Web sites, while evaluative analysis reveals a Web entity's popularity or quality level. According to (Zhou et al. 2005) which analyses link and content of Web sites owned by US domestic extremist groups, relational analysis works well for terrorism research because it illuminates the relations between extremist Web sites and organizations. Analyzing hyperlink structures sheds light on extremist and hate site infrastructures. It also reveals hidden communities in the relationships

among different Web sites for the same group and the interactions with other extremist group sites. In addition, hyperlinks between sites constitute an important cue for estimating the content similarity of any Web site pair in a collection.

Web content analysis is the systematic study of site content. Demchak, C. et al. proposed a well-defined methodology for analyzing communicative content in government Web sites (Demchak 2000). They developed a Web site attribute system tool to support their work, which basically consists of a set of high-level attributes, such as transparency and interactivity. Each high-level attribute is associated with a second layer of more refined low-level attributes. To better understand domestic extremists' uses and goals for the Web, Zhou et al. developed a similar attribute-based coding scheme for methodically capturing the content of Web pages (Zhou et al. 2005).

News Article

Bradford provided an example of identifying relationships among terrorist related entities from news articles in (Bradford 2006). Entities may include people, organizations, and locations. Relationships may include communications, financial transactions, and physical proximity. Items of interest may consist of complex combinations of entities and relations, such as events. The entities analyzed in (Bradford 2006) are individual terrorists, terrorist groups, targets, and weapons.

To identify information of interest in large collections of news articles, entity extraction and the matrix decomposition technique of latent semantic indexing (LSI) can be combined to allow direct analysis of entity-entity relationships. LSI is a well-established method for extracting relationship information from large collections of text (Berry 1999, Deerwester 1988). For any two entities present in the text collection of interest, the proximity of their representation vectors in the LSI space provides a direct measure of their degree of contextual association in the collection.

This feature can be exploited to provide rapid overviews of the aggregate implications of the relations present in large collections of unstructured information. In (Bradford 2006), two-dimensional cross-correlation matrices are used to highlight potentially interesting associations between entities. Identification of such associations allows users to focus their attention on information in the collection that may be of particular interest. This is of great utility in facilitating rapid overview of large quantities of text.

Abnormal Detection

Abnormal detection tries to find out objects which appear to be inconsistent with the remainder of the object set. It can be used to detect illicit activities or false identities to assist police and intelligence investigations. There are many algorithms for abnormal detection which can be classified into three categories (Han et al. 2006): the first category is analogous to unsupervised clustering, like *k-NN*, *k-means*, *CLARANS*, unsupervised neural network etc.; the second category is analogous to supervised classification which requires a *priori* data knowledge, like regression method, *PCA*, *SVM*, supervised neural networks, etc.; and the third category is analogous to semi-supervised recognition or detection, which is usually the combination of the first two type of methods. An example of applying text mining in abnormal detection is described next.

Web Page Access Analysis

By monitoring and analysis of Web pages accessed by Web surfers, it is possible to infer a surfer's areas of interest. Thus terrorists may be identified by some real time Web traffic monitor when they access terrorist–related information on the internet.

Some behavior-based anomaly detection model (Elovici et al. 2004, Elovici et al. 2005, Last et al. 2003) were proposed to use the content of Web pages browsed by a specific group of users as an input for detecting abnormal activities. The basic idea is to maintain information about the interests of "normal" users in a certain environment (such as a campus), and detect users that are dissimilar to the normal group under a defined threshold of similarity. The models have two phases, the learning phase and the detection phase:

During the learning phase, the Web traffic of a group of users is recorded and transformed to an efficient representation for further analysis. The learning phase is applied in the same environment where the detection would later be applied in order to learn the "normal" content of users in the environment. The collected data is used to derive and represent the group's areas of interest by applying a clustering technique.

During the detection phase, users dissimilar to the normal users are detected. The detection is performed by transforming the content of each page accessed by a user to a vector representation that can be compared against the representation of the groups for dissimilarity. The minimum number of suspicious accesses required in order to issue an alarm about a user are defined by the detection algorithm. The detection is performed on-line and should therefore be efficient and scalable.

Topic Discovery

The text corpus to be mined is usually very large, containing thousands to billions of documents. To prevent or alleviate security severity, topic discovery may identify the theme of documents so investigators can acquire the most desired documents without literally reading them. Topic discovery techniques include summarization, classification, clustering, and information retrieval. Summarization can greatly reduce the length of a document while keeping its main points. Classification methods (e.g. *decision tree*, *Bayes*, *SVM*, etc.) group a document to one of the predefined categories according to its word frequency. Clustering methods group similar documents without any *priori* knowledge about the documents. Typical clustering methods include *k-means*, *BIRCH*, *DBSCAN*, *CLIQUE*, etc. Readers may refer to (Han et al. 2006) for details of the aforementioned classification and clustering methods. Information retrieval accesses the documents based on user queries. Latent Semantic Indexing (Berry 1999, Deerwester 1988) is one of the widely used information retrieval methods. We use two examples to illustrate techniques used in security applications.

E-Mail Surveillance

Berry et al. applied a non-negative matrix factorization approach for the extraction and detection of concepts or topics from e-mail messages (Berry 2005). Given an e-mail collection, Berry et al. encoded sparse term-by-message matrices and used a low rank non-negative matrix factorization algorithm to preserve natural data non-negativity and avoid subtractive basis vector and encoding interactions present in techniques such as principal component analysis.

Non-negative matrix factorization (NMF) has recently been shown to be a very useful technique in approximating high dimensional data where the data are comprised of non-negative components (Lee and Seung 1999, Paatero and Tapper 1994). Given a collection of e-mail messages expressed as an $m \times n$ term by-message matrix X, where each column is an m- dimensional non-negative vector of the original collection (n vectors), the standard NMF problem is to find two new reduced-dimensional matrices W and H, in order to approximate the original matrix X by the product WH in terms of some metric. Each column of W contains a basis vector while each column of H contains the weights needed to approximate the corresponding column in X using the basis from W. The dimensions of matrices W and H are $m \times r$ and $r \times n$, respectively. Usually, the number of columns in the new (basis) matrix W is chosen so that r ≪ n.

Berry et al. have demonstrated how a parts-based representation of corporate e-mail can facilitate the observation of electronic message discussions without requiring human intervention or the reading of individual messages (Berry 2005). Such surveillance enables corporate leaders to monitor discussions without the need to isolate individual employees.

Terrorism Information Extraction

Sun et al. proposed the task of extracting information about terrorism related events hidden in a large document collection gathered from news websites (Sun et al. 2005). The task assumes that a terrorism related event can be described by a set of entity and relation instances. The objective is to select as few documents as possible to construct such entity and relation instances. Several document selection strategies based on information extraction patterns were proposed. Each strategy attempts to select one document at a time such that the gain of event related instance information is maximized.

Identity Detection

Efficiently identifying terrorists, extremists, and criminals becomes a hot topic after the terrorist attacks on Sep. 11 2001 (Wang et al. 2004). However, at the same time, terrorists, extremists, and criminals would like to conceal their identities and content of their communications as much as possible (Fong et al. 2006). In this section we discuss the techniques used to identify authorships from text documents.

Authorship Analysis

The e-mail, website and internet forums are important communication channels for criminal and terrorist organizations because of their speed, ubiquity and potential anonymity (Abbasi 2005). Authorship analysis can automatically extract linguistic features from online messages and evaluate stylistic details for patterns of terrorist communication. There are two major approaches to authorship analysis (Zheng et al. 2006): *Authorship identification* deals with attributing authorship of unidentified writing on the basis of stylistic similarities between the author's known works and the unidentified piece; it deals with classification problems. *Authorship characterization* attempts to formulate an author profile by making inferences about gender, education, and cultural backgrounds on the basis of writing style.

Abbasi et al. introduced an online authorship identification process, which consisted of three main steps: collection, extraction, and experimentation (Abbasi 2005). Collection programs crawled through the Internet searching for forums relate to cyber crime and homeland security issues. Once the process recognized such forums, programs stored the messages in text and HTML format. Extraction programs then derived writing style characteristics identified in the feature sets from each message. Classifiers like decision tree (Han et al. 2006) and Support Vector Machine (SVM) (Vapnik 1998) are used to identify each message's author according to the feature sets.

PRIVACY ISSUES OF TEXT MINING

Despite its capability of discovering hidden patterns from large amounts of information, text mining can also pose a threat to privacy and information security if not leveraged appropriately. The issue of privacy violation and information security threat is dependent on the extent to which the textual information is retrieved and used. Certainly, privacy issues in text mining cannot simply be eradicated by restricting text collection or even the use of information technology. Homeland security measures are increasing the amount of both data and textual information collected, processed and mined. In the meantime, individual owners of the data might raise legiti-

mate concern about their privacy and potential abuses of the data collected. Undoubtedly, there is a tradeoff between accuracy of text mining results and information privacy and security. Therefore, privacy-preserving text mining techniques and regulations are needed to balance privacy and information inquiry.

Privacy risks that could apply to text mining include the potential for erroneous association of individuals with crime and terrorism through textual data that are not accurate, the misidentification of individuals with similar names, and the use of texts that were collected for other purposes. The use of the text mining tools in conjunction with personal information raises concerns about a number of privacy risks that could potentially have an adverse impact on individuals. In general, potential privacy risks can be categorized in three perspectives, in relation to the relevant principles of Privacy Act. First, security safeguards principle, which states that personal information should be protected against risks such as loss or unauthorized access, destruction, use, modification, or disclosure, is related to the potential for personal information to be improperly accessed or disclosed. Second, the potential for individuals to be misidentified or erroneously associated with inappropriate activities is inconsistent with the data quality principle that requires that personal data should be accurate, complete, and current for a given purpose. Third, the risk that information could be used beyond the scope originally specified in based on the purpose specification and use limitation principles which states that personal information should only be collected and used for a specific purpose and that such use should be limited to the specified purpose and compatible purposes.

As public concern about the personal information is growing, governments and law enforcing agencies have introduced and implemented new privacy protecting laws and regulations. US Executive Order 2000 protects federal employees from being discriminated on the basis of protected genetic information for employment purposes. In addition, the establishment of E-Government Act of 2002 and related federal guidance requires governmental officials or law enforcing agencies to determine what specific controls are needed to mitigate the privacy risks. The inclusion of the controls is a key step in guarding against unauthorized access, use, disclosure, and modification. For instance, the controls could be implemented to ensure that personal information is used only for a legitimately specified purpose and could provide disambiguation, a process through which similar individual names can be distinguished, to address the risk of misidentification. In details, software controls could be implemented that require an analyst to specify an allowable purpose and check that purpose against the specified purposes of the databases being accessed. Yet, such controls alone cannot effectively mitigate potential privacy risks. We think that federal guidance can also play an important role in this regard, because the need to evaluate the privacy risks early in the development of information technology is consistently reflected in the E-Government Act of 2002.

FUTURE ANALYSIS

(Li et al. 2006) indicated that analysis in structured data can lead to questions that cannot be answered by just working on numbers; and sole research on unstructured data may raise questions that need to be checked against the structure data. They posited that a new term "*information mining*" is appropriate to refer to the integration of data mining and text mining technologies to provide better decision-making. Their contention is consistent with (Fan et al. 2006) in that a future trend is likely to involve a combination of quantitative and qualitative information analysis. Based on the theoretical underpinning of (Li et al. 2006), we believe that the future trend of text mining development for Information System Security will be inevitably associated with data mining. As

such, we propose that the ideal information mining taxonomy for ISS anti-terrorism intelligence involves both quantitative and qualitative analysis of collected information, as listed in Figure 2.

This unified platform which consolidates both text mining and data mining represents the future development trend in which ISS anti-terrorism experts can more effectively and efficiently extract the desired information toward hardened homeland security. This information mining taxonomy is useful in that anti-terrorism experts can further explore a question using different types of technology in another system when they encounter the question in one system. By deriving both quantitative and qualitative information, experts can fathom the underlying connections between the structured data and textual data and further create and maintain anti-terrorism intelligence for better decision making. Practically in business settings, (Fan et al. 2006) have found that this combination of data mining and text mining technologies has proved useful in banking and credit card customer relationship management in which decision-makers can analyze not only the transaction data but also can add call logs associated with customer service to better further analyze customer spending patterns from the text mining side.

Notwithstanding the promising benefits, the future advance of information mining undeniably will be confronted by several challenges. First, the immature or even slow development of text mining technologies makes the establishment of text mining management system a rather uneasy task for organizations to deploy and implement. Second, without a centralized management system to unify the information mining process, communication channels across the organization might be affected because different organizational units might have different approaches to build their data mining and/or text mining taxonomies. Therefore, the consolidation process remains a technological and managerial challenge. Last, it shall be an exigent task to integrate all the data and textual

Figure 2. Taxonomy of information mining for ISS (Adapted from (Li et al. 2006))

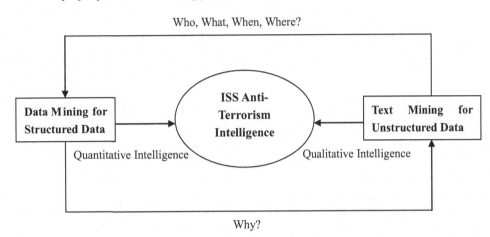

systems because of the various structures of the databases across the whole organization.

REFERENCES

Abbasi, A., & Chen, H. (2005). Applying Authorship Analysis to Extremist Group Web Forum Messages. *IEEE Intelligent Systems*, September/October 2005, pp. 67 -75.

Albertsen, K. (2003). The Paradigma Web Harvesting Environment. *Proceeding of 3rd European Conf. Research and Advanced Tech. for Digital Libraries Workshop on Web Archives*, 2003.

Borgman, C. L. & Furner J. (2002). Scholarly Communication and Bibliometrics. *Ann. Rev. Information Science and Technology*, (36), 2002.

Berry, M.W., & Browne, M. (2005). E-mail Surveillance Using Nonnegative Matrix Factorization. *Computational & Mathematical Organization Theory, 11*,(3), 2005, pp. 249-264.

Berry, M.W., Drmac, Z., & Jessup, E. R. (1999). Matrix, Vector Space, and Information Retrieval. *SIAM Rev, 41*, 335 – 362, 1999.

Bradford, R. B. (2006). Relationship Discovery in Large Text Collections Using Latent Semantic Indexing. *The proceedings of the Fourth Workshop on Link Analysis, Counterterrorism and Security*, Bethesda, Maryland, 2006.

Chapanond, A., Krishnamoorthy, & M., Yener, B. (2005). Graph Theoretic and Spectral Analysis of Enron E-mail Data. *Workshop on Link Analysis, Counterterrorism and Security, at the SIAM International Conference on Data Mining*. California, USA, 2005, pp. 15 - 22.

Deerwester, S., et al. (1988). Improving Information Retrieval with Latent Semantic Indexing, *Proceedings of the 51st Annual Meeting of the American Society for Information Science*, 1988, pp. 36-40.

Demchak, C. C., Friis, C., & La Porte, T. M. (2000). Webbing Governance: National Differences in Constructing the Face of Public Organizations. *Handbook of Public Information Systems*, Marcel Dekker, 2000.

Diesner, J., & Carley, K.M., (2005). Exploration of Communication Networks from the Enron E-mail Corpus. *Workshop on Link Analysis, Counterterrorism and Security, at the SIAM International Conference on Data Mining*. California, USA, 2005, pp. 3 – 14.

Dörre, J., Gerstl, P., & Seiffert, R. (1999). Text mining: Finding Nuggets in Mountains of Textual Data. *The Fifth ACM SIGKDD International Conference on Knowledge Discovery and Data Mining, ACM.* San Diego, California, 1999, pp. 398-401.

Durfee, A.V. (2006). Text Mining Promise and Reality. *Twelfth Americas Conference on Information Systems.* Acapulco, Mexico, 2006, pp. 1449-1460.

Elovici,Y., Shapira, B., Last, M., Kandell, A., & Zaafrany, O. (2004). Using Data Mining Techniques for Detecting Terror-Related Activities on the Web. *J of Information Warfare*, 3(1), 17-28.

Elvici, Y. et al. (2005). Content-Based Detection of Terrorists Browsing the Web Using an Advanced Terror Detection System (ATDS). *ISI 2005, LNCS* 3495, pp. 244-255, 2005.

European Parliament. (2001). European Parliament report on ECHELON. Retrieved from http://www.fas.org/irp/program/process/rapport_echelon_en.pdf, 2001

Fan, W., Wallace, L., Rich, S., & Zhang, Z. (2006). Tapping the Power of Text Mining. *Communications of the ACM* (49:9) 2006, pp 77-82.

Fong, S. W., Skillicorn, D. B., & Roussinov, D. (2006). Detecting Word Substitution in Adversarial Communication. *The proceedings of the Fourth Workshop on Link Analysis, Counterterrorism and Security.* Bethesda, Maryland, 2006.

Gibson, D., Kleinberg, J., & Raghavan, P. (1998). Inferring Web Communities from Link Topology. *Proc. 9th ACM Conference on Hypertext and Hypermedia*, 1998, pp. 225-234.

Han, J. & Kamber, M. (2006). Data Mining: Concepts and Techniques. 2006, 2nd Edition, Mogan Kaufmann Publishers.

Last, M. Elovici, Y. Shapira, B. Zaafrany, O, & Kandel, A. (2003). Using Data Mining for Detecting Terror-Related Activities on the Web. *ECIW Proceedings*, 2003, pp. 271-280.

Lee, D. & Seung, H. (1999). Learning the Parts of Objects by Non-Negative Matrix Factorization. *Nature*, Vol 401, 1999, pp. 788-791.

Li, Q., & Wu, Y.-F.B. (2006). Information Mining: Integrating Data Mining and Text Mining for Business Intelligence. Twelfth Americas Conference on Information Systems, Acapulco, Mexico, 2006, pp. 1410-1416.

Krebs, V. E. (2002). Mapping networks of Terrorist Cells. *Connections*, 24 (3), 2002, 43-52.

McCallum, A., Corrada-Emmannel, A., & Wang, X. (2005). The Author-Recipient-Topic Model for Topic and Role Discovery in Social Networks, with Application to Enron and Academic E-mail. Workshop on Link Analysis, Counterterrorism and Security, at the SIAM International Conference on Data Mining, California, USA, 2005, pp. 33 - 44.

Paatero, P., & Tapper, U. (1994). Positive Matrix Factorization: A Non-Negative Factor Model with Optimal Utilization of Error Estimates of Data Values. *Environmetrics*, 5:111–126, 1994.

Reid, E., Qin, J., & et al. (2005). Collecting and Analyzing the Presence of Terrorists on the Web: A Case Study of Jihad Websites. *ISI 2005, LNCS* 3495, pp. 402-411, 2005.

Sun, Z. et al. (2005). Event-Driven Document Selection for Terrorism Information Extraction. *ISI 2005, LNCS* 3495, pp. 37-48, 2005.

Vapnik, V. N. (1998). *Statistical Learning Theory.* John Wiley and Sons, New York, 1998.

Wang, G., Chen, H., & Atabakhsh, H. (2004). Automatically Detecting Deceptive Criminal Identities, *Communications of the ACM* 47, (3), 2004, 71-76.

Wasserman, S., & Faust, K. (1994). *Social Network Analysis: Methods and Applications.* Cambridge University Press, 1994.

Xu, J., & Chen, H. (2005). Criminal Network Analysis and Visualization. *Communications of the ACM, 28*, (6), 2005, 101-107.

Zheng, R. et al. (2006). A Framework of Authorship Identification for Online Messages: Writing Style Features and Classification Techniques. *Journal of the American Society for Information Science and Technology*, 57(3), 378-393, 2006.

Zhou, Y., Reid, E., & et al. (2005). US Domestic Extremist Groups on the Web: Link and Content Analysis. *IEEE Intelligent Systems*. September/October 2005, pp. 44 -51.

KEY TERMS

Abnormal Detection: Tries to find out objects which appear to be inconsistent with the remainder of the object set.

Authorship Characterization: Attempts to formulate an author profile by making inferences about gender, education, and cultural backgrounds on the basis of writing style.

Authorship Identification: Deals with attributing authorship of unidentified writing on the basis of stylistic similarities between the author's known works and the unidentified piece; it deals with classification problems.

Social Network Analysis: is the study of mathematical models for interactions among people, groups, and objects.

Text Mining: is the discovery by computer of new, previously unknown, information by automatically extracting information from different written resources.

Web Content Analysis: Is the systematic study of site content

Web Link Analysis: is based on hyperlink structure and is used to discover hidden relationships among communities.

Chapter XI
Data Mining in Aviation Safety Data Analysis

Reima Suomi
Turku School of Economics, Finland

Olli Sjöblom
Turku School of Economics, Finland

ABSTRACT

This chapter introduces aviation safety data analysis as an important application area for data mining. In the beginning of the chapter, the reader is introduced to the basic concepts of data mining. After that, the field of aviation safety management is discussed, and in that connection data mining is identified as a key technology to study through flight incidents reports. Afterwards the test runs for four data mining products, for possible use in the Finnish civil aviation authority, are described in detail. However, before the testing of tools the preparation of the test data for the tools is described in detail. The chapter ends with conclusions that tell that even sophisticated data mining tools are just tools: they do not provide any automatic tools, but skilled users can use them for searching clues in the data.

INTRODUCTION

Since the very beginning of aviation history there has been some kind of investigation after accidents as well as other, less fatal events and incidents. However, the incredible rapid development in huge volume of air travel, mainly because of jet airliners, created the need of systematic research for aviation safety. Different interest groups in aviation, like airlines and aviation authori-

ties, began to collect data about air traffic. The consequences of this development have been a significant reduction in incidents and occurrences as well as aviation accidents, especially during the sixties. It has now been widely recognised among aviation safety experts that the global rate of accidents is stabilising. The situation can now be regarded as satisfactory, but because of the growth in air traffic, the absolute number of fatal accidents per year might increase, if the flight safety is not improved. The collection of data and reporting systems have reached their top level. The focal point in this context is analysis. The source of aviation safety data are the incident reports that include both structured and narrative fields. The structured data can be analysed easily using queries from databases and running their results through graphic tools. Among narrative data the situation is totally different. There were no tools to analyse textual data until data mining tools have been developed. Still their use, at least among aviation, is at a moderate level. Flight safety can be significantly improved through the development of data analysis. Narrative text mining is demanding also because of the multiplicity of languages spoken in the world. Especially languages with small user groups have to wait for efficient tools longer than big languages such as English.

AVIATION SAFETY DATA MANAGEMENT

It is widely recognised that air transport is among the safest modes of transport. The global rate of accidents is stabilising. If nothing is done to improve it, the growth in air traffic will lead to an increase in the absolute number of fatal accidents per year. This kind of development would be, clearly, totally unacceptable and therefore new ways of improving air safety need to be explored (European Commission, 2000). Fundamental to every Safety Management System is the principle of collecting and analysing operational data (GAIN Working Group B, 2004). Aviation industry has placed significant investments into collecting aviation safety information from multiple sources. As a result of this process large databases exist, and at the same time, enormous challenges have appeared in analysing the information (Megaputer Intelligence, 2004c).

To improve air safety, the significant allocation of the newest research resources and data

processing techniques are unavoidable. Data has been collected, more or less, in different forms during the whole history of aviation. The data collected can roughly be divided into two types: structured data and unstructured, narrative data. The exactness of the incident and accident reports using structured data depends on the number of details and alternatives of the system classification. So, with structured data the explanation of the case usually tells the truth till a certain rate, but completed with narrative data it can reach the level of 100 per cent, at least theoretically. During the execution of various operational and support processes among operations of aircraft fleets large volumes of data are collected. Analysis and review of data is typically complicated requiring human involvement significantly. Usually the data accumulates faster than it can be processed (Wang, Huang, Cao, Shi, & Shu, 2007). The need for automated means to process the data is also increasing rapidly, because the amount of generated and stored unstructured data is increasing fast (Delen & Crossland, 2008).

Till the end of the 1990s, there have not been, at least in a wide range, other tools than report generators using queries with data stored into a relational database. Narrative data were practically not been processed with computing. Finding trends from structured data has never been a problem, but from narrative data it has required huge amounts of work made by man. Successful analysis work for aviation safety has been done during decades: In Finland, since beginning of the 1960s till today, through systematic safety work the accident rate has been reduced to a very small percentage from what it was. This trend seems to be global, at least among developed aviation countries: almost every statistics about this theme shows the same development. If one looks at different commercial airlines' statistics or even military aviation operation/accident rates, the view is very similar.

However, airlines and other operators use at large extent "normal" analytical tools, Excel and database reporting tools to be mentioned as an example, to perform flight data analysis, but the use of more specialised analytical capabilities appears more limited. The safety data analysis process is typically not very automated. Additional to the tool mentioned before there might be query tools for specific issues of database systems, but for more comprehensive analysis which could reveal underlying patterns in the data, there are usually few or no tools available. Thus, the analysis process and its possible results rely on the skills and experiences as well as the memory of the safety officer (Nazeri, 2003). Several types of specific analysis tools can be mentioned in this context. Process oriented tools are typically used on a day-to-day basis to manage and analyse safety information and to identify trends of safety performance in broad measures. Investigative tools are used when the target is to understand why something happened, rather than what happened. Exploratory tools, such as text mining and data visualisation tools are used to find not self evident relationships and to identify issues of concern. Decision support tools are used to help assess the effectiveness of alternative safety management actions as well as strategies (GAIN Working Group B, 2004).

DATA MINING

The significant development in database and software technologies, i.e., warehousing of transaction data has enabled the organisations to build the foundation for knowledge discovery in databases (KDD) which consists of such phases as selection, pre-processing. transformation, data mining and interpretation/evaluation (Blake, Singh, Williams, Norman, & Sliva, 2006). Data Mining cannot be considered as one method and it cannot be described very easily. In fact, there are several different methods that can be placed under the name of data mining. As well a data mining system can use several of these methods

as a combination. A rather good definition among many of them is that by Parsaye who regards data mining as *"a decision support process in which we search for patterns of information in data"* (Parsaye, 1997: p. 3). Regardless of whether the solution environment is in business or among governmental or other non-profit activities, the target of data mining is to search for relationships and global patterns that exist in large databases but are *hidden* in the vast amounts of data (Watson, 1999).

Watson continues as well that with conventional techniques it might take years to find these meaningful relationships, so-called nuggets of knowledge that are hidden in the data. Using data mining software, knowledge of data is combined by an analyst with advanced *machine learning* technologies to discover the relationships. In this discovery process for finding hidden patterns, there are no hypotheses or any other predetermined ideas about the existence or characteristics of the patterns. It is obvious that large databases, like those containing aviation incidents and other deviations, contain a large number of patterns, so that the user of the discovery system can practically never have an idea of asking the right question.

Among the commonly used tools in data mining are the systems that construct classifiers. As input they take a collection of cases, each of them are described by their values for a fixed set of attributes and so belongs to one of few classes. As an output they predict the class to which a new case belongs. Many pattern finding algorithms frequently used in data mining like decision tree, classification rules and clustering techniques are based on machine learning (Wu et al., 2007). The data mining process contains several steps or phases that must be gone through to form knowledge from raw data. It is obvious, that information has some value only when its users understand it. Therefore the information must be presented with reports, graphs or in another suitable form once it is found. The chain from data to knowledge is presented in Figure 1.

Figure 1. The Knowledge Discovery in Database process (adapted from (Fayyad, Piatetsky-Shapiro, & Smyth, 1996); (Han & Kamber, 2001))

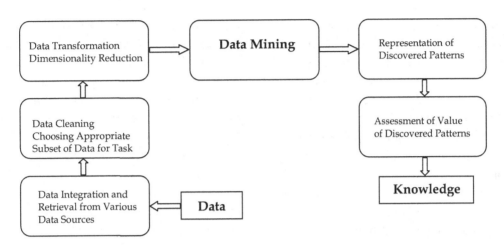

The first results of data mining process after representing the discovered patterns need to be evaluated carefully by consolidating them with the existing domain knowledge. This step requires large amount of experience among the problem area which is investigated and it can be stated to be more a combination of art and common sense than science (Kloptchenko, 2003). Data mining process does not give straight answer to questions, but its role is purely a decision support system. Experience has shown that the importance of good text mining ability is the first one for the applicable system. Text mining is one subclass of data mining (Visa et al., 2001).

Many security initiatives have chosen data mining as one of the key features because it produces among currently available analytical tools a significant advance as a means for assessing risk and detecting fraud. Despite of this, there are limitations to its capacity. Although data mining can help reveal relationships and patterns, the value or significance of these cannot be produced. So, this is one of the processes that involves human participation. The causal relationships are also to be discovered by human analysts. That is why to structure the analysis and interpret the created output successfully, skilled analytical and techni-

cal specialists are still required (Kutais, 2006).

One of the important roles in text mining and document management is searching for similar document. It generally focus in similar document search or in other text mining applications is classification which is based onto determining the class or category the document belongs to. Encouraging results have been achieved by applying methods that distinguish the documents belonging to more than one category. These results have primarily proved that this kind of systems have better performance than the traditional approach (Saracoglu, Tütünkü, & Allahverdi, 2008). Clustering is a commonly used method in data mining that explores the data set and determines the structure of natural groupings. Compared to classification, cluster analysis can be considered somewhat more primitive because using this method no assumption is made about the structure of the data set or the amount of underlying groups. As for classification techniques, they pertain to a known number of groups assigning new observations to one of these groups (Painter, Erraguntla, Hogg, & Beachkofski, 2006). However, some data mining systems allow the user to define the amount of clusters and hereby refine the clustering results to find out the optimum point.

DATA MINING IN AVIATION SAFETY ANALYSIS

Simply expressed, the goal of data mining process is extracting high-level knowledge from low-level data. Especially from the point of view of processing collected flight safety data, the main target is to find hazardous trends and patterns. The analysis of safety data is usually processed manually, as already mentioned before, thus it is not very automated. In many cases the safety officer operates with available query tools in safety report databases for specific issues, but most airlines are lacking, some of them totally, tools to help them undertake a more comprehensive analysis for revealing underlying patterns in the data. The safety officer's memory and past experiences build the base for the professional analysis process.

However, it is worth noticing that data mining tools do not replace the human analysts but help them with their analytical tasks. The greatest benefit comes from time saving in presenting results which could have otherwise been obtained through repeating queries, and, from the data mining systems' ability to make discoveries that could not be accomplished by using only queries. In addition to that, queries alone do not accomplish by making discoveries that data mining tools are able to. Discovery process often begins with making a hypothesis or taking previous knowledge as starting point, but using data mining this is not necessary. The safety officers are highly skilled specialists among their area with good knowledge on their domain and know how to examine the data. Still, data mining can discover patterns and anomalies that have not been thought before (Nazeri, 2003).

It has been widely estimated that the main part (over 80%) of the information in reporting is written in the unstructured and textual format. This information could contain nuggets of valuable knowledge. Data Mining has been an analysis method already for longer time but it has been

capable for analysing numerical data only. That is why text mining has appeared as an analysis method much later. Already, data mining has been used successfully for several years among a couple of airlines and other players of aviation industry. Two projects from year 2003 can be mentioned here as significant examples, although other successful attempts has been done as well: Southwest Airlines project in co-operation with Megaputer's PolyAnalyst and American Airlines' project with MITRE's Aviation Safety Data Mining Workbench. Both projects involved data and text mining of pilot narratives. As a bottom line these two projects produced a statement: "Very encouraging and very promising; more work to be done (Muir, 2004: p. 23)." These example projects processed text written in English. Text mining tools convert the text into numeric form in different ways and some of them are language dependant. For these reasons, among others, text mining in Finnish has not been used very widely. To find a suitable tool for a Finnish user, testing several products with the same data material might give remarkable support in choosing process.

DATA MINING IN FINNISH: TESTING FOUR TOOLS

The Finnish Civil Aviation Authority (FCAA), like other aviation authorities throughout the world, is in charge of issuing instructions and regulations on flight safety and security, and assumes other regulatory duties in civil aviation. The purpose of the FCAA can be simply expressed as, to maintain and further develop flight safety in Finland through monitoring and overseeing civil aviation safety. In doing so, it needs statistics and other information to be able to update aviation regulation, to meet the needs of flight safety requirements. One of the main sources of critical safety data is analysing and investigating safety reports collected from air operators and anyone with duties affecting flight safety as well as sports aviation. The investigation aims to determine why the incident occurred, and gives recommendations to prevent similar incidents from recurring. Where necessary, on the basis of these reports suggestions are made to improve aviation safety.

In this context, appropriate tools for analysis and investigation are unavoidable. The FCAA has used "normal" tools like Excel and report generators of database systems. It still lacks a tool that could process narratives that are important part of safety reports besides the structured data on it. Using flight safety reports from years 1994-1996 as test material, finally three systems for text mining were tested. One of the three systems was totally language independent, the other had a specific configuration for Finnish and the third was originally created for English, but encouraging results had been achieved with Spanish and that is why a Finnish test was also undertaken. All systems provided some encouraging results, as well as proved challenges still to be met. At the end, none of the system was selected for daily operative routine use because no single enough satisfying system was found, even though the need still is there. Anyway, the study was interesting to execute and it produced a lot of experience and knowledge about data mining and especially text mining. The study can be considered as a jump to the unknown, because, as far as the authors' knowledge, text mining in Finnish has been generally made only to some extent and nobody has applied text mining to Finnish flight safety reports before.

RESEACH PROCESS

VASA (VAaratilanteiden SeurantAjärjestelmä, System for Monitoring Dangerous Situations) is a database system constructed to replace the former database NORDAIDS during the period when European Coordination Centre for Accident and Incident Reporting System (ECCAIRS) was under construction and tested for implementation in production usage. VASA is a typical database system based on relational model consisting of 24 tables and eleven queries as well as three forms; each of them a separate routine, built using Visual Basic, for inputting, browsing and changing data in the records. The system is based on Microsoft Access 97. The base contains about 16 000 rows and includes cases since 1994, when NORDAIDS was put aside as active system.

VASA has theoretically multi-user capabilities, but most because of Access, practically it is a personal tool for one single user. That is one reason why it cannot be used as a widely allocated data source. The lack of reporting tools in Access improved the need to replace it totally as soon as possible. The basis for the change was created through directive 2003/42/EC on Occurrence Reporting ("DIRECTIVE 2003/42/EC OF THE EUROPEAN PARLIAMENT AND OF THE COUNCIL on occurrence reporting in civil aviation," 2003). It obliged the Member States of the European Union to collect and exchange the information about incidents and other occurrences since July 2005. The production use of the ECCAIRS system began at the Finnish CAA as well on the date mentioned. Tests have been carried out during years before, but without results good enough to replace VASA that remained the database for accidents and incidents at the FCAA. It was used as a parallel system with ECCAIRS till the end of summer 2005, when the changing period was practically over and ECCAIRS could satisfy the knowledge needs producing the necessary reports for internal, as well as for external use.

Referring to the knowledge discovery and data mining process presented in Figure 1, there are several important phases before the core mining action can be executed. The research process was planned to follow the process presented in it. Its first phase is Data Integration and Retrieval from various data sources which required the definition of data needs for testing. Period of three years seemed to create "a critical mass", which in this case means more than 1000 cases. The flight safety reports from years 1994-1996 were chosen. This set consisted of 345 cases from 1994, 421 cases from 1995 and 474 cases from the year 1996, thus 1240 incidents together, which amount can be considered as sufficient in this phase of the study. Another factor that determined the choosing of the data was its age. Hereby the material was old enough (more than 10 years). This guaranteed that the data was already statute-barred and there were no open cases. The main principle is that all the decisions and cases are public. This is in concordance with the law and practices adopted by the governmental organisations in Finland, that the documents and decisions of the authorities are public.

However, several exceptions from this basic rule can be recognised. Some of them were to be taken into the consideration when determining the cases that would be taken within to the test material. The first one, which is general practise among authorities, was that cases in this process (the investigation in this context) which are not closed will be excluded. Because the material is almost ten years old, no more open cases were found among these years. The other one is the appearance of military aircraft in the reports, so these reports were excluded. The third restriction is connected with the identity of persons in connection with the incident or accident. This required minute investigation for finding any names which all should be replaced with N.N. or other expressions that totally avoided the possibility to identify the person mentioned in the narrative. These cases could be included to the test data, although after the modification mentioned.

As for data retrieval, there was no need for collecting data from various data sources because all the data needed was accessible from one data base system. The data was extracted from VASA in .csv form which enabled rather easy manual processing. All the cases were checked immediately after the extraction process to be sure, that they contained no classified data such as person identification or cases about military aircraft.

Because of confirming the sufficient level of data protection, the researcher controlled the cases once again before the data was given to co-operators for processing. In contrast to a single case, that cannot be regarded to be classified, with the data as a mass the situation is totally different. The co-operators were required to write an engagement to guarantee that there was access to the data only for those whose job it belongs to and the data will neither delivered nor displayed others.

The next fields were taken into the test material: Year, report number, date, type of aircraft, register of aircraft, place where the incident happened or the vicinity of it, phase of flight, operator, place of departure (in case the incident happened during flight), route identification, destination (or planned destination) and narrative description of what happened. Excluded were also the status (pilot in command or co-pilot of the aircraft, air traffic controller, mechanic etc.) of the person who wrote the report, the authority which investigates the case (for example Civil Aviation Authority or Accident Investigation Board). The classification of the case decided by the officer saving the case into the database was excluded as well because it was in English. This was shown on one of the columns and this came from the system that is based on ADREP87. This data can later be used successfully in the estimating process of the achieved results.

This can be done from two points of view. The first is to see whether the system has classified the cases somehow in the same way and the second is to control whether the officer handling the data and saving the case into the database has used the right classification code. Another excluded column was the same classification in Finnish, but this data was available only in couple of cases, so it had no contribution for this purpose. The third phase in the process displayed Figure 1, data transformation and dimensionality reduction was realised before the second phase, but this did not make any difference in the whole process.

The narratives only were chosen, but no transformation was needed, as mentioned before about the source of the data. From the very beginning of this study the aim was to process the narratives, so, the other fields were regarded somehow unnecessary from this point of view. They were taken with into the material by thinking the future with the possibility to combine narrative text and categorical or coded data.

The second phase according to Figure-1 is data cleaning and choosing appropriate subset of data for task. Taking the narratives only for final test material can be regarded as choosing appropriate subset of data. The processing of the incident reports' narratives faces linguistic problems because they contain lots of domain-specific jargon expressions.

The processing systems are normally built with capabilities for recognising formal language only and that is why a specific dictionary on abbreviations and synonyms must be created. This requires a list of words that the system does not recognise. These are either acronyms or misspelled words and they create the basis for a collection of rules that are used for correcting misspelled words and expanding acronyms. Especially in this context, it is important to notice that abbreviations for airport codes and navigation fixes encountering frequently in pilot narratives must be sifted out in addition to misspelled words and acronyms. As an example the following can be provided: w/o → without, a/c → aircraft, RWY → runway and VFR → Visual Flight Rules. To get accurate results, the inseparable word combinations must be taken into account as well.

This kind of list of such phrases (word sequences) that are of particular interest, as Altitude Conflict, ATC Clearance, Logbook Error or Bird Strike, is created and imported in the system as a dictionary of phrases. A list of ignored terms, i.e., those unconditionally excluded from further analysis, products one more piece of useful information summarising either the results of iterative analysis of data or the background knowledge of the investigated domain. The project being undertaken determines the content of this list. As an example, in the case all safety events happened during take-off are investigated, the term 'runway' would be suitable to be added to the dictionary because this term obviously occurs in nearly every description of take-off events and thus does not help in categorisation of these events.

However, it is worth noticing that when studying other sets of safety reports, the term 'runway' by itself might contain lots of significant information (Megaputer Intelligence, 2004c). The length of the reports in the basic data varied remarkably. Therefore, the question about data quality that means data accuracy and completeness emerges as one of the biggest challenges for data mining. More complex data mining techniques are sensitive to subtle differences possibly existing in the data. These might be duplicate records, lack of data standards, timeliness of updates, including anomalous data points and human errors. Due to this, data needs to be cleaned frequently from these inaccuracies (Seifert, 2006).

The research continued to determine the number of tools that would be taken into the process. Three different systems seemed to be appropriate enough to compare the expected results as benchmarking. The author was aware of two prototypes, which seemed to be very interesting. One of the aims of this research is to find new methods and products for analysis and that is why two prototypes were considered in this process. In addition to these, one commercial product was taken into the process to be able to better compare the systems. Among aviation, one of them seems to be written about and evaluated more than others. So, it was chosen to be one of the evaluated systems. The demo of it was easily applicable from the Internet, which helped a lot. However, some changes were made during the process.

Another commercial tool with larger independence of languages appeared to be worth of evaluating and the first chosen commercial product was confirmed by the representatives of the company not to be able to process text written in Finnish. The first chosen system was totally language dependent, no exceptions could be found. It was still taken within the study, especially in the role of a so-called reference system, because material and users experiences were widely available.

The originally planned testing of this was cancelled and replaced with another commercial product that would not be as language dependent. This system has never been tested with Finnish, but the representative of the company declared encouraging results with many languages, especially Spanish, so, its ability with Finnish was estimated to be possible and thus it seemed to be a very interesting case from this point of view. Thus the original goal to test the material with three different systems was achieved. For scarce comparison, the first planned tool was taken to the table as well, although no data was tested with it.

The practical text processing began with tools #3 and #4 that was utilised for filtering the cleaned data. The shortest of the narratives consisted of 4 words only, as others might have put together using many sentences. The filtered data contained a total amount of 10572 words, numbers and special characters as well as other expressions, like call signs, headings, temperatures, etc. The amount could be, however, reduced to 8294 when parentheses and other similar characters were removed. The filtering process produced the frequency of each occurrence that varied between 767 and 1. The biggest frequencies (>100) with corresponding words alone were:

767 *'and'*
457 *'was'*   *859*
336 'aircraft'   753
311 *'no'*   *381*
304 *'after'*
244 'pilot'   337
187 'of the aircraft'   (synonym <'aircraft')
148 *'according to'*   *171*
144 'came'   202

138 'on the route'   235
131 *'about'*
129 'engine'   299
121 'so that'
116 *'during'*

After the words are listed the total amounts of occurrences of the words with all its synonyms and cases were available. The first 421 had the frequency 10 or more and the first 1710 had at least 2, all the rest only 1. The distribution of frequencies displays how important the usage of synonyms and stop words is, especially when Finnish will be mined. Its significance was confirmed later during the mining process. Of the 14 frequencies exceeding 100 listed above, clear stop words written in italics are 8 having cumulated frequency of 2355, thus creating a bit more than one fourth of the total amount of words.

After having the cleaned list of words the lists of stop words, synonyms and concepts were possible to create. Stop words list includes words that will be ignored. These are the ones that do not provide any insight. Examples of these are:

```
a
able
about
above
across
after
afterwards
again
all
almost
alone
along
already
also
although
always
```

Stop words list was created manually using the filtered list of words. From the total amount of more than 8000 words 446 stop words were listed. The principles were the same in Finnish as in English.

In addition to that, the verb 'to be' in all its forms was defined as a stop word, because it appears rather often in the reports and it can freely be ignored without losing any information.

List of synonyms is mapping multiple synonyms to one word. Misspellings and abbreviations can be fixed here, too. Optionally, non-alphabet and non-number characters are mapped to 'blank', and numbers are mapped to 'delete'. The format/layout of the list is as follows: 'word or phrase' tab 'word'. Some examples of these are:

```
t/o              takeoff
anti-icing       deice
re-issued        reissued
a/c              air _ craft
"                <blank>"
`                <blank>
'                <delete>
apparent         appear
apparently       appear
gnd              ground
hdg              heading
kts              knots
rwy              runway
sw               Southwest
stby             standby
taxied           taxi
taxiway          taxi
taxiways         taxi
twr              tower
rejected         reject
Reject Takeoff   RTO
```

The list of synonyms, like stop words, was created manually from filtered list of words and it contained 2048 words. The amount is rather high, mostly due to the big amount of cases in Finnish. Because of the same reason, stop words with synonyms were considered when the lists were created. As a good example is the verb 'to be' in all its different forms and tenses.

Concepts of interests are used to pick up ideas to achieve more accurate results through understanding the existing words differently according to their position compared to other words. It means that words alone do not have the same

information value as combined with other. More significant words the value of which, however, depend on the context they are being expressed. The format/layout of the expression is:

'word or phrase' tab 'word or phrase' tab 'number of words in between' tab 'concept' tab 'weight'.

The first row from the examples in explained form is as follows:

If 'alert' and 'box' are within '10' words of each other then create a concept called 'altitude_deviation' and give it a weight of '10'.

Some examples of these are shown in Box 1.

This action was skipped because of two reasons. First, because there was no experience in mining Finnish, the test arrangement was planned to be as simple as possible. Creating a complete list of concepts of interests did not seem to be appropriate at that time when not even preliminary mining results would be available, but later during the iterative process. This turned out to be the right decision. It is much easier to find concepts of interests when some mining results are available. Second, in connection with the first one, it would have taken too much time to write the list and achieving first results with even weaker basis was more important. In addition to this, the concepts should be determined before using the lists of stop words and synonyms, because after this process the words were in their basic forms and because of the structure of Finnish in that case it would have been impossible to find these concepts anymore. The process for creating lists mentioned before was not completely needed for tool #2, because it contains modules for Finnish which produces the ability to process separate stop words and synonyms. However, a list of special synonyms and acronyms depending on the context might be needed because they do not exist in the thesaurus of the mining system.

Box 1.

```
alert           box            10    altitude _ deviation    10
challenge       captain        10    crew _ issue            10
flight _ attendant  cockpit    10    distraction _ issue     10
not cleared     descend        10    altitude _ deviation    10
not hear        initial check  10    communication _ issue   10
traffic         tcas           15    altitude _ deviation    10
trouble         descend        10    descend _ problem       10
unusual         flight         10    unusual _ issue         10
very            busy           10    distraction _ issue     10
```

EVALUATION OF THE TOOLS

Four different tools of different type were tested for the data mining purpose. Because there were practically no experiences mining this kind of data in Finnish, clustering was the only function chosen to be used in the real mining process. Another reason for this was that English literature gives several examples about using especially clustering in mining this sort of reports. The characteristics to be studied for each product based on (Muir, 2004), as well as a summary of the findings are displayed in Table-1. Afterwards, each tool is discussed in more detail.

TOOL #1

Tool #1 is a commercial product of Megaputer Intelligence, Illinois USA, called PolyAnalyst. It was first planned to be one of the systems to be evaluated but was replaced later with tool #4. It aroused great interest because it had been carefully evaluated by Southwest Airlines in analysis of flight safety reports. A good demo was also available in the Internet and it would have been possible to have a reduced demo version for computing personal data for a limited time. According to the information available, it has several capabilities and is used throughout the world and its customers can be counted in hundreds.

After examining the characteristics of the system it seemed impossible to use it in this context. The tool was language sensitive concerning the parts of speech, i.e., nouns, verbs, etc. It would have been possible to use text analyzing component with other languages as those it had been constructed to process, but in that case the results would not have been filtered. So, very common terms would exist in the results and they would have been marked as delete words in the dictionary. The system incorporated about 10 major European languages, even Swedish that is the second domestic language in Finland, but that capability did not bring any solution to the language problem. Tool #1 was taken within the study only as a reference system to help in searching for evaluation criteria, because it was rather easy to find users' experiences as well as technical characteristics about this system.

TOOL #2

The Tool #2 is also from American origin. Xerox laboratories primarily began the development of it. Nowadays it is developed and represented by a French company Text Mining Solutions, TEMIS. The company was founded in 2000. The connection with Xerox began with signing an initial licensing agreement for XeLDA® linguistic engine. This agreement led later TEMIS management to acquire Xerox linguistic operations (TEMIS, 2005). The agent of the system in Finland is a company named Lingsoft Oy. It is located in Turku. In March 2005 TEMIS and

Table 1. Characteristics of evaluated data mining systems[1]

Characteristics	Evaluated systems			
	Tool #1	Tool #2	Tool #3	Tool #4
Commercial product/prototype	Commercial product	Commercial product	Prototype	Commercial product
System based on	Several tools in-built	Different algorithms	Vector model	Several techno-logies used
Appropriate analysis modules/ capabilities	Complete capabilities	Complete capabili-ties	Vector model	Complete capabilities
Clustering available	Yes	Yes	Yes	Yes
Needed languages supported	English	English, Finnish	Any	English (Spa-nish tested)
Visualisation and graphic tools capabilities	Yes	Yes	Through SOM	Yes
Amount of information needed for valid results	Small	Small	Small	Small
Users' experiences available widely	Yes	Yes (English) No (Finnish)	No commercial	Yes
Form of applicable data	Database, sequential file	Database, Sequential file	Sequential file	Database, ASCII files
Database products supported	Oracle, SQL Server	Oracle, Access, SQL Server	No	MS Access, SQL Server
Platform supported	Win2000, Win XP	Windows	Linux	Windows
Text and structured data mining capabilities	Yes	Yes	Yes	Yes
Accurate mining results	Yes	Yes	Yes	Yes
Reduced need for manual review of results	Moderate	Yes		Yes
Ease-of-use (interface and outputs)	Moderate; requires skills	Moderate; requires skills	Not in commercial use	Moderate; requires skills
Customisation needed	Little	Little	None	Little
System training available	Yes (not in Finland)	Yes	No commercial	Yes (not in Finland)
Purchase costs	Very high	High	Prototype	High, hiring possible
Operating costs	High	Low	Prototype	Low
Requires pre-processing	Much	Moderately	Little	Moderately
Thesaurus available	Yes	Yes	No	Yes
IT resources requirement	High	Moderate	Low	Moderate
Ease of acceptance and imple-mentation by IT dep.	n/a	Low	Low	n/a

Lingsoft signed a Bilateral Collaboration Agreement. Through this agreement TEMIS expanded its linguistic coverage to support 16 languages. The TEMIS products will now integrate the Lingsoft set of Northern European languages. Lingsoft, for one's part, will provide TEMIS with Finnish, Swedish, Norwegian Bokmal, and Danish Natural Language Processing software. The TEMIS core technology XeLDA® will have these multilingual software packages integrated in it. It is a multilingual linguistic engine for modelling and standardising unstructured documents in order to automatically exploit their content. Alongside with this agreement, Lingsoft will become a VAR (Value-Added Reseller) for TEMIS products for the Scandinavian area (Lingsoft Oy, 2005).

A preliminary test was run before the main test with real aviation safety incident data. The test began with choosing a suitable sample of data. Because aviation safety data is very often classified, the web was used. Applicable data was found in the site of NASA Aviation Safety Reporting System (ASRS). It contains twenty-eight (28) ASRS Database Report Sets on topics of interest to the aviation community in pdf-format. Each Report Set consists of fifty ASRS Database records, preceded by a note of introduction and caveats on use of ASRS data. All Report Sets have been pre-screened to assure their relevance to the pre-selected topic description. The reports sets will be updated quarterly (NASA, 2004). In this case the dataset Recreational Aviation Incidents was chosen. It is a sampling of reports from recreational aviation, including balloons and ultra light aircraft'. This was chosen, because all the others are classed into similar cases, so, clusters were more obvious to find in this set because it contained different types of incidents.

In the first phase the material was simplified to contain only text in two fields: Narrative and Synopsis. All the other information concerning date, time, environment, number of aircraft, assessments etc. was left away to be taken into the process later. The first process was clustering

with text mining functions. The system found 17 clusters, the first two of them containing five cases, the next 3 containing three cases, the next two cases and the rest of them containing one single case. Three cases were dropped out by the system; the obvious reason could be that the system did not find any components of these three cases to create a cluster. The problem appeared to be the abbreviations that are widely used in flight safety reports, but those seemed to follow a certain formula, so, they could have been added to the lexicon. In English version it would have been possible to 'open' the abbreviations and replace them with clear words and expressions.

The results of this preliminary test encouraged to continue with the real test material in Finnish. This can somehow be considered as prototyping, because while the tool had already been in production use, though the module for processing Finnish was quite new and there were no experiences in a wider range. The system was originally built to process larger texts but despite of that it also appeared to be capable in mining shorter texts like flight safety reports. The clustering test was in this case the most important and that is why the process began performing it.

The system has web based interface and provides good performance for examining the results. TEMIS decided to create 26 clusters leaving out 8 reports as unclassified documents, so 1232 reports were clustered. The size of the clusters varied from 109 to 21. The system was allowed by the operator to create sub clusters in the case the size of the cluster exceeds 100 reports and, therefore, the first cluster was divided into two sub clusters with 58 and 50 documents. The system handled each report as a document. Each cluster displayed also the five nearest clusters with their percentage of correspondence. These numbers varied between 5 and 1 percent, in most cases they were 2 or 3. This shows that the clusters are not at all close to each other and it is possible to come to the conclusion that clustering method in this context is usable. Inside the clusters every document is listed with its percentage explaining the cluster. The highest percentage was 27 which can be seen to significantly explain why especially the certain documents were placed to a certain cluster. An interesting observation was that in many cases the percentage of the first half was high and then it dropped notably.

The results also contain other features. One of them is the list containing the 30 most frequent features, which lists all the most significant words in the cluster and declares frequency of each feature. The smallest clusters began to produce some applicable information which indicates that the size of the clusters using this tool as well play a significant role in the applicability of results. This must, however, be scaled with the amount of production data, and it is also worth noticing, that a couple of similar cases do not automatically create a dangerous trend, but the way and the reasons causing them and it can only be estimated in thorough examination and investigation by human analysts. Compared to other tested tools, this might be easiest to use, at least as for data preparation, because in fact no problems appeared in analysing this kind of Finnish text. So, the new language module worked properly. Iteration in the use of this tool would also produce more accurate results and the ascertainment of its right tuning could only happen through repeating the mining process.

TOOL #3

The tool #3 is developed at Tampere Technical University, Signal Processing Laboratory as one of the results of the project called GILTA (manaGIng Large Text mAsses) between 1999 and 2003. The Gilta Project is a part of TEKES (Teknologian kehittämiskeskus, the National Technology Agency of Finland) USIX technology program. The main objective of the Gilta research project is to develop auxiliary means for finding and administering information in the mass of text documents. The scientific objective is to find out if it is possible to find the desired things in a mass of documents by using self-organising maps (SOM) or similar methods combined with linguistic sentence analysis.

According to Oard & Marchionini (1996) as well as Gey (2000), the information retrieval in text documents has been realised through grammars, language theories, fuzzy logic, automata theories, natural language processing, or latent semantic analysis. The usage of keywords is a common approach to topic detection and tracking because they given by the authors can be assumed characterising the text well. Compared to other methods, like using all the words of document and their frequency distribution, its accuracy, however, can be neglected. According to Manning and Schütze (1999) there are theories presenting that rare words enable distinguishing documents in histograms. Anyway, comparison of frequency distributions is complicated (Manning & Schütze, 1999). In Gilta project, the idea is utilised in a peculiar way applying the method to process the text on word, sentence and paragraph level.

After pre-processing the original text omitting extra spaces and carriage returns, the filtered text is translated into suitable form for encoding for which there are several approaches:

1. The word is recognised and replaced with a code. This approach is sensitive to new words.
2. The succeeding words are replaced with a code. This method is language sensitive.
3. Each word is analysed character by character and based on the characters a key entry to a code table is calculated. This approach is sensitive to capital letters and conjugation if the code table is not arranged in a special way.

In the Gilta Project, the last alternative is chosen, because it is accurate and suitable for statistical analysis. A word *w* is transformed into a number in the following manner (Toivonen, Visa, Vesanen, Back, & Vanharanta, 2001):

$$y = \sum_{i=0}^{L-1} k^i * c_{L-i}$$

where L is the length of the character string (the Word), ci is the ASCII value of a character within a word w, and k is a constant. Example: word is "c a t".

$$y = k^2 * ascii(c) + k * ascii(a) + ascii(t)$$

Different numbers will be assigned for each different word and only the same words can have equal numbers. The methods are similar on the paragraph level, so, all the paragraphs in the document are converted to vectors using the code numbers of sentences. In fact, this method includes several other procedures, but in this context it is sufficient to mention that expressed in very simplified form, the main principle is that documents are converted into vector form. The vectors determine the similarity of the documents through using Euclidean distance. The shorter the distance, the more similar the documents are. This method provides total language independence. The user can have all the similar documents when using this method as well as a number to the difference or clusters containing similar documents. Using systems training the methodology can easily be adapted to any application field (Toivonen et al., 2001).

As mentioned before, the tool was used in filtering the words to create lists of stop words and synonyms. The results were close to those processed with tool #4. The clustering results were produced in Excel form listing the most important words and their frequencies which made it clear and simple to analyse and interpret. The system itself decided to share the data into 100 clusters when the amount of most significant words was

chosen to be 9. The size of the clusters varied between 158 and 1. The biggest cluster consisting of 158 reports can be regarded as an aberration because the second biggest cluster contains 55 reports and the next ones 49 and 47. The reason for the enormous size of the cluster compared to the others was easily detectable. The word '(air)plane' in its all forms appeared 158 times as the most significant word as for the second most significant word 'flight' had frequency of 31 close to the rest the frequencies of which was about 20.

In the case the word mentioned had been ignored the size of this cluster would have been at least theoretically diminished to 31 which could have been an analysable size. The mentioning theoretically refers to the fact that the distribution of all reports would change if the word mentioned is ignored, so everything depends on everything. The system left out 4 reports belonging to no defined cluster. This was logical because these contained only one word. These single words had sufficient information in their reports because the other data in those clarified what happened and the narrative part was for example an explanation like 'engine failure (one word in Finnish)', but to text mining of narratives these do not bring any contribution. It is worth mentioning here that when all the data of the reports including structured data is mined, the situation might be different.

63 classes contained less than 10 reports. These are easily analysable by human analyst. These can already be considered as accurate mining results because several classes quickly analysed consisted similar reports. This proves that clustering is a utilisable function at least among this data. Some of the bigger classes having more than 10 reports could be interpreted to be real clusters, but according to experiences the sizes should be reduced to be less than 20. One finding among the bigger classes confirms, however, the utility of clustering and that is class 34 which consists of 32 reports that all are written about air space related cases. In the same way, class 55 consists of 25 reports which handle passenger related

cases. The clearly displayed results enabled their comprehensible analysis and comparison of them between other tools.

The mining process produced two special points worth noticing, which caused inaccuracies in the results. One of them was a simple mistake: the word 'jälkeen (after)' was left out from stop words list. The other one was kind of surprise. As mentioned before, the frequency of word 'kone (plane)' with all its forms and synonyms was very high. This was obvious due to the context in which the reports are written but it caused the growth of one cluster. The question about what explained before is somehow twofold: words 'before' and 'after' are themselves clear stop words and thus ignored, but as a part of a concept, for example, 'after landing' or 'before take-off' they could have valuable information. As for the word 'plane', it is obvious that it appears often in the reports, but could it be ignored or not? The amount of the clusters can be considered to be appropriate in this context, but the distribution of reports should be more uniform. The synonyms and stop words should be controlled and specified as well as the concepts should be utilised. According to the experiences received from analysing this tool it could be carefully estimated that the process should be iterated with different parameter determinations about 5 to 10 times.

TOOL #4

The tool #4 is a commercial product of American origin called PolyVista. The company is located in Houston, Texas. It is a full-capable data mining system with several components and technologies built-in having ability for mining both numerical and text data. The test material followed by the lists of stop words and synonyms was delivered to the company that performed the processing of the data. In this case only clustering was performed using different amounts of clusters that could be determined by the user. This was the first time when Finnish text was mined. The tool is built

to be used in English context, but tests had been made with Spanish achieved good and encouraging results and that is why the company dared to test its applicability for Finnish. This seemed to be successful as well.

The results were returned to the researcher in form of pictures taken from the Cluster Browser window. The first run was kind of a preliminary one made without any pre-processing. The results are illustrated in Figure 2.

This is how one would read the output:

- 1st cluster has 205 records
- Most important word in the 1st cluster is "oli" (was) with a score of 100
- 2nd most important word in the 1st cluster is "etta" (so that) with a score of 16, this implies that the rest of the words are not significant

Number of clusters 15 is just a guess, this is strictly dependent on data and it can be refined through some iterations. Number of words to describe a cluster is 10 starting from the left, and the first word describes the cluster best with a score of 100. The importance of words decreases left to right. The last word on the right has least significance in the cluster. The numeric score after a word gives an idea about the significance of that word in a cluster. Scoring is done from 0 (minimum) to 100 (maximum). The preliminary results declare the importance of using stop words. The most important word of clusters 1, 2, 5, 8, 11, 12, 14 and 15 can be considered as stop words. When all the most important words from each cluster are considered, the percentage of stop words is as high as almost 35 varying from 10 to 70.

As for the distribution, the amount of stop words among the 10 most important words does not seem to have any correlation with the size of cluster. The role of stop words appears also second time when the results of the first test are observed minutely. As available in the figure, the most important word with the score of 100 as

Figure 2. Mining results without pre-processing of the words

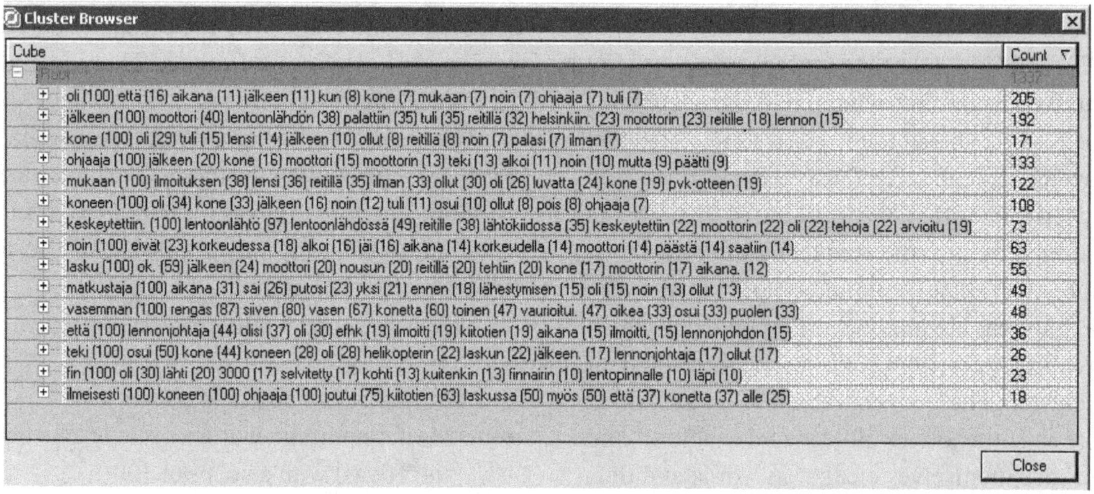

well as the second important word with score 16 of the first cluster are stop words. According to the reading instructions, the rest of the words are not significant. Because stop words are regarded as words without any significance and the rest of the words are not significant, the whole cluster with its 205 reports, which represents about 17 per cent of the test data, can be regarded having no significance and thus could be deleted.

It is obvious that the reports of the cluster include valuable information and that is why the usage of stop words and also synonyms is of great importance. The amount of synonyms is somewhat smaller, less than 23 per cent only. The amount of synonyms in the 10 most important words results have the values 0, 2 or 4 and that makes the percentage of the synonyms smaller the bigger the cluster is. Also in this case, the distribution does not seem to have any correlation with the size of the cluster.

After using stop words the results look different. They are illustrated in Figure 3. The synonyms are not defined in this case, that is why they appear often on the rows describing the clusters. The amount of clusters is 35 and their size varies from 131 to 1. One report does not create alone a cluster, so, the three last ones are

deleted from the observation process. Every tool has found a couple of reports that do not belong to any cluster and this does not make any exception. The smallest clusters contain three reports and that can already be taken within the observation. There is, however, an interesting point among these three reports left out. In two of them, all the words have the score 100 and in one of the first has 100 and the rest have 50.

The most important word has the score of 100 as before, but in contrast to observations before, the amount of second most important words is much higher. This indicates that the cluster is obviously more homogenous, that means, the cases are closer to each other. Using stop words there are 20 clusters of the observed 32 clusters where the score of second most important at least 50. Thus more than half of the cases, 62 per cent, can be stated to be more homogenous than the others. Using the same way of observation, compared to the results before, when mining was done without using stop words, the correspondent amount was only 4 clusters of the total amount of 15 clusters. This means that only 27 per cent of the clusters can be stated to be as homogenous as in the case stop words are used. The comparison illustrates the direction towards more minute mining results

Figure 3. Mining results with using stop words

when stop words are used. The clusters having about less than 40 reports seem to give some information according to the importance of the words and their content.

The process continued by taking synonyms with. The data was processed determining the number of clusters first to be 6 and then raising it up to 20 with step of 2. With 6 clusters their size varied from 117 to 410. The alteration of cluster amount did not cause any remarkable change in distribution or other factors. The only difference was the arithmetical fact that the number of reports in clusters diminished. A significant change compared to what happened before taking both stop words and synonyms was that the importance of second most important word was high in fairly more than half of the clusters. When there were 20 clusters, the smallest of them contained 10 reports and the biggest 232. The size of the biggest 5 was between 96 and 232, which means

that it is necessary to split them into smaller units. The rest contained 67 reports or less. It is worth noticing that in the case of 20 clusters, in 11 of them, i.e., a bit more than a half the scores of the three most important words were more than 50. In the last cluster containing 10 reports, of the 10 most important words, the score of 8 ones are 50 or more. This can already be considered as an accurate mining result.

All the research phases in the process of estimating this tool have produced some kind of good and applicable results, especially when the smallest clusters are observed. The scores of most important words are high and quickly estimated the words seem to be of significant character. These results, like those of the other estimated tools, were achieved by using no iteration, in which case the lists of stop words and synonyms could have been refined and thus the mining results would have been more accurate. The utilisation of concepts could have brought a significant contribution to the mining process.

FUTURE RESEARCH DIRECTIONS

Complex environments, that need description both in structured and unstructured ways, are many in this contemporary society, and aviation safely management is surely one of those environments. When data mining is performed, tools that provide integrated information from the data available both in structured (e.g., numerical values), semi-structured (e.g., text and other narratives) and unstructured (e.g., figures) ways are needed. Text mining is one challenging task in data mining. Any natural language as such is hard to interpret, but the challenge is even bigger in the case of small language groups, where tools for text mining are scarcer than in big languages like English, Spanish or German.

Anyway the results are very encouraging to develop the study further. The aim of the researcher is to continue the process and achieve more accurate and usable results. These results are interesting and encouraging themselves and they have proved, at least preliminary, the applicability of text mining tools in Finnish. One of the next steps would be the combination of mining both structured and textual data, which could move the test arrangements towards applicable tool that could in daily use serve the goal: improving the flight safety.

Data mining and text mining tools are decision support systems and that is why directly applicable results cannot be expected. One remarkable point is that although the results themselves do not directly discover any lethal trends in the reports, they could expose the existence of a couple of somehow similar cases, which should be examined further. Finding for example a few interesting cases reveals the existence of those and this might raise questions of their amount in larger scale in which case other tools might

be utilised like report generators of databases. They allow the user to determine a wide scale of criteria to access the cases searched. This kind of process could be as well performed with the same tool using another function than clustering only or combining many functions, e.g., finding words or expressions to discover reports in which same components may exist.

CONCLUSION

All the tested system confirmed the fact that data mining and especially text mining should be an iterative process. The number of clusters proved to be significant in the process: the more clusters, the better results. However, an optimum point would be important to find, because theoretically the number of clusters could be raised to the amount of cases which makes, of course, no sense. The size of clusters should be at maximum about 30, maybe somewhat higher depending on the type of reports. If the clusters contain less than 15 reports they are rather easy to analyse and find common factors creating the cluster. If their size is greater than 20, it is possible to estimate the similarity of them by finding describing words or expressions. Increasing the amount of clusters is not directly the only way to achieve better mining results. The stop words and synonyms should be controlled and updated if needed. Iterating the process only reveals the possible shortcomings and mistakes made during the creation process of the lists.

One obvious problem appears when the validity of the sample will be estimated. The lists of stop words and synonyms, for example, are created using the test material but the production data can contain a significant amount of both that could have not been defined on the basis of that. Because there are practically almost as many writers as received reports, they do not have any fixed form but each one is somehow unique. Positive exceptions of these are the reports written by airline pilots who are trained to do this and have a special way of expressing the cases. As mentioned before, data mining tools are decision support systems and they can be utilised in scarce retrieval of information.

Different tools had somewhat different functions and ways to process the data which produces valuable experiences to add and improve the requirements for an utilisable mining tool. All the estimated tools produced somehow similar results, which proved that the research is on right tracks, which also means that it does not seem difficult to refine the results by iterating the process several times. The study could have been slightly easier and more accurate if the researcher would not have been dependent on the operators of the systems. In that case the researcher could have changed the test arrangements himself along with the mining process.

REFERENCES

Blake, M. B., Singh, L., Williams, A. B., Norman, W., & Sliva, A. L. (2006). A Component-Based Data Management and Knowledge Discovery Framework for Aviation Studies. *International Journal of Technology and Web Engineering, 1*(1).

Delen, D., & Crossland, M. D. (2008). Seeding the survey and analysis of research literature with text mining. *Expert Systems with Applications: An International Journal, 34*(3), 1707-1720.

DIRECTIVE 2003/42/EC OF THE EUROPEAN PARLIAMENT AND OF THE COUNCIL on occurrence reporting in civil aviation, DIRECTIVE 2003/42/EC (2003).

European Commission. (2000). *Proposal for a DIRECTIVE OF THE EUROPEAN PARLIAMENT AND OF THE COUNCIL on occurrence reporting in civil aviation*. Brussels.

Fayyad, U., Piatetsky-Shapiro, G., & Smyth, P. (1996). *Knowledge Discovery and Data Mining: Towards a Unifying Framework*. Paper presented at the Second International Conference on Knowledge History and Data Mining (KDD-96), Portland, Oregon.

GAIN Working Group B. (2004). *Role of Analytical Tools in Airline Flight Safety Management Systems* (No. Second Edition): Global Aviation Information Network.

Gey, F. C. (2000, January 4-7 2000). *Information Retrieval: Theory, Application, Evaluation*. Paper presented at the Thirty-Third Annual Hawaii International Conference on System Sciences (HICSS-33), Hawaii.

Han, J., & Kamber, M. (2001). *Data Mining: Concepts and Techniques*: Morgan Kaufmann Publishers.

Kloptchenko, A. (2003). *Text Mining Based on the Prototype Matching Method*. Unpublished Doctoral Dissertation, Åbo Akademi University, Turku.

Kutais, B. G. (Ed.). (2006). *Focus on the Internet*: Nova Science Publishers, Inc.

Lingsoft Oy. (2005). *Lingsoft and TEMIS Announce Partnership to Expand Text Mining Coverage to Northern European languages and countries*. Retrieved 3.5.2005, 2005, from http://www.lingsoft.fi/news/2005/temis.html

Manning, C. D., & Schütze, H. (1999). *Foundations of Statistical Natural Language Processing*. Cambridge, Massachusetts: The MIT Press.

Megaputer Intelligence. (2004c). *Application of PolyAnalyst to Flight Safety Data of Southwest Airlines*. Bloomington, IN: Megaputer Intelligence.

Muir, A. (2004, September 28-30). *Fundamentals of Data and Text Mining*. Paper presented at the Seventh GAIN World Conference, Montreal, Canada.

NASA. (2004, 17 December 2004). *ASRS Database Report Sets.* Retrieved 18 October, 2004, from http://asrs.arc.nasa.gov/report_sets_nf.htm

Nazeri, Z. (2003). *Application of Aviation Safety Data Mining Workbench at American Airlines. Proof-of-Concept Demonstration of Data and Text Mining.* McLean, Virginia, US: Center for Advanced Aviation Systems Development, MITRE Corporation Inc.

Oard, D. W., & Marchionini, G. (1996). *A conceptual framework for text filtering* (Technical Report CS-TR3643): University of Maryland.

Painter, M. K., Erraguntla, M., Hogg, J., Gary L., & Beachkofski, B. (2006). *Using simulation, data mining, and knowledge discovery techniques for optimized aircraft engine fleet management.* Paper presented at the 2006 Winter Simulation Conference, Monterey, California.

Parsaye, K. (1997). A Characterization of Data Mining Technologies and Processes. *Journal of Data Warehousing, 2*(3), 2-15.

Saracoglu, R., Tütünkü, K., & Allahverdi, N. (2008). A new approach on search for similar documents with multiple categories using fuzzy clustering. *Expert Systems with Applications: An International Journal, 34*(4), 2545-2554.

Seifert, J. W. (2006). Data Mining: An Overview. In B. G. Kutais (Ed.), *Focus on the Internet* (pp. 101-118): Nova Science Publishers, Inc.

TEMIS. (2005). *Text Mining Solutions, TEMIS.* Retrieved 2.5.2005, 2005, from http://www.temis-group.com

Toivonen, J., Visa, A., Vesanen, T., Back, B., & Vanharanta, H. (2001). *Prototype Based Information Retrieval in Multilanguage Bibles.* Paper presented at the WIAMIS 2001.

Wang, X., Huang, S., Cao, L., Shi, D., & Shu, P. (2007). LSSVM with Fuzzy Pre-processing Model Based Aero Engine Data Mining Technology. In *Advanced Data Mining and Applications* (Vol. Tuesday, August 14, 2007, pp. 100-109). Heidelberg: Springer Berlin / Heidelberg.

Watson, R. T. (1999). *Data Management: Databases and Organizations* (2nd Edition ed.): John Wiley & Sons.

Visa, A., Toivonen, J., Autio, S., Mäkinen, J., Back, B., & Vanharanta, H. (2001, 16-17 April). *Data mining of text as a tool in authorship attribution.* Paper presented at the Data Mining and Knowledge Discovery: Theory, Tools and Technology III, Orlando, USA.

Wu, X., Kumar, V., Quinlan, J. R., Ghosh, J., Yang, Q., Motoda, H., et al. (2007). *Top 10 algorithms in data mining* (Survey paper). London: Springer-Verlag London Limited.

ENDNOTE

[1] In this table only the characteristics important among the planned using context are considered.

Section IV
E–Governance and Artificial Intelligence

Chapter XII
Applying Dynamic Causal Mining in E-Government Modeling

Yi Wang
Nottingham Trent University, UK

ABSTRACT

Electronic government or digital government is not a simple or well-defined theoretical construct. Electronic government is a complex phenomenon which involves technical, organizational, institutional and environmental aspects. Researchers from different disciplines are trying to model the E-government using combinations of methods from different areas which can help to deal with complexity and obtain more comprehensive explanations. This chapter uses Dynamics Causal Mining as the technique for modeling and analyzes E-government. Dynamics Causal Mining is a combination of System Dynamics and Data Mining.

INTRODUCTION

Causality plays a central role in E-government and decision-making by making the observation and recognition of the causality. A common scientific approach in recognizing causality is by manipulating attributes through experimentation. However, real world events are often affected by a large number of potential factors and many of these factors are hidden. For example, in manufacturing, many factors such as cost, labor, weather, social events, etc., can all affect the final product. Some of factors, such as cost and labor, have a clear causality with the final product. Other factors, such as weather and social events may not have a clear causality with the final product.

This chapter suggests an integration of *System Dynamics* and *Association Mining* for identifying causality and expanding the application area of both techniques. This gives an improved description of the target system represented by a database; it can also improve strategy selection and other forms of decision making. Such a combination extracts important dynamic causality. This type of causality is very common in daily life. For example, "an increase of productivity in a factory might cause an increase of pollution in the environment" and "the increasing pollution will cause a decreasing level of human health and welfare". In the real world, an occurrence of an event is often affected by a large number of potential factors. The aim is to identify causal factors hidden in the data and discover the underlying causality between the observed data.

In E-government, it is essential to understand the causality between entities, such as investment, human behavior, and revenue, in order to properly manage and understand it. Causality is not the same as correlation. Correlation can be classified as association and none association. Association between two attributes means that there exist a relationship between two attribute where the existence of one attribute lead to the existence of the other. Association can then be classified as cointegration and causality, where cointegration represents a weaker relationship. Causality can

then be classified as static causality and dynamic causality as it depicted in Figure 1. This chapter focuses on the dynamic causality and how it can assist in modeling, understanding and manage E-government.

This chapter first reviews the exiting research in E-government with focus on Data Mining and System Dynamics. Then details of Dynamic causal mining are presented. The chapter ends with a practical example and a conclusion.

Literature Review

The Dynamic Casual Mining (DCM) algorithm was discovered in 2005 (Pham et. al, 2005) using only counting algorithm to integrate with *Game theory*. It was extended in 2006 (Pham et. al, 2006) with delay and feedback analysis, and was further improved for the analysis in *Game theory* with *Formal Concept* analysis (Wang, 2007). *DCM* enables the generation of *dynamic causal rules* from data sets by integrating the concepts of *Systems Thinking (*Senge et al., 1994) and *System dynamics* (Forrester, 1961) with *Association mining* (Agrewal et al., 1996). The algorithm can process data sets with both categorical

Figure 1. Classification of causality

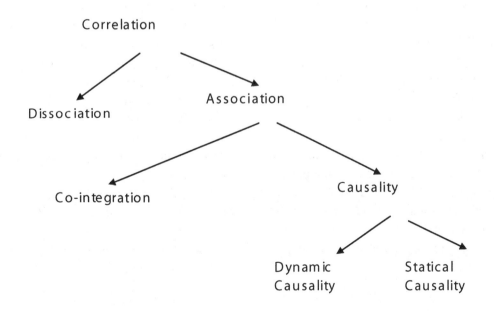

and numerical attributes. Compared with other *Association mining* algorithms, *DCM* rule sets are smaller and more dynamically focused. The pruning is carried out based on polarities. This reduces the size of the pruned data set and still maintains the accuracy of the generated rule sets. The rules extracted can be joined to create dynamic policy, which can be simulated through software for future decision making. The rest of this section gives a brief review of *Association mining* and *System Dynamics*.

Association Mining

Association mining was discovered by Agrawal (Agrewal et al., 1996). It was further improved in various ways, such as in speed (Agrewal et al., 1996 and Cheung et al., 1996). and with parallelism (Zaki et al., 1997) to find interesting associations and/or correlation relationships among large sets of data items. It shows attributes value conditions that occur frequently together in a given dataset. It generates the candidate *itemsets* by joining the large *itemsets* of the previous pass and deleting those subsets which are small in the previous pass without considering the transactions in the database. By only considering large *itemsets* of the previous pass, the number of candidate in large *itemsets* is significantly reduced.

System Thinking

System thinking is based on the belief that the component parts of a system will act differently when isolated from its environment or other parts of the system. Systems thinking is about the interrelated actions which provide a conceptual framework or a body of knowledge that makes the pattern clearer (Senge et al., 1994). It is a combination of many theories such as soft systems approach and system theory (Coyle, 1996). Systems thinking seeks to explore things as a whole, through patterns of interrelated actions.

System Dynamics

System Dynamics can be defined as "*a qualitative and quantitative approach to describe model and design structures for managed systems in order to understand how delays, feedback, and interrelationships among attributes influence the behavior of the systems over time*"(Coyle, 1996: pp.132), or "*the purpose of the model is to solve a problem, not simply to model a system. The model must simplify the system to a point where the model replicates a specific problem.*"(Sterman 1994:pp287).

System dynamics is a tool to visualize and understand such patterns of dynamic complexity, which is build up from a set of system archetypes based on principles in *System thinking* (Sterman, 2000). *System dynamics* visualizes complex systems through causal loop diagrams. A causal loop diagram consists of a few basic shapes, that together describes the action modeled.

System dynamics addresses two types of behavior, *sympathetic* and *antipathetic* [Pham et al., 2005]. *Sympathetic behavior* indicates an initial quantity of a target attributes starts to grow, and the rate of growth increases. *Antipathetic behavior* indicates an initial quantity of a target attributes that starts either above or below a goal level and over time moves toward the goal.

E-government consists of complex and recursive relationships between factors related to technology, management, and policy (Dawes & Pardo, 2002; Fountain, 2001; Gil-Garcia, 2005). Single methods (either quantitative or qualitative) are suitable for understanding specific aspects of E-government and information systems in general. However, authors from different disciplines have identified the desirability of using multiple methods and adding different disciplinary perspectives to the research endeavor (Bennet, 2002; Creswell, 2003; Newman & Benz, 1998).

According to Gil-Garcia & Pardo (2006), at least three different approaches to understanding

E- government exist in the academic literature (Gil-Garcia & Luna-Reyes, 2003; 2006). The first approach constructs a concrete definition or a list of elements that contains the main characteristics of what is, or what should be, electronic government (ASPA, 2001; M. Cook & LaVigne, 2002; UNPAN, 2002). A second approach is to list the different variants or applications of electronic government as a way to clarify this concept (Hiller & Bélanger, 2001; Holmes, 2001). A third conceptual approach to electronic government takes an evolutionary perspective; electronic government is defined by making reference to the different stages that appear to exist in its development (Gil-Garcia & Martinez-Moyano, 2005; Layne & Lee, 2001; Martinez-Moyano & Gil-García, 2003; Reddick, 2004; UN & ASPA, 2002).

E-government has been recognized as capable of promoting change in government settings (Heeks, 1999; Kraemer & King, 2003). Information technologies have the potential not only to improve the quality of services, but also to produce cost savings and make government policies and programs more effective (Bourquard, 2003; Dawes *et al.*, 1999; Garson, 2004; Gartner, 2000). However, scholars and practitioners think information technologies (IT) in general and electronic government in particular have not yet accomplished the promise of a more efficient, effective, and democratic public administration (M. E. Cook *et al.*, 2002; Davies, 2004; Garson, 2004). In fact, the failure rate of these projects is extremely high. Heeks (2003) estimates that the failure rate of e-government projects could be as high as 85%. Despite the high rate of failure, government spending in E-government projects has continually increased in the last few years and is estimated to surpass $5.8 billion in 2009 (Pulliam, 2005).

DATA MINING APPLIED IN E-GOVERNMENT ANALYSIS

Most data mining initiatives in government are for fraud and abuse prevention purposes. An example is cross checking tax bills and payments from various departments to see if taxes are refunded from one system, while outstanding balances are due in another. Data mining capability should extend across Enterprise Resource Planning (ERP) systems and e-commerce sites so user has a grasp of how enterprise is actually functioning as a whole. This capability provides a whole new management resource across government.

The limitations of data mining are primarily data or personnel related, rather than technology-related (Seifert, 2007). Although data mining can help reveal patterns and relationships, it does not tell the user the value or significance of these patterns. These types of determinations must be made by the user. Similarly, the validity of the patterns discovered is dependent on how they compare to "real world" circumstances. Another limitation of data mining is that while it can identify connections between behaviors and/or variables, it does not necessarily identify a causal relationship.

The effectiveness of this approach can be limited by the creativity of the user to develop various hypotheses, as well as the structure of the software being used (Makulowich, 1999). Moreover, such a robust data set can still lead to false positives. In contrast, a CATO Institute report suggests that the relatively small number of terrorist incidents or attempts each year are too few and individually unique "to enable the creation of valid predictive models."(Jonas and Harper, 2006) Several effective data mining techniques for detecting intrusions have been developed (Warrender et al., 1999), many of which perform close to or better than systems engineered by domain experts.

The work most similar to unsupervised model generation is a technique developed at SRI in the Emerald system (Javitz and Valdes, 1998). Emerald uses historical records to build normal detection models and compares distributions of new instances to historical distributions. Discrepancies between the distributions signify an intrusion. One problem with this approach is that intrusions present in the historical distributions may cause the system to not detect similar intrusions in unseen data.

Related to automatic model generation is adaptive intrusion detection. Teng et al. (1990) perform adaptive real time anomaly detection by using inductively generated sequential patterns. Also relevant is Sobirey's work on adaptive intrusion detection using an expert system to collect data from audit sources (Sobirey, 1996).

In this aspect, many different approaches have been proposed to build anomaly detection models have been proposed. A survey and comparison of anomaly detection techniques is given in (warrender, 1999). Stephanie Forrest presents an approach for modeling normal sequences using look ahead pairs (Forrester, 1996) and contiguous sequences (Hofmeyr, 1998). Helman and Bhangoo (1997) present a statistical method to determine sequences which occur more frequently in intrusion data as opposed to normal data. Lee et al. (Lee et al., 1997; 1998) uses a prediction model trained by a decision tree applied over the normal data. Ghosh and Schwartzbard (1999) use neural networks to model normal data. Lane and Brodley (1997; 1998; 1999) examine unlabeled data for anomaly detection by looking at user profiles and comparing the activity during an intrusion to the activity under normal use. Researchers have previously successfully developed data mining approaches for credit card fraud detection (Chan & Fan, 1999; Stolfo, 2000; 1997).

SYSTEM DYNAMICS IN E-GOVERNMENT ANALYSIS

System dynamics provides a way to explore feedback-rich systems in which the nature of the relationships among the elements. It allows the researcher to investigate the effect of changes in one variable on other variables over time.

System dynamics is a computer-aided approach to policy analysis and design that applies to dynamic problems arising in complex social, managerial, economic, or ecological systems (Richardson, 1996). The aim of a system dynamics modeling is to study and understand structurally-based behavior by generating insights that will allow the finding of leverage points of intervention.

System dynamics provides a framework for investigating the effect of changes in one variable on other variables over time. System dynamics, a computer-aided approach to policy analysis and design, applies to dynamic problems arising in complex social, managerial, economic, or ecological systems (Sterman, 2000) as is the case in digital government.

System dynamics approach to study the evolution of E-Government (Martinez-Moyano & Gil-Garcia, 2004). E-Government dynamics can be understood based on observed behavior conditions the system of rules present in an organization or enterprise. Over time, E-Government could become an operational standard of a legal requirement. (Courty & Marschke, 97).

System dynamics modeling is a simplified version of group model building variant. Group model building deals with "the processes and techniques designed to handle the tangle of problems that arise in trying to involve a large number of people in model construction." (Richardson, 1999;pp 375). Research that deals with the specifics of this method has been termed 'group model building' (Andersen & Richardson, 1997; Andersen, et al., 1997; Richardson & Andersen, 1995).

The literature in group model building continues to grow and gives specific guidelines and scripts for carrying out these processes (Andersen & Richardson, 1997; Andersen, et al., 1997; Vennix 1999). According to Zagonel (2002), two main types of models may arise in group model building: micro-world and boundary-object models. Micro-world models try to capture objective reality, whereas boundary-object models are artifacts that help in understanding diverse views about the world. In these models, a composite view of reality emerges as a result of the interaction of the individuals that build it.

DYNAMIC CAUSAL MINING

This section provides a general framework for *DCM*. It is an iterative and continual process of mining rules, formulating policies, testing, and revision of the models. DCM may have five stages.

Stage 1: Problem definition. In this phase, the problem is identified and the key variables are given. Also, the time horizon is defined so that the cause and effects can be identified.

Stage 2: Data preparation. Data are collected from various sources and a homogeneous data source is created to eliminate the representation and encoding differences.

Stage 3: Data mining. This stage involves transforming data into rules. This thesis suggests using *DCM* as a data mining tool. The details of *DCM* are explained in the following sections.

Stage 4: Policy formulation. Policies are groups of the rules extracted by mining techniques. Policies improve the understanding of the system. The interactions of different policies must also be considered since the impact of combined policies is usually not the sum of their impacts alone. These interactions may reinforce each other or have an opposite effect. The policy can be used for behaviour simulation to predict the future outcome.

Stage 5: Model Simulation. This stage tests the accuracy of the policies. The policies will predict results for new cases so the managers can alter the policy to improve future behavior of the system. It is necessary to capture the appropriate data and generate a prediction in real time, so that a decision can be made directly, quickly, and accurately.

Dataset

To find dynamic causality among a set of attributes means to identify correlation and interdependencies between them. The *DCM* algorithm is a way of describing the state of a target system as it evolves in time. It discovers dynamic causality in a data set by matching the dynamic behavior between separated attributes.

Time Stamp

Definition 1. *A dynamic time stamp is created from two time stamps. Consider two time stamps t_i and t_{i+1}. The dynamic time stamp Δt_i is equal to the difference between two consecutive time stamps.*

$$\Delta t_i = t_{i+1} - t_i \tag{1}$$

Time stamps are used for identifying the range of variables. The size of each time stamp is selected by the specific need and may vary in different situations. For instance, a time stamp for an increase in production may be in the order of months, while for a change in a cell may be in the order of milliseconds. The time stamp also can help to determine how detailed the variables need to be. The attribute may increase or decrease dramatically if the time stamp is in the order of seconds, however it may be assumed to be constant if the time stamp is in the order of years. All the time stamps should be of uniform length. In order to carry out *DCM*, the time stamps are summarized or partitioned into equal-sized time stamps. A time stamp is useful for describing and prescribing changes to the systems and objects.

Data

Definition 2. A *dynamic attribute is the change or the difference between two attribute values with consecutive time stamps. The two types of value do not have the same nature. Let D denote a data set which contains a set of n records with attributes {A$_1$, A$_2$, A$_3$,... A$_m$}, where each attribute is of a unique type (for example;, sale price, production volume, inventory volume, etc). Each attribute is associated with a time stamp t$_i$, where i ={1,2,3,...n}. Let D$_{new}$ be a new database constructed from D such that dynamic attribute $\Delta A_{m,\Delta t_i}$ in D$_{new}$ is given by:*

$$\Delta A_{m,\Delta t_i} = A_{m,t_{i+1}} - A_{m,t_i} \qquad (2)$$

where m identifies the attribute of interest.

Table 1. Original database D

Time	A$_1$	A$_2$
1	9	2
2	17	3
3	10	12
4	4	16
5	7	24

The classical *Association Mining* algorithms can be applied only to data in the original form (attribute form), e.g. in the market basket problem (Agrawal, et. al., 1993) the focus is on the items of each purchase. On the other hand, *DCM* is interested in the dynamic changes between data. To apply *DCM*, the records are arranged in a temporal sequence (*t = 1, 2 ,..., n*). Definition 2 is only for numerical attributes and the causality between categorical attributes in *D* can be identified by examining the differences of corresponding changes in attribute values. An example of

such a database is shown in Table 1. A$_1$ and A$_2$ represent attributes, such as from a tax database like income and tax.

Table 2. Derived database D$_{new}$

Δt	ΔA_1	ΔA_2
Δt_1	+8	+1
Δt_2	-7	+9
Δt_3	-6	+4
Δt_4	+3	+8

Definition 3. *In the case of categorical attributes, the dynamic causal attributes can be identified by joining the polarities of corresponding changes in attribute values. Let D$_{new}$ be a new data set constructed from D such that attribute $\Delta A_{m,\Delta t_i}$ in D$_{new}$ is given by:*

$$\Delta A_{m,\Delta t_i} = \mathrm{join}(A_{m,t_{i+1}}, A_{m,t_i}) \qquad (3)$$

where join is a function combining $A_{m,t_{i+1}}$ and A_{m,t_i} For example, (t=1, $A_{m,t_{i+1}}$ = Red) and (t=2, A_{m,t_i} = Blue) then ($\Delta t =1$, $\Delta A_{m,\Delta t_i}$ = RedBlue).

The *attribute* is gathered first and the *dynamic attribute* is derived from the *attribute* (see Table-2). The *dynamic attribute* identifies the significant relationship between the dynamics of the *attribute*.

Measurements

Since the input of the *DCM* algorithm can be quite large, it is important to prune away the redundant attributes.

Definition 4. *A polarity indicates the direction of a change of an attribute. There are three types of polarity (+, -, 0); where + indicates an increase, - indicates a decrease, and 0 indicates neutrality, i.e. no change at all.*

Definition 5. *A polarity combination is a joint set of two or more polarities. The simultaneous presence of combinations (+,+) and (-,-) indicates sympathetic changes and will produce a sympathetic rule. The simultaneous presence of combinations (+,-) and (-,+) indicates antipathetic changes and produces antipathetic rules. There are four different combinations of polarity (+,-) (antipathetic negative), (+,+) (sympathetic positive), (-,+) (antipathetic positive) and (-,-) (sympathetic positive) to indicate the degree of causality.*

This differs from the classical causal loops relation which has only + and -, due to a simultaneous increase of an attribute set not automatically leading to a simultaneous decrease of the same set.

Definition 6. *A support is the ratio of records of a certain polarity combination over the total number of records in the dynamic attributes. Three supports are applied in DCM; sympathetic support, antipathetic support, and single support. For data set D_{new} and any two attributes $\Delta A_{1,\Delta t_i}$ and $\Delta A_{2,\Delta t_i}$ the three kinds of supports are defined as follows.*

Sympathetic Support

$$(\Delta A_{1,\Delta t_i}, \Delta A_{2,\Delta t_i}) = \frac{freq\,(+,+)}{n} \qquad (4a)$$

$$\text{or} \quad \frac{freq\,(-,-)}{n} \qquad (4b)$$

Antipathetic Support

$$(\Delta A_{1,\Delta t_i}, \Delta A_{2,\Delta t_i}) = \frac{freq\,(+,-)}{n} \qquad (5.a)$$

$$\text{or} \quad \frac{freq\,(-,+)}{n} \qquad (5.b)$$

Single Attribute Support

$$(\Delta A_{m,\Delta t_i}) = \frac{freq(+)}{n} \qquad (6.a)$$

$$\text{or} \quad \frac{freq(-)}{n} \qquad (6.b)$$

$$\text{or} \quad \frac{freq(0)}{n} \qquad (7.c)$$

Where freq $(+,+)$ is a function counting the number of times where an increase in $\Delta A_{1,\Delta t_i}$ is associated with a simultaneous increase in $\Delta A_{2,\Delta t_i}$, freq $(-,-)$ is a function counting the number of times where an decrease in $\Delta A_{1,\Delta t_i}$ is associated with a simultaneous decrease in $\Delta A_{2,\Delta t_i}$, freq $(-,+)$ is a function counting the number of times where an decrease in $\Delta A_{1,\Delta t_i}$ is associated with a simultaneous increase in $\Delta A_{2,\Delta t_i}$, freq $(+,-)$ is a function counting the number of times where an decrease in $\Delta A_{1,\Delta t_i}$ is associated with a simultaneous decrease in $\Delta A_{2,\Delta t_i}$.

All *supports* relate to the frequencies of the occurring patterns. For a given user specified *support*, the problem of *DCM* is to find all rules where the support is greater than the user defined *support*. The *support* is the frequency of occurrences of attribute sets that support a rule.

Figure 2 shows the results of the comparison between two dynamic attributes. The *X*-axis represents the time stamp and the *Y*-axis represents the value of the dynamic attributes. Figure 3 shows the graphical representation of two dynamic attributes, where the polarity combination is indicated.

Definition 7. *A support level is the value threshold for each dynamic attribute. Every record in a dynamic attribute must have an absolute value larger or equal to the support level in order to be considered as candidate for the dynamic rule.*

For a given *support level*, a positive and negative value of the *support level* can be then drawn as

Figure 2. Graph of two dynamic attributes(X-axis: Time stamps, Y-axis: Dynamic attribute value, D.attr: Dynamic attributes)

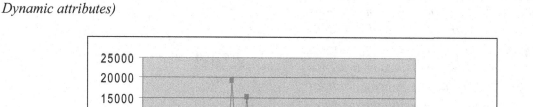

Figure 3. Illustration of polarity combination

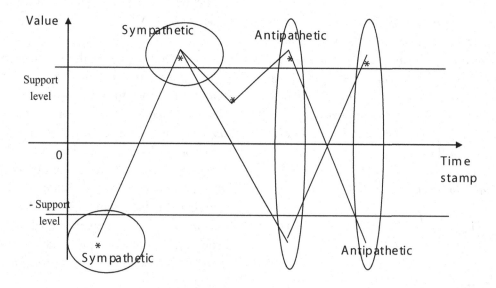

shown in Figure 3. The support is the occurrence of the polarity combination above the value of the support level.

Definition 8. *A frequent dynamic set is a pair of dynamic attributes which contain a polarity combination with frequency occurrence above a user-defined support threshold.*

Theorem 1. *If a pair of dynamic attributes (ΔA_1, ΔA_2) is infrequent, then either one individual dynamic attribute is infrequent or both dynamic attributes are infrequent.*

Proof: If a dynamic attribute set is frequent, then this indicates that both the dynamic attributes *are above the user-defined threshold* (see Table-3).

Table 3. Derived database D_{new} with arrows indicating support counting direction

Δt	ΔA_1	ΔA_2
Δt_1	+8	+1
Δt_2	-7	+9
Δt_3	-6	+4
Δt_4	+3	+8

The above theorem is a consequence of definition 7 for the frequent dynamic set. This observation forms the basis of the pruning strategy in the search procedure for frequent dynamic sets, which has been leveraged in many Association Mining algorithms (Zaki, 2000), that only the single dynamic attribute found to be frequent needs to be extended as candidate for the rule.

Theorem 2. *Confidence measure is not useful in DCM analysis.*

Proof: *The confidence measure is not used here because the total numbers of records in an attribute is equal to the total number of time stamps. Thus it makes the confidence equal to the support. Instead, multiple supports are introduced to further reduce the running time and size of the relevant rules.*

Rule Representation

A *dynamic causal rule* consists of variables connected by arrows denoting the causal influences among the attributes. Figure 4 shows an example of the notation. Two attributes, A_1 and A_2 are linked by a causal arrow. Each causal link is assigned a polarity and the link indicates the direction of the change.

In *System Dynamics,* a symbol $x \rightarrow^+ y$ can be interpreted as $\delta y/\delta x > 0$ and $x \rightarrow^- y$ can be interpreted as $\delta y/\delta x < 0$. This analogy is applied in *DCM* and the *dynamic causal rules* produced by *DCM* can form causal diagrams, which will be used to simulate future behavior.

Table 4. Counting result

	(+,+)	(-,-)	(+,-,)	(-,+,)
Supports(ΔA_1, ΔA_2)	2/4	0	0	2/4

Figure 4. Notation of a dynamic causal rule

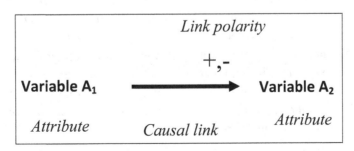

Definition 9. *A dynamic causal rule is derived from a frequent dynamic attribute set. A dynamic causal rule can be either strong or weak. A weak rule is a set of attributes with polarity that partially fulfils equation (4), (5), or (6). A strong rule is a set of attributes with polarity that completely fulfils equation (4), (5), or (6). There are two types of strong rule, sympathetic and antipathetic.*

Figure 2 shows that variables A_1 and A_2 are causally dependent. If *any* two variables A_1 and A_2 are truly causally related, then a change of A_1 causes a change of A_2. This paper focuses on the discovery of the causality with no time delay, which means that attributes are in same time period or interval. This implies that attributes should occur within the same time stamp.

Theorem 3. *The support for a strong rule is less than or equal to the half of the total time stamps.*

Proof: *Each dynamic attribute can have only one type of polarity at one time stamp. If the occurrence of one polarity is huge, the occurrence of the other two polarities will diminish. Following the definition of strong rules, the occurrence of the polarities + and – have both to be highly frequent. Since support indicates the times each polarity pair occurred over the total time stamp, the support cannot be more than ½ of the total time stamps.*

A *sympathetic* rule causes an increase or decrease in the output of a target system. It reinforces a change with more change in the same direction. An *antipathetic* rule represents an adjustment to achieve a certain goal or objective. It indicates a system attempting to change from its current state to a goal state. This implies that if the current state is above the goal state, then the system forces it down. If the current state is below the goal state, the system pushes it up. An *antipathetic* rule provides useful stability but resists external changes.

Dynamic Policy

Definition 10. *A dynamic policy consists of one or more dynamic causal rules. In a dynamic policy with several dynamic causal rules, each rule should share at least one dynamic attribute with other rules.*

Definition 11. *A dynamic policy is single if it consists only of one rule and if that rule does not share any common attribute with other rules in a dynamic policy.*

Given a *single dynamic policy* where an attribute A_1 is dynamically causally related to another attribute A_2, then such a rule can be represented as the following function.

$$\Delta A_2 = k \Delta A_1 \qquad (8)$$

where

$$k_t = \frac{\Delta A_{2,t}}{\Delta A_{1,t}} \qquad (9)$$

Given A_1^{new} indicating new values added in A_1, a ΔA_1^{new} can be calculated based on A_1^{new}, and based on equation 8 a ΔA_2^{new} can be calculated. If given a value $A_{2,t=0}$ a new set of A_2 can be derived, where $A_{2,t=2} = A_{2,t=1} + \Delta A_{2,t=1}^{new}$, $A_{2,t=3} = A_{2,t=2} + \Delta A_{2,t=2}^{new}$, etc.

Definition 12. *A dynamic policy is serial if each rule shares only one attribute with one other rule in a dynamic policy. A serial dynamic policy is open if each attribute in the policy has only one causal link, in other words, if there is a start and an ending attribute. A serial dynamic policy is closed if there is no start or ending attribute.*

Given an *open serial dynamic policy* where an attribute A_1 is dynamically causally related to another attribute A_2, and A_2 is dynamically causally related to another attribute A_3, then such a rule can be represented as the following function.

$$A_{2,T} = k_{1,T}A_{1,T} \text{ and } A_{3,T} = k_{2,T}A_{2,T} = k_{2,T}k_{1,T}A_{1,T} \tag{10}$$

where

$$T = (1, 2, 3, ...t), \quad k_{1,t} = \frac{A_{2,t}}{A_{1,t}}$$

$$\text{and } k_{2,t} = \frac{A_{3,t}}{A_{2,t}} \tag{11}$$

Definition 15. *A dynamic policy is complex if the policy consists of a mixture of open and closed serial dynamic policies.*

For a complex or closed dynamic policy there are attributes which are connected with more than one attribute. For instance, A_1 is connected with A_2, A_3, and A_4. A_2, A_3 and A_4 are not connected. Then A_1 can be represented with:

$$A_{2,T} * A_{3,T} * A_{4,T} = C_T$$

where

$$T = (1, 2, 3, ...t) \text{ and } C_t = A_{2,t} * A_{3,t} * A_{4,t}$$

MINING ALGORITHM

Problem Formulation

Let D denote a database which contains a set of n records with attributes $\{A_1, A_2, A_3, ... A_n\}$, where each attribute is of a unique type (sale price, production quantity, inventory volume, etc). Each attribute is linked to a time stamp t. To apply *DCM*, the records are arranged in a temporal sequence ($t = 1, 2, ..., n$). The causality between attributes in D can be identified by examining the polarities of corresponding changes in attribute values. Let D_{new} be a new data set constructed from D. A generalized dynamic association rule is an implication of the form $A_1 \rightarrow^p A_2$, where $A_1 \subset D$, $A_1 \subset D$, $A_1 \cap A_2 = f$ and p is the polarity.

The implementation of the *DCM* algorithm must support the following operations:

(1) To add new attributes.
(2) To maintain a counter for each polarity with respect to every dynamic value set. While making a pass, one dynamic set is read at a time and the polarity count of candidates supported by the dynamic sets is incremented. The counting process must be very fast as it is the bottleneck of the whole process.

Algorithm Description

DCM makes two passes over the data as shown in Figures 7 and 8. In the first pass, the *support* of individual attributes is counted and the frequent attributes are determined. The dynamic values are used for generating new potentially frequent sets and the actual *support* of these sets is counted during the pass over the data. In subsequent passes, the algorithm initializes with dynamic value sets based on dynamic values found to be frequent in the previous pass. After the second of the passes, the *causal rules* are determined and they become the candidates for the dynamic policy. In the *DCM* process, the main goal is to find the strong dynamic causal rule in order to form a policy. It also represents a filtering process that prunes away static attributes, which reduces the size of the data set for further mining.

The process time would be n^2-n, where n is the number of attributes. This becomes a huge problem if n becomes too large. It is obvious that the task becomes much simpler if the size of n could be reduced before the search.

Figure 7. The steps of DCM

Part 1: – Preprocessing: Removal of the "least" causal data from database
Part 2: – Mining: Formation of a rule set that covers all training examples with minimum number of rules
Part 3: – Checking: Check if an attribute pair is self contradicting (sympathetic and antipathetic at the same time)

Input: The original database, the values of the pruning threshold for the neutral, sympathetic and antipathetic *supports*.
Output: Dynamic sets
Step 1: Check the nature of the attributes in the original database (numerical or categorical). Initialize a new database with dynamic attributes based on the attributes and time stamps from original database.

Step 2: Initialize a counter for each of the three polarities.

Step3: Prune away all the dynamic attributes with *supports* above the input thresholds.

Figure 8. The checking step of DCM

Input: The mined database, the values of the pruning threshold for the supports of the polarity combinations.
Output: Dynamic sets
Step 1. Check weather a rule is self-contradictory (a rule is both sympathetic and antipathetic).
Step 2. If step 1 returns true then
Retrieve the attribute pair form the preprocessed database
Step Initialize a counter that includes polarity combination
Step 4. For the pair of attributes
Count the occurrence of polarity combination with two records each time.
Prune away the pairs if the counted support is below the input threshold.

EXPERIMENT

Data Preparation

The overall aim is to identify hidden dynamic changes. The original data was given as shown in Table 11. The only data of interest are the data with changes, for example sale amounts of a product, the time stamp, etc,. The rest of the static data, such as the weight and the cost of the product can be removed.

After cleaning the data, the *dynamic attributes* are found as shown in Figure 9. The *dynamic attribute* is calculated by finding the difference between sales amounts in one month and sales amounts in the previous month.#

In the next step, the neutral attributes are pruned. The idea of pruning is to remove redundant dynamic attributes; thus fewer sets of attributes are required when generating rules. The first pruning is based on the single attribute *support*. In this case, the single attribute *support* is defined to be 0.5, which means that if an attribute with polarity +, -, or 0 occurs in more than half of total time stamps, it will be pruned. In this case, 429 attributes remain for the rule generation.

In this experiment, dynamic sets are compared based on a simultaneous *time stamp*. Then the support of *sympathetic* and *antipathetic* rules for each dynamic set is calculated. The *support* is used as the threshold to eliminate unsatisfac-

Applying Dynamic Causal Mining in E-Government Modeling

Table 11. Original data sets

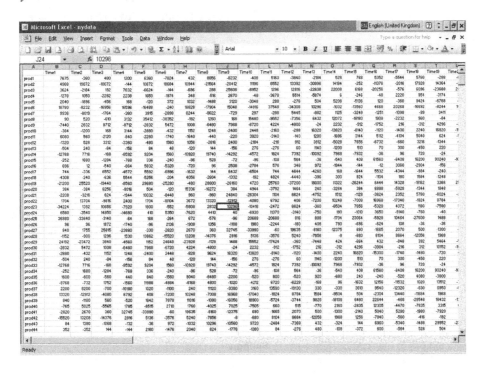

Table 12. Dynamic attributes

213

Figure 9. Rule plot with support level = 0

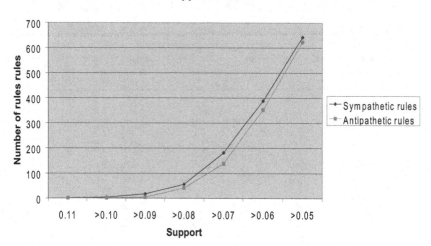

tory dynamic sets and to obtain the rules from the satisfactory sets.

Evaluation and Results

The algorithm was run based on the procedures described in previous sections. Figure 9 shows the plot of sympathetic and antipathetic support.

The x –axis represents the support and the y-axis represents the number of rules. This database shows that there are more sympathetic rules than antipathetic rules. The figure shows that increasing support will lead to exponential growth of the rules. As the support reaches 0.05 or 5, as it indicates on the figure, the number of rules is 630. Most of these rules are redundant and have no meaning due to the low support. Figure 10

Figure 10. Rule plot with support level equal to the average value

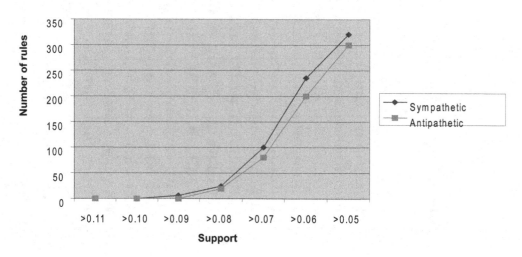

Table 13. Result generated by the algorithm

Strong Rules	Support
Sympathetic	
{C15276179, F030008}	0,093
{J08008008, F060010}	0,089
{A04004004, A05005005}	0,086
{A05005006, C10251104}	0,084
{A04004004, F100020}	0,082
Antipathetic	
{A05005008, C15276179}	0.092
{C10251104, F070010}	0.083
{A05005008, F030008}	0.082

shows the rule plot with support equal to average value, where the +support = the average of all positive records and −support = the average of all negative records. The number of rules has decreased by applying the support level.

Table 13 shows the extracted strong rules with support level equal to average value and support larger than 0.08. There are only dynamic pairs so there is no need to do the simulation

DISCUSSION

Apriori provides some form of causal information, i.e. suggesting a possible direction of causation between two attributes, but there is no basis to conclude that the arrow indicates direct or even indirect causation. The *DCM* algorithm, on the other hand, shows causality between attributes. Thus, where association rule generation techniques find surface associations, causal inference algorithms identify the structure underlying such associations.

Each type of relationship generated by the *DCM* algorithm provides additional information. The *DCM* algorithm finds four kinds of relationships, each of which deepens the user's understanding of their target system by constructing the possible models. For example, $A_1 \rightarrow^+ A_2$

provides more information than $A_1 \rightarrow A_2$ because the latter indicates that A_1 coexists with A_2. The condition of the rule is not stated (whether sympathetic or antipathetic). A genuine causality such as $A_1 \rightarrow^+ A_2$ provides useful information because it indicates that the relationship from A_1 to A_2 is strictly sympathetic causal.

The *rules* extracted by *DCM* can be simulated by using software to model the future behavior. The *rules* extracted by association algorithm cannot be simulated.

FUTURE RESEARCH DIRECTIONS

A number of aspects of the algorithms developed in this research could be improved. Parallel techniques, such as those based on lattices, can be introduced to *DCM* to reduce the time needed by the algorithm to find dynamic causal rules for a list of objects.

Another possible area of work might be to study different kinds of fuzzy relations that can be necessary in order to apply DCM to the analysis of fuzzy databases, in particular, when different ways to represent uncertainty and imprecision are employed in the database model.

The thesis has presented one type of measure based on the support of the rules. Alternative measures may be useful for some applications. An example might be partial completeness measure based on the range of the attributes in the rules.

Visualizing the output is an interesting research problem, since standard techniques do not scale beyond a few hundred attributes and very simple DCM rules. A problem is developing high-quality, easy-to-generate domain-specific or application-specific, visualizations.

CONCLUSION

This chapter provides insight into how to use dynamic causal mining approaches to E-government research can be addressed through management strategies specifically designed to respond.

The algorithm shows opportunities for more extensive examination of E-government as well as produces a framework for such analysis. A mining framework will provide E-government researchers, as well as researchers interested in other complex social phenomena, with insights into determining the best research design given a specific context.

This chapter addresses important and challenging issues of causal analysis within E-government and implementation of causality extraction and construction algorithms for E-government data. This chapter also studied the computational costs of causal, and has implemented a multi pruning approach for building models that incurs minimal computational cost while maintaining accuracy and unsupervised causality extraction algorithms to reduce the reliance on E-government data.

The work presented in this chapter is the first step towards constructing and managing e-government based on one of data mining techniques. There lacks a proper user friendly interface. And there are other techniques such as clustering and classification to explore.

REFERENCES

Agrawal, R., Mannila, H., Srikant, R., Toivonen, H., & Inkeri. A. (1996). *Fast Discovery of Association Rules, Advances in Knowledge Discovery and Data Mining*. The Association for the Advancement of Artificial Intelligence and The MIT Press, 307–328.

Andersen, D.F. and Richardson, G.P. (1997) Scripts for Group model Building. *System Dynamics Review, 13* 2, 107-129.

Andersen, D.F., Richardson, G.P. and Vennix, J.A.M. (1997) Group Model Building: Adding More Science to the Craft. *System Dynamics Review, 13* 2. , 187-201.

ASPA. (2001). *American society for public administration home page*. Retrieved May 12, 2002, from www.aspanet.org

Bennet, A. (2002). *Where the model frequently meets the road: Combining statistical, formal, and case study methods*. Paper presented at the American Political Science Association Conference, Boston, MA.

Bourquard, J. A. (2003). What's up with e-government? Retrieved April 6, 2005, from http://www.ncsl.org/programs/pubs/slmag/2003/303egov.htm

Cheung, D., Han, J., Ng, V. T. & Fu, A.W. (1996). Fast distributed algorithm for mining association rules. In *International Conference on Parallel and Distributed Information Systems*, Tokyo, Japan, 31–42.

Cook, M., & LaVigne, M. (2002). Making the local e-gov connection. Retrieved May 24, 2002, from www.urbanicity.org/FullDoc.asp?ID=36

Courty, P. and Marschke, G.: (1997) Measuring Government Performance: Lessons from a Federal Job-Training Program. The American Economic Review 87 383–388

Chan, P., Fan W., Prodromidis, A. and Stolfo, S.(1999) Distributed data mining in credit card fraud detection. *IEEE Intelligent Systems*, pages 67–74, Nov/Dec.

Coyle, R. G. (1996). *System dynamics Modelling: A Practical Approach*, London, Chapman and Hall.

Creswell, J. W. (2003). *Research design. Qualitative, quantitative, and mixed methods approaches.* Thousand Oaks, CA: SAGE Publications.

Dawes, S. S., Pardo, T., & DiCaterino, A. (1999). Crossing the threshold: Practical foundations for government services on the world wide web. *Journal of the American Society for Information Science, 50*(4), 346-35.

Dawes, S. S., & Pardo, T. A. (2002). Building collaborative digital government systems. Systematic constraints and effective practices. In W. J. McIver & A. K. Elmagarmid (Eds.), *Advances in digital government. Technology, human factors, and policy* (pp. 259- 273). Norwell, MA: Kluwer Academic Publishers.

Davies, T. R. (2004). Bypassing the revolution. Could it be that e-gov was never on track to transform the performance of state and local governments? Retrieved April 6, 2005, from http://governing.com/articles/10tech.htm.

Eskin. E. (2000)Anomaly detection over noisy data using learned probability distributions. In *Proceedings of the Seventeenth International Conference on Machine Learning (ICML- 2000).*

Flood, R. (1999). *Rethinking the fifth discipline. Learning within the unknowable*, Ruthledge, London

Forrester, J. W. (1961). Industrial Dynamics: A Major Breakthrough for Decision Makers. *Harvard Business Review*, July-August, 37-66.Fountain, J. E. (2001).

Forrest, S., Hofmeyr, S. A. , Somayaji, A. and Longstaff. (1996)T. A. A sense of self for unix processes. In *In 1996 IEEE Symposium on Security and Privacy*, pages 120–128. IEEE Computer Society.*Building the virtual state. Information technology and institutional change.* Washington, D.C.: Brookings Institution Press.

Garson, G. D. (2004). The promise of digital government. In A. Pavlichev & G. D. Garson (Eds.), *Digital government: Principles and best practices* (pp. 2-15). Hershey, PA: Idea Group Publishing.

Gartner. (2000). Gartner says u.S. E-government spending to surpass $6.2 billion by 2005. Retrieved April 6, 2005, from http://www.gartner.com/5_about/press_room/pr20000411c.html

Gil-Garcia, J. R. (2005). *Enacting state websites: A mixed method study exploring e-government success in multi-organizational settings.* Unpublished Doctoral Dissertation, University at Albany, State University of New York, Albany, NY.

Gil-García, J. R., Luna-Reyes, L.F.(2003): Towards a Definition of Electronic Government: A Comparative Review. In: Mendez-Vilas, A., et al. (eds.): Techno-legal Aspects of the Information Society and New Economy: An Overview. Formatex. Badajoz, Spain.

Gil-Garcia, J. R., & Martinez-Moyano, I. J. (2005). *Exploring e-government evolution: The influence of systems of rules on organizational action.* Cambridge, MA: National Center for Digital Government, Kennedy School of Government, Harvard University, Working Paper No. 05-001.

Gil-Garcia, J. R., & Luna-Reyes, L. F. (2006). Integrating conceptual approaches to e-government. In M. Khosrow-Pour (Ed.), *Encyclopedia of e-commerce, e-government and mobile commerce.* Hershey, PA: Idea Group Inc.

Gil-Garcia J. R.and Pardo , T. A. (2006). Multimethod Approaches to Understanding the Complexity of e-government. *International Journal of Computers, Systems and Signals, Vol.7, No.2*

Ghosh A.and Schwartzbard A. (1999) A study in using neural networks for anomaly and misuse detection. In *Proceedings of the Eighth USENIX Security Symposium.*

Heeks, R. (2003). Success and failure rates of egovernment in developing/transitional countries: Overview. from www.egov4dev.org/sfoverview.htm

Helman P. and Bhangoo. J. (1997) A stiatistically base system for prioritizing information exploration under uncertainty. *IEEE Transactions on Systems, Man and Cybernetics, Part A: Systems and Humans*, 27(4):449–466.

Hiller, J. S., & Bélanger, F. (2001). Privacy strategies for electronic government. In M. A. Abramson & G. E. Means (Eds.), *E-government 2001* (pp. 162-198). Lanham, Maryland: Rowman & Littlefield Publishers.

Hofmeyr, S. A., Forrest, S. and Somayaji. A. (1998) Intrusion detect using sequences of system calls. *Journal of Computer Security*, 6:151–180.

Holmes, D. (2001). *E.Gov. E-business strategies for government.* London: Nicholas Brealey Publishing.

Javitz H. S. and Valdes. A. (1998) The nides statistical component: description and justification. In *Technical Report, Computer Science Labratory, SRI International.*

Jonas, J.and Harper, J. (2006), *Effective Counterterrorism and the Limited Role of Predictive Data Mining*, CATO Institute Policy Analysis No. 584, December11, [http://www.cato.org/pubs/pas/pa584.pdf].

Kraemer, K. L., & King, J. L. (2003, September 29). *Information technology and administrative reform: Will the time after e-government be different?* Paper presented at the HeinrichReinermann

Schrift fest, Post Graduate School of Administration, Speyer, Germany.

Lane T. and Brodley. C. E. (1999) Temporal sequence learning and data reduction for anomaly detection. *ACM Transactions on Information and System Security*, 2:295–331.

Lane T. and Brodley. C. E. (1997) Sequence matching and learning in anomaly detection for computer security. In *Proceedings of the AAAI-97 Workshop on AI Approaches to Fraud Detection and Risk Management*, pages 43–49. Menlo Park, CA: AAAI Press..

Layne, K., & Lee, J. (2001). Developing fully functional e-government: A four stage model. *Government Information Quarterly, 18*(2), 122-136.

Lee W. and Stolfo. S. J. (1998) Data mining approaches for intrusion detection. In *In Proceedings of the 1998 USENIX Security Symposium.*

Lee, W. Stolfo, S. J. and Chan. P. K. (1997) Learning patterns from unix processes execution traces for intrusion detection. In *In AAAI Workshop on AI Approaches to Fraud Detection and Risk Management*, pages 50–56. AAAI Press.

Lee,W., Stolfo, S. J. and Mok. K. (1999). Data mining in work flow environments: Experiences in intrusion detection. In *Proceedings of the 1999 Conference on Knowledge Discovery and Data Mining (KDD-99).*

Makulowich, J. (1999) "Government Data Mining Systems Defy Definition," *Washington Technology*, 22 February, [http://www.washingtontechnology.com/news/13_22/tech_ features/393-html].

Martinez-Moyano, I. J. and Gil-Garcia, J. R. (2004) Rules, Norms, and Individual Preferences for Action: An Institutional Framework to Understand the Dynamics of e-Government Evolution, November 05, Springer Berlin / Heidelberg.

Newman, I., & Benz, C. R. (1998). *Qualitative-quantitative research methodology. Exploring the interactive continuum.* Carbondale and Edwardsville, IL: Southern Illinois University Press.

Pham, D.T., Wang, Y. & Dimov, S. (2005). Intelligfent Manufacturing strategy selection. *Proc 1st Int Virtual Conf on Intelligent Production Machines and Systems* Oxford: Elsevier. 312-318.

Pham, D.T., Wang, Y., & Dimov, S. (2006). Incorporating delay and feedback in intelligent manufacturing strategy selection. *Proc 2nd Int Virtual Conf on Intelligent Production Machines and Systems.* Oxford: Elsevier. 246-252.

Pulliam, D. (2005). E-gov spending expected to rise, despite congressional dissatisfaction. Retrieved December 11, 2006, from http://www.govexec.com/dailyfed/1204/010605p1.htm

Reddick, C. G. (2004). A two-stage model of e-government growth: Theories and empirical evidence for u.S. Cities. *Government Information Quarterly, 21*, 51-64.

Richardson, G. P.(1996) System Dynamics. In: Gass, S.I., Harris, C.M. (eds.): Encyclopedia of Operations Research and Management Science. Kluwer Academic Publishers. Boston 656-660.

Richardson, G.P. (1999) Citation for winner of the 1999 Jay W Forrester Award: Jac Vennix. *System Dynamics Review, 15* 4., 375-377.

Richardson, G.P. and Andersen, D.F. Teamwork in group model building. *System Dynamics Review, 11* 2. (1995), 113-137.

Seifert, J W. (2007)Data Mining and Homeland Security: An Overview. Crs report for congress. June 5.

Senge, P., Kleiner, A., Roberts, C., Ross, R., & Smith, B. (1994). *The fifth discipline fieldbook.* New York: Doubleday.

Sobirey, M., Richter, B. and Konig. M. (1996) The intrusion detection system aid. architecture, and experiences in automated audit analysis. In *Proc. of the IFIP TC6 / TC11 International Conference on Communications and Multimedia Security,* pages 278 – 290, Essen, Germany.

Sterman, J. D. (1994). Learning in and about Complex Systems. *System dynamics Review.* Volume 10 (2-3), 291-330.

Sterman, J. D. (2000). Business Dynamics: Systems Thinking and Modelling for a Complex World, Irwin McGraw-Hill, Boston, MA

Stolfo, S. J., Prodromidis, A. L., Tselepis, S., Lee, W. Fan, D. W. and Chan. P. K. (1997) JAM: Java agents for meta-learning over distributed databases. In *Proceedings of the 3rd International Conference on Knowledge Discovery and Data Mining,* pages 74–81, Newport Beach, CA, August. AAAI Press.

Stolfo, S. J., Fan, W. Lee, W., Prodromidis, A. and Chan. P. (2000) Cost-sensitive modeling for fraud and intrusion detection: Results from the JAM project. In *Proceedings of the 2000 DARPA Information Survivability Conference and Exposition,* January.

Teng, H. S., Chen, K. and Lu. S. C. (1990)Adaptive real-time anomaly detection using inductively generated sequential patterns. In *Proceedings of the IEEE Symposium on Research in Security and Privacy,* pages 278–284, Oakland CA, May.

UN & ASPA. (2002). *Benchmarking e-government: A global perspective.* New York: United Nations Division of Public Economics and Public Administration and the American Society for Public Administration.

UNPAN. (2002). Unpan e-government. Retrieved July 8, 2002, from www.unpan.org/egovernment.asp

Vennix, J.A.M. (1999) Group Model-Building: Tackling Messy Problems. *System Dynamics Review, 15* 4., 379-401.

Wang, Y. (2007). Integration of data mining with *Game theory, Journal of International Federation for Information Processing,* Volume 207/2006, Boston: Springer, pp 275-280.

Warrender, C., Forrest, S. and Pearlmutter. B. (1999) Detecting intrusions using system calls: alternative data models. In *In 1999 IEEE Symposium on Security and Privacy*, pages 133– 145. IEEE Computer Society.

Zagonel, A.S.(2002)., Model Conceptualization in Group Model Building: A Review of the Literature Exploring the Tension Between Representing Reality and Negotiating a Social Order. in *Proceedings of the 20th International Conference of the System Dynamics Society*, Palermo. Italy,

Zaki, M. J., Parthasarathy, S., Ogihara, M. & Li, W. (1997). New Parallel Algorithms for Fast Discovery of Association Rules, *Data Mining and Knowledge Discovery*, Vol. 1, No. 4, 343-37.

Chapter XIII
Ontology-Based Management of e-Government Knowledge

Yannis Charalabidis
National Technical University of Athens, Greece

Kostas Metaxiotis
National Technical University of Athens, Greece

ABSTRACT

In an effort to follow the new public administration roadmap but also invest in the sharing of knowledge, governmental organizations appear in a crossroad: a lot of knowledge has been created, organized and even digitized but still it cannot be considered available anywhere, anytime, for any citizen, business or other organization. The more scientists and managers study the issue, the more they realize that it is a question of "crossing the desert" than "jumping over the gap". Making governmental knowledge available to its final beneficiaries requires the design, development and deployment of a Federated Knowledge Registry, as the platform to cater for the formal description, composition and publishing of the governmental services canvas. Such a system will manage traditional or web services, together with the relevant electronic documents and the process descriptions, in an integrated schema. Touching upon all knowledge management processes from knowledge capture, knowledge sharing, to knowledge creation, the chapter goes beyond the methodology and tools used for developing such a system for the Greek Government, to the integration and the diffusion of eGovernment knowledge with the help of formal ontology definitions - capturing the core elements of the domain together with their main relationships.

INTRODUCTION

Today's private and public organizations come across a vast volume of knowledge and information. Public administrations are knowledge-intensive organizations. They host a particularly high percentage of professionals and specialized staff who command important domains of knowledge. This is particularly the case in ministerial departments, in the judiciary and in regulatory agencies. The necessity of efficient knowledge management is not only derived from this fact, but also from the high knowledge intensity of products and services, the continuous transformation and the special requirements and constraints of the public sector.

The concept of knowledge management (KM) is not new to the public sector; either intentionally or unintentionally, KM initiatives have always been integrated in government tasks, inseparable from strategy, planning, consultation and implementation (Metaxiotis et al., 2005a). More and more governments are realizing the importance of KM to its policy-making and service delivery to the public and some of the government departments are beginning to put KM high on their agenda. Societal responsibilities, for delivering public policy that benefit the common good further enhance the importance of effective KM in public services (Wiig, 2002). Furthermore, governments are under continual pressure from the society to increase their effectiveness and quality with fewer resources and better systems, by making use of ICT and web technologies (Metaxiotis et al., 2005b). E-Government is presented as a key solution towards this societal pressure for better public services delivery.

E-Government implies fundamental knowledge redistribution and requires a careful rethinking of the management of information resources and knowledge bases. Ample access to remote information and knowledge resources is needed in order to facilitate:

- Citizens' and businesses' oriented service delivery including one-stop service provision,
- Inter-organisational co-operation among governmental agencies
- Cross-border support for complex administrative decision making.

In this chapter, the authors, recognizing the importance of eGovernment and KM to devolve into the public administration sector, present a conceptual analysis of ontology-based management of eGovernment knowledge, define the ontological context of eGovernment knowledge, throw light on important aspects of this field and build avenues for future research.

The overall purpose of the presented approach is to provide for effective knowledge management within and during eGovernment transformation projects. Based on the fact that eGovernment transformation is engaging vast amount of diverse knowledge sources and elements, the presented approach is aiming to act as a propagation mechanism that would automatically diffuse the necessary knowledge, both within the public sector organisations and towards the final users of services. Such a mechanism would be able to provide citizens, businesses and public sector employees with the necessary pieces of knowledge in order to identify and use, but also compose and manage electronic services.

Touching upon all knowledge management processes from knowledge capture, to knowledge sharing, the chapter goes beyond the methodology and tools used for developing such a system for the Greek Government, to the integration and the diffusion of eGovernment knowledge with the help of formal ontology definitions - capturing the core elements of the domain together with their main relationships. Lessons learned include areas where technology meets society, such as the definition of eGovernment service category lists, life events and business episodes, government metadata standards and service orientation in the everyday operation of administrations.

MANAGEMENT OF PUBLIC ADMINISTRATION KNOWLEDGE

Managing knowledge to provide better public administration is not new. Building personal expertise in public servants is traditional; training programs, certifications and other approaches have long been used successfully (Wiig, 1993). However, in the current knowledge-based economy modernization and re-organization of public administration's and governmental work and responsibilities imply significant changes to knowledge resources. Most "products" of public administration's and governance's work are delivered in the shape of information and knowledge themselves. This mainly applies to policies, management, regulation and monitoring of society, market and environment. Besides, retirement of civil servants and frequent transfer of knowledge workers across government departments create new needs for the retention of knowledge and preservation of institutional memory and the training of new staff.

In an effort to follow the new public administration roadmap and also invest in the sharing of knowledge, governmental organizations appear in a crossroad: a lot of knowledge has been created, organized and even digitized but still it cannot be considered available anywhere, anytime, for any citizen, business or other organization. Nowadays it is widely recognized (Bresciani et al., 2003; Palkovits et al., 2003) that in order to efficiently manage public administration knowledge it is fundamental to transform the public administration into a learning organization, characterized by a high sharing, reuse and strategic application of the acquired knowledge and lessons learnt. A learning organization is an organization which facilitates the learning of all its members and continuously transforms itself. The basic idea

behind it is to create a knowledge chain (collection, production, customization and delivery), suitable to support and improve the whole organization functioning. In this context, the public administration knowledge to be managed can be used for the following:

- Transformation of Governmental services and processes
- Composition of new services
- Training of Public Administration officials
- Setting up goals and metrics for measuring e-Government progress
- Achievement of Interoperability and one-stop services composition
- Building or transforming information systems
- Assisting user access to electronic services
- Diffusion of new electronic services towards citizens and enterprises
- Setting up large initiatives (such as the Digital Strategy of a country, lighthouse projects involving Public Administration and IT companies)
- New research approaches in eGovernment

Administrations feel that the rapid reuse and overall exploitation of any relevant piece of quality information can significantly speed up implementations or reduce risks during eGovernment transformation at operational level. The more scientists and managers study the issue, the more they realize that it is a question of "crossing the desert" than "jumping over the gap". Towards this need for a systematic approach to managing knowledge coming from numerous, ever-changing organizations, several new approaches are emerging (Charalabidis et al., 2008): semantic enrichment, eGovernment ontologies, knowledge management and service orientation are currently spotlighted - as they extend their scope at theoretical and practical level, with the view to oppose the tendency of reinventing the wheel at the public sector and to gain from relevant business examples.

Due to the fact that public administrations - and their organizational environment – are characterized by the presence of very diverse kinds of actors (e.g. citizens, employees, businesses, politicians and decision-makers), the critical point for applying a KM concept to eGovernment is principally to build a suitable knowledge model and then to find the materials appropriate to feed the knowledge chain. On this basis, Metaxiotis (2007) proposed a framework for the application of KM in eGovernment, as presented in Table 1; the current authors' conceptual analysis of ontology-based management of eGovernment knowledge which is presented in the following sections is regarded as a step forward to this research.

DEFINING THE ONTOLOGICAL CONTEXT OF E-GOVERNMENT KNOWLEDGE

The main categorizations of knowledge found within the eGovernment domain, the space where public administrations and their systems meet citizens and businesses during service provision and interaction, take in mind the form, origin and characteristics of the knowledge to be modeled. Different levels of organisation and digitization are quite important as they demand for relevant input, access and retrieval facilities. Driven by generic knowledge management classification (Davenport et al. 1998, Guarino et al. 1999), initial public administration knowledge analysis (Lenk, 2003) and recent approaches of the eGovernment era (Eyob, 2004), such categorization yields the following broad groupings:

Table 1. The application of KM in e-Government

E-Government Phases	Application of Knowledge Management
1. PUBLISH These actions use ICT to expand access to government information, so that citizens and businesses do not have to travel to governmental offices and stand in long queue. This phase serves as the leading edge of e-government.	Knowledge is required on how to present information clearly online, how to manage its publication and how customers are likely to use the information. Knowledge is also required and can be transferred concerning the design, completion and processing of forms and other documents.
2. INTERACT The objective of these actions is to broaden civic participation in government (e.g. communication among government officials and citizens about various issues, creation of citizen/government forums, etc.).	Knowledge is required on how to react "electronically" to requests from "customers". This may include knowledge on how government officials or citizens search for information and like to receive it; or how to accept and maintain "customer" information. Issues of security are also important.
3. TRANSACT The objective of these actions is to make government services available on line. By automating specific procedures and processes, such as tax and fine collection, governments can achieve to stem corruption and increase citizen's trust in government. In addition, these actions can increase productivity in both the public and private sector.	The knowledge required is concerned with the security and efficiency of the transactions (e.g. taxes, registration fees and licenses). Efficiency is achieved by smoothly interfacing the online system with back-office processing systems. Issues of trust are very important.

Figure 1. Trends within the e-Government knowledge space

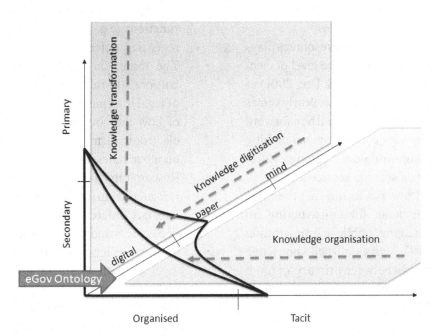

- Knowledge can be primary or secondary, depending on whereas a source is self-standing or it succeeds and extends pre-existing knowledge.
- Knowledge can be found in digital form, in paper or not captured and illustrated at all.
- Knowledge bears a level of "self organization", ranging from fully organized (indexed, searchable, interoperable) to tacit.

It is worth to be noted that, during eGovernment transformation, the tendency of the stakeholders is to manage the shift towards "digital" and "organized" forms of knowledge representation. Concerning the Primary-Secondary axis, web technologies offer now a way to instantly reuse content created elsewhere, allowing for unique descriptions of elements with a clear owner.

So, as indicated in Figure 1, it can be claimed that valid approaches for creating an ontology for managing eGovernment knowledge should at least start form the designated – core – area. In such a way, an ontology can provide the basis

for indexing, retrieving and reusing knowledge as knowledge pours from brains into systems, moving from tacit to organized.

SOURCES OF E-GOVERNMENT KNOWLEDGE

Going further in analyzing the sources and nature of knowledge elements in the public administration domain, as also in Wimmer (2000), Grossman (1995) and Deakins et al. (2002), one can identify the following artifacts:

- Governmental information concerning the structure and operation of the state, such as legal elements, organizational descriptions, communications, service descriptions, even press releases.
- Electronic government related information, such as electronic forms, services, systems and data bases.
- More generic supporting resources, such as best practice databases, books, research papers or other publication.

- Information on specific public administration offices, enterprises or citizens.

Each of the above sources and resources plays an important role, according to the level of electronic service provision (Layne & Lee, 2001) as depicted in Table 2. This illustration clearly shows that knowledge management should be a forward looking activity, always classifying and making available the most up-to-date and complex information elements at a specific service level.

Going further, towards identifying the main informational elements for constructing an ontology for managing public administration knowledge, up to 17 sources of such knowledge can be identified, split between primary, or more primitive, sources and secondary or derived ones, as depicted in Figure 2:

- Citizen, Enterprise and Public Administration recognition information, either as existing registrations and systems or as on-coming fully digital identification infrastructures, play a vital role. Such knowledge can be complex enough, since the information needed during eGovernment service provision usually has to provide for multiple

roles or the citizen or the enterprise, within different contexts in Public Administration functions (e.g. finance, health, civil order, registries, defense, etc).

- The main, large Public Administration corpora still relies among several millions of legal information pages and descriptions of how the government works – lately in electronic form in many European Union member states and US.

- Research and literature also provides useful information in the form of Books, Research Papers, Conference Proceedings, Best Practice reports and relevant documentation.

- Public services, documents, data forms together with their annotation metadata and the corresponding process descriptions certainly are in the core of knowledge management processes – especially when targeting eGovernment service provision.

- Finally, data and knowledge bases, together with back-office and front-office systems offer their share as dynamic sources of supportive knowledge in organized or indexed digital form.

Table 2. Importance of various knowledge resources, per level of services

	L1 Information Only	L2 Information & Downloads	L3 Full electronic application	L4 Complete transaction
Static Government Information	Critical	Important	Already there	Already there
e-Government Knowledge and Systems	Important	Critical	Critical	Important
Research and Practice Resources	Not needed	Important.	Important	Critical
Citizen and Enterprise knowledge	Not needed	Not needed	Important	Critical

Figure 2. Sources of e-Government knowledge

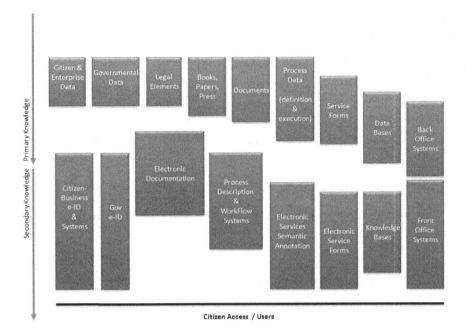

AN ONTOLOGY FOR E-GOVERNMNET KNOWLEDGE

The representation means of the proposed ontology should first capture the core elements of the domain, together with their main relationships. Most existing approaches for e-government ontologies cover neighboring domains, such as Public Administration Knowledge (Fraser et al 2003, Wimmer 2003), Argumentation in Service Provision (DIP Project, 2004), eGovernment project implementation (DAML, 2006), or types and actors in national governments (US Government 2002). As depicted in Figure 3, the proposed high level eGovernment Ontology provides for the representation of the following core elements:

- Policy related knowledge, such as legal elements, directives, policy programmes for eGovernment transformation and so on.
- Administration related knowledge elements, containing subclasses for Documents and Services Descriptions, ProcessMaps, Organogrammes, or codifications of Public

Administration Organisations and Operations.
- Implementation related information, consisting of documentation of public tenders for IT eGovernment projects, project deliverables or resulting systems, being back-office, front-office or web portals providing the electronic services.
- Practice-related information, containing descriptions of Best Practices, Methodologies or more generic Surveys and Reports.
- Research related knowledge elements, in the forms of Books, Scientific Papers, Research Prototypes, Surveys or Studies.

All the above are sub-classes of the main Class Knowledge Element, which holds the main attributes for classifying and indexing knowledge, shown in Table 3.

As further shown in Figure 2, the Core Ontology Layer of the a generic eGovernment Ontology should be extendible and easy to populate with real examples. Based on the application, deep-level metadata attributes may be inserted, as analysed

Figure 3. Classes of the core e-Government ontology layer

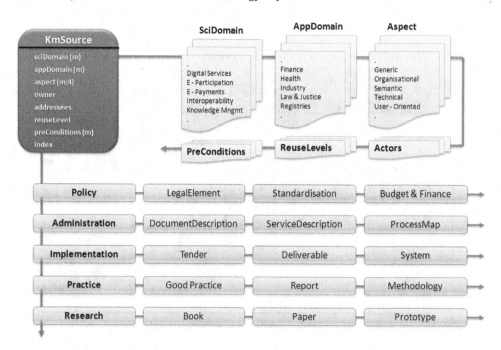

Table 3. Attributes of knowledge element class

Attribute	Description
sciDomain (m)	Scientific Domain of the element (values from the SciDomain tree)
appDomain (m)	Application Domain of the element (values from the AppDomain tree)
aspect (m:4)	Organisational, Semantic, Technical or Generic
owner	The owner Organisation.
addressees	The groups where the knowledge element may be addressed to.
reuseLevel	The estimated reusability level for the resource (high, medium, low).
preConditions (m)	The necessary preconditions for the re-application of the resource.
index	Indexing information for retrieving purposes (electronic or paper storage).

in the next section. Such applications may contain information on:

- Administrations, nested at infinite hierarchical levels, being ministries, regions, municipalities, organizations or their divisions and departments.
- Web Services, being electronically provided services, either final or intermediate ones (contributing to the provision of final services).
- Various formal representaions, such as XML (eXtensible Markup Language) Schema Definitions, BPMN (Business Process Modelling Notation) Models, or WSDL (Web Services Definition Language) Descriptions, linking Web Services with the respective systematic, machine readable description of their behavior.

Finally, additional rules and methods applicable to an eGovernment related ontology may be related to collaborative design (Holsapple et al., 2002), data access and search functions

(Hovy, 2003) or broader suggestions on formal definition, population and transformation (Jones et al, 1998).

APPLICATIONS

A case on ontology-based management of eGovernment is being introduced in this section. For sake of illustration, various activities and service characteristics of the Ministry of Public Administration of Greece have been discussed.

Initial Population of the eGovernment Ontology was greatly assisted by the existence of data in electronic form, through the Greek Ministry of Public Administration. As shown in Table 4, even for a country close to the average European Union Member State population (11,000,000 citizens), the size of the domain is significant, involving thousands of governmental points, services and document types.

Furthermore, a plethora of information systems are currently under development, during the new Greek Digital Strategy plan, aiming to

Table 4. Size of the domain in Greece

Organisational Aspect
18 ministries, 13 prefectures, 52 districts, 1,024 municipalities, 690 public sector organizations
2,500 Governmental "Points of Service"
Services and Data Aspect
3,000 non-interoperable Service Types (Government to Citizens and Businesses)
4,500 Document Types exchanged between Administrations
Systems Aspect
300 Central Government Internet Portals
1,000 Municipal Government Internet Portals
2,500 Public Administration Back Office Systems
Users Aspect
750,000 Enterprises (small, medium and large)
11,000,000 Citizens
18,000,000 Tourists per year
1,000 IT products and services companies

achieve full electronic operation of the State by 2013 (Charalabidis et al, 2007).

Population of the ontology was achieved through the following automated and semi-automated activities:

- Automated import of 1,797 administrations including ministries, prefectures, districts, municipalities and public sector organisations.
- Automated import of 1,009 public services definitions, with core metadata descriptions and frequency indications, stemming out of 3,000,000 service requests by citizens and businesses during the last year.
- Modelling of the core-100 governmental services (including all i2010 services and the services amounting to 85% of the yearly service requests),
- Modelling of the core XML schemas and WSDL for Web Services to be developed – an activity that is still going on.
- Representation and indexing of hundreds of books, papers, documents and best practice descriptions, found either in libraries or in publicly available web sites.
- Representation and indexing of hundreds of eGovernment administration project tenders and relevant deliverables.

The resulting platform is now being maintained and further populated with the assistance of engaged public administrations. Already, crucial questions of administrations can be answered, like:

- What is the formal description of the Birth Certificate Issuing service ?
- Which services are depending on identity card provision ?
- What are the most needed services by other services (interoperability request) ?
- What are the needed documents and their XML definitions for issuing a residence permit ?

- Which services pertaining to civil registries are already electronic at level 2 or 3 ?
- What are the existing Web Services from the Tax Authorities – Ministry of Finance ?
- Where can evidence be found for the current status of electronic service provision in Greece and the rest 24 EU Member States for the last 3 years ?

The acceptance of the eGovernment Ontology by the Greek Public Administration is following a three-stage approach, involving: (a) the core ontology development team, including the Ministry of Public Administration and the National eGovernment Framework team, (b) the main Public Sector stakeholders, including key ministries, organisations and local administrations and (c) eGovernment project managers and implementation teams, from the public and private sector.

As previously presented, specific metadata are inserted for each specific subclass of Knowledge Element. An example of extended characteristics, needed for the categorisation of a Public Service is shown in Table 5.

FUTURE RESEARCH DIRECTIONS

Current research results bearing significant applications worldwide, show that eGovernment knowledge ontologies can assist in constructing truly semantically enriched repositories for distributed management and cross-utilization of public administration knowledge; provided of course that application is performed with care: knowledge should be constantly maintained, updated and assessed - and these tasks cannot be fully automated, yet.

Future work in the domain should be expected to follow a multi-direction approach: ontological definition and formalization should dive further into the elements of knowledge, providing for

Table 5. Public service characteristics (metadata) and values

Field	Description, Type	Data
Code	The Service Code, Unique, String	00_18
Title	The Service Title, Unique, String	Passport Issuance
Providing Administration	The Administration (organization, department or office providing the service), Element	Ministry of Interior / Passports
Engaged Administration	Other Administrations, taking part in the service provision, Multi-Element	Ministry of Interior / Municipality Acc. Photographer
Final Service	Yes/No, if it is a final service, giving output to the citizens or businesses, List	Yes
Beneficiary	Citizens or Businesses or subtypes of them, Element	Citizens
Type	The Service Type, (e.g. Registration, Benefit, Application, Payment, etc), List	Certificates
Category	Service Category, according to GCL (e.g. social service, taxation, education), Element	Civil Services \ Certificate Services \ Passport Issuance
Life Event	The associated Life Event, Element	Gain ability to travel
Business Event	The associated Business Event, Multi-Element	Null
Legal Framework	The applying legal framework for the service, Multi-Element	Gr. Law 3103/2003
Ways of Provision	Manual, Internet, SMS, I-TV, etc., Multi-List	Manual
Electronic Provision Level	Level of electronic provision (1 to 4), according with the EC standardization	2
Multilingual Content	Languages in which the content for the service exists, Multi-List	Greek English
Manual Authentication Type	Type of Authentication needed when the service is provided in a manual way (e.g. presence in person, id-card, proxy), Multi List	Presence, ID-Card
Electronic Authentication Type	Type of Authentication needed when the service is provided electronically (e.g. username/passwd, token, digital signature), List	Null
Frequency	Frequency the service is requested, by means of Requests per year	600,000
Web Site	The URL of the portal providing the service, String	www.passport.gov.gr
International Policy	Yes / No, if the service is included in the i2010 services set, List	Yes
National Policy	Yes / No, if the service is included in the Greek Digital Strategy, List	Yes
Information Source	The source(s) of information for the service, String	Greek Government / Ministry of Interior
Date of last Update	The date of last sampling, Date	01.11.2007

fresh metadata, semantic matching and fuzzy approaches; systemic approaches should provide for viewing, querying and transforming such ontologies according to diverse user needs and towards multiple end-point ICT systems; knowledge management approaches for this new field of practice should be combined with the new, social-Web oriented challenges of enhanced citizen participation. Towards these directions, the following future research challenges are foreseen:

- Codification and definition of taxonomies of values for common categorization of public sector services and documents. Such common codelists shall provide for automated semantic matching during service provision, as values for public sector organisations, officials roles, types of documents and services will be shared among all collaborating systems.
- Extension of the eGovernment Ontology towards covering additional knowledge elements of the domain, such as specialised document, system or service types.
- Creation of web services interfaces for the automated population, modification or querying of the ontology repository, allowing for semantic assistance during service provision by collaborating eGovernment systems.
- Application of the methodology in other countries, so that the overall approach can be tested and properly enhanced: initial applications in the public sector in Lithuania and Czech Republic are currently being investigated by national officials.

CONCLUSION

As shown in everyday practice, knowledge management in the public sector can be a challenging task, especially when the state services evolve towards higher levels of electronic government. Public documents, legal elements, service descriptions and all forms of information stored in back-office and front-office systems, together with RTD results and components should be organized with a view towards managing change and constant evolution.

Further analysis of knowledge elements of the Public Administration domain, heavily impacted by eGovernment transformation, is revealing important aspects and usually hidden characteristics for them: the level of organisation and digitization is crucially important as to their immediate avail-

ability; the primary or secondary nature that poses coherence constraints; their relation to the level of digitization of a service or an administration that shows their importance.

The management and utilization of these knowledge artifacts can be greatly assisted by an ontology-based approach, covering the depth and width of the domain, resulting in better knowledge organization and soon in federated systems for managing governmental knowledge. Gathering resources from existing relevant ontologies, an eGovernment ontology is presented that can cover most aspects of knowledge elements. With a initial set of extendible class and instance structures, such an ontology can provide for indexing, searching for and accessing knowledge with extended semantic aids.

On the application area, an example population with information and knowledge artifacts from the Greek Public Administration is presented, exceeding 10,000 classes and instances in volume and catering for providing assistance to more than 50 government officials. Specific examples of automated population show that some time-consuming tasks have to be tackled with a systematic approach.

REFERENCES

Bresciani, P., Donzelli, P. and Forte, A. (2003). Requirements Engineering for Knowledge Management in eGovernment. *Proceedings of 4th Working Conference on Knowledge Management in Electronic Government*, Rhodes Island, Greece.

Charalabidis, Y., Askounis D., (2008). Interoperability Registries in eGovernment: Developing a Semantically Rich Repository for Electronic Services and Documents of the new Public Administration. *Hawaiian International Conference of System Sciences, HICCS-08*, January 7-10, 2008, Hawaii.

Charalabidis Y., Lampathaki F., Stassis A. (2007). A Second-Generation e-Government Interoperability Framework. *5th Eastern European e|Gov Days 2007* in Prague, Austrian Computer Society, 2007.

DAML Government R&D Ontology, http://www. daml.org/projects/integration/ projects-20010811, 2006.

Davenport, T. and Prusak, L. (1998). *Working Knowledge: Managing What Your Organisation Knows*. Harvard Business School Press, Boston, MA.

DIP project eGovernment Ontology http://dip. semanticweb.org/documents/D9-3-improved-eGovernment.pdf, 2004.

Eyob, E. (2004). E-government: breaking the frontiers of inefficiencies in the public sector. *Electronic Government*, 1(1), 107-114.

Fraser J., Adams N., A. Macintosh, A. McKay-Hubbard, T. Pariente Lobo, P. Fernandez Pardo, R. Cañadas Martínez and J.Sobrado Vallecillo (2003). Knowledge Management Applied to E-government Services: The Use of an Ontology. *KMGov 2003, LNAI 2645*, pp. 116–126.

Grossman, L. (1995).*The Electronic Republic: Reshaping Democracy in the Information Age.* Viking, New York, NY.

Guarino, N., Giaretta, P. (1999). *Ontologies and Knowledge Bases: Towards a Terminological Clarification*. ISO Press, 1999.

Holsapple, C. W., Joshi, K. D. (2002). A collaborative approach to ontology design. *Communications of the ACM 45*, 1/2002, pp. 42–47

Hovy, E. (2003). Using an Ontology to Simplify Data Access. *Communications of the ACM 46*, 47–49.

Jones, D. M., Bench-Capon, T. J. M., Visser, P. R. S. (1998). Methodologies for Ontology Develop-

ment. *Proceedings of Information Technology and Knowledge*, IT&KNOWs, 1998.

K. Layne and J.W. Lee (2001). Developing fully functional e-government: A four stage model. *Government Information Quarterly* 18 (2), 122–136.

Lenk, K. (2003). Relating Knowledge Management in the Public Sector to Decision-Making and Administrative Action. *Proceedings of 4th Working Conference on Knowledge Management in Electronic Government*, Rhodes Island, Greece.

Metaxiotis, K. (2007). A Framework for the Application of Knowledge Management in E-Government. in the book *"Encyclopedia of Public Information Technology"* edited by Prof. Kristin Klinger, IDEA Publishing.

Metaxiotis, K. and Psarras, J. (2005b). A Conceptual Analysis of Knowledge Management in E-Government. *Electronic Government: An International Journal*, 2(1), 77-86.

Metaxiotis, K., Ergazakis, K. and Psarras, J. (2005a). Exploring the World of Knowledge Management: Agreements and Disagreements in the Research Community. *Journal of Knowledge Management*, 9(2), 6-18.

Palkovits, S., Woitsch, R. and Karagiannis, D. (2003). Process-Based Knowledge Management and Modelling in E-government – An Inevitable Combination. *Proceedings of 4th Working Conference on Knowledge Management in Electronic Government*, Rhodes Island, Greece.

US Government, CIA World Fact Book: "The Government type Ontology" http://reliant.teknowledge.com/DAML/Government.owl, 2002.

Wiig, K. (1993).*Knowledge management foundations: Thinking about thinking-how people and organizations create, represent and use knowledge*. Arlington, TX: Schema Press.

Wiig, K. (2002). Knowledge management in public administration. *Journal of Knowledge Management.* 6(3), 224-239.

Wimmer M. and Roland Traunmuller (2000). Trends in Electronic Government: Managing Distributed Knowledge. *11th International Workshop on Database and Expert Systems Applications (DEXA'00)*, pp. 340-352.

Wimmer, M. (2006). Implementing a Knowledge Portal for e-Government Based on Semantic Modeling: The e-Government Intelligent Portal (eip.at). *Proceedings of the 39th Annual Hawaii International Conference on System Sciences (HICSS'06) Track 4*, pp. 82-90.

FURTHER READINGS

Deakins, E. and Dillon, S. (2002). E-government in New Zealand: the local authority perspective. *The International Journal of Public Sector Management*, 15(5), 375-398.

Donzelli, P., Bresciani, P. (2003). Goal Oriented requirements Engineering: a case Study in eGovernment. *Proceedings of the 15th Conference on Advanced Information Systems Engineering (CAISE'03)*, Klagenfurt, Austria, 16-20 June, 2003.

Leonard, D. (1999). *Wellsprings of Knowledge – Building and Sustaining the Sources of Innovation*. Harvard Business School Press, Boston, MA.

Liebowitz, J. (2004). Will knowledge management work in the government?. *Electronic Government*, 1(1), 1-7.

Luling, D. (2001). Taking it online: anyway, anyplace, anytime. *Journal of Government Financial Management*, 50(1) 42-49.

Malhotra, Y. (2000). Knowledge Management for E-Business Performance. *Information Strategy: The Executives Journal*, 16(4), 5-16.

Margetts, H. and Dunleavy, P. (2002). Better Public Services through e-Government. *National Audit Office, HC 704-III Session 2001-2002*, 4 April 2002.

Scheer, A.W. (1999). *Electronic Business und Knowledge Management*. Neue Dimensionen fur den Untemehmungserfolg, Physica-Verlag, Heidelberg, 1999.

Sharma, S. (2004). Assessing e-government implementations. *Electronic Government*, 1(2), 198-212.

Stracke, J. (2002). Ë-Government: Supporting Knowledge and Information Flows with Supply Chain Management. *Proceedings of 3rd Working Conference on Knowledge Management in Electronic Government*, Copenhagen, Denmark.

Traunmuller, R. and Lenk, K. (2000). E-Commerce as a Stimulus for e-Government. *Proceedings of the XIII. Bled Conference on Electronic Commerce: The End of the Beginning*, Bled, June 19 - 21, 2000.

Yu E., Mylopoulos, J. (1996). Using Goals, Rules, and Methods to Support Reasoning in Business Process Reengineering. *International Journal of Intelligent Systems in Accounting, Finance and Management.* 5(1),12-18.

Chapter XIV
Data Mining in Decision Support for Bioenergy Production

Nasser Ayoub
Tokyo Institute of Technology, Japan
Helwan University, Egypt

Yuji Naka
Tokyo Institute of Technology, Japan

ABSTRACT

This chapter presents Data Mining, DM, as a planning and decision support tool for biomass resources management to produce bioenergy. Furthermore, the decision making problem for bioenergy production is defined. A Decision Support System, DSS that utilizes a DM technique, e.g. clustering, integrated with other group of techniques and tools, such as Genetic Algorithms, GA, Life Cycle Assessment, Geographical Information System, GIS, etc, is presented. A case study that shows how to tackle the decision making problem is also shown.

INTRODUCTION

Vast quantities of data and information are captured and stored through the available information technologies. Moreover, the data available are changing rapidly that force the planners, in governmental and private sectors to think differently in order to face market challenges and predict future trends. The DM is one of the important tools that can master this data explosion and provide usable knowledge from them. The use of data mining in developing DSS is popular in medical science, information technology, (Chae, Ho, Cho, Lee, & Ji, 2001; Wang, 1997) and recently in environmental applications, (Gibert, Sanchez-Marre, & Rodriguez-Roda, 2006). However, in the field of biomass planning and utilization the work presented here is pioneer. To the best knowledge of the authors, no similar work is conducted in the field. Here DM is used to help in deciding the economical bioenergy production resources and the hot spots of energy production facilities by applying clustering methods to the available biomass resources data. Then Life Cycle Inventory, LCI, analysis is used to estimate the CO_2 emission from bioenergy production. As biomass materials distribution is diverse, from one location to another, GIS is used to allocate biomass resources to its real location. The GA is used, as a powerful combinatorial algorithm, to solve the optimization problem in the local level of gBEDS. However, LCI and GA works are not explained here as they are beyond the topic of this chapter. However, for interested reader, a detailed explanation can be found in (Ayoub, 2007).

In this chapter, the multilevel decision problem for bioenergy production has been considered to help local and national planners in deciding about the economical bioenergy resources quantities, energy production methods, facilities locations, annual investments, environmental and social impacts. The solution methods and strategies for such complicated problem including the use of DM as the main part in solving the problem are also discussed in this work. Furthermore a DSS called general Bioenergy Decision System, gBEDS that is used in realizing the solution methods has been explained with a case study.

DECISION MAKING PROBLEMS

Planning and decision-making processes are in most, if not all, cases take a multidisciplinary course of actions; as the decisions have to address many involved stakeholders. Consequently, decisions are seen from multiple perspectives that mostly have tradeoff nature. In addition, the methods of applying the decisions are of prime importance to the overall project efficiency (Basson & Petrie, 2007; Hoskinson, Rope, & Fink, 2007; Marquez & Blanchar, 2006). This means that the success of the decisions made lies, primarily, on their follow up and evaluation rather than their

appropriateness only. The decisions assessments, always, provide an aid in judging their suitability for specific actions and, mostly, help in stimulating better results by changing or modifying their drawbacks at early stages of bringing them into reality. The data being analyzed are often historical in nature: daily, weekly and yearly results (Chau, Cao, Anson, & Zhang, 2003) that is a fertile land for DM to be applied.

Although it is a sound solution, environmentally, for energy production, bioenergy is still less attractive, from economical point of view. Therefore, most of the bioenergy production projects are completely or, at least, partly funded by the government in all levels. That makes the communication between different governmental levels, i.e., national, regional, local, and operative; through electronic media (DSS) is a typical example of the E-Government problems where decision making and follow up need to be flexible and quick. All communications between different planners can be performed through automated plans (files with different formats) that can be discussed simultaneously using any communication media, such as video conferencing. That may clarify many misunderstanding between planners in each level. The misinterpretation exist because national level plans are strategic for the whole country and considered as a challenge for the following levels planners to understand strategic decisions and adjust them to the local factors. Some of these factors are regulation / deregulation, the competition in different energy and emissions markets or the competition between different energy carriers in satisfying the local energy demand (Catrinu, 2006; Rozakis, Soldatos, Kallivroussis, & Nicolaou, 2001).

Furthermore, bioenergy local systems planning should operate with measures and designs similar to those applied nationally in order to harmonize the local and national strategies. Although vertical linkages among planning levels are very important, there is rarity of integrated economic and environmental plans at the different levels (King, Annandale, & Bailey, 2000). Special attention is given to the analysis and development of a multilevel decision making life cycle strategy to support the E-Government promotion where different levels of decision making and analysis are exist i.e., decisions have to be made in multilevel.

MULTILEVEL DECISION MAKING LIFE CYCLE (MLDMLC)

When designing a DSS for a multilevel decision making problem in E-Government, such as bioenergy planning problem, the system developer has to keep in mind the possible interactions between the different decision levels through the analysis of Decision Making Life Cycle, DMLC and Decisions Life Cycle, DLC. Life cycle as defined in the dictionary is "the progression through a series of differing stages of development". From this prospective, the DLC in bioenergy multilevel decision making framework is defined as:

The track of developmental changes or approval of decision(s) throughout a hierarchy of subsequent bioenergy decision-making levels with increasing

intensity of details starting from the top national level, aiming at determining the best way to solve a prespecified bioenergy problem.

On the other hand, the DMLC as defined by (Ayoub, 2007, p.14) is:

The trip taken by the system designer and bioenergy decision makers until reaching a satisfactory Decision Support Tool(s) that help in the quick making of optimal or near optimal decisions, about establishing the bioenergy facilities or systems, based on the current constraint, starting from problem definition and ending at providing the results to the decision makers, in all levels, in an easy and understandable format.

Here, the MLDMLC shown as Figure 1 is proposed, for handling the bioenergy planning problem, by integrating the formal DMLC defined elsewhere (Borges, Pino, & Valle, 2005; Delen & Pratt, 2006) with the DLC and can be applied in the following steps:

- Problem definition and structuring based on a given set of indications or wish for change by an individual or group of responsible people in a firm or a country;

Figure 1. The multilevel decision making life cycle

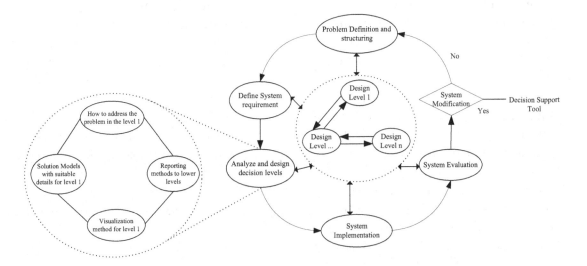

- Define the prospective decision levels i.e., national, regional, local, etc;
- Determine the best way to address the problem under study for each decision level;
- Develop the solution models with diverse details and appropriate to carry out the analysis at each level;
- Provide the results to the decision maker in an easily understandable format to allow exchange of decisions information and evaluation between different decision makers' levels as well as other concerned stakeholders.

Considering the MLDMLC while designing and developing the bioenergy DSS together with the appropriate Data Mining and Visualization techniques, will surely increase the cost and time of system development as the number of levels increases due to the task complexity of data collection and analysis, (Ayoub, 2007). However, this raise in cost will be recovered soon, as the system reinforces the robustness and effectiveness of decisions by overcoming several decision making weaknesses by:

- The ability to provide the decision makers in different levels with the suitable level of details that will save time and money for decision making procedure and their follow up, especially in the upper level.
- Ensure high communication performance through the mutual advantage of decisions visualization and semantics standardization.
- Increasing the possibilities of supporting future decisions of the same type through minor changes to system structure and data, that may reduce future costs.

By applying the bioenergy MLDMLC, it is recognized that the scope of a national planner, who proposes a biomass exploitation strategy for the whole country, is different from those of regional planners and executors who are applying policies in a small scale with specific requirements and limitations, e.g., resources availability, topological restrictions, energy needs, as shown in Figure 2. Such differences in scope must be taken into account when developing systems for decisions and planning support for the exploitation of biomass as a bioenergy resource.

For a macro-level of planning, such as that of national planners, a rough cost and simulation models are enough, since their main concerns are defining: the available biomass materials in the whole country; the available classes of energy conversion technologies for converting different biomass materials to different bioenergy; approximate economic effects, such as the cost of energy production or the potential legislative benefits; and the benefit in applying emission prevention legislation, e.g., Emission Taxation, Renewable Portfolio Standard and Fossil Fuel Taxation (Hakkila, 2006; Rozakis et al., 2001). The planning process in the two levels can be performed in four steps as given below:

- National level planning session is performed as shown by numbers 1 to 4 in Figure 2. The result of the national plan is the localities that considered as hot areas for energy production, type of institution, and specific supply chains.
- The national plans for the local areas are passed to the local levels in a form of proposal supply chains that have definite resources inputs, possible unit processes, potential products and the institution to be applied e.g., Renewable Portfolio Standard, number 5 in Figure 2.
- The local level planners evaluate the proposed plan by the national level, number 6 in Figure 2.
- The evaluation results, at the local level, can be one of three cases, number 7 in Figure 2;

Figure 2. Two levels with different objective

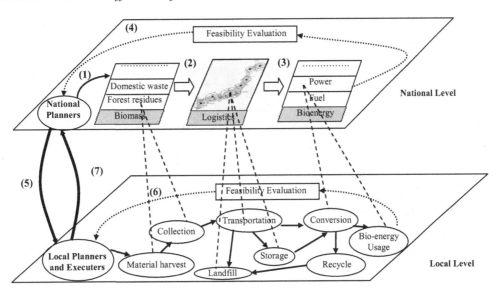

- ○ Agree and apply: the application results are reported back to the national level with the same level of details.
- ○ Modify and apply: define the modifications, the reason for making the modifications, the methods of applying the modifications.
- ○ Reject: the reason(s) for rejection, suggestions for new plan(s) to be approved by the upper level and the advantages of the proposed plan are reported by the local level.

The results of one planning cycle can be applied, with moderate modifications, to the local areas with similar situation.

DATA MANIPULATION AND CLUSTERING

The data of biomass resources are collected to the city level in the national planning session and to the county level in local planning session. This means that in case of the national level, the exact locations for the resources production

points are not known in certain. Furthermore, to define the collection places and the production facilities certain type of data clustering is needed to allocate the resources production points to bioenergy facility.

Clustering is a data mining technique and can be defined as "the process of grouping a collection of N patterns into distinct segments or clusters based on a suitable notion of closeness or similarity among these patterns". Good clusters show high similarity within a group and low similarity between patterns belonging to two different groups (Ye, 2003). Now a method on bioenergy resources data preparation is discussed next.

Bioenergy Resources Data Preparation and Clustering

A method for converting the available bioenergy resources quantities into resources production points is shown in Figure 3. The biomass resources quantities distribution are converted to weight points, or collection points, that are spread randomly around the centroid of the production area as seen in the right part of the figure. The resulted collection points are projected to the road

Figure 3. Converting the available bioenergy resources quantities into points.

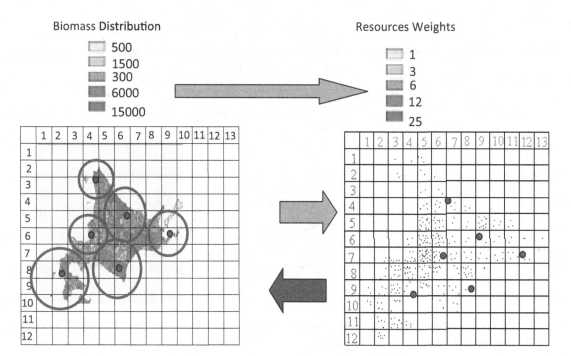

network of the country or the region to define the economical collection points as seen in Figure 4. Then the clustering technique is used to cluster the collection points based on their attributes to define the location of storage place or bioenergy plants. In case of using the bioenergy plants locations, the electricity grid is used to define the best choice of the provided alternatives. Once the locations of storage places and production plants are defined the procurement area for each cluster is defined and the supply chain optimization part can start as will be explained later.

To integrate all the above mentioned techniques and methods, and in order to achieve the optimal solution for the decision problem a DSS is developed and introduced in the following sections including the use of the system in planning for real situation.

GENERAL BIOENERGY DECISION SYSTEM (gBEDS)

The gBEDS is a DSS for planning and implementing bioenergy systems in national and local decision levels. It uses the functions of data management, processing, and visualization through combining a group of methods and tools in one platform to present meaningful results that support the decision makers in planning for bioenergy projects. The planning session involves, clustering, managing and optimizing the flow of biomass materials and properties from supply sources to the energy network. This system is used to design the Bioenergy Supply Chain defined as "the series of physically interconnected handling processes of biomass from production until energy production (generation), transmission and distribution facilities". The gBEDS is used as a tool to guide the decision maker through the process of choosing the sources and technologies needed for different

Figure 4. Schematic representation for estimating the locations of bioenergy facilities

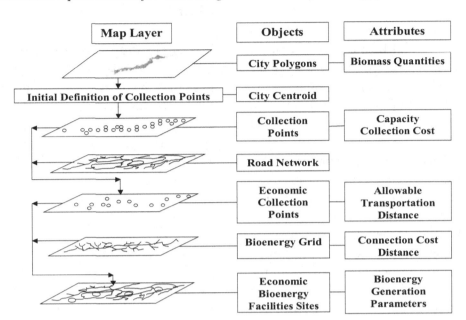

processes to realize the supply chain and their locations to satisfy community need.

The gBEDS Conceptual Structure

The gBEDS, as shown in Figure 5, consists of five parts; a common database; a Unit Process simu-lation or optimization module; the Data Mining engine; an in-line domain knowledge evaluation module; and a user interface. For more detailed explanation about the system components, the reader is directed to (Ayoub, Martins, Wang, Seki, & Naka, 2007; Ayoub, Seki, & Naka, 2007; Ayoub, Wang, Kagiyama, Seki, & Naka, 2006).

Figure 5. The conceptual structure of the gBEDS

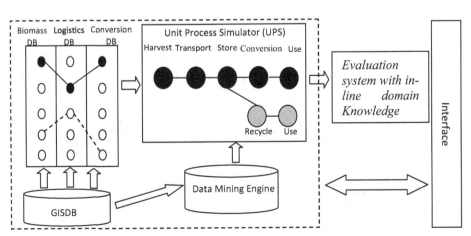

How gBEDS Works?

A general description of how DM Engine works with the modules of gBEDS is shown in Figure 6. It is clear that DM together with GIS are the heart of the gBEDS, as they are used to supply the subsequent modules with the necessary data for optimization calculations, e.g. locations and distances.

The GIS Database is prepared for the country or the region giving the data of biomass resources. By data clustering, of the GIS Database, we determine the feasible bioenergy resources quantities and their allocation to their calculated locations of bioenergy facilities and storage places, based on the spatial distribution of resources. In the Unit Process Simulator, UPS, the user defines a bioenergy supply chain. Depending on the planning level, the simulation or optimization model is used to calculate the different parameters of storage places and bioenergy facilities. The calculated parameters and impacts are, then, shown as maps on the GIS screen, figures, or spread sheet data for further analysis (Ayoub, Martins, Wang, Seki, & Naka, 2007).

HOW DATA MINING IS USED IN gBEDS

Fuzzy *C*-means Clustering

In gBEDS the fuzzy *C*-means clustering, which is a non-hierarchical clustering method, is used and designed to cluster data points into *C* clusters by minimizing the distance function. It is defined by Equation-1.

Equation-1:

$$E_c = \sum_{p=1}^{P_c} \sum_{i=1}^{n} \left(x_{cpi} - \overline{x}_{\dot{c}} \right)^2$$

where

c = index of the cluster, $c=1, 2, ...,C$.
P_c = collection points belong to cluster c
x_{cpi} = location of the p_{th} point of Pc data points on the i_{th} dimension of n-dimension variables for in the c_{th} cluster in standard dimension units (m)
x_{ci} = location of the centroid on the i_{th}-dimension in the c_{th} cluster in standard dimension units (m)
E_c = error sum of squares of distances for cluster c.

Figure 6. How gBEDS works?

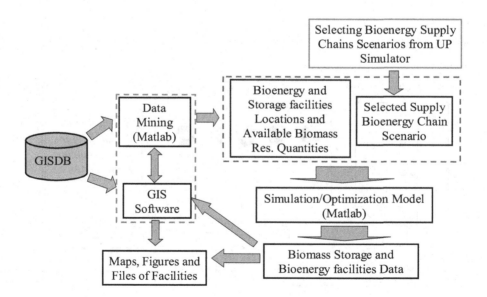

The data clustering methods may be applied for one or two times in the system depending on the supply chain defined by the user. That means if the supply chain includes storage, the clustering method will be applied first to define the potential location of the storage points by clustering the collection points considering the storage places as clusters centroids.

To locate the bioenergy conversion plants the resulted storage points, centroids of the first clustering iteration, are clustered to determine each bioenergy conversion plant location, assuming that it will be located at the centroid of the C-cluster. That means the transportation costs between the collection points to storage and from storage to conversion plants are optimized by the fuzzy C-means clustering at the same time.

Number of Clusters

In local planning level the number of clusters, storage and facilities, is small and defined by the decision makers based on the local inputs. On the other hand, at the national level, the numbers of storage places and bioenergy production facilities are defined automatically by a criterion known as cluster Validity Index, VI, that is measured for the input data set, (Shen, Chang, Lee, Deng, & Brown, 2005). The VI defines how well the clustering algorithm can partition the given data sets. In gBEDS the validity index to obtain the optimal number of clusters is represented by Equation-2 (Shen., 2005):

Equation-2, 3 and 4:

$$VI = \frac{Intra}{Inter}$$

$$Intra = \frac{1}{N} \sum_{i=1}^{C} \sum_{x \in U_i} \|x - z_i\|^2$$

$$Inter = \min_{i,j} \left(\|z_i - z_j\| \right)^2$$

Where

VI = Validity Index
C = number of clusters,
i = Cluster index, $i = 1, 2, \ldots, C-1$
j = Cluster index, $j = i + 1, i + 2, \ldots, C$
N = the number of collection points
z_i = spatial location of the i_{th} cluster center
z_j = spatial location of the j_{th} cluster center
x = spatial location of the storage or Plant U that belong to cluster i

The objective is to minimize the *intra*-value (as defined by Equation-3), which is average distance between the data points and the center of cluster and at the same time maximize the *inter*-value (see Equation-4) which is the inter distance between the clusters centers. The VI for C is obtained by minimizing the *intra–inter* ratio. The Validity Index table prepared for the specified data set as a pre-knowledge in the gBEDS and provided to the user. A sample of VI table prepared by the system for the Japanese forestry residues storage is shown, in Table 1, for the national level.

The gBEDS also provides an option to allow the calculation of the VI by the user, however, the computation cost of the algorithm is high, 48 hours to establish VI table of 500 clusters for 6195 collection points in a Pentium 3- 1500 MHz CPU. A sample of VI table prepared by the system for the Japanese forestry residues storage is shown, in Table 1, for the national level.

Using the VI table, the numbers of clusters, e.g., storages and bioenergy conversion plants that meet users requirements are defined. It is important to refer that the number of clusters and the maximum feasible amount of utilized biomass are not inter-related as shown in Table 1. If 450 storage places are considered, the feasible quantity is more than that of 500 storage places. Based on the optimal results by the fuzzy C-means clustering of the collection points all bioenergy conversion plants attributes such as locations, capacities, number of workers, etc. can be evaluated easily.

Table 1. Validity Index table provided to the user (storage locations)

Number of clusters	VI	Intra (m2)	Inter (m2)	Feasible biomass quantity (Ton)
10	0.086482	1.67E+09	1.93E+10	86568
50	0.51151	9.60E+08	1.88E+09	236250
100	0.76462	5.77E+08	7.55E+08	245740
150	1.3007	4.07E+08	3.13E+08	247200
200	1.5765	3.11E+08	1.97E+08	247770
250	2.4332	2.64E+08	1.08E+08	247610
300	4.1897	2.17E+08	5.18E+07	247690
350	3.6349	2.12E+08	5.83E+07	247570
450	4.3634	1.64E+08	3.75E+07	247770
500	10.178	1.57E+08	1.54E+07	247610

Collection Points Clustering and Impacts Estimation

The desired Validity Index is defined from the table or according to user requirements and the system is ready to estimate the biomass utilization impacts along the selected supply chains by applying the clustering method to the collection points data. In case of forest and others, the system asks the user to define some site-specific inputs required for the impacts calculations such as, type of bioenergy required; efficiencies of available bioenergy conversion plants, average access distance from transportations routs, etc. Default values are provided for system users who do not have sufficient information about the required inputs.

The data related with the required storages, locations, areas, costs, etc., are calculated and saved in a matrix. In order to establish the storage layer in the GIS interface, database is stored in dbf files. Furthermore, the system defines the different impacts, environmental, economical and social, of bioenergy production from the input type biomass, costs, CO_2 emissions per amount of electricity produced, number of men-labor per the supply chain, total investments required for estab-

lishing the business, and others, for constructing a matrix of all data related to bioenergy production for each plant as a database file. In addition to these, at the national level, the optimization is performed by calculating the minimum distance only and the different impacts, from the selected bioenergy supply chain, are calculated as the sum of impacts produced from their Unit Process, UP, models defined for this level. However, at the local level the optimization model is used for further impacts reduction through investigating the different technologies defined in the UP models (Ayoub, 2007).

CASE STUDY

Now, a case study is being described by illustrating the above mentioned methods. This case study is performed for an integrated system of bioenergy resources with different supply chains to produce electricity in a Japanese city called Iida. Nine bioenergy resources have been chosen with their supply chains as shown in Figure 7. The quantities used in are given in Table 2. The bioenergy production plan includes; defining the locations of the new facilities; biomass resources quantities al-

Figure 7. Supply chains for integrated biomass resources

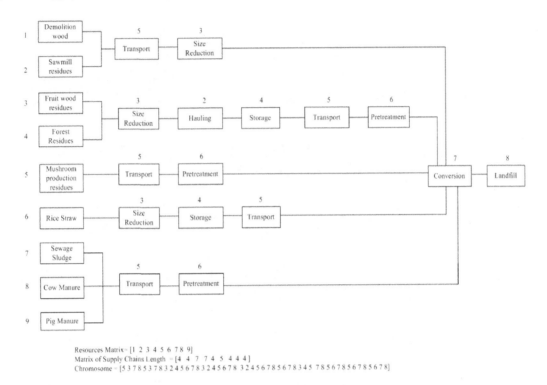

Resources Matrix = [1 2 3 4 5 6 7 8 9]
Matrix of Supply Chains Length = [4 4 7 7 4 5 4 4 4]
Chromosome = [5 3 7 8 5 3 7 8 3 2 4 5 6 7 8 3 2 4 5 6 7 8 3 2 4 5 6 7 8 5 6 7 8 3 4 5 7 8 5 6 7 8 5 6 7 8 5 6 7 8]

located for each bioenergy plant and its production capacities; annual investments, costs, emissions, energy and number of labor hours needed per year for bioenergy production. The output of applying this scenario may be considered as a future blueprint for the possible locations, capacities, types, etc. of bioenergy conversion plants.

Study Area

The planning session for Iida city, in Nagano prefecture, the Middle part of Japan, is selected here as a model for local level planning. The gross area of the city is 325.68 km^2 and a total population of 107,384 citizens. The city area is divided into 265 counties with population density ranges from 0 citizens/km^2 where the county area is all forests to 9941.22 citizens/km^2 in the center of city. The city is served by a water treatment facility, an animal manure facility, 25 sawmills, and 3 wood chipping facilities.

Scenario Results

The planning for integrated bioenergy system tested here starts in gBEDS by first clustering the bioenergy resources to the number of facilities and defining the desired supply chain (see Figure 7).

Clustering Session

The output of the data clustering session, of the nine-biomass resources, is the location of potential facilities with the county name where they are located, and the quantities of bioenergy resources allocated to each bioenergy production plant are shown in Figure 8. It has been observed that, the locations of conversion facilities are found close to the areas of average and high population. This result is expected as the production of resources utilized depends on the number of population except the forestry residues that found to be of

Figure 8. The potential location of bioenergy production facilities in Iida city.

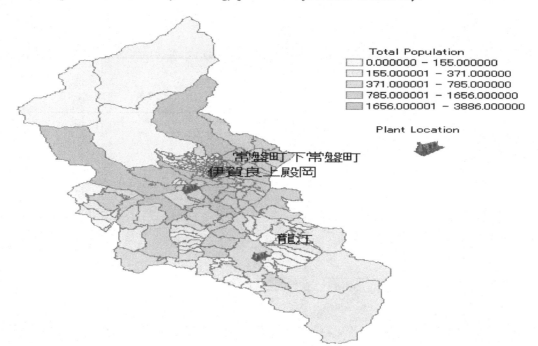

small amounts as seen in the resulted resources allocation quantities to each facility of Table 3.

Data Mining and Optimization

Once the locations of the bioenergy production facilities is decided the different impacts of establishing the facilities are calculated and visualized on the country map that enables the user to navigate the different impacts of establishing the bioenergy production facilities. For example, gBEDS, in the data mining session, calculates optimal sizes, capacities of the storage place (if it is included), the bioenergy conversion plants capacity, the minimum traveling distance between collection points and the storage, minimum distance from the storage to bioenergy conversion plant for minimizing the transportation costs, CO2 emissions and number of workers. In the following sub-sections, an introduction about data mining and clustering techniques is given and followed by explaining the clustering method applied to GIS data in this work.

Based on a selected scenario, the optimization session is conducted for the three facilities to minimize the cost of bioenergy production. As a result, the bioenergy plants capacities, cost of one MWh in each plant, and annual investments are calculated. The average data, of the optimization solution for the three plants are shown in Table 3.

The data shown in Table 3 are computed by optimizing the three supply chains based on the cost and resulted a specific UP models, where each model belongs to a specific technology type, that work as a blue print for the coming level. Table 4 shows an example of UP models suggested by the system for three bioenergy production plants to produce bioenergy from the specified resources.

CONCLUSION

In this chapter a description for Data Mining as an effective tool for decision support is presented.

Table 2.The bioenergy resources data used in solving the optimization problem

Biomass resources data

Optimization Parameters	Forest Residues ton/year	Rice Straw ton/year	Mushroom Residues ton/year	Fruit Tree residues ton/year	Damaged Wood ton/year	Pig Manure ton/year	Cow Manure ton/year	Sewage Sludge ton/year	Demolition Wood ton/year	Bioenergy plant operating hours ton/year	Distance to electricity network km
Bioenergy production plant 1	3129	647.35	3393.8	622.26	553.68	40241	0	9329.4	1805	4000	5
Bioenergy production plant 2	9105.8	2083.1	491.8	122.26	51.181	10238	0	0	156.75	4000	5
Bioenergy production plant 3	5298.3	2134.1	1513.8	291.97	204.72	22516	1.27E+05	447.09	1008	4000	5

A two level system called, general BioEnergy Decision System, gBEDS, as an effective tool in planning for bioenergy supply chains is introduced with the core part of Data Mining techniques, i.e. clustering. The gBEDS is integration of ideas and methods used for the first time in the research field of bioenergy planning and decision making. The Multilevel Decision Making Life Cycle concept has been applied, both, in the analysis of data required for the specified decision level as well as explaining the differences in prospective between the two decision levels. A general explanation about the proposed DM method used in this work is presented and followed by detailed explanation of the specific use of DM in the gBEDS prototype.

Special attention was given to the clustering techniques used to tackle the problem of distributed nature of biomass and identifying locations of the biomass utilization facilities that is considered a preliminary optimization based on distance and the integration between GIS and DM in defining the feasible biomass quantity is also explained. It is also, demonstrated by a case study how gBEDS helps the decision makers to establish, design, and evaluate a system of bioenergy production, starting from location determination via DM and ending to suggesting specific technologies for the specified Unit Process.

The authors, believe that this research results, which for the first time approach the biomass planning process via non-conventional optimization techniques, e.g., Data Mining, GA and GIS, may provide vital footing for the development of DSS in the bioenergy planning field and other similar fields.

FUTURE RESEARCH DIRECTIONS

The results of this work open several opportunities for further research and improvement via different Data Mining techniques and can be summarized in the following paragraphs. To overcome

Table 3. The bioenergy optimization problem results based on cost criteria

Bioenergy planning parameters	Bioenergy supply chains		
	Plant 1	Plant 2	Plant 3
Plant Capacity MW	4.85	2.46	11.11
Annual Investment (Myen/year)	290.39	245.97	547.19
Supply Chain Cost Per MWh (yen/MWh)	14962	25040	12308
Supply Chain Emission Per MWh (KgCO2eq/MWh)	37.39	43.15	37.50
Supply Chain Energy Per MWh (MJ/MWh)	1212.49	1264.23	1245.84
Supply Chain Labor (L.h/year)	46632.93	47139.32	88530.09
I/O Energy Ratio	0.105	0.076	0.161
Forest Residues (ton/year)	2254.28	8570.29	4071.62
Rice Straw (ton/year)	553.72	1742.21	1622.60
Mushroom Residues (ton/year)	3326.26	486.88	1483.68
Fruit Tree residues (ton/year)	537.97	105.70	210.35
Damaged Wood (ton/year)	542.66	50.16	200.65
Pig Manure (ton/year)	39440.20	10034.26	22290.84
Cow Manure (ton/year)	0	0	124423.70
Sewage Sludge (ton/year)	9143.75	0	438.19
Demolition Wood (ton/year)	1770.87	153.63	987.94

Table 4. The UP models recommended by the optimization model based on cost criteria

| Biomass resources | Bioenergy supply chain UPs technologies | | |
	Plant 1	Plant 2	Plant 3
Forest residues			
	Road side Hammer mill	Road Side Disk Drum Chipper	Road Side Disk Drum Chipper
	(12 ton/h)	(9 ton/h)	(9 ton/h)
	Self propelled forwarder	Self propelled forwarder	Self propelled forwarder
	(1.688 ton/h)	(1.688 ton/h)	(1.688 ton/h)
	Unprotected on crushed rock	Pole framed Structure on crushed rock	Poly Tarp Cover on crushed rock
	Dump Truck Diesel (15 ton)	Dump Truck Bio-Diesel (10 ton)	Dump Truck Diesel (10 ton)
	Tube bundle dryer (B) - Saturated steam	Tube bundle dryer (A) - Saturated steam	Tube bundle dryer (B) - Saturated steam
	160 KW, (3 t.ev.w/h)[a]	94 KW, (3 t.ev.w/h)	160 KW, (3 t.ev.w/h)
	Coal Co-firing	Coal Co-firing	Coal Co-firing
	Landfill without gas recovery system	Landfill without gas recovery system	Landfill with gas recovery system
Rice straw			
	Hesston 5800 Round Baler (3.3 ton/h)	John Deer Model 346 Square Baler (6 ton/h)	Hesston 5800 Round Baler (10 ton/h)
	Poly Tarp Cover on crushed rock	Pole framed Structure on crushed rock	Poly Tarp Cover on crushed rock
	Dump Truck Bio-Diesel (15 ton)	Dump Truck Bio-Diesel (15 ton)	Dump Truck Diesel (4 ton)
	Coal Co-firing	Coal Co-firing	Coal Co-firing
	Landfill without gas recovery system	Landfill without gas recovery system	Landfill with gas recovery system
Sewage sludge			
	Dump Truck Bio-Diesel (4 ton)	NA[b]	Dump Truck Diesel (4 ton)

continued on following page

Table 4. continued

Tube bundle dryer (B) - Saturated steam 160 KW, (3 t.ev.w/h)	NA		Tube bundle dryer (A) - Saturated steam 94 KW, (3 t.ev.w/h)
Landfill without gas recovery system	NA		Landfill with gas recovery system
Coal Co-firing	NA		Coal Co-firing

a) t.ev.w : ton evaporated water per hour
b) NA: not applicable

Figure 9. The structure of data manipulation for the two levels of decision making

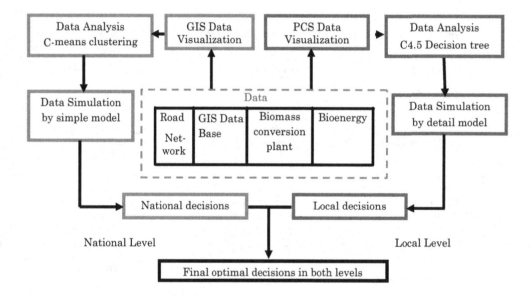

the differences in nature between localities it is important to establish standard classes of localities that share similar characteristics, i.e., land, weather, locations, etc., which is a typical DM task. In this case, applying an institution or plan on one instance of specific class can be applied to other instances with moderate effort, time and resources.

The possible collaboration between the localities at the same level, such as material transportation and supply, is not considered in the gBEDS where planning is made for only one local area at a time. Therefore, this point, as well as the resources exchange between succeeding localities, is considered challenging tasks to be added in the local level planning. For example, if resources shortage has been occurred, there should be a procurement strategy from the nearest local area within certain distance for safe feed supply and this can be supported by the popular DM technique Decision Trees.

In the current DSS authors used one DM technique and the same data visualization method for both decision making levels which needs to be revisited and modified in the future versions of gBEDS. As seen in Figure 9, the structure of data manipulation in both DM and data visualization can be modified to include more detailed techniques, i.e., C4.5 Decision tree and PCS Data visualization techniques in the local level planning.

NOTE

Two figures (2, 5), one table (1) and some text are reproduced from our previous publication "Ayoub, N., Martins, R., Wang, K., Seki, H., & Naka, Y. (2007). Two levels decision system for efficient planning and implementation of bioenergy production. *Energy Conversion and Management, 48*(3), 709-723" under the permission of Elsevier Limited}.

REFERENCES

Ayoub, N. (2007). *A Multilevel Decision Making Strategy for Designing and Evaluating Sustainable Bioenergy Supply Chains*. Unpublished doctoral dissertation, Tokyo Institute of Technology, Yokohama, Japan.

Ayoub, N., Martins, R., Wang, K., Seki, H., & Naka, Y. (2007). Two levels decision system for efficient planning and implementation of bioenergy production. *Energy Conversion and Management, 48*(3), 709-723.

Ayoub, N., Wang, K., Kagiyama, T., Seki, H., & Naka, Y. (2006). A Planning Support System for Biomass-based Power Generation. In W. Marquardt & C.Pantelides (Eds.), *16th European Symposium on Computer Aided Process Engineering and 9th International Symposium on Process Systems Engineering Vol. 21B.* (pp. 1899-1904). Garmisch-Partenkirchen, Germany.

Basson, L., & Petrie, J. G. (2007). An integrated approach for the consideration of uncertainty in decision making supported by Life Cycle Assessment. *Environmental Modelling & Software Environmental Decision Support Systems, 22*(2), 167-176.

Borges, M. R. S., Pino, J. A., & Valle, C. (2005). Support for decision implementation and follow-up. *European Journal of Operational Research Decision Support Systems in the Internet Age, 160*(2), 336-352.

Catrinu, M. D. (2006). *Decision Aid for Planning Local Energy Systems: Application of Multi-Criteria Decision Analysis*. Unpublished doctoral dissertation, Norwegian University of Science and Technology, Trondheim, Norway.

Chae, Y. M., Ho, S. H., Cho, K. W., Lee, D. H., & Ji, S. H. (2001). Data mining approach to policy analysis in a health insurance domain. *International Journal of Medical Informatics, 62*(2-3), 103-111.

Chau, K. W., Cao, Y., Anson, M., & Zhang, J. (2003). Application of data warehouse and Decision Support System in construction management. *Automation in Construction, 12*(2), 213-224.

Delen, D., & Pratt, D. B. (2006). An integrated and intelligent DSS for manufacturing systems. *Expert Systems with Applications, 30*(2), 325-336.

Gibert, K., Sanchez-Marre, M., & Rodriguez-Roda, I. (2006). GESCONDA: An intelligent data analysis system for knowledge discovery and management in environmental databases. *Environmental Modelling & Software, 21*(1), 115-120.

Hakkila, P. (2006). Factors driving the development of forest energy in Finland. *Biomass and Bioenergy*: Proceedings of the third annual workshop of Task 31 'Systainable production systems for bioenergy: Impacts on forest resources and utilization of wood for energy' October 2003, Flagstaff, Arizona, USA, *30*(4), 281-288.

Hoskinson, R. L., Rope, R. C., & Fink, R. K. (2007). Using a decision support system to optimize production of agricultural crop residue Biofeedstock. *Biomass and Bioenergy, 31*(4), 186-194.

King, P., Annandale, D., & Bailey, J. (2000). A Conceptual Framework for Integrated Economic and Environmental Planning in Asia - A Literature Review. *Journal of Environmental Assessment Policy and Management, 2*(3), 279-315.

Marquez, A. C., & Blanchar, C. (2006). A Decision Support System for evaluating operations investments in high-technology business. *Decision Support Systems, 41*(2), 472-487.

Rozakis, S., Soldatos, P. G., Kallivroussis, L., & Nicolaou, I. (2001). Multiple Criteria Analysis of Bio-energy Projects: Evaluation of Bio-Electricity Production in Farsala Plain, Greece. *Journal of Geographic Information and Decision Analysis, 5*(1), 49-64.

Shen, J., Chang, S. I., Lee, E. S., Deng, Y., & Brown, S. J. (2005). Determination of cluster number in clustering microarray data. *Applied Mathematics and Computation, 169*(2), 1172-1185.

Wang, H. (1997). Intelligent agent-assisted decision support systems: Integration of knowledge discovery, knowledge analysis, and group decision support. *Expert Systems with Applications, 12*(3), 323-335.

Ye, N. (2003). *The Handbook of Data Mining.* London: Lawrence Erlbaum Associates, Publishers.

ADDITIONAL READINGS

Anderson, B. F. (2002). *The Three Secrets of Wise Decision Making.* Portland, Oregon: Single Reef Press.

Anttiroiko, A. V., & Malkia, M. (Eds.). (2007). *Encyclopedia of digital government.* Hershey. London. Melbourne. Singapore: Idea Group Publishing.

Bigus, J. P. (1996). *Data mining with neural networks: Solving business problems:from application development to decision support.* McGraw-Hill.

Chinese, D., & Meneghetti, A. (2005). Optimisation models for decision support in the development of biomass-based industrial district-heating networks in Italy. *Applied Energy, 82*(3), 228-254.

Cios, K. J., Pedrycz, W., Swiniarski, R. W., & Kurgan, L. A. (2007). *Data Mining: A Knowledge Discovery Approach. New York,: Springer Science+Business Media, LLC.*

Courtney, J. F. (2001). Decision making and knowledge management in inquiring organizations: toward a new decision-making paradigm for DSS. *Decision Support Systems, 31*(1), 17-38.

Dornburg, V., Faaij, A. P. C., & Meuleman, B. (2006). Optimising waste treatment systems: Part A: Methodology and technological data for optimising energy production and economic performance. *Resources, Conservation and Recycling, 49*(1), 68-88.

Freppaz, D., Minciardi, R., Robba, M., Rovatti, M., Sacile, R., & Taramasso, A. (2004). Optimizing forest biomass exploitation for energy supply at a regional level. *Biomass and Bioenergy, 26*(1), 15-25.

Gibert, K., Sanchez-Marre, M., & Rodriguez-Roda, I. (2006). GESCONDA: An intelligent data analysis system for knowledge discovery and management in environmental databases. *Environmental Modelling & Software, 21*(1), 115-120.

Larichev, O. (1999). Normative and descriptive aspects of decision making. In T. Gal, T. Stewart

& T. Hanne (Eds.), *Multicriteria decision making: Advances in MCDM models, algorithms, theory and applications* (pp. 5.1-5.24). Boston: Kluwer Academic Publishers.

Larose, D. T. (2006). *Data mining methods and models*. Hoboken, New Jersey: John Wiley & Sons, Inc.

Lin, F. r., Huang, K. j., & Chen, N. (2006). Integrating information retrieval and data mining to discover project team coordination patterns. *Decision Support Systems, 42*(2), 745-758.

Makaila, M., Anttiroiko, A. V., & Savolaine, R. (2004). *E-Transformation in Governance: New Directions in Government and Politics*. Hershey: Idea Group Publishing.

Min, H., Ko, C. S., & Ko, H. J. (2006). The spatial and temporal consolidation of returned products in a closed-loop supply chain network. *Computers & Industrial Engineering: Special Issue: Logistics and Supply Chain Management, Selected Papers from The 33rd. ICC&IE, 51*(2), 309-320.

Mitchell, C. P. (2000). Development of decision support systems for bioenergy applications. *Biomass and Bioenergy, 18*(4), 265-278.

Myatt, G. J. (2007). *A Practical Guide to Exploratory Data Analysis and Data Mining*. New Jersey: John Wiley & Sons, Inc.

Ramachandra, T. V., & Shruthi, B. V. (2007). Spatial mapping of renewable energy potential. *Renewable and Sustainable Energy Reviews, 11*(7), 1460-1480.

Taniar, D. (2007 .). *Research and trends in data mining technologies and applications*. Hershey: Idea Group Publishing.

Tonn, B., & Martin, M. (2000). Industrial energy efficiency decision making. *Energy Policy, 28*(12), 831-843.

Wang, J. (Ed.). (2003). *Data Mining: Opportunities and Challenges*. London: Idea Group Publishing.

Witten, I. H., & Frank, E. (2005). *Data Mining: Practical Machine Learning Tools and Techniques* (Second Edition ed.): Morgan Kaufmann.

Section V
Virtual Communities and Cases

Chapter XV
Virtual Assistants for E–Government Interaction

Rodrigo Sandoval-Almazán
Autonomous University of the State of Mexico, Mexico

Mario Arturo Gutiérrez Alonso
Tecnológico de Monterrey Campus Morelia, Mexico

ABSTRACT

The objective of this chapter is to provide an example of a user-friendly interface for knowledge management and information retrieval, through the use of virtual assistants in E-government applications. The chapter is going to provide a short state of the art on virtual assistants technology, highlighting the knowledge management aspects. Two case studies: the Mexican state of Guanajuato, and the Federal Government Citizen's Web Page will be presented and discussed. These case studies provide new insights into access methods, interfaces and ways to query and present information in e-government applications.

INTRODUCTION

E-government portals are improving the way citizens interact with government. However the government officials are not always aware of the users needs and expectations; many e-government portals start as an unidirectional communication channel designed to provide general information about bureaucratic processes and transactions.

The new trend of e-government portals is to establish a bidirectional communication to better address the citizens needs and expectations, becoming more friendly sites. According to this goal, the governments – local, state and federal – are increasing their efforts to assess their portals and improve them. The search for better communication and interaction paradigms has led to the use of virtual assistants as an important element in the user interface of an e-government portal.

The aim of this chapter is to explain how virtual assistants can be used to facilitate the interaction of citizens with e-government portals and analyze their effectiveness in a real situation (e-government portal of the Guanajuato state). virtual assistants are usually presented in the form of virtual characters that can have a realistic or a cartoon-like appearance. They are visualized using video or 3D graphics and are able to answer questions asked in a written or even oral form. Furthermore, the chapter will try to relate the implications of virtual assistants in the e-government processes. Eventually, it would justify the insinuation of data mining in the knowledge management system, utilizing virtual assistants.

This chapter will be divided in the following sections:

A review of the e-government concepts required to understand the use and potential benefits of virtual assistants in e-government portals. A brief introduction to virtual assistants technology. Role of virtual assistants in the knowledge management processes and effectiveness of virtual assistants in the e-governance systems. Two case studies representing the use of a virtual assistant in the e-government portal of the Mexican state of Guanajuato. The description will include: history about internet achievements in government, process of implementation, analysis of recently obtained data concerning the performance and user acceptance of the technology.

Discussion and conclusions, providing a set of best practices and other recommendations concerning the use of virtual assistants in e-government portals.

The Methodology of the chapter will contain two kinds of information: Theory about the virtual assistants research and e-government. Data collected by the authors directly from the sources, including: interviews with the systems director in charge of the virtual assistant, and statistics from the governmental source: number of visits, number of questions answered, costs, etc. The final section is on future research.

BACKGROUND

E-Government Theoretical Framework

There are numerous conceptualizations about electronic government. West and Berman (2001) state that the electronic government "... refers to the delivery of information and services online through the internet" that implies the use of web pages – Internet- to deliver government information and services to the citizens.

Araujo (2004) understand e-government as: "the way in which the government employs the new technologies to offer the people a better access to the information and the government services, to improve the quality of public services and to provide more opportunities to participate in the democratic institution and the processes".

Gil-Garcia and Luna (2003) tried to integrate the concept and understand the electronic government from more administrative or organizational perspectives. They have also studied the evolution of the concept. On the other hand, the concept proposed by Holmes (2001) is the closest one to this study and complements the concepts of West and Berman:

Electronic government is the use of information technology, in particular intern, to deliver public services in a much more convenient, customer oriented, cost effective, and altogether different and better way

From a more institutional perspective, the World Bank (2008) states that e-government

refers to the use by government agencies of information technologies (such as Wide Area Networks, the Internet, and mobile computing) that have the ability to transform relations with citizens, businesses, and other arms of government. These technologies can serve a variety of different ends: better delivery of government services to citizens, improved interactions with business and industry, citizen empowerment through access to information, or more efficient government management. The resulting benefits can be less corruption, increased transparency, greater convenience, revenue growth, and/or cost reductions.

Finally, it can be considered that the growing popularity of e-government "is determined by a frame of three factors: the technology evolution, the adaptation of new capacities in the local government and the legitimization of the same political systems" (Ficarra, 2004).

These definitions agree on the use of technology in the e-government services. Their main difference relies on the degree of involvement in government activities; some definitions are more focused on processes (World Bank 2008) some others are focused on politics (Ficarra 2004, Gil-Garcia and Luna 2003), and very few are focused on the citizens perspective (Holmes 2001 and Araujo (2004). This research adopts the last perspective, and the main goal is to provide a better services and accessibility for citizens. As it will be shown with two case studies, the use of virtual assistants are a promising alternative.

If one would like to relate the role of virtual assistants in e-governance improvement processes, it has been observed that this recent technology addition has put forward advantages in pursuing e-government systems. Campbell (2008) rightfully indicated that a virtual assistant frequently does work that is similar to an administrative assistant, only working "virtually" — i.e., at a distance and not at the premises. The role reflects the distributed way so many of these work today, from "anywhere." Furthermore, virtual assistants can work from anywhere, giving individuals and small businesses that extra set of hands that is so often needed around the office, without actually taking up any office space (Free Press Release, 2008). This way, e-governance processes can be enhanced in a more sophisticated techniques. However, this immense set of data may result

in handling huge data sets. To cope up with the extended data search, rapid access and tackle the growing database, data mining techniques may be applied.

Virtual Assistant Framework

A virtual assistant (VA) is a preliminary outcome of a technology to come and a field of research that is ongoing. Virtual assistants are interactive virtual characters that can perform a dialog with the user. Commonly, users write questions or comments that are answered in a written or oral form by the virtual character. Virtual assistants are usually limited to an animated face with realistic or cartoon-like appearance. There are a few works targeted at exploiting full-body animation such as the animation engine proposed by Gutierrez et. al (2002), or the virtual assistants included in some versions of the Microsoft Office suite. Most of the efforts have been focused on animating virtual faces. This research can be traced back to the work on real time face interaction by Kalra (1993) and Pandzic et. al (1994). Later, Magnenat-Thalmann et. al. (1995) developed a more complex application to allow communication between virtual and real humans.

Nowadays, virtual faces are 3D or 2D shapes carefully designed by digital artists or based on photographies and/or video of real persons. Virtual faces can have various skills. They can be accessed through the Internet and display a set of facial expressions, and a synthetic voice, a good example is the work of Kshirsagar et al. (2001). The work of Goto et al. (2001a;b) included speech recognition to ease the interaction.

Animated faces have evolved into conversational agents. Egges et al. (2004) show how animated faces can be complemented by different technologies, including Artificial Intelligence to simulate personality, emotions and implement basic cognitive skills such as natural language processing. In this way, virtual characters turn into appealing agents with enough skills to establish a dialog or conversation and help users in a variety of tasks such a information search and retrieval. But until now this technology was used only for experimental purposes and very few enterprises have introduced it to the market of online applications.

Foglia et.al (2007) conducted a research to asses the impact of virtual assistants technology for governmental purposes. The findings reveal that people benefit from virtual assistants when they need to find new information or when they need to learn how to perform a specific transaction or procedure in the e-government portal. On the other hand, virtual assistants can be annoying if they speak for too long, or can be an obstacle when users know exactly what they need to do in the web portal. From this study, it can be concluded that virtual assistants technology should be used carefully, since it can also produce negative effects on the user. In the next sections, the deployment process of a virtual assistant in an e-government portal has been described.

VIRTUAL ASSISTANTS FOR E-GOVERNMENT PORTALS: TWO CASE STUDIES

Case 1

On October 2006, the Public Information Access Unit (IAU) of the Guanajuato State in Mexico, launched a virtual assistant as interface for their e-government portal. This is a conversational agent, which acts as an online interactive tool for the exchange of information. The system focuses on the dissemination of public information concerning the government of the state of Guanajuato. It is regarded as cutting-edge technology that provides a friendly interface to the Internet. (see Figure 1)

This system is part of the technological infrastructure owned by the IAU of the Guanajuato State Government, and has two main objectives:

- Improve the amount and quality of information available online,
- Diversify the modalities to access and search for information.

Figure 1. Interactive virtual assistant at the Transparency Portal (Notations and corresponding activities indicated in the figure)

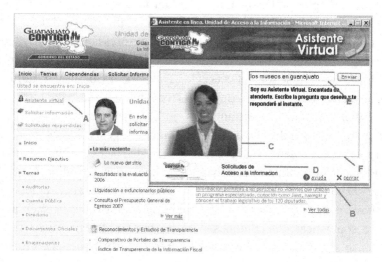

The purpose of the virtual assistant system is to facilitate direct interaction with citizens, as well as to strength the transparency philosophy of the state government. The virtual assistant allows users to "talk" with an automatic entity, express their information needs and get relevant answers. At the same time the system provides links to Web pages containing related or complementary information.

A. **Link to access the virtual assistant**
    Opens the application window
B. **Virtual assistant Interface**
    A new window appears
C. **Image of the virtual assistant**
    Image of public officers.
D. **Proactive Messages**
    Random messages or images that appear within the window system, providing users with direct access to related information.
E. **Input Text Box**
    Access to the conversation with the assistant.
F. **Scoreboard Response**
    In this space the assistant will provide answers and links where the user can find related information.

The virtual assistant, as conversational agent, has a knowledge base with information linked to natural language formulas. This helps it to understand questions formulated in colloquial language. Ideally, the system would answer to any given question according to its own interpretation and understanding of the information that the citizen is looking for. The virtual assistant is not a simple information searcher which provides a list of pages containing the search terms. The assistant analyses the questions formulated in natural language and tries to define the user intentions concerning the information required. The system can ask further questions in order to clarify the user needs and provide better answers. Whenever the assistant is unable to answer a question, due to unavailability of information or failure in the process and interpretation of the question, it presents the user with the options of Intelligent Search and the Requests Module. Such tools offer the user alternative means to search for the required information.

Interactivity between users and system derives on increased efficiency and encourages people to use the technological tool more often. All conversations are recorded, this offers good scaling and updating mechanisms. The records are send to specialized agents who analyze the context and contents of the talks. This constitutes a framework for supervision and continuous update of the system.

Summarizing, a virtual agent gives support to citizens during their visit to the Web site of the Government of the Guanajuato State. Interaction is done through direct conversation, using natural language, this software system provides better service for citizens and 24/7 attention to all people who uses internet to interact with the government. The following sub-sections provide more details on the system architecture and implementation details.

System Architecture

The virtual assistant system is installed on an Intel XEON server at 3 Ghz, 2 Gb Ram and 70 Gb of Hard Drive, using Windows 2000 Server as operating system. Two subsystems work in parallel in order to update information and control the performance: the Talk Reporting System and the Content Control System.

*   Talk Reporting System: Allows human supervisors to review the talks or conversations that the virtual assistant has established with the citizens. This helps to identify information that does not exist within the database. This operation is done through a Web-based interface and does not require any special platform for its operation (see Figure 2).

Figure 2. Talk reporting system (Notations and corresponding activities indicated in the figure)

- Content Control System: Controls the flow of information and keeps the virtual assistant updated and online. The virtual assistant keeps in touch with public officers via e-mail and sends information requests to the responsible officers.

Keeping the virtual assistant efficiency requires timely review of the new questions that are received, in order to identify information needs, send information requests and update the database.

A. **Dates Log**
   Shows conversations recorded in a given date.
B. **Talks Log**
   Shows conversations recorded at a specific time.
C. **Individual Conversation**
   Contents of the conversation.

The virtual assistant was developed by the Spanish company "Asistentes Virtuales" (http://www.asistentesvirtuales.com), who has deployed Virtual Assistans for Spanish banks and other companies. Their counterpart in Mexico was Digital Data, and both developed Neuro-Script, a programming language used to create the subsystem that understands – parse – and interprets natural language conversations and identifies questions that the software can answer.

System Capabilities

- The system can keep thousands of simultaneous conversations, without continuous monitoring.
- It can take advantage of various communication channels such as chat, collaborative navigation, etc.
- It allows to customize the talks according to customer profiles and other information available, and be proactive in the dialog.
- It has a feedback mechanisms that allows for answering to new questions using questions that have been already asked by other users.
- The information database can be easily updated and extended.

Statistics of Use

The virtual assistant has been visited 2,711 times since March, 2008. The assistant performs between 9 and 16 conversations per day. Omar Alberto Ortiz Vázquez from IAU office mentioned in an interview that visits are not measured by hit, but only by conversation or completed query, this can explain why the numbers are relatively low. Figure 3 shows a conversation sample.

The most frequently asked subjects are:

- Name of certain minister or public officer.
- Governor's and other minister's salary
- Sponsors of governmental programs

Conversation subjects are also related to the season of the year. For example, from January to February the most recurrent subject is tax payment; mid-June questions are more related to scholarships, information about schools, or financial systems for education; September is related to real state and heritage.

A. **Scoreboard response.**
    The information is displayed inside the box once the user specifies a query sent to the system, giving the impression that it is in a chat-like conversation.

B. **Link associated with the response.**
    Website containing information related to the question.

Case 2

There is another example of the use of virtual assistants in the Web Portal of the Federal Government (www.gob.mx) (See Figure 4), This virtual assistant reports 15 queries per day and answers 2.40 questions daily. The average conversation time is 2.40 mins. Questions without answers usually last only 2 mins. ☒According to the data provided by the service supplier "Integración de Negocios en Tecnología de Información" (INTI), the number of queries of this virtual assistant from January to July was 1,105,238. From this, 539,698 are blank hits, and the rest belong to the categories listed on Table 1.

The report from INTI, the service provider, states that the average response time on June was 108 .24 seconds, this was caused by two reasons: empty queries that affect the search engine, and complexity of taxonomies involved in the query.

Figure 3. virtual assistant query (Notations and corresponding activities indicated in the figure)

Table 1. Most frequently requested subjects on June 2008

Query	Amount	Percentage
Scholarships	5361	0.91%
Car Ownership Tax	4223	0.71%
Civil Registry	3466	0.59%
Birth Certificate	3261	0.55%
Fines	1254	0.21%
Sum	**17565**	**2.97%**

Table 2 shows the expanded list of the subjects involved in the queries.

The virtual assistant of the Federal Government's website makes an online survey to evaluate its performance, one of the questions is: the information provided by the VA was useful? 57 percent answered No and only 42 percent said yes.

To the question: Information was… sufficient, fair and not enough?. 60 percent mentioned that not enough information was provided; 24 percent said they got a fair amount of information, and 15 percent considered they received sufficient information. The queries that according to the users, were answered with not enough information or with only a fair amount of data concerned the following topics: Government Programs, education, law and civil rights.

Last question was about the visual arrangement of the information, the evaluation categories

Figure 4. Mexican Federal Government's virtual assistant

Table 2. Detailed queries

Query	Amount	Percentage
National Registry	195	0.00033
Property Tax	194	0.00033
Official Newspaper	132	0.00022
House Mortage	128	0.00022
Plates	119	0.00020
Tobbaco General Law	112	0.00019
Official Newspaper from July 14	109	0.00018
antecedentes penales	88	0.00015
Social Security Institute	85	0.00014
legal record	83	0.00014
employment	83	0.00014
passport	83	0.00014
Social Security Institute for Federal Workers	73	0.00012
National Development Plan	69	0.00012
Official News paper	67	0.00011
Tobbaco law	65	0.00011
Music work at queretaro state	64	0.00011
Car Verification	61	0.00010
Energy Reform debate	58	0.00010
Organization Plan	57	0.00010

were: good, fair, bad. 40 percent mentioned the information arrangement was good, but 39 percent mentioned it was bad, only 20 percent mentioned it was a fair visual arrangement. Topics that were considered to have a bad visual arrangement included: Laws, transportation, Federal Registry Carnet, education.

Data provided from this Virtual Assistant offers additional elements to analyze who the technology is used and perceived by the citizens. Next section elaborates on this matter.

PROBLEMS AND ADVANTAGES OF A VIRTUAL ASSISTANT IN AN E-GOVERNMENT CONTEXT

Despite the technological advance that a virtual assistant represents, in Mexico, very few government web sites use one. Our research found two more web sites with a VA. The Veracruz Tourism web site (www.veracruz.gob.mx) and the Mexican Government citizens portal (www.gob.mx).

In a recent interview with Carlos Patiño, webmaster of the citizens portal told that their VA is at the bottom of the page and hidden from the average user of the site. Patiño mentioned that this was due to the fact that the virtual assistant was considered as a toy and many people asked silly questions, for such reason they reduced the presence of the online assistant. Further studies are required to evaluate and understand the user acceptance of this kind of technology.

The use of VA in government websites has several advantages and disadvantages. According to former director of the AIU, Jorge Loyola:

the VA addresses directly to the citizens using natural language. It is able to answer questions immediately, it can also provide web links to complement the information and this usually leaves citizens completely satisfied

If the virtual assistant has access to the whole information from the government services, it can help citizens to limit their search, direct comments or questions and establish communication with government 24/7.

VA have the following advantages over conventional web sites and common search engines:

- Time saving for the citizen
- Query in natural language, avoiding the use of logical operators (e.g. if, and, or)
- The use of natural language promotes communication
- Answers in natural language are enriched with links to web sites containing related information
- Helps to limit the search to specific boundaries.
- Online presence 24/7

- Cost reductions, minimizing the time public officers spend answering emails or phone calls.

This research and interview with developers, rose several arguments that give elements to solve the question about the problems involved in deploying VA technology in an e-government portal.

1. **Questions Database:** According to Jorge Loyola, the questions database started with 10,000 questions and capturing this data took two or three months. Creating such a large Database is a challenge that not many governments are not willing to take. The amount of questions in the database is a key element for success because it maximizes the possibility that the citizen will find the answer he/she was looking for. The VA should have answers even for unusual questions such as "do you have a boyfriend?". If the citizen does not get an answer or it takes too long he/she gets frustrated and won't use the system anymore.

2. **Information Quality or specialized information:** The VA of the Information Access Unit has the commitment to ensure transparency and free access to government data. For such reason its knowledge database is specialized in government information, in particular from the executive branch. Other kind of information, like wages of the Congressman or Major's salary is not completely specified in the database. Information sharing among governmental agencies is a big problem to establish an efficient VA. The dilemma is whether to provide large amounts of general information or high level of details on specific subjects.

3. **Government expectations of the web site:** If the objective of the government web site is to provide information, promote tax payment, and increase the governor's popularity,

a VA would not help too much. On the other hand, if the web site is citizen-oriented and is intended to provide services and value to its citizens, then a virtual assistant is a good instrument to achieve its goal. However, very few governmental portals share this view.

Of course the main problem of deploying a virtual assistant is the cost. The main justification for such an expense is to provide the citizens with an alternative modality for communication with the government. As a side effect, it can promote cost reduction of the government personnel solving doubts of the community. The investment could be profitable in the long term.

CONCLUSION

The purpose of this chapter was to present virtual assistants as an alternative tool to communicate with citizens. One of the main goals was to show how virtual assistants are useful as interfaces for querying knowledge bases for e-government. Authors developed an e-government and virtual assistant theoretical framework, analyzed two case studies and provided some explanations about the advantages and problems of this technology.

VA technology is still rarely used in e-government portals, and authors believe that this is due to several reasons. In first place, this technology is not well known. A few webmasters know about it and very few of them are willing or able to deploy it. A second reason could be the cost. Currently, these tools are not sold as commercial out-of-the-box solutions. They have high requirements in terms of development time and personnel specialization. However, a small state like Guanajuato in Mexico could afford it.

A third reason, and could be the most logical one, is that VA is difficult to use efficiently. Conversations about government data and services, may not be very attractive for the citizens. Patiño – webmaster of Federal Government portal

– mentioned that people use VA to make fun of the government. This means that people do not know how to use it, or they underestimate the benefits of this technology.

Virtual assistants could be used for different purposes besides providing government information. For example, VA could help on the tax payment process. The virtual assistant technology could be afforded by any small or medium sized government if they help on the tax payment by reducing time spend by citizens, and improving the experience with the government services. Online tax payment interfaces usually have FAQs, and they provide information about exemptions, calculations, and so on. An efficient VA could be used to solve such questions in a more user-friendly way. It could provide extra feedback or give advice while users interact with the system. The latter has been tried before, with the already cited example of the Microsoft Office assistants, but with doubtful results. One of the reasons VA are not used or accepted as expected is that they may display a clumsy behavior, e.g. misunderstand questions or fail to interpret user's actions or intentions while using an application. Research should focus on improving natural language and user behavior understanding.

With this chapter authors tried to provide a first approach to virtual assistants technology and how it can be used in e-government. The technology is still in an early stage of maturity and much work should be done before it can be as efficient as a real human assistant. However, we believe governments can be excellent users and contributors to advance this technology, for the well being of their citizens.

FUTURE RESEARCH

In this preliminary approach to the virtual assistant technology for e-government, authors identified at least five research topics: 1) Assess User Experience; 2) Improve the VA technology; 3) Develop

VAs for other specific areas or services; 4) Collect data from other VA government experiences and 5) Assess Cost Reduction Impact on bureaucracy through the use of a VA.

1. **Assess user experience:** The information provided in this chapter shows the government perspective. The citizen's point of view is missing: What do they think about VAs? Is it good for solving their information needs? What improvements they can identify? How can we measure the impact of the VA in the government portal?

2. **Improve the VA technology:** As mentioned before, improving the VA skills on natural language and user behavior understanding, among others are essential requirements to consolidate VAs as a tool. Web 2.0 technologies such as interactive and collaborative web sites, e.g. wikis, blogs and so on, provide tools that can be exploited by virtual assistants and help them to achieve their goals. For instance, users could be directly involved in the expansion and maintenance of the knowledge base, using wiki-inspired technology. It is important to explore such ideas through systematic research.

3. **Develop virtual assistants for specific areas or services:** As it is mentioned in the previous section, VA benefits can be consolidated if they are deployed in other areas that provide more added value for the citizens. Authors propose to explore other areas of application such as tax payment, e-congress initiatives, and e-voting, this could help citizens to take better decisions.

4. **Collect data from other virtual assistant government experiences:** Experiences like the Federal Portal of Mexico (www.gob.mx) and other mexican state governments have not been documented or analyzed yet. The case studies were presented is not a unique experience. In order to provide a systematic analysis this research need to collect more

information about these cases. The next step on this research is to explore more cases at a national and international level. Furthermore, incorporation of data mining algorithms and techniques can improve the queuing and searching processes.

5. **Assess cost reduction impact on bureaucracy through the use of a VA:** The question of, How good is a VA to reduce costs?, is a very important one. Is it true that investment on this technology impacts bureaucracy? How to quantify such impact? Understanding the impact and consequences of this new technology on public administration is a widely open research topic.

Virtual assistant technology is the top of the iceberg. More developments and technology to come will help governments to achieve their goals. VAs will be the new competitor of the traditional search engine, and they may replace this useful and iconic tool of the Internet Era in the near future.

ACKNOWLEDGMENT

Authors particularly thank Jorge Loyola, former director of the Public Information Access Unit (IAU) who provided them with a detailed description of the Virtual Assistant and encouraged them to believe in this alternative communication channel for the citizen. They also like to thank Omar Alberto Ortiz Vázquez personnel of the IAU, for the information he provided. This research was partially sponsored by the Autonomous University of the State of Mexico.

REFERENCES

Araujo, R. M. (2004). El gobierno electrónico en el ámbito local del país Vasco: del discurso tecnológico a la realidad institucional. Ninth International Congress of Public Administration-CLAD. Madrid, Spain 2-5 de November, Spain. Retrieved March 29, 2007 from http://www.edonostia.net/@mentxu/RAMILO_CLAD.pdf

Campbell, A. (2008). From Secretaries to Virtual Assistants to … Social Media Assistants? Retrieved July 25, 2008 from http://www.theappgap.com/virtual-assistants-social-media.html

Free Press Release (2008). Reliable and Convenient Support for Business Owners, Retrieved August 30, 2008 from http://www.free-press-release.com/news/200802/1201891752.html

Magnenat-Thalmann, N., Kalra, P. & Pandzic, I.S. (1995). Direct Face-to-Face Communication Between Real and Virtual Humans. International Journal of Information Technology, 1(2), 145-157.

Pandzic, I.S., Kalra, P., Magnenat-Thalmann, N. & Thalmann, D. (1994). Real-Time Facial Interaction. Displays (Butterworth-Heinemann), 15(3).

Goto, T., Kshirsagar, S. & Magnenat-Thalmann, N. (2001a). Real-Time Facial Feature Tracking and Speech Acquisition for Cloned Head. IEEE Signal Processing Magazine, 18(3), pp 17-25. May.

Goto, T., Kshirsagar, S. & Magnenat-Thalmann, N. (2001b). Automatic Face Cloning and Animation. IEEE Signal Processing Magazine, 18(3), 17-25.

Ficarra, F. (2004). Internet en la gestión pública y municipal. Revista Latinoamericana de Comunicación CHASQUI, 88.

Holmes, D. (2001). eGov : eBusiness strategies for government. Naperville, Ill.: Nicholas Brealey Pub.

Gutierrez, M., Vexo, F., Thalmann, D. (2002). A MPEG-4 virtual human animation engine for interactive web based applications, Robot and Human Interactive Communication. Proceedings. 11th IEEE International Workshop on, 554-559.

Gil-Garcia, J. R., & Luna-Reyes, L. F. (2003). Towards a Definition of Electronic Government: A Comparative Review. In A. Mendez-Vilas, J. A. Mesa Gonzalez, J. Mesa Gonzalez, V. Guerrero Bote & F. Zapico Alonso (Eds.), Techno-legal Aspects of the Information Society and New Economy: An Overview. Badajoz, Spain: Formatex.

Kalra, P.K. (1993). An interactive multimodal facial animation system. Doctoral dissertation (No. 1183), École Polytechnique Fédérale de Lausanne, Switzerland.

Kshirsagar, S., Joslin, C., Lee, W. & Magnenat-Thalmann, N. (2001). Personalized Face and Speech Communication over the Internet. IEEE Signal Processing Magazine, 18(3), 17-25.

Kshirsagar, E.S. & Magnenat-Thalmann, N. (2004). Generic Personality and Emotion Simulation for Conversational Agents. Computer Animation and Virtual Worlds. 15(1),1-13.

West, J. P., & Berman, E. M. (2001). The Impact of Revitalized Management Practices on the Adoption of Information Technology: A National Survey of Local Governments. Pubic Performance & Management Review, 24(3), 233 - 253.

World Bank (2008). E-government operational definition. Retrieved April 30, 2008, from http://go.worldbank.org/M1JHE0Z280

Chapter XVI
Digital Divide and its Implication on Malaysian E-Government:
Policy Initiatives

Abdul Raufu Ambali
University Technology MARA (UiTM), Malaysia

ABSTRACT

*There is no doubt that e-government application in public administration and its productive use of information technologies (ICTs) would improve the interface between respective governments and their citizens in both service deliveries and provisions of basic needs. However, it is recognized that while there are many benefits that have been obtained by implementing e-government, there are many sectors of society that are not part of this growing electronic culture. Perhaps, economics, lack of access to the Internet and other technologies, low literacy levels and often lack of interest or willingness to use the new technologies, contributes to a country's disparities in e-government practices. It is argued that the concept of citizen's disparities in e-government application in **public sectors** is based on the hypothesis that there are both "information-haves and information-have-nots" in the ICT Era. In addition, the basis for such division may include demographic characteristics such as income, educations, ethnicity, regions and locality. Most of the governments all over the world recognized these fundamental divisional issues but fail to include them along the implementation of their e-government programs. Therefore, from a public policy perspective, the research questions to be asked are: does citizen's disparity matter in a successful application of e-government **in public sectors**? How much do these fundamental disparities (such as illiteracy, economic conditions of individual citizens, family and groups, disabilities and lack of interest or willingness levels) prevent citizens from appreciating the application of e-government? How much do these issues impact on the relationship between government and the citizenry in relation to the thesis of e-government programs? What kinds of policies might be needed by governments to ensure that* *large segments of the citizens are included in the e-government implementations? This chapter seeks to address the digital divide associated with e-government, which can serve as impediment for application of ICT. As a case study, the chapter explores the various initiatives that have been undertaken by the Malaysian government to bridge the gap.*

INTRODUCTION

Science and technology have undergone revolutionary changes in the past century and only a few decades ago that all telecommunications services were delivered over copper wires. More recently, the world has witnessed the exponential growth of mobile telephony and the widespread commercial development of the Internet. Today, the dazzling array of new technologies, services and applications has led to a digital age of information communications technology (ICT) in which access has become a key component of people's lives. These changes brought so much promise. The convergence of technologies, its rapid rate of change and its importance in the development of the economic, social, financial, administration and educational sectors, is opening new opportunities from e-commerce, e-government to tele-education and tele-medicine (Ambali, 2007).

It could be argued that the changes brought about by the Information Age are revolutionary in nature. Malaysian government, towards its vision 2020, welcomes the advent of the information communication technology (ICT) with its opportunities and promises of a new world order and globalization. As such, the country has created a Multimedia Supper Corridor flagship (MSC) in 1996. The MSC has accelerated the country's entry into ICT applications in **public sector** to enhance its services for citizens. In other words, e-government application seeks to reinvent how government works and how it delivers services to the people as can be envisaged in the objective of the whole program. At the same time, the changes brought by ICT applications in **public sectors** pose fresh challenges especially to the

people in the developing world such as Malaysia (see: Ambali, 2007). A number of citizens have been completely shut out of the digital revolution and the promise it holds. As the pace of the technological revolution increases, so does the digital disparity in e-government agenda of the country. The disparity in e-government concerns Malaysian government and governments elsewhere in the world, private sector, multi-lateral organizations, financial institutions, non-governmental organizations and the citizens themselves.

THEORETICAL BACKGROUND TO ICT APPLICATION AND DIGITAL DIVIDE

Diffusion of Innovation Theory and Digital Divide

The Diffusion of Innovations theorists such as Compaine (2001) hold to a belief that the nature of the marketplace dynamics will eventually close the digital divide gaps between **haves and haves-not** without interference from policy-makers. The fundamental root of their thoughts relies on eventual widespread adoption of technologies such as television, radios and the telephone. Compaine established his argument in line with Roger's Diffusion of Innovations Theory (1986) that technologies initially are adopted by those with plentiful resources, and that these early adopters drive the cost down for those with fewer resources, making access an increasingly viable option for those who cannot afford the initial costs of technology. While appreciating the existence of digital gaps among haves and haves not, Compaine has drawn out his view from the dramatic decreases in the cost of computers and Internet services in recent years as well as the increases in the number of minority groups online to support his argument. To the conclusion of this theorist, such a tremendous increase in the number of minority groups or "haves not" online and a drastically drop in the costs of computer is a manifestation that the Digital Divide really is not a problem but rather, a natural progression of the market that would resolve itself over time.

However, in this chapter it is argued that Internet and information technology (IT) in general are incomparable to previous communication media used as a baseline for argument by the Diffusion Innovation theorists. For example, it could be observed that though the early adopters drive the cost down for those with fewer resources, making access an increasingly viable option for those who cannot afford the initial costs of technology as claimed by Diffusion theorists. However, while advances in telephones, radio and television fall along the lines of improved quality, advances in IT allow for increasingly complex tasks, requiring a cumulative set of sophisticated digital skills. In the same line of this observation, Rogers (1986) has also pointed that the adoption of interactive communication technologies such as IT systems incomparable to the older communication technologies such as television for several reasons that include new digital divide problem.

In addition, by a critical assessment of Diffusion Theory of Innovation, one may also argue that IT and the Internet may create a series of dependent S-curves due to their rapidly-evolving nature and the cumulative digital skills required in putting them into effective use. According to Rogers, the rapid evolution of technology may serve to increase existing information gaps. In essence, those who have been using the Internet are developing an increasingly sophisticated set of information seeking and processing skills, and gaps between these advanced users and the late adopters who possess only basic skills are likely

to expand. Thus, instead of a single S-curve of adoption there are successive S-curves based upon skills, not just access to equipment (Rogers 1986). In line with the concept of Digital Divide, Roger's view has been reinforced by Van Dijk (1999) under his discussion on usage gaps in IT technologies. To Dijk, the advancements in technology create situations in which those who are limited to a very basic level of skills now will be outpaced by those who are ahead in the ability to select and process information.

Knowledge Gap Theory and Digital Divide

The views brought out by both Rogers and Van Dijk in addressing the flaws in Diffusion Innovation Theory are seemed to be related to knowledge differentials among high and low educated people in Knowledge Gap Theory of Digital Divide. As far as back in the late 1970s, theorists of Knowledge Gap has hypothesized that an increase in knowledge flow on any given topic would always accompanied by a greater acquisition of knowledge about that topic among the most educated ones (see: Tichenor, Donohue and Olien 1970). This implies that even if everyone become more knowledgeable about a topic, the expansion of knowledge is still relatively greater for the most educated and thus the gaps between those who are highly educated and those with low education increase. In critical assessment of this theory in relation to Digital Divide issue, one can attribute such gap in knowledge between highly educated (the haves) and less educated (the haves–not) show differences in communication skills, stored knowledge, **social network**s and selective exposure. Hence, according to the Knowledge Gap Thesis people with higher levels of education have better abilities to gain information, comprehend such information, and have better chance to discuss any chosen topic with other people all over the world at the expense of the less educated people within the same community, society, locality and country at large. Additionally, Gaziano (1983 and 1997) contended that as more information circulates via IT or any other media devices through society, those in higher education categories acquire them at faster rates than those at lower levels. However, at a later part of the day with more vigorous research activities, Gaziano noted that knowledge inequalities appear to be an enduring phenomenon that can be eroded as technology evolves. In contrast to Gaziano's erosion of knowledge inequalities as technology evolves over time, Van Dijk (1999) holds to a belief that the inability to process information under current technological information age will continue to impede the less educated users. To Dijk, those who are currently able to create and share content online would maintain a learning pace consistent with technological evolution, while those ordinary learning to search for and/or retrieve information on the Internet will forever be playing catch-up which must be seen as an additional gaps beyond basic access. These gaps can be seen in terms of frequency of use of IT due to basic knowledge and skills. Dijk (1997b) indicates that Internet skill level affects level of usage. Along the same line of argument, Hacker and Steiner (2001) contended that having access to the Internet do not necessitate the usage of it unless there is combination of skills and comfort therein. Thus knowledge, skills are prerequisites to the likelihood and frequency of usage. In other words, a large amount of effort may be made to increase the opportunities for Internet access by making it available at all locations to decrease cost of access, yet skill and comfort gaps persist in societies and escalate the existing Digital Divide in E-government.

Structuration Theory and Digital Divide

In the context of Digital Divide, this theory argues that those with power and resources outside of the IT context are the primary early adopters of the technology. Such power and resources have helped them use the technology to meet their needs, to further enhance their resources as well as the rules they brought into the IT. Thus, IT application seems to reproduce the existing power-relation gaps in the social system as it opens up a new channel from which those without power and resources (haves-not) are further excluded. The theory suggests that the rapid evolution of IT to meet the increasing demand for the more sophisticated and efficient processing of information is determined by those who negotiate what has value in society. Those who are possessing sophisticated resources and skills continue to shape the technology. The outcome is a technology that primarily meets the needs of those who adopted it first, while the consequential outcome is that those already excluded fall further behind. For example, Castells (1996; and 2000) argues that those with the resources to effectively utilize information technology to network are the negotiators of a society, while those without these resources are excluded from another opportunity for social influence.

It could also be seen that certain members of society have access to the information and benefits that the Internet provides, the technical skills to use the access optimally to improve their life situations and/or the ability to alter social structures that produce change in social institutions, while other members of society do not. Obviously, this is nothing but a new status division that emerges in society between those who have and can use the technology and those who are excluded (Tranter and Willis 2002). For example, IT users are able to build **social network**s, connect with others without concern for geography, and influence existing elements of society, such as governments and organizations at the expense of those who cannot afford to use it (Tranter and Willis 2002). This is the networking ability that Castells (2006) refers to, and it is the key to the creation of structured inequality if there is no effective policy in place to bring equality in IT adoption among **haves and haves-not** in society.

The work of Dijk (1999) provides further insight into the structural inequalities that may be the unexpected consequence of unequal IT adoption in society. According to Dijk (1999), modern society is in the process of becoming a society which organizes its relationships around connections among members of society and its structures. In other words, application of IT in general is a context in which multiple types of social interaction occur, making it an intricate part of societal organization and may intensify the existing societal stratification, especially the existing information inequalities, as those who have the resources to adopt the technology shape it and those without fall behind. Finally, the arguments made by Castells, and Dijk are useful in understanding the societal implications of the Digital Divide. Although they approach the problems of technological exclusion in distinct ways, but they share a common theme that application of ICT can be used to unintended or unconsciously create, alter, maintain, reproduce or escalate the existing Digital Divide in society if care is not taken by policy-makers.

E-GOVERNMENT IN MALAYSIA

Objectives of E-Government

In any country or in Malaysia, e-government is being regarded as one of the ICT applications in the **public sector**. The principle objectives of e-government in Malaysia are to offer efficient, high quality administrative on-line services to citizens and businesses. It also includes an effort to streamline government's internal processes to improve quality of services, reduce costs and increase productivity. In addition, the objective is to strengthen data security and protect privacy as well as to increase citizen's participation in governance. Above all, the e-government application also aims to create transparency through good documentation, effective communication

and traceability. In other words, the primary objectives are to bring dramatic improvements in the quality of government's interactions with its citizens and business by enhancing conveniences, accessibility and efficiency of its services and also to make government more responsive to the needs of its citizens (Anwar and Soon, 1999, p.168; Karim and Khairuddin, 1999, p.185, MAMPU, 1997, p.2).

Focus Areas of E-Government Applications

The vision of Malaysian e-government sought the business and civil service collaboratively working together using the ICT as tools for the benefit of all Malaysians. Thus, e-government has been implemented in five different areas that engage all the citizens in one way or the other. The areas of e-government include: electronic delivery of driver and vehicle registration and/or licensing and summons services, utility bill payments, on-line health information, electronic procurement, human resource management **information systems** and project monitoring system (Karim and Khairuddin, 1999, p.192, MAMPU, 1997, p.5).

The Progress of E-Government in Malaysia

Application of e-Government has been introduced into various aspects of **public sectors** in Malaysia such as, licensing and related vehicle services and utility payments, electronic procurement, generic office environment of the Prime Minister's Office, human resource management **information system** and project monitoring system as stated earlier. The application of e-Government to licensing and related vehicle services and utility payment enables the public to transact with the government and other utility companies using variety of access methods. With the one-stop e-service's window provided by the government, public are able to carry out **transaction**s relating to renewing of license, registration of new vehicle of all kinds, paying electricity and/or telephone bills and obtain health information through a kiosk in shopping mall or Internet through the PC at home. The application of electronic government in these areas was firstly introduced in the Klang Valley in February 1998 as pilot project. Today, its successful application has been extended to a large number of urban cities throughout the country.

In another application, the electronic procurement allows the government agencies to select items to be procured from the network electronically. The procurement of goods and services through the Central Contract are automated with connection facilities between the buyers and suppliers. This application involves direct purchase, quotation and tenders. Similarly, the application of generic office environment (GOE) has provided a full integration and scaleable paperless office environment for the Prime Minister's Office using the multimedia technology. Hence, the GOE accommodates various types of business functional components, which closely reflect any organization's business processes to deal with the government directly. The GOE encompasses an enterprise-wide information management system (EIMS), enterprise-wide communication management system (ECMS) and enterprise-wide collaboration management **system**. Generally, the EIMS, as part of e-government, provides a universal interface for business citizen to manage, find, retrieve and compose information that are needed for their day to day operations. Since the establishment of GOE in 1998, the current status of operation has been extended to the office of the Prime Minister, the Deputy Prime Minister, the Chief Secretary to the government, the Cabinet Division and MAMPU and other government agencies. Thus, information flows and processes within the government were also improved thereby speeding up the policy development and proper coordination among the government agencies (Ibrahim, 2003).

Malaysian e-government application in **public sector** has reached a progressive point in relation to project monitoring system. The implementation has started with pilot project since 1998 with full grown today and rolled-out since March 2000 to support decision-making system. It was designed as a mechanism for improving efficiency and effectiveness of government development projects. It enables the concerned government agencies to work in a collaborative environment characterized by workgroup computing, workflow management systems, common database access and messaging services. Operationally, it enriches the agencies with project status information as well as ministries to consolidate and/or produce report analysis for evaluation. Hence, it has improved managerial functions with services relating to data mining, statistical trend analysis, forecasting and simulation. The trend and the progress in e-government have benefited many citizens across a wide range of spectrum of government functions.

Hence, the rapid advance of ICT application in **public sector** has created more opportunities for citizens and businesses to deal directly with the government for different services. Currently, many new subschemes under e-government program have taken place in Malaysia. These include My-Kad, and e-Perolehan which have benefited some citizens widely. E-Perolehan has been designed as an official and secure online marketplace to build the interface between suppliers and government agencies for business deals. Today, My-Kad scheme in e-government application has given the citizens opportunity to obtain their national identity electronically as well as cashless financial **transaction**s. My-Kad replaces the functions of passport in terms efficient entry and exit of Malaysian citizens at immigration checkpoints as well as prompt retrieval of health and personal data during emergency cases (Karim, 2003). However, it has been observed that the Digital Divide has widened the gap between "haves" and "haves-not" and deprive certain segment of people from enjoying the benefit of e-government in Malaysia.

DIGITAL DIVIDE'S IMPLICATION ON MALAYSIAN E-GOVERNMENT

While the implementation of e-government policy in Malaysia has benefited a wide number of citizens in the country, quite a number of digital divide issues have associated with its applications in various aspects of public services. The central theme of the issue in e-government applications to provide the basic services to the people lies in separation between "haves and have-nots". On one side of the equation are the people who can afford or who have access to computer, a high-speed broadband connection and plethora of services provided by the government. On the other side are people who cannot afford the technology or cannot get broadband access due to their location. In addition, there are majority of citizens who have learning and/or cultural limitations to the usage of technology devices in carrying out their basic needs activities and **transaction** with government. This segment of the population is at a serious disadvantage of availing the e-government services. Thus, lack of access to networked technology results in a substantial segment of society having neither the skills nor the mean to participate in a progressively "knowledge-based" Malaysian e-government schemes. The concentration of ICT infrastructure in urban areas of the country has widened the disparity among the rural and urban dwellers of peninsular Malaysia. Geographically, the rural states of Sabah and Sarawak are far short of the national average in digital infrastructure distribution by the government.

According to Marhaini and Asiyah (2007), "out of 136 districts that make up the country, 89 have been identified as underserved areas', (p.11). It is an obvious fact that access to e-government services normally involves investment in a computer, various types of software, a phone line and even a printer or fax machine. A study on Internet subscriber in 2002 has shown that more than 90% of the subscribers of TM.Net were located in the Klang Valley areas and urban cities of Johor Bharu in the southern part of Peninsular, Penang Kuantan, Kota Kinabalu and Ipoh; living the rural poor behind the digital access to government information and services. In addition, 73% of subscribers of Malaysian second largest ICT providers (ISP.Jaring) were from the capital cities and urbanized states of Selangor, Johor and Pulau Penang. Apart from urban-rural disparities in ICT facilities for e-government services, there are disparities in ICT infrastructure among city dwellers themselves due to economic reason. Economic disparities have been reflected in Personal Computer (PCs) ownerships.

Taking from diffusion innovation theory, the information in Figure 1 has shown that the Digital Divide issue is obvious and has a big implication for e-government applications in Malaysia. The diagram reflects different level of ICT gaps such as access, adoption and impact gaps among people. These gaps are fundamental issues that need to be addressed before a successful e-government can be achieved by the Government. For example, the PCs ownerships have been concentrated in large urban cities compared to the rural areas. In other words, 65% of the distribution of PCs ownership concentrated in the Federal Territories, Penang, Selangor and capital cities of other states at the expense of the rural areas or concentrated in the hands of the rich at the expense of the poor people in the country. Research has also shown that the rate of PC penetration into poor household is as low as 5% of the whole country. Another potential digital divide issue that is hindering the spill-over of e-government service benefits to the people is the low rate of Internet penetration at 6% for every 100 household populations in the rural poor areas as compared to urban and the rich dweller's households (Marhaini and Asiyah, 2007, p.11).

Besides, digital literacy among the people is another disparity that challenges the e-govern-

Figure 1. *The Digital Divide status (Source: Adapted from Bridging Digital Divide, Access. Adoption and Value, Kuala Lumpur, 5 Dec., 2006)*

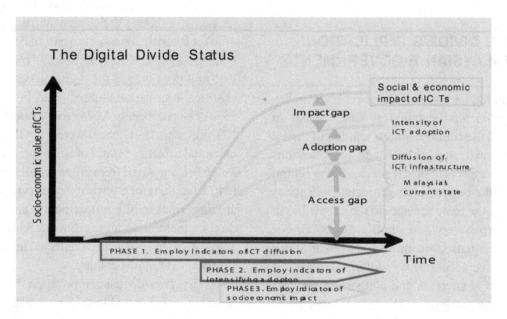

ment thesis in Malaysia. In other words, there exists a policy issue of digital information rich and digital information poor among Malaysian citizens in relation to the degree of literacy. While in urban areas of the country and/or within the rich communities one could witness a high level of information rich, and the information poor characterized the rural areas and its dwellers. This disparity is similar to the incidence of poverty scenario. Perhaps, this is due to high cost that must be incurred in installing and maintaining telecommunications services in poor areas. In addition, a host of obstacles stand in the way of many poor Malaysian citizens, particularly in Sabah and Sarawak. Many people live scattered in the midst of dense rainforest, often hilly terrain that obscures line of sight and complicates telecommunications infrastructure development. This makes it difficult for many of them to have access to e-government services. Hence, it places them at a big disadvantage of benefiting much, if at all, from the national e-government policy implementation in the country.

Moreover, in a study conducted by Sharifah (2004), digital divide is evident from Tumpat area, a fishermen district located in Kelantan state on the east coast of west Malaysia with about 25,000 households. The result of the empirical study shows that out of the total male respondents, 59 percent are non-computer users and among the female, 41 percent are non-computer users in terms of personal computer user as shown in Table 1.

In Sharifah's study, an in-depth observation has shown that those in the age group of 15 to 20 years are the dominant computer users as indicated in Table 2. In addition, as age increases, computer usage is seen to be decreased proportionately and that the older population with age above 50 years "has only seen computers from a far". (p.2)

One may argue that the question of PC usage and non-usage to carry out **transactions** with government via E-government programs has to do with accessibility as well as connectivity, which can be examined through the number of PC ownerships and rate/level of **Internet connectivity** in a given community. Digital divide becomes an obvious evident Tumpat area of Kelantan for

Table 1. Personal computer (PC) users by gender (Source: Sharifah (2004), p.2

Category	Male %	Female %	Total %
None PC user	59	41	100
PC user	60	40	100

Table 2. Age, PC users and education level (Source: Sharifah (2004), p.2)

Education Level	Age	PC Users		
		No (%)	Yes (%)	Total (%)
Primary	10 to 12	4.5	7.8	7.0
Secondary	13 to 17	9.1	34.0	28.1
Tertiary / Working	18 to 55	59.1	58.2	58.4
Pensioner	56 & above	27.3	0	6.5
Total		144 (100)	241 (100)	385 (100)

example. Empirical results from survey study by Sharifah have shown that out of the total surveyed sample of 207 respondents in that community, 46 percent have no PC at home. As reported, "Majority of the PC belongs to a family member, who is usually working or studying at a higher learning institution", (p. 3). Hence, computer sharing is obvious within these households. But with some controls it becomes a big implication for those who have to rely on others computers for carrying out any forms of e-government **transactions**. As such, large majority members of community have to solely depend on cyber-café due to lack of **Internet connectivity** at home as well as possession of a PC.

Looking at connectivity on a national level-base, the data from the Household Use of the Internet Survey, 2005 conducted by the Malaysian Communication and Multimedia Commission (MCMC) have shown that Digital Divide exists on several observable manifestations in terms of disparity between top and bottom groups including age, educational attainment, marital status,

employment status, purchase via Internet, number of personal computers in household and monthly income category as well as growing percentage point trails between top and bottom ranked groups for each category in significant terms (see Tables 3, 4, 5, 6, 7, 8, and 9).

Table 3. Distribution of household users of the Internet by age (Source: MCMC, (2005), Household Use of the Internet Survey, p. 13)

Age	Percent %
Below 15	6.5
15-19	18.6
20-24	17.2
25-29	12.5
30-34	12.2
35-39	9.9
40-44	9.6
45-49	5.1
Above 50	8.4

Table 4. Distribution of household users of the Internet by educational attainment (Source: MCMC, (2005), Household Use of the Internet Survey, p. 13)

Educational Attainment	Percent %
None	*0.1
Primary	1.4
Secondary	37.7
Diploma	25.4
Degree and higher	35.4

*Note: *Among those no longer schooling*

Table 5. Distribution of household users of the Internet by marital status (Source: MCMC, (2005), Household Use of the Internet Survey, p. 14)

Marital Status	Percent %
Single	55.0
Married	44.3
Divorce/widowed	0.7

Table 6. Distribution of household users of the Internet by employment status (Source: MCMC, (2005), Household Use of the Internet Survey, p. 14)

Employment Status	Percent %
Employer	5
Employed	37.7
Self Employed	8.6
Unemployed	12.0
Student	36.5

Table 7. Distribution of household users of the Internet by purchase via Internet (Source: MCMC, (2005), Household Use of the Internet Survey, p. 17)

Purchase via Internet	Percent %
Yes	9.3
No	90.7

Table 8. Distribution of household users of the Internet by No of PC in household (Source: MCMC, (2005), Household Use of the Internet Survey, p. 18)

No of PC	Percent %
1	62.8
2	26.0
3	7.8
4	2.3
5	0.5
More than 5	0.6

Table 9. Distribution of household users of the Internet by monthly income (Source: MCMC, (2005), Household Use of the Internet Survey, p. 19)

Monthly Income	Percent %
No income	43.9
Less than RM1,000	7.9
RM1,000 but less than RM3,000	30.5
RM 3,000 but less than RM5,000	11.1
RM5,000 and above	0.5
More than 5	6.6

Again, as seen from the above tables there are parities between each category types and reciprocal displacement of top-ranked groups. Therefore, it is impossible to dispute the historic lag among each category of Digital Divide incidence found with Internet users in all tables. From an analytical perspective, it is therefore not supportable to suggest that the Digital Divide is gone, or going soon. In fact, as one may combined the data and understanding of this phenomenon, it is getting wider. As a matter of simple fact one can see that historically under-serviced groups, particularly young people in primary education, are being left behind more privileged sectors of society. Findings from those tables demonstrates that usage and **Internet connectivity** is inversely related to income, age, number of PC per houses, education, employment status and marital status for a given group and that these variables may function independently of one another with severe implications for a successful e-Government program. It seems clearly that anything less than a continued and determined effort to improve access for all Malaysians and most particularly our nation's children as they prepare for future responsibility is imperative.

Overall, a relative comparison of information in the above tables reflects the magnitude of barriers to **Internet connectivity** in terms of education, age and income, and household in line with the thesis of the Digital Divide issues. From the standpoint of the optimistic view of solving problem of the Digital Divide, in terms of quality, e-Government program should have resulted in a greater level of **Internet connectivity** in the country, but not. Current connectivity levels means that legacy systems and processes may have to be perpetuated indefinitely. This will at best delay many of the benefits and savings associated with e-Government program, leading to potentially increased stakeholder costs and inconveniences. A societal saturation point may underlie this outcome, whereby once **Internet connectivity** has reached a certain level in particular environments

or social structural mixes, diminishing returns on incremental investment to increase it may apply. This will have a big impact on e-Government applications as the level of readiness in society is not up to the expectation.

A close examination of the nature of these identified issues were the existing policy problems of Digital Divide before the inception of e-government application in **public sectors** and/or services, which needed to be addressed by the government ever before the move to or draft along the e-government policy formulation and implementation.

GOVERNMENT POLICY AND STRATEGY FOR DIGITAL DIVIDE

In line with the effort to narrow Digital Divide that can jeopardize the e-Government program in the country, the government has came up with a policy of up-grading the ICT infrastructure through several initiatives including increasing the capacity of the transmission backbone up to 10 gigabits per second and introducing the Network Management System for better service availability under the Eighth and Ninth Malaysia Plans. According to policy effort, the ICT infrastructure will be extended to the rural areas to reduce the digital divide. Among the programs to be implemented include Infodesa and Internet Desa, which will offer awareness and training courses and facilitate the introduction of new and innovative services in the communication industry. In relation to that, Ministry of Communication and Multimedia Industries has developed three principles of universal service to all Malaysians, which include availability, **equitable access** and affordability of ICT device.

Availability means that coverage of network services such as telephone, Internet, etc. must be made available nationwide, when and where they are needed. While **equitable access** means all people regardless of age, educational status, income and race should be given equal treatment; there must be no discrimination in terms of price, service and quality, regardless of geographical location. Affordability is translated as network services that must be affordable to all people of Malaysia. The policy aims to achieve balance between areas and groups of people so as to bridge the Digital Divide between those who are 'information rich' and 'information poor'. In order to ensure the availability of and **equitable access** to network infrastructure and services, the Government contended that there is need to provide wider and more even coverage between the different areas and groups in the society. The provision of infrastructure through 'network rollout' to enhance both computer and Internet penetration can bridge the digital divide between areas and groups of people in the country, (see: Ministry of Energy and Communication, 2007). According to Zaiton and Barbara (2005), "the government has removed all taxes on computers and related items, with the intension of bringing their prices down" to support the policy efforts on the one hand and to assist the citizens on the other hand (p.8). In addition, the UNDP Project Document on Malaysia's National Framework for Bridging Digital Divide in October 2004, has shown that the policy, legal and regulatory framework have been reformed to substantially expand people's connectivity to information and communication technologies (ICT). In addition, a national "e-readiness" assessment has been carried out on connectivity, policy frameworks and human and institutional capacity. On top of that legislative framework adopted and being implemented to foster ICT use (see, UNDP: A National Strategic Framework for Bridging the Digital Divide). In preparation of the strategies and plan of action, the National Framework for Bridging Digital Divide, inline with the UNDP Project Document includes the following outline tasks:

1. Measuring the state of the spatial Digital Divide;

2. Developing a framework including relevant indicators for the government

3. Review of current government policies and strategies for Bridging the digital divide (BDD);

4. Review current initiatives undertaken by both the Government and non-government organizations (NGOs) and status of implementation of BDD;

5. Develop a framework including relevant indicators for government to regularly assess progress and performance towards bridging the digital divide;

6. Analyze and assess the impact of existing BDD programs and projects on target groups;

7. Analyze the problems and issues involved in implementing BDD programs and projects among the target groups;

8. Establish benchmarks based on international and regional best practices in BDD; and

9. Propose specific strategies and a plan of action to further improve and enhance the effectiveness of BDD programs, (see: Government of Malaysia/UNDP Project Document, 2004, p.5).

Given the fact that income disparities among people is a fundamental issue in Digital Divide and big implication for e-Government program in the country, the Government continues to address the issues of income imbalance between and within ethnic groups, income groups, economic sectors, regions and even the states. With the expected high economic growth in the nearest future 2020, the middle income group is expected to increase in size and share of income. As part of a major long-term income distribution objective, the Government will create a bigger and more prosperous middle-income group in addition to increasing income of the lower income group. Various measures will be implemented to reduce income imbalances between the rural and urban areas as well as between the less developed and the more developed states. In addition, the Government has come up with measures to encourage smallholders and farmers, particularly those with small and uneconomical land size, to diversify into activities such as aquaculture and livestock farming as well as in non-agricultural income generating activities regardless of gender status, (see: Ninth Malaysia Plan).

POLICY INITIATIVES TO ADDRESS DIGITAL DIVIDE

The Malaysian government has shown a sense of concern and awareness of various disparities, in its multifaceted dimensions, that could jeopardize the e-government application in **public sector** of the country. Thus, in light of the issues of access, literacy and others in diverse communities, many strategies have been developed at the federal, state governments, private and/or corporate philanthropic; computer and Internet design industry levels as well as community initiative level.

The state governments have developed local programs and initiatives to address digital divide through (a) each state's public utility commission, (b) franchise agreements with national and international telecommunications providers, (c) infrastructure investments and (d) the Ministry of Education's initiatives.

In the Third Outline Perspective Plan 2001-2010 (OPP3), the Malaysian government stressed the need for increased use of information and communication technology, Since then, Malaysian government has taken positive strides to build an administration based on information technology starting with the creation of a high-tech multimedia zone, research agencies and an intelligent cybercity about 50 kilometers South of Kuala Lumpur. The new initiative of e-school project aimed to further enable Malaysia government to narrow the digital disparities and its impact on e-government applications between rural and urban society. It also aims to empower every pupil

in both rural and urban area, after completing school to become a contributing member of the 'K' generation facing the challenges of the K-Economy promoted by the Prime Minister. Thus, the government with its introduction of e-school believes that closing the *knowledge gap* is one of the country's two main challenges in the IT field. The other is to increase the overall number of people with knowledge of using the Internet and other e-government enablers in rural areas.

In addition, the Kedah State Development Cooperation has joint ventured with One-Ed Dot Com, Ericsson, Widuri Canggih Sdn Bhd and Virtual Applications Technology Sdn Bhd to provide digital education nationwide for youth, students and citizens at large. Unimas researchers recently loaded computer onto buffaloes for the final stretch of their voyage to *e-Bario*, an isolated community in Sarawak's Kelabit highlands. The initiative known as *e-Bario* involves wiring a 'smart' school to introduce students of the rural area to IT. The second objectives was to make the residents of the community of scattered villages use wired technologies for social development, especially to reverse the outflow of young people lured by jobs to Malaysia's towns and cities. The Kuala Lumpur City Hall (DBKL) has recently launched *e-Warga Kota* (e-City Residents) with aim to use ICT as enablers not only for bridging the digital divide but to improve the socio-economic well-being of Malaysia's urban poor. This initiative project introduces ICT training and access to residents in Public Housing Sri Perak Bandar Baru Sentul and Public Housing Jalan Jelatek, through the upgrading of local ICT resource centers. In year 2003, Malaysian Grid for learning (MyGfL) was endorsed by the Prime Minister of Malaysia YAB Datuk Seri Abdullai Ahmad Badawi as the national *e-Learning* initiative to promote and support the lifelong learning agenda in Malaysia to accelerate the spill-over of e-government benefits and/or e-services to the people especially the poor through the use of ICT. The initiative project was aimed to connect the Malaysian learning community, schools and educational institutions, industry, communities, individuals and online learning resources into one integrated platform. Thus, the program is an integrated online learning platform catering to Malaysians of every age, from kindergarten children to adult learners in both rural and urban areas of the country. It will become a one-stop center for all existing e-learning projects by providing online learning resources and services to all (http://www.mygfl. net.my, accessed 24 July, 2007).

Other initiatives include some collaborative activities between Sabah State Library, Unit Kemajuan IT Negeri (KIT), Chief Minister's Department, Jabatan Perkhidatan Komputer Negeri, Jabatan Pendidkan, KKIP Communications Sdn Bhd and Des@Net computer training center to promote the effective use and awareness of ICT to improve standards of living, learning, work and recreation among the rural Sabah people and students as well as the people access to government services. The initiative has grown faster to capture 10 schools in the rural district of Papar, Kudat and Kota Belud in Sabah. For example, each school is visited once every fortnight for full day training in basic computing skills, usage of Internet browsing and e-mail, word processing and homepage creation. This collaborative initiative via Des@Net has also been used as training workshops in ICT for women in Sipitang by Sabah Women Advisory Council. In peninsular Malaysia, ICT hubs have been set up in semi-urban and rural areas of Klang, Muar, Terengganu, Tampin in Negeri Sembilan and Perlis primarily to gain access to e-government services and training in ICT under a project called *e-Learning for Life*. Similar initiative project was formulated by UNDP through the support of Coca Cola in January 2002 and the Malaysian Ministry of Education. This initiative project in Malaysia is the latest in a series of communication partnerships that Coca Cola has launched in Asia to support local efforts to bridge the so-called digital divide and disparities. Another potential policy initiative to

bridge e-government disparities among Malaysian citizens was the establishment of a Community Communications Development Program (CCDP) in December 2002 by the government. The initiative was a collaborative effort between Maxis Communications, Time dotcom and the State Economic Planning Units (EPUs) to build capacity as well as to introduce and encourage growth in the usage of communications and multimedia-based e-services to communities all over Malaysia, which have limited access to communications networks and services. The first phase of the program introduced a range of communications and multimedia services to facilitate Internet access, e-commerce and e-learning, e-government with five sites per district in Pahang, Perak, Kedah, Perlis and Malacca. The remaining States were included in the second phase of the project initiative. The Selangor state government has embarked on another potential initiative to close the e-government disparities between poor and rich, rural and urban dwellers. The Selangor state government in collaboration with Coca Cola, and Ministry of Education has established 64 ICT centers of which 46 were located in rural areas of the state. The focus on rural communities is based on computer literacy rates of 20% in contrast to 80% in urban areas. From the year 2002 until the present period, the state government of Selangor has introduced computers to rural children through Community Development Department's KEMAS Kindergartens as well as giving the local village heads a three-month computer training course (http://www.selangor. gov.my/suk/prodnews.php?cod=60, accessed on 28 of Aug., 2007).

ASSESSMENT AND PROSPECTS FOR FUTURE

The Malaysian government, in its Ninth Malaysia Plan, has come up with some constructive and productive initiatives of addressing socio-economic inequalities among citizens in the country in order to pave way for a successful e-Government program in the country. The efforts include eradication of hardcore poverty as well as reducing disparities between rural and urban population by improving access to basic needs that facilitate the e-government services for poor people. Thus, under the Ninth Malaysia Plan, the government has allocated about RM368.2 million for the advancement towards bridging the e-government disparities and/or digital divide. The National IT Council (NITC) together with several ministries and agencies were tasked monitoring and running of this policy initiative over the stipulated period in most of the rural areas (Mid-Term Review of Eighth Malaysia Plan 2001-2005, p.296).

In line with the Ninth Malaysia Plan, the Ministry of Energy, Water and Communication has initiated a comprehensive program of solving Digital Divide problem in the country with much focus to rural people. With the support from Federal Government of Malaysia, the Ministry has adopted various strategies for enhancing the rate of computer and Internet penetration across the nation. The strategies taken by the Ministry include: Universal Service Provision (USP), PC Ownership Campaign, Rural Internet Centers Programs, e-Community and Community Awareness Program.

The Ministry has embanked on the implementation of its strategies especially USP for solving digital Divide with the following objectives:

1. Preparing the communication infrastructure services and internet access services at rural area, urban fringe area, and inland area;
2. Bridging the digital divide between urban community, rural community, and underserved community;
3. Preparing the ICT practice and skills for rural community, urban fringe community, and inland community; and
4. Bridging the mind divide between urban community and rural community through internet access.

The USP implementation has been scheduled to undergo four phases as shown in Table 10.

The implementations of the USP project works in partnership with other ministry and government agency like a Ministry of Health Malaysia, Ministry of Education Malaysia, National Library and Rural Libraries. Various Ministries and agencies were employed to suggest schools, rural clinics and rural libraries especially at rural territory, urban fringe and inland that are lack of tool facilities such as computer, internet cable, communications cable following the equable criteria. Computer facilities and internet cable has been served for free for trainees and community territory. The strategic implementation progress of the USP was carried out through open tender to Telecommunications Company to:

Provide, sender, install, give commission and maintenance communications tools and data using suitable technology and also given training for trainee and community delegate from every locations. The locations available with 2-4 computers together with internet cable, printer, scanner or digital camera (for rural clinic). Service maintenance are about (5) years. JKR (ICT Branch) has constituted as a Project Management Consultant, (See: MEWC, 2007).

Upon the implementation of these strategies, many potential prospects for future begun to emanate among the rural community in terms of access to information, improvement in computer skills, rate of Internet penetration and connectivity at large. The findings of the report about this initiative have proven a high potential and prospects for future success of Digital Divide program and spill-over of e-Government benefits to all people in Malaysia.

The implementation of USP project first phase has started since 2002. Between the period 2002 and 2007, the project has embraced 110 schools in Sarawak and Sabah making a total of 220 schools with Internet, computer facilities. In fact

Table 10. Implementation of usp project phases (Source: Ministry of Energy, Water and Communication, 2007)

Phase 1:
Started on year 2002
Service and maintenance are about 5 year (2002-2007);
Location : 220 schools; 110 in Sarawak and 110 in Sabah;
Direct negotiation with TMB by Ministry of Financial;
Note: Already integrated to 10,000 school under SchoolNet Project

Phase 2:
Started on year 2003;
Service and maintenance are about 5 year (2003 – 2008) ;
Location : 226 rural libraries and rural clinics/clinics; 50 rural clinics/clinics and 176 rural libraries all over the country;
ICT training for trainee and community representative of about 972 people;
Accomplished by Maxis Company through open tender.

Phase 3:
Started on year 2004;
Service and maintenance are about 5 year (2004 – 2009) ;
496 rural clinics/clinics and rural libraries; 309 rural clinics/clinics and 187 rural libraries all over the country;
ICT basic practice for trainee and community representative about 972 people;
Network Monitoring System (NMS) instalment;
Accomplished by TM Company through open tender.

Phase 4:
Started on year 2005;
Term of period for services and maintenances are for 5 years (2005 – 2010) ;
Location : 147 rural/branch/ and district libraries all over the country;
ICT basics and practice for trainee and community representative from Phase 2 until Phase 4, about 2000 peoples;
9 CSKC - (Community Service and Knowledge) pioneer project locations, at the selected USP project locations;
1 pioneer project location served home line phone and Internet using VSAT technology that already have at the selected USP project locations;
Central Monitoring System (CMS) instalment for all phase;
Developing Network Operation Centre - (NOC);
Integrating all phases in one USP project network;
Developing 'Bridging the Digital Divide' portal;
Producing 'Aspirasi Digital' - the bulletin every twice a month;
Implementing by TM through open tender.

Table 11. Summary of overall USP location by school, clinic, and library (Source: Ministry of Energy, Water and Communication, 2007)

Phase	Year	School	Clinic	Library	Total
1	2002	220	-	-	**220**
2	2003	-	50	176	**226**
3	2004	-	309	187	**496**
4	2005	-	-	147	**147**

it has been integrated to 10,000 schools under a hybrid project called SchoolNet. In terms of rural location and coverage, USP implementation of the second phase in 2003 has covered 174 rural libraries and 50 rural clinics all over the country bringing the total to 226 equipped with various facilities such as Internet and computers to build the information gaps in rural areas (Table 11). Table 12 shows the distribution according to state. Within the second phase of the project, 972 ICT training for trainee and community representative accomplished by Maxis Company through an open tender was implemented for people in the rural areas to close the information access gaps as well as skills in ICT. The second phase of USP project implementation is expected to finish by 2008. The third phase of the project has started since 2004 and estimated to finish by 2009 with a target of 496 rural clinics and rural libraries to be covered with ICT facilities. So far, 309 rural clinics and 187 rural libraries have been equipped with computer and Internet facilities all over

the country (Table 10; and Table 11 according to state). The third phase of the project has also covered a Network Monitoring System (NMS) instalment accomplished TM Company through an open tender.

The implementation of the fourth phase of the USP project has also started in year 2005 with location of more 147 rural branch and district libraries all over the country to be equipped facilities. It is expected to continue till 2010. Moreover, ICT basics and practice trainings have been given to trainees and community representatives from Phase 2 until Phase 4 and about 2000 peoples have gained enough skills. As indicated in Table 13, 9 Community Service and Knowledge have been established at the selected USP project locations. There is one pioneer project location that served home line phone and Internet using VSAT technology at the selected USP project locations. In addition, a Central Monitoring System (CMS) instalment for all phases was established. The phase four (2005-2010) implementation has

Table 12. Total library under USP project according to state (Source: Ministry of Energy, Water and Communication, 2007)

State	USP 2	USP 3	USP 4	Total
Perlis	12	3	2	17
Kedah	18	10	11	39
P.Pinang	14	6	1	21
Perak	18	14	20	52
Selangor	15	17	9	41
Kuala Lumpur	-	-	5	5
Negeri Sembilan	9	5	9	23
Melaka	14	6	6	26
Johor	15	29	3	47
Pahang	19	5	15	39
Terengganu	2	24	12	38
Kelantan	2	1	6	9
Sabah	18	24	5	47
Sarawak	20	43	41	104
W.P.Labuan	-	-	2	2
Total	**176**	**187**	**147**	**510**

committed to Developing Network Operation Centre - (NOC); integrating all phases in one USP project network; developing 'Bridging the Digital Divide' portal and producing 'Aspirasi Digital' - the bulletin every twice a month which is being accomplished by TM through an open tender.

RECOMMENDATION

This study puts forward a few recommendations for better implementation of e-government initiatives:

1. Government should take measure of enhancing affordability of ICT components that are needed for absorbing the benefits of e-government services by poor people. This may include an appropriate policy measure needed to lower the cost hardware and all online access tools like PCs, laptops, mobile phone and other digital devices associated with e-government enhancement.

2. There is an urgent need to improvement of network and provision of better electricity in underserved areas. This is critical for achievement of e-government goals in rural areas of the country as this can make the rural residents unconnected with ICT that would help benefit them from e-government mission.

3. Government should encourage more commercial expansion to rural areas and corporate responsibility among ICT and/or service providers.

4. Government should be cautioned of grant-making framework brought by many ICT service providers to address the problem of disparities among the people. These types of organizations often come to digital divide

Table 13. RMK9 - Service Centre and Knowledge Community (PPIK) (Source: Ministry of Energy, Water and Communication, 2007)

State	USP Location	USP Location Phase 5	Total PPIK Location
Perlis	22	5	8
Kedah	57	18	19
P.Pinang	40	19	14
Perak	76	24	26
Selangor	59	18	20
Kuala Lumpur	5	-	1
Negeri Sembilan	34	10	12
Melaka	45	19	15
Johor	69	22	23
Pahang	61	22	21
Terengganu	61	28	21
Kelantan	23	14	8
Sabah	77	30	26
Sarawak	104	69	35
W.P.Labuan	2	-	1
TOTAL	**735**	**298**	**250**

table with their own business agenda. They are often concerned about their own survival in very fast and ever-changing business environment. They would like to expand their markets with a primary aim of self-serving that is necessary aligned with community needs. In this context, government should be aware that some of these private companies may be bringing more problems than solutions to the existing digital disparities facing the rural and urban poor communities.

5. The replication of the successes of the universal design model for access remains elusive to the underserved communities with e-government thesis. Therefore, to make a design solution for access truly inclusive of all citizens, there is a need to encompass more of the diversity of human experience such as the lack of education and media literacy training, political participation, culture or gender.

CONCLUSION

As discussed in the study, the Malaysian government has recognized the importance of ICT as an essential component for enhancing the interface between the government agencies, citizens and the business under the e-government policy implementation. The implementation of e-government policy in public services using ICT that is capable of storing, sorting, transmitting information rapidly through an electronic device has opened up new possibilities for Malaysian government to deliver more efficient, effective and convenient services to a wide range of its citizens. As seen in the study, the e-government has, to some extent, provided many high-income groups of people and/or well-to-do in the country with access to information, and services without any barrier of time and distance. At the same time, innovative use of ICT in improving the day-to-day operations of the public services is preparing the civil

service for the next century to meet the nation's aspiration of becoming a developed country by the year 2020. The e-government application in **public sector** has covered a wide range of services in Malaysia and many are still underway to increase the efficiency and responsiveness of government to its people.

However, many issues have emerged in e-government applications. These include urban-rural disparities in terms of access to information, PCs ownership rate, telecommunication infrastructure development, regional and geographical disparities between citizens in Peninsular, Sabah and Sarawak as well as disparities in degree of digital literacy. Generally, the Government has a good standard of e-Government **strategy** and implementation and the necessary structural and legislation enabling factors. In addition to these, the findings from literature review and results from empirical survey have shown some weaknesses in the e-Government program in the areas of infrastructure, general readiness for e-Government due to the existing Digital Divide, which needs to be addressed first. However, the Government expects its e-Government program to achieve a material level of narrowing the Digital Divide in the country.

This overall result does not auger well for the expectation of the Government that their modern and proactive approach to e-Government should have an identifiable and material positive in mitigating the impact of this Divide. Thus, Malaysian Government has recognized that while the technology is available there is an urgent need to formulate a coherent plan to tap the potential area of disparities among the citizens in relation to benefits and services of e-government scheme in the country. In this context, the study has revealed various policy initiatives, which have been taken by federal, state, and local governments in the country. In addition many philanthropic organizations from local and international bodies such as UNDP, Coca Cola, etc., have come to play vital roles in collaboration with government agencies to facilitate the avenue for bridging Digital Divide in the country. Finally, it is expected that government body and agencies charged with policy of narrowing Digital Divide as well as e-Government implementation in the country would pay due attention to the various recommendations in this study.

REFERENCES

Ambali, A.R (2007, February 21). E-government in public administration: Benefits and challenges. *The E-Government Magazine for Asia & the Middle East, 3*(2), 20-31.

Castells, M. (1996). *The rise of the network society.* Oxford: Basil Blackwell.

Castells, M. (2000). *End of millennium: The information age, economy, society and culture.* Wiley-Blackwell.

Castells, M. (2006). *Mobile communication and society: A global perspective.* Wiley-Blackwell.

Compaine, M. B. (2001). *Digital divide: Facing a crisis or creating a myth.* MIT Press.

Dijk, J.A.G.M van (1999). *The network society.* London: Sage Publications.

Dijk, J.A.G.M.van (1997b). The reality of virtual communities: Trends in communication 1997/1. *New Media Developments*, 39-61.

Gaziano, C. (1983). The knowledge gap: An analytical review of media effects. *Communication Research*, 10, 447-486.

Gaziano, E., & Gaziano, C. (1995). Social control, social change and the knowledge gap hypothesis. In D. Demers, K. Viswanath (Eds.), *Mass media social control, and social change: A macrosocial perspective.* Iowa State Press.

Gaziano, C. (1997). Forecast 2000: Widening knowledge gaps. *Journalism and Mass Communications Quarterly*, 74, 237-264.

Government of Malaysia, (2003). *Mid-term review of the Eighth Malaysia Plan 2001-2005.* Kuala Lumpur: Government Printer.

Government of Malaysia, (2005). *Ninth Malaysia Plan 2006-2010.* Kuala Lumpur: Government Printer.

Government of Malaysia, & UNDP Project Document (October, 2004): *A national strategic framework for bridging the digital divide.*

Ibrahim, O. (2003). *Information system planning approach: A Malaysian electronic case study,* Ph.D, Dissertation. University of Salford.

Karim, A.M. R. (2003). Technology and improved service delivery: Learning points from the Malaysian experience. *International Review of Administrative Sciences, 69*(2), 191-204.

Karim, M. R. (1999). *Reengineering the public service: Leadership and change in an electronic ag.,* Suban Jaya: Pelanduk.

Karim, M. R., & Salmah, K. (1999). *E-government: Reinventing service delivery.* (M.R. Karim Ed). Suban Jaya: Pelanduk.

Marhaini M. N., & Asiyah, K. (2007, February 21). Digital literacy: Urban vs. rural areas in Malaysia. *The E-Government Magazine for Asia & the Middle East, 3*(2), 8-12.

MAMPU, (1997). *Towards a vision for a new electronic government.* Kuala Lumpur: Malaysian Administrative Modernization and Management Planning Unit.

MAMPU, (1997). *Electronic government information technology policy and standards (EGIT).* Kuala Lumpur: Malaysian Administrative Modernization and Management Planning Unit.

MAMPU, (1997). *Electronic government blueprint for implementation.* Kuala Lumpur: Malaysian Administrative Modernization and Management Planning Unit.

Anwar, M., & Soon T. K. (1999), The MSC and E-Government: Ensuring Interoperability. In Karim M. R. (Ed.), *Reengineering the Public Service*: *Leadership and Change in an Electronic Age,* Suban Jaya: Pelanduk.

MyGfL (Malaysian Grid for Learning) About MyGfL Initiative. July 24th, 2007, from http://www.mygfl.net.my; http://www.selangor.gov.my/suk/prodnews.php?cod=60 on 28th August, 2007.

Rogers, E. (1986). Communication technology: The new media in society. *The Free Press.*

Sharifah, M. S. M. A. (2004). Bridging digital divide in marginalized areas: A focus on IT policy, planning and implementation issues in Malaysia, *ITDC Newsletter*, *4*(1), 1-14.

Tichenor, P.J., Donohue, G.A., & Olien, C.N. (1970). Mass media flow and differential growth in knowledge. *Public Opinion Quarterly 34*: Colombia University Press.

Willis, S., & Tranter, B. (2006). Beyond the digital divide: Internet diffusion and inequality in Australia. *Journal of Sociology, 42*(1): 43 – 59.

Zaitun A. B. & Barbara, C. (2005). Overcoming the digital divide: A proposal on how institutions of higher education can play a role. *Malaysian Online Journal of Instructional Technology*, *2*(1), 1-11.

Chapter XVII
Digitization Initiatives and Knowledge Management:
Institutionalization of E–Governance in Teaching, Learning and Research in East African Universities

A. M. Chailla
Sokoine University of Agriculture, Tanzania

F. W. Dulle
Sokoine University of Agriculture, Tanzania

A. W. Malekani
Sokoine University of Agriculture, Tanzania

ABSTRACT

Digitization initiatives and Knowledge Management have become a part and parcel of each other in the changing global information society. Where as Knowledge Management (KM) comprises a range of practices used by organizations to identify, create, represent, and distribute knowledge, digitization initiatives refer to either jointly or collaborative efforts to translate existing library holdings whether in print, graphical, audio or combination of all, into digital format commonly known as electronic resources. Digitization initiatives have become a corner stone for KM in today's electronic environment. The term 'digital library' emanates from 'digitization' referring to the libraries where some or all of the information sources are available in electronic format and are made available electronically over the Internet for user access. East African university libraries, through digitization should provide coordinated access to digital information contained within their libraries creating conducive electronic environment in all universities for access to e-resources and provision of universities' generated literature on-line to users outside campuses. Furthermore, incorporating data mining techniques, access to these resources could be improved and the system could be made more efficient in making intelligent decision. The chapter discusses the problems of digitization, challenges and future opportunities for East African university libraries with focus on collaborative efforts and strategies backed up with policies for investments in ICTs training and integration of ICTs into the core university activities for effective Knowledge Management (KM) and information dissemination. It is argued in the chapter that digitization of library information will add value to more effective university KM, information access and use in multidisciplinary fields including local content.

INTRODUCTION

Knowledge Management (KM) (which according to Wikipedia comprises a range of practices used by organizations to identify, create, represent, and distribute knowledge) activities are worldwide; in industries, organizations, institutions and involve building databases, establishing libraries, building intranet, developing training program fostering collaboration and sharing of resources and best practices among institutions and organizations. The ICTs being the major facilitators in KM, university libraries have undertaken some of the most significant digitization initiatives in the past 25 years (Haule, 2007) for better management and dissemination of resources. The application of ICTs in KM has also been integrated in national strategies, policies and implementations processes as part of e-governance practices. The acquisitions of computers and associated software, faxes and modems, scanners, creation of intranets, and searchable Online Public Access Catalogues (OPACs) particularly in university libraries signified the beginning of advanced knowledge management and implementation of e-governance in higher learning institutions in East Africa. Developments in the aforesaid aspects have enabled the higher learning institutions to implement digitization of both implicit and explicit knowledge in libraries. The intranets for example in many universities have become powerful tools of communication of knowledge and knowledge base. They have become portals for sharing information among universities, forums for discussions and so on.

As stated above, KM comprises of elements of information acquisition, creation, renewal, archival, organizational, dissemination and sharing. KM in higher learning institutions focuses on the sharing of information among themselves and other institutions and community outside them for the purpose of enhancing learning, research, consultancy and outreach activities. To meet these capabilities ICTs have bridged the gap that existed before in the accomplishment of these tasks. One development that has been made possible in the path to achieve the information sharing has been the possibility to turn implicit and explicit knowledge into electronic formats for easy of archival, processing, dissemination and sharing. This is digitization.

There have been many digitization projects and initiatives running over the world and many initiatives have provided digital information in different formats. There are also private digital collections such as those being maintained by DIALOG[1], Mead Data[2] and Micro media[3] that could offer a lot of opportunities in information access. East African Universities and research institutions together can explore the potentials of accessing and subscribing to world scientific and social databases offered by DIALOG, Mead Data and Micro media companies. DIALOG offers online information and retrievable databases to private, academic and business corporations. Individually though it is unlikely for East African higher learning institutions to afford subscriptions to full text information compiled by DIALOG, Mead Data and Micro media companies. Hence the need for a consortium of East African Universities and research institutions is critical to exploit the electronic resources offered by such companies. For instance the two primary services of Mead Data (LEXIS and NEXIS) could create the capacity of East African University Libraries to join the global information search unit and benefit from legal research services of LEXIS and full text news and business information from NEXIS. Use of digital resources has increased following the rapid advancement in technology development. The developments have had a greater influence than expected on the current trend of establishment of digital libraries to contain materials that are born digital such as e-journals, e-books, Internet resources, databases and other materials originally produced in another form but subsequently digitized to become part of digital library collection. Access to digital resources to a greater extent, has brought about the development of high quality teaching and research, and added value to traditional teaching in institutions of higher learning in Africa.

The use of computers in information management opened the door to new ways of accessing and using information, making it possible to create and access electronic resources such as indexes, bibliographical databases, online journals and conference papers. The developments have to-day led to digitization which has become one of the core activities in facilitating KM in academic and research institutions. Moreover, adopting innovative techniques, as such data mining access, search, maintenance and management of these potential content could be improved far better than currently available digitization techniques. However, currently available digitization techniques. However, this chapter will not provide adequate discussion on data mining methods and techniques. Rather, it will emphasize on available digitization techniques, their applications in East

African universities, the challenges by these applications and a few hints on further research.

One of the main purposes of this chapter is to give a historical background to digital libraries as tools for KM provide an overall view on digital library development in East African universities and emphasize on the need for digitization for effective KM and information sharing nationally, regionally and globally. The chapter also deliberates on challenges and future strategies for East African universities in digitization of their information resources and concludes with initiatives currently being undertaken by the libraries to embark on collaborative activities towards effective KM through digitization and online information sharing. Before conclusion this chapter will provide a few hints on adoption of data mining techniques in digitization processes.

BACKGROUND TO DIGITAL LIBRARY DEVELOPMENT

Historically, digital libraries date as far back as 1940's when academic libraries with large bibliographical databases became familiar with online retrieval and public access systems. Since then, digital technology continues to evolve with advancements in ICTs, connection of computers to large networks and eventually to Internet so much as to be conceptualized to-day as a gateway to easy, finger tip access to information. There are many definitions for the term 'digital library.For example, the Educational Technology Collaborative defines a digital library as "An organized collection stored in digital/electronic format and accessible online" (ETC, 2005).

Rosenberg (2007) state that "a Digital Library is one where users access resources by electronic means and where information is delivered to users electronically". For the purpose of this chapter, a definition given by Rosenberg (2007) is adopted.

From the definitions given above, a digital library should have the following characteristics among many others:

- Electronic digital formats which may include converted materials from printed works; original electronic publications; resources in a wide variety of types such as reference works, visual materials, sound recordings, moving pictures etc. (Chapman and Klemperer, 1997) cited in Haule, (2007).
- The digital library collection should be organized in a way that enables users to find it easy to access the information contained within it.
- They should evolve in an electronic network environment and have the capacity to provide hyperlinks to resources held in other libraries.
- Digital libraries require both the skills of librarians as well as those of IT scientists and technicians.

The basic building blocks of a digital library include automation of library systems, sufficient ICT facilities (computers and networks), and adequate connectivity (Rosenberg, 2006).

The 'term digital library' is used interchangeably with 'electronic collections', as an end product of the process of digitization. Despite the diverse definitions, it is the authors' strong view that a digital library apart from being exclusively electronic, it could be a supplement or an extension of an already existing physical library or library collection.

Buckland (1992) tried to categorize libraries into three categories, based on the collections and the extent to which technology has been adopted and used: - the paper library containing most paper materials and administered primarily via paper; the automated library containing primarily paper but administered electronically; and electronic e-library in which both the collection and the administration are electronic. The

paper libraries in industrialized countries are almost non-existent and most libraries in less industrialized countries to-day offer electronic access to digital collections in addition to their physical collections. However most scholars are of the opinion that "the electronic library is yet to come. Many libraries maintain digital collections, but there are few entirely digital libraries with no physical counterpart".

Some of the institutions that have effectively utilized data mining techniques to digitize their collections are the leading Yugoslav research and cultural institutions, which through National Center of Digitization (NCD) have managed to digitize scientific and cultural heritage information. The NCD brings together several scientific and cultural heritage information in Serbia in the culture of digitization. During the digitization process the NCD focused mainly in publishing, organization of conferences and participation in South-Eastern European Digitization Initiatives (SEEDI) (NCD, n.d). Other institutions with a vast of information in digital contents include Digital Library Federation which is a consortium of many university libraries in the US, networked to many other consortia (http://www.diglib.org/about.htm).

Information in East African University Libraries can be more easily accessible through data mining techniques like clustering, statistics, and neighborhood and so on. The East African University Libraries and Research Institutions should embark on research on their information needs so as to prioritize the information mostly demanded by clients in the region and apply international standards and protocols so that data mined can be accessed globally.

Another distinction between types of digital libraries is given by Greenstein and Thorin (2002). They made a distinction between three types of digital libraries based on age and sophistication: The 'young digital library' being launched; the 'maturing digital library' and 'adult digital library'. Greenstein and Thorin point that the young digital library is in the planning and experimental stage (the stage at which most of the young university libraries in East Africa are), while the maturing digital library has already acquired core competencies and technical know how in keeping up with advancements in ICTs (this is a stage we can include few universities like University of Dar es Salaam, Sokoine University of Agriculture, Nairobi University, Makerere University and few other in East Africa). The authors put it in this way:-"the maturing digital library is no longer as experimental as in its younger days. It has acquired core competencies and technical understanding and is focused primarily on integrating digital materials into the library's collections and on developing the policies, technical capacities and professional skills needed to sustain it". At this juncture it can be ascertained that most university libraries in East Africa including the most affluent ones in research institutions are at the young stage of' development. The assumption is confirmed by Diana Rosenberg's survey of libraries in Sub-Sahara Anglophone Africa (2004) in which she concluded that few East African University Libraries can be said to be at the 'maturing' stage while digital libraries which in which services are performed electronically, and has an entire electronic collection in its holdings, is an extremely rare type in low developing countries.

ISSUES, CONTROVERSIES, PROBLEMS

There are as many definitions of 'digitization' as there are for a 'digital library'. Many scholars have defined the term 'digitization' as the process of translating a piece of information such as a book, sound recording, picture, video, into bits. Harrods' Librarians dictionary defines 'digitization' as the process of translating information content from traditional format into a digital readable version (Prythern (1945). Despite numerous definitions, digitization is not only for text format but im-

ages and musical scores. The main and overall objective of digitization is to provide a better management, improvement and accessibility to valuable information resources in libraries as well as preservation of rare historical materials. In East Africa, many digital libraries are either academic, research or affluent business documentation units focused on generating information/data and making it freely available to potential users in electronic format. This could be achieved by employing various data mining techniques such as classical techniques (clustering, statistics, e.t.c), next generation techniques (trees, networks and rules) which have been used in other institutions in the world In this chapter the term data mining is the same as one defined by Grossman, *et al* (1998), which states that "data mining is the semi-automatic discovery of patterns, associations, changes, anomalies, rules, and statistically significant structures and events in data".

DIGITAL LIBRARY DEVELOPMENTS IN EAST AFRICAN UNIVERSITIES: AN OVERALL VIEW

The International Network for the Availability of Scientific Publications (INASP) commissioned Diana Rosenberg in 2004 to carry out a survey of the 'current status' of library digitization in Sub-Sahara Anglophone Africa; South Africa exempted, so as to determine the countries' progress and future potentials in terms of development in ICTs. Tanzania, Kenya and Uganda were included. The survey questionnaire according to Rosenberg (2006) covered all aspects of digitization that is; automation, ICT facilities, e-resources, local content, finances, management, training user education and future plans in place.

The findings revealed that 65% of university libraries in Africa are 'young digital libraries' still in the planning and experimental stage while 15% university libraries could be considered fully automated that is:- 'maturing digital libraries'.

An average of 21% had not begun the digitization process at all. On electronic resources, the study found out that most university libraries in Sub-Sahara Anglophone Africa have a long way to go. Thirty Five percent had developed library Web pages, 45% had online Public Access Catalogs (OPACs) and of which only 16% were accessible from the Web. Furthermore, institutional local contents were not made available electronically. Full text digitization and the establishment of Institutional Repositories (IRs) were very few.

Currently, East African Community member states have taken bold stapes to implement the Information and Communications Technology (ICT) development objectives laid out in the World Summit on Information Society (WSIS) plan of Action. Thus the three countries have formulated policies and legislative frameworks in place to guide the implementation. However, the implementation is being constrained by a number of factors, including the rural/urban divide, a lack of awareness about the advantages of ICTs and a low level of skills in addition to technical problems like low band width.

The universities within these countries have also responded to the need to have policies in place to integrate ICT in their core university activities. Thus, there have been a number of ICT projects within the university units including libraries. However, there have been a varying degree level of the extent to which ICT integration have been achieved depending on the kind of assistance that each university gets from the donors.

However, the avenues provided by enabling policies to integrate ICTs in national development activities by the regions in the bloc should be harnessed by university libraries for digitization of their collections. This will provide an opportunity to manage and promote access and use of local content to enhance effective teaching, research, and consultancy and outreach activities in East African Universities.

NEED FOR DIGITIZATION IN EAST AFRICAN UNIVERSITIES

There are three particular factors in academic communities in East Africa, which inspire digitization process; namely the need to make information more easily accessible for use; need to increase availability of current as well as archive information in multidisciplinary fields including local content; the need to minimize duplication of efforts in developing/generating information and learning resources through establishment of Institutional Repositories (IRs) and other resource sharing mechanisms within and beyond the region. Thus, through digitization of physical university library materials, a lot of current publications will be timely available online, thereby, making research, teaching and learning more current. To-day's situation in Low Developed Countries (LDCs) pertaining to easy access and availability of current information to academic communities particularly in scientific fields is discouraging compared to the developed world.

There is evidence that scholars in LDCs face problems both in accessing and disseminating scholarly information. There are numerous factors contributing to the crisis such as underdeveloped ICT infrastructures, lack of information search skills (Lwoga et al, 2006; Pain-Ramchan and Dave, 2006), low research funding and low staff morale (Kapange, 2006; Moller, 2006)). Non-accessibility to renowned scientific journals and literature is aggravated by exorbitant costs to journal subscriptions and the growing volume of literature that has made it difficult if not impossible for LDCs to subscribe to adequate information resources. For example Aronson as cited by Chan and Costa (2005), reports on a survey conducted by the World Health Organization (WHO) indicating that *"of the 75 countries with a Gross National Product (GNP) per capita per year of less than US$ 1,000, 56 percent of institutions have had no subscriptions to journals over the last five years; of countries with a GNP between US$*

1000 - 3,000, 34 percent have had no subscriptions and a further 34 percent have an average of two subscriptions per year" Aronson (2004). Limited accessibility to information in Tanzania is supported by research findings by Dulle *et al* (2001) and Chailla (2001) in which researchers in the National Agricultural Research Institutes (NARI) are reported to have experienced problems in accessing scientific literature.

Contribution to global scholarly literature by Less Developed Countries is also said to be negligible. According to Chan and Costa (2005) new knowledge is largely created in richer countries. They cite an example given by King (2004), indicating that, researchers in eight countries led by the United States, the United Kingdom, Germany and Japan produce almost 85 percent to the world's most cited publications, while 163 other countries, mostly developing ones, account for less than 2.5 percent. The documentation of research output in Eastern, Central and Southern Africa region also reveal some deficiencies likely to contribute to the low level of accessible scholarly literature (Chailla and Matovelo, 1999, Mook et al 2005, Tanzania Agricultural Research Project Report, 2005). The above sources indicate a large percentage of researchers' output is documented as grey literature characterized with limited dissemination of its contents particularly when printed and archived in print format (Chailla, 2001, Chisenga, 2006). As a result it is quite difficult to access information generated from the region even for individuals within same institutions where such information has been generated.

The above factors among many others are rightful reasons as to why East African Universities should embark on collaborative digitization to establish Institutional Repositories (IRs) and other digital library collections. It is a matter of fact that many East Africa Universities are already investing in the acquisition of e-resources and making bibliographic information of their catalogues available online. Such initiatives are commendable and should be sustained for more access and

use of knowledge contained within the university libraries. However, little achievement has been made with respect to the accessibility of locally generated information. Creation of institutional repositories could lead to a much more access to locally generated information and such repositories could become part of regional and global library. This means that our locally generated information could not only be accessible at regional level but also globally. According to Heery and Anderson (2005) Institutional Repositories (IRs) should have the following characteristics:

- Contents should be deposited in a repository by the content creator/author/ owner or third party.
- Contents should be managed by repository institution
- The repository should offer a minimum set of basic services such as search and access control
- The repository must be sustainable, well supported and managed

Institutional Repositories (IRs) though a relatively recent development, provide access to the contents and materials produced by member institutions. Through digitization, East African Universities will have an opportunity to establish institutional repositories in which information shall be captured, stored and disseminated to other institutions online. Such information includes institutional journal articles, research outputs, complete and on-going research projects and consultancy reports and other alumni academic publications. As stated by Lynch (2003); " Open Access Archives (OAAs) are electronic repositories (data repositories) that may include already published articles (post-prints), pre-published articles (pre-prints), theses, manuals, teaching materials or other documents that the authors or their institutions wish to make publicly available without financial or other access barriers". There are many benefits for institutional repositories (data repositories) making it justifiable for our universities to consider it seriously in investing in such ventures. According to Chan et al (2005), an institutional repository (data repositories) provides and promotes:

- *Access to International research output-* research that is currently inaccessible due to cost barrier becomes globally accessible. As more and more International institutes establish archives, a growing body of published research becomes available to any one with Internet access;

- *International access to research generated in developing countries-* papers published by developing countries' researchers in foreign journals which are not accessible to researchers in their home countries may be easily accessible if universities and science academics in these countries set up archives to be populated immediately with a great number of papers published by their researchers;

- *Institutional research output-* By showing their faculty's research outputs, institutional archives can bring prestige to both staff and institutional research as well as provide a better picture of country's research outputs and areas of specialization. Papers published by researchers in LDCs in foreign journals can be easily accessible if universities set up repositories.. This is also true for gray literature emanating from such countries but remains invisible in the conventional publishing system. Institutional research will therefore provide a better picture of institutional and country's research out puts and areas of specialization;

- *Improved citation and research impact-* the most persuasive reason for institutions to set up interoperable open access archives, both in developed and developing countries. There is the growing evidence that citation and the impact of papers that are openly accessible are far greater than non-OA publications. A study by Broady and Harnard (2004) reveal that compared with articles that have not been made openly accessible, open access papers were cited much more often.

- *Improved access to subsidiary data-* repositories of materials such as theses and dissertations, technical reports and other forms of publications that do not have regular publishing outlets but are important for research and teaching purposes (Chan *et al*, 2005).

DIGITIZATION DRAWBACKS

Despite the many advantages of digitization, there are several drawbacks that need to be addressed. Although not exhaustive the following are some of the most important factors hindering digitization project more so in LDCs:

(i) The digitization process involves an extensive budget, staff training, movement of physical items, copyright clearance, creation of record and indexes. Getting started on the process and keeping up with the technology is a challenge to most university libraries in East Africa. Above all digitization is a technology that needs a state of the art expertise for implementation.

(ii) Prioritizing material for digitization can prove a deterring factor in university libraries if user needs assessment has not been carried out.

(iii) Teaching, learning and researching using the current technologies can be overwhelming for some academicians in most academic institutions. It is also challenging to libraries to choose and decide on the use of an appropriate user friendly yet moderately stable software for digitization.

(iv) Some university teaching and research staff need inspiration and literacy programs in place to dare learn the skills necessary for access and use of digital resources.

Despite the above hindering factors, higher learning institutions are encouraged to take advantage of the worldwide developments in ICTs and make a start on digitization process for more effective KM for enhancement of research, teaching, consultancy and extension services. Furthermore, continued researches are being carried out in the field of data mining for improved content archiving, management and dissemination, including incorporation of intelligent search.

DIGITIZATION: CHALLENGES AND FUTURE STRATEGIES FOR EAST AFRICAN UNIVERSITIES

The above setbacks in digitization pose challenges in digital library development in almost all university libraries in East Africa.

Experiences from Sokoine National Agricultural Library (SNAL) and Nairobi University (NU)

At SNAL developments of digital library started with a gradual introduction of ICT facilities in the university. The university began to use computers way back in 1990s through donor support. It laid down a fiber optic Local Area Network (LAN) and installed a Very Small Aperture Terminal (VSAT) dish for ground satellite connection to the Internet in 1998 (SUA computer center, 2002). At SNAL, ICT projects and hence digital collection development, largely funded by donors started in 1996. Among the developments made at that time include establishment of connectivity between library users through the LAN and access to other electronic information via the Internet. Other developments that have taken place since

then include establishment of OPAC and acquisitions of a Web Based Library Integrated System (WEBLIS) that offers several specialized modules to manage library automations. Thus, it has been possible to enter various documents in the module at bibliographic levels (so far more than 7000 books and journals can be accessible through OPAC), some activities like circulations and ordering of documents is being done online.

Moreover, a database to manage special projects for undergraduate students has been created. This keeps records up to abstract level and more that 1500 projects have been entered in the database. The major means of data capture from hard documents has been through typing assisted with a small scanner available in the library. The library has developed its web page from which links to various online databases, free and subscribed can be accessed.

At NU, electronic information sharing information is strongly advocated for, and the university is committed to strengthen access to information, increased use of ICT and e-resources and the diversification of methods of access to information resources. To be more efficient and in access and usage of e-resources, NU is a member of Kenya Libraries Services Consortium. (KLISC). One of the major objectives of KLISC is to create the capacity of university libraries and other institutions to purchase and subscribe to e-databases, and journals through cost–sharing mechanisms, so as to ensure sustainable availability of e-resources to meet user needs. The NU library is at advanced level (mature) digital library. The library facilitates access to all types of contemporary information resources including electronic resources. The library is automated using VUBIS (Vrije Universiteit .Integrated System). The library has a website for access to its catalogue (http://library. unonbi.ac.ke/website/index.html).

Some of the challenges common to all the east African Libraries in managing and sustaining the digitization in their libraries include:

- *Lack of adequate number of competent library ICT staff:* Currently ICT infrastructures in most young universities and even in well established ones are underdeveloped and are constrained in IT trained staff. It is also difficult to retain highly trained personnel in ICT because of their high demand elsewhere with more pay and fringe benefits than in libraries.

- *The academic staff attitude/mindset:* The attitude of some researchers and academicians are unfortunately still traditional. The library staff has to work much harder to raise the level of awareness on the importance, and convenience of using the e-resources. There has to be a training program in place for library staff, researchers and management.

- *Care and handling of digital materials:* The CD-ROMs and magnetic tapes and cassettes should be kept in special constructed racks in well air-conditioned rooms. The computers should also be maintained within the same temperature range. Care in handling delicate digital materials should be communicated to users during training sessions.

- *Information literacy skills:* Electronic resources in some university libraries are not fully utilized both by students and academic staff due to lack of awareness and knowledge on how to use them. The Sokoine National Agricultural library for instance, has been organizing Information Literacy (IL) seminars for a long time now. Such seminars have not been successful in terms of attendance and impact due to several reasons such as; lack of official recognition by the University, lack of support by the students and time factor. SNAL is currently working toward convincing the management to include IL in the university curriculum.

- *Lack of funds:* Decision makers at the university managerial levels do not accord the University Libraries the priority they deserve in funding. Marketing and publicity of the Library services need money. There has to be a strategic plan in place to secure more funding for the university libraries.

- *Inconsistent supply of power and low bandwidth:* This leads to unreliable Internet connectivity. In one of INASP workshops on Bandwidth Optimization and Management Training Support (http://www.inasp.info/training/bandwidth), it was noted with much concern that research and education in developing countries are faced with major obstacles in their usage of networked information resources because the cost of bandwidth is high. It was however agreed that a key feature of increasing bandwidth availability for research and educational purposes is effective management which entails having a skilled e-resource manager for management and optimization of bandwidth.

FUTURE STRATEGIES AND OPPORTUNITIES

One of the objectives of International Network for the Availability of Scientific Publications (INSP) through Program for Enhancement of Research Information (PERI) is to support country collaboration and network. As argued by INASP: "There is a need for organizations and information providers to collaborate to pull resources and jointly provide access and services that people need" (http://www.inasp.inf/peri/collaboration.shtml). This can be a case in point justifying for a functional COTUL. The universities in Tanzania have one national goal that is to accelerate development through training and research. To realize the goal, access to desired information worldwide is essential. It is nevertheless doubtful if this can be achieved individually by university libraries.

Another opportunity for creation of digital libraries in the region is through use of the available open source software for adoption by respective universities wishing to establish institutional repositories. According to Chan *et al.* (2005), where the technical infrastructure for setting up institutional archives is in existence, it is not prohibitive to establish such repositories due to freely available software. The best known and most widely used open source software are E-prints made available by the US-based Massachusetts institute of technology (Chan *et al.* (2005). Many Universities in the region have the capacity to support institutional repositories and put in place other cooperation mechanisms to ensure that the resources are pulled together and shared through networking activities.

The co-operation will be viable through an established Consortium of East African University Libraries which jointly can:

- Promote establishment of digital libraries.
- Overcome individual institutional costs for e-resources through collective subscriptions.
- Enhance training in ICT and access skills to electronic resources.
- Encourage and support digital Institutional Repositories.
- Increase capacity building in digitization in young university libraries.
- Establish resource sharing mechanisms.
- Share professional and ICT expertise.
- Undertake research in digital library development in East African University Libraries.

DATA MINING RESEARCH

Data mining or knowledge discovery is a new concept in most university libraries in Sub-saharan Africa and indeed in east Africa. It draws upon several tools as stated by Grossman *et al* (1998).

These tools include statistics, machine learning, databases, and high performance computing. A report of three NSSF workshops on mining large, massive and distributed data held in January, 21st 1998 (draft 8.4.5) acknowledge that the field of data mining and knowledge discovery is emerging as a new "fundamental research area with important applications to science, engineering, medicine, and education.

However, the hindrance to research in these area lies on three factors, namely, the amount of digital data that has exploded over the past decades while the number of experts has remained static, lack of support from government to embark on data mining research and requirements of special systems and computing infrastructure in some cases in data mining (Grossman *et al*, 1998). These are same areas that East African Universities can affect data mining research in East African Universities.

Research data mining challenges identified by the workshop, which are also applicable to east African Universities and research institutions, are:

- the daily increase of information, particularly research records in scientific records,
- increase in number of attributes,
- increase in the number of models or rules set for data analysis.

CONCLUSION

Given the importance of access and use of current information in academic institutions, the need for East Africa Universities libraries to adopt digitization along with its merits and demerits, is more crucial today because scholarly communication is technologically driven globally, for free access to information. Publishing is no longer the private domain of publishers, and distance learning has become cost effective than classroom teaching. Furthermore, digitization of university library collections can be a solution to optimization and effective learning, teaching and research. It is a platform through which local contents can be promoted. Digitization could also be an answer to standardization and for online e-resource sharing. Many studies however, have found that the current status of digitization in university libraries in Sub-Sahara Anglophone have progressed at different speeds and levels. Libraries of newly established universities are much more at a disadvantage and lag behind due to inadequate ICT infrastructure including ICT facilities, trained staff and users, reliable Internet connectivity and institutional ICT policy in place. Given the high costs associated with acquisition and development of Digital Libraries, the East African University Libraries should collaborate with each other for the success of such projects. Moreover, adoption of innovative data access techniques, like data mining to improve their overall operations, will remain another future challenge.

REFERENCES

Buckland, M. (1992). *Redesigning Library Services: A Manifesto.* Chicago: America Library Association.

Chailla, A.M. (2001). *Implementation of Policies and Strategies for Agricultural Information Access and Use in Tanzania.* Unpublished doctoral dissertation, University of Natal, Pietermaritzburg.

Chan, L. Kirsop, B. & Arunachalam, S (2005). *Open Access Archiving: the fast track to building research capacity in developing countries.* Science and Development Network. Retrieved July, 25, 2007 from http://www.scidev.net/open_access/files/open%20Archiving.pdf

Chapman, S. & Klemperer, K (1997). *Digital libraries: A selected resource guide.* Retrieved on 21st June, 2008 from http:/www.lita.org/ital/1603 klemperer.htm

Chisenga, J. (2006). *The development and use of digital libraries, institutional repositories, digital repositories, and open access archives for research and national development in Africa: opportunities and challenges.* [Online]: Retrieved on 2nd Nov. 2006 from http://www.uneca.org/disd/events/2006/wsis-library/presentations/development~

Dulle, F. W., Lwehabura, M.J.F., Mulimila, R.T. & Matovelo D.S. (2001). Researchers' perspectives on agricultural libraries as information sources in Tanzania. *Library Review, 50*(4), 187-192.

Educational Technology Collaborative (2005). *Digital Treasures, exploring new research sources on the internet.* Retrieved 16th July, 2008 from http://edtech.tennessee.edu/set/2005/set33/extra/glossary.html

Harnad, S. & Brody, T. (2004). Comparing the impact of open access (OA) versus NON-OA articles in the same journals. *D-Lib Magazine.* Online: Retrieved on 15th January, 2007 from http://dlib.org/june04/hanard/06hanard.html

Greenstein, D., & Thorn, S. E. (2002). The digital Library: A Bibliography (Technical Report 109). Washington, D.C.: Digital Library Federation Council on Library and Information Resources. Retrieved on 12nd May, 2008 from http://www.clir.org/pubs/reports/pub109/pub109.pdf

Grossman, R.(Ed.), Kasif, S., Moore, R., Rocke, D. & Ullman, J. (1998). *Data Mining Research: Opportunities and Challenges. A Report of three NSF Workshops on Mining Large, Massive, and Distributed Data.* Retrieved 16th July, 2008 from http://www.rgrossman.com/epapers/dmr-v8-4-5.htm*

Haule, L. (2007). Digitization concept and types of digitization: texts and images. Paper presented at the Tanzania Library Association's Workshop on *'Sustainable Digital Library Development in Tanzania: challenges, prospects and strategies'.* Iringa, Tanzania – 20 – 23 February 2007.

Heery, R. & Anderson, S. (2005). Digital Repositories Review, UKOLN-AHDS. Retrieved February 19, 2005 from http://www.jisc.ac.uk/uploaded_documents/digital-repositories-revew-

Hitchcock, S., et al. (2007). Digital Preservation Services provider Models for institutional Repositories: *D-lib Magazine* May/June 2007, Vol. 13, No. 5/6.

Kapange, B. (1999). *ICTs and National Agricultural Research Systems-the case of Tanzania.* Retrieved August 08, 2006 from http://www.isnar.cgiar.org/pdf/inars/tanzania.pdf

King, D. (2004). The Scientific Impact of nations. *Nature,* 430, 311-316.

Klampere, K. & Chapman, S. (1997). Digital Libraries: a Selected Resource Guide: Retrieved on 2nd August, 2008 from http://www.lita.org/ital/1603 klempere.htm.

Krause, J. (2004). University of Koblenz-landau and Social Science Information. Bonn, Germany. Retrieved on 3rd September from http://www.uni_koblenz.de/-krause/

Leriviere, J. (2000). *Guidelines for legal deposit legislations. Paris: UNESCO.* Retrieved on 3rd September from http://www.ifla.org/VII/s1/gnl/legaldep1.htm

Lor, P. (1995). Legal deposit: some issues in the international science. *Musaion, 13*(1/2), 94 –111.

Lor, P. (2003). What prospects for national libraries in East Africa? *A South African perspective. Alexandria, 15*(3), 141–150.

Lwoga, E.T., Forzi, T., Laing, P. & Mjema, E. (2006). KM in the agricultural field: an ICT-based approach to promote the development and sharing of knowledge among agricultural researchers in Africa. In Cunningham, P. and Cunngham, M. (Eds) *IST-AFRICA conference proceedings.* [Online]: Retrieved on 1st Aug. 2006 from http://www.IST-Africa.org/conference2006

Malekani, A. & Grace E. (2007). *Development and status of Digital Libraries in Agricultural Information Systems: Experiences with Sokoine National Agricultural Library.* Paper presented at a Workshop on "Sustainable digital development in Tanzania: challenges, prospects and strategies". Iringa. Tanzania.

Matovelo, D. S. & Chailla, A. M. (1999). Documentation and dissemination of agricultural research results in Tanzania: avenues and challenges. *Tanzania Journal of Agricultural Sciences, 2*(1), 99-106.

Moller, A.M. (2006). *The open access publishing, with a special reference to open access journal and their prospects in South Africa.* MA Dissertation (Unpublished), University of Western Cape. [Online]: Retrieved on 2nd September, 2006 from http://eprints.rclis.org/archive/000518/01/MollerThesis.pdf

Mook, B., Munyua, H. & Nampala, P. (2005). *Report on the baseline study of agricultural information in the Eastern and Central Africa Region.* Unpublished, consultants' report submitted to the Regional Agricultural Information Network (RAIN), Entebbe, Uganda.

National Center for Digitization (NCD) (n.d). Retrieved on 16th July, 2008 from http://www.ncd.matf.bg.ac.yu/

Papin-Ramchan, J.I. & Dawe, R.A. (2006). Open Access Publishing: A developing country view. *First Monday, 11*(6). [Online]: Retrieved on 1st Sept. 2006 from http://firstmonday.org/issues/issue11-6/papin/index.html

Pomerantz, J. (2003). Integrating Digital Reference Services into the Digital Library Environment. In: R.D. Lankes, S. Nicholson & A. Goodrum (Eds), *The Digital Reference Research Agenda* (pp. 23-47). Chicago Association of College and Research Libraries.

Rosenberg, D. (2006). Towards the digital library in Africa. *The Electronic Library, 24*(3), 289 -293. Retrieved on 01August,2007 from http://www. emeraldinsight.com.Insight/ViewContentSevle t?Filename=/published/emeraldfulltextarticle/ pdf/2630240301.pdf)

Unsworth, J. (2004). *The value of digitization of libraries: The Newberry library,* May 2004 (An Innodata Isogen Symposium).

Warren P. & Alsmeyer D. (n.d). *The digital Library: A case study in intelligent content management.*

ADDITIONAL READINGS

Arms, W. Y. (2000). Digital Libraries, MIT Press, Cambridge, MA.

Klemperer, K. & Chapman, S. (1997). Digital Libraries: a Selected Resource Guide. Retrieved on 18/01/2007 from the World Wide Web: http:// www.lita.org/ital/1603_klemperer.htm

Krishnamurthy, M. (2005). Digital library services at the Indian Statistical Institute. *The Electronic Library, Vol. 23, No. 2. pp. 200-203.* Retrieved on 19/01/2007 from: http://www.emeraldinsight. com/10.1108/02640470510592898

Online Computer Library Centre (2006). OpenURL and LinkServer Basics. Retrieved January 25, 2007 from http://openly.oclc.org/ 1cate/basics.html

Reich, V. & Winograd, T. (1995). Working Assumptions about the Digital Library. Retrieved on January 18, 2007 from http://www-diglib. stanford.edu/diglib/WP/PUBLIC/DOC10.html

Rosenberg, D. (2006). Towards the digital library in Africa. *The Electronic Library, Vol. 24, No. 3. pp. 289-293.* Retrieved on January 19, 2007 from http://www.emeraldinsight.com/Insight/ ViewContentServlet?Filename=/published/em- eraldfulltextarticle/pdf/2630240301.pdf

Translation Bureau (2008). *Handbook of Terminology.* Retrieved 16th July, 2008 from http://www. translationbureau.gc.ca/index.php?cont=700&l ang=english

SUA computer centre. (2002). ICT Policy Guidelines.

University of Minnesota Libraries, (2006). What is Open URL? Retrieved January 18, 2007 from http://faq.lib.umn.edu/public/showRecord. pl?kbrecordid=5821&mode=public

ENDNOTES

[1] DIALOG-: Is a Thompson corporation business that offers online information and retrievable databases in areas of business, science and law. It was the first information retrieval system created by Rodger summit in 1967 and launched its services in 1972.

[2] Mead Data Inc: Is a leading database service headquartered near Dayton, Ohio, with 50 sales offices in the USA and overseas. The company's primary services, LEXIS and NEXIS, serve over 650,000 active subscribers through 5,000 databases.

[3] Micro media: is a term for characterizing, analyzing and understanding recent developments both in the "Mobile Web" and in the so-called "Web 2.0".

[4] LEXIS: is a legal research service of Mead Data Central, Inc.

[5] NEXIS: Is a full text news and business information service of Mead Data Central Inc.

Chapter XVIII
Data Mining in Public Administration

John Wang
Montclair State University, USA

Xiaohua Hu
Drexel University, USA

Dan Zhu
Iowa State University, USA

INTRODUCTION

Data mining involves searching through databases for potentially useful information such as knowledge rules, patterns, regularities, and other trends hidden in the data. In order to complete these tasks, the contemporary data mining packages offer techniques such as neural networks, inductive learning decision trees, cluster analysis, link analysis, genetic algorithms, visualization, and so forth (Hand, Mannila, & Smyth, 2001; Wang, 2006). In general, data mining is a data analytical technique that assists businesses in learning and understanding their customers so that decisions and strategies can be implemented most accurately and effectively to maximize profitability.

Data mining is not general data analysis, but a comprehensive technique that requires analytical skills, information construction, and professional knowledge.

Businesses are now facing globalized competition and are being forced to deal with an enormous amount of data. The vast amounts of data and the increasing technological ability to store them also facilitated data mining. In order to gain a certain level of competitive advantage, businesses now commonly adopt a data analytical technology called data mining. Nowadays, data mining is more widely used than ever before, not only by businesses who seek profits, but also by nonprofit organizations, government agencies, private groups, and other institutions in the public sector. Organizations use data mining as a tool to forecast customer behavior, reduce fraud and waste, and assist in medical research.

BACKGROUND

Data mining uses statistical analysis, artificial intelligence, and machine-learning technologies to identify patterns that cannot be found by manual analysis alone. The primary function of data mining has already amazed many people and is now considered one of the most critical issues toward a business's success. However, data mining was not born all of a sudden. The earliest usage of data mining can be traced back to the World War II years. Data analytical methods such as model prediction, database segmentation, link analysis, and deviation detection were used for military affairs and demographic purposes by the U.S. government, but data mining had not been seriously promoted until the 1990s.

Gramatikov (2006) compares statistical methods to data mining, differentiating them by the ultimate focus of these two tools. Statistical methods use data that are collected with a pre-defined set of questions. Statisticians are either looking for describing parameters of data or making inferences through statistics within intervals. With data mining, knowledge is generated from hidden relations, rules, trends, and patterns that emerge as the data are mined.

The reason that data mining has been developed enormously again in the last few years is that a huge amount of information was demanded by modern enterprises due to globalization. Important information regarding markets, customers, competitors, and future opportunities were collected in the form of data to be put in databases, and businesses needed data mining to unearth useful information and knowledge. Otherwise, a huge, overloaded, and unstructured database could just make it very difficult for companies

to utilize it, and it would in turn mislead the database users.

Public administration is, broadly speaking, the study and implementation of policy. The term may apply to government, private-sector organizations and groups, and individuals. The adjective *public* often denotes government at federal, state, and local levels, though it increasingly encompasses nonprofit organizations such as those of civil society or any not specifically acting in self-interest. Then, a long list exists, including colleges and universities, health care organizations, and charities, as well as postal offices, libraries, prisons, and so forth.

In the public sector, data mining initially was used as a means to detect fraud and waste, but has since grown for purposes such as measuring and improving program performance. Data mining has been increasingly cited as an important tool for homeland security efforts, crime prevention, and medical and educational applications to increase efficiency, reduce costs, and enhance research.

BENEFITS OF DATA MINING IN PUBLIC ADMINISTRATION

Data mining techniques offer public-sector opportunities to optimize decisions based on general trends extracted from historical data. With the knowledge that can be extracted from the data, public organizations can level up its knowledge accumulation strategies and steps. The knowledge that can be derived with the data mining could serve first as a tool for better governance and second as a means for sustaining the organizational knowledge. Data mining technology is applied in different aspects of public administration such as health care, immigration, law enforcement, and other public sectors to solve specific business or research problems. Examples of application areas follow.

Improving Service or Performance

The purpose of SBA's (Small Business Administration) lender and loan monitoring system is to improve service and performance. The system was developed by Dun and Bradstreet. SBA uses the system to identify, measure, and manage risk in its business loan programs. Its outputs include reports that identify the total amount of loans outstanding for a particular lender and estimate the likelihood of loans becoming delinquent in the future based on predefined patterns (U.S. Government Accounting Office [GAO], 2005).

Hospitals are currently using data mining to save money in the long run by reducing medication errors and the cost of transcribing doctors' dictation. For example, a family practitioner at UW Health's Meadowood clinic uses the Epic System to order a drug; the computer automatically checks a database of potential cross-reactions with other medications that the patient is currently taking. This system makes it easier for doctors to do their job very well, and at the same time, this system makes it easier for patients to see their information and interact with doctors. Also, with the growing rate of infections in hospitals in the United States, some hospitals are adopting data mining techniques to inform doctors of problems they might miss. MedMined of Birmingham is a company that has sold its data analysis services to hospitals to help detect infection in its early stage. Hospitals transmit encrypted data from patients' records to MedMined, which then uses its data mining algorithms to detect unusual patterns and correlations. At first only a few hospitals used this system, but now it is becoming a necessity in hospitals (Lok, 2004).

Cahlink (2000) reported that data mining techniques are used by health organizations and hospitals to improve upon work processes. The Center for Disease Control and Prevention National Immunization Program in Atlanta implemented data mining software to allow better tracking of reactions to vaccine. The program has a huge database of adverse reactions to vaccines reported by physicians, clinics, hospitals, patients, and pharmaceutical companies across the nation. Statisticians and federal researchers monitor the data regularly to find problems caused by a single vaccine or vaccine combinations.

Through a cooperative agreement, the FDA's (Food and Drug Administration) Division of Drug Risk Evaluation in the Office of Drug Safety has been working for almost 2 years to implement a desktop data mining software system. This data mining tool will help to evaluate the hundreds of thousands of reports submitted annually to the Adverse Events Reporting System (AERS), a system that has become more widely available to the public (Anonymous, 2005).

Delavari, Shirazi, and Beikzadeh (2004) showed that higher educational institutes use data mining models to identify which part of their processes can be improved by data mining technology and how they can achieve their goals. Data mining is used in the educational system to allocate resources and staff more efficiently, manage student relations, and enhance the performance of the institution and its students and faculty. Databases include information on students and teachers, course schedules, academic performance, test scores, extracurricular activities, postgraduation activities, and so forth, all of which can guide an institution on how to improve.

Helping Customer Relations Management

Studying consumer behavior is the primary purpose of data mining. Data mining has enabled businesses to provide better customer service through the use of CRM (customer relations management) technology. Most federal agencies have different customers such as citizens, businesses, other government agencies, and even offices within agencies, and each customer interaction provides extensive data that are used to develop new channels of service for customers. CRM is a conglomeration of technologies and management strategies that is used by organizations to control the operational side of their businesses. CRM is implemented in every department that deals with customers, be it in sales, technical support, customer service, or marketing. CRM combines all customer data derived from these departments into one place such that the information can be accessed anywhere. This will enable the company to see the snapshot of a customer's history whenever a customer is contacted.

According to Dean (2001), the government's use of CRM technologies is very different from the private sector's benefits. Businesses use CRM to weed out customers that are costly to serve while the government uses CRM as a tool to help them acquire customers. All the same agencies use CRM to learn about customer habits to create efficiency and cost-savings solutions. The Internal Revenue Service (IRS) uses CRM as a federal tax payment system; it uses this system to facilitate the collection of tax payments from corporations. Also, this system is incorporated in the IRS's call center and helps customer service representatives to have access to taxpayers' data to help resolve any issues they may have with their tax payments. This system has been said to help reduce the time it takes taxpayers to phone in payments by more than 40%, and the number of taxpayer requests have dropped by 90%. The average payment now takes just 2 minutes and 20 seconds, and it happens 100,000 times a day.

CRM has helped governments and businesses to take an inventory of their customers, identify the products and services provided to customers, identify the methods of providing the products and services, and measure the effectiveness of communications with the customers through service channels.

Analyzing Scientific and Research Information

The increasing amount of data accumulated in the health care industry creates databases that can serve as the basis for data mining. As the health care industry continues its work to enhance the quality of care, promote services, and reduce cost, undiscovered patterns of care will become increasingly transparent, first for physicians, nurses and other clinicians, and ultimately for all consumers of health care. Providers are now beginning to recognize the value of data mining as a tool to analyze patient care and clinical outcomes. As providers deploy advanced clinical data systems, more granular, primary data are becoming available for analysis.

In health care, increased access to data and information has facilitated the development of new drugs that seem to be produced at ever-increasing speeds, as Boire (2005) claims. By being able to quickly analyze volumes of data from all kinds of different tests and during different time periods, data mining represents a critical cog within the drug development process. What was once a few years ago almost considered impossible entered the realm of the possible through access to these newfound capabilities due in large part to data mining. According to scientists, the breakthrough discovery of being able to map the DNA genome offers limitless possibilities in the development of new drugs now that specific genes can be isolated.

Data mining gives an opportunity to analyze the actual impact of one variable on another. The analysis of data mining results enables the health care industry to discover new approaches in care delivery that consider a multitude of data points. A big step forward was achieved in medical research with the help of data mining. Children's Memorial Research Center, a leading U.S. pediatric hospital and research institute, has gained unique insights into tumor classification and treatment strategies with the help of SPSS predictive analysis. The automated extraction of information from biomedical literature promises to play an increasingly important role in text-based knowledge discovery processes ("SPSS Predictive Analytics Accelerating Cancer Research at Children's Memorial Research Center," 2005).

Managing Human Resources

According to Ashbaugh and Miranda (2002), the human resource management system (HRMS) is an integral part of the digital government that streamlines government processes in accounting, payroll, and personnel administration. The underlying architecture for digital government is the Internet and integrated administrative systems commonly known as enterprise resource planning (ERP) systems. ERP systems are built on software that integrates information from different applications into a common database. The ERP system and HRM system are the linkage between financial and human resources applications through a single database in a software application that is both rigid and flexible. The rigidity comes from the need to standardize processes and deter customers from modifying the underlying software source code. Flexibility refers to the customer's ability to configure the software to collect specific data and other business goals. Business intelligence is a new concept in the public sector that uses advanced analytical tools such as data mining to provide insights into organizations' trends and patterns, and helps organizations to improve their decision-making skills. HRMS and business intelligence can be used to support personnel management decisions, including turnover analysis, recruitment, training analysis, and salary and workforce planning.

The U.S. Air Force uses data mining to manage its human resources. It has signed an $88.5 million multiyear contract with the Oracle Corp., which includes a closely watched deal to build a new logistics system for the organization. The Air Force's Expeditionary Combat Support System

(ECSS) is intended to replace more than 500 legacy IT systems with one integrated commercial supply chain management system. Oracle was competing against other enterprise resource planning vendors for the ECSS contract. Oracle uses data mining to provide information on promotions, pay grades, clearances, and other information relevant to human resources planning (Cowley, 2005).

Detecting Fraud, Waste, and Abuse

In the government, data mining was initially used to detect financial fraud, waste, and abuse. The Department of Agriculture's Risk Management Agency (RMA) uses data mining methods to identify potential abusers, improve program policies and guidance, and improve program performance and data quality. RMA uses information collected from insurance applicants as well as from insurance agents and claims adjusters. The department produces several types of output, including lists of names of individuals whose behavior matches patterns of anomalous behavior, which are provided to program investigators and sometimes insurance agencies. In addition, it also produces programmatic information, such as how a procedural change in the federal crop insurance program's policy manual would impact the overall effectiveness of the program, and information on data quality and program performance, both of which are used by program managers (U.S. GAO, 2005).

Fraud in health care is controlled by the use of data mining by federal agencies. The agency can compare costs charged for medical services and find health care providers overcharging their patients. Data mining is used to compare treatments for different medical conditions to determine if a patient is receiving inadequate or excessive care. Researchers are currently using data mining to review records of infants stored in the database to compare the effectiveness and safety of the narcotics morphine and fentanyl in easing pain. The need to mine existing data is very important in newborn intensive care units, where different treatments cannot always be studied in large-scale randomized clinical trials (Landro, 2006).

Instead of insurance companies continuing to rely on the medical expertise of physicians as well as other trained clinicians, to manually review insurance claims to detect health care fraud and abuse, companies can now use a data mining framework that assesses clinical pathways to construct an adaptable and extensible detection model. Clinical pathways are driven by physician orders as well as industry and local standards of clinical care. Pathways provide the medical community with algorithms of the decisions to be made and the care to be provided to a particular patient population. The use of clinical pathways in detecting insurance fraud and abuse by service providers shows significant promise. A care activity is highly likely to be fraudulent if it orders suspiciously. For example, a typical pattern of physicians is that of ordering noninvasive tests before ordering more invasive ones. Therefore, there is a high probability that the same set of medical activities ordered in a different order is fraudulent or abusive (Yang & Hwang, 2006).

Detecting Criminal Activities

Data mining is also used by federal and state agencies to identify criminal activities, fraudulent misuse of governmental credit cards, and Medicaid and Medicare abuse. The SPSS predictive analytics software is used for crime prevention. This software's ability to detect unusual activity patterns has aided in the detection of credit card and Medicare fraud. In Richmond, Virginia, police use data mining to help them predict where to put patrols for crime prevention. An arm of the U.S. Army's homeland security uses the SPSS software to fight cybercrime. The Army aims at protecting the databases of utility companies from hackers bent on shutting down these systems (Van, 2005).

The IRS uses the system to identify financial crime, including individual and corporate tax fraud. Its outputs include reports containing names, social security numbers, addresses, and other personal information of individuals suspected of financial crime. Reports are shared with IRS field office personnel, who conduct investigations based on the report's results (U.S. GAO, 2005).

In line with Boire (2005), the murder rate in New York City was reduced from 2,200 in the late 1970s to between 600 to 700 murders a year over time under Mayor Giuliani's leadership. Some other factors like Bill Clinton's bill to increase the number of police officers and the zero-tolerance policy, initiated by Giuliani, resulted in the full prosecution of even minor crimes such as the illegal placement of graffiti on public property. Giuliani used technology and data mining to analyze data concerning crimes in all sectors of his city. Data mining made it possible to analyze massive amounts of data that allowed uncovering trends and patterns concerning future crime behavior within high-risk areas.

Detecting Terrorist Activities

Following the terrorist attacks of September 11, 2001, data mining has been used increasingly as a tool to help detect terrorist threats through the collection and analysis of public- and private-sector data. Data mining has become one of the key features of many homeland security initiatives and its use has also expanded to other purposes.

In the context of homeland security, data mining can be a potential means to identify terrorist activities, such as money transfers and communications, and to identify and track individual terrorists themselves, such as through travel and immigration records. Some of the homeland security data mining applications represent a significant expansion in the quantity and scope of data to be analyzed. Some efforts that have attracted a higher level of congressional interest include the

Terrorism Information Awareness (TIA) project (now discontinued) and the Computer-Assisted Passenger Prescreening System II (CAPPS II) project (now canceled and replaced by Secure Flight; Seifert, 2006). Other initiatives that have been the subject of recent congressional interest include the Multi-State Anti-Terrorism Information Exchange (MATRIX), the Able Danger program, and data collection and analysis projects being conducted by the National Security Agency (NSA; "MATRIX Pilot Project Concludes," 2005).

Other government data mining projects include Talon, a program run by the Pentagon's Counterintelligence Field Activity, which collects reports on demonstrators outside U.S. military bases. Thousands of such reports are stored in a database called Cornerstone and are shared with other intelligence agencies. The Pentagon's Advanced Research and Development Activity based at Fort Meade, Maryland, runs a research program whose goal is to develop better ways to mine huge databases to help the nation avoid strategic surprises such as those of September 11, 2001 (Boyd, 2006).

BARRIERS OF DATA MINING IN PUBLIC ADMINISTRATION

Two precursors are necessary for a successful data mining expedition: a clear formulation of the problem to be solved, and access to relevant data. Complicating the formulations of the problems to be solved and inherent in the public sectors are constraints raised by political opposition, privacy considerations, and concerns arising from the inherent limitations of the technology itself and the competency and hidden agendas of those who would implement the data mining projects and interpret its outputs. The most potent threat to privacy interests created by data mining technology arises from efforts to prevent terrorism in this country and overseas. As a result of anguished inquiries into the failure of the Unites States

military and intelligence branches to detect the risk, and to intercept at least one previously identified terrorist before he boarded the airplane at Newark Airport and participated in the attacks, it became more politically acceptable for politicians and public servants to procure and develop more effective and potentially intrusive data mining techniques in the interest of public safety.

Building on the U.S. Patriot Act was the Total Information Awareness Project (TIA) developed by the Department of Defense. TIA was designed to collect information on individuals' financial transactions, travel records, medical records, and other activities from a wide variety of public and private databases. The data mined from these sources were to be used to prevent terrorism. Unlike the Patriot Act, which passed through Congress with little opposition, two bills were introduced in Congress to prevent TIA from moving forward. TIA was much broader in scope than the Patriot Act and focused on collecting information about ordinary Americans rather than terror suspects. Because TIA was seen as a greater threat to with less return in security, Congress was widely against it. The TIA project has since been scrapped (Bagner, Evansburg, Watson, & Welch, 2003).

FUTURE TRENDS

The world is fast becoming a global village and with this comes the urgent need for a new generation of computational tools to assist humans in extracting useful information from the rapidly growing volumes of digital data. The future of data mining lies in predictive analysis or one-click data mining, accomplished through the simplification and automation of the entire data mining process.

Despite the limitations, data mining will have a tremendous impact on how business is done in the future. As a technology, data mining will become more embedded in a growing number of business applications, making it more readily available to a wider market segment. The developers of data mining applications therefore need to develop it into something that most users can work with and that can provide and add value to our every day lives. Easier interfaces will allow end user analysts with limited technical skills to achieve good results.

CONCLUSION

Data mining has become an indispensable technology for businesses and researchers in many fields including public administration. Since public-sector organizations and decision makers are dealing with a large amount of information from the public, a systematic way of collecting and reading data is necessary. This solution would not only find the similarities in one case to another, but also would identify unique cases and extreme values. Decision makers, service providers, and researchers would then be able to launch the next action based on the knowledge discovered from the database, and this increases their chances of being right. When the target market is the entire human population in the universe instead of a specific business market, data mining means more than making money for one's self. Exercising data mining in public administration is done to help the public, improve people's lives, and hence benefit the public as a whole.

FUTURE RESEARCH DIRECTIONS

Predictive Analysis

Augusta (2004) suggested that predictive analysis is one of the major future trends for data mining. Rather than being just about mining large amounts of data, predictive analytics looks to actually understand the data content. They forecast based on the contents of the data. However,

this requires complex programming and a great amount of business acumen. They do more than simply archive data, which is what data mining is currently known for. Organizations aim not just to process data, but understand them more clearly, which will in turn allow them to make better predictions about future behavior. With predictive analytics you have the program scour the data and try to form, or help form, a new hypothesis. This shows great promise and would be a boon for public administration everywhere.

Diversity of Application Domains

In data mining and the "X" phenomenon, as Tuzhilin (2005) coined it, X constitutes a broad range of fields in which data mining is used for analyzing the data. This has resulted in a process of the cross-fertilization of ideas generated within this diverse population of researchers interacting across the traditional boundaries of their disciplines. The next generation of data mining applications covers a large number of different fields from traditional businesses to advanced scientific research. Kantardzic and Zurada (2005) observed that with new tools, methodologies, and infrastructure, this trend of diversification will continue each year.

REFERENCES

Anonymous. (2005). FDA drug safety reviewers to use data mining tool. *Washington Drug Letter, 37*(5).

Ashbaugh, S., & Miranda, R. (2002). Technology for human resources management: Seven questions and answers. *Public Personnel Management, 31*(1), 7-19.

Augusta, L. (2004). The future of data mining: Predictive analytics. *DM Review, 14*(8), 16-20, 37.

Bagner, J., Evansburg, A., Watson, V. K., & Welch, J. B. (2003). Senators seek limits on DoD mining of personal data. *Intellectual Property & Technology Law Journal, 15*(5), 19-20.

Boire, R. (2005, October). Future of data mining in marketing: Part 1. *Direct Marketing News.*

Boyd, R. S. (2006, February 2). Data mining tells government and business a lot about you. *Knight Ridder Washington Bureau.*

Cahlink, G. (2000). Data mining taps trends. *Government Executive, 32*(12), 85-87.

Cowley, S. (2005, October 24). Oracle wins $88.5 million Air Force contract. *IDG News Service.*

Dean, J. (2001). Better business through customers. *Government Executive, 33*(1), 58-60.

Delavari, N., Shirazi, M. R. A., & Beikzadeh, M. R. (2004). A new model for using data mining technology in higher educational systems. *5th International Conference on Information Technology Based Higher Education and Training* (pp. 319-324).

Gramatikov, M. (2006). *Data mining techniques and the decision making process in the Bulgarian public administration.* Retrieved March 8, 2007, from http://unpan1.un.org/intradoc/groups/public/documents/nispacee/unpan009209.pdf

Hand, D. J., Mannila, H., & Smyth, P. (2001). *Principles of data mining.* Cambridge, MA: MIT Press.

Kantardzic, M. M., & Zurada, J. (Eds.). (2005). *Next generation of data-mining applications.* IEEE Press, Wiley-Interscience.

Landro, L. (2006, January 26). The informed patient: Infant monitors yield new clues. Studies of digital records are used to identify problems with medications: Practices. *Wall Street Journal,* p. D5.

Lok, C. (2004, October). Fighting infections with data. *Technology Review,* p. 24.

MATRIX pilot project concludes. (2005). Retrieved March 8, 2007, from http://www.fdle.state.fl.us/press_releases/expired/2005/20050415_matrix_project.html

SPSS predictive analytics accelerating cancer research at Children's Memorial Research Center, Chicago. (2005, March 7). *Business Wire.*

Tuzhilin, A. (2005). Foreword. In J. Wang (Ed.), *Encyclopedia of data warehousing and mining* (1st ed.). Hershey, PA: Idea Group Reference.

U.S. Government Accounting Office (GAO). (2005). *Data mining: Agencies have taken key steps to protect privacy in selected efforts, but significant compliance issues remain* (GAO-05-866). Author.

Van, J. (2005, October 17). Cybercrime being fought in new ways. *Knight Ridder Tribune Business News,* p. 1.

Wang, J. (Ed.). (2006). *Encyclopedia of data warehousing and mining* (1st ed.). Hershey, PA: Idea Group Reference.

Yang, W. S., & Hwang, S. Y. (2006). A process-mining framework for the detection of healthcare fraud and abuse. *Expert Systems with Applications, 31*(1), 56-68.

FURTHER READING

Agard, B., & Kusiak, A. (2004). Data-mining-based methodology for the design of product families. *International Journal of Production Research, 42*(15), 2955-2969.

Álvarez-Macilas, J. L., Mata-Vázquez, J., & Riquelme-Santos, J. C. (2004). Data mining for the management of software development process. *International Journal of Software Engineering & Knowledge Engineering, 14*(6), 665-695.

Berberidis, C., & Vlahavas, I. (2005). Mining for weak periodic signals in time series databases. *Intelligent Data Analysis, 9*(1), 29-42.

Besson, J., Robardet, C., Boulicaut, J. F., & Rome, S. (2005). Constraint-based concept mining and its application to microarray data analysis. *Intelligent Data Analysis, 9*(1), 59-82.

Brito, P., & Malerba, D. (2003). Mining official data. *Intelligent Data Analysis, 7*(6), 497-500.

Calders, T., Lakshmanan, L. V. S., Ng, R. T., & Paredaens, J. (2006). Expressive power of an algebra for data mining. *ACM Transactions on Database Systems, 31*(4), 1169-1214.

Ceglar, A., & Roddick, J. F. (2006). Association mining. *ACM Computing Surveys, 38*(2), 1-42.

Cheng, B.W., Chang, C. L., & Liu, I. S. (2005). Enhancing care services quality of nursing homes using data mining. *Total Quality Management & Business Excellence, 16*(5), 575-596.

Cheng, D., Kannan, R., Vempala, S., & Wang, G. (2006). A divide-and-merge methodology for clustering. *ACM Transactions on Database Systems, 31*(4), 1499-1525.

Cho, S. B., & Won, H. H. (2003). Data mining for gene expression profiles from DNA microarray. *International Journal of Software Engineering & Knowledge Engineering, 13*(6), 593-608.

Churilov, L., Bagirov, A., Schwartz, D., Smith, K., & Dally, M. (2005). Data mining with combined use of optimization techniques and self-organizing maps for improving risk grouping rules: Application to prostate cancer patients. *Journal of Management Information Systems, 21*(4), 85-100.

Chye, K. H., Chin, T. W., & Peng, G. C. (2004). Credit scoring using data mining techniques. *Singapore Management Review, 26*(2), 25-47.

Czerwinski, M., Gage, D. W., Gemmell, J., Marshall, C. C., Pérez-Quiñonesis, M. A., Skeels, M. M., et al. (2006). Digital memories in an era of ubiquitous computing and abundant storage. *Communications of the ACM, 49*(1), 44-50.

Dumouchel, B., & Demaine, J. (2006). Knowledge discovery in the digital library: Access tools for mining science. *Information Services & Use, 26*(1), 39-44.

Fan, W., Wallace, L., Rich, S., & Zhang, Z. (2006). Tapping the power of text mining. *Communications of the ACM, 49*(9), 77-82.

Fatemieh, S. O. (2006). A review of "Discovering knowledge in data: An introduction to data mining." *Journal of Biopharmaceutical Statistics, 16*(1), 127-130.

Feng, C. X. J., & Wang, X. F. (2004). Data mining techniques applied to predictive modeling of the knurling process. *IIE Transactions, 36*(3), 253-263.

Firestone, J. M. (2005). Mining for information gold. *Information Management Journal, 39*(5), 47-52.

Ford, J. M. (2005). Data and text mining: A business applications approach. *Personnel Psychology, 58*(1), 267-271.

Gama, J., Fernandes, R., & Rocha, R. (2006). Decision trees for mining data streams. *Intelligent Data Analysis, 10*(1), 23-45.

Garatti, S., Savaresi, S. M., Bittanti, S., & Brocca, L. L. (2004). On the relationships between user profiles and navigation sessions in virtual communities: A data-mining approach. *Intelligent Data Analysis, 8*(6), 579-600.

Gibert, K., Sànchez-Marrè, M., & Flores, X. (2005). Cluster discovery in environmental databases using GESCONDA: The added value of comparisons. *AI Communications, 18*(4), 319-331.

Guo, G., & Neagu, D. (2005). Fuzzy knnmodel applied to predictive toxicology data mining.

International Journal of Computational Intelligence & Application, 5(3), 321-333.

He, B., Chang, C. C., & Kevin. (2006). Automatic complex schema matching across Web query interfaces: A correlation mining approach. *ACM Transactions on Database Systems, 31*(1), 346-395.

Holzman, L. E., Fisher, T. A., Galitsky, L. M., Kontostathis, A., & Pottenger, W. M. (2004). A software infrastructure for research in textual data mining. *International Journal on Artificial Intelligence Tools, 13*(4), 829-849.

Hormozi, A. M., & Giles, S. (2004). Data mining: A competitive weapon for banking and retail industries. *Information Systems Management, 21*(2), 62-71.

Hou, J. L., Yu, F. J., & Lin, R. K. (2006). A knowledge component analysis model based on term frequency and correlation analysis. *Journal of Computer Information Systems, 46*(4), 64-77.

Hu, Y. C. (2005). Finding simplified fuzzy if-then rules for function approximation problems using a fuzzy data mining approach. *Applied Artificial Intelligence, 19*(6), 601-619.

Jones, K. (2006). Knowledge management as a foundation for decision support systems. *Journal of Computer Information Systems, 46*(4), 116-124.

Kajko-Mattsson, M., & Chapin, N. (2004). Data mining for validation in software engineering: An example. *International Journal of Software Engineering & Knowledge Engineering, 14*(4), 407-427.

Kersten, G. E., & Zhang, G. (2003). Mining inspire data for the determinants of successful Internet negotiations. *Central European Journal of Operations Research, 11*(3), 297-316.

Last, M., Friedman, M., & Kandel, A. (2004). Using data mining for automated software testing.

International Journal of Software Engineering & Knowledge Engineering, 14(4), 369-393.

Macdonell, C. (2005). Easy data mining for school libraries. *Library Media Connection, 24*(1), 38-39.

Morbitzer, C., Strachan, P., & Simpson, C. (2004). Data mining analysis of building simulation performance data. *Building Services Engineering Research & Technology, 25*(3), 253-267.

Nayak, R., & Qiu, T. (2005). A data mining application: Analysis of problems occurring during a software project development process. *International Journal of Software Engineering & Knowledge Engineering, 15*(4), 647-663.

Neaga, E. I., & Harding, J. A. (2005). An enterprise modeling and integration framework based on knowledge discovery and data mining. *International Journal of Production Research, 43*(6), 1089-1108.

Padmanabhan, B., & Tuzhilin, A. (2003). On the use of optimization for data mining: Theoretical interactions and eCRM opportunities. *Management Science, 49*(10), 1327-1343.

Perng, Y. H., & Chang, C. L. (2004). Data mining for government construction procurement. *Building Research & Information, 32*(4), 329-338.

Qian, G., Zhu, Q., Xue, Q., & Pramanik, S. (2006). Dynamic indexing for multidimensional non-ordered discrete data spaces using a data-partitioning approach. *ACM Transactions on Database Systems, 31*(2), 439-484.

Ren, Y., Ding, Y., & Zhou, S. (2006). A data mining approach to study the significance of nonlinearity in multistation assembly processes. *IIE Transactions, 38*(12), 1069-1083.

Riquelme, J. C., Polo, M., Aguilar-Ruiz, J. S., Piattini, M., Ferrer-Troyano, F. J., & Ruiz, F. (2006). A comparison of effort estimation methods for 4 GL programs: Experiences with statistics and data mining. *International Journal of Software Engineering & Knowledge Engineering, 16*(1), 127-140.

Šcf, T., & Gams, M. (2004). Data mining for creating accentuation rules. *Applied Artificial Intelligence, 18*(5), 395-410.

Sinha, A. P., & May, J. H. (2005). Evaluating and timing predictive data mining models using receiver operating characteristic curves. *Journal of Management Information Systems, 21*(3), 249-280.

Spangler, W. E., Gal-Or, M., & May, J. H. (2003). Using data mining to profile TV viewers. *Communications of the ACM, 46*(12), 66-72.

Spangler, W. S., Kreulen, J. T., & Newswanger, J. F. (2006). Machines in the conversation: Detecting themes and trends in informal communication streams. *IBM Systems Journal, 45*(4), 785-799.

Subramanyam, R. B. V., & Goswami, A. (2005). A fuzzy data mining algorithm for incremental mining of quantitative sequential patterns. *International Journal of Uncertainty, 13*(6), 633-652.

Toussaint, G. (2005). Geometric proximity graphs for improving nearest neighbor methods in instance-based learning and data mining. *International Journal of Computational Geometry & Applications, 15*(2), 101-150.

Vason, B. J. (2004). Mine data to discover infection control trends. *Nursing Management, 35*(6), 46-47.

Wang, S., Chung, K. F. L., & Shen, H. (2005). Fuzzy taxonomy, quantitative database and mining generalized association rules. *Intelligent Data Analysis, 9*(2), 207-217.

Wood, C. A., & Ow, T. T. (2005). Corporate data to data derived from the Web. *Communications of the ACM, 48*(9), 99-104.

Wu, R. C., Chen, R. S., & Chian, S. S. (2006). Design of a product quality control system based on the use of data mining techniques. *IIE Transactions, 38*(1), 39-51.

Xing, Z., & Stroulia, E. (2006). Understanding the evolution and co-evolution of classes in object-oriented systems. *International Journal of Software Engineering & Knowledge Engineering, 16*(1), 23-51.

Zhong, N., Hu, J., Motomura, S., Wu, J. L., & Liu, C. (2005). Building a data-mining grid for multiple human brain data analysis. *Computational Intelligence, 21*(2), 177-196.

Zurada, J., Karwowski, W., & Marras, W. (2004). Classification of jobs with risk of low back disorders by applying data mining techniques. *Occupational Ergonomics, 4*(4), 291-305.

KEY TERMS

Business Intelligence: Business intelligence is a new concept in the public sector that uses advanced analytical tools such as data mining to provide insights into organization trends, patterns, and decision making.

Customer Relations Management (CRM): CRM is a conglomeration of technologies and management strategies used by organizations to control the operational side of the business, and this is the domain for human resources and financial systems.

Data Mining: This is a process of sifting through the mass of organizational data to identify patterns critical for decision support.

Data Quality: This refers to the accuracy and completeness of data.

Enterprise Resource Planning Systems (ERPS): This is a system built on software that integrates information from different applications into a common database.

Interoperability: This is the ability of a computer system and/or data to work with other systems using common standards.

Public Administration: The term may apply to government, private-sector organizations and groups, or individuals.

This work was previously published in Handbook of Research on Public Information Technology, edited by G. Garson and M. Khosrow-Pour, pp. 556-567, copyright 2008 by Information Science Reference (an imprint of IGI Global).

Compilation of References

Abecker, A., Bernardi, A., Hinkelmann, K., Kuhn, O., & Sintek, M. (1998). *Techniques for Organizational Memory Information Systems*. DFKI GmbH: DFKI Document D-98-02.

Abbasi, A., & Chen, H. (2005). Applying Authorship Analysis to Extremist Group Web Forum Messages. *IEEE Intelligent Systems*, September/October 2005, pp. 67 -75.

Abrazhevich, D. (2004). Electronic Payment Systems: A User-Centered Perspective and Interaction Design, Dennis Abrazhevich publication.

ACC & AHA, "ACC/AHA/NASPE 2002 Guideline Update for Implantation of Cardiac Pacemakers and Antiarrhythmia Devices", (2002). American College of Cardiology Foundation and the American Heart Association, 106:2145-2161, URL: http://www.americanheart.org/downloadable/heart/1032981283481CleanPacemakerFinalFT.pdf

Adler, P.S. & Heckscher, C. (2006). Towards Collaborative Community, In The Firm as a Collaborative Community. In Charles Heckscher and Paul S. Adler (Eds.) *Reconstructing Trust in the Knowledge Economy*, 11-101.

Agosta, Lou. (2005). Data Warehousing Lessons Learned: Hub-and-Spoke Architecture Favored. *DM Review*, March 2005.

Agrawal, R., Mannila, H., Srikant, R., Toivonen, H., & Inkeri. A. (1996). *Fast Discovery of Association Rules, Advances in Knowledge Discovery and Data Mining*. The Association for the Advancement of Artificial Intelligence and The MIT Press, 307–328.

Agresti, A. (1990). *Categorical Data Analysis*. New York: John Wiley & Sons.

Albertsen, K. (2003). The Paradigma Web Harvesting Environment. *Proceeding of 3rd European Conf. Research and Advanced Tech. for Digital Libraries Workshop on Web Archives*, 2003.

Alexander, J.A, Ye, Y., Lee, S.D., Weiner, B.J. (2006). The Effects of Governing Board Configuration on Profound Organizational Change in Hospitals. *Journal of Health and Social Behavior*, 47(3), 291-308.

Alexander, J.A., Weiner, B.J. (1998). The Adoption of the Corporate Governance Model by Nonprofit Organizations. *Nonprofit Management & Leadership*, 8(3), 223-242.

Al-Hakim, L. (2006). Global E-government: Theory, Applications and Benchmarking, Idea Group Publication.

Alley, M., Alonso, PJ., Womack, C & Yao, Y. (2006). Star or Dimensional Modeling. Assignment in Data Warehousing and Data Mining, *Term Paper*, WEHCBA, Roosevelt University, Summer 2006.

Altschuler, A. & Zegans, M. (1997). Innovation and Public Management: Notes from the State House to City Hall. in A. Altschuler and R. Behn (Eds.), *Innovation in American Government*, Washington D.C.: Brookings Institution.

Amaravadi, C. (2005). Digital repositories for e-government. *Electronic Government: An International Journal*, 2(2), 205-218.

Ambali, A.R (2007, February 21). E-government in public administration: Benefits and challenges. *The E-Government Magazine for Asia & the Middle East*, 3(2), 20-31..

American Productivity & Quality Center (APQC). (2004, April). *Measuring the impact of knowledge management*. Proceedings of the E-Gov Institute Knowledge Management 2004 Conference.

Andersen, D.F. and Richardson, G.P. (1997) Scripts for Group model Building. *System Dynamics Review*, 13 2, 107-129.

Andersen, D.F., Richardson, G.P. and Vennix, J.A.M. (1997). Group Model Building: Adding More Science to the Craft. *System Dynamics Review*, 13 2. , 187-201.

Anderson, Richard (1997). Intelligence-Led Policing: A British Perspective. In *Intelligence Led Policing: International Perspectives on Policing in the 21st Century.* Lawrenceville, NJ: International Association of Law Enforcement Intelligence Analysts.

Anik, A.A. & Pathan, Al-Mukaddim K. (2004). A Framework for Managing Cost Effective and Easy Electronic Payment System in the Developing Countries, In Proceedings of International Conference on Intelligent Agents, Web Technology and Internet Commerce (IAWTIC'04), Gold Coast-Australia, 12-14 July, 2004. pp. 112-119.

Anonymous. (2005). FDA drug safety reviewers to use data mining tool. *Washington Drug Letter, 37*(5).

Anwar, M., & Soon T. K. (1999), The MSC and E-Government: Ensuring Interoperability. In Karim M. R. (Ed.), *Reengineering the Public Service: Leadership and Change in an Electronic Age,* Suban Jaya: Pelanduk.

Araujo, R. M. (2004). El gobierno electrónico en el ámbito local del país Vasco: del discurso tecnológico a la realidad institucional. Ninth International Congress of Public Administration-CLAD. Madrid, Spain 2-5 de November, Spain. Retrieved March 29, 2007 from http://www.edonostia.net/@mentxu/RAMILO_CLAD.pdf.

Arden Syntax for Medical Logic Systems, web site: http://cslxinfmtcs.csmc.edu/hl7/arden

Ardichvilli, A., Page, V. & Wentling, T. (2003). Motivation and barriers to participation in virtual knowledge-sharing communities of practice. *Journal of Knowledge Management, 7*(1)*,* 64-77.

Argüello, M., El-Hasia, A. & Lees, M. (2006). A Semantic Web Portal to construction knowledge exchange, In Zanasi, A., Brebria, C.A. & Ebecken, N.F.F. (Eds.). *Data Mining VII: Data, Text and Web Mining and their Business Applications* 417-427, WIT Transactions on Information and Communication Technologies, Vol 37, WIT Press.

Arrow, K. (2003), Reflections on the Reflections. In: Hammer, P.J., Haas-Wilson, D., Peterson, M.A., Sage, W.M., editors. *Kenneth Arrow and the changing economics of health care.* Durham: Duke University Press.

Ashbaugh, S., & Miranda, R. (2002). Technology for human resources management: Seven questions and answers. *Public Personnel Management, 31*(1), 7-19.

ASPA. (2001). *American society for public administration home page.* Retrieved May 12, 2002, from www.aspanet.org

Atkins, R.D. (1995) (Ed.), The Alleged Transnational Criminal: The Second Biennial, Martinus Nijhoff Publishers.

Atre, S. (2003). The Top 10 Critical Challenges for Business Intelligence Success; *Computerworld;* June 30, 2003.

Atre, S. (2003). Business Intelligence Success is Never an Accident; *Computerworld*; September 15, 2003.

Augusta, L. (2004). The future of data mining: Predictive analytics. *DM Review, 14*(8), 16-20, 37.

Austin, M.P. (1976). On nonlinear species response models in ordination. *Vegetatio, 33*, 33-41.

Avery, J.P. (2008). A different kind of Web-based knowledge management: "Little A" Principles Apply to "Big A" Portals, Defense AT&L, May-June 2008: 30-33.

Awazu, Y. (2004). Knowledge Management in Distributed Environments: Roles of Informal Network Players, A Proceedings of the 37th Hawaii International Conference on System Sciences, Hawaii.

Ayoub, N. (2007). *A Multilevel Decision Making Strategy for Designing and Evaluating Sustainable Bioenergy Supply Chains.* Unpublished doctoral dissertation, Tokyo Institute of Technology, Yokohama, Japan.

Ayoub, N., Martins, R., Wang, K., Seki, H., & Naka, Y. (2007). Two levels decision system for efficient planning and implementation of bioenergy production. *Energy Conversion and Management, 48*(3), 709-723.

Ayoub, N., Wang, K., Kagiyama, T., Seki, H., & Naka, Y. (2006). A Planning Support System for Biomass-based Power Generation. In W. Marquardt & C.Pantelides (Eds.), *16th European Symposium on Computer Aided Process Engineering and 9th International Symposium on Process Systems Engineering Vol. 21B.* (pp. 1899-1904). Garmisch-Partenkirchen, Germany.

Bagner, J., Evansburg, A., Watson, V. K., & Welch, J. B. (2003). Senators seek limits on DoD mining of personal data. *Intellectual Property & Technology Law Journal, 15*(5), 19-20.

Bannister, F. (2005). E-government and administrative power: The one-stop-shop meets the turf war. *Electronic Government: An International Journal, 2*(2), 160-176.

Barnard, G. (2003). Knowledge Sharing in Development Agencies: Knowledge Fortress or Knowledge Pool?, a paper presented at the EADI/MWG Conference, Dublin.

Basson, L., & Petrie, J. G. (2007). An integrated approach for the consideration of uncertainty in decision making supported by Life Cycle Assessment. *Environmental Modelling & Software Environmental Decision Support Systems, 22*(2), 167-176.

Batra, S. (2006). Impact of information technology on organizational effectiveness: a conceptual framework incorporating organizational flexibility. *Global Journal of Flexible Systems Management 7*(1/2), 15-25.

Bauknecht, K., Madria, S.K. & Pernul, G. (2000). (Eds.) Electronic Commerce and Web Technologies: First International Conference on Electronic Commerce and Web Technologies, EC-Web 2000, Springer.

Baum, L.E. (2003) "Hidden Markov Models and the Baum-Welch Algorithm", IEEE Information Theory Society Newsletter, Vol. 53, No.4, December 2003, pp. 1-1

BEA (2006). NHS24: Knowledge Management Portal Delivers High Quality Healthcare Information, BEA Systems, Inc., CA, USA.

Beekun, R.I., Stedham, Y., Young, G.J. (1998). Board Characteristics, Managerial Controls and Corporate Strategy: A Study of U.S. Hospitals. *Journal of Management, 24*(1), 3-19.

Bei, A., De Luca, S., Ruscitti, G. and Salamon, D. (2005) Health-Mining: a Disease Management Support Service based on Data Mining and Rule Extraction. In *Proceedings of the 2005 IEEE Engineering in Medicine and Biology 27th Annual Conference Shanghai, China,* IEEE.

Bennet, A. (2002). *Where the model frequently meets the road: Combining statistical, formal, and case study methods.* Paper presented at the American Political Science Association Conference, Boston, MA.

Berry, M.J.A. & Linoff G.S. (2004). *Data Mining Techniques: For Marketing, Sales, and Customer Relationship Management* (paperback), 2nd Edition. ISBN: 0-471-47064-3, Wiley.

Berry, M.J.A. & Linoff, G.S. (2004). Data Mining Techniques: For Marketing, Sales, and Customer Relationship Management. Wiley Computer Publishing, 2004.

Berry, M.J.A., & Linoff, G. (1996). *Data Mining Techniques: for marketing, sales, and customer support.* New York: John Wiley and Sons.

Berry, M.W., & Browne, M. (2005). E-mail Surveillance Using Nonnegative Matrix Factorization. *Computational & Mathematical Organization Theory, 11,*(3), 2005, pp. 249-264.

Berry, M.W., Drmac, Z., & Jessup, E. R. (1999). Matrix, Vector Space, and Information Retrieval. *SIAM Rev, 41,* 335 – 362.

Besouw, S.M., Noordman, T.B.J. (2005). *Non-Profit Governance. Zicht op de stand van zaken.* Delft: Eburon.

Bhatnagar, S.C. (2004). E-government: From Vision to Implementation : a Practical Guide with Cases, Sage Publications

Bion, J.F., Heffner, J.E. (2004). Challenges in the care of the acutely ill. *Lancet, 363,* 970-7.

Blake, M. B., Singh, L., Williams, A. B., Norman, W., & Sliva, A. L. (2006). A Component-Based Data Management and Knowledge Discovery Framework for Aviation Studies. *International Journal of Technology and Web Engineering, 1*(1).

Blomqvist K., & Levy, J. (2006). Collaboration Capability – A Focal Concept in Collaborative Knowledge Creation And Innovation in Networks. *International Journal of Management Concepts and Philosophy* 2: 1, 31-48.

Blomqvist, K., Miles, G., Miles, R.E. & Snow, C.C. (2007). *Critical Factors and Organizational Processes in Continuous Collaborative Innovation.* Paper submitted to the Copenhagen Conference on Partnerships: Achieving Collaborative Advantage, 30th - 31st of August 2007, Copenhagen Business School, Denmark.

Blundell, R.W. (1988). Consumer Behaviour: Theory and Empirical Evidence – A Survey. *The Economic Journal, 98,*16-65.

Böhle, K. (2002). Integration of Electronic Payment Systems into B2C Internet Commerce: Problems and Perspectives, Background Paper#8, European Communities.

Böhle, K., Rader, M. & Riehm, U. (1999). (Eds.) Electronic Payment Systems in European Countries: Country Synthesis Report, European Commission, ECSC-EEC-EAEC, Brussels, Luxembourg.

Boire, R. (2005, October). Future of data mining in marketing: Part 1. *Direct Marketing News.*

Borges, M. R. S., Pino, J. A., & Valle, C. (2005). Support for decision implementation and follow-up. *European Journal of Operational Research Decision Support Systems in the Internet Age, 160*(2), 336-352.

Borgman, C. L. & Furner J. (2002). Scholarly Communication and Bibliometrics. *Ann. Rev. Information Science and Technology,* (36), 2002.

Bose, R. (2002). Customer relationship management: key components for IT success. *Industrial Management & Data Systems*, *102*(2), 89-97.

Bosh, X. (2004), French health system on verge of collapse, says report. *Lancet*, 363, 376.

Bourquard, J. A. (2003). What's up with e-government? Retrieved April 6, 2005, from http://www.ncsl.org/programs/pubs/slmag/2003/303egov.htm

Boyd, R. S. (2006, February 2). Data mining tells government and business a lot about you. *Knight Ridder Washington Bureau.*

Bozdogan, H. (2003). (Ed.). Statistical Data Mining and Knowledge Discovery, Chapman & Hall/CRC.

Bradford, R. B. (2006). Relationship Discovery in Large Text Collections Using Latent Semantic Indexing. *The proceedings of the Fourth Workshop on Link Analysis, Counterterrorism and Security*, Bethesda, Maryland, 2006.

Brancheorganisaties Zorg. (2005). *Zorgbrede Governancecode*. Utrecht: BoZ.

Breiman, L., Friedman, J. (1985). Estimating Optimal transformations for Multiple Regression and Correlation, *Journal of the American Statistical Association*, 80(394), 580-598.

Breiman, L., Friedman, J. H., Olshen, R., & Stone, C. J. (1984). *Classification and Regression Trees*. Pacific Grove, CA: Wadsworth & Brooks.

Brenner, P. DeCoster & Brenner, P. (2006). Central America: Structural Foundations for Regional Financial Integration, International Monetary Fund, World Bank. International Monetary Fund.

Bresciani, P., Donzelli, P. and Forte, A. (2003). Requirements Engineering for Knowledge Management in eGovernment. *Proceedings of 4th Working Conference on Knowledge Management in Electronic Government*, Rhodes Island, Greece.

Bresciani, P., Donzelli, P., & Forte, A. (2003). *Requirements engineering for knowledge management in egovernment*. Proceedings of the Fourth Working Conference on Knowledge Management in Electronic Government, Rhodes Island, Greece.

Breslin, M. (2004). Data Warehousing: Battle of the Giants; *Business Intelligence Journal*, pp 6-20; Winter 2004.

Brickley, J.A., Van Horn, L. (2002). Managerial incentives in nonprofit organizations: evidence from hospitals. *J Law Econ*, 45, 227-249.

Brin S., Motwani R., Ullman J.D., Tsur S.(1997, May) *Dynamic itemset counting and implication rules for market basket data*. Paper presented at the ACM SIGMOD International Conference on Management of Data, Tucson, Arizona.

Brint dot com (2007). Retrieved December 28, 2007 from http://www.brint.com/km/

Britt, P. (2007). Government gets a grip on knowledge sharing. *KMWorld*, April 1. Retrieved September 3, 2007, from http://www.kmworld.com/Articles/ReadArticle.aspx?ArticleID=35777&PageNum=1

Bruecher, H. (2003). *Requirement analysis for a knowledge management system in egovernment*. Proceedings of the Fourth Working Conference on Knowledge Management in Electronic Government, Rhodes Island, Greece.

Buckland, M. (1992). *Redesigning Library Services: A Manifesto*. Chicago: America Library Association.

Bugajski, J., Grossman, R., Sumner, E. & Zhang, T. (2005). A Methodology for Establishing Information Quality Baselines for Complex, Distributed Systems, 10th International Conference on Information Quality (ICIQ), November 4th - 6th 2005, MIT, Cambridge, MA.

Busse, R., Schlette, S., Weinbrenner, S., editors. (2005). *Health Policy Developments. Issue 4. Focus on Acces, Primary Care, Health Care Organization*. Gütersloh: Verlag Bertelmann Stiftung.

Cadbury, A. (1992). *Report of the Committee on the Financial Aspects of Corporate Governance*. London: Gee.

Cahlink, G. (2000). Data mining taps trends. *Government Executive, 32*(12), 85-87.

Campbell, A. (2008). From Secretaries to Virtual Assistants to … Social Media Assistants? Retrieved July 25, 2008 from http://www.theappgap.com/virtual-assistants-social-media.html

Cantu, et. al. (2005). A Knowledge-based entrepreneurial approach for business intelligence in strategic technologies: Bio-MEMS, *Proceedings of the Eleventh Americas Conference on Information Systems,* Omaha, NE, USA August 11th-14th 2005: pp: 1327-1340.

Carbonaro, G. (1985). *La Povertà in Italia – Studi di Base: Nota Sulle Scale di Equivalenza*. Roma, IT: Istituto Poligrafico dello Stato.

Cardinaels, E., Roodhooft, F., Van Herck, G. (2004). Drivers of cost system development in hospitals: results of a survey. *Health Policy*, 69(2), 239-52.

Cardoso, J. & Sheth, A. (2006). Semantic Web Services, Processes and Applications, Springer, 2006.

Cardoso, J. (2007). Semantic Web Services: Theory, Tools and Applications, Idea Group.

Caribbean KD Center (2008). Accessed February 02, 2008 from http://ckmportal.eclacpos.org/;

Caribbean KD Center (2008). Accessed February 02, 2008 from http://eceeg.dec.uwi.edu/drupal/

Caribbean KD Center (2008). Accessed February 02, 2008 from http://ckmportal.eclacpos.org/dev/suriname

Carter, L. & Belanger, F. (2004). Citizen Adoption of Electronic Government Initiatives, A Proceedings of the 37th Hawaii International Conference on System Sciences, Hawaii.

Carver, J. (2006). *Boards That Make a Difference. 3th edition*. San Francisco: Jossey-Bass.

Castells, M. (1996). *The rise of the network society*. Oxford: Basil Blackwell.

Castells, M. (2000). *End of millennium: The information age, economy, society and culture*. Wiley-Blackwell.

Castells, M. (2006). *Mobile communication and society: A global perspective*. Wiley-Blackwell.

Catrinu, M. D. (2006). *Decision Aid for Planning Local Energy Systems: Application of Multi-Criteria Decision Analysis*. Unpublished doctoral dissertation, Norwegian University of Science and Technology, Trondheim, Norway.

Center for Democracy and Technology. (2002). *2002 digital state survey*. Retrieved from http://centerdigitalgov.com

Chae, Y. M., Ho, S. H., Cho, K. W., Lee, D. H., & Ji, S. H. (2001). Data mining approach to policy analysis in a health insurance domain. *International Journal of Medical Informatics, 62*(2-3), 103-111.

Chailla, A.M. (2001). *Implementation of Policies and Strategies for Agricultural Information Access and Use in Tanzania*. Unpublished doctoral dissertation, University of Natal, Pietermaritzburg.

Chan, J and Chowdhury, S. (2005). Enhancing Customer Services using Case-based Reasoning. Published in the communications of the ICISA – *the official journal of the International Chinese Information Systems Association*, Vol VII. Number 1, pp 53-61.

Chan, J., Witte, C. & Chowdhury, S. (2004). *Information Architecture for Electronic Customer Relationship Management*. Paper presented at the American Society of Business and Behavioral Sciences (ASBBS) conference, 2004.

Chan, L. Kirsop, B. & Arunachalam, S (2005). *Open Access Archiving: the fast track to building research capacity in developing countries*. Science and Development Network. Retrieved July, 25, 2007 from http://www.scidev.net/open_access/files/open%20Archiving.pdf

Chan, P., Fan W., Prodromidis, A. and Stolfo, S.(1999) Distributed data mining in credit card fraud detection. *IEEE Intelligent Systems*, pages 67–74, Nov/Dec.

Chapanond, A., Krishnamoorthy, & M., Yener, B. (2005). Graph Theoretic and Spectral Analysis of Enron E-mail Data. *Workshop on Link Analysis, Counterterrorism and Security, at the SIAM International Conference on Data Mining*. California, USA, 2005, pp. 15 - 22.

Chapman, S. & Klemperer, K (1997). *Digital libraries: A selected resource guide*. Retrieved on 21st June, 2008 from http:/www.lita.org/ital/1603 klemperer.htm

Charalabidis Y., Lampathaki F., Stassis A. (2007). A Second-Generation e-Government Interoperability Framework. *5th Eastern European e|Gov Days 2007* in Prague, Austrian Computer Society, 2007

Charalabidis, Y., Askounis D., (2008). Interoperability Registries in eGovernment: Developing a Semantically Rich Repository for Electronic Services and Documents of the new Public Administration. *Hawaiian International Conference of System Sciences, HICCS-08*, January 7-10, 2008, Hawaii.

Chau, K. W., Cao, Y., Anson, M., & Zhang, J. (2003). Application of data warehouse and Decision Support System in construction management. *Automation in Construction, 12*(2), 213-224.

Chenoweth, T., David, S & Robert SL. (2003). A Method for Developing Dimensional Data Marts. *Communications of the ACM*, Vol. 45, No. 12, pp.93-98.

Cheung, D., Han, J., Ng, V. T. & Fu, A.W. (1996).Fast distributed algorithm for mining association rules. In *International Conference on Parallel and Distributed Information Systems*, Tokyo, Japan, 31–42.

Chisenga, J. (2006). *The development and use of digital libraries, institutional repositories, digital repositories, and open access archives for research and national development in Africa: opportunities and challenges.* [Online]: Retrieved on 2nd Nov. 2006 from http://www.uneca.org/disd/events/2006/wsis-library/presentations/development~

Choi, B. & Jong, A.M., (2005). An Examination of KM Strategies and the Market Value of the Firm: Based on the Event Study Methodology, A proceedings of Knowledge Management in Asia-Pacific 2005, Building a Knowledge Society: Linking Government, Business, Academia and the Community, Victoria University of Wellington, New Zealand.

Chow, C.W., Ganulin, D., Teknika, O., Haddad, K., Williamson, J. (1998). The balanced scorecard: a potent tool for energizing and focusing healthcare organization management. *Journal of Healhtcare Management*, 43, 263-80.

Chow, W. S. (2001). Ethical belief and behavior of managers using information technology for decision making in Hong Kong. *Journal of Managerial Psychology, 16*(4), 258-267.

Chowdhury S. (2007). A Research Proposal on Model Conversion: E-R to Star Model. Roosevelt University, Spring 2007.

Chowdhury, S and Chan, J. (2007). *Data Warehousing And Data Mining: A Course In MBA And MSIS Program From Uses Perspective.* Paper presented at the 18th Annual Conference of IIMA (International Information Management Association), Beijing, China, October, 2007.

Chowdhury, S. (2001). From Databases to Case-bases: What, Why and How?" presented at the MBAA (Midwest Business Administration Association) *–SAIS (Society for the Advancement of Information System)* Conference, 2001.

Chowdhury, S. (2005). Lecture Notes on *A course on Data Warehousing and Data Mining*, WEHCBA, Roosevelt University, 2005.

Chowdhury, S. (2005). Tools and Techniques for Exploring Business Problems and Solutions and Attaining as well as Retaining Business Intelligence. presented at the MBAA (Midwest Business Administration Association) *–SAIS (Society for the Advancement of Information System)* Conference, 2005.

Chowdhury, S. (2006). *Project description in Data Warehousing and Data Mining Course*, WEHCBA, Roosevelt University, Summer 2006.

Chowdhury, S. (2007). Methodology for Ensuring Data Quality in Data Warehouses, *Paper published in the Proceedings of the MBAA-SAIS (Midwest Business Administration Association - Society for the Advancement of Information System)*, March 28-30, 2007.

Chowdhury, S. (2007). From ER to Star Data Modeling - A Methodology, Paper accepted for publication in the *Journal of American Society of Business and Behavioral Sciences* (ASBBS). Fall2007.

Chowdhury, S. (2007). Trends in Database Tools and Technologies, paper accepted for publication in the *Journal of The Business Review*, Cambridge, Vol. 7, No. 1, Summer 2007.

Chowdhury, S.I. (1990). Computer-Based Support for Knowledge Extraction from Clinical Databases, *Linköpings Studies in Science & Technology.* Dissertations No. 240, Linköping University.

Churilov, L., Bagirov, A. M. , Schwartz, D. , Smith, K. A. & Dally. M. (2004) "Improving risk grouping rules for prostate cancer patients with optimization". In *HICSS*, 2004.

Cirasino, M. (2007). Reforming Payments and Securities Settlement Systems in Latin America and the Caribbean, World Bank Publications.

Clarke, K.R., & Warwick, R.M. (1994). *Change in Marine Communities: an Approach to Statistical Analysis and Interpretation.* Plymouth, UK: Plymouth Marine Laboratory, Natural Environment Research Council.

Clausen, S.E. (1998). *Applied Correspondence Analysis. An Introduction.* Thousand Oaks, CA: SAGE Publications, Inc.

Clement, J.M. (2004). *Hôpital 2007: Les répercussions dans le champ du droit hospitalier.* Bordeaux: Les études hospitalières.

Compaine, M. B. (2001). *Digital divide: Facing a crisis or creating a myth.* MIT Press.

Computer Science and Telecommunications Board. (2002). *Information technology research, innovation, and e-government.* Retrieved May 14, 2008, from http://books.nap.edu/openbook.php?record_id=10355&page=R1

Cong, X., & Pandya, K. (2003). Issues of knowledge management in the public sector. *Electronic Journal of Knowledge Management, 1*(2), 25-33.

Cook, M., & LaVigne, M. (2002). Making the local e-gov connection. Retrieved May 24, 2002, from www.urbanicity.org/FullDoc.asp?ID=36

Courty, P. and Marschke, G.: (1997) Measuring Government Performance: Lessons from a Federal Job-Training Program. The American Economic Review 87 383–388

Cowley, S. (2005, October 24). Oracle wins $88.5 million Air Force contract. *IDG News Service*.

Cox, T.F., Cox, M. (2001), *Multidimensional Scaling*. London: Chapman and Hall.

Coyle, R. G. (1996). *System dynamics Modelling: A Practical Approach*, London, Chapman and Hall.

Crean, M. (2003). *A Weblog Recommender using Machine Learning and Semantic Web Technologies*, White paper, University of Bristol, UK.

Creswell, J. W. (2003). *Research design. Qualitative, quantitative, and mixed methods approaches*. Thousand Oaks, CA: SAGE Publications.

Cummings, Joanne. (2007). How e-discovery can save you big bucks. *Network World*, May 22. Retrieved September 6, 2007, from http://www.itworldcanada.com/Pages/Docbase/ViewArticle.aspx?id=idgml-5ae90c98-4918-4e2d-b8aa-9be1611fe6f2

Cyert, R. & March, J. (1963). *A Behavioral Theory of the Firm*. Englewod Cliffs: Prentice Hall.

Daconta, M.C., Obrst, L.J., & Smith, K.T. (2003). The Semantic Web: A Guide to the Future of XML, John Wiley & Sons.

DAML Government R&D Ontology, http://www.daml.org/projects/integration/ projects-20010811, 2006

Data Mining Group, PMML, web site: http://www.dmg.org/v3-1/GeneralStructure.html

Davenport, T. and Prusak, L. (1998). *Working Knowledge: Managing What Your Organisation Knows*. Harvard Business School Press, Boston, MA.

Davies, J., Studer, R. & Warren, P. (2006). Semantic Web Technologies: Trends and Research in Ontology-based Systems, Wiley.

Davies, T. R. (2004). Bypassing the revolution. Could it be that e-gov was never on track to transform the performance of state and local governments? Retrieved April 6, 2005, from http://governing.com/articles/10tech.htm.

Dawes, S. S., & Pardo, T. A. (2002). Building collaborative digital government systems. Systematic constraints and effective practices. In W. J. McIver & A. K. Elmagarmid (Eds.), *Advances in digital government. Technology, human factors, and policy* (pp. 259- 273). Norwell, MA: Kluwer Academic Publishers.

Dawes, S. S., Pardo, T., & DiCaterino, A. (1999). Crossing the threshold: Practical foundations for government services on the world wide web. *Journal of the American Society for Information Science, 50*(4), 346-35

De Bleser, L., Depreitere, R., De Waele, K., Vanhaecht, K., Vlayen, J., Sermeus, W. (2006). Defining pathways. *Journal of Nursing Management, 14*(7), 553-63.

De Luca, S., Memo, E., Santesso. E. et al.(2005) *L'appropriatezza dei ricoveri ospedalieri: analisi e proposte*, (in Italian: *Appropriateness of hospital admissions: analysis and proposals*), 2005 Libreria Editrice Cafoscarina (Venice).

Dean, J. (2001). Better business through customers. *Government Executive, 33*(1), 58-60.

Debrosse, D. (2006). New Governance. Creation of an executive committee and regrouping by centres. *Hospital, 8*(2), 45-6.

Deerwester, S., et al. (1988). Improving Information Retrieval with Latent Semantic Indexing, *Proceedings of the 51st Annual Meeting of the American Society for Information Science,* 1988, pp. 36-40.

Delavari, N., Shirazi, M. R. A., & Beikzadeh, M. R. (2004). A new model for using data mining technology in higher educational systems. *5th International Conference on Information Technology Based Higher Education and Training* (pp. 319-324).

Delen, D., & Crossland, M. D. (2008). Seeding the survey and analysis of research literature with text mining. *Expert Systems with Applications: An International Journal, 34*(3), 1707-1720.

Delen, D., & Pratt, D. B. (2006). An integrated and intelligent DSS for manufacturing systems. *Expert Systems with Applications, 30*(2), 325-336.

Delen, D., Walker, G. & Kadam, A. (2005) "Predicting breast cancer survivability: a comparison of three data mining methods", in *Artificial Intelligence in Medicine* (2005) 34, pp. 113—127

Demchak, C. C., Friis, C., & La Porte, T. M. (2000). Webbing Governance: National Differences in Constructing the Face of Public Organizations. *Handbook of Public Information Systems*, Marcel Dekker, 2000.

Department of Health. (2005). *A Short Guide to NHS Foundation Trusts*. London: Department of Health.

Desai, N. and Chowdhury, S. (2003). Data Mining for Competitive Business Advantages: Present and Future Implications. Published in the *Journal of American Society of Business and Behavioral Sciences* (ASBBS). Vol. 10, N0. 1, pp62-71, Spring 2003.

Diesner, J., & Carley, K.M., (2005). Exploration of Communication Networks from the Enron E-mail Corpus. *Workshop on Link Analysis, Counterterrorism and Security, at the SIAM International Conference on Data Mining*. California, USA, 2005, pp. 3 – 14.

Dijk, J.A.G.M van (1999). *The network society*. London: Sage Publications.

Dijk, J.A.G.M.van (1997). The reality of virtual communities: Trends in communication 1997/1. *New Media Developments*, 39-61.

DIP project eGovernment Ontology http://dip.semanticweb.org/documents/D9-3-improved-eGovernment.pdf, 2004

Direction de l'hospitalisation et de l'organisation des soins. (2004). *Circulaire DHOS/E1 n°61 du 13 février 2004 relative à la mise en place par anticipation de la nouvelle gouvernance hospitalière.*

DIRECTIVE 2003/42/EC OF THE EUROPEAN PARLIAMENT AND OF THE COUNCIL on occurrence reporting in civil aviation, DIRECTIVE 2003/42/EC (2003).

Ditzel, E., Štrach, P., Pirozek, P. (2006). An inquiry into good hospital governance: A New Zealand-Czech comparison. *Health Research Policy and Systems*, 4, 2.

Dixon, J. (2002) Foundation hospitals. *Lancet*, 360, 1900-1.

Djellal, F., Gallouj, F. (2005). Mapping innovation dynamics in hospitals. *Res Pol*, 34, 817-35.

Dörre, J., Gerstl, P., & Seiffert, R. (1999). Text mining: Finding Nuggets in Mountains of Textual Data. *The Fifth ACM SIGKDD International Conference on Knowledge Discovery and Data Mining, ACM*. San Diego, California, 1999, pp. 398-401.

Downes, J. & Goodman, J.E. (2006). Dictionary of Finance and Investment Terms, Barron's Educational Series, Incorporated.

Dulle, F. W., Lwehabura, M.J.F., Mulimila, R.T. & Matovelo D.S. (2001). Researchers' perspectives on agricultural libraries as information sources in Tanzania. *Library Review*, 50(4), 187-192.

Durfee, A.V. (2006). Text Mining Promise and Reality. *Twelfth Americas Conference on Information Systems*. Acapulco, Mexico, 2006, pp. 1449-1460.

Ebrahim, Z. & Irani, Z. (2005). E-government adoption: architecture and barriers. *Business Process Management Journal, 11*(5), 58-611.

ECA (1999). Economic Commission for Africa (ECA), 1999 available at http://www.uneca.org/adf99/theway-forward.htm

Eden, S. (2007). Vendors jump on e-discovery bandwagon. *Intelligent Enterprise, 10*(1), 9.

Educational Technology Collaborative (2005). *Digital Treasures, exploring new research sources on the internet.* Retrieved 16th July, 2008 from http://edtech.tennessee.edu/set/2005/set33/extra/glossary.html

Eeckloo, K., Delesie, L., Vleugels, A. (2007). Hospital Governance: Exploring the European Scene – Part I, *Hospital*, 9(2), 14-16.

Eeckloo, K., Delesie, L., Vleugels, A. (2007). Hospital Governance: Exploring the European Scene – Part II, *Hospital*, 9(3), 30-32.

Eeckloo, K., Van Herck, G., Van Hulle, C., Vleugels, A. (2004). From Corporate Governance To Hospital Governance. Authority, transparency and accountability of Belgian non-profit hospitals' board and management. *Health Policy*, 68, 1-15.

Elo, M. (2005). *SME Internationalization from Network Perspective – Empirical Study on a Finnish-Greek Business Network.* A doctoral dissertation, Publications of Åbo Akademi University, Finland.

Elovici, Y., Shapira, B., Last, M., Kandell, A., & Zaafrany, O. (2004). Using Data Mining Techniques for Detecting Terror-Related Activities on the Web. *J of Information Warfare*, 3(1), 17-28.

Elvici, Y. et al. (2005). Content-Based Detection of Terrorists Browsing the Web Using an Advanced Terror Detection System (ATDS). *ISI 2005, LNCS 3495*, pp. 244-255, 2005.

EMCC (European Monitoring Centre on Change) (2003), *The future of health and social services in Europe*, European Foundation for the Improvement of Living and Working Conditions. URL: http://www.eurofound.europa.eu/emcc/publications/2003/sf_hss_1.pdf

ePSO (2001). Electronic Payments Systems Observatory, ePSO Newsletter Issues no. 1-8, July 2000-September 2001, Institute for Prospective Technological Studies, European Commission, pp.3

Eskin. E. (2000)Anomaly detection over noisy data using learned probability distributions. In *Proceedings of the Seventeenth International Conference on Machine Learning (ICML- 2000).*

European Commission (2001). *White paper on European governance.* Brussels: European Commission of the European Union.

European Commission. (2000). *Proposal for a DIRECTIVE OF THE EUROPEAN PARLIAMENT AND OF THE COUNCIL on occurrence reporting in civil aviation.* Brussels.

European Parliament. (2001). European Parliament report on ECHELON. Retrieved from http://www.fas.org/irp/program/process/rapport_echelon_en.pdf, 2001

Eyob, E. (2004). E-government: Breaking the frontiers of inefficiencies in the public sector. *Electronic Government: An International Journal, 1*(1), 107-114.

Fan, W., Wallace, L., Rich, S., & Zhang, Z. (2006). Tapping the Power of Text Mining. *Communications of the ACM* (49:9) 2006, pp 77-82.

Fang, R., & Tuladhar, S. (2006). Teaching Data Warehousing and Data Mining in a Graduate Program of Information Technology. In *The Consortium for Computing Sciences in Colleges*, pp.137-144.

Fayyad, U., Piatetsky-Shapiro, G., & Smyth, P. (1996). *Knowledge Discovery and Data Mining: Towards a Unifying Framework.* Paper presented at the Second International Conference on Knowledge History and Data Mining (KDD-96), Portland, Oregon.

Federal Reserve Bank of Boston (2002). The Future of Retail Electronic Payments Systems: Industry Interviews and Analysis, Staff Study #175, Federal Reserve Staff for the Payments System Development Committee, Board of Governors of the Federal Reserve System, Federal Reserve Bank of Boston, USA.

Feldman, R., & Sanger, J. (2006). The Text Mining Handbook: Advanced Approaches in Analyzing Unstructured Data, Cambridge University Press.

Feng, Y., Wu, Z., Zhou, X., Zhou, Z., Fan, W. (2006) "Knowledge discovery in traditional Chinese medicine: State of the art and perspectives", in *Artificial Intelligence in Medicine* (2006) 38, pp. 219—236

Fensel, D., Wahlster, W., Lieberman, H. & Handler, J. (2002). Spinning the Semantic Web: Bringing the World Wide Web to Its Full Potential, MIT Press.

Ferguson, R.W. Jr. & Minehan, C.E. (2002). In Foreword: The Future of Retail Electronic Payments Systems: Industry Interviews and Analysis, Staff Study #175, Federal Reserve Staff for the Payments System Development Committee, Board of Governors of the Federal Reserve System, Federal Reserve Bank of Boston, USA.

Ferraro, K. F. & LaGrange, R. (1987). The measurement of fear of crime. *Sociological Inquiry* 57, 70–101.

Ficarra, F. (2004). Internet en la gestión pública y municipal. Revista Latinoamericana de Comunicación CHASQUI, 88

Field M., Lohr K. (1992) Clinical Practice Guidelines: Directions for a New Program, I.o.M., editor. Committee to Advise the Public Health Service on Clinical Practice Guidelines; 1992.

Flood, R. (1999). *Rethinking the fifth discipline. Learning within the unknowable*, Ruthledge, London

Fong, S. W., Skillicorn, D. B., & Roussinov, D. (2006). Detecting Word Substitution in Adversarial Communication. *The proceedings of the Fourth Workshop on Link Analysis, Counterterrorism and Security.* Bethesda, Maryland, 2006.

Forcht, Karen A., & Thomas, Daphyne S. (1994). Information compilation and disbursement: moral, legal and ethical considerations. *Information Management and Computer Security, 2*(2), 23-28.

Forrest, S., Hofmeyr, S. A. , Somayaji, A. and Longstaff. (1996)T. A. A sense of self for unix processes. In *In 1996 IEEE Symposium on Security and Privacy*, pages 120–128. IEEE Computer Society.*Building the virtual state. Information technology and institutional change.* Washington, D.C.: Brookings Institution Press.

Forrester, J. W. (1961). Industrial Dynamics: A Major Breakthrough for Decision Makers. *Harvard Business Review*, July-August, 37-66.Fountain, J. E. (2001).

Forthman, M.T., Dove, H.G., Wooster, L.D. "Episode Treatment Groups (ETGs): A Patient Classification System for Measuring Outcomes Performance by Episode of Illness", *Top Health Inform Manage*, 2000, 21(2), 51–61

Fox J., Johns N., Rahmanzadeh A. (1998) Disseminating medical knowledge: the PROforma approach. Artificial Intelligence in Medicine 1998;14:157–81.

Francis, D. & Bessant, J. (2005). Targeting innovation and implications for capability development. *Technovation*, 25, 171–183.

Frank, D. (2002). *E-gov theme: "Collect once, use many."* Retrieved from http://www.fcw.com/fcw/articles

Fraser J., Adams N., A. Macintosh, A. McKay-Hubbard, T. Pariente Lobo, P. Fernandez Pardo, R. Cañadas Martínez and J.Sobrado Vallecillo (2003). Knowledge Management Applied to E-government Services: The Use of an Ontology. *KMGov 2003, LNAI 2645*, pp. 116–126.

Free Press Release (2008). Reliable and Convenient Support for Business Owners, Retrieved August 30, 2008 from http://www.free-press-release.com/news/200802/1201891752.html

Fry, M.J. et. al. (1999). Payment Systems in Global Perspective. Routledge.

Fust, W. (2003). Knowledge Society, Knowledge Management and ICT, an Editorial contribution to a publication edited by the Community Development Library, Dhaka, Bangladesh.

GAIN Working Group B. (2004). *Role of Analytical Tools in Airline Flight Safety Management Systems* (No. Second Edition): Global Aviation Information Network.

Galvan M. (2006). *Active Data Warehousing*. Term-paper in INFS413-X5: Data Warehousing and Data Mining, Roosevelt University, summer 2006.

Gao, F., Li, M. & Nakamori, Y. (2002). Systems thinking on knowledge and its management: systems methodology for knowledge management. *Journal of Knowledge Management*, 6(1), 7-17.

Garcia, C., Janjua, T. & Galvan, M. (2006). *Northwind Traders Star Schema Model. Assignment in Data Warehousing and Data Mining*, Term Paper, WEHCBA, Roosevelt University.

Garson, G. D. (2004). The promise of digital government. In A. Pavlichev & G. D. Garson (Eds.), *Digital government: Principles and best practices* (pp. 2-15). Hershey, PA: Idea Group Publishing.

Gartner. (2000). Gartner says u.S. E-government spending to surpass $6.2 billion by 2005. Retrieved April 6, 2005, from http://www.gartner.com/5_about/press_room/pr20000411c.html

Gasson, S. & Shelfer, K.M. (2007). IT-based knowledge management to support organizational learning Visa application screening at the INS. *Information Technology & People*, 20(4), 376-399.

Gauch, H.G.Jr (1982). Noise reduction by eigenvector ordinations. *Ecology*, 63(6), 1643-1649.

Gaziano, C. (1983). The knowledge gap: An analytical review of media effects. *Communication Research*, 10, 447-486.

Gaziano, C. (1997). Forecast 2000: Widening knowledge gaps. *Journalism and Mass Communications Quarterly*, 74, 237-264.

Gaziano, E., & Gaziano, C. (1995). Social control, social change and the knowledge gap hypothesis. In D. Demers, K. Viswanath (Eds.), *Mass media social control, and social change: A macrosocial perspective.* Iowa State Press.

Geva, B. (2001). Bank Collections and Payment Transactions: Comparative Study of Legal Aspects, Oxford University Press.

Gey, F. C. (2000, January 4-7 2000). *Information Retrieval: Theory, Application, Evaluation.* Paper presented at the Thirty-Third Annual Hawaii International Conference on System Sciences (HICSS-33), Hawaii.

Ghosh A.and Schwartzbard A. (1999) A study in using neural networks for anomaly and misuse detection. In *Proceedings of the Eighth USENIX Security Symposium.*

Gibert, K., Sanchez-Marre, M., & Rodriguez-Roda, I. (2006). GESCONDA: An intelligent data analysis system for knowledge discovery and management in environmental databases. *Environmental Modelling & Software, 21*(1), 115-120.

Gibson, D., Kleinberg, J., & Raghavan, P. (1998). Inferring Web Communities from Link Topology. *Proc. 9th ACM Conference on Hypertext and Hypermedia*, 1998, pp. 225-234.

Gibson, S. (2006). The urgent need for e-data management at the enterprise level: the impending implosion of electronic stored information. *Computer and Internet Lawyer, 23*(8), 5-8.

Gil-Garcia J. R.and Pardo , T. A. (2006). Multi-method Approaches to Understanding the Complexity of e-government. *International Journal of Computers, Systems and Signals, Vol.7, No.2*

Gil-Garcia, J. R. (2005). *Enacting state websites: A mixed method study exploring e-government success in multi-organizational settings.* Unpublished Doctoral Dissertation, University at Albany, State University of New York, Albany, NY.

Gil-Garcia, J. R., & Luna-Reyes, L. F. (2003). Towards a Definition of Electronic Government: A Comparative Review. In A. Mendez-Vilas, J. A. Mesa Gonzalez, J. Mesa Gonzalez, V. Guerrero Bote & F. Zapico Alonso

(Eds.), Techno-legal Aspects of the Information Society and New Economy: An Overview. Badajoz, Spain: Formatex.

Gil-Garcia, J. R., & Luna-Reyes, L. F. (2006). Integrating conceptual approaches to e-government. In M. Khosrow-Pour (Ed.), *Encyclopedia of e-commerce, e-government and mobile commerce*. Hershey, PA: Idea Group Inc.

Gil-Garcia, J. R., & Martinez-Moyano, I. J. (2005). *Exploring e-government evolution: The influence of systems of rules on organizational action.* Cambridge, MA: National Center for Digital Government, Kennedy School of Government, Harvard University, Working Paper No. 05-001.

Gil-García, J. R., Luna-Reyes, L.F.(2003): Towards a Definition of Electronic Government: A Comparative Review. In: Mendez-Vilas, A., et al. (eds.): Techno-legal Aspects of the Information Society and New Economy: An Overview. Formatex. Badajoz, Spain

Gillenson, M. (2005). *Database Processing: Fundamentals of Database Management Systems*, ISBN – 0-471-26297-8, Wiley.

Glouberman, S., Mintzberg, H. (2001). Managing the Care of Health and the Cure of Disease. Part I: Differentiation & Part II: Integration. *Health Care Management Review*, 26(1), 56-84.

Gödel K., *Über formal unentscheidbare Sätze der Principia Mathematica und verwandter Systeme*, Monatshefte für Mathematik und Physik, vol. 38 (1931).

Goto, T., Kshirsagar, S. & Magnenat-Thalmann, N. (2001). Real-Time Facial Feature Tracking and Speech Acquisition for Cloned Head. IEEE Signal Processing Magazine, 18(3), pp 17-25. May.

Goto, T., Kshirsagar, S. & Magnenat-Thalmann, N. (2001). Automatic Face Cloning and Animation. IEEE Signal Processing Magazine, 18(3), 17-25.

Government of Malaysia, & UNDP Project Document (October, 2004): *A national strategic framework for bridging the digital divide.*

Government of Malaysia, (2003). *Mid-term review of the Eighth Malaysia Plan 2001-2005.* Kuala Lumpur: Government Printer.

Government of Malaysia, (2005). *Ninth Malaysia Plan 2006-2010.* Kuala Lumpur: Government Printer.

Gramatikov, M. (2006). *Data mining techniques and the decision making process in the Bulgarian public administration.* Retrieved March 8, 2007, from http://unpan1.un.org/intradoc/groups/public/documents/nispacee/unpan009209.pdf

Greenacre, M. J.(1984). *Theory and Applications of Correspondence Analysis.* London: Academic Press.

Greenstein, D., & Thorn, S. E. (2002). The digital Library: A Bibliography (Technical Report 109). Washington, D.C.: Digital Library Federation Council on Library and Information Resources. Retrieved on 12nd May, 2008 from http://www.clir.org/pubs/reports/pub109/pub109.pdf.

Groppelli, A.A. & Nikbakht, E. (2006). Finance, Published 2006, Barron's Educational Series, Inc.

Grossman, L. (1995).*The Electronic Republic: Reshaping Democracy in the Information Age.* Viking, New York, NY.

Grossman, R.(Ed.), Kasif, S., Moore, R., Rocke, D. & Ullman, J.(1998). *Data Mining Research: Opportunities and Challenges. A Report of three NSF Workshops on Mining Large, Massive, and Distributed Data.* Retrieved 16th July, 2008 from http://www.rgrossman.com/epapers/dmr-v8-4-5.htm*

Groth, R. (2000). *Data Mining: Building Competitive Advantage.* New Jersey : Prentice Hall PTR.

Guarino, N., Giaretta, P. (1999). *Ontologies and Knowledge Bases: Towards a Terminological Clarification.* ISO Press, 1999.

Gutierrez, M., Vexo, F., Thalmann, D. (2002). A MPEG-4 virtual human animation engine for interactive web based applications, Robot and Human Interactive Communication. Proceedings. 11th IEEE International Workshop on, 554-559.

Hakkila, P. (2006). Factors driving the development of forest energy in Finland. *Biomass and Bioenergy*: Proceedings of the third annual workshop of Task 31 'Sustainable production systems for bioenergy: Impacts on forest resources and utilization of wood for energy' October 2003, Flagstaff, Arizona, USA, *30*(4), 281-288.

Han, J. & Kamber, M. (2006). Data Mining: Concepts and Techniques. 2006, 2nd Edition, Mogan Kaufmann Publishers.

Han, J., & Kamber, M. (2001). *Data Mining: Concepts and Techniques*: Morgan Kaufmann Publishers.

Hand, D. J., Mannila, H., & Smyth, P. (2001). *Principles of data mining.* Cambridge, MA: MIT Press.

Hand, D., Mannila, H., Smyth, P. (2001). *Principles of Data Mining (Adaptive Computation and Machine Learning).* Massachusetts: MIT Press.

Harnad, S. & Brody, T. (2004). Comparing the impact of open access (OA) versus NON-OA articles in the same journals. *D-Lib Magazine*. Online: Retrieved on 15th January, 2007 from http://dlib.org/june04/hanard/06hanard.html

Harris, M. (1993). Exploring the Role of Boards Using Total Activities Analysis. *Nonprofit Management & Leadership*, 3(3), 269-281.

Hastie, T., Tibshirani, R., & Friedman, J. (2001). *The Elements of Statistical Learning: data mining, inference and prediction*. New York: Springer-Verlag.

Haule, L. (2007). Digitization concept and types of digitization: texts and images. Paper presented at the Tanzania Library Association's Workshop on *'Sustainable Digital Library Development in Tanzania: challenges, prospects and strategies'*. Iringa, Tanzania – 20 – 23 February 2007

Hazzan, O., Impagliazzo, J., Lister, R. & Schocken, S. (2005). Using history of computing to address problems and opportunities. In J. Dougherty (Ed.), *Proceedings of the 36th SIGCSE technical symposium on computer science education* (pp.126-127). New York, NY: Association for Computing Machinery, Inc.

Healthcare Commission. (2005). *The Healthcare Commission's review of NHS foundation trusts*. London: Commission for Healthcare Audit and Inspection.

Heeks, R. (2003). Success and failure rates of egovernment in developing/transitional countries: Overview. from www.egov4dev.org/sfoverview.htm

Heery, R. & Anderson, S. (2005). Digital Repositories Review, UKOLN-AHDS. Retrieved February 19, 2005 from http://www.jisc.ac.uk/uploaded_documents/digital-repositories-revew-

Helman P. and Bhangoo. J. (1997) A stiatistically base system for prioritizing information exploration under uncertainty. *1EEE Transactions on Systems, Man and Cybernetics, Part A: Systems and Humans*, 27(4):449–466.

Hendrikse, G.W.J., Schut, F.T. (2004). Naar nieuwe beheersstructuren in de Nederlandse gezondheidszorg? *Acta Hospitalia*, 44(1), 5-20.

Hewett, W. G. & Whitaker, J. (2002). Data protection and privacy: the Australian legislation and its implications for IT professionals. *Logistics Information Management*, 15 (5/6), 369-76.

Hiller, J. S., & Bélanger, F. (2001). Privacy strategies for electronic government. In M. A. Abramson & G. E.

Means (Eds.), *E-government 2001* (pp. 162-198). Lanham, Maryland: Rowman & Littlefield Publishers.

Himma, K. E. (2007). Foundational issues in information ethics. *Library Hi Tech, 25*(1), 79-94.

Hindle, D., Yazbeck, A.M. (2005). Clinical pathways in 17 European Union countries: a purposive survey. *Aust Health Rev*, 29, 94-104.

Hitchcock, S., et al. (2007). Digital Preservation Services provider Models for institutional Repositories: *D-lib Magazine* May/June 2007, Vol. 13, No. 5/6.

Hnatyuk, Y., Marur, M. & Patrzalek, E. (2001). Money Mover, Electronic Payment System, available from http://www.telono.com/research/MOMO.pdf

Hoek, H. (1999). The art of governance of Dutch hospitals. *World Hosp Health Serv*, 35(3), 5-7.

Hofmeyr, S. A., Forrest, S. and Somayaji. A. (1998) Intrusion detect using sequences of system calls. *Journal of Computer Security*, 6:151–180.

Hollway, W. and Jefferson, T. (2000). The role of anxiety in fear of crime. In T. Hope and R. Sparks (Eds.) *Crime, risk and insecurity*. London: Routledge.

Holmes, D. (2001). *E.Gov. E-business strategies for government*. London: Nicholas Brealey Publishing.

Holsapple, C. W., Joshi, K. D. (2002). A collaborative approach to ontology design. *Communications of the ACM 45*, 1/2002, pp. 42–47

Holt, N., Johnson, A., de Belder, M. (2000). Patient empowerment in secondary prevention of coronary heart disease. *Lancet*, 356, 314.

Hong, J. & Ståhle, P. (2005). The Coevolution of Knowledge and Competence Management, Int. J. *Management Concepts and Philosophy*, Vol. 1, No. 2.

Hoskinson, R. L., Rope, R. C., & Fink, R. K. (2007). Using a decision support system to optimize production of agricultural crop residue Biofeedstock. *Biomass and Bioenergy, 31*(4), 186-194.

Hovy, E. (2003). Using an Ontology to Simplify Data Access. *Communications of the ACM 46*, 47–49.

Howell, B. (2004). Lessons from New Zealand for England's NHS Foundation Trusts. *J Health Serv Res Policy*, 9(2), 104-9.

Huang, Y., McCullagh, P., Black, N & Harper, R. (2007) "Feature selection and classification model construction on type 2 diabetic patients' data", in *Artificial Intelligence in Medicine*, Volume 41, Issue 3, November 2007, Pages 251-262

Humphrey, D.B. (1995). Payment Systems: Principles, Practice, and Improvements, World Bank Technical Paper #260, World Bank, World Bank Publications.

Hunter, J., Drennan, J. & Little, S. (2004). Realizing the Hydrogen Economy through Semantic Web Technologies, E-Science, IEEE Intelligent System, January-February 2004, pp. 1-9.

Ibrahim, O. (2003). *Information system planning approach: A Malaysian electronic case study*, Ph.D, Dissertation. University of Salford

Information for Development Programme (InfoDev). (2004). *E-government handbook for developing countries*. Retrieved from http://www.infodev.org

Inmon, Bill. (2004). Information Management: Charting the Course: The Virtual Data Warehouse – Transparent and Superficial. *DM Review* March 2004.

Inmon, W. (2002*). Building the Data Warehouse*. 3rd ed. John Wiley and Sons.

Jain, A., Duin, R., Mao, J. (2000). Statistical Pattern Recognition: A Review, *IEEE Transactions on Pattern Analysis And Machine Intelligence*, 22, 4-37.

Javitz H. S. and Valdes. A. (1998) The nides statistical component: description and justification. In *Technical Report, Computer Science Labratory, SRI International.*

Jeffery, K.G. (2000). The Grid for e-Science: e-Commerce Benefits, Information technology Department, CLRC, ITD.

Jin, R. & Agrawal, G. (2003). Efficient Decision Tree Construction on Streaming Data, in the Proceedings of 9th International Conference on Knowledge Discovery and Data Mining (SIGKDD), August.

Johnson, C. & Tesch, B. (2005). Forrester Research, (2005). US eCommerce: 2005 To 2010, A Five-Year Forecast And Analysis Of US Online Retail Sales, Retrieved June 16, 2008 from http://www.forrester.com/Research/Document/Excerpt/0,7211,37626,00.html

Johnson, Omotunde E. G. (1998). Payment Systems, Monetary Policy, and the Role of the Central Bank, International Monetary Fund.

Joi, L. (2004). Bridging the digital divide: Some initiatives in Brazil. *Electronic Government: An International Journal, 1*(3), 300-315.

Jonas, J.and Harper, J. (2006). *Effective Counterterrorism and the Limited Role ofPredictive Data Mining*, CATO Institute Policy Analysis No. 584, December11, [http://www.cato.org/pubs/pas/pa584.pdf].

Jones, D. M., Bench-Capon, T. J. M., Visser, P. R. S. (1998). Methodologies for Ontology Development. *Proceedings of Information Technology and Knowledge*, IT&KNOWs, 1998.

Jongman, R.H.G., Ter Braak, C.J.F., & Van Tongeren, O.F.R. (1995). *Data Analysis in Community and Landscape Ecology*, Cambridge, UK: Cambridge University Press.

Joshi, M.S., Hines, S.C. (2006). Getting the board on board: Engaging hospital boards in quality and patient safety, *Jt Comm J Qual Improv*, 32(4), 179-187.

Jovanović, et. al. (2007). Using Semantic Web Technologies to Analyze Learning Content, In *Internet Computing*, September/October 2007 (Vol. 11, No. 5): 45-53.

Judge W.Q., Zeithaml C.P. (1992). An Empirical Comparison between the Board's Strategic Role in Nonprofit Hospitals and in For-Profit Industrial Firms. *Health Services Research*, 27(1), 47-64.

Jukic, N. (2006). Modeling Strategies and Alternatives for Data Warehousing Projects. *Communications of the ACM*, Vol. 49, No. 4, pp. 83-88.

Juntunen, A. (2005). *The emergence of a new business through collaborative networks: a longitudinal study in the ICT sector*. Acta Universitatis Oeconomicae Helsingiensis. Printed in HSEPrint. A-series, no 256, ISSN 1237-556X. ISBN: 951-791-957-3/1.

K. Layne and J.W. Lee (2001). Developing fully functional e-government: A four stage model. *Government Information Quarterly* 18 (2), 122–136.

Kalra, P.K. (1993). An interactive multimodal facial animation system. Doctoral dissertation (No. 1183), École Polytechnique Fédérale de Lausanne, Switzerland.

Kantardzic, M. M., & Zurada, J. (Eds.). (2005). *Next generation of data-mining applications*. IEEE Press, Wiley-Interscience.

Kapange, B. (1999). *ICTs and National Agricultural Research Systems-the case of Tanzania*. Retrieved August 08, 2006 from http://www.isnar.cgiar.org/pdf/inars/tanzania.pdf

Karim, A.M.R. (2003). Technology and improved service delivery: Learning points from the Malaysian experience. *International Review of Administrative Sciences, 69*(2), 191-204.

Karim, M. R. (1999). *Reengineering the public service*: *Leadership and change in an electronic ag.,* Suban Jaya: Pelanduk.

Karim, M. R., & Salmah, K. (1999). *E-government: Reinventing service delivery.* (M.R. Karim Ed). Suban Jaya: Pelanduk

Kazemzadeh, R.S. and Sartipi, K. (2006), Incoporating Data Mining Applications into Clinical Guildelines. In *Proceedings of the 19th IEEE Symposium on Computer-Based Medical Systems (CBMS'06)*, IEEE.

Kenett, R., & Thyregod, P. (2006) Aspects of statistical consulting not taught by academia. *Statistica Neerlandica 60*(3), 396-411.

Khosrowpour, M. (1995). Managing Information and Communications in a Changing Global Environment, International Conference of Management Association, Information Resources Management Association, Idea Group Inc (IGI).

Khosrowpour, M. (2005). Practicing e-government: A Global Perspective, Organisation for Economic Co-operation and Development, 2005, Idea Group Publication.

Khosrowpour, M. (2005). Advanced Topics in Electronic Commerce: V. 1., 2005, Idea Group Publication.

Kimball, R and Ross, M. (2002). *The Data Warehouse Toolkit.* 2nd ed. John Wiley & Sons.

Kimball, R. & Merz, R. (2000). The Data Webhouse Toolkit: Building the Web-Enabled Data Warehouse. Wiley.

King, D. (2004). The Scientific Impact of nations. *Nature, 430,* 311-316.

King, P., Annandale, D., & Bailey, J. (2000). A Conceptual Framework for Integrated Economic and Environmental Planning in Asia - A Literature Review. *Journal of Environmental Assessment Policy and Management, 2*(3), 279-315.

Kissan (2008). Accessed February 02, 2008 from http://www.igovernment.in/site/KISSAN-to-offer-agri-portal-platform-to-other-indian-states/).

Klampere, K. & Chapman, S. (1997). Digital Libraries: a Selected Resource Guide: Retrieved on 2nd August, 2008 from http://www.lita.org/ital/1603 klempere.htm.

Klein R. (2004). The first wave of NHS foundation trusts. *BMJ,* 328, 1332.

Klein, R. (2003). Governance for NHS foundation trusts. *BMJ,* 326, 174-5.

Klischewski, R. & Jeenicke, M. (2004). Semantic Web Technologies for Information Management within e-Government Services, In *Proceedings of the 37th Annual Hawaii International Conference on System Sciences (HICSS'04) - Track 5 p. 50119b,* Hawaii.

Kloptchenko, A. (2003). *Text Mining Based on the Prototype Matching Method.* Unpublished Doctoral Dissertation, Åbo Akademi University, Turku.

Kogut, B. & Zander, U. (1992). Knowledge of the Firm, combinative capabilities and the replication of technology. *Organization Science* 3(3): 383-397.

Koh, C. E., Ryan, S. & Prybutok, V. R. (2005). Creating value through managing knowledge in an e-government to constituency environment. *The Journal of Computer Information Systems, 45*(4), 32-42.

Kondratova, I. & Goldfarb, I. (2003). Design concepts for Virtual Research and Collaborative Environments, in J. Cha, R. Jardim-Gonçalves, & A. Steiger-Garção (Eds.) *Knowledge Management in Architectural, Engineering and Construction, 10th ISPE International Conference on Concurrent Engineering: The Vision for Future Generation in Research and Applications.* Madeira Island, 26-30 July 2003. Portugal, A.A. Balkema Publishers, 797-803.

Kraemer, K. L., & King, J. L. (2003, September 29). *Information technology and administrative reform: Will the time after e-government be different?* Paper presented at the Heinrich Reinermann Schrift fest, Post Graduate School of Administration, Speyer, Germany.

Krause, J. (2004). University of Koblenz-landau and Social Science Information. Bonn, Germany. Retrieved on 3rd September from http://www.uni_koblenz.de/-krause/

Krause, J. (2007). E-discovery gets real. *ABA Journal, 93,* 44-51.

Krebs, V. E. (2002). Mapping networks of Terrorist Cells. *Connections,* 24 (3), 2002, 43-52.

Kroenke, D. (2002). Database Processing – *Fundamentals, Design and Implementation* (8th ed.). Pearson Education, Inc.

Kruijthof, K. (2005). *Doctors' Orders. Specialists' Day to Day Work and their jurisdictional Claims in Dutch Hospitals.* Rotterdam: Erasmus Universiteit Rotterdam.

Kshirsagar, E.S. & Magnenat-Thalmann, N. (2004). Generic Personality and Emotion Simulation for Conversational Agents. Computer Animation and Virtual Worlds. 15(1),1-13.

Kshirsagar, S., Joslin, C., Lee, W. & Magnenat-Thalmann, N. (2001). Personalized Face and Speech Communication over the Internet. IEEE Signal Processing Magazine, 18(3), 17-25.

Kullback, S. (1959) *Information Theory and Statistics*, New York: Wiley.

Kutais, B. G. (Ed.). (2006). *Focus on the Internet*: Nova Science Publishers, Inc.

Kwong, S., Chau, C.W., Man, K.F., Tang, K.S, (2001) "Optimisation of HMM topology and its model parameters by genetic algorithms", Elsevier, *Pattern Recognition* 34 (2001), pp. 509 – 522

Lacy, L.W. (2005). OWI: Representing Information Using the Web Ontology Language, Tratfford Press, 2005.

Landro, L. (2006, January 26). The informed patient: Infant monitors yield new clues. Studies of digital records are used to identify problems with medications: Practices. *Wall Street Journal*, p. D5.

Lane T. and Brodley. C. E. (1997). Sequence matching and learning in anomaly detection for computer security. In *Proceedings of the AAAI-97 Workshop on AI Approaches to Fraud Detection and Risk Management*, pages 43–49. Menlo Park, CA: AAAI Press.

Lane T. and Brodley. C. E. (1999). Temporal sequence learning and data reduction for anomaly detection. *ACM Transactions on Information and System Security*, 2:295–331.

Langley, L.L., editor. (1973). *Homeostasis: origins of the concept*. Stroudsburg: Dowden, Hutchinson and Ross.

Last, M. Elovici, Y. Shapira, B. Zaafrany, O, & Kandel, A. (2003). Using Data Mining for Detecting Terror-Related Activities on the Web. *ECIW Proceedings*, 2003, pp. 271-280.

Laudon, K.C and Laudon, J.P. (2004). *Managing the Digital Firm*, Eigth Edition, Prentice Hall, Upper Saddle River, New Jersey.

Laudon, K.C and Laudon, J.P. (2006). *Managing the Digital Firm*, Tenth Edition, Prentice Hall, Upper Saddle River, New Jersey.

Laudon, K.C. & Traver, C.G. (2001). E-commerce: Business, Technology, Society, 2001, Addison Wesley.

Lave, J. & Wenger, E. (1991). *Situated Learning: Legitimate Peripheral Participation*. New York, NY: Cambridge University Press.

Lavrač, N. (1999) "Selected techniques for data mining in medicine", in *Artificial Intelligence in Medicine* Vol. 16 (1999) pp. 3–23.

Lawyer, J and Chowdhury, S. (2005). Data Warehousing Practices – A success Story. *Published in GESTS (Global Engineering, Science and Technology Society) International Transactions on Computer Science and Engineering*, Paper field: Computer and its Application. Vol. 21 and No. 1. Nov. 2005.

Laxman, S. Sastry, P.S., Unnikrishnan, K.P. (2005) "Discovering Frequent Episodes and Learning Hidden Markov Models: A Formal Connection", in *IEEE Transactions On Knowledge And Data Engineering*, vol. 17, no. 11, November 2005, pp. 1505 – 1517

Layne, K., & Lee, J. (2001). Developing fully functional e-government: A four stage model. *Government Information Quarterly, 18*(2), 122-136.

Lee W. and Stolfo. S. J. (1998) Data mining approaches for intrusion detection. In *In Proceedings of the 1998 USENIX Security Symposium*.

Lee, D. & Seung, H. (1999). Learning the Parts of Objects by Non-Negative Matrix Factorization. *Nature*, Vol 401, 1999, pp. 788-791.

Lee, W. Stolfo, S. J. and Chan. P. K. (1997) Learning patterns from unix processes execution traces for intrusion detection. In *In AAAI Workshop on AI Approaches to Fraud Detection and Risk Management*, pages 50–56. AAAI Press.

Lee,W., Stolfo, S. J. and Mok. K. (1999).Data mining in work flow environments: Experiences in intrusion detection. In *Proceedings of the 1999 Conference on Knowledge Discovery and Data Mining (KDD-99)*.

Lega, F., DePietro, C. (2005). Converging patterns in hospital organization: beyond the professional bureaucracy. *Health Policy*, 74(3), 261-81.

Lenk, K. (2003). Relating Knowledge Management in the Public Sector to Decision-Making and Administrative Action. *Proceedings of 4th Working Conference on Knowledge Management in Electronic Government*, Rhodes Island, Greece.

Lenk, K. (2003). *Relating knowledge management in the public sector to decision-making and administrative action*. Proceedings of the Fourth Working Conference on Knowledge Management in Electronic Government, Rhodes Island, Greece.

Leriviere, J. (2000). *Guidelines for legal deposit legislations. Paris: UNESCO.* Retrieved on 3rd September from http://www.ifla.org/VII/s1/gnl/legaldep1.htm

Lewis, R. (2005) NHS foundation trusts. The Healthcare Commission's review offers something for both proponents and detractors. *BMJ*, 331, 59-60.

Li, Q., & Wu, Y.-F.B. (2006). Information Mining: Integrating Data Mining and Text Mining for Business Intelligence. Twelfth Americas Conference on Information Systems, Acapulco, Mexico, 2006, pp. 1410-1416.

Liebowitz, J. (2004). Will knowledge management work in the government? *Electronic Government: An International Journal, 1*(1), 1-7.

Lingsoft Oy. (2005). *Lingsoft and TEMIS Announce Partnership to Expand Text Mining Coverage to Northern European languages and countries.* Retrieved 3.5.2005, 2005, from http://www.lingsoft.fi/news/2005/temis.html

Lok, C. (2004, October). Fighting infections with data. *Technology Review*, p. 24.

Lor, P. (1995). Legal deposit: some issues in the international science. *Musaion, 13*(1/2), 94 –111.

Lor, P. (2003). What prospects for national libraries in East Africa? *A South African perspective. Alexandria, 15*(3), 141–150.

Loshin, P. & Vacca, J.R. (2003). Electronic Commerce, Charles River Media.

Lousiana (2002). *The State IT Master Plan*, Office of Information technology, State of Lousiana, Baton Rouge, Lousiana.

Lowe, P. (2006), 'Payment Systems Developments and Architecture: Some Background', speech to the Australian Bankers' Association and APCA Forum on 'Payment Systems Evolution: Where to From Here?', 27 September.

Lwoga, E.T., Forzi, T., Laing, P. & Mjema, E. (2006). KM in the agricultural field: an ICT-based approach to promote the development and sharing of knowledge among agricultural researchers in Africa. In Cunningham, P. and Cunngham, M. (Eds) *IST-AFRICA conference proceedings*. [Online]: Retrieved on 1st Aug. 2006 from http://www.IST-Africa.org/conference2006

Lyman, P. & Varian, H.R. (2003). *How much information?* Retrieved September 6, 2007, from http://www2.sims.berkeley.edu/research/projects/

Lynn, L.E., Heinrich, C.J., Hill, C.J. (2001). *Improving Governance: A New Logic for Empirical Research.* Washington DC: Georgetown University Press.

Mädche, A. & Staab, S. (2003).The Karlsruhe Ontology and Semantic Web Meta Project, KAON: The Karlsruhe Ontology and Semantic Web Meta Project, Special issue on Semantic Web, *Künstliche Intelligenz* (3): 27-30.

Mädche, A., & Staab, S. (2002). Applying Semantic Web Technologies for Tourism Information Systems,. In: K.Wöber, A. Frew, M. Hitz (eds*.), Proceedings of the 9thInternational Conference for Information and Communication Technologies in Tourism, ENTER 2002.* Springer Verlag, Innsbruck, Austria, 23 - 25th January 2002, pp. 311-319

Magnenat-Thalmann, N., Kalra, P. & Pandzic, I.S. (1995). Direct Face-to-Face Communication Between Real and Virtual Humans. International Journal of Information Technology, 1(2), 145-157.

Mainz, J. (2003). Developing evidence-based clinical indicators: a state of the art methods primer. *Int J Qual Health Care*, 15(Suppl 1), i5-i11.

Makarenkov, V., & Legendre, P. (2002). Nonlinear redundancy analysis and canonical correspondence analysis based on polynomial regression. *Ecology, 83*(4), 1146-1161.

Makulowich, J. (1999). "Government Data Mining Systems Defy Definition," *Washington Technology*, 22 February , [http://www.washingtontechnology.com/news/13_22/tech_features/393-html].

Malekani, A. & Grace E. (2007). *Development and status of Digital Libraries in Agricultural Information Systems: Experiences with Sokoine National Agricultural Library.* Paper presented at a Workshop on "Sustainable digital development in Tanzania: challenges, prospects and strategies". Iringa. Tanzania.

Malhotra, Y. & Galletta, F.D. (2003). Role of commitment and motivation in knowledge management systems implementation: theory, conceptualization, and measurement of antecedents of success. In R.H. Sprague (Ed.), *IEEE Computer Society Proceedings of the 36th Annual Hawaii International Conference on System Sciences (HICSS'03)* (Track 4, Volume 4, page 115.1) Washington, D.C.: IEEE Computer Society.

Malhotra, Y. (2000). Knowledge Management and New Organization Forms: A Framework for Business Model Innovation, *Information Resources Management Journal*, 13(1), January-March, 2000, pp. 5-14.

Malhotra, Y. (2000). Knowledge management for e-business performance. *Information Strategy: The Executives Journal, 16*(4), 5-16.

MAMPU, (1997). *Electronic government information technology policy and standards (EGIT)*. Kuala Lumpur: Malaysian Administrative Modernization and Management Planning Unit.

MAMPU, (1997). *Towards a vision for a new electronic government*. Kuala Lumpur: Malaysian Administrative Modernization and Management Planning Unit.

Mann, C.L. (2000). Electronic Commerce in Developing Countries: Issues for Domestic Policy and WTO Negotiations, Peterson Institute Working Paper Series #WP00-3, Peterson Institute for International Economics, Washington, DC.

Mann, C.L., Eckert, S.E. & Knight, S.C. (2000). Global Electronic Commerce: A Policy Primer, Institute for International Economics, Washington, DC.

Manning, C. D., & Schütze, H. (1999). *Foundations of Statistical Natural Language Processing*. Cambridge, Massachusetts: The MIT Press.

Manuel, P. (2005). A model of e-governance based on knowledge management. *Journal of Knowledge Management Practice*, pp. 1-10.

Mardia, K.V., Kent, J.T., & Bibby, J.M. (1979). *Multivariate Analysis*. San Diego, U.S.:Academic Press, INC.

Marhaini M. N., & Asiyah, K. (2007, February 21). Digital literacy: Urban vs. rural areas in Malaysia. *The E-Government Magazine for Asia & the Middle East, 3*(2), 8-12.

Mark, T.L., Evans, W.N., Schur, C.L., Guterman, S.M.A. (1998). Hospital-Physician Arrangements and Hospital Financial Performance. *Med Care, 36*(1), 67-78.

Marquez, A. C., & Blanchar, C. (2006). A Decision Support System for evaluating operations investments in high-technology business. *Decision Support Systems, 41*(2), 472-487.

Martinez-Moyano, I. J. and Gil-Garcia, J. R. (2004) Rules, Norms, and Individual Preferences for Action: An Institutional Framework to Understand the Dynamics of e-Government Evolution, November 05, Springer Berlin / Heidelberg.

Matovelo, D. S. & Chailla, A. M. (1999). Documentation and dissemination of agricultural research results in Tanzania: avenues and challenges. *Tanzania Journal of Agricultural Sciences, 2*(1), 99-106.

MATRIX pilot project concludes. (2005). Retrieved March 8, 2007, from http://www.fdle.state.fl.us/press_releases/expired/2005/20050415_matrix_project.html

Mattke, S., Seid, M. & Ma, S. (2007) "Evidence for the Effect of Disease Management: Is $1 Billion a Year a Good Investment?" in *The American Journal Of Managed Care*, Vol. 13, No. 12, pp. 670–6

Mawby, R. I., Brunt, P. & Hambly, Z. (2000). Fear of crime among British holidaymakers. *British Journal of Criminology* 40, 468–79.

May, J. (2006) DMAA: Defining Quality in Health Care Coordination. In Disease Management, vol. 9, n. 6., pp 371-375.

May, P. (2000). The business of ecommerce: from corporate strategy to technology, Cambridge University Press.

Mazzi, G.B. (2006). The European Vision for digital payment systems. In: Pacifici, G., Pozzi, P. (Eds.), Money-On-Line.eu: The European Scenario of Digital Payment Systems and Smart Cards, FrancoAgneli, Milan, Italy.

McCallum, A., Corrada-Emmannel, A., & Wang, X. (2005). The Author-Recipient-Topic Model for Topic and Role Discovery in Social Networks, with Application to Enron and Academic E-mail. Workshop on Link Analysis, Counterterrorism and Security, at the SIAM International Conference on Data Mining, California, USA, 2005, pp. 33 - 44.

McDonagh, K.J. (2006). Hospital governing boards: a study of their effectiveness in relation to organizational performance. *Journal of Healthcare Management*, 51, 377-391.

McKee, M., Healy, J., Edwards, N., Harrison, A. (2002). Pressures for change. In: McKee, M., Healy J., editors. *Hospitals in a changing Europe*. Buckingham: Open University Press.

McLaren, C.H. & McLaren, B.J. (2000). E-commerce: Business on the Internet, 2000, South-Western, Educational Publishing.

McLure, W. & Faraj, S. (2000). It is what one does: why people participate and help others in electronic communities of practice. *The Journal of Strategic Information Systems, 9*(2/3), 155-73.

Megaputer Intelligence. (2004c). *Application of Poly-Analyst to Flight Safety Data of Southwest Airlines*. Bloomington, IN: Megaputer Intelligence.

Metaxiotis, K. (2007). A Framework for the Application of Knowledge Management in E-Government. in the book *"Encyclopedia of Public Information Technology"* edited by Prof. Kristin Klinger, IDEA Publishing.

Metaxiotis, K. and Psarras, J. (2005b). A Conceptual Analysis of Knowledge Management in E-Government. *Electronic Government: An International Journal*, 2(1), 77-86.

Metaxiotis, K., & Psarras, J. (2004). E-government: New concept, big challenge, success stories. *Electronic Government: An International Journal, 1*(2), 141-151.

Metaxiotis, K., & Psarras, J. (2005). A conceptual analysis of knowledge management in e-government. *Electronic Government: An International Journal, 2*(1), 77-86.

Metaxiotis, K., Ergazakis, K. and Psarras, J. (2005). Exploring the World of Knowledge Management: Agreements and Disagreements in the Research Community. *Journal of Knowledge Management*, 9(2), 6-18.

Metaxiotis, K., Ergazakis, K., & Psarras, J. (2005). Exploring the world of knowledge management: Agreements & disagreements in the research community. *Journal of Knowledge Management, 9*(2), 6-18.

METI (2004). Towards eQuality: Global E-Commerce Presents Digital Opportunity to Close the Divide Between Developed and Developing Countries, METI's Proposal for WTO E-Commerce Initiative, Ministry of Economy, Trade and Industry, Japan.

Miller, J.L. (2002). The Board as a Monitor of Organizational Activity. The Applicability of Agency Theory to Nonprofit Boards. *Nonprofit Management & Leadership*, 12, 429-450

Ministry of the Interior (2004). *A Safer Community. Internal Security Programme Summary.* Ministry of the Interior publications 2004. Retrieved August 13, 2007, from www.intermin.fi

Mintzberg, H., Ahlstrand, B. & Lampe, J. (1998). *Strategy Safari. The complete guide through the wilds of strategic management.* Prentice Hall Financial Times. London.

Moeller J. (2001). The EFQM Excellence Model. German experiences with the EFQM approach in health care. *Int J Qual Health Care*, 13(1), 45-9.

Moffett, S., McAdam, R. & Parkinson, S. (2003). An empirical analysis of knowledge management applications. *Journal of Knowledge Management*, 7(3), 6-26.

Mohamed, M., Stankosky, M. & Murray, A. (2006). Knowledge management and information technology:

can they work in perfect harmony? *Journal of Knowledge Management, 10*(3), 103 – 116.

Molinié, E. (2005). *L'Hôpital public en France: Bilan et perspectives.* Paris: Conseil Economique et Social.

Moller, A.M. (2006). *The open access publishing, with a special reference to open access journal and their prospects in South Africa.* MA Dissertation (Unpublished), University of Western Cape. [Online]: Retrieved on 2nd September, 2006 from http://eprints.rclis.org/archive/000518/01/MollerThesis.pdf

Montalbano, J.P & Chowdhury, S.I. (2006). Business Intelligence Systems: Critical Considerations. Paper published in the *Proceedings of the MBAA-SAIS (Midwest Business Administration Association - Society for the Advancement of Information System).*

Mook, B., Munyua, H. & Nampala, P. (2005). *Report on the baseline study of agricultural information in the Eastern and Central Africa Region.* Unpublished, consultants' report submitted to the Regional Agricultural Information Network (RAIN), Entebbe, Uganda.

Mörchen, F. (2006) "Algorithms for time series knowledge mining". In Eliassi-Rad, T., Ungar, L. H. , Craven, M., Gunopulos, D. editors, *Proceedings The Twelveth ACM SIGKDD International Conference on Knowledge Discovery and Data Mining,* pages 668–673, 2006.

Mörchen, F. (2007), "Unsupervised pattern mining from symbolic temporal data", in *SIGKDD Explorations* Volume 9, Issue 1, pp. 41 – 55.

Mueller, J.P. (2004). Mining Amazon Web Services: Building Application with the Amazon API, Sybex.

Muir, A. (2004, September 28-30). *Fundamentals of Data and Text Mining.* Paper presented at the Seventh GAIN World Conference, Montreal, Canada.

MyGfL (Malaysian Grid for Learning) About MyGfL Initiative. July 24th, 2007, from http://www.mygfl.net.my; http://www.selangor.gov.my/suk/prodnews.php?cod=60 on 28th August, 2007.

Nabitz, U., Klazinga, N., Walburg, J. (2000). The EFQM excellence model: European and Dutch experiences with the EFQM approach in health care. *Int J Qual Health Care*, 12(3), 191-201.

NASA. (2004, 17 December 2004). *ASRS Database Report Sets.* Retrieved 18 October, 2004, from http://asrs.arc.nasa.gov/report_sets_nf.htm

National Center for Digitization (NCD) (n.d). Retrieved on 16th July, 2008 from http://www.ncd.matf.bg.ac.yu/

Nazeri, Z. (2003). *Application of Aviation Safety Data Mining Workbench at American Airlines. Proof-of-Concept Demonstration of Data and Text Mining.* McLean, Virginia, US: Center for Advanced Aviation Systems Development, MITRE Corporation Inc.

Nemati, H.R. & Barko, C.D. (2003). Key factors for achieving organizational data-mining success. *Industrial Management & Data Systems, 103*(4), 282-292.

Newman, I., & Benz, C. R. (1998). *Qualitative-quantitative research methodology. Exploring the interactive continuum.* Carbondale and Edwardsville, IL: Southern Illinois University Press.

Nissen, M.E., & Levitt, R.E. (2004). Agent-based modeling of knowledge dynamics. *Knowledge Management Research & Practice, 2*(3), 169-183.

Oard, D. W., & Marchionini, G. (1996). *A conceptual framework for text filtering* (Technical Report CS-TR3643): University of Maryland.

Observatório Português dos Sistemas de Saúdo. (2006). *Um Ano de Governação em Saúdo.* Coimbra: CEIS-UC.

OECD - Organization for Economic Co-operation and development (2007), *OECD Health Data 2007 - Frequently Requested Data,* URL: http://www.oecd.org/document/16/0,2340,en_2649_34631_2085200_1_1_1_1,00.html

Oliveira, J. (2001). The balanced scorecard: an integrative approach to performance evaluation. *Healthc Financ Manage, 55*(5), 42-6.

Oliver, S. & Kandadi, K.R. (2006). How to develop knowledge cultures in organizations? A multiple case of large distributed organizations. *Journal of Knowledge Management, 10*(4), p. 6-24.

Openclinical, clinical Practice Guidelines, web site: http://openclinical.org/guidelines.html

Osborne, D. & Gaebler. T. (1992). Reinventing Government: How the entrepreneurial spirit is transforming the public sector. *Plume,* 1992. p. 87.

Paatero, P., & Tapper, U. (1994). Positive Matrix Factorization: A Non-Negative Factor Model with Optimal Utilization of Error Estimates of Data Values. *Environmetrics,* 5:111–126, 1994.

Painter, M. K., Erraguntla, M., Hogg, J., Gary L., & Beachkofski, B. (2006). *Using simulation, data mining, and knowledge discovery techniques for optimized aircraft engine fleet management.* Paper presented at the 2006 Winter Simulation Conference, Monterey, California.

Palkovits, S., Woitsch, R. and Karagiannis, D. (2003). Process-Based Knowledge Management and Modelling in E-government – An Inevitable Combination. *Proceedings of 4th Working Conference on Knowledge Management in Electronic Government,* Rhodes Island, Greece.

Pan, J.Z. & Thomas, E. (2007). Approximating OWL-DL Ontologies. *Proceedings of the Twenty-Second AAAI Conference on Artificial Intelligence,* July 22-26, 2007, Vancouver, British Columbia, Canada. AAAI Press 2007: 1434-1439.

Pandzic, I.S., Kalra, P., Magnenat-Thalmann, N. & Thalmann, D. (1994). Real-Time Facial Interaction. Displays (Butterworth-Heinemann), 15(3), 1994

Pape, T.M. (2003). Applying airline safety practices to medication administration. *Medurg Nurs,* 12(2), 77-93.

Papin-Ramchan, J.I. & Dawe, R.A. (2006). Open Access Publishing: A developing country view. *First Monday,* 11(6). [Online]: Retrieved on 1st Sept. 2006 from http://firstmonday.org/issues/issue11-6/papin/index.html

Parsaye, K. (1997). A Characterization of Data Mining Technologies and Processes. *Journal of Data Warehousing, 2*(3), 2-15.

Pastor, F.G. (2002). *Knowledge Management: A Trip Round Europe, Knowledge Management and Information Technology,* UPGRADE Vol. III, No. 1, February 2002, pp. 66-71.

Paul, L.G. (2003). Why three heads are better than one: how to create a know-it-all company. *CIO Magazine,* 17(5), 94-106.

Peleg M, Boxwala A. A., Omolola O., Zeng Q., Tu, S.W, Lacson R., Bernstam, E., Ash, N., Mork, P., Ohno-Machado, L., Shortliffe, E.H., and Greenes, R.A. (2000). "GLIF3: The Evolution of a Guideline Representation Format" In Overhage M.J.,, Ed., *Proceedings of the 2000 AMIA Annual Symposium (Los Angeles, CA, 2000),* Hanley & Belfus, Philadelphia.

Perner, P.(2002). *Advances in Data Mining.* Berlin-Heidelberg: Springer Verlag.

Perry, Chad (1998). Processes of a case study methodology for postgraduate research in marketing, *European Journal of Marketing.* Vol. 32: 9/10.

Peterson, Marilyn (2005). Intelligence-Led Policing: The New Intelligence Architecture. NCJ 210681. September 2005.

Pham, D.T., Wang, Y. & Dimov, S. (2005). Intelligfent Manufacturing strategy selection. *Proc 1st Int Virtual Conf on Intelligent Production Machines and Systems* Oxford: Elsevier. 312-318.

Pham, D.T., Wang, Y., & Dimov, S. (2006). Incorporating delay and feedback in intelligent manufacturing strategy selection. *Proc 2nd Int Virtual Conf on Intelligent Production Machines and Systems.* Oxford: Elsevier. 246-252.

Piquemal, M. (2002). *Rapport de mission.* Paris: Mission Nationale d'Evaluation de la mise en place de la R.T.T. dans les établissements de santé.

Pollach, I. (2007). What's wrong with online privacy policies? *Communications of the ACM 50*(9), 103-108.

Pomerantz, J. (2003). Integrating Digital Reference Services into the Digital Library Environment. In: R.D. Lankes, S. Nicholson & A: Goodrum (Eds), *The Digital Reference Research Agenda* (pp. 23-47). Chicago Association of College and Research Libraries.

Porter, M. (1985). *Competitive Advantage. Creating and Sustaining Superior Performance.* The Free Press. NY.

Powers, T.L., & Bendall, D. (2003). Improving health outcomes through patient empowerment. *J Hosp Mark Public Rel*, 15(1), 45-59.

Prabhu, C.S.R. (2006). E-governance: Concepts and Case Studies, 2006, Prentice Hall of India.

Preker, A.S., Harding, A. (2003). *Innovations in Health Service Delivery: The Corporatization of Public Hospitals.* Washington DC: The World Bank.

Prentice, I.C. (1977). Non-metric ordination methods in ecology. *The Journal of Ecology*, *65*(1), 85-94.

Prins, J.E.J. & Prins, C. (2001). Designing E-government: On the Crossroads of Technological Innovation and Institutional Change, Published 2001, Kluwer Law International.

Proforma, web site: http://www.acl.icnet.uk/lab/proforma.html

Prybil, L.D. (2006). Size, composition, and culture of high-performing hospital boards. *American Journal of Medical Quality*, 21, 224-229.

Pulliam, D. (2005). E-gov spending expected to rise, despite congressional dissatisfaction. Retrieved December 11, 2006, from http://www.govexec.com/dailyfed/1204/010605p1.htm

Quetzal Tritter, J., McCallum, A. (2006). The snakes and ladders of user involvement: Moving beyond Arnstein. *Health Policy*, 76(2), 156-68.

Rabiner, L. R. (1989) "A tutorial on hidden Markov models and selected applications in speech recognition," *Proc. IEEE*, vol. 77, no. 2, pp. 257–286, Feb. 1989.

Rafalski, E. & Mullner, R. (2003). Ensuring HIPAA compliance using data warehouses for healthcare marketing. *Journal of Consumer Marketing, 20*(7), 29-633.

Rahman, H. (2008). Prospects and Scopes of Data Mining Applications in Society Development Activities, In Rahman, H. (Ed.) Data Mining Applications for Empowering Knowledge Societies, IGI Global, Information Science Reference, Hershey: pp. 159-185.

Rahman, H. (2008). Application of Data Mining Algorithms for Measuring Performance Impact of Social Development Activities, In: Rahman, H. (Ed.). *Data Mining Applications for Empowering Knowledge Societies*, IGI References, Hershey, PA, USA: 135-158.

Ramswamy, S. (2004). Changing the learning curve, accessed from http://www.tata.com/0_our_commitment/employee_relations/articles/20040629_tmtc.htm on March 04, 2008.

Rao, C.R. (1964). The use and interpretation of principal component analysis in applied research. *Sankhyaá, A 26*, 329-358.

Ratcliffe, Jerry (2003). Intelligence-led policing. *Australian Institute of Criminology – trends and issues in crime and criminal justice*, no 248.

Ray, S. & Mukherjee, A. (2007). Development of a framework towards successful implementation of e-governance initiatives in health sector in India. *International Journal of Health Care Quality Assurance*, 20(6), 464-483.

Reddick, C. G. (2004). A two-stage model of e-government growth: Theories and empirical evidence for u.S. Cities. *Government Information Quarterly, 21*, 51-64.

Reid, E., Qin, J., & et al. (2005). Collecting and Analyzing the Presence of Terrorists on the Web: A Case Study of Jihad Websites. *ISI 2005, LNCS* 3495, pp. 402-411, 2005.

Reinhardt, R. (2005). Implementation of an intellectual capital management system: advantages of a "bottom-up" approach. *Journal of Universal Knowledge Management, 0*(1), 67-73.

Reserve Bank of Australia (2006). Payment Systems Developments and Architecture: Some Background, Payments Policy Department, Reserve Bank of Australia.

Richardson, G. P.(1996). System Dynamics. In: Gass, S.I., Harris, C.M. (eds.): Encyclopedia of Operations Research and Management Science. Kluwer Academic Publishers. Boston 656-660.

Richardson, G.P. (1999). Citation for winner of the 1999 Jay W Forrester Award: Jac Vennix. *System Dynamics Review, 15* 4., 375-377.

Richardson, G.P. and Andersen, D.F. Teamwork in group model building. *System Dynamics Review, 11* 2. (1995), 113-137.

Riege, A. & Lindsay, N. (2006). Knowledge management in the public sector: stakeholder partnerships in the public policy development. *Journal of Knowledge Management, 10*(3), 24-39.

Rieger, M. L. (2006). *Star Database Model: A comparison of 3 Alternatives with a Recommended Solution.* Assignment in Data Warehousing and Data Mining, Term Paper WEHCBA, Roosevelt University.

Robertson, S. & Powell, P. (1999). Exploiting the benefits of Y2K preparation. *Communications of the ACM, 42*(9), 42-48.

Roddick, J.F., Fule, P., Graco, W.J., (2003) "Exploratory Medical Knowledge Discovery Experiences and Issues", in *ACM SIGKDD Explorations Newsletter*, Volume 5 , Issue 1 (July 2003), pp. 94 – 99

Rodier, M. (2007). E-Discovery: a daunting task -- as electronic data proliferates, complying with e-discovery rules becomes more difficult - and more costly. *Wall Street & Technology, 25*(9), 23.

Rogers, E. (1986). Communication technology: The new media in society. *The Free Press.*

Rogerson, S., Weckert, J. & Simpson, C. (2000). An ethical review of information systems development – the Australian computer society's code of ethics and SSADM. *Information Technology & People, 13*(2), 121-136.

Rohan. B., Graham. W., and Hongxing, H. (2001) Feature Selection for Temporal Health Records. In Cheung, D., Williams, G.J. and Li, Q. (Eds.): *PAKDD 2001, LNAI 2035*, pp. 198-209.

Rosenberg, D. (2006). Towards the digital library in Africa. *The Electronic Library, 24*(3), 289 -293. Retrieved on 01 August, 2007 from http://www.emeraldinsight.com. Insight/ViewContentSevlet?Filename=/published/emer-aldfulltextarticle/pdf/2630240301.pdf)

Rowe, R., Bond, M. (2003). Foundation trusts. Hitting the big time. *Health Serv J*, 113, 30-1.

Rozakis, S., Soldatos, P. G., Kallivroussis, L., & Nicolaou, I. (2001). Multiple Criteria Analysis of Bio-energy Projects: Evaluation of Bio-Electricity Production in Farsala Plain, Greece. *Journal of Geographic Information and Decision Analysis, 5*(1), 49-64.

Rozman, R. (2000). The organizational function of governance: development, problems, and possible changes. *Management,* 5(2), 94-110.

Rubin, E.L. & Cooter, R. (1994). The Payment System: Cases, Materials, and Issues, 1994, West Publishing Company.

Sankar K. Pal, S. & Shiu C. K. (2004). *Foundations of Soft Case-Based Reasoning.* Wiley-IEEE, ISBN 0471086355.

Saracoglu, R., Tütünkü, K., & Allahverdi, N. (2008). A new approach on search for similar documents with multiple categories using fuzzy clustering. *Expert Systems with Applications: An International Journal, 34*(4), 2545-2554.

Sato, S. & Humphrey, D.B. (1995). Transforming Payment Systems: Meeting the Needs of Emerging Market Economies, World Bank Publications.

Saxena, K.B.C. (2005). Towards excellence in e-governance. *International Journal of Public Sector Management 18*(6), 498-513.

Scalise, D. (2004). Evidence-based medicine. *Hosp Health Netw*, 78(12), 32-7, 2.

Scherlis, W., & Eisenberg, J. (2003). IT research, innovation and e-government. *Communications of the ACM, 46*(1), 67-68.

Scholten, G.R.M., van der Grinten, T.E.D. (2005). The integration of medical specialists in hospitals. Dutch hospitals and medical specialists on the road to joint regulation. *Health Policy*, 72, 165-73.

Schwaig, K. S., Kane, G. C., & Storey, V. C. (2005). Privacy, fair information practices and the fortune 500: the virtual reality of compliance. *SIGMIS Database 36*(1), 49-63.

Seifert, J W. (2007)Data Mining and Homeland Security: An Overview. Crs report for congress. June 5.

Seifert, J. W. (2006). Data Mining: An Overview. In B. G. Kutais (Ed.), *Focus on the Internet* (pp. 101-118): Nova Science Publishers, Inc.

Seifert, J.W. (2004). Data mining: an overview. *CRS Report for Congress, December 16.* Retrieved December 1, 2007, from http://www.fas.org/irp/crs/RL31798.pdf

Sen, A. & Sinha, AP. (2005). A Comparison of Data Warehousing Methodologies. *Communications of the ACM*, Vol. 48, No. 3, pp. 79-84.

Senge, P., Kleiner, A., Roberts, C., Ross, R., & Smith, B. (1994). *The fifth discipline fieldbook*. New York: Doubleday.

Sengupta, A., Mazumdar, C. & Barik, M.S. (2005). e-Commerce security – A life cycle approach, *Sadhana* Vol. 30, Parts 2 & 3, April/June 2005, pp. 119–140, India.

Servant, François-Paul (2007). Semantic Web Technologies in Technical Automotive Documentation, Proceedings of the OWLED 2007 Workshop on OWL: Experiences and Directions, Vol. 258, Innsbruck, Austria, June 6-7, 2007. Edited by Christine Golbreich, Aditya Kalyanpur, & Bijan Parsia, Technical University of Aachen, Germany.

Shahar, Y., Miksch, S., Johnson, P., (2006) "A task-specific ontology for the application and critiquing of time-oriented clinical guidelines", in *Artificial Intelligence in Medicine*, Springer, Lecture Notes in Computer Science, Volume 1211/1997

Shahar, Y., Young. O, Shalom, E., Galperin, M., Mayaffit, A., Moskovitch, R., Hessing, A., (2004) "A framework for a distributed, hybrid, multiple-ontology clinical-guideline library, and automated guideline-support tools", Elsevier, Journal of Biomedical Informatics 37 (2004) 325–344

Sharifah, M. S. M. A. (2004). Bridging digital divide in marginalized areas: A focus on IT policy, planning and implementation issues in Malaysia, *ITDC Newsletter, 4*(1), 1-14.

Sharma, S. (2004). E-Governance: An Approach to Manage Bureaucratic Impediments, in the *Proceedings of the E-Governance: challenges and opportunities for democracy, administration and law*, Seoul, S. Korea, p. 11.

Sharp, D. (2003). Knowledge Management Today: Challenges and Opportunities, Information Systems Management, Vol. 20, Issue 2, pp. 32-37.

Shen, J., Chang, S. I., Lee, E. S., Deng, Y., & Brown, S. J. (2005). Determination of cluster number in clustering microarray data. *Applied Mathematics and Computation, 169*(2), 1172-1185.

Shiffman, R.N, Michel, G., Essaihi, A., Thornquist, E, (2004), "Bridging the Guideline Implementation Gap: A Systematic, Document-Centered Approach to Guideline Implementation", in *Journal of the American Medical Informatics Association* Volume 11 Number 5 Sep / Oct 2004.

Silverman, E., Skinner, J. (2004). Medicare upcoding and hospital ownership. *J Health Econ*, 23(2), 369-89.

Singh, R., Saleemi, A., Walsh, K., Popert, R., O'Brien, T. (2003). Near misses in bladder cancer – an airline safety approach to urology. *Ann R Coll Surg Engl*, 85, 378-81.

Smith, B.W. (2001). *E-Commerce: Financial Products and Services*, 2001, Law Journal Press.

Smith, H., McKeen, J., & Singh, S. (2006). Making knowledge work: five principles for action-oriented knowledge management. *Knowledge Management Research and Practice, 4*(2), 116 – 124.

Sobirey, M., Richter, B. and Konig. M. (1996) The intrusion detection system aid. architecture, and experiences in automated audit analysis. In *Proc. of the IFIP TC6 / TC11 International Conference on Communications and Multimedia Security*, pages 278 – 290, Essen, Germany.

Solon, J.A., Feeney, S.H., Jones, S.H., Rigg, R.D., Sheps, C.G. (1967) "Delineating episodes of medical care". *American Journal of Public Health*, 57 (1967) 401–408.

Solon, J.A., Feeney, S.H., Jones, S.H., Rigg, R.D., Sheps, C.G. "Delineating episodes of medical care" in *American Journal of Public Health*, 57 (1967) pp. 401–408.

Sperley, E. (1999). *The Enterprise Data Warehouse: The Planning, Building & Implementation*. Volume I: 1st edition, ISBN 0139058451, Prentice Hall.

SPSS predictive analytics accelerating cancer research at Children's Memorial Research Center, Chicago. (2005, March 7). *Business Wire*.

Staab, S., & Studer, R. (2004). Handbook on Ontologies, Heidelberg: Springer Verlag.

Sterman, J. D. (1994). Learning in and about Complex Systems. *System dynamics Review*. Volume 10 (2-3), 291-330.

Sterman, J. D. (2000). Business Dynamics: Systems Thinking and Modelling for a Complex World, Irwin McGraw-Hill, Boston, MA

Stewart, T.A. (2001). *The Wealth of Knowledge: Intellectual Capital and the Twenty First Century Organization*. First edition. New York, NY: A Currency Book: Doubleday; A division of Random House, Inc.

Stolfo, S. J., Fan, W. Lee, W., Prodromidis, A. and Chan. P. (2000) Cost-sensitive modeling for fraud and intrusion detection: Results from the JAM project. In *Proceedings of the 2000 DARPA Information Survivability Conference and Exposition*, January.

Stolfo, S. J., Prodromidis, A. L., Tselepis, S., Lee, W. Fan, D. W. and Chan. P. K. (1997). JAM: Java agents for meta-learning over distributed databases. In *Proceedings of the 3rd International Conference on Knowledge Discovery and Data Mining*, pages 74–81, Newport Beach, CA, August. AAAI Press.

Stracke, J. (2002). *E-government: Supporting knowledge and information flows with supply chain management.* Proceedings of the Third Working Conference on Knowledge Management in Electronic Government, Copenhagen, Denmark.

Sun, Z. et al. (2005). Event-Driven Document Selection for Terrorism Information Extraction. *ISI 2005, LNCS 3495*, pp. 37-48.

Suzlon Energy (2008). Accessed on February 02, 2008 from http://www.tech2.com/biz/india/casestudies/computing/suzlon-energy-knowledge-management-portal-energises-employees/1522/0

Taipale, K. (2003). Data mining and domestic security: connecting the dots to make sense of data. *Columbia Science & Technology Law Review, 5(2)*. Retrieved September 11, 2007, from http://www.stlr.org/html/volume5/taipaleintro.php

Takeuchi, K., Yanai, H., & Mukherjee, B. N. (1982). *The Foundations of Multivariate Analysis.* New Delhi: Wiley Eastern Limited.

Tan, Pang-Ning, Steinbach, M., Kumar, V. (2005). Introduction to Data Mining, Addison Wesley.

TEMIS. (2005). *Text Mining Solutions, TEMIS*. Retrieved 2.5.2005, 2005, from http://www.temis-group.com

Teng, H. S., Chen, K. and Lu. S. C. (1990)Adaptive real-time anomaly detection using inductively generated sequential patterns. In *Proceedings of the IEEE Symposium on Research in Security and Privacy*, pages 278–284, Oakland CA, May.

ter Braak, C.J.F. (1986). Canonical correspondence analysis: a new eigenvector technique for multivariate direct gradient analysis. *Ecology 67*, 1176-1179.

ter Braak, C.J.F., & Verdonschot, P.F.M. (1995) Canonical Correspondence Analysis and related multivariate methods in aquatic ecology. *Aquatic Sciences, 3*, 255–289.

Terplan, K. (2003). Electronic Bill Presentment and Payment, CRC Press.

The World Bank Group (2008). E-Government Definitions. Retrieved May 10, 2008, from http://go.worldbank.org/M1JHE0Z280.

Thorpe, R. & Horman, G. (2000). Strategic Reward Systems, Financial Times.

Tichenor, P.J., Donohue, G.A., & Olien, C.N. (1970). Mass media flow and differential growth in knowledge. *Public Opinion Quarterly 34*: Colombia University Press.

Todman, C. (2001). *Designing a Data Warehouse: Supporting Customer Relationship Management (Paperback)*. ISBN: 0-13-089712-4. Prentice Hall.

Toivonen, J., Visa, A., Vesanen, T., Back, B., & Vanharanta, H. (2001). *Prototype Based Information Retrieval in Multilanguage Bibles.* Paper presented at the WIAMIS 2001.

Tomes, N. (2006). The patient as a policy factor: a historical case study of the consumer/survivor movement in mental health. *Health Aff*, 25(3), 720-9.

Trask, C. (2002). The lot of airline pilots and consultants is not so different. *BMJ*, 13, 105.

Traylor, N.T. et.al. (1998) Payments, Clearance, & Settlement: A Guide to the Systems, Published 1998, DIANE Publishing.

Tserng, H.P. & Lin, Yu-Cheng (2004). *Developing an activity-based knowledge management system for contractors*, Automation in Construction Volume 13, Issue 6, November 2004, Pages 781-802, Elsevier B.V.

Tu, S. W., Kahn, M. G., Musen, M. A., Ferguson, J. C., Shortliffe, E. H., and Fagan, L. M. (1989). "Episodic Skeletal-Plan Refinement on Temporal Data". *Communications of ACM*, 32:1439-1455.

Tuohy, C.H. (2003). Agency, Contract, and Governance: Shifting Shapes of Accountability in the Health Care Arena. *Journal of Health Politics, Policy and Law*, 28(2-3), 195-215.

Tuomi, I. (1999). *Corporate Knowledge: Theory and Practice of Intelligent Organizations.* Helsinki: Metaxis.

Tuomi, I. (2002). *Networks of Innovation: Change and Meaning in the Age of the Internet.* Oxford: Oxford University Press.

Turban, E., Aronson, J.E., & Liang T.P. (2005). *Decision Support Systems and Intelligent Systems*, 7th Edition. Upper Saddle River, NJ: Prentice Hall.

Tushman, Michael L., & Anderson, Philip (2004). (Eds.) *Managing Strategic Innovation and Change: A Collection of Readings*. 2nd ed. N.Y.: Oxford University Press.

Tuzhilin, A. (2005). Foreword. In J. Wang (Ed.), *Encyclopedia of data warehousing and mining* (1st ed.). Hershey, PA: Idea Group Reference.

Tyson, E. (2006). Personal Finance for Dummies, Published 2006, John Wiley & Sons.

U.S. General Accounting Office (GAO) (2004), *"Data Mining: Federal Efforts Cover a Wide Range of Uses,"* GAO-04-548, May 2004.

U.S. Government Accounting Office (GAO). (2005). *Data mining: Agencies have taken key steps to protect privacy in selected efforts, but significant compliance issues remain* (GAO-05-866). Author.

U.S. Judicial Conference. (2005). *Report of the Civil Rules Advisory Committee 40 (amended July 25, 2005)*. Washington, D.C.: Reprinted in Communications on the Rules of Practice and Procedure of the Judicial Conference of the U.S., Summary of Committee on Rules of Practice and Procedure: Agenda E-i8 app. C.

Umar, A. (2003). E-Business and Distributed Systems Handbook: Architecture, NGE Solutions, Inc., USA.

UN & ASPA. (2002). *Benchmarking e-government: A global perspective*. New York: United Nations Division of Public Economics and Public Administration and the American Society for Public Administration.

UN (2005). Information and Communication technologies for development: Progress in the implementation of General Assembly resolution 57/295, report of the Secretary-General, General Assembly, A/60/323, United Nations.

UNPAN. (2002). Unpan e-government. Retrieved July 8, 2002, from www.unpan.org/egovernment.asp

Unsworth, J. (2004). *The value of digitization of libraries: The Newberry library,* May 2004 (An Innodata Isogen Symposium).

U.S. Government, CIA World Fact Book: "The Government type Ontology" http://reliant.teknowledge.com/DAML/Government.owl, 2002

USCH (1995). The Future of Money: Hearing Before the Subcommittee on Domestic and International Monetary Policy, Trade, and Technology, Committee on Banking and Financial Services, Subcommittee on Domestic and International Monetary Policy, United States Congressional House, Congressional Sales Office, United States.

Van Hulle, C., Eeckloo, K., Van Herck, G., Vleugels, A. (2002). Governance bij Belgische ziekenhuizen: analyse en optimalisering. In: Peeters, L., Matthyssens, P., Vereeck, L., editors. *Stakeholder Synergie*. Leuven: Garant.

Van, J. (2005, October 17). Cybercrime being fought in new ways. *Knight Ridder Tribune Business News*, p. 1.

Vanhaecht, K., Bollmann, M., Bower, K., Gallagher, C., Gardini, A., Guezo, J. et al. (2006). Prevalence and use of clinical pathways in 23 countries - an international survey by the European Pathway Association (www.E-P-A.org). *J Integ Care Pathways*, 10, 28-34.

Vapnik, V. N. (1998). *Statistical Learning Theory*. John Wiley and Sons, New York, 1998.

Vaughn, T., Koepke, M., Kroch, E., Lehrman, W., Sinha, S., Levey, S. (2006), Engagement of leadership in quality improvement initiatives: executive quality improvement survey results. Journal of patient safety, 2, 2-9.

Vennix, J.A.M. (1999) Group Model-Building: Tackling Messy Problems. *System Dynamics Review, 15* 4., 379-401.

Verschoor, C. (2000). Can an ethics code change behavior? *Strategic Finance, 82*(1), 26-28.

ViciDocs (2008). Accessed on February 02, 2008 from http://www.vicidocs.com/govtpub.asp

Viglioni, G.M.C. (2007). *Methodology for Railway Demand Forecasting using Data Mining*, SAS paper 161-2007, SAS Institute Inc., USA.

Vincze, Z. (2004). *A Grounded Theory Approach to Foreign market expansion in newly emerging market. Two Finnish Companies in the Visegrád countries*. Series A-4:2004. Doctoral dissertation. Publications of the Turku School of Economics and Business Administration, Turku, Finland.

Visa, A., Toivonen, J., Autio, S., Mäkinen, J., Back, B., & Vanharanta, H. (2001, 16-17 April). *Data mining of text as a tool in authorship attribution*. Paper presented at the Data Mining and Knowledge Discovery: Theory, Tools and Technology III, Orlando, USA.

Vouros, G.A. (2003). Technological issues towards knowledge-powered organizations. *Journal of Knowledge Management, 7*(2), 114-127.

Wagner, C., Cheung, K., Lee, F., & Ip, R. (2003). Enhancing e-government in developing countries: managing knowledge through virtual communities. *The Electronic Journal on Information Systems in Developing Countries 14*(4), 1-20.

Walsh, J.P. (1995). Managerial and organizational cognition: Notes from a trip down memory lane. *Organization Science*, 6: 280-321.

Wang, G., Chen, H., & Atabakhsh, H. (2004). Automatically Detecting Deceptive Criminal Identities, *Communications of the ACM* 47, (3), 2004, 71-76.

Wang, H. (1997). Intelligent agent-assisted decision support systems: Integration of knowledge discovery, knowledge analysis, and group decision support. *Expert Systems with Applications, 12*(3), 323-335.

Wang, J. (Ed.). (2006). *Encyclopedia of data warehousing and mining* (1st ed.). Hershey, PA: Idea Group Reference.

Wang, X., Huang, S., Cao, L., Shi, D., & Shu, P. (2007). LSSVM with Fuzzy Pre-processing Model Based Aero Engine Data Mining Technology. In *Advanced Data Mining and Applications* (Vol. Tuesday, August 14, 2007, pp. 100-109). Heidelberg: Springer Berlin / Heidelberg.

Wang, Y. (2007). Integration of data mining with *Game theory, Journal of International Federation for Information Processing,* Volume 207/2006, Boston: Springer, pp 275-280

Warren P. & Alsmeyer D. (n.d). *The digital Library: A case study in intelligent content management.*

Warrender, C., Forrest, S. and Pearlmutter. B. (1999) Detecting intrusions using system calls: alternative data models. In *In 1999 IEEE Symposium on Security and Privacy*, pages 133– 145. IEEE Computer Society.

Wasem, J., Greβ, S., Okma, K.G.H. (2004). The role of private health insurance in social health insurance countries. In: Saltman, R.B., Busse, R., Figueras, J., editors. *Social health insurance systems in western Europe.* Berkshire: Open University Press.

Wasserman, S., & Faust, K. (1994). *Social Network Analysis: Methods and Applications.* Cambridge University Press, 1994.

Watson, R. T. (1999). *Data Management: Databases and Organizations* (2nd Edition ed.): John Wiley & Sons.

Watts D. J. (2003). *Six Degrees: The Science of a Connected Age.* New York: Norton.

Wearing, R. (2005). *Cases in corporate governance.* London: SAGE Publication.

Weiss, L. M. (1998). *Collection and Connection: Rationalized and Embedded Knowledge in Knowledge-Intensive Organizations (Rationalized Knowledge).* Ph.D dissertation, Harvard University.

Welch, W.P., Bazarko, D., Ritten, K., Burgess, Y., Harmon, R., Sandy, L.G., (2007). "Electronic Health Records in Four Community Physician Practices: Impact on Quality and Cost of Care", *Journal of the American Medical Informatics Association*, Volume 14, Issue 3, May-June 2007, Pages 320-328

Wenger, E. (2004). Knowledge management as a doughnut: shaping your knowledge strategy through communities of practice. *Ivey Business Journal, 68*, 1-7.

Wenger, E., McDermott, R. & Snyder, W.M. (2002). *Cultivating Communities of Practice.* Boston, MA: Harvard Business School Press.

West, J. P., & Berman, E. M. (2001). The Impact of Revitalized Management Practices on the Adoption of Information Technology: A National Survey of Local Governments. Pubic Performance & Management Review, 24(3), 233-253.

White, K.R. (2000). Hospitals sponsored by the Roman Catholic Church: separate, equal, and distinct? Milbank Q, 78(2), 213-39.

Wiig, K. (1993). *Knowledge management foundations: Thinking about thinking-how people and organizations create, represent and use knowledge.* Arlington, TX: Schema Press.

Wiig, K. (1993). *Knowledge management foundations: Thinking about thinking. How people and organizations create, represent and use knowledge.* Arlington, TX: Schema Press.

Wiig, K. (2002). Knowledge management in public administration. *Journal of Knowledge Management.* 6(3), 224-239.

Williams, G., Baxter. R., Kelman, C., Rainsford, C., He, H., Gu, L., Vickers, D., Hawkins, S., (2002), "Estimating Episodes of Care Using Linked Medical Claims Data", in R.I. McKay and J. Slaney (Eds.): *AI 2002*, LNAI 2557, Springer, pp. 660–671, 2002.

Williamson, O.E. (1999). *The Mechanisms of Governance.* New York: Oxford University Press.

Willis, S., & Tranter, B. (2006). Beyond the digital divide: Internet diffusion and inequality in Australia. *Journal of Sociology, 42*(1), 43–59.

Wilmoth, S. (2004). Foundation trusts and the problem of legitimacy. *Health Care Anal, 12*(2), 157-69.

Wimmer M. and Roland Traunmuller (2000). Trends in Electronic Government: Managing Distributed Knowledge. *11th International Workshop on Database and Expert Systems Applications (DEXA'00)*, pp. 340-352.

Wimmer, M. (2006). Implementing a Knowledge Portal for e-Government Based on Semantic Modeling: The e-Government Intelligent Portal (eip.at). *Proceedings of the 39th Annual Hawaii International Conference on System Sciences (HICSS'06) Track 4*, pp. 82-90.

Witte, R., Zhang, Y. & Rilling, J., (2007). Empowering Software Maintainers with Semantic Web Technologies, In Franconi, E., Kifer, M. & May, W. (Eds.), *The Semantic Web: Research and Applications*, 4th European Semantic Web Conference, ESWC 2007, Innsbruck, Austria, June 3-7, 2007, Proceedings of, Springer, pp. 37-52.

Witten, I.H. & Frank, E. (2005). Data Mining: Practical Machine Learning Tools and Techniques, Morgan Kaufmann.

Won, K-J., Prügel-Bennett, A., Krogh, A., (2006). Evolving the Structure of Hidden Markov Models, *IEEE Transactions on Evolutionary Computation*, vol. 10, no. 1, February 2006, pp. 39–49.

World Bank (2008). E-government operational definition. Retrieved April 30, 2008, from http://go.worldbank.org/M1JHE0Z280

Wu, X., Kumar, V., Quinlan, J. R., Ghosh, J., Yang, Q., Motoda, H., et al. (2007). *Top 10 algorithms in data mining* (Survey paper). London: Springer-Verlag London Limited.

Xu, J., & Chen, H. (2005). Criminal Network Analysis and Visualization. *Communications of the ACM, 28*, (6), 2005, 101-107.

Yang, W. S., & Hwang, S. Y. (2006). A process-mining framework for the detection of healthcare fraud and abuse. *Expert Systems with Applications, 31*(1), 56-68.

Ye, N. (2003). *The Handbook of Data Mining*. London: Lawrence Erlbaum Associates, Publishers.

York, S., Tunkel, D., Chia, K. & Edge, H.S. (2000). E-commerce: A Guide to the Law of Electronic Business, Butterworths.

Young, G.J. (1996), Insider Representation on the governing boards of nonprofit hospitals: trends and implications for charitable care. *Inquiry*, 33(4), 352-362.

Young, G.J., Stedham, Y., Beekun, R.I. (2000), Boards of Directors and the Adoption of a CEO Performance Evaluation Process. *Journal of Management Studies*, 37(2), 277-296.

Yuen, P. (2005). *Compendium of health statistics. 17th edition*. London: Office of Health Economics.

Zagonel, A.S.(2002). Model Conceptualization in Group Model Building: A Review of the Literature Exploring the Tension Between Representing Reality and Negotiating a Social Order. In *Proceedings of the 20th International Conference of the System Dynamics Society*, Palermo, Italy.

Zaitun A. B. & Barbara, C. (2005). Overcoming the digital divide: A proposal on how institutions of higher education can play a role. *Malaysian Online Journal of Instructional Technology*, 2(1), 1-11.

Zaki, M. J., Parthasarathy, S., Ogihara, M. & Li, W. (1997). New Parallel Algorithms for Fast Discovery of Association Rules, *Data Mining and Knowledge Discovery*, Vol. 1, No. 4, 343-37.

Zheng, R. et al. (2006). A Framework of Authorship Identification for Online Messages: Writing Style Features and Classification Techniques. *Journal of the American Society for Information Science and Technology*, 57(3), 378-393.

Zhou, Y., Reid, E., & et al. (2005). US Domestic Extremist Groups on the Web: Link and Content Analysis. *IEEE Intelligent Systems*. September/October 2005, pp. 44-51.

About the Contributors

Hakikur Rahman, PhD, is the principal, Institute of Computer Management & Science (ICMS), and President of ICMS Foundation. He is currently serving Bangabandhu Sheikh Mujibur Rahman Agricultural University as an Adjunct Faculty, and the South Asia Foundation Bangladesh Chapter as the Secretary. He served Sustainable Development Networking Foundation (SDNF) as its executive director (CEO) from January 2007 to December 2007, the transformed entity of the Sustainable Development Networking Programme (SDNP) in Bangladesh where he was working as the National Project coordinator since December 1999. SDNP is a global initiative of UNDP and it completed its activity in Bangladesh on December 31, 2006. Before joining SDNP he worked as the director, Computer Division, Bangladesh Open University. Graduating from the Bangladesh University of Engineering and Technology in 1981, he has done his Master's of Engineering from the American University of Beirut in 1986 and completed his PhD in computer engineering from the Ansted University, UK in 2001.

* * *

Rodrigo Sandoval-Almazán is an assistant professor in the Research Center of Business Collge in the Autonomous State University of Mexico, in Toluca City and a research fellow at the Center for Development of Information Technologies and Electronics of the ITESM. Dr. Sandoval-Almazán is the author or co-author of articles in *Handbook of research on Public Information Technology*; *Journal of Information Technology for Development*; *Espiral: Estudios sobre Estado y Sociedad, and Espacios Públicos*. His research interests include electronic government, information technologies and organizations, digital divide technology, online political marketing, new public management, and multi-method research approaches. Dr. Sandoval-Almazán has a bachelors degree in political science and public administration, a masters in management focused on marketing, and he received the PhD in management with information systems in Technology Institute of Monterrey.

Abdul Raufu Ambali obtained his PhD from International Islamic University Malaysia, Department of Political Science in year 2005 and joined University Technology MARA (UiTM), Shah Alam, Malaysia. The author is a prolific writer in public policy, public administration, e-government and governance issues. He is a senior lecturer and coordinator of research methodology and data analysis as well as supervisor for both undergraduate and post-graduate students at Faculty of Administrative Science and Policy Studies in UiTM. With his interdisciplinary research background and experience, he has tremendously contributed to international and local journals, chapters in books as well as conferences within and outside Asia.

Paola Annoni is a research fellow at the Dept. of Economics, Business and Statistics of the University of Milan (IT). For a decade she worked as a physicist in the Environmental Dept. of an Italian research centre where she primarily dealt with problems of open and ground water dynamics, pollution dispersion and analysis of environmental data. Later she got a PhD in statistics at the University of Milano-Bicocca and her late research interests include: linear and non-linear multivariate statistics, statistical models for species-abundance relationships, environmental statistics, optimal scaling, treatment of qualitative variables, discrete mathematics and ranking techniques.

Nasser M. Ayoub received the BSc degree in mechanical engineering from the department of Industrial and Production Engineering Department, Zagazig University in 1993, the MSc degree in engineering from Eindhoven University of Technology and Fontyes University, Netherlands, in 1999, and the PhD degree from the Department of Environmental Chemistry and Engineering from Tokyo Institute of Technology, Japan, in 2007. He is a full time assistant professor in Production Technology Department, Helwan University, Egypt. Since January 2008 he joined the Process Systems Engineering Division of Tokyo Institute of Technology, Japan as research associate. His current research interests are Socio-technical systems, regulation generation schemes development, decision support for biomass utilization networks, data mining approaches to decision-making, and e-government decision support systems.

Judith Barlow, PhD, Dr. Barlow joined the College of Business as an associate professor of Management Information Systems (MIS) in 2000. She has a PhD in information systems from the University of Colorado-Boulder and an MS in mineral economics/operations research at the Colorado School of Mines. Her research interests include technology-supported teaching and learning, integrated enterprise systems, supply chain management, data warehousing, and data mining.

LuAnn Bean, PhD, CPA, CIA, CFE, FCPA. Dr. Bean is professor of Accounting at the College of Business, Florida Institute of Technology, Melbourne, Florida. She has published articles in *The Journal of Computer Information Systems, The CPA Journal, The Accounting Historians Journal, The Ohio CPA Journal, Internal Auditing, The Petroleum Accounting and Financial Management Journal, Thunderbird International Business Review, The Journal of Corporate Accounting and Finance, The Journal of Business and Behavioral Sciences*, and other professional journals. She is active in many professional organizations, including the Florida Institute of CPAs, American Accounting Association, and the Institute of Internal Auditors.

Deborah Carstens, PhD, PMP. Dr. Carstens is an associate professor in Management Information Systems (MIS) and joined Florida Institute of Technology in Fall 2003. She has a PhD in industrial engineering from the University of Central Florida, an MBA from Florida Institute of Technology, and a Bachelor of Science degree in business administration from the University of Central Florida. Previously, she worked for NASA Kennedy Space Center (KSC) from 1992 through 2003. She currently instructs undergraduate and graduate courses and conducts research in human error analysis research resulting in the optimization of systems, safety and processes.

Angela Mashauri Chailla has completed her BA (Ed) from University of Dar es Salaam, PGD (LIS) from Aberystwyth College of Librarianship-University of Wales, MA (LIS) from Loughborough

University of Technology, and PhD (agricultural information management) from University of Natal, RSA. Dr. Chailla is the senior librarian at the Sokoine University of Agriculture (SUA).

Yannis Charalabidis is a computer engineer and holds a PhD in information systems engineering from National Technical University of Athens. He has been employed as an executive director in Singular Group, occupying the positions of project director, development director, strategy director and deputy general manager. He has also been the managing director of Baan Eastern Europe Localisation Centre SA, based in Poland and Netherlands. Previous employments include Siemens-Nixdorf GmbH and Bull SA. Currently he is heading e-government & e-business research in the Decision Support Systems Laboratory - National Technical University of Athens, planning and coordinating high-level policy making, research and pilot application projects for Governments and Administrations Worldwide. His scientific and technological interests include e-government information systems, interoperability and standardization, e-participation and government transformation.

Shamsul Chowdhury is currently a full-time faculty in Information System at Roosevelt University. He has taught at the Linköping University and Jönköping International Business School in Sweden for many years as an assistant/associate professor. He has a broad interest and expertise in database systems and database oriented system development & management, knowledge-based systems, knowledge discovery in databases, data mining and data ware housing, CBR (case-based reasoning) systems and applications. He has more than 90 publications in well-reputed journals, books and proceedings. One of his works, namely: Evaluation and Validation of decision support systems in medicine appeared in the yearbook on the 1992 Medical Informatics.

Lucas Delesie is MSc from the Catholic University of Leuven, Belgium and MSc and PhD in operations research from the University of Pennsylvania. His field is exact, in contrast to assumption based or simplified, information management, data mining and visualisation. He worked in a hospital federation, hospital group and now university hospital. He is also part-time professor at the School of Public Health of the Catholic University of Leuven.

Frank W. Dulle is a senior librarian at the Sokoine National Agricultural Library, Sokoine university of Agriculture. He holds a BSc agriculture from same university and masters degree in library and information studies from the University of Botswana. He is currently a doctoral student at the University of South Africa. His research interests include: ICTs application in education and research; scholarly communication; Information management; and Community information services.

Kristof Eeckloo is a research fellow at the School of Public Health of the Catholic University of Leuven, Belgium. He holds a master's degree in law and prepares a PhD in social health sciences. His field of interest is healthcare management and governance. He is the coordinator of a European study on hospital governance. In this study, data mining and information visualisation are used as methods of data analysis.

Pieralda Ferrari is full professor of Statistics at the Department of Economics, Business and Statistics at the University of Milan, Italy. Her main research interests are: multivariate statistical analysis, multilevel models, applications of statistics to sociology and economics.

Mario Gutiérrez leads the Digital Animation Research Center of Tecnológico de Monterrey, Campus Morelia in Mexico. He received his PhD in computer science from the École Polytechnique Fédérale de Lausanne, Switzerland. Dr. Gutiérrez is co-author of the book, *Stepping into Virtual Reality* (Springer, 2008). He has published serveral papers in refereed international conferences in the field of virtual reality, computer graphics and human-machine interfaces such as IEEE VR, IEEE RO-MAN, IEEE Cyberworlds, ACM VRST, ACM VRCIA, WorldHaptics, etc. He has published articles in the following journals: *IEEE Computer Graphics and Applications*, *IEEE Multimedia*, *The Visual Computer*, *Computers & Graphics*, and *International Journal of Computer Applications in Technology*.

Arla Juntunen has a PhD in marketing at the Helsinki School of Economics (HSE), Marketing and Management Department, Finland and a master's degree in administrative information systems at the University of Helsinki. She is a post-doc researcher at the University of Helsinki, researcher at the HSE and a Senior Advisor in Finland's Supreme Command of the Police. Her research interests focus on strategic management, innovation and business networks, and management information systems (MIS).

Stefano De Luca is the CEO of Evodevo s.r.l, an innovation company specialized in semantic web technologies, electronics, sensor networks and homeland security. He realized products as a logic-based middleware, a semantic web enabled CMS, agent-based hazard simulators. He has a degree in Philosophy with specialization in mathematical logic and philosophy of science, and teaches Artificial Intelligence and Multi-Agent Systems at Rome University "Tor Vergata". Before founding Evodevo, he worked as R&D manager in multinational companies. He has published books on agent-based modeling and simulation, process optimization in health care, and papers on intelligent adaptive systems. His research interests ranges in nature inspired computing, evolutionary computation, semantic web, homeland security, intelligent agents.

Andrew W. Malekani was born on 14th August, 1971 in Sumbawanga, Rukwa Region in Tanzania, completed primary school in 1987, completed ordinary level secondary school in 1991 and advanced level studies in 1994. In 1995 Malekani joined Sokoine University of Agriculture to pursue a four year degree program in agricultural sciences, and completed that in 1999. In October 2004 he joined the University of Dar es Salaam to pursue a two year MA degree in information studies, and completed that in June 2006. Currently, Malekani is employed as a librarian at Sokoine National Agricultural Library.

Kostas Metaxiotis is assistant professor in the University of Piraeus and senior advisor to the Secretary for the Information Society in the Greek Ministry of Economy and Finance. He has wide experience in knowledge management, artificial intelligence, knowledge cities, artificial intelligence, decision support systems, e-government. He has published more than 60 scientific papers in various journals, such as *Journal of Knowledge Management*, *Journal of Information and Knowledge Management*, *Knowledge Management & Practice*, *Journal of Intelligent Manufacturing*, *Applied Artificial Intelligence*, *Industrial Management & Data Systems*, *Journal of Computer Information Systems*, etc. He is a member of editorial boards of several leading journals in the field and is a member of Program Committee at international conferences. Since 1996 he has been participating in various EC-funded projects within Tacis, Phare, MEDA and IST Programmes as senior ICT consultant and manager.

Enrico Memo is a consultant and researcher for public administrations, non profit organizations and Health Institutions. He collaborates as a researcher with Ca' Foscari University in Venice. In the last 15 years he worked with SDA Bocconi Business School's Quantitative Methods Area, developing his statistical skills. After that he has been statistical official for Assifact (Italian Factoring Association), Business analyst for Finantix srl and now he is developing human resources management skills.

Yuji Naka, received the B.Eng the M.Eng from Osaka University in 1968 and 1970 respectively. From 1971-1981 Kyoto University Research assistant in the Department of Engineering where he obtained his PhD degrees. From 1979 to1980 he joined Leeds University as research associate. From 1981-1993 he worked as a full time associate professor in Chemical Resources Laboratory, Tokyo Institute of Technology. From 1993 until now he is a full professor and Group leader of The Process Systems Engineering Division, Tokyo Institute of Technology. He is the recipient of the Best Paper Award from Ecodesign 2001. He is now leading a group of long term projects funded by the Japanese government where he developed a wide concept on the development of Technological Information Infrastructure and socio-technical systems development. His current research interests are knowledge integration to support lifecycle engineering. He is a member of SCEJ, AIChE, SICE, JPI, and JSWME.

A.M.M. Safiullah is the vice chancellor of the Bangladesh University of Engineering and technology (BUET). Obtaining PhD in 1981 from the University of Strathclyde, UK he is serving in BUET at various capacities, as professor, dean and head of the Department of Civil Engineering; director of Planning and Development, and Directorate of Continuing Education. Currently he is the president of the Bangladesh Society for Geotechnical Engineering; member-secretary of the Board of Accreditation for Engineering and technical Education; and member of the Bangladesh Professional Engineers' Registration Board. Among various other past involvements, he was the chairman of Civil Engineering Division, Institute of Engineers, Bangladesh and chairman of the Organizing Committee for International Symposium on 'Scour of Foundations' held in Melbourne, November 2000 under the auspices of ISMGE TC-33. Dr. Safiullah has contributed to over 50 publications as research journals, conference proceedings, and book chapters. He has attended many conferences in home and abroad for his research and academic interests.

Silvia Salini holds a degree in statistics from the Catholic University of Milan and a Phd in statistics from the University of Milan Bicocca. Currently she is an assistant professor of Statistics in the Department of Economics, Business and Statistics at the University of Milan. Her main research interests are multivariate statistical analysis, data mining and statistics for social science.

Olli Sjöblom was born in 1956 in Turku, Finland. He has graduated from Turku School of Economics 1985 having international marketing as main subject. After a couple of years he continued his studies among information systems science aiming to become a doctoral student changing the main subject. Since 2001 he has been employed by the Finnish Civil Aviation Authority having a variety of positions during his career, Information Systems Officer to be mentioned as an example. His current position is inspector at the Investigation and Analysis Unit. He is completing his thesis in information systems science at Turku School of Economics.

Reima Suomi is a professor of Information Systems Science at Turku School of Economics and Business Administration, Finland since 1994. He is a docent for the universities of Turku and Oulu, Finland. During years 1992-93 he spent as a "Vollamtlicher Dozent" in the University of St. Gallen, Switzerland, where he led a research project on business process re-engineering. Reima Suomi has together over 300 publications, and has published in journals such as *Information & Management, Information Services & Use, Technology Analysis & Strategic Management, The Journal of Strategic Information Systems, Behaviour & Information Technology, Journal of Management History and Information Resources Management Journal.* For the academic year 2001-2002 he was a senior researcher "varttunut tutkija" for the academy of Finland. With Paul Jackson he has published the book, *Virtual Organization and Workplace Development*, with Routhledge, London.

Arthur Vleugels, medical doctor, is full professor at the School of Public Health of the Catholic University of Leuven and director of the Centre for Health Services and Nursing Research. He is advisor to various Belgian health authorities. The research interests of the Centre are in clinical nursing, care for the elderly, healthcare policy, healthcare governance and healthcare management.

Yi Wang is a lecturer of Nottingham business school, Nottingham Trent University. He got his masters from the Norwegian University of Science and technology and PhD from Cardiff University. Dr. Wang has been working in Southampton as a research fellow. His special interests are in operations management, health care management, game theory, semantic and ontology analysis.

Index

K

KDD process 75
KM portal, social implications 47
KM portals, cases 53
KM portals, challenges 55
KM portals, social responsibilities 47
KM portals and data mining 50
KM practices, maximizing 30
knowledge discovery 24
knowledge discovery in database (KDD) 70
knowledge discovery in databases (KDD) 7, 180
knowledge gap theory, and digital divide 269
knowledge management (KM) 43, 222, 289
knowledge management (KM), e-government 28–41
knowledge management, and e-government 16–27
knowledge management, conceptual framework 1–15
knowledge management portals 42–64

L

low developed countries (LDCs) 293

M

Malaysian e-government, digital divide implication 267–287
Markov chains 79
memory, organizational 24
mining algorithm 211
mobile payment 140
multidimensional scaling (MDS) 97
multilevel decision making life cycle (MLDMLC) 237

N

Nairobi University (NU) 296
National Center of Digitization (NCD) 291
national health services (NHS) trusts 93
national quality registers, Swedish model 67

O

on-line transaction processing (OLTP) 4
ontology-based management of e-government 221–234

P

principal component analysis (PCA) 116
profiling households 106–125
public administration knowledge, management 223
public government, data mining to advance knowledge 106–125

R

redundancy analysis (RDA) 116

S

Semantic Web technologies 50
social advancement system, data mining 49
social network analysis 168, 169, 176, 177, 339
Sokoine National Agricultural Library (SNAL) 296
structuration theory and digital divide 270
system dynamics 200, 202
system dynamics in e-government analysis 204
system thinking 202

T

terrorist attacks 307
third party billing systems 140
total activities analysis approach (TAA) 97

U

universal payment system 139

V

virtual account 140
virtual assistant (VA) 257
virtual assistant in an e-government, pros and cons 262
virtual assistants for e-government interaction 255–266

W

Web content analysis 177
Web link analysis 177